MID-CONTINENT PUBLIC LIBRARY
3 0000 13259326 4

D0845579

How Sex Became a Civil Liberty

How Sex Became a Civil Liberty

LEIGH ANN WHEELER

OXFORD
UNIVERSITY PRESS

Oxford University Press is a department of the University of Oxford. It furthers the University's objective of excellence in research, scholarship, and education by publishing worldwide

Oxford New York
Auckland Cape Town Dar es Salaam Hong Kong Karachi
Kuala Lumpur Madrid Melbourne Mexico City Nairobi
New Delhi Shanghai Taipei Toronto

With offices in
Argentina Austria Brazil Chile Czech Republic France Greece
Guatemala Hungary Italy Japan Poland Portugal Singapore
South Korea Switzerland Thailand Turkey Ukraine Vietnam

Published in the United States of America by
Oxford University Press
198 Madison Avenue, New York, New York 10016

Library of Congress Cataloging-in-Publication Data
Wheeler, Leigh Ann, 1967–
How sex became a civil liberty / Leigh Ann Wheeler.
p. cm.
Includes bibliographical references and index.
ISBN 978-0-19-975423-6 (hbk. : alk. paper)
1. Sex—United States—History—20th century. 2. Sexual rights—United States—History—20th century. I. Title.
HQ18.U5W49 2012
306.70973'0904—dc23 2012012448

1 3 5 7 9 8 6 4 2
Printed in the United States of America
on acid-free paper

For Don and Brady

Stu's Views
© Stu All Rights Reserved www.STUS.com
STU
Are you in the mood to exercise our Constitutional rights?

CONTENTS

ACKNOWLEDGMENTS

In 1997 I taught an interdisciplinary honors seminar, Rethinking Pornography and Hate Speech, at the University of Minnesota. To get a sense of where my students were coming from on the issues, I began the course with an informal survey that included the following questions: How would you feel if your partner or spouse brought pornography into your home? How would you respond? One by one, nearly every female student first assumed a heterosexual identity and then explained that, while pornography made her personally uncomfortable, she would not demand that her boyfriend or husband remove it from her home for fear of violating his right to free speech. At the end of the twentieth century, these students equated criticizing pornography and exercising control over their private space with advocating censorship, eliding, in the process, critical distinctions between private conduct and state action. Why, I wondered, did they think this way? How and why did they conflate categories that seemed to me so separate: personal opinions, private relationships, and civil liberties? After reading *Defending Pornography: Free Speech, Sex, and the Fight for Women's Rights* (2000) by Nadine Strossen, president of the American Civil Liberties Union at the time, I saw striking similarities between my students' thinking on these issues and Strossen's. This was not, I realized, because they had read her book—they hadn't—but I wondered if it was an indication that they inhabited a civic and sexual culture profoundly shaped by values popularized by the ACLU. Recurring experiences like this one ensured that questions about these matters continued to gnaw at me, and they gave rise to this project.

Beginning my acknowledgments to *How Sex Became a Civil Liberty* with a classroom experience seems fitting not only because the book was conceived through interactions with students, but also because teaching is crucial to my work as a historian. I am inspired by students who are genuinely curious about the past, and also by those who are indifferent to it. From all of them I learn more about how to make history matter to young people today; that makes me a better teacher and also a better writer. So I thank the students I taught in Minnesota fifteen years ago, as well as the many who have endured and those who have honestly enjoyed my courses since then. They have all influenced this book more than they know.

Several students deserve specific mention. Jon Halverstadt and Amy Gresham both worked as my research assistants when they were still undergraduate students; more recently, as a law student at Ohio State University, Jon helped me locate legal materials. Many graduate students provided me with research assistance for this project; they include Meredith Clark-Wiltz, Seneca Vaught, Rachel Ayers, Kyle Smith, Peter Kuebeck, Eva Manney, Andrew Smith, and Don Eberley. Students and individuals at other institutions also assisted me by accessing archival collections I could not personally visit; a special thanks to Aaron Bell, Nick Speth, Nicholas Cizek, Mike Massey, and Linda Morrison, each of whom discovered valuable documents for this project. An especially talented group of Binghamton University graduate students in my spring 2011 seminar on Women in the Modern United States read the entire book manuscript when it was double the size it is now and offered encouragement and useful suggestions for slimming it down.

I am also indebted to a number of institutions that funded my travel and awarded me fellowships that provided crucial time to focus on research and writing. They include Binghamton University; the National Endowment for the Humanities; the Harry Ransom Center at the University of Texas at Austin; the Seeley G. Mudd Manuscript Library at Princeton University; the Sophia Smith Collection at Smith College, and the Institute for the Study of Culture and Society at Bowling Green State University.

Patient and generous archivists and librarians are a historian's best friend and I have more to thank than I can name, but I am especially grateful to Dan Linke at Princeton University's Seeley G. Mudd Manuscript Library; Richard Workman at the University of Texas at Austin's Harry Ransom Center; Helen Fisher at the American Nudist Research Library in Kissimmee, Florida; David Klaassen at the Social Welfare History Archives at the University of Minnesota; Amy Hague at the Sophia Smith Collection at Smith College; Kausalya Padmaraj and Mary Beth Zachary at Bowling Green State University's William T. Jerome Library; and Jesslynn Shafer at Binghamton University's Glenn G. Bartle Library.

A number of scholars have put aside their own work to help me with mine—an act of supreme generosity. Years before I met my esteemed colleague Sam Walker in person, he became a dear friend. I thank him not only for his friendship, encouragement, and hilarious e-mail banter, but also for reading my work with the keen eye of *the* expert on ACLU history. In addition, Sam shared chapters from his own book, *Presidents and Civil Liberties from Wilson to Obama*—released by Cambridge University Press in 2012—and exchanged with me the joys and woes of bringing a book manuscript to completion. Claire Potter and an anonymous reviewer for Oxford University Press offered a close, critical, and encouraging reading of my work that helped me to sharpen the arguments and reduce the verbiage. Johanna Schoen, Margot Canaday, and Lynn Chancer read and commented on an early version of the proposal for this book project. (Margot also allowed my five-year-old son and me to occupy her apartment for several weeks while I worked at Princeton's Mudd Library and he went to day camp.) Frank Couvares, Andrea Friedman, David Garrow, Brian Hoffman, Catherine Jacquet, Rebecca Kluchin, Philippa Strum, David Rabban, John Semonche, Diane Sommerville, and Laura Wittern-Keller read and commented on various chapters. Paul Boyer, Don Eberley, Brett Gary, David Garrow, Brian Hoffman, Natalie E. H. Hull, Nan Levinson, Chadwick Roberts, and Sam Walker all shared materials from their own research. I thank all of you for offering me encouragement, providing insightful criticism, and helping me fix embarrassing mistakes that would have been even more so had they shown up here. I know that some errors remain, and I take full responsibility for them even as I acknowledge that the strengths of this book owe a great deal to your helpful suggestions and timely interventions.

I am also grateful to the many people who have commented on my conference presentations, invited me to speak, served as anonymous reviewers for my articles, attended my presentations, and asked probing questions that sent me back to my files. In particular, I thank John D'Emilio, Joanne Meyerowitz, George Chauncey, Andrea Friedman, Alison Parker, Carol Faulkner, Rickie Solinger, Chadwick Roberts, and Lisa Heineman. Parts of this book have appeared elsewhere or will soon, and I thank the anonymous readers for the *Journal of the History of Sexuality*—which published chapter 1 in a different form in volume 21, issue 1 (January 2012): 60–92—and also the readers for Duke University Press, which will publish a version of chapter 3 in *Sex Scene: Media and the Sexual Revolution*, a forthcoming anthology edited by Erik Schaefer.

That the book tells many undocumented stories and extends into the 1990s is due to the kindness of strangers. Many people—central players in these stories and, in some cases, their children—spoke with me in person or on the telephone, answering my questions for hours and often on more than one occasion. Many retrieved documents and photos from attics, basements, storage lockers, and old computer files, and then enlisted the help of friends, spouses, and secretaries to send them to me. ACLU records for recent decades are sealed for at least twenty years and sometimes longer, though more will be open by the time this book comes out. Without the privately held collections these individuals shared with me, this book could not have even considered the crucial issues of rape and sexual harassment that make up the final chapter. It is with heartfelt gratitude that I thank Judith and Alan Appelbaum, Jeanne Baker, Janet Benshoof, Mitchell

Bernard, Mark Blassius, Robyn Blumner, Susan Brownmiller, Thomas Coleman, Mary Coombs, Susan Deller Ross, Brenda Feigen (Fasteau), Mary Ellen Gale, Marilyn Haft, Chris Hansen, Trudy Hayden, Lawrence Herman, Nan Hunter, Wendy Kaminer, Joan E. Mahoney, Judith Mears, Michael Meyers, Aryeh Neier, Isabelle Katz Pinzler, Joseph Ronsely, Karen Sauvigne, Joel Sprayregen, Nadine Strossen, Melvin Wulf, and Linda, Lannie, and David Watts. I also thank Alexander Polikoff, Anthony Amsterdam, Barbara Babcock, Estelle Freedman, Andrew Hacker, Kathleen McCabe, Margaret Russell, Barbara Sommer, and Ruth Jane Zuckerman for corresponding with me by e-mail about various topics covered in this book.

My editor, Susan Ferber, is every author's dream. I was hooked after our first meeting and have not been disappointed. Susan has responded to distressed e-mails in the middle of the night, kept my manuscript on track even when circumstances made that difficult, and edited my prose in a way that is funny but clear and helpful. "I'm not loving this" is my favorite comment; it cracked me up, and after reading it, I wasn't loving that paragraph so much any more either. I have been well served by others at Oxford University Press, including my copy editor, Richard Isomaki, and my responsive and patient production editor, Marc Schneider.

Writing is lonely. It is also, in many ways, a stunningly selfish act that requires one to withdraw from the world for hours, days, and months at a time. Throughout the eight years that I have behaved this way, my family and friends have been supportive, patient, and nurturing. For filling my life with fun, love, encouragement, and interesting conversation, I thank Andy and Deborah Schocket, Renee and Stephen Ortiz, Lisa Yun and Rick Laremont, Wendy Wall and Andy Robertson, Roger and Mary Thibault, Pepi and Kim Levene, Diane Sommerville, Howard Brown, Liz Rosenberg, Michelle Mouton, Annette Mahoney, and Rachel Buff. I am looking forward to spending more time with all of you now that the book is done.

My friendship with Jean Quataert began only four years ago when I accepted a job at Binghamton University, but it seems as if we have already bonded over a life's worth of joys and sorrows. Thank you Jean for your candor, amazing energy, wise advice, faith in me, and, with your precious Don, for opening your arms and your hearts to my family. We love you, and we thank you for helping to bring us to this wonderful place.

At Binghamton University I have found what I've always wanted—a vibrant and productive intellectual community of fun and caring people. In addition to colleagues already mentioned, thanks to Benita Roth, Elisa Camiscioli, Kitty Sklar, Tom Dublin, Doug Bradburn, Richard Mackenney, Anne Bailey, Elizabeth Casteen, Adam Laats, and Nancy Appelbaum for making this such a delightful place to work.

Several loved ones who are very important to me slipped out of my life for a time, and I am thrilled to have them back. Years ago, my uncle, David Strome, loaned me his clarinet and showed me how to get a Ph.D.—both were crucial to my ability to do what I do today. My aunt, Nancy Miller, set a feisty example for a shy little girl, showing her how to break some rules, be strong, make things, and have fun—I draw daily on what she taught me about how to live life to the fullest. Gordon Rogers touched my young heart, stirred my soul, and reappeared in my life at a crucial moment in the writing of this book. Thank you, Gordon, for remembering me, and most of all for blessing me with your unforgettable charisma, irreverent humor, timely encouragement, unshakeable faith, sustaining friendship, and abiding love.

My mom, Shirley Hoden, and brother, Todd Wheeler, are truly two of my very best friends. They consistently cheer for me when I've accomplished the slightest little thing, console and help me recover from my miserable failures, and are always, always in my corner. Some people post the minutiae of their lives on Facebook, hoping that someone out there cares; I call my mom with my daily trivia knowing that it matters to her even when it wouldn't to anyone else. Her wise counsel and reasonable approach to life help to balance my tilt toward the dramatic. Todd has helped with this book in so many ways; he has conducted research in medical archives, diagnosed computer problems over the phone, coached me through a variety of emotional crises, and swept me away from it all to a decadent spa-resort in Maine where we dined on lobster, drank Prosecco, and ran on the beach. What a brother!

I began this project with a nursing baby. That important detail made the microfilmed records of the American Civil Liberties Union a gold mine for me, because they allowed me to get started on this project without leaving town. By the time my son Brady turned four, he was weaned, of course, and he had also developed the outgoing personality, adventuresome spirit, and remarkable self-confidence that made it possible for me to take him on the road. I thank the Northampton Montessori in Northampton, Massachusetts; Harmony School in Princeton, New Jersey; and Child's Day in Austin, Texas, for providing outstanding care for him while I worked in the archives. And I thank Brady for his loving companionship, delightful sense of humor, and amazing cooperation on these journeys. Exhausting though they were, we had lots of fun and made great memories while I did the research for this book.

Don Nieman, my husband, made all of this possible—the career, the child, the trips, the books, the happiness—and has provided constant support and love. Don does not just read my chapters over and over again. He also co-teaches jumbo U.S. history courses with me. Moreover, during the past four years he has served as such an effective dean of Harpur College of Arts and Sciences that he was just appointed provost and vice president for academic affairs at Binghamton

University. Not only that but he washes and folds laundry, grocery shops and cooks, and tells me repeatedly that this book is important. His investment in it is nearly as great as mine but far more selfless. Don is also an exemplary father who plays catch, golf, and basketball, lines up babysitters, helps with homework, and supervises play dates. Thank you, Don, for all of this and more. Most of all, thank you for always being there to catch me when I fall, for pulling me back up, and for persuading me to begin again. My goal was to be able to say to my child, "You are just like your father," and mean it as a compliment, not an insult. Happily, I have succeeded. I dedicate this book to both of you.

How Sex Became a Civil Liberty

Introduction

"What possible relevance could the Constitution have to sexual behavior?" Walter Barnett asked in the introduction to his 1973 book *Sexual Freedom and the Constitution*. As a legal scholar and longtime member of the movement for homosexual rights, Barnett had already devoted many years to composing an answer.[1] In 1973 the idea that civil liberties might include sexual behavior was still a new one. Today, just four decades later, legal scholars write about "sexual rights" and "sexual citizenship," while judges, lawyers, activists, popular media, and members of the general public treat sexual behavior as constitutionally protected. Indeed, a majority of Americans polled in 2011 acknowledged the importance of sexual rights by opposing laws against gay sex, supporting legal abortion, and condemning censorship.[2] But as late as 1973, few Americans could conceive of the possibility that the U.S. Constitution might protect sexual rights and provide for sexual citizenship. Such a possibility was even more inconceivable to Americans early in the twentieth century.

This book explains how we got from there to here—how we moved from a time when sexual behavior and even sexual expression seemed irrelevant to the U.S. Constitution, to the present, an era in which declarations of sexual civil liberties are the order of the day. Sexuality, a term both historical and contemporary, encompasses at different moments and for different people behaviors or identities related to procreation, coition, genital and erotic pleasure, and/or biological and cultural differences between women and men. Issues of sexuality became matters of civil liberties largely due to the work of the American Civil Liberties Union (ACLU), a major and stunningly successful advocacy group. The ACLU played a pivotal role in drawing the parameters of this nation's disputes over sexuality, not just by bringing carefully crafted lawsuits and presenting sharply argued legal briefs but by reaching well beyond the courtroom to lobby public officials, inspire and shape grassroots activism, assist and advise individuals in need, implement far-reaching public education campaigns, create new organizations, and build coalitions with existing ones. This study shows how, why, and with what results ACLU activists gradually adopted sexual expression, practice, and privacy as civil liberties; persuaded courts to do the same; and joined with their own state affiliates, commercial media, and other advocacy groups to promote to the broader public a civil liberties perspective on sexuality. By influencing public discourse as well as law, the ACLU helped to shape a distinctive and also polarized American sexual culture even as it contributed to the emergence of a broad consensus on the sanctity of freedom of speech and sexual privacy.

By no means did the ACLU accomplish this single-handedly. Indeed, because the ACLU addressed a full range of issues related to sexuality, it was rarely in the vanguard on any particular one. That position was generally occupied by far more specialized single-issue organizations. But, by building coalitions with other organizations and becoming a significant force behind a wide range of issues related to sexuality, the ACLU helped to frame discussion and debate in civil libertarian terms. It used the idiom of civil liberties and the Constitution to shape public and legal discourse on sexuality even as it rode the waves of broader cultural shifts.

This story starts in the early 1900s, when the individuals who would found the ACLU came of age politically and otherwise. Examining the personal values, interconnecting relationships, intimate behavior, and often profoundly gendered experiences that lay behind the choices ACLU leaders made reveals much about the compromises they negotiated and the policies they ultimately developed. Patterns in their experience reveal the workings of gender, showing how individual women and men, acting collectively, shaped major transformations in legal thought and practice with regard to sexuality. They also expose the flesh-and-bone origins of a now-iconic organization.

The so-called sexual revolutions—one in the 1910s and 1920s and the other in the 1960s and 1970s—anchor this story, but this book also implicitly questions the characterization of these revolutions as discrete historical events.[3] Individuals who helped to forge the first sexual revolution, in part through their unconventional sexual relationships, founded the ACLU and became, in many ways, an institutional hub for the sexually experimental, bohemian Left of Greenwich Village. By surviving, thriving, and gradually developing a full-blown sexual civil liberties agenda, the ACLU helped to stretch the first sexual revolution across the twentieth century, connecting it with the second in ways that we are only beginning to understand.

Individual women influenced ACLU policies and positions from the outset as founders, board members, benefactors, clients, and spouses of male leaders.[4] Women, like men, did not speak in a unified voice about how civil liberties principles should apply to birth control and intimate relationships in the 1920s and 1930s, nudism in the 1930s and 1940s, abortion and obscenity from the 1950s through the 1970s, *Playboy* and prostitution in the 1970s and 1980s, or rape and sexual harassment in the 1980s and 1990s. Some highlighted pragmatism over idealism; others worried about the racial and class implications of various feminist proposals, and still others insisted that feminist demands must bow to older civil libertarian principles. Women's voices, in all their diversity, became more plentiful as the century wore on, and the emergence of the women's rights movement bolstered the authority of all women in the ACLU.

No organization is a monolith, and the ACLU may be even less so than most, given how heavily it has relied on the contributions of genuine mavericks—strong and independent-minded volunteers who staff its boards and committees and represent its clients. An examination only of the ACLU's policy or legal arguments would miss the contested origins, negotiated nature, and contingent character of its positions, obscuring how and why, over time, ACLU leaders fit birth control information, nudism, contraceptive devices, abortion, prostitution, homosexuality, sexual harassment, rape, and many other sexual issues into a civil liberties paradigm.

The phrase *ACLU leaders* occurs frequently in this book. It should be read as a catchall term for individuals who guided and implemented the national ACLU's policies as directors, cooperating attorneys, and members of the board, staff, and various committees. In the ACLU's first decades of existence, these positions were held, overwhelmingly, by individuals who lived in New York City. Over time, as the ACLU developed a national network of affiliates, broadened its reach and membership base, and diversified its policymaking committees and executive boards, many of the individuals who occupied these positions rose to leadership in their local affiliates before being elected or appointed to a board or committee position with the national ACLU.

Unlike many histories of civil liberties, freedom of speech, and sexuality, this one is not a history of inevitability or even progress, per se. Its protagonists do not, for example, gradually recognize that the First Amendment was meant, from the beginning, to protect all expression or that the Constitution necessarily embraced sexual privacy. This story is, rather, one of contingency—of roads not taken, roads tentatively explored, and roads hacked out through uncharted territory. It shows how transformations in sexual civil liberties did not just establish greater freedom through modern rights to privacy but also how they disregarded older understandings of privacy and, in the process, hindered the establishment of new protections from unwanted sex. Rather than evaluating the work of various entities according to a particular civil liberties standard, this book considers the elasticity of civil liberties concepts and examines how the ACLU and its opponents employed the same language for very different ends. One group, for example, invoked a right to privacy to defend unfettered access to any and all sexual material, while another called on privacy rights to prevent unwanted exposure to sexual displays. Some groups relied on the First Amendment and consumer rights to legitimize their boycott of *Playboy* vendors, while others argued that such boycotts violated the First Amendment rights of *Playboy*'s consumers.

Consumer rights became profoundly important early on. Through them, ACLU leaders reinterpreted the First Amendment to protect not only the right to speak but also the right to consume speech—a stealthily executed innovation that expanded the amendment's potential beneficiaries to include not just orators, authors, publishers, and filmmakers, but *anyone* who might want to listen to a particular speech, read a particular book, subscribe to a particular magazine, or watch a particular movie. This new approach to the First Amendment also recast as censorship a number of conventionally acceptable activities and regulations, from zoning ordinances to age restrictions, from boycotts to workplace policies. Evidence that the ACLU's reinterpretation of the First Amendment changed the ways Americans think about rights—including the right to consume sexually oriented material—is plentiful in court decisions and the popular discourse employed by leaders of civic organizations, the media, and individual citizens. So well has the argument resonated with the individualistic ethos of a culture in which consumption has become a fundamental right that it has become almost an article of faith.

This is a history not merely of how sexual speech became a civil liberty but of how sexual civil liberties came to embrace conduct as well. It shows, then, how defending nudist literature and practice planted seeds that rooted protections for sexual conduct in a right to privacy as early as the 1930s. Those seeds would flower decades later when a new generation of ACLU leaders joined birth control advocates to formulate a constitutional right to privacy, one they would, in the ensuing years, stretch to include the right to use contraceptives, to perform and undergo abortions, and to engage in any and all private, adult, consensual sexual behavior. ACLU leaders did not embrace these sexual rights readily or easily. Rather, they struggled over various competing civil liberties and battled over how to prioritize them.

Regular infusions of new blood played a role in how these disputes were resolved. Activists from the civil rights and women's rights movements who entered the ACLU in growing numbers in the 1960s and 1970s profoundly altered discussions of sexual issues and influenced resulting policies and litigation strategies. By then, support for sexual and reproductive freedom came relatively easily; protection for victims of unwanted sexual expression and behavior did not. So feminist demands for a Reproductive Freedom Project and a Sexual Privacy Project dedicated to expanding rights for homosexuals gained widespread support and funding. But feminist efforts to position the ACLU behind rape law reform that would benefit the complainant met strong and effective opposition. Feminist concerns about unwanted exposure to pornography and sexual harassment also encountered resistance. When it came to sexuality, a civil liberties approach tilted toward freedom *to* and against freedom *from*.

In this and other ways, the ACLU helped to set in motion a mutually constitutive reshaping of modern sexuality and liberalism. Scholars have pondered the ways that American liberalism has erected a wall around sexual practice within the private sphere by insulating it from government intrusion. But they have also noted an associated erasure of borders between public and private such that images, messages, and behaviors once considered private increasingly saturate public culture.[5] These seemingly contradictory developments occurred simultaneously as products of the ACLU-assisted process of making sex a civil liberty.

This book does not argue or assume that full sexual rights and sexual citizenship have been achieved. Indeed, the ongoing culture wars and polarizing debates over "moral values" show that rights to sexual activity and expression remain contested. In political campaigns around the country, supporters of sex education and of gay and reproductive rights continue to line up against defenders of abstinence, heterosexual marriage, and "life." Sexuality coded as morality inflects American party politics even as it shapes a uniquely contradictory and polarized sexual culture, one characterized by buttoned-up prudery—the modesty behind many efforts to revise censorship laws—and bare-it-all prurience—the gratuitous, commodified sex that permeates the popular media and now enjoys broad First Amendment protection. The roots of these disputes over sexual issues can be found in the uneven and contested development of sexual civil liberties as they relate to two very different kinds of privacy—the constitutional construct that establishes freedom from state intrusion and the more general freedom from the intrusion of private individuals and commercial entities. Concerns about both kinds of privacy have inspired a wave of scholarship lamenting the disappearance of privacy, questioning the ascendancy of individual privacy rights over the common good, and calling for equality considerations to temper privacy rights. To the extent that sexual civil liberties rest on an understanding of privacy that values protection from the government above all, they aggravate individuals who resent it when their sexual privacy is invaded by individual citizens and commercial sources—like the "erection stimulant" advertiser who sent an unsolicited and very graphic e-mail to my inbox even as I typed this sentence.[6]

This is a story of personal experiences, contested understandings, collaborative undertakings, and turning points. It does not attempt to provide an exhaustive history of the ACLU's involvement with obscenity law, abortion rights, or any of the other sexual issues considered here. Nor is this book a traditional legal or constitutional history; it does not take a comprehensive case-by-case approach, delve deeply into evolutions in judicial interpretation, or provide a comprehensive examination of the precedents established along the way. Instead it identifies and examines key moments—some of which involved pivotal legal cases—in the development of sexual civil liberties to explain how and why the ACLU first took on particular sexual issues and how it transformed them into matters of civil liberties. It scrutinizes the organization's initial forays into defending advocates, distributors, and consumers of birth control, sex education, abortion services, nudist literature, nudism, *Playboy*, and other sexually oriented material. It also investigates ACLU leaders' growing support for homosexual rights and reproductive freedom—including freedom from coerced sterilization—as well as their positions on sexual harassment and rape law reform. It also seeks to understand why the ACLU rejected particular cases. Going well beyond litigation and legal strategies, it considers the many ways that ACLU leaders influenced the broader culture by advising individuals, engaging in direct action, endeavoring to shape public opinion, and applying behind-the-scenes pressure on private citizens and public officials.[7]

Such a sweeping yet deep and intimate study relies on a wide range of sources. The ACLU's archives contain correspondence, legal briefs, minutes, and often transcripts of entire meetings. I rely heavily on these records while keeping in mind the cautionary advice of one ACLU board member who pointed out to me that the documentary record does not always capture the personal beliefs of individual participants, some of whom played devil's advocate as a strategy for pushing colleagues to explore the outer dimensions of civil liberties questions.[8] Much of the biographical texture and substance comes from the personal papers of and oral interviews with individual ACLU leaders.

While my goal is to show how the U.S. Constitution became central to discourse on sexual expression and behavior, I also hope that this book will encourage a more critical perspective on how treating sex as a civil liberty has shaped law, policy, and the ways we think about and experience sexuality. Certainly, it has nurtured greater personal autonomy and freed individuals to make choices about the most intimate matters in their lives, including whether and when to bear children and with whom they will have sexual relations. The right to privacy has erected constitutional protections around these intimate personal choices. But in the process of constitutionalizing protections for sexual choices, the boundaries between public and private have been redrawn, advancing some forms of sexual privacy while eroding others and privileging sexual expression over freedom from unwanted sex. This has had profound and controversial consequences even as it has given rise to a hegemonic discourse that provides people who disagree on ends with a common commitment to means through freedom of speech and privacy rights. By recognizing the highly contingent and socially constructed nature of rights many now see as inevitable, absolute, and firmly grounded in the Constitution, perhaps this book will promote more civil discussion of the difficult choices inherent in determining what sexual matters are kept private and which ones enter the public world we share.

Many of the issues addressed here are deeply personal. It is fitting, then, that the book begins with a brief journey into the intimate lives of those who founded the early ACLU. The private dilemmas they faced and decisions they made would have important consequences for the organization they founded, as well as for the American law and culture they shaped.

1

"Where Else but Greenwich Village?"

Taking Sexual Liberties, 1910s–1920s

In 1921, the ACLU was only a year old. Leaders of the fledgling organization worked out of temporary offices in a four-story West Village building, quibbled over their letterhead design, and responded to victims of postwar crackdowns who turned to them in desperation. The office phone rang incessantly with callers reporting police raids of labor union meetings, courts upholding labor injunctions, judges approving the incarceration of conscientious objectors, and mobs attacking blacks, Socialists, and union organizers.[1] Busy as they were with these pressing issues, ACLU leaders did not hesitate to act when police interfered with a birth control meeting.

It was not just any birth control meeting but the crowning event of the first American Birth Control Conference, hosted by Margaret Sanger. Booked at the Town Hall, a new, privately owned structure billed as the "uptown Cooper Union," the meeting tested the venue's purpose of fostering civic participation and "free speech." But the morning after the scheduled event, ACLU leaders read, with outrage, that police had stopped the meeting and arrested the speakers, possibly at the behest of Catholic Church officials. They flew into action, offering Sanger full support, urging her to file a civil suit against municipal authorities, and exhorting the police commissioner to conduct a full investigation of the incident. By all accounts, police officers had truly misbehaved. After locking the half-empty hall so that those who had been admitted could not leave and ticket-holders outside could not enter, they arrested Sanger and another woman on charges of "disorderly conduct." Other public officials hoped the case would go away quickly; indeed, after only a few minutes, the Police Court judge released the women and dismissed all charges against them. But ACLU leaders pressed the issue. They demanded that Catholic Church officials disclose their involvement, called for an investigation into police behavior, and recommended that public officials responsible for the debacle be removed. "Until we came to her defense," recalled the ACLU's field secretary, Lucille Milner, Sanger fought for the right to speak about birth control "almost single-handed[ly]."[2]

The ACLU was created to defend opponents of war and critics of capitalism. Why then did its leaders come so readily to the aid of birth control activist Margaret Sanger just months after its founding? What sexual experiences and values did ACLU founders, who would pioneer the creation of sexual civil liberties, bring to their work? Answering these questions requires visiting the social and cultural milieu inhabited by the men and women who created and led the early ACLU. Peeking into their daily and intimate lives reveals the profoundly gendered personal relations and politics from which the organization emerged and highlights some of the contingencies that gave rise to sexual civil liberties early in the twentieth century.[3]

Long before they founded the ACLU, Crystal Eastman, Roger Baldwin, his wife Madeleine Zabriskie Doty, and others who shaped the ACLU's first policies on matters related to sexuality participated in the sexual experimentation that characterized Greenwich Village's bohemian culture in the early twentieth century. As their lives show, the rapidly changing cultural environment opened new opportunities for sexual expression even as it sustained sharply gendered differences in experience.

Catherine Crystal Eastman was born in 1881 into a family steeped in the ideals of nineteenth-century reform. Her parents, Annis Ford and Samuel Eastman, both Congregationalist ministers, lived in Glenora, New York, with their daughter and three sons. In a bout with scarlet fever in 1884, Eastman lost her eldest brother and suffered permanent damage to her own health. By 1889, the family moved to Elmira, New York, where Eastman's parents replaced Thomas Beecher as pastors of Park Church. The Eastmans were less prominent than the church's longtime minister—brother of novelist Harriet Beecher Stowe, educator Catharine Beecher, and clergyman Henry Ward Beecher—but their abolitionist roots and embrace of women's rights assured that their pastorate would continue the Beecher family tradition. This unconventional and intellectually vibrant community imbued Eastman with a commitment to individual freedom and a determination to chart her own course in life. After earning her B.A. at Vassar College, she moved to Greenwich Village to attend New York University Law School, one of the few to admit women. Despite, however, graduating second in the class of 1907, she found herself unable to find work as an attorney.[4]

Eastman's friend and roommate, Madeleine Zabriskie Doty, also endured frustrating personal and professional setbacks. Born in 1877, Doty and her brothers grew up moving back and forth between the New Jersey countryside to please her father Sam, and New York City, which better suited her mother Lottie.

Luxurious dolls, silk stockings, a pony, indulgent governesses, European tours, and long summers in Saratoga Springs left Doty with memories of a princess-like childhood. When, as a teenager, Doty watched her family's export business in cheese and butter decline and her beloved mother become addicted to alcohol and stimulants, she developed chronic digestive problems that would plague her throughout adulthood. But intellectual ambitions and feminist aspirations prevented Doty, like Eastman, from surrendering to her physical ailments.[5]

By 1892, Doty's parents were forced by financial circumstances to sell the family home and move into an apartment in New York City. "I was 15 but still an innocent," Doty recalled before explaining, "I didn't know how babies came into this world." Four years later, as a student at Smith College, Doty would begin to shed that innocence when a man accosted her and two friends while they picnicked in the countryside. Naive and trusting, Doty did not feel endangered until her friends chased the man away and explained to her what he wanted. Infuriated but chastened, Doty developed a more cautious and defensive posture toward men, one that constrained her relations with them even as it enhanced her sense of identity and intimacy with other women. Throughout her college years, Doty hung a sign over her door that announced, "Man delights not me." Like many of her classmates, Doty developed crushes on women, including a particularly intense and long-lived infatuation with Harriet Seelye, daughter of the college's president. After Seelye married, Doty decided to attend NYU Law School.[6]

By fits and starts, Doty became enamored of the bohemian culture of the Village, though she was initially unsettled by the mixed-sex gatherings in which women smoked, booze flowed, and sexual overtures were casual and common. After meeting one particular woman who possessed "a weird, magnetic fascination" for her, Doty wrote, "I try to keep away, but I feel myself drawn toward her. I think I am beginning to understand more about physical attraction." But, she continued, "this knowledge makes me sick." Doty resisted when the seductive woman tried to kiss her, repelled, admittedly, mostly by the smell of liquor on her breath. Several months later, Doty ended a brief relationship with a fellow law student, a man who held her hand a little too long, gazed into her eyes a little too intensely, and trembled with desire a little too perceptibly. Noting that she "had no corresponding emotion" toward him, she sent him on his way, insisting later to her brother, "I *do* like men." The note of defensiveness might have been prompted by what Doty wrote next. As a law student she had finally learned about "the relation between men and women, the meaning of sex. I had learned about the misuse of sex and the impure relation that can exist between women. I was appalled and upset." After that discovery, Doty took care to redirect her romantic interests rather deliberately toward men.[7]

Following graduation in 1902, Doty secured an unpaid apprenticeship with a law firm, but illness and the ongoing deterioration of her father's business forced her to find paid work as a teacher. Three years later, she passed the New York bar exam and, with two female friends, set up Ashley, Pope, and Doty, Attorneys and Counselors at Law. When their Fifth Avenue office failed to attract the wealthy society women they sought, they found themselves looking for work once again.[8]

Doty and Eastman met at Greenwich House, a new settlement house that offered each of them part-time employment, networking opportunities in local reform circles, intellectual stimulation, and an opportunity to help the less fortunate tenement dwellers of the Village. The women were among the first wave of middle-class radicals whose unconventional tastes and aspirations would transform the area from a low-rent, working-class ghetto of immigrants, racial minorities, and factories to a trendy enclave of artists and intellectuals. Ironically, even as Doty, Eastman, and their peers flocked to the area for its cheap rents and opportunities to rub elbows with people unlike themselves, they helped to turn the Village into an exclusive plot of prime real estate.[9]

While Doty and Eastman tried to cobble together careers, they became roommates in 1906. Doty enjoyed an amusing and fabulously successful effort to get a job when she persuaded the *New York Times* to hire her as a freelance book reviewer by agreeing to write under a masculine name, Otis Notman (which "really meant 'O tis not man,'" she confided with glee). Still struggling to cover the rent, the two women invited Doty's law school friend, Ida Rauh, to move in. Their apartment became one of the first Village salons, a meeting space for labor activists, social reformers, and feminists, among them suffragist Inez Milholland, social reformer and journalist Paul Kellogg, Greenwich House founder Mary Simkhovitch, philosopher John Dewey, and Eastman's brother and *The Masses* editor Max Eastman.[10]

During the year Doty lived with Crystal Eastman, she began what would become a long, painful struggle to reconcile her sexual desires, emotional needs, spiritual values, and feminist politics.

Doty met noted novelist and muckraker David Graham Phillips when she interviewed him in 1906 for one of her book reviews. Her encounter with this "extraordinarily good looking" man initiated an alternately traumatic and exhilarating relationship of frustrated mutual attraction. Enchanting dinners, extended conversations, and vigorous outings soon became exhausting tug-of-war games as Phillips chided Doty for not doing "what we both want" and Doty fought hard against her own desires. Phillips did not want to marry; that was clear. Either ignorant of birth control, unable to acquire it, or unwilling to use it, Doty concluded that, under those circumstances, she must not yield to Phillips's advances unless she was "ready to have an illegitimate child." After one particularly difficult evening with Phillips, Doty wrote: "We nearly wrecked each other. One night when I was alone in my flat he remained until 3 a.m., without the ultimate union." In the spring of 1908, the two decided to end the relationship, but Phillips had the last word. "What you want is a husband and a flat and a family," he wrote, and I have "a horror of bonds and burdens."[11]

Doty fled with a friend to Europe, returning four months later to try unsuccessfully to reopen her law office, only to find herself incapacitated by colitis. Attributing her digestive ailments to emotional problems, feelings of helplessness, and sexual tensions, she realized that she could have neither Phillips nor a legal career. With great relief and gratitude, she accepted her father's offer to subsidize her stay in a rest home for Smith alumnae. There she read Havelock Ellis's four volumes on sex as well as August Forel's *Sex and Psychology*, all without finding solutions to her inner turmoil. But her life began to pivot after her first appointment with the renowned Boston internist Dr. Richard Cabot, who advised her to turn her attentions outward toward the needs of others rather than obsessing about her own. In 1910, she found meaningful employment working with the New York Health Department and Child Welfare Committee. Her job—traveling the country to collect comparative data on juvenile delinquency—occasioned her first meeting with Judge Ben Lindsey, leader in the children's court movement, and Roger Baldwin, a charming and "very attractive young man."[12]

Meanwhile, she reconnected with Phillips and, feeling more independent and sure of herself at thirty-two than she had earlier, she harbored a faint hope. Perhaps his forty-four years, graying temples, stiffening joints, and deepening wrinkles would change his attitude toward marriage. Or maybe he would appreciate the changes in her, including the inner peace she had obtained by devoting herself to the needs of children, and would consider making a commitment. On a cold January day in 1911, Doty was staffing the first Child Welfare Exhibit at the U.S. Armory in New York City and looking forward to Phillips's visit later that day when she glimpsed her father hurrying toward her. She wondered at his obvious distress and the newspaper clutched tightly to his chest but soon discovered the cause. Phillips had been shot six times, the victim of an insane man with a gun. He died before Doty could reach him.[13]

Widowed by the death of a dream if not a spouse, Doty coped by throwing herself into work with the Children's Court Committee of the Russell Sage Foundation and abandoning many of the inhibitions that had so troubled her relationship with Phillips. She became involved with a married man. His name goes unmentioned in her unpublished autobiography, but it was almost certainly Hugh Cabot, brother of Richard Cabot, the physician who had prescribed service to others as a remedy for Doty's stomach complaints.[14] The thirty-nine-year-old Cabot had just assumed leadership of the new Massachusetts General Hospital genitourinary surgery unit when his brother introduced him to Doty. After diagnosing her with an acute case of appendicitis, Hugh operated on her, and they began to develop a close personal relationship during his long daily visits to her hospital room and monthly calls after she returned home to New York City. They started "something that should never have been," Doty noted decades later. Hugh Cabot was no genteel intellectual, no graceful linguist, no tall, dark-haired athlete—in other words, no David Graham Phillips. Nor did he resemble his saintly older brother, Richard. Hugh Cabot was "a *he* man," a balding, strong-featured, coarse and blunt-spoken man of science. He was, in Doty's reflections, her opposite. But his attentions delighted her, and she marveled at the thrill she felt when he tried to dominate and also protect her.[15]

Eventually, the two decided that Doty would visit Cabot's home for ten days and the two would confess their love to Cabot's wife, Mary Anderson Boit Cabot, and ask for her forbearance. Doty reassured Mary that she did not want to steal, only to share her husband—only to enjoy "a little of his love"—but the meeting did not go well. Devastated, Mary turned frantically to Doty, sobbing that Cabot gave Doty "all the things he never gave me"—his confidence, respect, friendship, and affection. Mary Cabot refused to accept the triangular love affair. Hugh Cabot feared for his thriving career, knowing that his relationship with Doty could jeopardize it, bring scandal to his prominent family, tarnish Doty's reputation, and ultimately make ugly what had seemed beautiful, uplifting, and precious. Doty and Cabot agreed to end their relationship. They would continue to correspond sporadically until 1920 but would see each other only once more.[16]

Doty destroyed most of Cabot's letters and dedicated herself to investigating prisons and reformatories. By 1913, she had become an official New York State prison commissioner, an unpaid position that, nonetheless, granted her an impressive amount of freedom and influence. Suspecting that no one could understand prison life without experiencing it firsthand, she and a friend obtained permission to go undercover as convicted criminals. As a prison inmate, she again encountered "lady lovers," but explained their behavior as "perverted love" aroused by the suppression of normal sexual outlets. The report Doty wrote after spending a week of incarceration as "Maggie Martin #933" in the State Prison for Women in Auburn exposed inhumane aspects of prison life, galvanized the public, and propelled Doty into intensive reform work on behalf of prisoners and probationers. The outbreak of war, however, redirected her energies toward peace, drawing her in 1915 to The Hague for the international conference of women for peace. Her thirst for understanding, hunger for an end to the carnage, and eagerness for adventure led her, first, behind German lines, where she engaged in reporting equivalent to espionage and, later, to Russia, where she witnessed the first days of the Bolshevik regime. Back on board a ship bound for home in 1918, fears of submarine attack kept the excitement at a fever pitch that morphed into erotic exploration when a male war correspondent, just back from the front, approached Doty, "pressed close and asked for something more than talk." Tempted, feeling the "weakness of desire," Doty nevertheless resisted what she called "the evil in both of us, lust without love."[17] Meanwhile, her deepening pacifist activism set her on course to reconnect with Roger Baldwin.

Doty's departure from the Greenwich Village apartment caused Eastman no hardship; the perfect roommate situation had lost its luster long ago. Doty's determination to avoid romantic entanglements with women may have led her to erect an emotional barrier that chilled the friendship. Meanwhile, Eastman accepted a short-term job to investigate industrial accidents for what would become a model of sociological research in the service of legal reform, the famous Pittsburgh Survey. Within a year, she accepted an appointment to New York's Wainwright Commission to perform similar studies and make legislative recommendations. The work proved extraordinarily satisfying until a workmen's compensation law based on it was struck down by the New York Supreme Court in 1911, one day before fire broke out at the Triangle Shirt-Waist factory only blocks from her apartment. Locked doors and inadequate fire escapes—the very abuses that workmen's compensation laws were designed to discourage and remedy—produced an inferno that took the lives of 146 workers, most of them women. Eastman was devastated. She and Doty had provided free legal advice to many of the victims when they were arrested for striking just two years earlier. Her faith in law, the state, and reform was shaken to the core, and a month later, she married.[18]

Like Doty, Eastman wrestled with her own sexual desires. Her biographer calls her a "woman-identified woman" but does so less because she expressed sexual or romantic interest in other women than because she "delighted" in their company and oriented her life and work toward their needs. Some historians have also speculated that Eastman and her brother Max shared a strong incestuous attraction to each other. But more generalized sexual cravings seemed to trouble Eastman, leading her to consult popular Freudian psychoanalyst Dr. A. A. Brill in hopes that he could help bring her "libido" down. While Doty tried premarital celibacy, then an affair with a married man, Eastman opted for marriage, first to Wallace Benedict, an insurance agent from Milwaukee, Wisconsin. Where Brill failed, marriage seems to have succeeded. Eastman later recommended that married couples live separately, in part to preserve the erotic desire destroyed by shared domesticity.[19]

Disillusionment and preoccupation with personal issues did not remove Eastman from the field of reform for long. During her honeymoon in Europe, she became involved in the international woman suffrage movement and returned to her husband's home in Wisconsin to lead the fight for suffrage there.

Undeterred by the 1912 defeat of suffrage in Wisconsin but fearful of being trapped in the Midwest, Eastman persuaded Benedict to move to New York. There she collaborated with Alice Paul, Lucy Burns, and other feminists to establish the Congressional Union for Woman Suffrage, predecessor to the National Woman's Party. The outbreak of war in Europe in 1914 returned her to international concerns, temporarily strengthening her ties with Progressive reformers around the country as they mobilized for peace amid shared horror at European bloodshed and American preparations to join it. Indefatigable despite ongoing medical complaints and a faltering marriage, Eastman collaborated with Lillian Wald, Paul Kellogg, and others to found and lead the American Union Against Militarism (AUAM) in 1914 and the New York branch of the Women's Peace Party in 1915.[20] It was as director of the AUAM that Eastman met Roger Baldwin, the man with whom she would launch the American Civil Liberties Union.

Born in 1884 to newlyweds Frank Fenno and Lucy Cushing Baldwin, Roger Baldwin grew up in a fashionable Boston suburb, the son of a leather merchant and eldest of seven children. Generations of wealth and a family tree laced with Mayflower Pilgrims secured the Baldwins' status among the "better" sort. Unitarians for generations, the family was also respectably nonconformist. Baldwin described his childhood home as a "happy place" where he learned to love nature, appreciate art, and value people of different races, ethnicities, and religious convictions. Despite the family's prominence and rank, Baldwin insisted that his father "had no sense of social superiority," as indicated by his Jewish best friend, Negro houseguests, and well-treated Catholic servants. "A kind of feminis[m]" might be noted in his mother's support for woman suffrage, but it seems to have made little impression on the family's internal dynamics. Baldwin's mother—"quiet," "self-effacing," and "compliant"—supervised the domestic realm, while his entrepreneurial father "exuded authority," functioned as the ultimate "boss," and left his children "fearful of crossing him."[21] Like Doty, Baldwin grew up with every privilege and luxury, but in his case, family finances remained secure.

Years before Eastman and Doty wrestled with their own sexual desires, Baldwin indulged his. At the young age of only twelve or thirteen, he began a sexual affair with an Irish servant employed by his family, probably Mary Crowley, listed on the 1900 census as Baldwin's senior by five years. "She seduced me," he insisted, after seeing him taking a bath and observing that he was "ready for business." Adjoining bedrooms on the top floor facilitated their activities. In an effort to explain the liaison, Baldwin recalled that "she was pretty enough," but "I don't think I was making such distinctions." Despite two to three years of regular sexual contact, Baldwin remembered their relationship as without "emotion, a purely physical thing." Although it was a first for him, Baldwin boasted that he knew "everything that was to be known, even how to prevent getting her pregnant." His encounters with Crowley took place "right under the nose" of his parents, though he averred that perhaps it was "a mistake to put boys up in the attic with the maids."[22]

In many ways, Baldwin did exactly what was expected of him. He attended Harvard, earned high grades, sharpened his social skills, refined his connections, and capped his graduation with a yearlong tour around Europe where he visited famous sites, studied Italian, and caroused with friends. On his twenty-second birthday, Baldwin joined several other men in what sounds, to all intents and purposes, like a sexual orgy with a "professional lady." As a college student, Baldwin had denounced men who patronized prostitutes, though he acknowledged the problem of finding sexual partners, because "at that time nice girls wouldn't go to bed with you." What made this sex-for-hire encounter different—that it was a group experience, part of a European adventure, a requirement of masculine heterosexuality?[23] Baldwin left the question unanswered, but in contrast to his female peers, he was not haunted by fears that an evening of illicit sexual pleasure could derail his life or his career.

Shortly after returning from Europe, Baldwin began casting about for a job that would take him away from Boston. His decision to leave the area was motivated by advice from Louis Brandeis, an attorney at his father's firm, but also by disturbing developments on the home front. Baldwin Sr. was involved in an affair with his own niece. Baldwin learned of it from his mother, who tearfully showed him a letter from her niece confirming the affair. Deeply disturbed, Baldwin confronted not his father but his cousin, begging her to end the relationship "for the sake of the children" and the family. But the affair continued, only to be followed by another. This time, Baldwin Sr. moved in with his lover, while at the same time pursuing a sexual relationship with yet another woman and, simultaneously, her daughter. Baldwin's parents lived apart for the rest of their lives but, to avoid scandal and keep up "appearances," they did not divorce. In fact, Baldwin Sr. remained a "gentleman," visiting his wife, flowers in hand, as late as 1943. Angry on behalf of his beloved mother, Baldwin refused to speak to his father and developed for a time what he called a "certain horror of adultery." The unpleasant family drama also deepened his desire to strike out on his own.[24]

Thanks to his extensive social networks and a Harvard degree, Baldwin received a number of attractive job offers and eventually accepted positions as a sociology instructor at Washington University and a settlement house director at Self-Culture Hall in St. Louis, Missouri. Before departing, he consulted with Lillian Wald, founder and director of the Henry Street Settlement, beginning a professional relationship that would later pave his way back to the East Coast and propel him into civil liberties work. Between 1906 and 1917, Baldwin joined a wide array of Progressive reform projects in the "rather shabby, mediocre town" that had become his home. Many of these reforms relied on expanding the reach and power of government agencies. As director of Self-Culture Hall, Baldwin created educational and social programs for a crowded, conflict-ridden neighborhood of poor immigrants, including Catholics from Ireland and Jews from eastern Europe. A forty-minute trolley ride took Baldwin from the unpaved streets, high-rise tenements, and rampant juvenile delinquency associated with his job on the East Side, across the Mississippi River, to the courtyards, stone edifices, and privileged students he taught at Washington University. Frequent trips to juvenile court with boys from his neighborhood persuaded him to add supervision of young probationers to his job description. Within a year he was appointed chief probation officer of the Juvenile Court and stitched together a state-sponsored mantle of protection that brought local government into the daily lives of children and their families.[25]

Reform work did not deprive Baldwin of an active social life among St. Louis's rich and famous. Evenings one might find him in black tie, hurrying to a debutante party or pursuing Anna Louise Strong, a visiting social worker and consultant on child labor issues. Strong, who had earned her Ph.D. from the University of Chicago, was fast on her way to becoming a radical Socialist. She had recently extricated herself from a painful relationship with a married man and arrived in St. Louis wary of men but eager for romance. It was not long before she met and fell for the dashing and eligible Baldwin. The attraction was mutual. The two shared a commitment to helping young people, fighting poverty and injustice, and leading unconventional domestic lives. They soon embarked on what would become a tempestuous engagement, with Baldwin urging Strong toward ever greater physical intimacy and Strong resisting and demanding that Baldwin give up cigarettes and alcohol. Behind the scenes, Strong's father, Sydney Dix Strong, a Congregational minister, objected to the relationship for the simple reason that Baldwin was not a Christian. In the end, Strong's and Baldwin's differences over morals and personal freedom proved irreconcilable. "I loved her," Baldwin recalled later, "but I loved my independence more."[26]

Baldwin soon set his romantic sights on Ann Drew, daughter of a prominent local bank president, officer in the Women's Trade Union League, suffragist, and activist in the Catholic Church. For several years the two met in the Drew family drawing room, where they talked, read poetry and literature, danced, and fell in love. The local scandal sheet endorsed the match, describing "Roger and Annie" as "well suited in their tastes and ideas," and noting that "both are blessed with plenty of this world's goods." But Drew's father would not approve of marriage between his daughter and a non-Catholic, and the Unitarian-agnostic Baldwin refused to convert.[27]

Figure 1.1 Roger Baldwin at Washington University in St. Louis, 1906. (Courtesy, Princeton University Library)

Romantic pursuits and disappointments did not hinder Baldwin's professional success or damage his social status. Through his juvenile court work, Baldwin gained a national reputation among social workers, including Jane Addams and Florence Kelley, who nominated him for a position with the National Consumers' League. He declined this and other attractive job offers to become, in 1910, the executive secretary of the city's most effective reform group, the St. Louis Civic League. The post allowed him to shape a new charter for the city, one that included basic Progressive reforms such as the initiative, referendum, and recall.[28] It also solidified his position as a respected civic leader.

Roger Baldwin was no radical, but he became increasingly interested in radical issues, even as he hobnobbed with the local elite and collaborated with other social workers and reformers. After hearing the notorious anarchist and leader of the Free Speech League Emma Goldman speak in St. Louis around 1909, Baldwin was so impressed with her that he committed to obtaining public space for her lectures and invitations for her to speak at private ladies clubs. It was Goldman who began to reorient Baldwin's attitude toward the state. Whereas much of his career had involved using the state to achieve social reform, Goldman considered the state a tool of coercion and repression—an entity that persecuted its opponents, repressed labor, prohibited birth control, and punished sexual nonconformists. Even as Baldwin grew increasingly enamored of Goldman and intrigued by her free love agenda, he became disillusioned with democracy. A group of citizens, using reforms he had established through the new city charter, initiated a law that would segregate housing in St. Louis by race. The city council would not have approved such a law, but the democratic majority passed it handily, oppressing a vulnerable minority and throwing Baldwin's democratic ideals into question. When the federal courts declared St. Louis's efforts to segregate unconstitutional, Baldwin concluded that perhaps judicial review was the proper check on the tyranny of the majority. But Goldman's anarchy also offered a solution, one that inspired Baldwin's emerging libertarianism and his goal of "a society with a minimum of compulsion, a maximum of individual freedom and of voluntary association, and the abolition of exploitation and poverty." These early encounters in St. Louis would provide Baldwin and Goldman with the foundation for what would become a lifelong correspondence and friendship.[29]

In January 1916, Baldwin received a circular sent by Sanger to "Friends and Comrades" urging them to assist her as she faced prosecution for publishing articles on birth control in the *Woman Rebel*. Exhorting her readers to help "raise the entire question of birth control out of the gutter of obscenity and into the light of human understanding," Sanger suggested they write to the judge assigned to her case, organize protest meetings, and send moral and financial support. "I am thoroughly with you in this cause," Baldwin wrote Sanger, and although he questioned the "propriety" of contacting a judge during an ongoing trial, he agreed to "take a chance in a case like this." Hundreds of others followed suit and by the end of February, Judge Henry D. Clayton dismissed the charges against Sanger, who then launched a massive speaking tour across the middle and western states.[30]

Baldwin bristled when he read the morning edition of the *St. Louis Globe-Democrat* and learned that Sanger had been barred from fulfilling her scheduled speaking engagement at a privately owned hall in downtown St. Louis. As a civic leader and "guardian of good government," Baldwin felt duty-bound to defend Sanger's right to speak. He asked Sanger to join him in holding a meeting to protest police interference with Sanger's lecture. Amid a throng of thousands arrayed on the street, Baldwin signaled for silence and introduced Sanger in front of a locked theater. Rather than relying on the police to quiet her, Sanger's organized Catholic opponents had persuaded the theater owner to close down and leave town. The entire meeting took only three minutes; the police behaved; no one was injured. Nonetheless, it marked the last banning of a birth control meeting in St. Louis and prompted a local newspaper to announce that "To throttle free speech is to give it a megaphone," and led the St. Louis Men's City Club and the Women's Town Club to invite Sanger to speak to their members. Even more important, the brief assembly on behalf of Sanger marked the first of many free speech meetings hosted by Baldwin and the beginning of his efforts to apply civil liberties guarantees to birth control.[31]

Energized by his effective defense of Sanger, Baldwin was nonetheless becoming disillusioned by reform in St. Louis as citizens continued to turn Progressive tools toward antidemocratic ends. The war in Europe brought additional sources of disenchantment as well as new job opportunities. After rejecting a number of offers from organizations devoted to the Allied cause, Baldwin connected with the American Union Against Militarism (AUAM), the organization Crystal Eastman had helped to create in 1915, after the Great War broke out in Europe.

The AUAM's goal was to protest compulsory military training, conscription, and other efforts to prepare for war. Under the leadership of such prominent reformers as Henry Street Settlement founder Lillian Wald, editor of *The Survey* Paul Kellogg, Crystal and Max Eastman, and Hull House founder Jane Addams, the AUAM issued masses of propaganda, held public lectures, staged spectacular parades, lobbied congressmen and President Wilson, and, with a determination that ultimately proved its undoing, refused to prepare for war. Baldwin feared that male pacifists would feel alienated by the AUAM's close association with women's organizations and strategies and urged it to develop a distinctively masculine antiwar sentiment. AUAM leaders, including Baldwin's old friends Wald and Addams, remained committed to their gender-neutral, gender-inclusive organization and approach, but they appreciated Baldwin's ambition and ingenuity and invited him to lead the AUAM during Eastman's maternity leave. Momentarily free of romantic entanglements and eager to return to the radical pacifist communities of the East Coast, Baldwin jumped at the opportunity. During his first year in New York City, the United States declared war on Germany and the AUAM collapsed when its leaders could not agree on a wartime agenda. Some wanted to endorse the Allies and use the government's expanding powers to accomplish their own reform goals. Others, including Eastman and Baldwin, continued to oppose war altogether. They had grown skeptical of the state and its increasingly repressive apparatus.[32]

In the wake of the AUAM's demise, Baldwin and Eastman created a Civil Liberties Bureau to aid conscientious objectors and defend American liberties. Their activities smacked of treason in a time of war, and Baldwin suffered a Justice Department raid on his office, followed by arrest and incarceration for refusing to comply with the conscription law. Eastman escaped imprisonment but emerged from the war branded a radical and blacklisted by the FBI.[33] Eastman, Baldwin, and others who branched off to found the National Civil Liberties Bureau (NCLB)—soon to be reorganized as the American Civil Liberties Union (ACLU)—entered the 1920s with special cause to distrust state and federal power. Within their wartime experiences lay seeds of their emerging civil libertarianism.[34]

If the federal government suspended many civil liberties when it entered World War I, it threatened to destroy them at war's end. The Supreme Court upheld wartime convictions of antiwar protesters like Eugene Debs, who was imprisoned for denouncing the draft and encouraging young men to resist it. Meanwhile, the triumph of the Bolshevik Revolution inspired a full-blown Red Scare that left American Communists and ideological leftists of all stripes more vulnerable than ever. When, in addition, postwar economic instability triggered an unparalleled wave of protests by laborers, domestic terrorists, and political radicals, federal authorities targeted radicals across the country for arrest, incarceration, and deportation. Race riots and the revival of the Ku Klux Klan added to the chaos.[35] After ACLU leaders defended draft dodgers, antiwar activists, and others caught in the web of sedition laws, they began to address new and ongoing encroachments on civil liberties, bringing Progressive values to civil libertarianism and transforming reigning interpretations of the U.S. Constitution.[36]

ACLU founders located their headquarters in Greenwich Village, just blocks from Mabel Dodge's salon, the Provincetown Playhouse, and the Liberal Club at Polly's, famous Village haunts where leftist scholars, political radicals, and avant-garde artists met for mutual inspiration and intellectual exchange. The Village community included writers who deemed their work art, artists who married their fauve painting to anarchism, anarchists who embraced birth control and free love, birth controllers and free lovers who identified with Socialism, and Socialists who championed free speech. Such a heady time and place as Greenwich Village in the twenties attracted the attention of moral censors who brought charges of obscenity against Village authors, performers, painters, publishers, and sex radicals. At the same time, political radicals, critics of the government, and labor leaders in the Village, as elsewhere, suffered increased state repression. Support for freedom of speech forged bonds of sympathy and grounds for collaboration among them, linking otherwise disparate groups in common cause. Indeed, early ACLU meetings at the Civic Club on West Twelfth Street brought together an impressively eclectic group—religious leaders, labor activists, attorneys, social workers, authors, and artists—all committed to expanding freedom of speech on "matters of public concern."[37]

The ACLU's odyssey into the realm of sexual expression began with birth control, a controversial practice that occupied a dubious legal status in the United States of the 1920s. Federal obscenity law forbade circulating information about birth control by mail. Twenty-four states criminalized selling or advertising contraceptives. Connecticut went so far as to make it illegal to *use* birth control. Many individuals escaped or defied the law by selling condoms to prevent disease, marketing pessaries to support a prolapsed uterus, and simply peddling a variety of over-the-counter, under-the-table, or homemade items to reduce the chances of conception.[38]

From the ACLU's earliest days, leaders protested church and state disruption of birth control meetings and harassment of birth control advocates in New York City. They were especially incensed when Sanger, a central figure in the cultural and intellectual life of Greenwich Village, was silenced by police at the first American Birth Control Conference at the Town Hall in 1921, and they urged her to let them sue the police on her behalf. Sanger, however, engaged her own attorney and declined to file suit after police allowed her to hold another meeting at a larger venue that attracted thousands of people and raised thousands of dollars. In the meantime, the ACLU remained actively involved in the investigation it helped to initiate, attending the hearings, recruiting and advising witnesses, and protesting when the hearings became, in the hands of investigators, yet another tool to intimidate birth control activists. Throughout, ACLU leaders maintained that they had no particular interest in birth control, but wanted to protect the rights of assembly and free speech. They celebrated the conclusion of the hearings which, although it brought no formal reprimands or removals from office, nonetheless condemned the actions of the police and vindicated birth control activists.[39]

The ACLU then worked to open more public venues to birth control advocates. When, in 1922, trustees denied birth control activists use of Cooper Union, the central Greenwich Village meeting place popularly associated with the exercise of free speech, ACLU counsel Albert DeSilver protested, appealing directly to individual trustees and sharing his correspondence with the press. "A great social question like birth control," DeSilver declared, "should be fully and freely discussed." The ACLU threatened legal action and arranged another birth control meeting that included ACLU attorney Arthur Garfield Hays a year later when the mayor of Albany, New York, prevented Sanger from addressing a meeting of birth control activists. When the Syracuse City Council banned discussion of birth control in 1924, Sanger turned immediately to the ACLU, which distributed press releases and letters to Mayor John H. Walrath. Within a week, Walrath vetoed the new ordinance in a ringing affirmation of rights to free speech and assembly that buoyed the ACLU's reputation among birth control activists.[40]

After their victories in New York state, ACLU leaders initiated efforts in Boston, where Mayor James Curley prohibited public advocacy of birth control. Baldwin confessed to taking "a sort of personal delight in baiting the [New England] censors with test cases."[41] Indeed, since 1923, ACLU leaders had struggled to find a local organization to host Sanger at a Boston public birth control meeting, offering to coordinate the event, cover all related legal expenses, and provide the entertainment. Baldwin maintained that the ACLU could not

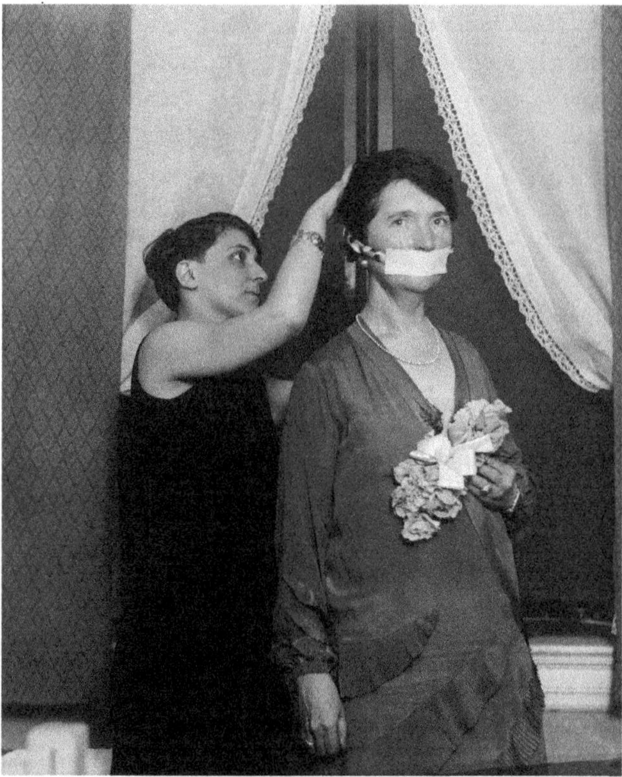

Figure 1.2 Margaret Sanger dramatizes the relationship between laws against birth control and censorship, Boston, Massachusetts, April 17, 1929. (Courtesy, ©Bettmann/ CORBIS)

publicly sponsor such a meeting, because civil liberties activists "cannot appear as the prime movers" in these cases. "Our business is to help those whose rights are attacked," he insisted, not to advocate any particular cause. Behind the scenes, though, ACLU leaders *were* the prime movers, as indicated by their dogged efforts to find a sponsor for a birth control meeting in Boston. Baldwin's requests for active partners to host the meeting became pleas for little more than names and bodies as he pared his requirements down to a bare minimum: "a good presiding officer, a group of people to sit on the platform, and a committee to sign the speaking arrangements." ACLU leaders would handle everything else, but they needed birth control activists "on the ground," Bostonians willing at least to *appear* to lead the meeting. One individual agreed to host the meeting in a private space "without any fuss," but Baldwin insisted that it take place in a public hall in order to confront the mayor directly by meeting in a venue under his control. In February 1925, a frustrated Baldwin finally traveled to Boston to arrange the meeting himself.[42]

Unwilling to associate himself publicly with the birth control movement and unable to secure a public meeting hall, Baldwin settled for a "Free Speech Meeting" in the Old South Meeting House, a private building that had served as a staging ground for such crucial historical events as the Boston Tea Party. This compromise signaled a victory for Mayor Curley, who had intimidated local activists and managers of public buildings. Still, the mayor seethed over the affront to his authority represented by the ACLU's meeting, and he issued a public statement skewering the ACLU as a "pestilent aggregation of parlor Bolshevists... engaged in the playful pastime of destroying society." The mayor was joined by leaders of the Veterans of Foreign Wars, who condemned Baldwin for resisting military service during the war and urging women to become "slackers" by refusing to "give birth to children." ACLU leaders accused Mayor Curley of violating the First Amendment and failing to maintain separation between church and state because he allowed birth control opponents to hold public meetings but denied that right to proponents. Hoping to annoy Curley further, ACLU leaders also announced their intention to defend the rights of the anti-Catholic Ku Klux Klan to meet in public spaces, but they made no attempt to collaborate with the KKK or to construct a test case of its activities. Indeed, even as ACLU leaders encouraged birth control meetings, they denounced the KKK.[43]

The aggravations Baldwin experienced in his efforts to organize birth control gatherings in Boston stemmed in part from the fact that activists in the birth control and civil liberties movements brought different goals and strategies to their work. Whereas birth control activists were content to hold private meetings for the benefit of their own members, ACLU leaders preferred to test the reach of the First Amendment by holding public meetings, provoking arrests, challenging censorious municipal authorities, and, if necessary, filing lawsuits. To bring suit, one must demonstrate standing to sue by showing harm, so ACLU leaders could not take legal action without the cooperation of birth control activists whose rights had been violated. ACLU leaders offered legal assistance, but because Sanger and her colleagues retained their own attorneys, the ACLU was limited to registering protests with public officials and the press, observing procedures and offering advice, recruiting supporters, organizing meetings, and, perhaps most important of all, repeatedly framing the issue as one of constitutional rights. The question was not, ACLU leaders insisted, whether birth control was a social good or a social evil but whether prohibitions on advocating it violated rights of assembly and freedom of speech.[44]

In 1923 the ACLU intervened on behalf of Carlo Tresca after he was arrested for sending obscenity through the mail. Tresca, a popular Village personality and the lover of board member Elizabeth Gurley Flynn, had mailed copies of his Italian anarchist newspaper, *Il Martello,* which included a two-line advertisement for a book about birth control methods. ACLU leaders denounced the obscenity charges against Tresca as a trumped-up pretext for harassing a political radical and issued a press release proclaiming his innocence. Failing to save Tresca from conviction, they applied for and obtained a presidential commutation of his sentence.[45]

The ACLU's birth control activism faded briefly in 1926 due to developments in the cases of Niccola Sacco and Bartolomeo Vanzetti, immigrant anarchists charged with murder. ACLU leaders' interest stemmed from their own personal connections, through Flynn and Tresca, to Sacco and Vanzetti and their fear that the case would be determined less by the men's actual guilt or innocence than their political convictions. Riveted to the case by the life-and-death urgency it had assumed, ACLU officials temporarily suspended their challenges to censorship and repression of birth control activism in Boston as Sacco and Vanzetti exhausted their appeals. But the day after the men were executed, ACLU interim director Forrest Bailey shifted gears. Fighting for free speech seemed "out of place at a time when there was a far more important fight making claim upon all of us," he admitted. But "now that the Sacco-Vanzetti story has come to its tragic conclusion, we feel here that it is time to set ourselves right with reference to the general Boston situation."[46]

The ACLU had maintained a relatively low public profile in the cases of Sanger and Tresca—both of which were handled by private attorneys—and it tried to maintain a public distance from birth control, but this did not prevent many observers from associating the organization with sex radicalism. The Federal Bureau of Investigation (FBI), for example, filed a thirty-one-page report in 1924 accusing the ACLU of attacking American "institutions in every form" by defending "immoral or lewd writings and speech." Chief among the FBI's concerns were "Bolshevism" and anarchism, but also the ACLU's efforts to erode obscenity law and thereby undermine the nation's mainstream sexual values.[47]

Indeed, many ACLU leaders did not just defend sex radicals; they also partook of the sexual experimentation for which Villagers became famous. Indeed, Village men and women participated in a variety of unconventional sexual relationships, defended as expressions of equality and individual liberty, but gendered bodies, expectations, and opportunities shaped their experiences and determined the limits of their freedom. Despite these differences, the unconventional sexual lives led by many of the ACLU's founders and leaders inclined them toward incorporating protections for sexual expression into their civil liberties agenda.[48]

As a cofounder, Eastman exercised a profound influence on the ACLU, one that would be short-lived but powerful, deriving from the force of her personality and the individuals she attracted to the new organization. In the early 1920s, internationalist concerns, feminist goals, and Bolshevik sympathies redirected Eastman toward writing and reporting for radical publications in the United States and abroad.[49] Baldwin, however, would go on to lead the organization for more than three decades, bringing to it a newfound devotion to civil liberties and individual rights that permeated his private no less than his public life.

In 1918, after leading the AUAM, founding the NCLB-cum-ACLU, sustaining a Justice Department raid on his offices, and serving time in prison for resisting the draft, Baldwin reconnected with Madeleine Doty. A mutual interest in social work, prison reform, and nature drew them together; "then it became emotional," Baldwin recalled, and "we fell in love." They also developed "a very interesting sexual relationship," Baldwin remembered, one that "worked out very well for awhile." During Baldwin's year in prison, separation from Doty led Baldwin to write, "It's hell to be away from you now when for the first time we understand and love together. I feel like—a hunk of dynamite—ready to explode." Recognizing that Doty, too, struggled with the constraints on their privacy, Baldwin wrote, "I hate to see you suffer at all—and you do if we can't have it *all* together. Of course we can't. I am never free of a guardian." Even as Baldwin yearned for Doty, he delighted in anticipating their future together. "How I rejoice in the prospect of a free marriage. It is a sort of respectable free love!" he wrote. In the summer of 1919, soon after his release from prison, Baldwin and Doty married. Eschewing contemporary wedding conventions—no veil, no white gown, no names changed, no rings exchanged, no promises of obedience or fidelity—the bride and groom celebrated individuality and autonomy in vows that expressed Doty's generosity and "feminist principles" and Baldwin's "ideas of freedom." Baldwin concentrated on independence and self-fulfillment, recognizing that living a "creative life" requires "many friendships, many loves shared together openly, honestly, and joyously." Doty, on the other hand, pledged to sacrifice for Baldwin's benefit. "My one desire," she declared, "is that our love may increase your power to live and to love. This it cannot do unless you are absolutely free, free to love whom you will, to go where you will, to be your own master total and absolute."[50]

As a feminist, Doty kept her own name. She also advocated for woman suffrage, protective legislation for workers, birth control, and peace, all issues that Baldwin supported. She expected equality as well as give-and-take in their marriage, but she struggled to define the sexual boundaries. Doty had enjoyed at least two affairs with married men, but after marrying Baldwin, she developed a new understanding of and regret about the pain experienced by her lovers' wives. She expected fidelity from Baldwin, but he chided her for allowing her "emotional reactions" to compromise her "intellectual convictions." When Baldwin pressed Doty about exploring his desires for other women "to their natural limit," she objected. "A union of spirit as well as body" should prevent the need for other sexual liaisons, she explained. Baldwin accused Doty of trying to dominate him; she criticized him for applying his "ideal of freedom to everything." He demanded "unadulterated and unconditional freedom"; she yearned for something larger, "a freedom shared." At one point, Baldwin apologized for being "a bum husband," but then suggested that Doty take a lover of her own, thinking, perhaps, that doing so would reconcile her to his demands. Still, Doty resisted.[51]

Baldwin's failure to convince Doty to permit extramarital sexual relationships did not impede him. "I wasn't always faithful," Baldwin confessed, but he dismissed his wanderings as "incidental affairs," too trivial to qualify as infidelity. His friends remembered things differently. Many knew—and several thought *everyone* knew—about his long-term affair with one woman who thought Baldwin would marry her if only Doty would agree to a divorce. Doty also worried about Baldwin's close relationships with old girlfriends, and probably with good reason. "I never break up with my women," Baldwin admitted later. Keen observers could see what was going on. Doty "was so madly in love with him," ACLU secretary Lucille Milner recalled, but it was "apparent to all of us that she was no longer in the running."[52]

Insecure about the marriage and aware that Baldwin would not be tied down by anyone, wife or child, Doty took great care to avoid becoming pregnant. Despite her efforts—and Baldwin's claims to have known, since the tender age of thirteen, how to avoid pregnancy—their contraceptive methods failed at least once. Agonizing over what to do, Doty contacted Hugh Cabot, her onetime doctor, longtime friend, and, most likely, former lover. After several letters and phone conversations, Cabot surmised that Baldwin's attitude toward the pregnancy must explain Doty's desperation to end it, and he urged

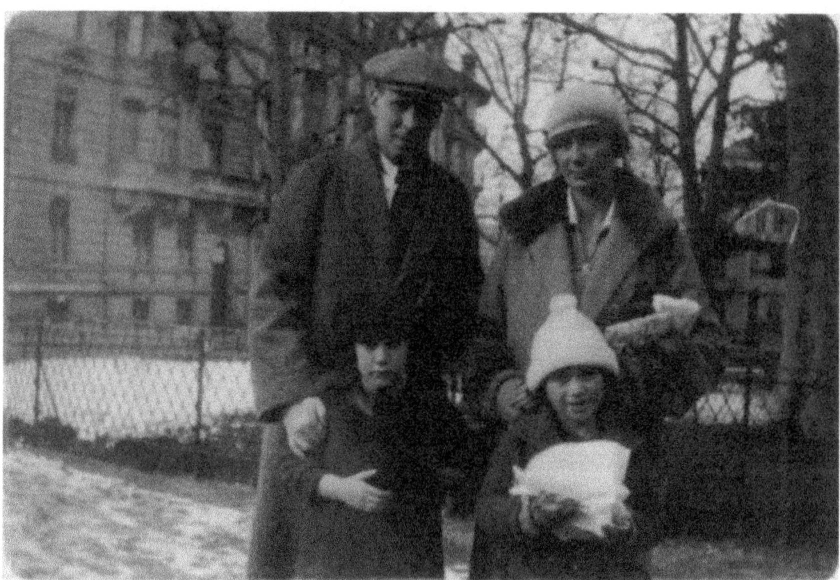

Figure 1.3 Roger Baldwin and Madeleine Doty, Geneva, Switzerland, 1927; children not identified. (Courtesy, Sophia Smith Collection, Smith College)

her to demand that Baldwin take responsibility. Cabot did not consider abortion legitimate on any grounds, and he doubted that Doty could find a reputable obstetrician to perform it. Furthermore, he warned, allowing Baldwin to continue in his irresponsible ways would damage Doty's feminist goals. "It is too bad an example of the relations between men and women which you want so deeply and wisely to improve," he noted. You cannot "help women by exemplifying inequality" in your own marriage. Nor, he argued, would Baldwin advance his own civil liberties work by showing so little consideration for his mate. Nevertheless, Doty ended at least one pregnancy. She also persuaded Baldwin to see a psychiatrist, and even experimented with a transcontinental "marriage under two roofs," to use Eastman's phrase—all to no avail. In 1934, after she discovered that Baldwin had become deeply involved with another woman, they divorced. Doty remained single for the rest of her life. Baldwin immediately married his lover, Evelyn Preston, another Villager and wealthy divorcee who proved more tolerant than Doty of Baldwin's ongoing infidelities.[53]

Baldwin was not alone; many men who helped to lead the ACLU or were involved with female ACLU leaders imported their ideals about individual freedom into their sexual and romantic relationships, and did so frankly.[54] In many ways, their private lives became laboratories for experimenting with sexual civil liberties.

Wolcott H. Pitkin, Jr., former attorney general of Puerto Rico and one of the ACLU's first lawyers, enjoyed intimate relationships with two women simultaneously—Dorothy Kenyon, a single attorney who worked in his law office, and Gertrude King, a married mother of five and public intellectual whose husband, Stanley King, became president of Amherst College. In the spirit of honesty and openness popular among free love proponents of the day, Pitkin informed the women about the nature of his relationship with each of them, introduced them, and urged them to cooperate with each other so that jealousy would not impede their relations with him.

Voluminous correspondence between King and Kenyon documents the women's herculean, idealistic, and often heartbreaking efforts to comply with his wishes. They visited, wrote letters back and forth, tried to love each other, apologized for the "inevitable hurts" each caused the other, and exchanged compliments, advice, and information about how best to care for their mutual love interest. For five years, they struggled to align their desires with each other's and, most importantly, with Pitkin's. "Our primary interests are not in conflict," King wrote to Kenyon, as long as we both want, first and foremost, "his blooming, his maximum freedom & health and poised strength." Later, she wrote, "the important thing is to be dedicated to his interests what*ever* the conditions. The important thing is to start with *his* assumptions,—otherwise self gets into it somehow to spoil the game." Even as the two women strove to be generous with Pitkin, he focused on his own freedom and independence. When Kenyon demanded his time and attention, tried to plan for a future together, or pressured Pitkin to fulfill her expectations, he chastised her for straying from his ideal of "a FREE

Figure 1.4 Dorothy Kenyon, no date. (Courtesy, Sophia Smith Collection, Smith College)

relationship." Kenyon—who would never marry and, by the 1960s, established an international reputation as an independent, no-nonsense advocate of women's rights—nonetheless strove in 1921, at the age of thirty-three, to adapt to Pitkin's desires, writing apologetically, "Do I stick too close?... Do you want to hit me—the way I do the cur dog... ? I *want* to have things the way you like 'em." After King died suddenly in 1923, Pitkin grew increasingly impatient with Kenyon's growing demands. Reminding her of King's lessons in selflessness and his own need for freedom had little impact. In 1924, Pitkin ended their relationship, explaining to Kenyon that she clearly could not be satisfied with "the kind of association I can really give you and which I enjoy." Several years later, Pitkin married, and a devastated Kenyon rededicated herself to a legal career and civil liberties. She joined the ACLU board in 1930, after Pitkin left his position as the organization's legal counsel. Throughout her forty-two years on the ACLU board, she prevailed upon colleagues to defend women's rights to birth control and abortion. Between 1930 and her death in 1972, Kenyon enjoyed a number of intense love affairs with men but never married.[55]

Elmer Rice, a Pulitzer Prize–winning playwright who guided the ACLU's anticensorship agenda for several decades, met Baldwin through the Civic Club founded by ACLU pioneer Mary Ware Dennett. Like Baldwin, Rice's early sexual explorations included hiring a prostitute while exercising restraint with the women he courted. "I was personally puritanical," he wrote in his autobiography. "I could not have brought myself to make advances to a 'nice girl'... though I had the most advanced views about sexual freedom in general." Like Baldwin, Rice's "puritanism," such as it was, allowed and even encouraged sexual encounters with servants and prostitutes but discouraged sexual overtures to female peers. Unlike Baldwin, Rice neither wrote his views about freedom into his vows nor let them hinder his becoming a father, but he did bring them into his marriage to Hazel Levy.[56]

Sex figured prominently in Rice's life. "The regular gratification of the sex appetite," he wrote a friend, "is a long step towards happiness." Rice whetted and satisfied his appetite in a number of ways, attending revues "full of naked girls," reading literature such as James Joyce's widely censored *Ulysses*—a book that exercised a "stimulating effect," Rice wrote, "upon my erectile tissue"—and engaging in a variety of sexual liaisons. Inhibited by "no moral compulsion to monogamy" and believing, in fact, that "among men monogamy is exceptional," Rice sustained a number of long-term affairs with women, both married and single. Admitting that he was rarely without an extramarital sexual relationship, Rice allowed his wife Hazel "the same freedom I demanded for myself" even as he acknowledged that fears of pregnancy and social censure necessarily limited a woman's sexual freedom. Hazel—who worked for many years as an unpaid secretary for the ACLU—complained about Rice's "pathological raving for privacy," his insistence on maintaining a separate apartment, and his "propensity to

Figure 1.5 Elmer and Hazel Rice, 1933. (Courtesy, Harry Ransom Center, University of Texas at Austin)

become enamored of young and pretty girls." In 1941, Hazel was devastated and even suicidal when her husband of twenty-six years fled to Reno, Nevada, to file for a speedy divorce so he could marry screen and stage star Betty Field.[57]

After the divorce, Hazel left her volunteer position for paid war work while Rice remained active in the ACLU. Like Baldwin and Pitkin, Rice imported his civil libertarian values into his romantic relationships, declaring that, in private as in public life, "nothing is more important than independence of thought and freedom of action."[58]

The experiences of Rice, Pitkin, and Baldwin contrast markedly with those of their female peers. Like Madeleine Doty, Dorothy Kenyon, and Hazel Rice, board members Mary Ware Dennett and Elizabeth Gurley Flynn were also involved with men who, over their vigorous protests, insisted on sexually open relationships.

In 1907 and 1908, Dennett tried valiantly to adapt to the demands of her husband, Hartley, who argued that any limits on his relations with other women would violate his freedom and "individual sovereignty." He did not want a divorce, but he did want to spend nights, weeks, and even months with Margaret Chase, a socially prominent married woman. Mary felt betrayed, abandoned, and deeply hurt. Six years after the affair began, she finally obtained a divorce, joined the famed Greenwich Village women's group Heterodoxy, founded the Civic Club, and redoubled her commitment to a number of political causes, including civil liberties. Her work on behalf of birth control, women's rights, and sex education—responses, in many ways, to her traumatic marital experiences—would deepen the ACLU's commitment to legal and judicial defenses of sexual expression.[59]

In 1916, Elizabeth Gurley Flynn would have married Carlo Tresca, but because he could not persuade a court to grant him a divorce, the two lovers simply moved in together. Flynn was a prominent Socialist, but Tresca was a renowned anarchist—one whose relations with women mimicked his politics. Before Flynn, Tresca confronted statutory rape charges for sexual intercourse with a sixteen-year-old girl before being convicted of the lesser offense of adultery. Flynn believed that her great love would restrain Tresca's roving, even though he assured her that he could not be faithful. After Flynn learned that Tresca had fathered a child with her own sister, she plunged into a deep depression and physical illness that would remove her from New York radical politics for nearly a decade. In 1931, Tresca finally found a partner who would accept his infidelities, Margaret DeSilver, longtime ACLU member, benefactor, and widow of one of the organization's first attorneys. Flynn meanwhile found solace in the arms of a woman, the well-known physician Marie Equi.[60]

Women in sexually "free" relationships with men could hardly hope to participate as equals without, at the very least, reliable birth control. Perhaps it is unsurprising then that Eastman, Doty, Flynn, Kenyon, Mary Dennett, and Hazel Rice pressed the ACLU to defend birth control activists and literature. With access to birth control and even abortion, women of the middle and elite classes could more easily enjoy sexual intercourse and consummate illicit liaisons with men. For middle-class and elite men like Baldwin, Pitkin, Hartley Dennett, and Elmer Rice, greater availability and acceptability of birth control among women of their class promised opportunities for sexual encounters with female peers.

Even as these Greenwich Village bohemians guided the ACLU in its early years, they were joined by more conservative colleagues who nonetheless espoused many of the same views on birth control. John Haynes Holmes, an

ACLU founder and prominent Unitarian minister steeped in the Social Gospel tradition, declared birth control "one of the greatest causes of our day." As early as 1916, after the birth of two children with his wife Madeleine Hosmer Baker, Holmes denounced laws against contraception and soon thereafter declared himself "heartily in favor of birth control." He joined Dennett's Voluntary Parenthood League (VPL) in 1922. In 1925, he worked to persuade his Community Church to host a lecture by Sanger and in 1931, he named Sanger one of the "ten greatest women of today." What motivated Holmes to take this progressive stand on birth control? He had, after all, been reared in the Puritan tradition and was an outspoken critic of "free love" and an unapologetic defender of laws against obscenity who apparently remained faithfully married until his wife died more than a half century later.[61] Did Holmes embrace birth control, along with Unitarianism, in rebellion against a rigid upbringing? Or did he simply want to help less privileged people plan their families as he and his wife had?

And what of Margaret and Albert DeSilver, an independently wealthy couple that provided a substantial portion of the ACLU's early budget while also financing birth control activism? The DeSilvers, parents of three, offered able service and generous financial support to Dennett's National Birth Control League in 1918, rescued her Voluntary Parenthood League from financial failure with a munificent gift in 1922, and appealed to major foundations on her behalf. True, after Albert's tragic death in 1924, Margaret DeSilver plunged headlong into the Village cultural scene and, in the 1930s, married Carlo Tresca.[62] But why, years before, had the DeSilvers done so much to promote the birth control movement?

Answers to these questions remain a mystery. Not only are personal stories difficult to piece together, but determining motives is always tricky business. That so many ACLU founders worked diligently to align their public principles with their private practices eases the task somewhat. That so many of them pursued unconventional sexual relationships challenges scholars who portray them as "puritanical" or "squeamish about sex."[63]

The women and men who created the ACLU came to their work with dramatically different sexual experiences and histories that influenced their ideas about civil liberties. As participants—willing, unwilling, and ambivalent—in the twentieth century's first sexual revolution, Eastman, Dennett, Kenyon, Flynn, Doty, and Hazel Rice were frequently unhappy, but their male partners, opportunists in a rapidly changing sexual landscape, seemed perfectly content with the new terrain. While men happily incorporated civil liberties values into their intimate relationships, women struggled against the "conflicts and tensions" that emerged "between feminism and the sexual revolution." That so many individuals who worked together in the young ACLU were involved in such tangled, experimental, and often tormented intimate relationships is telling. That all retained a long-standing commitment to the birth control movement and later supported sex education suggests that civil libertarians' early attention to these issues may have grown out of and helped to bridge gender-related differences among them in the 1920s and 1930s.[64]

ACLU leaders did not simply discover the true meaning of the U.S. Constitution. Rather, they created that meaning in a long and painstaking process of negotiation and collaboration that resembled not so much scales falling from the eyes of the blind as stones being laid and turned this way and that to build a meandering path of uncertain destination. They began to construct sexual civil liberties in the unique cultural milieu that was Greenwich Village in the 1920s as they looked out for their own and their friends' interests. Although men and women in the ACLU often disagreed about the virtues of monogamy, with men more likely to champion sexual freedom and women more insistent on sexual fidelity, birth control mediated their experiences and values, providing women more opportunities to explore the former and men more chances to escape the latter. This is not to argue that ACLU founders fashioned an organization and formulated a civil liberties agenda merely to meet their own needs and fulfill their own desires. Nevertheless, many of the principles that they developed grew out of their personal experiences and collective cultural environment. A civil liberties focus alone, in other words, did not predestine the ACLU to identify birth control, explicit sex education, or suggestive plays as issues of free speech. Its Village roots did, however, incline it in this direction—a direction that would have profound implications for evolving understandings of the Constitution and its relationship to sexuality.

2

"Queer Business for the Civil Liberties Union"

Defending Unconventional Speech about Sex, 1920s–1930s

"The performance was thoroughly vulgar and indecent," the report began, "as most burlesque shows ordinarily are. While women wore tights as required by your rules, other parts of the body were naked, suggestive dancing was frequent, sexual jokes with double meanings were common, all the usual stunt appeals to sex interest and feelings were there." The disapproving tone and graphic description of this account echoes reports compiled by early-twentieth-century moral reformers, but this one was written by ACLU founder Roger Baldwin and submitted to Boston's Commissioner of Licenses.[1] So why would Baldwin, who delighted in taunting Boston censors with free speech challenges, have notified Boston public officials of a risqué burlesque show in 1931?

Baldwin's report came at a pivotal moment in the ACLU's evolving agenda regarding sexual speech. His comments did not reflect puritanism or squeamishness about sex, but a carefully calibrated strategy to expose the hypocrisy and potential unconstitutionality of censorship directed at different types of commercial entertainment.[2] By contrasting the graphic sexual display permitted on the burlesque stage with the more subtle sexual themes banned from serious plays, Baldwin called attention to the inconsistent standards applied to lowbrow and highbrow entertainment, hoping, thereby, to destabilize Boston's entire censorship regime.

Personal experiences and values may have predisposed ACLU leaders to defend birth control activists, but the path they followed to defending sexual expression more broadly was a circuitous and halting one. Over time, it led from providing covert assistance to engaging in public advocacy, from defending only noncommercial and educational speech to championing commercial entertainment, from representing only friends to taking on the cases of outright strangers, from employing strictly principled strategies to experimenting with more pragmatic approaches, and from focusing on civil liberties clearly articulated in the Constitution to gradually inferring others, including the right to privacy. By the end of the 1930s, the ACLU's defense of sexual expression would embrace not only birth control advocates but serious sex educators, nudists, theatrical producers, and even somewhat shady itinerant sex lecturers. The project of creating sexual civil liberties was well under way.

When it came to cases involving sexual matters, leaders of the young ACLU defended people they knew personally and trusted. That unwritten policy seemed especially sound when the ACLU executive committee reflected on its involvement with Warner Williams, a man arrested for distributing material that violated Boston's obscenity laws. Williams was an unknown quantity when he requested help in 1927, but ACLU leaders were eager to reenter the Boston censorship fight after a recent hiatus during which they focused on the Sacco-Vanzetti case. Williams turned out to be a publicity-seeking fanatic whose get-rich-quick schemes and rude, rambling letters betrayed questionable sanity. Within weeks, ACLU leaders lamented their haste and dropped Williams's case. On issues of censorship regarding sexuality in particular, they felt on much safer ground when defending friends and acquaintances.[3]

Moreover, ACLU leaders had yet to reach a consensus on how to deal with obscenity. Executive director Roger Baldwin and board members Mary Ware Dennett and John Haynes Holmes tended to support laws that maintained boundaries between public and private and to tolerate bans on public sexual expression that did not, in their opinion, address issues of public concern. Unlike some of their colleagues, they distinguished sexually explicit books and magazines that pandered to base desires from material that expressed serious if controversial ideas. Other board members, most notably Elmer Rice and Arthur Garfield Hays, were more concerned about protecting freedom of expression and public access to it.[4] Nevertheless, they all found common ground on a number of issues including sex education, nudism, and theater.

Mary Ware Dennett's sex education case served as a bridge between the ACLU's behind-the-scenes work on behalf of birth control in the 1920s and its growing interest in defending sexual expression more broadly. In 1922, the U.S. postmaster general declared Dennett's sex education pamphlet, "The Sex Side of Life," unmailable on grounds of obscenity, despite great demand for it by public welfare and social work agencies. Unable to ascertain the objectionable passages, Dennett ignored the ban and continued filling orders for her pamphlet—25,000, in fact—escaping prosecution by responding only to specific requests, always under the confidentiality of sealed envelopes and first-class postage. In 1928, after learning about the ban, attorney Morris Ernst urged Dennett to challenge it in court, offering to appeal her case all the way to the Supreme Court if necessary. Coincidentally, within two weeks of Ernst's proposal, Dennett was indicted and summoned before a federal district court for mailing obscene material. She had been entrapped by a postal inspector who ordered her pamphlet under the name of a female decoy.[5]

As an ACLU board member and a prominent activist on the Village's intellectual, political, and social scene, Dennett easily obtained ACLU support. Her timing was also fortuitous; the ACLU had recently announced plans to broaden its anticensorship agenda, and Dennett's case promised to extend the organization's reach into the areas of postal censorship and sex education. Moreover, Dennett believed that postal authorities had targeted her sex education pamphlet not because they considered it especially objectionable, but because it was written by a vocal opponent of laws against birth control. Thus, the specter of political bias raised by her case appealed to Rice and Hays, who had long contended that censors aimed not to quash obscenity per se, but to suppress unconventional ideas.[6]

The ACLU organized the Mary Ware Dennett Defense Committee to raise funds and orchestrate a public relations campaign, a move that strengthened its budding relationship with Morris Ernst. For the next decade and a half, Ernst would serve on the ACLU board and help to shape its policies around his belief that "personal freedom" must extend "into the realm of private relations." Like Hays and Rice, fellow attorneys and also "secularized Jews," Ernst also challenged the idea that sexual expression should be limited to the private sphere. He brought a resume rich with experience defending birth control and attacking censorship in court. A member of Dennett's Voluntary Parenthood League since 1923, Ernst had also long provided legal assistance to Sanger and became, in the 1930s, legal counsel for her American Birth Control League. By bringing Ernst on board and taking major responsibility for Dennett's case, the ACLU increased its commitment to litigate on behalf of serious authors ensnared by obscenity law.[7]

If ACLU leaders agreed to support Dennett's case, they nevertheless continued to wrangle over the issue of obscenity. Founding board member and minister of the Unitarian Community Church of New York John Haynes Holmes assured his congregation that Dennett was right and the law wrong. "It is not Mrs. Dennett but the absurd laws of this country which stand convicted," he declared.[8] Even so, neither he nor Dennett was ready to join Rice and Ernst in opposing obscenity law altogether.

Dennett considered employing obscenity law against Werber's Theater, a local exhibitor that tried to capitalize on the hype surrounding her case by hawking a combined stage and film show titled *The Sex Side of Life*. Advertisements for the show depicted Dennett and featured her name on a large canvas

Figure 2.1 Morris Ernst in his office, posing for a *Life Magazine* photo shoot, 1944. (Photographer, J. R. Eyerman, Courtesy, Time & Life Pictures)

that announced, "The Most Discussed Subject of To-day. 'Sex Side of Life.'" Bold signs fairly shouted: "WOMEN ONLY, SEX-SATIONAL THRILLING STAGE PRESENTATION, ACTUAL SCENES—THE NAKED TRUTH—SHOWS EVERYTHING." Dennett feared that this tawdry show would associate her name with smut, and she implored Ernst to stop the exhibit by invoking obscenity law if necessary. Ernst instead threatened a copyright infringement suit. The case was flimsy, but the exhibitor agreed to remove Dennett's image and name and change the title to *Sex View of Life*. Dennett was not satisfied. Although Ernst's resolution of the matter removed her name and image from advertising for this deliberately salacious show, it could not prevent commercial enterprises from distorting and profiting from the freer discussions of sex that her work set in motion.[9]

When Dennett's case finally went to trial in April 1929, neither ACLU support nor even Ernst's "magnificent argument," as Dennett characterized it, could prevent the all-male jury from returning a guilty verdict. Dennett refused to pay the resulting $300 fine, and she and Ernst entered another round of motions and appeals. The ACLU's Mary Ware Dennett Defense Committee, meanwhile, concentrated on public relations, fund-raising, and bolstering Dennett's morale. In May 1929, it held a meeting on sex education at New York's Town Hall, featuring Dennett and her chief defenders. The committee invited her most vocal detractors as well, but only one attended. John S. Sumner, secretary of the

New York Society for the Suppression of Vice, refused to participate on the grounds that holding a public meeting regarding an ongoing court case amounted to trying the case "on a public platform or in the newspapers." Tellingly, this is exactly what Ernst and Dennett's Defense Committee hoped to accomplish as they prepared for the next court date.[10]

The court saga of "The Sex Side of Life" finally ended on March 3, 1930. The U.S. Court of Appeals for the Second Circuit reversed Dennett's conviction in an opinion that affirmed the constitutionality of the obscenity statute in question but shortened its reach. "The sex impulses are present in everyone," wrote Judge Augustus Hand, one of the nation's most distinguished jurists. If the statute aimed to "bar from the mails everything which *might* stimulate sex impulses," it would surely exclude "much chaste poetry and fiction" as well as medical texts. Given the alternative—leaving children to "grope about in mystery and morbid curiosity," obtaining information "from ill-informed and often foul-minded companions"—Hand concluded that "The Sex Side of Life" was likely to do more good than harm. Its accuracy, "decent language," and "manifestly serious and disinterested spirit" rendered it an "intelligent and high-minded source" of information. Dennett's triumph was complete when the solicitor general of the post office bowed to the enthusiastic public support for Hand's decision and declined to appeal the case to the Supreme Court.[11] Victory left Dennett's defense committee with $1,402 and an agenda that would create more opportunities for the ACLU to incorporate sexuality into its emerging civil liberties paradigm.

The ACLU expanded its involvement in sexual issues by coming to the defense of nudists, a fringe group that treated nudity as a strategy for strengthening families and eroding the appeal of obscenity. Demystifying the nude human body would, nudists claimed, prevent it from serving as a source of titillation. Removing clothing would eliminate sartorial markers of class, gender, and sexuality, returning the body to its natural, wholesome state. Ideally, nudism would not stimulate sexual appetites but redirect them toward nature and activity. It would not lure curious voyeurs but attract satisfied participants. It would not cater only to men but engage entire families. Most important, nudism, like sex education, would provide an antidote to obscenity.[12]

Many ACLU leaders practiced "casual nudism." They vacationed on Martha's Vineyard, a sleepy, sparsely populated Massachusetts island where they gathered at Barn House, a Greenwich Village–inspired "cooperative, intellectual venture." In this "communal utopia" of rustic cottages spread over a forty-acre private complex, ACLU leaders relaxed, threw parties, discussed current events, recruited new members, negotiated complicated love affairs, and sunbathed together in the nude. At Barn House, Wolcott Pitkin, Dorothy Kenyon, and

Figure 2.2 Mary Ware Dennett at home, receiving congratulations from friends after her victory in the United States Circuit Court, March 3, 1930. (Courtesy, ©Bettmann/CORBIS)

Gertrude Besse King pursued their agonizing love triangle until King's untimely death in 1923. There too, Roger Baldwin began a romance with Evelyn Preston that ended his first marriage, began his second, and made him joint owner of 280 acres of beachfront property on Martha's Vineyard. There too ACLU attorney Corliss Lamont and his wife visited but tried to avoid the beach, where "we had to bathe in the nude which we really didn't like." The unique culture of the Vineyard facilitated nudism because most of its beaches were, in the 1920s as they are today, privately owned, restricted to residents, and/or simply inaccessible to the public. In memos written thirty years later for his children and grandchildren, Baldwin reminisced about his interest in nude sunbathing. "It was more fun," he admitted, but it also discouraged people from developing "a false sense of prudery about the body."[13]

Baldwin became chummy with leaders in the nudist movement whom he encountered through his settlement house network and the Greenwich Village cultural scene. At his urging, in 1929 the ACLU offered assistance to Maurice Parmelee, a prominent nudist leader who ran afoul of federal authorities when the Customs Bureau confiscated his book, *Nudism in Modern Life*. The ACLU represented Parmelee during a nearly decade-long journey through the courts. Nudists around the country heard about the ACLU's support for the case and submitted their own appeals for help when local authorities cracked down on their practises. The Reverend Ilsley Boone, another prominent nudist leader, called on the ACLU when newsdealer Maurice Fellerman was charged under obscenity law for selling *The Nudist,* a movement magazine. ACLU attorneys joined the case, but the State Supreme Court sustained Fellerman's conviction in *New York v. Fellerman* (1934).[14]

Even as ACLU leaders defended nudist literature, their work took a new turn when they began to treat the practice of nudism as a civil liberties matter. They did so for the first time in spring 1934, when the Olympian League rented Fred Topel's Swimming School, a gymnasium in Manhattan, to host its annual open-invitation recruitment event. Women and men paid one dollar and doffed their clothing in separate dressing rooms before joining each other for calisthenics, handball, gymnastics, basketball, and swimming. Police officers raided the event and arrested three men for "indecent exposure" and "outraging public decency," and the Court of Special Sessions of the City of New York convicted them of "willfully and lewdly expos[ing]" their "private parts" in a "public place." The League's founder, Vincent Burke, appealed the decision with the assistance of an ACLU attorney and triumphed in a New York State Supreme Court opinion that declared nudism in New York state legal.[15]

The decision in *New York v. Burke* (1934) turned out to be less important than the language in which it was rendered. The court declared the law under which the men were convicted insufficient to cover nudism, but it also called an

Figure 2.3 Ilsley Boone, no date. (Courtesy, American Nudist Research Library)

antinudist movement into being by encouraging the legislature to put a stop to the practice as soon as possible. Meanwhile, the national press explored the decision's implications for commercial entertainment, and a Manhattan magistrate cited *Burke* when he exonerated a group of burlesque dancers charged with an indecent performance on the grounds that "nudity, partial or complete, is not in and of itself lewd."[16]

In January 1935, just one week after *Burke*, New York State's Catholic Legion of Decency answered the State Supreme Court's challenge by drafting antinudist legislation and convincing Senator John T. McCall (D) to sponsor it.[17] The national Legion of Decency had been founded months earlier to reform motion pictures and magazines, but New York's Legion added nudism to its agenda under the prodding of former governor Alfred E. Smith. "It seems to us inconsistent to take a stand on the screen and ignore this latest challenge to the enforcement of decency in reality," the Legion explained. We cannot "appeal for cleanliness in motion pictures" but ignore "immorality in the flesh." Outraged that the *Burke* decision allowed women and men to swim together "without clothing," Smith and the local Legion drafted a bill that would make it a misdemeanor for a person to "expose his person, or the private parts thereof, in the presence of two or more persons of the opposite sex" who are similarly exposed. To Smith, nudity was indecency, whether filmed or witnessed, whether found in a magazine, a movie, or a gymnasium.[18]

After the Legion introduced its antinudist bill before the New York State Legislature, many others entered the debate. Opponents of the bill included Jewish leaders and Protestant clergy who actually supported laws against "indecent exposure of the body for any lewd purpose or for theatrical or commercial exploitation" but considered the nude human body a healthy and natural introduction to sex.[19] One man, who introduced himself as a "God-fearing" father of three, supported the Legion's motion picture reform but objected to laws against nudism. "The exposure of our bodies was only made to seem wrong by man in his ignorance centuries ago," he wrote. Meanwhile, a committee of nudists lobbied Smith, explaining that nudists shared the Legion's goal of advancing a moral and wholesome approach to sex but simply used different methods. While the Legion of Decency employed suppression and inculcated inhibitions to coerce moral behavior, nudists cultivated morality through "frankness, honesty and wholesome understanding between the sexes." Nudists did not admit spectators to their gatherings, they assured Smith, and "men are not aroused sexually under the circumstances of nudism."[20]

When the legislature called public hearings on the antinudist bill, nudist leaders appealed to the ACLU for help. The ACLU agreed, declaring the bill an invasion of "the privacy of the home," because it forbade mixed-sex nudism in private as well as in public. Testimony for the ACLU was given by Mary Ryskind, an ACLU member, office volunteer, wife of a prize-winning playwright, and a mother who "obviously was not a nudist." Ryskind opposed the antinudist bill as an affront to privacy and maternity. The bill would make parents who were nude in the company of their three-year-old child, whether in a swimming pool or a bathtub, guilty of a misdemeanor. "As a wife and mother of two children," Ryskind asserted, "I resent such an invasion of my private life by the state." More seriously, Ryskind warned, "this sweeping amendment would outlaw the practice of nudism," a movement of "thoughtful and high-minded persons without an impure thought." They might be "the only genuinely puritanical persons now living," Ryskind averred. The bill under consideration would not just prohibit public nudity but would penalize nudist practices everywhere, including in "private parks or sanitariums far removed from public view where no outsider could possibly be offended."[21]

Ryskind testified before legislators and a friendly crowd of more than two hundred people. No one appeared in support of the bill, and many spoke against it. One man joked that the bill would make it illegal for a woman to give birth to twin boys. Another critic called the bill "freak legislation" akin to the "anti-evolution bills" that led to the Scopes trial in Tennessee ten years earlier. A member of the Sunbathers League, a nudist group near Peekskill, New York, argued that nudism eliminated unhealthy curiosity about the human body. "If you go to Turkey and see a face veiled," he explained, "you are curious." But "you'd be surprised how quick you lose your curiosity in a nudist camp." After the laughter and applause died down, he assured his audience that nudism inspires respect for women. "One lady said she got more respect from the men in our nudist group" than she did in "church circles," he maintained. A woman testified against the bill on behalf of local artists who feared that its passage would endanger "art model classes." Meanwhile, Boone cited *Burke* when he pointed out that "the nude human body is distinct from the lewd human body." After the hearings, ACLU leaders considered the antinudist bill defeated but, as one noted prophetically, "you can never tell when things will begin to stir when nudists are around."[22]

The New York antinudist bill might have died an ignominious death had developments in Europe and around the nation not breathed new life into it. Especially crucial was the influence of the Legion of Decency and Catholic clergy. A month after the Albany hearings, newspapers headlined Pope Pius's denunciation of nudism as a wanton, pagan cult devoted to pleasure, amusement, and "the mania ... to see everything and enjoy everything to the full." Just two years earlier, Nazi leaders in Germany, the birthplace of organized nudism, accused nudists of threatening the morality of the *Volk* by deadening "women's natural feelings of shame" and destroying "men's respect for women." The German state police worked to destroy the nudist movement, because it was associated with Socialism and Marxism, political ideologies anathema to the Nazi regime.[23] By 1935, on both sides of the Atlantic, in countries governed democratically and others under fascist rule, nudists confronted determined efforts to eliminate their movement.

Ongoing efforts to outlaw nudism in New York were led by Catholics who addressed the privacy issue first raised by the ACLU. Just one month after public hearings put the original antinudist bill to rest, Smith and McCall introduced a revised version, one that responded to Ryskind's privacy claims by forbidding mixed-sex nudism only in public spaces, including rental property and any place that charged an entrance fee. According to its advocates, the law would prevent nudists from continuing to cavort naked before fee-paying observers as they had, presumably, at Burke's nudist event. Burke opposed the bill, arguing that it should not cover spaces rented for private use or open to fee-paying guests. ACLU leaders urged Governor Herbert H. Lehman to veto the bill because it represented a "serious violation of personal privacy." They opposed empowering the state "to regiment individual and family habits." The proposed law could be used against two brothers and a sister who skinny-dipped together, for example. "Families or friends who wish to practice nudism privately should be allowed to do so," they argued, whether at home or "in camps and sanitariums, far removed from the curious public."[24]

Governor Lehman rejected the notion that privacy rights should protect nudist practices and signed Smith's bill into law. Nudists questioned the constitutionality of the new law, but they also turned their sights to establishing a nudist camp outside the state. In 1936, Boone moved his operation to Mays Landing, New Jersey, where he built Sunshine Park to provide a natural setting for nudist recreation and set up Outdoor Publishing to produce *The Nudist* and other literature. Meanwhile, ACLU leaders challenged laws that hindered not only nudist publications but also, on grounds of privacy, "legitimate nudist activities"—conduct that many people considered sexual.[25]

The ACLU continued to defend Parmelee's *Nudism in Modern Life* in a case that required a constant flow of attention and funds though it had languished, since 1933, in the Washington, D.C., court system. Finally, in December 1938, the book was condemned as obscene on the basis of its illustrations alone. ACLU leaders believed the case could be won on appeal and, by 1940, they had the ruling they wanted. In *Parmelee v. U.S.*, the U.S. Court of Appeals recognized that the meaning of obscenity changed over time and held that social science should determine contemporary standards. "Civilization has advanced far enough," it concluded, "to permit picturization of the human body for scientific and educational purposes."[26]

Parmelee v. U.S. represented a resounding victory, and ACLU leaders circulated the opinion, celebrated their triumph, and watched eagerly to see how it would influence law and policy. Delighted by the outcome of the case, Boone contracted with Parmelee to issue a new edition of his book. The legal world took notice too, and courts at all levels, including the U.S. Supreme Court, cited the case with growing frequency. The victory became all the more sweet when the Customs Bureau announced that it would defer to *Parmelee* and permit books containing pictures of nudes to enter the country as long as they were accompanied by serious and relevant text. ACLU leaders appreciated the salutary impact of the case on their broader sexual civil liberties agenda and intensified their commitment to defending nudist practices and publications.[27]

Theatrical performances joined birth control, sex education, and nudism at the center of the ACLU's emergent sexual civil liberties agenda when Pulitzer Prize–winning playwright and board member Elmer Rice raised the issue in 1930. Legitimate theater faced imminent censorship at the hands of ministers and legislators who accused producers of staging obscene shows, but it also confronted threats of *self*-censorship proposed by the Actors' Equity Association, the major labor union for theater professionals. Rice linked theater censorship to the ACLU's traditional concerns by characterizing the obscenity charges as a smoke screen erected by "conservative and reactionary elements" determined to purge the theater of liberal ideas about marriage, divorce, and birth control.[28]

Efforts to censor the theater were far from new. Since the nation's colonial days, local authorities had prohibited or censored plays, and as recently as the early 1920s the theater community regulated its own productions through a play jury system made up of theater professionals, municipal officials, and "impartial citizens." Rice opposed the play jury from the start, seeing no meaningful distinction between it and state censorship. Whether voluntary or official, censorship boards were composed of "individuals whose judgments are determined by their particular prejudices, superstitions, illusions and repressions." Moreover, while censorship often began as a means of cleaning up "'salacious' plays," it was eventually used to persecute "the innovator and the iconoclast in art." Happily for Rice, New York City's first play jury system collapsed after just a few years.[29]

The play jury returned in response to changes in commercial entertainment and reform inspired by the Great Depression. Struggling owners of local amusements tried to attract audiences with ever more daring sexual displays even as antiobscenity reformers turned to the expanding state to regulate racy material. As the Depression deepened, motion picture producers drew theater professionals away from the floundering Broadway strip and out to Hollywood, where the "talkies" were new and profits continued to roll in. Burlesque and legitimate theater fought hard to stay in business and, less worried about government censorship than bankruptcy, they staged bolder shows that attracted harsh criticism from local opinion leaders. Meanwhile, antiobscenity reformers took advantage of the crippled economy and the national mood to demand an end to the "excesses of the twenties."[30] In this context, the theater community once again considered creating a play jury system to defend itself against state censorship.

When Rice requested that the ACLU help him ward off another play jury in 1930, leaders recognized a valuable opportunity to broaden the ACLU's First Amendment agenda to include protection for the theater and opposition to self-censorship. Building on their past success with the defense committee created for Dennett's "Sex Side of Life" case, they formed the Committee Against Stage Censorship (CASC) to challenge state, local, and also voluntary self-censorship. Such ad hoc committees helped the ACLU, a fledgling organization with limited resources and staff, respond to crisis situations by rallying the public and attracting prominent supporters. The CASC campaigned against censorship legislation as well as the new play jury system proposed by Actor's Equity.[31]

Responses to CASC recruitment letters revealed disturbing sources of potential conflict among those who joined. Helen Arthur, an attorney, theater producer, and stage manager, accepted the invitation, declaring that she was "unequivocally opposed to censorship." But she also complained about the theater's treatment of sexual themes and hoped that the CASC would urge theater associations to discourage their members from writing and appearing in "dirty plays." By contrast, when Dorothy Kenyon became a member, she announced her opposition to all forms of censorship and her sincere wish that the CASC would free the theater of all "puritanic leading strings." Rabbi Sidney Goldstein, director of the Social Service Department of New York City's Free Synagogue, joined because he opposed "the appointment of police to serve as the moral censors of the community." Still, like Arthur, he hoped that the CASC would also direct attention to "sanitation" by exploring noncensorious ways to clean up the "cesspools" of modern theater.[32]

Within one month, the CASC boasted a varied membership of one hundred, most of them Villagers, including theater professionals, such as Pulitzer Prize–winning playwright Eugene O'Neill. The ACLU did not hide the CASC's internal disagreements but used them to attract attention and educate the public by holding a public debate between two board members, John Haynes Holmes and Elmer Rice. Holmes endorsed the play jury as a counterweight to the current profit-based system. "The temple of theatrical art has been captured by commercialism," he declared, but the theater is too important to be left in the hands of those who would use it "only for the purposes of making money." Rice, who resisted any form of regulation, countered with arguments about the relativism of "decency" and the importance to artistic creativity of allowing playwrights and producers to follow their own standards.[33]

Newspapers declared Rice the victor in these debates, although he and the Dramatists' Guild, the professional association for playwrights, soon acceded to a resurrection of the play jury system through the newly formed Conference Board of Theatres on Censorship (CBTC). By promising to clean up the theater, the CBTC foiled legislative efforts to pass more restrictive censorship laws as well as Equity's efforts to impose a more coercive play jury system. After the immediate danger passed, however, Rice led the Dramatists' Guild in withdrawing from the CBTC. ACLU leaders who opposed censorship of all kinds, voluntary and self-imposed as well as official and state-sponsored, supported Rice's eleventh-hour support for—and subsequent denunciation of—the new CBTC play jury system, because it helped to thwart pending theater censorship bills and Equity's self-censorship plan.[34]

By spring of 1931, ACLU leaders celebrated the defeat of theater censorship and laid plans for an organization that would protect not just theater but "the literary arts, the press, motion- and talking-pictures, the radio, and the scientific discussion of sex." The idea was to bring two successful but disbanded ACLU committees—the Mary Ware Dennett Defense Committee and the Committee Against Stage Censorship—together to create a new and much longer-lived entity, the National Council on Freedom from Censorship (NCFC).[35]

The NCFC defended a diverse array of material—mostly that produced for an elite audience—but cast its net widely in terms of geography. Even successful local anticensorship efforts, leaders realized, could not protect New York plays when they traveled beyond the city. Boston officials, for example, demanded that Broadway producers make changes before their shows appeared in the city's theaters. Two censored productions of particular concern to the ACLU were *The Captive,* a serious stage play about lesbianism defended by ACLU attorney Arthur Garfield Hays, and *Strange Interlude,* a drama by CASC member Eugene O'Neill, that addressed marital infidelity and abortion. ACLU leaders did not just perform central roles in the legal dramas surrounding each play; they were also enthusiastic patrons.[36]

Many liberal intellectuals accused Boston's censorship regime of being hostile to elite entertainment. "Why is it that the cheap and shoddy," asked prominent journalist Lewis Gannett, "the genuinely corrupt, seem to elude the censors with ease, while a work of art which seriously mirrors unpleasant" aspects of "life catches their attention at once?" Another wrote directly to Boston's license commissioner to ask why he failed to discipline burlesque theaters that regularly featured vulgarity and indecency but insisted on censoring the language and ideas expressed in serious stage plays. "I am content to let the Old Howard and Columbia go on serving their clientele with the fare they demand," he wrote, but "I wish ... that the playhouses serving the highest type of dramatic fare to Boston might be given the same freedom." Leading First Amendment scholar Zechariah Chafee agreed, pointing out that Boston censorship "is directed primarily to serious plays, not to the burlesque or leg-shows."[37]

The same suspicion inspired Roger Baldwin and his assistant Gordon Moss to visit Boston's Old Howard Theatre in 1931 with hopes of encountering a raunchy burlesque show. As Baldwin pointed out to the city's license commissioner, "every rule laid down was violated openly and frequently." Chiding officials for ignoring the "obvious indecency" in risqué burlesque shows while censoring the allegedly "indecent ideas" in legitimate stage plays, Baldwin accused them of deliberately applying stricter standards to entertainment for the elite than to the amusements of the masses. This pattern of censorship, he argued, exposed the real goal of municipal authorities; it was not to eradicate obscenity but to quash ideas, not to eliminate the ubiquitous "strip routine" of the burlesque house but to prohibit unconventional ideas about "marriage, sex relations and the social order." Baldwin's complaint had little immediate impact, but it put Boston authorities on notice regarding the ACLU's widening spheres of interest.[38]

Through the NCFC, ACLU leaders took an even more active role in defending theatrical productions in the 1930s. They arranged opportunities for censorship crackdowns on particular shows—as they had with birth control meetings—so that they could mount a vigorous protest. Often, they learned which plays were in jeopardy from Rice, their own in-house playwright, and through him they urged other playwrights and producers to take a risk by staging uncut shows. At Rice's behest, they also offered legal representation to Broadway producer Billy Rose when public officials in Minneapolis, Minnesota, banned his musical revue *Crazy Quilt*. Their efforts, which included pressuring the mayor, advising and encouraging theater owners, and publicly criticizing reformers, did little more than annoy local officials, but they also laid essential groundwork for the ACLU's expanding sexual civil liberties agenda.[39]

By 1931, ACLU leaders gladly called attention to indecency on the burlesque stage in an effort to expose the hypocrisy of local officials and protect avant-garde theater. That they made little headway against theater censorship mattered less in the end than that their anticensorship agenda had broadened beyond New York City and begun to embrace commercial entertainment, albeit entertainment for the elite. In addition, their support for the bait-and-switch technique Rice employed against the play jury system and their eagerness to expose risqué burlesque shows in an effort to exonerate highbrow ones indicated a new willingness to use strategies born more of pragmatism than principle.

ACLU leaders' growing willingness to use practical strategies and defend commercial material created new tensions in their work with birth control activists. In the early 1930s, the main issue of contention among birth control activists involved whether to demand, as Dennett did, a repeal of all birth control laws or push, along with Sanger, for legal reform that would grant the medical profession a monopoly over birth control. Considering the former approach ideal but the latter more practical, the ACLU tried to support both. At the same time, it brought a unique civil liberties perspective to the issue by opposing laws that could not be enforced without violating rights to due process. Because so many attempts to suppress birth control literature and devices—like Prohibition-era efforts to suppress alcohol—involved unlawful searches and seizures, ACLU leaders suggested, as early as 1932, that enforcing laws against birth control might necessarily violate the Constitution.[40]

When the ACLU supported Sanger's pragmatic approach in the 1930s, Dennett called Baldwin "an incorrigible wobbler" on the birth control issue. It is "queer business for the Civil Liberties Union" to sacrifice its principles by endorsing legal reform that would merely exchange governmental jurisdiction over birth control for the medical profession's, Dennett argued. "Establishing special privilege is hardly a step toward freedom or equality, is it? Legalizing class monopoly is not quite in line with the Union's general principles, is it?" In reply, Baldwin explained that the ACLU sometimes had to compromise principles for tactical advantage. "We have got to use any means we can find," he insisted, to weaken restrictions on birth control.[41]

The means that proved most effective changed over time, and the 1930s presented civil libertarians and birth control activists with unique opportunities. The Depression encouraged a reassessment of state responsibility for the welfare of citizens, including a rethinking of policy on birth control. Economic collapse encouraged policymakers to adopt arguments long made by birth control activists that working-class people in particular needed the ability to limit their families to a size they could support financially. Family limitation began to seem essential to economic survival in a world of scarcity. Some members of President Franklin Roosevelt's brain trust blamed the Depression on population pressures and advocated state intervention. Social workers employed by the Federal Emergency Relief Administration (FERA) confronted the issue directly when some states withheld and others provided information about contraception. ACLU leaders joined birth control activists in demanding that FERA require states to provide contraceptive information even though such a policy would increase the reach of federal authority. With the right people in power, perhaps the national government could actually advance efforts to enhance and ensure individual civil liberties, including the right to distribute information about birth control.[42]

As the public visibility and respectability of birth control surged in the 1930s, growing numbers of entrepreneurs began to exploit it. The ACLU's response to this development revealed a growing willingness to defend commercial enterprises and also highlighted a stark divergence between ACLU priorities and those of Sanger's birth control movement.[43]

Sanger and her colleagues focused ever more narrowly on their doctors-only agenda, a strategy that promised to attract support from the medical profession and to mobilize doctors against "sex bootleggers" who openly peddled potions that claimed to prevent conception. By 1931, after sixteen years of lobbying, they celebrated when the prestigious New York Academy of Medicine endorsed the removal of all restrictions on physicians regarding birth control information, urged medical schools to teach contraceptive methods, and argued that contraception "should be placed under highest-grade medical control."[44]

The ACLU, however, through its NCFC, intervened in a number of birth control cases that aimed to move birth control information beyond the medical community. One of these involved C. E. Midgard, a little-known book importer in Seattle, Washington, who contacted Dennett for advice after Customs officers seized 120 copies of *The Sexual Life in Its Biological Significance* because the book contained birth control information and had been ordered by a mere vendor rather than a physician. Dennett considered Midgard a principled advocate for birth control and sex education, and she urged the ACLU to assist him. Ernst and ACLU assistant director Forrest Bailey agreed that the case had merits but recommended that it be reopened under the name of an "eminent physician" who would order the same books. Dennett, however, pointed out that physicians were rarely prosecuted for violating birth control laws and that, in any case, a victory on behalf of a physician would not set a precedent for the masses. Ernst acquiesced and by 1931, with ACLU help, Midgard won his case in federal court on the grounds that the credentials of the purchaser mattered little when the book in question was "a serious biological work."[45]

Just a year later, an acquaintance called Baldwin's attention to another opportunity to fight for greater freedom to speak publicly about sex and birth control. M. Sayle Taylor, an itinerant speaker who marketed pamphlets and products for male prostate trouble and "feminine hygiene"—code in the 1920s for over-the-counter contraceptives—was barred from speaking by public officials in Lynchburg, Virginia. Dubbed the "Billy Sunday of the sex world," Taylor rented auditoriums, theaters, and tents where he lectured to "men-only" and "women-only" crowds on sexual issues. Like the Werber's Theater show, *The Sex Side of Life,* which took advantage of the excitement surrounding Mary Ware Dennett's court case, Taylor advertised his presentations under the title *Married Love* to exploit the celebrity of Marie Stopes's *Married Love,* a book about female sexuality that was also triumphantly defended in court by Morris Ernst. Taylor sometimes used human models or actors—including "International Beauties" and Samuel Olmstead, "the man with the perfect body"—and offered his pamphlets for sale. By 1928, the AMA began to receive skeptical queries about "Dr. Taylor," including several from Sanger's American Birth Control League (ABCL).[46] Critics described Taylor's pamphlets as "bolder and more pornographic" than Dennett's, and some suspected him of "quackery" and inquired about his medical credentials. An AMA staff investigation concluded that Taylor was indeed a "fake," because he used the title "Dr." without having earned the

Figure 2.4 Streetcar advertising a presentation by M. Sayle Taylor, 1931. (Courtesy, Tampa-Hillsborough County Public Library System)

degree.[47] Even so, by 1932 Taylor had become a national phenomenon who regularly commanded sold-out audiences numbering in the thousands.

Baldwin declared the case "right up our alley" and offered to help Taylor challenge the local ordinance under which he had been censored. ACLU leaders cared little about Taylor's credentials but a great deal about his right to speak publicly about sex. The AMA disagreed and, in an effort to dissuade the ACLU from defending Taylor, sent an urgent wire explaining that Taylor had no medical degree and was "ignorant and without scientific background," a swindler who uses "crude and nastily nauseating" messages to inspire a "commercialized morbid interest in sex." Likewise, ABCL leaders considered Taylor a threat to the respectability they had tried to establish for birth control, and they tried to demonstrate that Lynchburg authorities did not censor legitimate birth control lecturers by scheduling one of Sanger's speakers for a presentation in Lynchburg. ACLU leaders were not swayed and they strove, without success, to develop a test case with Taylor. The ACLU's cooperating attorneys refused to work pro bono for an enterprise as profitable as Taylor's. Moreover, after Taylor calculated the daily cost of remaining in Lynchburg to test the ordinance, he welcomed the opportunity to present his program in a tent erected just outside the city limits. Once again, ACLU efforts were frustrated by the divergence between its own goals and those of its would-be client.[48]

The AMA continued to criticize Taylor as an imposter who made money by representing himself as a medical doctor. But neither the AMA nor the ACLU addressed the issue that most worried birth control advocates—the efficacy of

Taylor's products, the accuracy of his information, and the respectability of his delivery. ACLU leaders, in contrast, cared less about Taylor's qualifications and profits than about the preemptive suppression he experienced at the hands of public officials.[49]

Neither Midgard nor Taylor exercised a significant impact on sex education or birth control in the 1930s. Together, though, their cases demonstrate ACLU leaders' growing eagerness to aid individuals censored for disseminating information about sex. They also expose meaningful differences in the priorities of the ACLU, AMA, and birth control activists.[50] Taylor's case in particular underscored the difficulties of distinguishing between educational and commercial speech, while exposing the frustrations experienced by ACLU leaders who tried to defend victims who were reluctant to challenge censorship.

Divergent perspectives also distinguished ACLU from ABCL approaches to the issue of obscenity. In 1932, for example, Hatcher Hughes, director of the ACLU's NCFC, asked the Birth Control League to endorse a bill that would limit the administrative censorship exercised by postal authorities. Stella Hanau, editor of the ABCL's *Birth Control Review,* urged her colleagues to support the bill, pointing out the *Review*'s vulnerability to postal censorship. But ABCL leaders ultimately followed the advice of their attorney, G. H. Dorr, who urged them to "vigorously oppose" the bill, explaining that under it "a professional purveyor of pornographic material of the foulest sort could" more easily "circulate clearly indecent material." Their decision was doubtless influenced by their desire to avoid disrepute and enhance the movement's respectability.[51]

ACLU attorneys' deepening involvement with the birth control movement nevertheless ensured that each group would continue to influence the other. By 1934, Ernst replaced Dorr as chief counsel for the ABCL, a position that brought him, along with the ACLU, into ever more birth control cases. A major court victory by Ernst and his colleague Harriet Pilpel in 1936 tilted civil libertarians more sharply toward the "doctors-only" strategy with regard to birth control devices. The case involved Hannah Stone, physician and director of Sanger's Birth Control Clinical Research Bureau who imported Japanese pessaries that were seized by U.S. Customs. Ernst sued on Stone's behalf and established the right of physicians to import contraceptive devices for "the health of their patients."[52]

Ernst and Pilpel aggressively marketed the opinion in *U.S. v. One Package* (1936) to the medical profession, calling it a veritable "Medical Bill of Rights." Physicians who attempted to downplay the decision's significance in hopes of minimizing its impact made little headway. Six months later, the AMA echoed Ernst and Pilpel, declaring *U.S. v. One Package* the medical profession's "bill of rights in the field of contraceptive medicine" and urging medical schools to assume responsibility for researching and teaching about contraception.

"Legislators are today more concerned with assuring a high standard of contraceptives," Pilpel crowed in 1937, "than with attempting to ban them entirely—a change from prohibition to regulation." This growing attention to the quality of birth control methods reflected the gradual triumph of the "doctors-only" approach associated with Sanger and increasingly adopted by ACLU attorneys.[53]

By the end of the 1930s, contraceptives had become sufficiently accessible to enough women, especially middle- and upper-class women with access to private medical care, that the national movement to legalize it began to sputter. Contributing to the decline, Sanger entered a period of semiretirement, and the national movement reoriented under male leadership and around the rights of physicians.[54] But the movement had already accomplished a great deal in the realm of public opinion. In 1936, 70 percent of those polled nationwide agreed that distribution of information on birth control should be legalized, and two years later a *Ladies Home Journal* survey found that 79 percent of its female readers favored birth control, citing economic factors as reasons for limiting the size of their families. Within a few years, 77 percent of those questioned in a Gallup Poll endorsed government dissemination of birth control information.[55] Clearly, the birth control movement benefited from a variety of developments during the depressed 1930s, including the fact that large families had become less economically viable. The radical edge of the birth control movement softened as it became associated less with Greenwich Village bohemians and free love radicals and more with respectable middle-class women and their physicians.[56] The patterns of change were uneven across the nation, as Massachusetts continued to outlaw distribution of birth control devices and information and Connecticut still prohibited the actual *use* of contraceptives; in these states, the birth control movement continued to thrive.

Birth control activism also gained new momentum with the rise of a population control movement designed to help "Third World" countries and territories resist Communism through economic progress aided by birth control. In Puerto Rico—an island whose poverty was attributed to overpopulation by U.S. officials—Ernst and local birth control activists handily toppled laws against government birth control clinics. It was a curious victory in a territory at least as Catholic as the state of Massachusetts but an understandable one given policymakers' fears that the country's poverty might invite Communist infiltration. The overpopulation scare would not play a prominent role in domestic birth control politics until after World War II, but by 1940 Ernst, Sanger, and others in the movement had already tapped concerns about overpopulation to gain support for birth control. Ernst, like other leaders in the birth control and civil liberties movements, was eager to take advantage of the political and economic climate to overturn not only laws against birth control but also to clear the way for the state to provide birth control services, first in Puerto Rico and eventually in the mainland United States.[57]

Baldwin's trip to Boston in 1931 and Morris Ernst's journey to Puerto Rico in 1940 marked important milestones on the road to developing sexual civil liberties, but neither followed a direct or preordained route. In deciding which cases to take up, Baldwin, Ernst, and other ACLU leaders looked first for seriousness of purpose, absence of commercial intent, evidence of political bias, and personal connections that traced a path, more often than not, through the streets, clubs, and bedrooms of Greenwich Village. Their approach evolved in the 1930s in response to developments in the birth control movement, theater censorship, nudist appeals for assistance, and changes associated with the Great Depression, among them concerns about overpopulation. By the end of the decade, ACLU leaders had begun to take very public roles on issues of censorship and legal repression related to sexuality. In addition, through the National Council on Freedom from Censorship, ACLU leaders reached beyond their web of friends and acquaintances to defend individuals with commercial intentions, including Broadway producers and popular sex lecturers, ensuring the ACLU an ever-widening arena for its anticensorship work.

Pragmatism characterized the ACLU's anticensorship agenda in the 1930s. Accordingly, ACLU leaders defended nudists after recognizing that the resonance between mainstream values and nudist ideals could make such cases especially powerful tools for overturning laws against sexual material. They also approved the bait-and-switch tactic by which the theater community agreed to a self-censorship regime just long enough to stave off the threat of state censorship, and they notified public officials of indecent burlesque shows in an effort to highlight the stricter standards applied to the legitimate theater. For tactical reasons, ACLU leaders also went against the wishes of their colleague, Mary Ware Dennett, to back Sanger's plan, advocating that birth control for women be placed under the control of physicians as a strategy for attracting support from the powerful medical profession. Finally, under the influence of the New Deal, they began to consider ways that state intervention might advance their broader goals.

ACLU founders were generally suspicious of state power and eager to champion individualistic solutions to social problems. With regard to sexually oriented material, including birth control information, sex education, nudism, and suggestive stage plays, they demanded freedom from state intervention. But as the Great Depression stoked fears of overpopulation and concerns about the fertility of the poor, it weakened opposition to birth control and also to state intervention. Under the New Deal, ACLU leaders began to encourage government distribution of birth control information and services, a reflection of their pragmatism but also a sign that they recognized the possibility that state power could advance the cause of sexual civil liberties. Serious questions about what role the state should play in providing reproductive options would not resurface until the 1960s and 1970s, but the ACLU had already begun to stretch its sexual civil liberties agenda to embrace state intervention some thirty years earlier.

Many early ACLU leaders were as eager to resist capitalist and commercial exploitation as to protect freedom of expression. But their defense of nudist magazines, popular sex lecturers, and legitimate theater in the 1930s eroded their bias against commercial speech as it highlighted the difficulties of distinguishing between serious-minded educational material and frivolous for-profit fare. As they became more comfortable defending expression designed for commercial purposes, ACLU leaders increasingly employed an idiom of commerce—the marketplace of ideas—that demanded unfettered consumers as well as producers of speech. This new emphasis on consumers also originated in pragmatic considerations, and it would fundamentally transform the ACLU's work on behalf of sexual civil liberties as well as popular understandings of freedom of speech for decades to come.

3

"Are You Free to Read, See, and Hear?"

Creating Consumer Rights out of the First Amendment, 1940s–1960s

On February 8, 1961, J. P. McGlynn, a diesel instructor with the Union Pacific Railroad, fretted over the latest achievements of the local Citizen's Committee for Decent Literature. The group had convinced several newsstands in Omaha, Nebraska, to stop selling *Playboy*, McGlynn's favorite magazine and one he enjoyed reading with his two teenage sons. Suspecting that Hugh Hefner, the magazine's editor, and Pat Malin, executive director of the American Civil Liberties Union, would share his frustration, McGlynn implored them to defend his "freedom to read." McGlynn's letter points to a budding relationship between the ACLU, *Playboy* magazine, and *Playboy* readers, one that signaled important developments in conceptions of the First Amendment. It also reflected a growing sense among many citizens that civil liberties included not just an individual right to speak but also rights as individual consumers to read, see, and hear.[1]

This story exposes an aspect of sexual civil liberties that many now take for granted—the idea that the First Amendment protects consumers as well as producers of speech. Political theorists had long linked citizens' access to information with democracy, but they did so by prioritizing communitarian values that treated citizens in the aggregate as a tool for achieving and sustaining democracy.[2] What the ACLU did, increasingly in partnership with commercial producers and other interest groups, was fundamentally different and designed to empower citizens to claim access to information and images as an individual right. As ACLU leaders and others reframed the First Amendment to include consumers' rights, they abandoned, once and for all, their earlier commitment to defending only matter created for educational, political, artistic, or intellectual purposes and increasingly defended material produced purely for profit and pleasure.

That the First Amendment underwent a consumer-driven reinterpretation in the postwar period is scarcely surprising given the era's celebration of economic prosperity and the consumer goods that promoted the superiority of American capitalism. But the roots of the ACLU's attention to consumer rights stretched back to prewar developments, including Depression-era attention to consumers and consumption as causes of the economic downturn; the rise of pressure groups that threatened consumer access to movies, books, and magazines; and ongoing concerns about corporate consolidation that had long troubled Progressives. On the eve of World War II, none of these matters had been resolved. The antitrust laws and policies Progressives championed had achieved limited effects at best and were, at worst, redirected against organized labor. The Great Depression provoked increased criticism of big business even as it inspired New Deal programs that allowed and encouraged the very consolidation and collusion that older antitrust laws aimed to prevent. Moreover, government spending during World War II exacerbated this trend by lavishing funds and favors on corporations large enough to meet military demands. The time was ripe for a new assessment of consumerism.

The postwar culture of consumption changed everything—from intimate relationships to public accommodations, from suburban domestic architecture to corporate urban planning, from neighborhood geography to geopolitical strategy.[3] This environment nurtured the ACLU's growing support for commercial producers of speech even as it impelled the ACLU to fight for the consumer's right to read, see, and hear—a right that would significantly expand the boundaries of sexual civil liberties.

ACLU leaders were not the first to develop a notion of media-related consumer rights. Radio reformers preceded them but focused on collective rather than individual consumer rights. Because radio was a public medium with scarce airwaves, it experienced an unprecedented level of government regulation designed to ensure that it fulfill the "public convenience, interest, or necessity." In the 1920s and 1930s, radio reformers took advantage of that public charge to demand that radio stations provide equal access to political candidates. ACLU leaders supported them, advocating in addition that broadcasters practice an "open door policy" that would allow discussion of controversial issues like birth control and Communism. During this period of vigorous radio reform, citizen groups formed "listeners' councils" to communicate their preferences to broadcasters and federal regulators, and in the 1940s the ACLU, led by Morris Ernst and Elmer Rice, began to consider the impact of media consolidation—such as single ownership of local radio stations and newspapers—on consumers. Their focus remained, however, on consumers' collective rather than individual rights.[4]

From the 1910s through the 1930s, many groups also employed collective consumer power to reduce the amount of public sexual display by pressuring theater owners to feature "moral" shows. The Catholic Theatre Movement,

Better Movie Movement, Legion of Decency, and other religious groups rated movies, administered a "pledge of decency" to church members, conducted boycotts, and distributed seals of approval to worthy businesses.[5] Because these activities did not rely on government coercion but focused on educating consumers, guiding their purchases, and giving them a voice, pressure group leaders argued that they did not exercise censorship. Rather, they defended consumer rights against media monopolies, brought democracy and deliberation to consumption, and created a form of commercial citizenship that mimicked American political life.

ACLU policy on this sort of pressure group activity did not emerge easily given the uncertain relevance of private collective action to civil liberties. Instead of relying on state coercion, groups like the Legion of Decency, for example, employed pickets and boycotts, using speech and consumer protest strategies that Progressive reformers and ACLU founders had long supported when employed on behalf of labor. But when these techniques allowed private groups to restrict the media, many ACLU leaders considered their work as dangerous as government censorship and issued public statements on the matter. Under Elmer Rice's leadership, the National Council on Freedom from Censorship (NCFC) publicly accused Catholic leaders of censorship in 1934, declaring that under the First Amendment "no superimposed authority may dictate what the adult may see or hear or read." Moderates in the ACLU framed their concerns about the Legion of Decency in terms of slippery slopes—the organization's activities might lay groundwork for state censorship. Alone on the ACLU board, John Haynes Holmes strenuously objected to ACLU charges against the Legion, accusing his colleagues of mistaking organized protests and consumer boycotts for censorship. Our business with the Legion of Decency, Holmes insisted, should "begin and end with guaranteeing them their full right under our Constitution to advocate their doctrines." Holmes lost this battle when the ACLU released a letter accusing Legion leaders of violating the free will of individual Catholics by requiring that they boycott motion pictures.[6] Beneath this rhetoric lay a nascent argument about consumer rights under the First Amendment, one that emerged with gusto in response to concerns about communications monopolies and the Catholic movement's growing influence over them.

For at least two decades, ACLU leaders had not considered it their business to condemn the emerging communications monopolies, such as the Associated Press (AP), the National Association of Broadcasters (NAB), and the Motion Picture Producers and Distributors of America (MPPDA). Created shortly after the ACLU's founding, in 1921, the MPPDA consisted of seventeen motion picture producers who collaborated to gain control over labor and stave off censorship through a studio system that determined what pictures were made and by whom, a public relations office that censored scripts and film, and a distribution arrangement that exerted control over independent exhibitors. They succeeded and, by the 1940s, the MPPDA dominated a consolidated industry that proudly joined the war effort with movies that romanticized combat, glamorized women war workers, demonized Germans and the Japanese, and otherwise promoted the Roosevelt administration's aims.[7]

The two most zealous critics of media monopolies on the ACLU Board of Directors were Elmer Rice and Morris Ernst. Rice resented what he called the "organized blackmail" that led motion picture executives in 1931 to purge his Pulitzer Prize–winning play *Street Scene* of images and language likely to offend pressure groups. Ernst developed a full-blown thesis against modern business monopolies, *Too Big* (1940), that introduced a civil libertarian critique of corporate media monopolies. Ernst spoke of a marketplace of ideas using concepts that echoed those articulated by classical theorists several centuries earlier. His vision was an old-style communitarian one of "the freest possible marketplace for thought" so that "truth will win out." But the adversaries he identified were new—the MPPDA, the NAB, and news syndicates like the AP—all instruments of media consolidation that restricted speakers' access and thus reduced the availability of diverse views. "While we [in the ACLU] are fighting a particular effort to suppress the freedom of thought or expression of a particular man," Ernst lamented, "the curse of bigness" ensures that "fewer and fewer people" dominate "the pipelines of thought—the newspapers, the radio and the movies." Ernst called for the ACLU to reorient its approach to civil liberties, demanding that it take affirmative steps to ensure a free marketplace of ideas. The ACLU could do this by holding the government responsible for guaranteeing that all points of view had access to media outlets.[8]

Ernst's colleagues were dubious but not dismissive. Some worried that tackling the problem of media consolidation would divert their energies into economic battles that were only tangentially related to civil liberties. Moreover, in the 1940s, the attention of the ACLU, like the rest of the country, was focused elsewhere as leaders struggled over whether to support the United States' entry into the war, allow Communists to serve on the board, defend conscientious objectors, or challenge Roosevelt's internment order. Even in the midst of these crises, many considered Ernst's critique of media consolidation, but they began to redirect it toward more conventional and individualistic ACLU goals.

In 1942, ACLU director Roger Baldwin suggested that, from "the audience point of view," communications monopolies raised civil liberties questions regarding the individual rights of consumers. ACLU attorneys began to incorporate these notions into legal briefs and even brought them to the attention of the

Supreme Court in *Martin v. City of Struthers* (1942), a case that would become foundational for consumers' rights under the First Amendment. On behalf of the ACLU, board member Dorothy Kenyon filed an amicus brief that argued for a right "to listen as well as to speak, to read as well as to write." Justice Hugo Black echoed her thoughts in his written opinion, declaring that the right to speak "necessarily protects the right to receive it." Jehovah's Witnesses must be allowed to canvass, he maintained, not only to protect their own rights but also the rights of those receiving their literature. Thus, a consumer's right that Rice and the NCFC alone invoked against pressure group censorship in the 1930s was transformed by ACLU attorneys in the 1940s into a constitutional theory that gained the imprimatur of the U.S. Supreme Court.[9]

Concerns about corporate monopoly, media consumers' rights, and freedom of speech acquired new urgency in the postwar years. Radio again became a focal point as the chair of the Federal Communications Commission, James Lawrence Fly, popularized the idea of listeners' rights in an address, "Freedom to Listen—a Universal Principle." Fly's ideas caught the attention of President Franklin Roosevelt, who advocated a postwar international broadcasting system premised on the "freedom to listen," a principle that guided Justice Department antitrust suits against the Associated Press and the motion picture industry. It also showed up in a report issued by the Commission of Inquiry on Freedom of the Press, a group of prominent citizens whose *Time*-funded study recognized the possibility of distinct rights for consumers under the First Amendment. Accordingly, citizens began to demand that these rights be honored. Labor union leaders, for example, challenged the NAB for withholding airtime from them, arguing that listeners had a right to hear organized labor's point of view. Media consumers' rights also appeared in the 1948 United Nations Declaration of Human Rights, whose drafting committee, chaired by Eleanor Roosevelt, recognized a right "to seek, receive, and impart information and ideas through any media."[10]

Suspicion of media conglomerates and receptiveness to consumers' rights to read, see, and hear approached high tide by the middle of the 1940s. In this new climate, Ernst substituted the language of consumer rights for his earlier rhetoric about corporate consolidation and thereby helped to initiate a new ACLU agenda that would have momentous consequences not only for the organization but also for juridical and popular understandings of consumer rights under the First Amendment.[11]

ACLU leaders treated the shift casually, using language such as "of course freedom of expression implies freedom to hear." That the shift was a real one, however, can be seen in leaders' own actions and the responses they elicited. ACLU leaders publicized the new approach in a formal resolution that curiously attempted to deny the reason for its existence by characterizing it as *not* new but as old as the First Amendment itself. "Freedom of speech, press and assembly," it declared, "imply freedom to hear, read and see without interference by public authorities" or by "private agencies." ACLU affiliates quickly picked up the new language and perspective, agreeing that the real victim of censorship had always been the consumer.[12]

The new consumer-oriented policy helped the ACLU inspire wider public interest in its work. Since the organization's earliest days, leaders complained that beyond those who stood to profit—producers, exhibitors, and publishers—few people protested the closing of a burlesque theater, censoring of a motion picture, banning of a nudist magazine, or seizure of a racy novel. But by shifting attention from producers to consumers the ACLU's new approach promised to persuade more people to take censorship personally. As ACLU member and censored author James Farrell explained to Baldwin, we need to "popularize the idea that censorship is not [only] an invasion of the rights of the author; it is also an invasion of the rights of the reader. If this idea is popularized in the minds of liberal readers it would then be possible to stir them" to protest against censorship on their own. Hoping for this very outcome, Baldwin issued a press release and a new ACLU pamphlet, "Are you FREE to READ—SEE—HEAR?" that pledged to support the rights of media consumers. ACLU members responded enthusiastically, one by writing simply, "I am glad to see the A.C.L.U on the side of the consumer-listener."[13]

The consumer-rights approach also sharpened the ACLU's criticism of private business practices that prevented "the public from seeing, hearing or reading." It implicated commercial vendors who deferred to pressure groups or declined to stock particular material by holding them responsible for guaranteeing the consumer's First Amendment rights. In defense of consumer rights, the ACLU denounced the local theater exhibitor who rejected *The Outlaw*, the druggist who refused to stock *Esquire*, and the community bookseller who removed Edmund Wilson's *Memoirs of Hecate County* from the shelf. Accordingly, ACLU leaders supported the federal government's antitrust suit against Paramount Pictures, arguing that producer ownership of theaters violated "the fundamental rights of motion picture audiences," who should be able to "see all films freely and on an equitable basis." On these same grounds, they considered initiating a lawsuit against the MPPDA for restricting the movies available to consumers through the Motion Picture Production Code.[14] Ironically though, the new policy also crystallized a shared interest between the ACLU and the MPPDA. Although the two organizations would continue to tangle over the MPPDA's own internal censorship apparatus, leaders of both organizations agreed that casting censorship as a violation of consumer rights could be quite useful.

Morris Ernst lost his bid to bring the ACLU into a full-blown war against media monopoly, but his efforts combined with broader legal and cultural developments to reorient ACLU policy around the rights of individual consumers in the marketplace of ideas. By 1948, the ACLU announced that it would consider

Here's A Cartoon That Will Help

THIS 3-column cartoon is one of a series of three provided for use in local publicity campaigns against motion picture censorship. It is issued in mat form and is suitable for use in any newspaper having its own casting plant. It costs you nothing. Order your mats through The American Recreation League, Riggs Building, Washington, D. C. This cartoon may be obtained in slide form at a cost of 20 cents, from the Standard Slide Corporation, 211 West 48th Street, New York City.

Figure 3.1 Undated cartoon produced by the American Recreation League. It depicts censorship as directed at motion picture consumers rather than producers. (Courtesy, Minnesota Historical Society)

any effort to prevent "the public from seeing, hearing or reading" a "form of attempted censorship." Ernst, meanwhile, circulated his ideas through scholarly articles, letters to public officials, a memoir, and conversations with publishers and motion picture moguls.[15]

Ernst had employed the language of consumer rights to obtain support for his campaign against media monopoly, but the ACLU took these ideas in a different direction. For Ernst, media consumers were a tool for opening up the marketplace to more producers of speech, but for the ACLU, the point became simply enhancing media consumers' rights to what had already been produced. Ernst wanted to initiate legislative investigations, draft bills, launch a massive public education campaign, and create alternative new media outlets with broad public access, but the ACLU board declined such a sweeping agenda, announcing simply that "restrictions on freedom in communication by private agencies are a proper field for the Union's activities where the right of the public to see, read and hear is clearly involved." In some ways, Ernst's approach reflected an older Progressive mind-set that prioritized the common good over individual rights and noncommercial over commercial speech, a mind-set that obtained decreasing support among the ACLU's newer generation of leaders.[16] But because Ernst's proposals were also current, they gained traction in the burgeoning postwar consumer economy that emerged alongside Cold War–inspired concerns about media monopolies, pressure group censorship, and freedom of speech. In this context, Ernst's broad communitarian arguments for an open marketplace of ideas would be channeled into a narrower theory of individual consumer rights under the First Amendment.

The year 1950 opened a new era for the ACLU. Founding executive director Roger Baldwin, distracted by international affairs and weary of managing the organization's internal politics and difficult personalities, retired and cast his sights overseas. Others claimed that the ACLU board ousted him. Many of Baldwin's colleagues thought his penchant for control hindered the organization's growth; his cult of personality stifled change and discouraged new leadership from emerging; his distaste for administrative tasks left important work undone, and his dictatorial and overbearing presence alienated talented staff. His replacement, Patrick Murphy Malin, could not compete with Baldwin's charisma, but he brought formidable administrative skills and ambitions to expand the ACLU into a mass-membership organization. During Malin's twelve-year tenure, the ACLU increased its membership sixfold, setting in motion what would become a twenty-four-year period of growth. It developed and staffed affiliate offices in major cities around the country, integrated national and affiliate memberships, and created, for the first time, "a truly national organizational structure." The ACLU's growth and maturation accompanied and encouraged its escalating involvement in national issues, including mass movements and commercial media. When ACLU leaders took on cases related to obscenity or sexuality, they no longer limited their defense work to their own members or acquaintances, but increasingly relied on cooperating attorneys and amicus briefs rather than direct involvement. At the same time they defended commercial entities and consumer rights against pressure groups as well as state censorship.[17]

ACLU support for a notorious pornographer in the 1950s signaled the shift. Samuel Roth might have been one of the least attractive but most flamboyant entrepreneurs to attract ACLU attention. A self-educated immigrant from Austria, he grew up on New York's Lower East Side, mixed with anarchists, attended Emma Goldman lectures, and later opened a bookshop in Greenwich Village—activities that might have brought him into contact with any number of the ACLU's founding members. However, he rose to local fame by dealing in material no other business would touch—books, pamphlets, and magazines with sexually explicit and libelous content. When Roth, who had served a number of jail sentences for violating obscenity laws, sought ACLU assistance in 1940, its leaders dismissed him as one of the many shameless commercial exploiters of sex whom they had for two decades proudly refused to defend.[18]

By 1955, ACLU leaders reconsidered assisting Roth, when the nation's leading publisher of mail-order erotica faced criminal charges related to a mass mailing that had generated a deluge of complaints from postal customers. But they were thinking strategically of their upcoming testimony against postal censorship

Figure 3.2 Founding director Roger Baldwin congratulates his successor, Patrick Malin, December 22, 1949. (Courtesy, Princeton University Library)

before a Senate subcommittee. Representing Roth and his "sexy come-on advertising for sexy stuff" at this moment could poison their public relations and jeopardize their legislative efforts. Ernst and Pilpel considered taking Roth's case as part of their private practice, but feared that their close relationship with one of the presiding judges, Judge Jerome Frank, a friend of civil liberties, could backfire if it led Frank to recuse himself.[19] It was without direct ACLU involvement that Roth pursued his appeal in the Second Circuit Court of Appeals, where he faced three judges, one of them Frank. A proponent of Sigmund Freud and pioneer in efforts to bring law to bear on social problems, Frank frequently consulted Ernst, his close friend of twenty years, and he did so on Roth's case—something he could not have done had Ernst represented Roth. In the end, Frank joined the majority in ruling against Roth, but he did so in a concurring opinion and only in deference to the Supreme Court. Frank's statement drew on Ernst's writings and Alfred Kinsey's sex research to urge the High Court to reopen the issue and consider the likelihood that obscenity laws violated the U.S. Constitution. The Court should no longer allow statutory suppression of material that merely provoked "undesirable sexual thoughts, feelings, or desires" but had not been proven to create a "clear and present danger."[20]

ACLU board members Herbert Levy, Elmer Rice, Harriet Pilpel, and Rowland Watts read Frank's concurrence with glee, but their sentiments were not shared by everyone in the ACLU. The president of the Louisiana Civil Liberties Union worried that Frank's reasoning would erase all barriers on public displays of pornography. His fears foreshadowed disagreements over obscenity that would soon break out when Rice demanded that the ACLU reconsider its obscenity policy. Lamenting that some board members "would go to the stake for the right to utter any political or religious heresy," Rice complained that many would nevertheless balk at the suggestion that sexual expression should be equally free. Heartened by Frank's opinion, Rice renewed his efforts to persuade the ACLU to renounce obscenity law once and for all.[21]

Rice's efforts instigated what would become a protracted battle, one waged throughout the ACLU national office and its affiliates. As with consumer rights to speech and other new approaches, leaders experimented before they began formulating policy, this time in an amicus brief filed on behalf of Roth's appeal to the U.S. Supreme Court. The postal hearings behind them, ACLU leaders happily used Roth's case as an opportunity to articulate a clearer position on obscenity, highlight ideas in Frank's concurrence, and honor Frank, who died suddenly of a heart attack just months after writing his momentous opinion. The ACLU brief explicitly extended to sexual expression the "clear and present danger" test long accepted for political speech, maintaining that "there is no special category of obscenity or pornography to which different constitutional tests apply." To be constitutional a statute may target only material proven "beyond a reasonable doubt" to induce criminal behavior in individuals who would not otherwise engage in such behavior. After setting a high bar, the brief went on to explain why it could not be cleared. Citing Alfred Kinsey's theory of "sensual receptiveness," it maintained that a specific book, movie, or magazine could not be blamed for stimulating sex impulses or actions because such material possessed no inherent ability to provoke sexual response; that response depended on an individual's unique receptivity to stimulation by the material in question.[22]

These arguments gained attention among the majority on the Supreme Court in *U.S. v. Roth* (1957). In private conference, one justice commented approvingly on Frank's lower-court opinion, and another agreed that literature should not be banned "merely because it produced lustful thoughts." Chief Justice Earl Warren embraced ACLU claims that readers' responses to sexual material vary, though he still supported punishing "the commercial exploitation of the morbid and shameful craving for materials with prurient effect." In two separate dissents, Justices John Marshall Harlan, Hugo Black, and William O. Douglas agreed with the ACLU that obscenity could not be singled out for differential treatment. Nor could the court define obscenity as material capable of "arousing sexual thoughts"—after all, sexual thoughts could be provoked by perfectly innocent material. Moreover, sexual thoughts did not necessarily lead to action, deviant or otherwise; so, while the government might proscribe public nudity, adultery, or other forms of sexual misbehavior, it could not censor speech about that behavior.[23]

Despite these gratifying nods, the Court as a whole rejected the ACLU's reasoning outright in a six-to-three decision upholding Roth's conviction. Writing for the majority, Justice William Brennan borrowed language and logic from the American Law Institute (ALI)—a private group of judges, attorneys, and legal scholars that had worked since 1923 to make penal law more uniform, effective, humane, and scientifically grounded. Indeed, even as the justices considered *Roth*, ALI members hastened to release a model obscenity law, hoping to influence the outcome of the first obscenity case to reach the U.S. Supreme Court. The ALI did not take as liberal a view of obscenity as the ACLU did, but it did employ ACLU ideas in its model code, criticizing current laws for purporting to address obscenity's effect on viewers—something "we know little or nothing about"—and focusing instead on qualities intrinsic to the material itself. It explicitly eliminated from the definition items the ACLU had long defended, including nudist and birth control literature, and it defined obscenity as material whose "predominant appeal" is to "prurient interest" in violation of "current community standards." Brennan echoed the ALI draft as he narrowed the definition of obscenity to material whose "dominant theme" appealed to the "prurient interest" of the "average person." Retooling the ALI's definition of obscenity as material that exceeds "customary limits of candor," Brennan created the "contemporary community standards" test. He defined obscenity as material "utterly without redeeming social importance" and affirmed the constitutionality of the federal obscenity statute that prohibited mailing it.[24] It was a decision that contained a little something for everyone—except Samuel Roth.

While Roth commenced a five-year prison sentence, antiobscenity pressure groups around the nation took courage from the Supreme Court's opinion. Not only did the court acknowledge the existence of obscenity and reaffirm the legitimacy of laws against it, community standards moved to the foreground. Determined to shape and represent those community standards, pressure groups intensified their activities, updated their methods, and diversified their ranks. Countless local decency groups joined the twenty-five-year-old Legion of Decency, the twenty-one-year-old National Organization of Decent Literature (NODL), and a new Churchmen's Commission for Decent Literature in calling for a war on obscenity. Statements released by these organizations claimed to recognize the importance of free speech and due process even as they exhorted the public and law enforcement officials to enforce existing obscenity laws. The ACLU's associate director, Alan Reitman, recognized NODL's rhetoric against censorship and for civil liberties as responses to ACLU campaigns, but he regretted that decency groups continued to direct, often with great success, obscenity law and pressure tactics against materials they found objectionable.[25]

Roth appealed his lengthy sentence as the ACLU became involved with two related cases—one involving a homosexual magazine and the other a nudist one—that advanced to the U.S. Supreme Court, where they benefited mightily from *Roth*. ACLU leaders planned to file an amicus brief on behalf of *ONE*, a four-year-old magazine published by an early homophile organization, the Mattachine Society, after the Los Angeles postmaster declared it obscene and unmailable. They lost the opportunity to do so, however, when the Supreme Court exonerated the magazine with one swift motion in a decision that offered no written opinion and simply cited *Roth*.[26] The nudist magazine *Sunshine & Health* also squeezed victory out of Samuel Roth's defeat. After a decade of litigation, in 1958 the U.S. Supreme Court also cited *Roth* when vindicating, without comment, the ACLU's longtime client, Ilsley Boone. Boone owed his victory not only to the ACLU and the hapless Roth, but also to the ACLU's vast network of excellent cooperating attorneys, who also helped Boone obtain second-class postal rates for his magazine. Baldwin celebrated Boone's triumphs, thanking his attorneys and proclaiming the right to "appear nude in the press without going to jail or running foul with the Post Office Department."[27]

Nudist practice also returned briefly to the top of the ACLU's agenda in the 1950s as Midwestern legislatures and law enforcement officials cracked down on nudist camps and films. National ACLU staff served as a clearinghouse, connecting individual plaintiffs with nearby affiliates and attorneys, sharing legal arguments, and standing ready to bring the national ACLU in as amicus—literally, "friend of the court"—when cases advanced to the U.S. Supreme Court. Behind the scenes, the ACLU contributed to a number of significant lower-court victories that reversed, on grounds of privacy, nudist losses from the 1930s. In *People v. Hildabridle* (1958), the Michigan Supreme Court acquitted Earl Hildabridle and his codefendants of violating indecent exposure laws, because they practiced nudism in private where the law had no right to intervene. In *Excelsior Pictures v. Regents of the University of the State of New York* (1957), the New York State Court of Appeals disarmed New York's 1935 antinudist law by interpreting it as a prohibition merely on "nudity in public or quasi-public places," not in private nudist camps.[28]

That nudists obtained these victories while a rash of obscenity cases found their way to the U.S. Supreme Court in the late 1950s signaled major changes in the nation's sexual culture. The U.S. military's provision of pinups for GIs, the infusion of those pinups into civilian life, and private publishers' eagerness to stimulate and meet demand for this material led to a proliferation of racy books and magazines. Business entrepreneurs' efforts to expand their consumer base by masculinizing consumption also played a role. New periodicals for men—*Esquire, Playboy,* and their imitators—used sexualized images of women to reassure male readers that reading magazines, throwing parties, and grooming themselves need not compromise their heterosexuality or their masculinity.[29] Meanwhile, the "paperback explosion" and direct-mail boom provided new vehicles for producing and circulating sexy material. All of these developments contributed to a tumultuous cultural environment that increased obscenity traffic in the court system. The arbitrary administrative censorship long employed by postal authorities and customs officials declined under pressure from the ACLU and the courts, but pressure group censorship and the number of obscenity prosecutions swelled. In this context, ACLU leaders revisited their policy on pressure groups and reconsidered their negotiated approach to obscenity.

Even as administrative censorship declined, pressure groups and congressional hearings on obscenity, pornography, and juvenile delinquency incited more calls for censorship. Sponsored by Congressman Ezekiel C. Gathings in 1952, Senator Estes Kefauver in 1954, and Congresswoman Kathryn E. Granahan in 1959, friendly witnesses cast pornography as a covert tool for subverting the United States' moral fiber and superiority in its Cold War against Communism.[30] When ACLU leaders testified, they too spoke in a Cold War idiom, urging legislators to recognize freedom of speech and consumer rights—rather than morality and Christianity—as the distinguishing features between "our way of life" and Communism. "It is not only the freedom of the publisher that is at stake," the ACLU's executive director explained. "It is also the freedom of 160,000,000 Americans whose Constitution guarantees them that no governmental official may tell them what they may or may not read." But ACLU testimony could not compete with findings that Americans spent $1 billion annually on mail-order pornography and millions of postal patrons received unwanted "lewd and obscene material." These reports inspired the creation of the Comics Code, gave rise to new obscenity laws, and provoked even greater pressure group activism.[31]

ACLU criticism of pressure groups extended back to its earliest days, but not until the 1950s did leaders begin to articulate a consistent criticism of pressure groups rooted in consumer rights. More specifically, they castigated pressure groups for employing economic boycotts, seals of approval, and other strategies that divested "citizens of their right to read." The national office issued press releases and pamphlets, challenged the congressional commissions' findings, lobbied against censorship bills, tried to influence media code authorities, and loudly condemned pressure groups as agents of censorship, all in the name of the consumer's rights. One ACLU radio announcement declared the importance of free expression "in the struggle against Communist tyranny" and directly asked listeners, "Are you being deprived of the chance to read, see, or hear things in the press, films, radio, theater, books and magazines?" The national office advised its affiliates to protect "the public's right to see, read and hear" by treating local exhibitors and booksellers as public servants with public obligations, offering them ACLU support in case of legal trouble, pressuring leaders of decency groups to denounce boycotts, and organizing counterprotests when necessary. The ACLU insisted that because motion picture interests and book publishers enjoyed a "special relationship to the public," they must take responsibility for maintaining the "public's freedom to see, read and hear everything." Many affiliates responded enthusiastically, joining the fight with gusto and issuing strong statements of their own.[32]

But the ACLU also confronted resistance to its position on pressure group censorship from within and beyond its own ranks. Many ACLU members wrote the national office, demanding to know why the organization opposed Congress's efforts to protect children from sexually explicit and violent comic books and mailings. One indignant woman refused to "stand by submissively when smut peddlers are *free* to send lewd pictures and literature in the mail to my children!" The ACLU replied that its job was to protect everyone's civil liberties and to prevent American literary culture from being reduced to the level of a child's nursery. But ACLU leaders struggled with the issue. Two board members, Norman Thomas and Dorothy Dunbar Bromley, implored the ACLU to recognize the need for laws to protect children. "The ACLU's position that freedom to read can be applied as logically to children as to adults," Bromley wrote, "is completely unrealistic." Influential elements of the popular press also scoffed at the ACLU's implicit treatment of juveniles as if they were grown-ups. The Northern California affiliate objected to what it considered an ACLU attack on the free speech of pressure groups. Meanwhile, most media industry leaders resisted ACLU offers to defend them against pressure group censorship.[33] ACLU leaders, frustrated with the ongoing effectiveness of pressure groups and the relative quiescence of motion picture producers, publishers, and others, became ever more committed to the project of convincing consumers of their rights and rallying them to defend those rights.

The ACLU also had powerful allies in its defense of the consumer's right to read, see, and hear. In 1951, *Redbook* published "What Censorship Keeps You From Knowing." An article later condensed for *Reader's Digest*, it refocused concerns about censorship on the consumer and encouraged readers to join the ACLU. The concept of a "right to read" took hold as librarians, teachers, publishers, lawyers, and judges used it to defend themselves against Red Scare–inspired censorship. Librarians fought for the "freedom to read" when confronted with demands that they withdraw "un-American" materials from circulation. The American Library Association (ALA) issued a widely publicized manifesto, "On Freedom to Read," in 1953 that condemned "private groups and public authorities" who banned books or otherwise aimed to restrict their availability to the public. "The freedom to read is guaranteed by the Constitution," the ALA declared in a statement that gladdened the hearts of ACLU colleagues. The American Book Publishers Council (ABPC) conducted its own spirited defense of "the freedom to read," initiating Right-to-Read committees around the country. Together, the ABPC and the ALA formed a Commission on the Freedom to Read made up of prestigious university professors who issued a report urging communities to form Right-to-Read committees against pressure group censorship. Meanwhile, Judge Curtis Bok, a prominent Pennsylvania judge, delivered a radio address entitled "The Freedom to Read," and the American Bar Association pronounced "the freedom to read" a "corollary of the constitutional guarantee of freedom of the press." Two years later, Paul Blanshard, a journalist and attorney who worked closely with the ACLU, published *The Right to Read: The Battle Against Censorship*. In the next few years, the ACLU and its affiliates helped Columbia Pictures advertise its new film, *Storm Center*, featuring Bette Davis as an embattled librarian who defended "the freedom to read!" An ACLU board member published *The Freedom to Read: Perspective and Program*, and ACLU staff advised citizens to form "Freedom to Read Committees" to recruit librarians, ministers, rabbis, publishers, lawyers, teachers, businessmen, and labor leaders into the campaign against censorship. ACLU leaders communicated regularly with these groups and individuals and celebrated the extensive alliance they formed for "readers' rights" and against censorship.[34]

By the middle of the 1950s, ACLU leaders had adopted a strong policy against pressure group censorship, but they still struggled to determine how it should influence the organization's rhetoric and legal strategies. Elmer Rice took various members to task for not adhering closely enough to his understanding of the new policy. When, for example, one of his ACLU colleagues published a letter to the editor of *The New Leader* admitting that he would withhold patronage from a store whose inventory he did not approve of, Rice accused him of issuing "an invitation to the public to organize a boycott." Some groups had become so skilled at using economic pressure to achieve their ends that several ACLU attorneys explored the possibility of suing groups that conducted effective boycotts on the grounds that they restrained trade. But the ACLU's endorsement of some boycotts and condemnation of others left it vulnerable to charges of hypocrisy. ACLU leaders responded to accusations of inconsistency for approving of "Negroes [who] boycott segregated bus companies" but condemning Catholics who boycott purveyors of "smut," by asserting that "the commodity of ideas" should receive "special protection in a democracy." Moreover, whereas boycotting an objectionable movie brought censorship, boycotting segregated buses brought justice.[35]

In response to these criticisms, ACLU leaders revised their policy to reflect their evolving efforts to single out boycotts waged against movies, books, and magazines as uniquely illegitimate. They did so by amplifying one phrase from their initial statement—"intimidation and reprisal have no place in the field of ideas"—and carefully, painstakingly distinguishing between acceptable and unacceptable boycotts. Under the new policy, the ACLU condemned any boycotts that would limit the freedom to read, see, and hear. ACLU leaders struggled to bring the Constitution to bear on the issue, arguing that such boycotts violate "the spirit of expression contained in the First Amendment" and the "principle of freedom" by exercising prior restraint and limiting "the freedom of choice of the whole community." They criticized all groups—religious, civil rights, labor, parent-teacher, and women's—that "engage in censorship activity" but reserved their harshest words for NODL precisely because so many public officials and private businesses consulted NODL lists to determine which titles to remove from shelves, newsstands, and marquees.[36]

In a sweeping call to arms signed by 160 writers, editors, and publishers, in 1957 the ACLU offered to assist not only producers of speech but also prospective consumers who have "the will to explore legal avenues for the maintenance of their freedom." The plea showed up in national-circulation magazines and newspapers and the ACLU's own widely circulated pamphlets with a cover letter by Morris Ernst titled "Your *Freedom to Read* is in Danger." ACLU leaders did not just offer assistance—they begged for an opportunity to provide it. For purposes of legal standing, they needed a complainant, but even without one they made legal threats, including empty ones, informing NODL officials, for example, that "some attorneys" considered their activities "a restraint in trade, punishable under the anti-trust laws." Because legal action against pressure groups was so difficult to execute, ACLU leaders concentrated on educational work, urging consumers to defend their rights to read, see, and hear—exhorting producers and distributors to hold the line against pressure groups, and prevailing upon pressure groups themselves to eschew activities the ACLU considered censorious.[37]

Reactions to the ACLU's new policy on pressure groups were quick and mixed. Many Catholics took the policy personally and wrote in to criticize it. "If we do not care to see filthy, lustful movies that is none of your business," one angry individual from Kansas City wrote. "We Catholics have free expression," the writer insisted, but we exercise it by "not having to see indecent movies." A man from Philadelphia spun the ACLU's language of freedom a different way when he declared himself "more free than you think, especially when I am divinely guided." A sister Philadelphian insisted that "freedom is not always a matter of being able to choose what we want to do, but rather peace of mind through knowing we are doing what is right." A couple of writers characterized the ACLU as an anti-Catholic organization of Jews whose primary goal was to help Jewish businesses make more money. A Catholic columnist complained that the ACLU did not appreciate the duty of citizens to safeguard the "common good" by persuading merchants to keep immoral literature out of public places frequented by children. An editorialist ridiculed the ACLU for defending children's rights "to read whatever they please." One woman insisted that the material attacked by decency groups did not disseminate ideas but operated "insidiously below the idea level, in a sub-cortical, thalamic region where morbid and degenerative emotional stimuli do far-reaching harm. A good idea," she agreed, "can combat a bad idea, but the most rational idea in the world sometimes cannot touch a complex emotional disturbance instigated knowingly by those who would pervert below the idea level."[38]

Many ACLU contributors and members also objected to the new policy, complaining also about the harsh and accusatory tone directed toward NODL and other pressure groups, and insisting on a dramatically different understanding of civil liberties. "Surely the right *not* to buy," one woman asserted, "is as important as the ability to purchase freely." An Indiana ACLU member criticized the organization for sending out anticensorship literature signed by producers—publishers, booksellers, authors, and playwrights—"persons who profit from such pandering." Claiming "the right as a consumer and as a parent" to fight the "pernicious influence" exerted by pornographic material, he insisted that scenes of "two humans copulating" should be confined to the "bedroom of married persons" and not placed in "the hands of my children.

I believe that I have a right to persuade others by all legal means to assist me in that endeavor. I believe that any attempt to curb me in that regard is a violation of my civil liberties."[39] The most damning criticism of the ACLU's position on pressure group censorship came from Alexander Meiklejohn, a respected authority on the First Amendment and founder of the ACLU's Northern California affiliate. Meiklejohn criticized the ACLU for conflating "official and private censorship" and treating both as violative of the First Amendment.[40]

The language of consumer rights surfaced often in statements of support for the ACLU's policy against pressure group censorship. Sometimes it was tinged with anti-Catholic sentiment. One woman, outraged to hear that "the Catholic group is censoring what Americans may read or write," applauded the ACLU. In her hometown of Orange, Texas, she admitted, Catholics "rule nearly everything," a problem she planned to address by using ACLU material as the basis of public talks against Catholic pressure groups. Two unexpected allies were *Presbyterian Life* and *The Churchman,* liberal Protestant journals that criticized pressure group censorship for denying the consumer's right to see and hear. Similarly, fifteen Protestant clergymen denounced Catholics who pressured local theaters to ban *Baby Doll* from the screen, asserting the "right to exercise our freedom of choice ... to see or not to see this film as we see fit." In applauding the ACLU's efforts, one woman condemned groups that try to "act as my censor on what I read and what movies I see." A man informed the ACLU that he was "thrilled by the speed with which you recognized the dangers" of economic boycotts that threaten "the American freedom to speak, read, and inquire."[41]

When popular television personality Mike Wallace interviewed Bennett Cerf, ACLU member and president of Random House, these arguments appeared before a national audience and inspired even more grassroots activism on behalf of consumer rights. Cerf explained the ACLU's case against pressure groups that exercised censorship, denouncing such groups as "self-appointed snoop hounds" who violate the "right to read." He praised the ACLU's statement against pressure group censorship and assured Wallace that the entire publishing industry agreed with it. A growing number of individuals—empowered by the concept of a right to read, see, and hear, and acting only in their capacity as consumers—contacted the ACLU to report on and seek advice regarding pressure group activity in their communities. They also created thousands of Right-to-Read committees that mobilized consumer influence to counter the pressure wielded by groups like NODL.[42]

ACLU leaders celebrated the results of their new initiative against pressure group censorship. Not only had their arguments attracted national attention and support, but they put NODL and other decency groups on the defensive. Catholic leaders, fearing for NODL's reputation, issued a statement disavowing censorship and commending freedom of speech, while NODL's executive secretary, Monsignor Thomas J. Fitzgerald, issued a public statement denying that NODL advocated censorship. He then asked that Malin inform him of any NODL-affiliated groups that engaged in "illegal boycott[s]" so that he could intervene—something he did at least twice. Other leaders of religious pressure groups consulted the ACLU to verify that their activities did not constitute censorship. Similarly, when the Southern California Council of Churches issued its 1959 report on "decency in literature and other mass media," it endorsed the ACLU's criticism of religious groups that imposed their judgment "upon the freedom of choice of the whole community."[43]

Even as the ACLU's efforts brought NODL to its knees, another influential pressure group emerged to fill the breach. Citizens for Decent Literature (CDL) shared NODL's vision and also exploited widespread concerns about juvenile delinquency and the nation's moral character along with the fever pitch of anti-Communism that gave a patriotic gloss to some forms of censorship. ACLU leaders responded by constructing an anti-Communist defense of freedom of speech and consumers' rights. In contrast to NODL, the CDL employed obscenity law and litigation rather than consumer pressure.[44] This development added urgency to a task the ACLU had already begun—an intensive reworking of its obscenity policy, one that would update its approach to obscenity law and advance its emerging sexual civil liberties agenda.

ACLU leaders saw great promise in the potential for recent cultural and judicial developments to liberate sexual expression. Some, like Elmer Rice, glimpsed the possibility of eliminating obscenity law entirely and urged the ACLU to deny "that *anything* is censorable." But as Rice initiated efforts to revise the ACLU's brokered obscenity policy, he discovered deep disagreements among members of the ACLU's Censorship Committee with regard to the potential impact of sexual material. The committee gathered and studied literature by social scientists, law enforcement officials, and psychiatrists on possible causal connections between sexually explicit material and behavior. Some members concluded that sexually explicit material could incite antisocial and even criminal actions; others remained skeptical. Some members declared the matter of causation irrelevant. Rice, for example, pointed out that the ACLU already defended a wide array of material that might lead to criminal behavior. "How about a book," he asked rhetorically, that "advocates homosexuality? Or advocates polygamy? Or pre-marital sexual relations among adolescents (statutory rape)?" Similarly, John Coons, a Northwestern University law professor, considered the issue of causation a distraction. Civil libertarians must *assume* causation, he argued. "The very raison d'etre of the First Amendment," Coons maintained, "is the tremendous impact of all speech on its hearers. Speech is protected, not because it is ineffective, but [because it is] effective." Joseph O'Meara, dean of Notre Dame Law School, took a different approach. He agreed that "the absence of a scientifically demonstrable relationship between exposure to obscene materials and anti-social conduct is beside the point," but maintained that the ACLU should pay attention to the type of media under consideration. Because radio and television use the public airwaves and "come into my own home at the turn of a knob," they must be regulated to prevent sexual content from entering private space.[45]

Many of these disagreements pivoted on tensions between public and private and implicated the ACLU's consumer-oriented approach to the First Amendment. Some ACLU leaders insisted that obscenity laws were less about controlling what individuals read, see, and think than safeguarding public culture by screening out the sexual and the private. The president of the Louisiana Civil Liberties Union, for example, argued that "the public should be protected from obscene sights as they are protected from excessive noises." Another wrote that in a democracy, citizens expect to be "protected *from* as well as protected *for*." Yet another ACLU leader regretted that some of his colleagues ridiculed "those of us still determined to protect ourselves and our culture" from obscenity.[46]

A few ACLU leaders drew on their own experiences with sexual material, revealing that conflicted opinions resided within individuals even as they permeated the organization as a whole. The president of Southern California's ACLU admitted that he viewed "hard-core pornography" but found it harmless and boring compared to his "own pornographic fantasies." The ACLU's legal director, Herbert Monte Levy, mused about his experience watching previews for *Teaserama,* admitting that "the gyrations and actions contributed to my normal male instincts." ACLU director George Soll acknowledged, "I saw a great deal of hard-core pornography as a child and I do not think it has harmed me at all." He wondered though whether exposure to this material might have affected him differently if it were openly available.[47]

Developing the ACLU's new obscenity policy took five years, some dubious deals, an ongoing push for obscenity law enforcement by pressure groups, the conspicuous absence of certain individuals at key meetings, and a sense among many that the time was ripe for a major change in the nation's obscenity laws. Harriet Pilpel drafted the final statement in 1962, opening with an unequivocal declaration that neatly glossed over years of acrimony and debate: "There can be no disagreement on the part of Civil Libertarians anywhere with the Union's position that all obscenity laws are unconstitutional." The statement admitted that several board members considered the ACLU's new uncompromising position on obscenity strategically unwise, but nowhere did it recognize that several board members opposed the policy formulation on other grounds, including sexual privacy, protection of children, or the quality of public culture. Acknowledging, however, the need for pragmatism in a judicial environment that had not ratified the ACLU's interpretation, Pilpel's statement insisted that no court could find an obscenity statute constitutional without proof "beyond a reasonable doubt" that the material in question deliberately targeted children or posed a "clear and present danger" of causing the commission of a crime.[48]

Even as the ACLU narrowed its definition of prosecutable obscenity to material proven to elicit criminal behavior, communications scholars debated media's effects on children and raised new concerns about privacy. Most scholars who conducted this research in the 1950s used quantitative methods and short-term studies and found little if any impact. But psychiatrists Fredric Wertham and Hilde L. Mosse employed clinical research and longitudinal studies that revealed disturbing effects. Mosse showed that crime comics portrayed women as "sexually seductive and deceitful" and as "objects of sadistic attacks." In addition to scenes of "near-rape," women were "shown being slapped, flogged, bound and gagged." Mosse and Wertham found that this material aroused "sado-masochistic erotic fantasies in many children . . . some of whom remained fixated on this type of pleasure, and their entire later sex life was affected." Of greatest concern to Mosse was the extent to which these images and messages about women "invaded the former privacy of the home." Wertham and Mosse's approach to privacy contrasted with the one taken by a majority of ACLU leaders. Whereas Wertham and Mosse sought to shield the home from unwelcome and seemingly harmful commercial media, the ACLU majority treated the individual and the home as most vulnerable to intrusion not by commercial media but by public officials and pressure groups that sought to restrict commercial media and thereby impede the consumer's right to "read, see, and hear."[49] As Wertham and Mosse's work began its long slide into obscurity, ACLU attorneys breathed new life into the consumer rights agenda that would underwrite the sexual civil liberties of American media.

It all began with a wave of lawsuits inspired by the 1961 publication of *Tropic of Cancer*, the blockbuster sex-capade by Henry Miller. The book itself was not new, having appeared originally in a 1934 French edition released by Obelisk Press. In it, Miller narrated a relentless litany of sexual encounters, many described in intimate, graphic, and shameless detail. Attempts to import the book or publish it in the United States attracted support from the ACLU's Northern California branch in the 1950s, but the novel failed in federal court. Grove Press founder Barney Rosset, whose own youth was inspired by a smuggled copy of *Tropic*, was determined to publish the book in the United States. He began to lay the legal groundwork and introduce American readers to Henry Miller, and in 1959 his magazine, *Evergreen Review*, published his passionate "Defense of the Freedom to Read," a piece designed to rally American readers to support his work by highlighting their victimization by censorship. Three years later, when Rosset released *Tropic of Cancer*, police confiscated the book, decency groups attacked it, librarians banned it, booksellers returned it, consumers demanded it, and Rosset was prepared to defend it. But he was not financially ready for the more than sixty lawsuits that took *Tropic* into court all over the country. ACLU attorneys were ready; they represented *Tropic* itself, book dealers who sold it, the press that published it, librarians who offered it to the public, and, eventually and even more significantly, prospective readers—would-be consumers who for the first time claimed standing—the right to sue—under the First Amendment.[50] The idea that a consumer might gain legal standing by demonstrating that she or he had been deleteriously affected by censorship in a way that legal action could resolve was new, but also timely, given that the notion of a right to read, hear, and see now saturated American culture.[51]

Proclamations of consumer rights to media showed up everywhere by the early 1960s. Editorials on "Who is to Censor What We See, Hear, Read?" and "Your Right to Read, to Know" appeared regularly in the press. "The Right to Read" and "The Students' Right to Read"—strong statements against pressure group censorship—were published in 1962 by the National Council of Teachers of English in cooperation with the ACLU and the American Book Publishers Council, whose regular newsletter *Censorship Bulletin* became *Freedom-to-Read Bulletin*. At the same time, a group of citizens formed Audience Unlimited to fight against censorship on behalf of consumers and *Freedom to Read* joined the federal government's Public Affairs Pamphlet series. The emerging homosexual press also made use of the new motto, announcing its efforts to "guarantee your freedom to read" and running articles on "Freedom to Read and the Law."[52]

Barney Rosset and Henry Miller took full advantage of the popularity of media consumer rights by crafting a high-profile, right-to-read defense of *Tropic of Cancer*. Rosset's hometown, Chicago, provided rich soil for the campaign; the city's police force was so widely reviled for brutality and excess that citizens were eager to mobilize against it. As one ACLU attorney remembered, police seizures of *Tropic of Cancer* were a "gift horse" for galvanizing public opinion against censorship. Taking full advantage of local sentiment against the police and national attention to the right to read, Rosset recruited prominent literary figures to sign a "Statement in Support of Freedom to Read" and used it to arouse the community further. Letters to the editor echoed Rosset's language as ordinary Chicagoans asserted their right to read *Tropic of Cancer*. Elites also picked up the language. As a top official at Bell & Howell wrote, "I haven't read [*Tropic of Cancer*] but I'll be darned if I want a policeman telling me I can't."[53] So even as decency groups advocated censorship in the press, in the courts, and behind the scenes in precinct offices, others—including Rosset, the ABPC, the ALA, the NCTE, and the ACLU—worked to delegitimize censorship of all kinds.

Joel Sprayregen and Burton Joseph, both general counsel for the ACLU's Illinois Division, took the idea of consumers' rights under the First Amendment to the next level by establishing prospective readers' standing to sue for access to banned material. Sprayregen, a "feisty young lawyer" fresh out of Yale Law School, and Joseph, a working-class graduate of DePaul University Law School, actually shared many qualities, including a Jewish heritage, frustration with the reluctance of booksellers, publishers, and distributors to challenge censorship, and an eagerness to take on the Chicago police. Together, they worked to institute the "new and unique principle that a private citizen, as a potential reader, has the right to challenge police censorship in the courts." The task of establishing standing for consumers was "formidable," Sprayregen acknowledged, given that the First Amendment referred only to producers, not consumers of speech. Nevertheless, he and Joseph assumed the job with gusto and optimism.[54]

The two firebrands found willing plaintiffs among their Northwestern University acquaintances. Franklyn Haiman, a communications professor and director of the Northern Illinois ACLU; Isabel Condit, Burt Joseph's friend and neighbor; and Joseph Ronsley, an ACLU member and graduate student in English literature, all agreed to participate. Their job was to canvass booksellers and confirm that they could not purchase *Tropic of Cancer* in Lake County, Illinois. They would then bring two separate suits against suburban police chiefs who confiscated *Tropic of Cancer,* ordered dealers not to sell it, or otherwise violated the public's right to read it.[55]

In *Haiman v. Morris,* Sprayregen argued before Samuel B. Epstein, chief judge of the Superior Court of Cook County, Illinois, that a prospective consumer must have standing to sue in order to protect the "constitutional right to read." "We frankly concede," his brief began, that "we know of no prior English or American decision presenting the precise question of the standing of citizens to sue against illegal official conduct which has deprived them of the right to read books of their choice." Even so, he argued, the ideas behind a prospective consumer's standing were deeply rooted in American history and democratic theory. The First Amendment was not designed primarily to protect a publisher's right to earn a profit but the American public's right to enjoy a free exchange of ideas. "It must surely follow," Sprayregen continued, "that American citizens have standing to sue against unlawful official interference with that access." Judge Epstein agreed and granted Haiman and Condit status to sue as consumers and prospective readers. That alone represented a significant victory. Epstein's final ruling brought yet another. Epstein came down firmly on the side of the consumer in an influential opinion that declared the "freedom to read" a "corollary to the freedom of speech and press." One without the other would be "useless," he asserted. To protect "the inherent constitutional rights and privileges of the reading public," the police must cease and desist from interfering with the "free distribution and sale" of *Tropic of Cancer.*[56]

All but forgotten now, Epstein's decision received a great deal of attention in its day. It was covered extensively in the national press and widely declared a landmark case in First Amendment jurisprudence. Sprayregen called it "the first English or American case in which the right of *readers* to sue to challenge censorship has been upheld." Meanwhile, Rosset worked to draw greater attention to the opinion's unique consumer orientation by recruiting 200 prominent authors and publishers to endorse it in a "Statement in Support of Freedom to Read" published on the front cover of his *Evergreen Review*.[57]

In the meantime, *Ronsley v. Stanczak* proceeded to the Circuit Court of Lake County, Illinois, where Joseph argued for the consumer's standing to sue public officials who demanded that bookstores remove *Tropic of Cancer* from their shelves. The "social value" of the First Amendment was not to protect "the right of the publisher to earn a profit," he argued, but the public's "free access to ideas and publications." Following the example set by Epstein two months earlier, Judge Bernard M. Decker affirmed Ronsley's standing to sue as a "prospective purchaser" and also proclaimed "the public's right to read and have access to books of their choice." Declaring that "the constitutional safeguards are designed not only to protect authors and publishers but the reading public as well," Decker issued an injunction against police interference with *Tropic*.[58]

The ACLU's consumer approach to freedom of speech carried the day. It circumvented the reluctance of commercial producers and distributors to sue and brought public pressure to bear on the judiciary in new ways. It also inspired members of the public, as consumers, to take censorship personally. After the success of *Haiman* and *Ronsley*, ACLU attorneys and others brought successful consumer-initiated suits against public officials in a number of places, including South Bend, Indiana; Los Angeles, California; and Montgomery County, Maryland. In addition, even when ACLU affiliates represented booksellers, distributors, or publishers, they couched their role as "defending the right of a free people to choose their own reading matter." The Supreme Court ended the three-year *Tropic* case craze in 1964 when it reversed a Florida court's holding that the book was obscene. The decision, *Grove Press v. Gerstein*, was handed down with no written opinion; the words would come one year later in *Lamont v. Postmaster General* when Justice William J. Brennan observed that "it would be a barren marketplace of ideas that had only sellers and no buyers." Meanwhile, John F. Kennedy fortified the relationship between consumerism and civil liberties when he issued what amounted to a consumer bill of rights, complete with presidential support for the right "to be informed" and "to choose."[59] Thus, by the middle of the 1960s, the ACLU's concept of consumer rights had moved to the center of the Supreme Court's First Amendment jurisprudence and received a presidential seal of approval.

Consumer rights also presented the ACLU with new ideas for membership recruitment. Leaders of the ACLU Illinois affiliate, for example, targeted buyers of *Playboy*, a Chicago-based, national-circulation magazine that faced frequent censorship threats. "*Playboy* readers," the local affiliate's development director explained, "are 'naturals' for the ACLU." After obtaining, without charge, names and addresses from *Playboy*'s subscriber list, the ACLU's Illinois affiliate sent out several mass mailings. "Sophisticated people like yourself," one recruitment letter began, "are not afraid to read whatever magazine or book you want to," including one that features "a picture of a divine figure with smasheroo legs." Another acknowledged that "most men who like to gaze at pictures of beautiful women in a magazine... couldn't care less about such stuffy business as civil liberties. After all, what has *that* got to do with a divine figure and elegant legs?" Turning to the First Amendment rights of consumers, the letter assured readers that "there are many people—you know the kind—who would do away with pictures of beautiful women" and censor books, movies, and magazines "though you have a right to read these—a right guaranteed by the Bill of Rights of the Constitution of the United States." In a final recruitment pitch, the letter pointed out that "a reader who enjoys reading what you enjoy reading about... should care enough to join the ACLU," the only organization that defends "the rights of readers, writers, and publishers."[60] Such membership-building strategies strengthened the growing tendency among civil libertarians to identify freedom of speech with consumption, adding a new dimension to that equation by treating consumers of cheesecake as especially laudable individuals whose rights to read represented the vanguard of First Amendment jurisprudence.

By the middle of the 1960s, the much-touted marketplace of ideas had taken on a character that would have been unrecognizable to the First Amendment's framers two centuries earlier. Thanks in part to the efforts of civil libertarians riding the wave of postwar cultural and political trends, the public arena was increasingly conceived of less as a forum for the exchange of ideas and information among citizens of a polity than as a marketplace of buyers and sellers, consumers and producers. No longer a community with aggregate needs, the marketplace hosted individuals with singular claims to speak, to publish, and to access all that was spoken and published. However, even as ACLU attorneys fashioned this new understanding of individual consumer rights under the First Amendment, opponents employed consumer rights in ways that threatened the ACLU's larger goals.

Consumerism could cut many ways. The ACLU used consumer rights to open up and diversify the marketplace in order to allow freer circulation of sexual material, but its opponents invoked consumer rights to restrict and even homogenize the media marketplace by reducing the flow of such material. In 1963 and again in 1967, Congress held hearings on a series of bills that would allow postal patrons to identify material as "obscene," "obnoxious," or "Communist propaganda" and demand to be removed from the sender's mailing list. Supporters of the bills argued that mass mailings violated the privacy and sanctity of the home by bringing into it unsolicited advertisements from "an outfit called EROS," "a homosexual group called the Mattachine Society," and "a full-sized vibrating rubber finger for women." In testimony replete with barbs directed at the ACLU, Charles Keating, founder of Citizens for Decent Literature (CDL), assured legislators that Soviet leaders did not permit the circulation of such "pornography," because they considered it "inimical to creativity and to a healthy, strong nation." For Keating, a nation's values and priorities, not differences between a command economy and a consumer-driven one, explained the relative absence of pornography from Soviet public life. Carol Trauth, a young woman associated with Keating's CDL, injected another perspective on consumerism into the hearings when she criticized *Playboy* and other magazines for treating women as consumer objects, "as a plaything for men—a toy to be used and discarded." Most friendly witnesses, however, emphasized the importance of preserving the sanctity and privacy of the home through postal legislation that would allow potential recipients to reject particular types of material. Many postal patrons received mail directly into their homes in the 1960s; through a slot in the front door, mass mailings crossed physical boundaries between public and private. A graphic ad for "Strippers School Book," "Men Only!" "Scanty Panties," or "Vibra Finger" might drop through the mail slot and hit the entryway floor, where they would await curious children and teens. Whereas earlier postal censorship hearings involved public officials, these showcased consumers who argued that without the postal bill they could not maintain their privacy by keeping offensive sexual literature out of their homes.[61]

Testifying for the ACLU, legal director Herbert Monte Levy argued against the bill. Mass mailings did not jeopardize domestic privacy, he insisted. Without any new laws at all, consumers could simply tear up unsolicited circulars and throw them away. Junk mail could be annoying, Levy admitted, though he had not been "fortunate enough...to get some of the salacious mail" others had described. After an extended debate over whether or not mass mailers targeted children and whether sexual immorality was more prevalent among Russians or Americans, the discussion turned again to privacy. Edward Roybal, a Democratic congressman from California, acknowledged "the right of the individual to solicit, to use the mails," but "on the other hand, there is also the right of privacy." Without missing a beat, Levy replied, "I would say that the right of privacy is not a constitutional right. The right of freedom of speech and press is."[62] Thus, in 1963, just two years before the ACLU would argue confidently and persuasively in *Griswold v. Connecticut* (1965) that a constitutional right to privacy protected the use of birth control, its legal director denied the existence of such a right when opposing postal bills that would empower consumers to refuse particular types of mail.

By 1967, constitutional rights to privacy were well established, but the debate over postal legislation raged on as each side faced off over the relative importance of privacy vis-à-vis freedom of speech. Postal officials demanded a law that would address the 200,000 complaints about unsolicited sexual mailings received in 1966 alone. Some were undoubtedly responses to the three million brochures for *Eros* recently mailed out by Ralph Ginzburg, who personally received at least 10,000 angry letters from recipients of his literature. The post office's general counsel testified that, when sexual displays are "thrust upon us... our privacy is invaded." Legislation allowing postal patrons to demand removal from certain mailing lists might thwart constitutionally protected speech, he admitted, but the patron must retain the "right to secure the privacy of his home." The ACLU's Washington, D.C., director, Lawrence Speiser, however, argued for the absolute primacy of the First Amendment, contending that privacy, though one of "the most precious rights of men... must yield when it comes in conflict with the paramount right of freedom of speech." Allowing mail recipients to refuse mail from any concern they deemed responsible for having sent, in the past, erotic or sexually arousing material would invite abuse. Individuals would reject mail from "any company that includes a shapely female in its mail advertisements," Speiser predicted, including creditors, the Internal Revenue Service, retail outlets, publishers, churches, charities, or political organizations. "The effect," he warned, would be "the sexual sterilization of American business and industry." Women's bodies figured prominently in Speiser's testimony as he concluded that, if enacted, this law would result in "a 20th Century Mother-Hubbard-gowning" of American culture.[63]

In the end, consumers who demanded privacy through protection from unsolicited sexual mailings won. Congress passed a number of laws enabling postal patrons to stop items from mailers who had, in the past, sent "erotically arousing or sexually provocative" material. By 1969, ACLU leaders realized that they were, for the foreseeable future, fighting a losing war. Given the "temper of the times," the presidential administration of Richard Nixon, and "the kind of Supreme Court which will be sitting two years from now," they expected the postal laws to stick. And they did. In 1970, the Supreme Court declared that "a mailer's right to communicate" must "stop at the mailbox of an unreceptive addressee" in order to "protect minors and the privacy of homes."[64] Here, the ACLU's arguments for freedom of speech failed, succumbing to the powerful case made by legislators and witnesses who effectively appropriated two civil liberties brought to life largely by the ACLU, consumer rights and privacy.

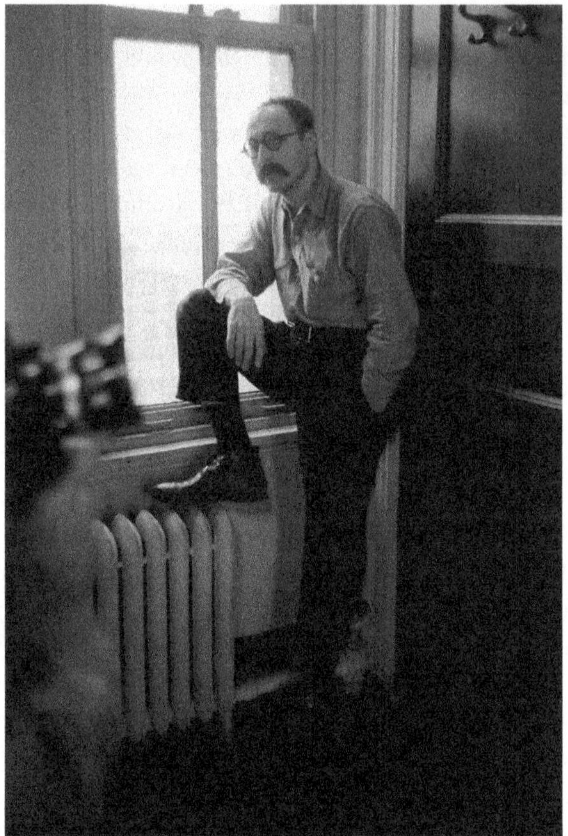

Figure 3.3 Ralph Ginzburg in his New York City office, preparing to serve a three-year prison term, February 13, 1972. (Courtesy, AP Photo)

Consumer rights also shaped the ACLU's ongoing battle with the motion picture industry over its self-censorship apparatus. ACLU leaders had long objected to the MPAA's Motion Picture Code as a restraint on trade, a form of private censorship, and a mechanism for pressure group blackmail.[65] The ACLU continued to attack both the Code and the handful of local movie censorship boards that hung on in several states and cities around the country, filing amicus briefs that highlighted consumer rights. In *Times Film Corp. v. Chicago* (1961), Sprayregen decried the censor's ability to determine "what is appropriate for the public to hear and to see," and in *Jacobellis v. Ohio* (1964), ACLU legal director Melvin Wulf accused film censors of violating "the right of members of the adult public to exercise their freedom of choice." Parents as consumers, not public officials, should supervise children's movie selections, they argued. A Supreme Court victory for the ACLU and its allies in *Jacobellis* left local censorship statutes in tatters. But the majority opinion approved of "laws aimed specifically at preventing distribution of objectionable material to children, rather than at totally prohibiting its dissemination." The decision inspired an explosion of grassroots demands for state-mandated classification systems to categorize movies by age group and require theater owners to bar juveniles from "adults only" movies. A deluge of movie classification laws followed.[66]

The ACLU and movie industry representatives condemned state-sponsored movie classification as censorship. Such systems would hold theater owners accountable for barring juveniles from movies rated for adults and also impinge on the rights of adults accompanied by children to attend movies of their choosing. "A mother with a babe in arms," one flier protested, "couldn't go into a theatre playing an 'adults only' motion picture." Together with motion picture interests, the ACLU insisted that state classification laws violated the rights of parents by usurping "the parent's judgment as to what is good or not good for the children."[67]

The trend toward classifying movies had deep roots, but it also grew from new sources. Pressure groups had long compiled lists of approved and condemned movies, denoting those recommended for family viewing, and inspiring the MPAA to sponsor its own lists. State-mandated movie classification grew out of these measures, but it was also a reaction to more recent developments, including heightened attention to consumers and individual consumer choice. More specifically, the emerging field of market research and the ability of many industries to meet consumer demand with limited product runs allowed producers of consumer goods to cater to a segmented market even as they helped to create it. Recognizing the emerging, independent buying power of teenagers, postwar businesses offered fashions, music, food, and magazines like *Seventeen* that further distinguished them as a unique age group with particular consumer needs. Meanwhile, television bypassed parents and advertised directly to children, using Tony the Tiger to sell cereal, promises of adventure to peddle space helmets, and dreams of glamour and domesticity to promote Barbie and the Easy-Bake Oven. Market segmentation also fueled and followed the tumultuous cultural and political climate that saw the rise of "identity politics" as individuals asserted group identities based on race, age, and gender. Thus, the Black Power movement emerged alongside Clairol hair treatments for Afros; the women's movement saw its ideals of independence echoed in Virginia Slims' "You've Come a Long Way, Baby" commercials, and as the Gray Panthers fought against "ageism," *Modern Maturity* advertised products to ease the pains and celebrate the freedom of the golden years. Thus, in the increasingly segmented cultural and political milieu of the 1960s and 1970s, motion pictures joined other commercial enterprises to direct products at particular and often identity-based groups of buyers.[68]

MPAA leaders worked closely with the ACLU as they developed a new movie rating system to replace their thirty-eight-year-old Production Code, take advantage of marketing trends, and stave off calls for state-mandated movie classification. The MPAA's general counsel, Barbara Scott, met several times with the ACLU's board of directors to seek advice, answer questions, and address civil liberties concerns. The rating system featured four categories—G for general audiences, M for mature audiences, R for audiences over the age of 16 (unless accompanied by a parent or guardian), and X for audiences over the age of 16 only. Scott assured the board that the MPAA's new rating system would be voluntary but admitted that, because the MPAA dominated the industry, participation would essentially become mandatory for all theaters. Board member Harriet Pilpel objected to "a small body making judgments for the entire film industry," a practice likely to "stifle diversity of opinion" and inhibit the creative work of artists. Scott replied that producers and artists actually approved of the new system because, by providing a range of rating options, it would free them from the restrictions of the Code and allow them to produce "films on a more mature level." Other committee members worried that the rating system violated the rights of parents by preventing them from taking their children to X-rated movies. At the conclusion of the final meeting, the ACLU board voted unanimously to oppose the MPAA's rating system and publicized the decision in a passionate defense of consumer rights.[69] When the industry determines who may and who may not see a particular film, the ACLU declared, "the public has lost its right of choice." Accordingly, "those who value highly the First Amendment guarantee of free expression should oppose the rating system."[70]

Over loud objections from the ACLU, in 1968 the MPAA unveiled its comprehensive movie rating system. The new system would allow moviegoers to make informed selections and parents to provide intelligent guidance to their children, the MPAA maintained. Unspoken was the usefulness of the rating system for defending the movies against pressure groups, obscenity law, state-mandated classification, and renegade movie producers who released films without the MPAA seal of approval. Indeed, the timely passage of the rating system helped the movie industry weather two important events at the federal level. The Supreme Court, in *Ginsberg v. New York* (1968), upheld a New York statute that created an audience-specific definition of obscenity—"variable obscenity"—outlawing the sale to minors of material considered sexually harmful to them alone. Just a few months later, the U.S. Senate held hearings to explore the possibility of creating a "Committee on Film Classification" to make recommendations regarding the creation of a federal film classification system. ACLU leaders actively opposed both of these developments, but it was the MPAA's rating system that protected movies against a federal film classification and child-oriented censorship laws inspired by *Ginsberg*.[71]

The MPAA's new rating system struck many as momentous and attracted widespread consumer support. "Social historians may someday write," opined

Vincent Canby for the *New York Times*, "that on November 1, 1968, for better or worse, the American movie industry inaugurated its voluntary film classification system, designed to bar children under 16 from seeing movies that the industry's code people deem to be too vulgar, violent, or sexy." The rating system met with widespread approval from Catholic Church officials, theater owners, and parents who praised the rating system as a major advance in private industry's responsiveness to consumer demands. The ACLU stood practically alone in sturdy opposition.[72] Once again, consumerism, however essential to the ACLU's campaign to erode restrictions on sexual expression, had proven slippery ground on which to stake a civil liberties agenda.

By some measures, the ACLU failed in its efforts to diversify and expand material available to consumers. The postal law passed, as did others like it, many still in effect today. Despite the ACLU's consistent opposition, the MPAA rating system survives through the Classification and Rating Administration (CARA). Although it is less effective at keeping adolescents from attending movies rated R, PG-13, or NC-17 than many might wish, it nevertheless influences the movie choices made by millions of people and functions to keep movies awarded an X out of mainstream theaters and inaccessible to many.[73] In these particular battles, the ACLU lost, trumped by consumer-based arguments that undermined its broader agenda of expanding and diversifying the media market.

However, despite the apocalyptic predictions of many ACLU leaders, no return to Victorianism ensued, and the expansion of sexual civil liberties proceeded apace. Indeed, *Playboy* reader J. P. McGlynn would have been pleased at the outcome. The ACLU may have lost its battle to free mass marketers from postal laws and save movies from rating systems, but there can be little doubt that it won the war. By establishing in law, jurisprudence, and the broader culture a consumerist approach to the First Amendment, the ACLU raised public concerns about censorship and heightened the sense of violation experienced by consumers denied access to particular media. Individual consumer demands, interpreted as an exercise of First Amendment rights, would drive media culture even as collective efforts to reshape media content were recast as censorship. Moreover, as ACLU attorneys chipped away at obscenity law, they left it standing but increasingly difficult to enforce.[74]

The ACLU piloted these transformations, advancing the cause of sexual civil liberties by bringing to sexual expression the gloss and respectability of constitutional rights and the crowd-pleasing allure of the buyer's choice even as it battled more conservative groups with vastly different agendas on the territory of privacy and consumer rights.

Moreover, the postal laws and rating system that withstood the ACLU's assault in the 1960s would soon matter little. Even as the ACLU helped make it possible for sexuality to enter the public realm in new ways, it reinforced the notion that privacy rights apply to sexual behavior and that such rights protect consumer access not only to sexual literature and images but also to sexual conduct and the means to control its reproductive consequences. As we will see, sex would become ever more public even as privacy rights trumped laws against many sexual practices, advancing the broader agenda of making sex a civil liberty.

4

"To Be Let Alone in the Bedroom"

Expanding Sexual Rights through Privacy, 1940s–1960s

"Nowhere is the lag between the law on the books and the mores of the American people more obvious," wrote Harriet Pilpel, a cooperating attorney with the ACLU, than in "legal restrictions touching on birth control." Laws against common sexual practices should be repealed, she argued as early as 1944, several years before her client, noted sex researcher Alfred Kinsey, made the same case. Pilpel's portfolio of clients reflected and also shaped her evolving perspective on civil liberties and sexuality. Indeed, Pilpel represented not just Kinsey and the ACLU; she also served as legal counsel for the American Birth Control League, the Planned Parenthood Federation, the Association for Voluntary Sterilization, and other organizations focused on reproduction and sexuality. Working with all of these groups simultaneously encouraged Pilpel to consider how sexual conduct might pertain to civil liberties, leading her to conclude that "the sex laws" responsible for criminalizing sexual "behavior in private between consenting adults" are "a dagger aimed at the heart of some of our most fundamental freedoms." After Pilpel became an ACLU board member in the 1960s, she urged her colleagues to recognize that laws against "birth control, abortion, . . . sterilization, prostitution, miscegenation, homosexuality, fornication, and adultery" led to violations of civil liberties every bit as unconstitutional as laws that restricted freedom of speech.[1]

By the 1940s, the ACLU had made a name for itself defending the First Amendment rights of birth control activists, authors, nudists, playwrights, and even consumers. With the exception of nudism, however—which remained a special but still peripheral issue for the ACLU—sexual conduct seemed another matter entirely.

The story of how, why, and with what effects the ACLU made the journey from defending speech to defending sexual practice as well is critical to understanding the evolution of sexual civil liberties. It reveals the ongoing importance of individual experiences and values, not only of ACLU leaders but also of the countless individuals who sought their assistance. It exposes a pattern of communication and mutual influence—of intellectual cross-pollination—among attorneys who served different organizations that shows how profoundly they influenced each other.[2] As Pilpel and other ACLU attorneys moved back and forth between and among their many client organizations, they revised their ideas. In the process, they brought civil liberties priorities and language to single-issue organizations and communicated the concerns of those groups back to the ACLU as it struggled to define new civil liberties, delineate public and private, and bring the Constitution to bear on issues of sexuality. Exploring how and why Pilpel and others stretched sexual civil liberties to include sexual behavior reveals heretofore unknown origins of the right to privacy that would transform the cultural and constitutional landscape.

Harriet Fleischl Pilpel was born in 1911, the first of three daughters to Ethel Loewy, a schoolteacher with fifteen siblings, and Julius Fleischl, a self-educated son of immigrants from Czechoslovakia. Pilpel grew up on the west side of the Bronx, where her father worked in his family's dairy and poultry business. He was "out of his mind with enthusiasm" at her birth, she was told, and treated her as the son he never had, investing in her education, and consulting her on business matters. Of her mother, Pilpel believed, "the sense of her own dependence somehow encouraged her to encourage *me* to be independent." Pilpel was a child when the ACLU defended Margaret Sanger's right to speak publicly about birth control at New York City's Town Hall in 1919, but she recalled her parents' displeasure that public officials had canceled the "great woman's" appearance. "I guess this was a kind of prophetic episode," Pilpel mused later, "because my chief interests include not only human reproduction and the law but civil liberties." The Fleischls supported the birth control movement, partly because they had friends and relatives who had resorted to illegal abortions, but also due to Ethel's personal experiences as one of sixteen children.[3]

Pilpel attended Vassar College, married Robert Cecil Pilpel, a recent graduate of New York University Law School, and matriculated at Columbia University Law School, where she was one of twelve women—only six of whom graduated—out of 260 students. Pilpel aimed to excel, make law review, delay becoming pregnant, retain her femininity, and—after reading work by Morris Ernst and hearing him speak at the Law School in the 1930s—secure a job at Greenbaum, Wolff & Ernst. After learning that the firm was not hiring, Pilpel donned a red wool dress, black coat, and velvet hat to try to persuade Ernst to make an exception. Ernst's secretary suspected that he might want to meet with this "pretty young woman" and ushered Pilpel into his office for a five-minute interview. That brief encounter would mark the beginning of a lifelong partnership. Beginning in 1936, Pilpel worked first on birth control issues and later added civil liberties, as well as literary and entertainment law. After establishing herself professionally, Pilpel had two children and struggled to juggle career and family with the help of a live-in nurse. For fifteen years, Pilpel "voluntarily reduced" her compensation on the presumption that motherhood lessened her contributions to the firm, though she later suspected that this arrangement had short-changed her. Meanwhile, male colleagues communicated additional gendered expectations, suggesting on occasion that Pilpel use her "womanly charms" with particularly difficult male clients.[4]

Throughout her legal career Pilpel, like her mentor Morris Ernst, provided pro bono assistance to nonprofit organizations whose goals she shared, including the American Birth Control League, Planned Parenthood Federation, Association for Voluntary Sterilization, and the Kinsey Institute. Pilpel and Ernst also participated in public discussions of law and civil liberties, especially as they pertained to women's rights and sexual matters, appearing on radio and later television shows, giving public lectures, writing books and pamphlets for lay readers, and publishing articles for the popular press. In 1937, Pilpel wrote a pamphlet to update Mary Ware Dennett's 1926 book on birth control laws and together with Ernst persuaded the medical profession to recognize birth control as an issue of physicians' rights.[5]

Figure 4.1 Harriet Pilpel, 1951. (Courtesy, Judith Appelbaum)

Pilpel and Ernst's approach to birth control did not at first accord with the ACLU's. Before the 1950s, the ACLU still addressed birth control primarily in terms of freedom of speech, a focus narrower than Pilpel's and the birth control movement's more generally because it ignored the sale and use of birth control devices themselves. Although the ACLU was slow to broaden its defense of contraception beyond information and advocacy, it nonetheless encouraged birth control activists to frame their issue in constitutional terms through, among others, cooperating attorney Harriet Pilpel and board member Morris Ernst. The inner workings of this process can be glimpsed in the origins of what would become the landmark birth control and privacy case, *Griswold v. Connecticut* (1965).

The Connecticut Birth Control League (CBCL) challenged state laws that criminalized the sale and use of birth control devices with the assistance of a number of ACLU attorneys. Pilpel and Ernst as well as Fowler Harper and Catherine Roraback, leaders in the ACLU's Connecticut affiliate, helped the CBCL draft legislation, lobby politicians, devise legal strategies, search for likely defendants, and arrange and litigate test cases. It enjoyed support from the national ACLU and its local affiliate only when it focused on laws against distributing information about birth control. But as the ACLU and the birth control movement shared attorneys, they funneled information and concepts back and forth, teaching leaders in each movement to think about their main issues in terms that incorporated the central concerns of the other. More specifically, when Ernst and Pilpel reported on birth control cases and legislative efforts to the ACLU board in the 1940s and 1950s, they prodded ACLU colleagues to consider how the sale and use of birth control devices might implicate civil liberties. They also brought ideas from the ACLU back to birth control activists who worked to develop a civil liberties framework for their cause.[6]

This process of cross-pollination did not bring sudden changes to the ACLU or to the birth control movement, but birth control activists adopted the language of civil liberties more readily than the ACLU embraced their aims. As early as the 1940s Sanger attempted to reinvent her movement's relationship to civil liberties in a series of talks and articles titled "Birth Control and Civil Liberties." Civil liberties must be defined more broadly than "freedom of speech, freedom of the press and freedom of worship," she argued. To be meaningful, they must include "the right of free men and free women to control, as best they may, their own destiny on earth; their right to undertake the deep and satisfying act of parenthood, not by chance or in ignorance, but in full knowledge of their responsibility—to the child, to themselves and to their nation." Sanger did not deny the importance of the First Amendment, pointing out that laws against birth control denied speakers a platform, publishers a market, and authors the means to distribute their material. But she declared laws against birth control a "direct and intimate invasion of personal rights and freedom of religious conscience."[7] In 1950 Molly Cunningham, executive director of the Connecticut Birth Control League's successor, the Planned Parenthood League of Connecticut (PPLC), echoed Sanger, declaring that "the fundamental issue of our fight to change the birth control law is that of civil liberties." Even so, throughout most of the decade, the ACLU maintained that civil liberties extended only to the dissemination of birth control information, not to conduct involved in the use or distribution of birth control devices.[8]

The civil liberties aspects of birth control received fresh attention when the PPLC's new executive director, Estelle Griswold, took office in the mid-1950s. Griswold worked to diversify the organization's base racially and economically even as she sought new ways to persuade middle- and upper-class women, who could obtain birth control through their private physicians, that their civil liberties too suffered under the Connecticut law. In 1955, the PPLC brought the message home in an advertisement that depicted police officers hiding beneath beds, pad and pencil ready to record any activity that might take place on the mattress above. "A policeman in every home is the only way to enforce this law," read the text, suggesting that all Connecticut residents were vulnerable to police intrusion into their bedrooms as long as state law forbade the use of contraceptives (See Figure 4.2).[9]

As birth control activists framed their work in ever broader civil liberties terms, they encouraged the ACLU to bring birth control more fully onto its own agenda. Sometimes they did this in very direct ways, such as in 1955 when the Planned Parenthood Federation of America (PPFA) invited ACLU director Patrick Malin to address its annual meeting. Malin's original text declared that state laws criminalizing the use of contraceptives and the circulation of information about how to obtain illegal contraceptives violated no civil liberties. PPFA officials objected to his draft and urged ACLU legal director Herbert Monte Levy to revise Malin's speech, if not his thinking. Levy suggested that Malin consider a "right of privacy and the possibility that it should protect a man and wife in the determination of whether or not they want to plan their families, have them haphazardly or have no families at all." The Connecticut birth control law "may be a violation of the most private of the rights of privacy," Levy claimed and, at the very least, "suppression of information which may lead to deprivation of life" would seem to violate civil liberties.[10] Levy's analysis led neither Malin nor the ACLU to embrace privacy as a fundamental right in 1955. But Malin did revise his speech. When he addressed a PPFA audience of eight hundred on the subject of "Civil Liberties and the American Family," he condemned any and all "suppression of free speech about planned parenthood," even when such speech constituted an incitement to crime as it did in Connecticut.[11]

Spring **SPECIAL LEGISLATIVE EDITION** *1955*

A POLICEMAN IN EVERY HOME IS THE ONLY WAY TO ENFORCE THIS LAW.... passed in 1879

Section 8568: "Any person who shall *use* any drug, medicinal article or instrument for the purpose of preventing conception, shall be fined not less than fifty dollars or imprisoned not less than sixty days nor more than one year or be both fined and imprisoned."

Section 8875: "Any person who shall assist, abet, *counsel*, cause, hire or command another to commit any offense may be prosecuted and punished as if he were the principal offender." (This means it is a criminal offense for a doctor to prescribe a contraceptive to a married woman, even if her life is endangered by pregnancy.)

REPEAL....AMEND....or ENFORCE?

BILLS NOW BEFORE THE LEGISLATURE

HB 1177 – To Repeal Section 8568 of the General Statutes.

HB 1182 – The provisions of Sections 8568 and 8875 of the General Statutes shall not be construed to prevent (a) any physician duly licensed to practice in accordance with Section 4634 of the General Statutes from prescribing any method or means for the temporary prevention of pregnancy in a married woman, when, in the opinion of such physician, pregnancy would endanger the life or seriously impair the health of such married woman; or (b) a married person from using the method or means so prescribed, or (c) duly licensed pharmacists and druggists from filling said prescription.

OPEN HEARING
before the
Public Health and Safety Committee

Date: **WED., APRIL 20**

Hour: **1:30 P.M.**

Place: State Capitol
House of Representatives

! COME TO THIS HEARING !

AN IMPRESSIVE SHOW OF SUPPORT FOR THESE BILLS IS VITAL

MEN and WOMEN of CONNECTICUT

Show Your Determination To Be Heard!!

46 States have liberal Maternal Health Laws....Why Can't We?

Figure 4.2 Cartoon depicting birth control laws as enforceable only through police surveillance of the bedroom. Planned Parenthood League of Connecticut, "Special Legislative Edition," Spring 1955. (Courtesy, Princeton University Library)

While national ACLU leaders quibbled, state affiliates mapped out a variety of new civil liberties approaches to birth control in response to local conditions. The New York Civil Liberties Union fought Catholic efforts to prevent public hospitals from providing birth control information, arguing against "morality censorship" and the intrusion of the state into doctor-patient relationships. The Niagara Frontier Branch demanded that tax-supported hospitals provide contraceptive advice to patients. The Ohio Civil Liberties Union launched an investigation of laws and policies that obstructed the dissemination of birth control information or discriminated against birth control clinics for tax purposes. Meanwhile, the Minnesota Civil Liberties Union and the Greater Pittsburgh chapter both challenged rules that prevented state caseworkers from referring needy clients to birth control clinics. The Pittsburgh chapter drew on the ACLU's consumer rights approach, objecting less to the abridgement of caseworkers' speech than to limits on "the right of free citizens to receive information."[12] Thus, even in the absence of clear leadership from the national office, state affiliates experimented with new ways of applying civil liberties principles to the issue of birth control.

The ACLU took a long leap toward expanding its approach to sexual civil liberties in 1958 when it hired Melvin Wulf as assistant legal director. A recent graduate of Columbia University Law School, Wulf came to the ACLU with experiences that prepared him to transform the organization's approach to a number of issues, including sexual rights. The son of a Latvian immigrant and a first-generation American whose parents immigrated from Poland, Wulf grew up in Troy, New York, where his family owned a clothing-manufacturing business. Wulf developed an early resentment of authority that emerged, as he remembers it, from a formative episode of parental interference with his adolescent longings for popularity, athletic accomplishment, and sexual opportunity. Wulf's mother and father prohibited him from playing football out of fear for his physical safety, and seventeen-year-old Wulf lost his dream to become a high school quarterback and "get all the girls." Despite his resentment of parental authority, he followed his father's advice and enrolled in the Lowell Textile Institute to prepare for entering the family clothing business. There he read "highfalutin literature," joined a Jewish fraternity that included Communist Party members, and spent summers at his father's factory, where he witnessed firsthand the chasm between those who owned the means of production and those who did not. "Even though I was the boss's son," he recalled, "I was for the worker." He was also on his way to becoming a lifelong Democratic Socialist. Wulf spent much of his young adulthood trying to avoid being drafted into "grunt" service in World War II and subsequently the Korean War, first by entering the New York State Maritime Academy—where resistance to authority earned him a wealth of demerits—and later by attending law school, then activating his naval commission. Throughout, there were "lots of girls" and Wulf stayed busy with them, sports, legal work for the navy, and later a job with a blue-chip law firm in Albany. All the while he cast about for a more fulfilling professional direction.[13]

Wulf had long thought of the ACLU as an organization that shared his values—defending the disadvantaged, advocating for civil rights, demanding a secular and limited government, and, more generally, challenging authority. From Albany, Wulf served as a cooperating ACLU attorney before making "one of the best decisions" of his life, quitting his job, moving to New York City, and offering his services to the ACLU pro bono. Soon ACLU legal director Rowland Watts obtained permission to hire an assistant and offered the job to Wulf. When he joined the ACLU staff in 1958 Wulf was single, living in Greenwich Village, "sexually active if not promiscuous," and possessed of "a personal commitment to birth control." Marrying Deirdre Howard in 1962 only deepened his commitment to the cause. Not only were his wife and mother-in-law both birth control activists, but the newly married Wulfs wanted to plan their own family. Thus, when a New Jersey attorney asked the ACLU to defend a drugstore clerk convicted of selling contraceptives, personal life experiences had primed Wulf to take the case seriously. He was disappointed to discover that the ACLU challenged only laws against the distribution of birth control information and not the sale of contraceptives. He joined Levy and others in pressing for a reconsideration of the issue.[14]

External and internal forces pressured the ACLU to revise its position on birth control. Birth control activists prodded ACLU leaders to extend their pol-

Figure 4.3 Melvin Wulf with client, former FBI agent John F. Shaw, January 27, 1971. (Courtesy, AP Photo/John Rous)

icy—which remained limited to defending "discussion and debate"—to take into account an emerging "deprivation of life constitutional claim." Meanwhile, ACLU board members worried that affiliates were getting out ahead of the national organization on birth control, thereby challenging its authority, and mapping out disparate civil liberties approaches united by no clear guiding principle. Many were eager to develop a more robust birth control policy in order to prevent the issue from being left to affiliates and a handful of renegade attorneys who did not represent the ACLU. In this context, Malin informed his staff that "we should immediately move, in cooperation with our Connecticut affiliate, to do whatever—if anything—we can do on this." He admitted that "there is considerable question as to whether civil liberties are at all involved," but urged his colleagues to think creatively about what possible rights might be violated by Connecticut's birth control laws. In 1959, the ACLU finally adopted a new birth control policy that declared restrictions on the "sale of contraceptive devices" a violation of the Fourteenth Amendment. The new policy received mixed reactions even from those who approved of it. To many observers—certainly to insiders in the birth control movement—the ACLU's new policy was hardly groundbreaking. Some leaders in the birth control movement seemed annoyed by the announcement, as if the ACLU might be trying to take advantage of its late entrance on the stage to claim the spotlight. Others, however, praised the ACLU's new birth control policy as a first step toward a significantly broader approach to sexual civil liberties. In any event, the new policy prepared the ACLU to join the Planned Parenthood League of Connecticut birth control case on the grounds that the Connecticut law violated not only the First but also the Fourteenth Amendment, because it denied married women whose health required that they avoid pregnancy the right to "life, liberty and property without due process of law."[15]

Throughout the long process of court appearances and appeals, attorneys for the PPLC, PPFA, and ACLU shared information, advice, and briefs, creating a sometimes collaborative, often competitive, and always intellectually dynamic legal team whose mutually influential work promised to expand the boundaries of sexual rights. Just as birth control activists encouraged ACLU leaders to articulate greater civil liberties protections for birth control, ACLU attorneys persuaded birth control activists to consider a wider range of civil liberties claims. Pilpel and Ernst in particular urged local attorneys for the Connecticut birth control activists to develop an argument that built on the recent U.S. Supreme Court decision in *Roth v. United States* (1957) by claiming that the widespread use of birth control in Connecticut indicated that community standards condoned it. Pilpel drew on the work of her client Alfred Kinsey to emphasize the damage produced by marital sexual abstinence, the only alternative legally available to Connecticut women whose health could not sustain a pregnancy. When, as expected, the case failed in the Connecticut courts, the legal team confidently prepared an appeal to the U.S. Supreme Court.[16]

Success seemed possible. Birth control was becoming more widely accepted than ever, with mainstream media outlets running features and publishing polls showing that most married couples used contraception. Questions were being raised about the inconsistency of laws that allowed the open sale of condoms for men but prohibited or restricted the availability of diaphragms for women. At the same time, public concern about the record levels of teenage pregnancy in the postwar era and also about fecundity among the poor, at home and abroad, prompted a more positive evaluation of contraception. Arguments about population pressures, although not new, gained greater traction by the end of the 1950s as they helped Cold War policymakers explain poverty in developing countries without having to acknowledge the colonialism that contributed to it. In addition, the Supreme Court, presided over by Chief Justice Earl Warren, was known for its eagerness to employ judicial review to overturn state statutes that violated the Bill of Rights.[17]

When the Supreme Court agreed to hear *Poe v. Ullman* in 1959, the ACLU joined the group representing the Connecticut and national Planned Parenthood organizations. Pilpel's brief for the PPFA focused on the state laws' failure both to serve a legitimate public purpose and to provide reasonable alternatives to wives for whom pregnancy could prove fatal. Abstaining from sexual intercourse, she argued, was neither a reasonable expectation nor one that would serve the public interest in preserving marriages. Citing Alfred Kinsey's research on the importance of "sexual satisfaction" to marital happiness, she declared that "abstinence doesn't work" for married couples.[18]

Wulf's argument in *Poe* on behalf of the ACLU pivoted on a multidimensional right to privacy, one he articulated in terms romantic as well as constitutional. Appellants simply want "legislators as well as policemen to stay out of their bedrooms," Wulf declared, using a memorable phrase that conjured up images from the PPLC's 1955 advertisement. "The 14th Amendment protects persons from invasions of their privacy by the states," he maintained. That privacy was violated by Connecticut statutes that denied appellants "the right to engage in sexual intercourse," a "natural expression of love" that touched "the marrow of human behavior" but one that could, under certain circumstances and without adequate contraception, threaten the "life and health of the female spouse." The brief went on to denounce the hypocrisy of a law designed ostensibly to encourage morality by preventing physicians from prescribing diaphragms for married women while allowing the free and open sale of condoms, devices easily procured by "one bent on immorality." Privacy also figured prominently in the brief Harper submitted for the PPLC's appellants, but whereas privacy occupied only five pages of the lengthy brief submitted by Harper, it dominated Wulf's relatively short twenty-one-page document. "When the long arm of the law reaches into the bedroom and regulates the most sacred relations between a man and his wife," Wulf declared, "it is going too far." Harper went on to celebrate "the privacy of the home," remind justices that "a man's home is his castle," assert that spouses simply want "to be let alone in the bedroom," and claim "a 'right' to consortium."[19]

When asked how he came up with the historic privacy angle in *Poe*, Wulf glibly attributed his thinking to "a very creative imagination" before recalling his preoccupation at the time with Fourth Amendment protections against unreasonable search and seizure. Indeed, even as *Poe*'s challenge to Connecticut birth control laws wended its way through the courts, another crucial and in many ways very similar case involving search and seizure commanded ACLU attention. Ohio statutes criminalized not only the sale and transport of obscene material, as most states did, but also mere possession of it. In 1957, three white Cleveland police officers without a warrant forcibly entered the home of Dollree Mapp, a young black mother and owner of a boardinghouse. Searching for evidence that Mapp was harboring a bombing suspect, the police confiscated pamphlets, books, and pictures that they considered obscene. Mapp sued. In 1959, when the case went before the Ohio State Supreme Court, the five-year-old Ohio Civil Liberties Union (OCLU) joined as amicus curiae in hopes of overturning the state's harsh obscenity law—a law that interfered, they argued in the day's popular idiom, with the "right to read." Mapp appealed the case to the U.S. Supreme Court, where it attracted the attention of Watts and Wulf. Unlike their OCLU colleagues, who focused narrowly on the state's obscenity law, Watts and Wulf saw great promise in *Mapp v. Ohio* for persuading the Court to prohibit the use of illegally seized evidence in federal cases through the exclusionary rule of the Fourth and Fourteenth Amendments. The same amendments protected Mapp's right to privacy, they argued. The ACLU brief helped to convince the Court to recognize a "right to privacy free from unreasonable state intrusion" and to declare evidence obtained by unconstitutional searches and seizures "inadmissible in court."[20]

Dollree Mapp was prosecuted for violating a law against possessing obscene material that had no relationship to birth control, but Wulf saw meaningful similarities between *Mapp* and *Poe*. Ohio's obscenity law and the Connecticut birth control law punished mere possession, and both laws imposed criminal sanctions on private sexual behavior. Because Wulf and other ACLU attorneys participated in so many different types of cases—always with civil liberties, broadly construed, uppermost in their minds—they were able to imagine a sweeping privacy claim that would stretch across incidents of search-and-seizure and the enforcement of laws against possessing obscenity and using contraceptives. By presenting variations on these privacy arguments to the High Court as they applied to different scenarios, ACLU attorneys began to develop a coherent approach to sexual issues that attracted ever more judicial support and promised to expand protections for sexual conduct that had long been criminalized. In the end, the privacy argument Wulf developed in *Poe*—and its eventual acceptance by the High Court—owed a great deal to *Mapp* and to the broad ACLU civil liberties agenda that brought the two cases together.[21]

But in 1961, the U.S. Supreme Court was not yet ready to overturn a state birth control law. Instead, it concluded that the case did not "present a justiciable question," because the appellants sued before they had actually been prosecuted. Even so, few doubted that the tide was moving in favor of birth control. Four justices dissented in *Poe*, and Justice John Marshall Harlan's dissent read like a ringing endorsement of a constitutional right to marital privacy. "It is difficult to imagine," Harlan wrote, anything "more private or more intimate than a husband and wife's marital relations." Nothing is more "grossly offensive" than subjecting those relations to "the enquiry of the criminal law." Citing the Fourth and Fourteenth Amendments, Harlan maintained that "the Constitution protects the privacy of the home against all unreasonable intrusion," though it does not prevent the state from forbidding "adultery, homosexuality and the like."[22] In Harlan, heterosexual marital privacy had gained a strong judicial advocate.

The tides of change were apparent elsewhere too as Pilpel maintained in her oral argument before the Court in *Poe*. Not only did sixty-six prominent physicians file an amicus brief on behalf of Poe, but even Catholic leaders had begun to denounce laws against birth control. In 1960, the Food and Drug Administration approved the first pill for contraceptive purposes. Moreover, the mass media joined an array of federal policymakers in calling for international population control, blaming population pressures for economic instability and the spread of Communism.[23] So even as the Supreme Court lagged behind in the early 1960s, the direction of ACLU policy, legal reform, social science research, and public opinion was clearly in favor of birth control and edging toward treating sexual behavior more generally as a civil liberty.

In addition, a trio of activist groups—civil libertarians, legal elites, and sexologists—had for several decades contributed to a penal law reform movement that aimed to decriminalize sexual activities between consenting adults. Their efforts instigated change at all levels of government from the state legislature to the Supreme Court, with privacy figuring prominently.

The movement to revise penal laws shared similar origins with the ACLU—the Progressive Era enthusiasm for reform coupled with World War I–inspired efforts to restore and maintain law and order. Many prominent attorneys and public officials worried about the destabilizing possibilities of domestic opposition to the war and capitalism, while others were troubled by the postwar government crackdown on dissenters. Consensus among them centered on dissatisfaction with the hodgepodge of more than fifty different state penal codes, most of them obsolete relics of English common law, and each more "ineffective, inhumane and thoroughly unscientific" than the last. After years of planning by participants in the Association of American Law Schools, several hundred leading lawyers and judges met in 1923 to found the American Law Institute (ALI) for the purpose of making law more predictable and consistent while reducing the possibility of discretionary abuse. In its first few decades, the ALI focused on collecting and restating state criminal codes, a process that magnified the need for reform and prompted the institute to turn to the task of drafting a Model Penal Code that would encourage states to revise their laws.[24]

By 1951 when the ALI began to work on a Model Penal Code, Alfred Kinsey's groundbreaking *Sexual Behavior in the Human Male* was just three years old and had attracted considerable interest among influential lawyers in addition to the ACLU's Ernst and Pilpel. As early as 1943, near the beginning of his research on human sexual behavior, Kinsey contacted Ernst to discuss "legal aspects" of his work on sex offenders. Ernst responded enthusiastically, offering to assist Kinsey at reduced fees or none at all. At their first meeting, Kinsey flattered Ernst and offered him inside information on the latest sex research; in return Ernst provided legal expertise and expressed avid interest in Kinsey's work; many would say that sex was Ernst's raison d'être, and that he assumed it was everyone else's as well.[25] Together, Ernst and Pilpel advised Kinsey and his staff on issues related to publication, copyright, film rights, obscenity law, libel, and defamation and even tried to help him obtain access to the stores of obscene materials reputedly warehoused by the Federal Bureau of Investigation.[26]

While Pilpel and Ernst handled Kinsey's mundane legal matters, Kinsey attacked laws against sexual practices. In *Sexual Behavior in the Human Male,* he exhorted legislators to liberalize the law so that American men would not be breaking the law when they engaged in such normal behavior as adultery, fornication, sodomy, and homosexual relations. Sexual acts that remained private and consensual ought to be decriminalized, Kinsey argued. Early in the 1950s, he took his argument to the California State Legislature, where he testified against stricter laws and harsher punishments for sex offenders.[27] Kinsey's efforts to use his research to reform sex laws also brought him into closer association with Ernst and Pilpel, who functioned as a bridge between social science and law.

Kinsey fought legal battles on his own behalf as well when customs authorities confiscated photographs and books that he tried to import from abroad for his own research. His landmark case, *United States v. 31 Photographs,* established a "conditional privilege" for "scientists and scholars to import material that would be obscene in the hands of the average person." Pilpel considered the decision, concluded a year after Kinsey's death, revolutionary. "From now on," she wrote Kinsey's successors, "nothing can be considered obscene until the circumstances of its projected use are known." It is, Pilpel assured them, "good law—and you and we made it." Indeed, the case confirmed the "variable obscenity" notion that some civil libertarians had long advocated, establishing a precedent for treating material as obscene or not according to its intended audience and purpose.[28]

Kinsey's influence over the law went far beyond the reach of this one case thanks to his own ambitions as well as the coordinated efforts of Pilpel, Ernst, the ALI, and the ACLU. Ernst worked to promote what he called Kinsey's "Research Magnificent," by providing marketing advice, urging Rockefeller Foundation officers to continue to support Kinsey, writing laudatory articles for *Redbook* and other popular magazines, and even condensing *Sexual Behavior in the Human Male*'s 824 pages of turgid, technical text to 175 pages of light prose for the lay reader. In *American Sexual Behavior and the Kinsey Report* (1948), Ernst and his coauthor David Loth discussed ways that American law should be changed given Kinsey's finding that 85 percent of males interviewed had violated one of the sex laws. They argued that just because laws against adultery, fornication, seduction, homosexual activity, and sodomy went largely unprosecuted did not negate the laws' effects. Rather, this allowed public officials to enforce sex laws according to personal whim, provided tools for blackmail, and instilled cynicism toward the law. Kinsey's findings should lead lawmakers to decriminalize and reclassify a number of common sexual acts, Ernst and Loth argued, removing, for example, adultery as grounds for divorce because its prevalence indicated its compatibility with marriage. "The State should keep out of the bedroom," Ernst and Loth concluded.[29]

Ernst led the charge to align the sex laws with Kinsey's recommendations, and he recruited others to the cause. In 1948, when Judge Curtis Bok consulted Ernst about an obscenity case, Ernst referred him to Kinsey's work, and Bok's decision cited Kinsey to exonerate the items in question. In 1956, when Judge Jerome Frank sought Ernst's assistance with Samuel Roth's case, the resulting concurrence relied heavily on Kinsey's research. Attorneys, plaintiffs, and judges quoted Kinsey in court cases, judicial opinions, and the popular press. A vocal minority took the legal reform question in a different direction, suggesting that Kinsey's findings indicated that the sex laws should not be abolished but more stringently enforced. In general though, legal professionals were among Kinsey's most ardent supporters and, encouraged by the indomitable Ernst, they brought Kinsey's data and conclusions into American law.[30]

Other ACLU leaders and staff joined Ernst and Pilpel, exchanging information and advice with Kinsey through correspondence, intermediaries, and face-to-face meetings in New York City. Shared concerns included censorship, obscenity, and nudism, and ACLU leaders hoped to gather data and possibly extract expert testimony from Kinsey on a number of matters related to obscenity cases. When the ACLU began to revise its own obscenity policy in 1959, the legal director in charge turned to Kinsey's staff for information on the causal relationship between viewing obscene material and committing an illegal or antisocial act. ACLU attorneys offered assistance when the Customs Office confiscated Kinsey's research materials. In addition, they protested when public officials threatened to ban Kinsey's books, and they distributed anticensorship literature at Kinsey's request.[31]

Not everyone considered Kinsey's work reliable, let alone definitive. Statisticians complained about Kinsey's sloppy use of data and failure to employ random sampling for his interviews. Anthropologist Margaret Mead and other social scientists questioned Kinsey's assumption that behaviors found to be common should necessarily be considered normal. Tooth decay is common, one pointed out, but it should not be considered normal, let alone desirable. Still others objected to the interpretive license evident in his book. Psychologists criticized Kinsey's narrow and exclusively physiological approach to sexuality—his definition of sex, for example, as merely an "outlet" for orgasm and his assumption that quantity and variety determined the quality of sexual experience. As one prominent scholar wrote, Kinsey has an "unconscious bias that in sexual matters, 'the more the merrier,'" but he took comfort in his belief that the American people will never adopt laws "which hold up compulsive sexual over-drives as a goal for all to emulate."[32]

Kinsey suffered severe scholarly criticism but enjoyed record book sales, both of which led the Rockefeller Foundation to terminate its generous support of his work. Some foundation officials doubted the quality of his research; others thought that his publishing success should underwrite his efforts. Drawing a close to this long relationship with Kinsey prompted the foundation's officers to consider the impact of their investment. Some worried that by awarding a majority of their funds to Kinsey for so many years running they had skewed the field of research on human sexuality and discouraged others from entering it. "It is always dangerous," wrote one, "to leave a field dominated by a very large or monumental set of studies which tend to scare off the competition." Those more optimistic about the value of Kinsey's studies eagerly anticipated their influence on laws regarding sexual behavior.[33]

The Rockefeller Foundation ensured that Kinsey's work would reshape the sex laws when it funded the ALI's Model Penal Code. Officers of the foundation approved the Code's leaders or "reporters" and advised them to draw on current social science as they drafted new laws. The four reporters, Herbert Wechsler (chief), Louis B. Schwartz, Morris Ploscowe, and Paul W. Tappan, worked for more than a decade with a number of special consultants and research associates who guided their multidisciplinary approach to law reform. Each of the reporters publicly supported Kinsey's findings, interpreted them as a call for liberalizing sex laws, and took up that call when they began to draft the Model Penal Code in 1951. Even so, debates emerged among them about how and whether to continue criminalizing sodomy, prostitution, obscenity, abortion, and illicit sexual intercourse. Eventually, the group developed a new legal paradigm that decriminalized most private sexual behavior between consenting adults. Citing Kinsey's finding that one-half of married men admitted to infidelity, the Model Penal Code advised that adultery be freed of legal censure as long as it remained private or was, in other words, conducted discreetly enough to avoid becoming a "public nuisance" or risking "public lewdness." Noting Kinsey's discovery that substantial numbers of men and women experimented sexually with members of their own sex, they recommended a zone of privacy that would shield homosexual and other consensual sexual behavior from the law. They also declined to include any regulation of contraceptives and established parameters for "justifiable abortion." Indeed, Schwartz admitted that the Code would have dealt with abortion even more leniently if not for fear that it would offend Catholic sensibilities and lose influence as a result. But when fears of Catholic opposition frustrated ALI efforts to reform the code's treatment of sodomy, Rowland Watts, the ACLU's legal director, intervened.[34]

The ACLU first considered issues of homosexuality when it defended victims of McCarthyism during the "Lavender Scare" of the 1950s. Its initial support for individuals charged with deviant sexual conduct came back to issues of due process—when individuals accused publicly were not allowed to answer charges, the ACLU cried foul. But beyond due process claims, assistant director Alan Reitman had difficulty finding civil liberties relevant and suspected that the persecution experienced by homosexuals could be addressed more effectively by medical professionals than by the Constitution. Accordingly, he urged Dr. William Menninger, cofounder of the world-renowned Menninger Institute, to persuade psychiatrists to remove homosexuality from the category of mental illness, thereby eliminating federal officials' justification for treating homosexuals as uniquely vulnerable to blackmail and therefore security risks.[35] ACLU leaders expressed concern about the wholesale persecution of homosexuals that grew in the shadow of Cold War witch hunts, but most did not consider it a civil liberties matter.

Even so, homosexual appeals for ACLU assistance grew throughout the decade as undesirable discharges from the military, dismissals from federal employment, and denials of security clearances increased. Many who appealed to the ACLU were members, and they acknowledged that the abuses they suffered might not qualify as civil liberties violations. One woman, an "Air Force girl," wrote the ACLU that she was questioned by military personnel, along with eleven others, about her alleged homosexual activities and told that if she confessed she would be discharged with no penalty. "I just hung myself out of fear," she wrote, but received an "undesirable discharge" anyway. She had been recruited into the military without being told that "lesbians are undesirable," offered no attorney when charged with homosexual conduct, given no consideration regarding the quality of her work, and not told the exact nature of her offense. They do not care, she wrote, "whether you seduce every girl in sight of [*sic*] whether you were once seduced and have since been dating and staying far away from the whole business." She was also encouraged to "spy on the other girls and to list girls who are friends and who *might* be engaged in homosexual relations." Worse, she discovered, "anyone with homosexual tendencies may be discharged—and who among us is without such?" The cost of this "rotten" policy was borne by many, she argued, including taxpayers, whose money was wasted on her training, and her parents, who suffered "personal heartbreak." In addition, she now faced discrimination in the civilian job market. I'm in "one hell of a mess," she wrote, begging the ACLU for advice.[36]

A friend of hers who was discharged from the air force under similar circumstances also wrote to the ACLU. She had broken off a lesbian relationship and begun to visit a base psychiatrist to get her "mental state straightened out" when she received notice that her former lover had reported her to the authorities. After confessing, she was granted an undesirable discharge and classified a "bad security risk." "It's too late to help me at all in this mess," she wrote, but she worried about "twenty girls left there at Wright-Patterson who live in constant terror." In an echo of her friend's letter, she lamented that she and her colleagues were given no "consideration as individuals." No one seemed to care about "my character, nobody asked my work unit if I did my work well. . . . I was a nonentity with a homosexual contact." The ACLU's legal director, Levy, informed the women that "there is no violation of civil liberties involved" in the army's discharge of homosexuals. He suggested that they seek "medical treatment if you really desire to abandon homosexual relations."[37]

The growing number of individuals, many of them members, who wrote to criticize the ACLU for ignoring homosexuals while defending southern blacks and other persecuted minorities in the 1950s received discouraging responses. One wrote, "My civil liberties are more completely denied than those of any of the groups which you defend. In my own country I am a criminal, classed with thieves and murderers, and ever more despised. I am at the mercy of blackmailers, politically inspired cleanup campaigns, and anyone looking for a scapegoat. If my painful façade of 'normality' ever slips I will stand to lose the whole life that I have managed to build up for myself." Levy assured this correspondent that the ACLU would defend homosexuals against due process violations if they would come forward. But he also affirmed that, because homosexuality was considered a mental illness, homosexuals were uniquely vulnerable to blackmail that could legitimately exclude them from federal employment as security risks. Private employers were within their rights, he explained, to refuse to hire criminals, including individuals who violated sodomy laws.[38]

By late 1956, persecution of homosexuals by the military, federal government, and the House Un-American Activities Committee had led to high-profile purges, suicides, growing public criticism, and greater attention from the legal and civil liberties communities. The ALI debated the issue of sodomy while drafting its Model Penal Code even as Britain's Wolfenden Report recommended the decriminalization of private homosexual acts between consenting adults. Moreover, the ACLU received daily pressure from homosexual victims of discrimination and ACLU affiliates, all of whom urged the organization to take a stand against the escalating persecution. The ACLU's top officers were deeply divided between Malin, Joughin, and the outgoing Levy, who were reluctant to become involved, and the incoming legal director, Rowland Watts, who was eager to address the discrimination experienced by homosexuals.[39]

Watts brought decades of experience as an activist to his work for the ACLU. Born in Baltimore, Maryland, in 1912, he grew up Methodist in a family dedicated to pacifism, the Social Gospel, and the life of the mind. After completing his B.A. at the University of Chicago in 1934, he earned a law degree from the University of Baltimore in 1938. During World War II, Watts accepted nonmilitary assignment as a conscientious objector, left the church due to its prowar stance, and married Fay Bennett, an antiwar activist; together they had three children. After the war, Watts moved with his family to Greenwich Village and took a job with the Workers' Defense League, an organization dedicated to defending labor rights. Through social and professional networks, Watts became friends with a number of homosexuals, including civil rights activists Bayard Rustin and Pauli Murray. Personal experiences as well as a general commitment to human rights and a deeply empathic nature primed Watts to pursue the matter of homosexual rights when he was hired as ACLU staff counsel in 1955 and replaced Levy as legal director in 1958.[40]

At Watts's urging, the ACLU studied the plight of homosexuals and began to draft its first policy on homosexuality. Watts laid groundwork by circulating educational material among his staff, including *One: The Homosexual Magazine* and Donald Webster Cory's *The Homosexual in America*, a pathbreaking book that called for an end to discrimination against homosexuals. Watts also consulted with Cory about how the ACLU could help victims of discrimination. The first policy statement drafted by the ACLU did little more than articulate the organization's commitment to defending due process rights, including those of homosexuals. "Like members of other socially heretical or deviant groups," it acknowledged, homosexuals are susceptible to persecution, entrapment, and denial of rights to due process and free speech, all "matters of proper concern for the Union." The ACLU will, the statement concluded, "support the defense of such cases that come to our attention."[41]

The ACLU may not have advocated strongly for homosexual rights in the 1950s, but as one of the few organizations to offer any support at all, it became a veritable networking hub and information clearinghouse for homosexual victims of discrimination. When, for example, the ACLU received a letter about the frequency of suicides among young women dismissed from the military for homosexual activity, it forwarded this information to Fredric Wertham, a psychiatrist researching the problem. Watts regretted that the ACLU could not offer more help to a very troubled young person who identified as a "true lesbian hermaphrodyte [*sic*]," but referred the individual to the George W. Henry Foundation, one of the earliest organizations devoted to helping "sexual deviants." With another correspondent, Watts discussed England's recently released Wolfenden Report on homosexuality and called its recommendations against state proscriptions on consensual sexual activity between adults in private "the enlightened view." Unable to provide legal assistance, under current ACLU policy, to homosexuals suffering discrimination that involved no rights to free speech or due process, he offered his correspondent information about subscribing to *ONE* and joining the Mattachine Society. When the Los Angeles postmaster declared *One* unmailable on grounds of obscenity, Watts assured its publisher that the ACLU would vigorously defend *ONE*'s access to the mails on First Amendment grounds. Later, when an individual wrote to ask whether he would be violating the law by subscribing to *ONE*, Watts affirmed that the ACLU would assist him if he encountered any difficulties. And as always, ACLU staff frequently referred individuals who contacted them for legal assistance to local cooperating attorneys.[42]

The ACLU itself had yet to take a firm civil liberties stand on any sexual behavior other than nudism and birth control, but that did not prevent Watts from using his position as legal director to criticize laws against sodomy. After recognizing inconsistencies in the ALI's treatment of sodomy in its 1958 draft of the Model Penal Code, Watts demanded to know why the ALI recommended that private, consensual sexual conduct be removed from penal law but continued to treat "sexual deviation"—code for homosexual sex—"as a criminal act." His question invited friendly ribbing from ACLU colleagues, but Watts pressed on. By 1962, when the Model Penal Code appeared in final form, Watts was pleased to see that it no longer criminalized consensual adult "sexual deviation," including sodomy.[43]

Watts's intervention with the ALI is unsurprising in light of his correspondence with individuals persecuted for homosexuality. More conscientiously than other ACLU attorneys, he read their letters, wrote thoughtful responses, and educated himself and his colleagues about homosexual concerns. Whereas Reitman often informed correspondents that the ACLU did not concern itself with homosexual issues because "the civil liberties aspects of the question of sexual deviation" are so minor, Watts characterized the ACLU as "very much concerned" about "the barbaric operation of the penal laws concerning sexual activities." Watts was so moved after reading an unsigned letter written by "a homosexual" and longtime ACLU member that he routed the letter to office staff. "Even though I have been undergoing psychiatric care for four and a half years now," the nameless author wrote, "I am not 'cured.'" Burdened by a police record, impoverished from paying blackmailers for protection, and demoralized by police beatings and "warnings," the writer closed with a heart-wrenching plea. "You ask me how you can help? Help me so that I can help. Let me serve... let my heart sing again, feeling that I am innocent in society... let me be free! How? I don't know. It's your society. The law does not consider me part of it."[44] Watts worked to change that by gently prodding his colleagues, forcefully confronting the ALI, and providing sympathetic and respectful advice to homosexuals who appealed to the ACLU for help.

With the arrival of Melvin Wulf in 1958, Watts gained not only an assistant legal director but also an ally in his efforts to roll back government regulation of sexual behavior. Wulf's expansive vision of sexual civil liberties encompassed contraception, homosexual conduct, and also abortion. Wulf admitted, in one of his first letters on the subject, that the ACLU considered sexual practice unrelated to civil liberties but suggested that he and his colleagues might reexamine that stance in light of Britain's popular Wolfenden Report, which seemed to indicate "growing social uneasiness concerning the intrusion of the state into the private behavior of its citizens."[45]

Meanwhile, the ACLU received ever more complaints relating to homosexuality, many involving postal officials who monitored mail, unsealed and inspected first-class packages and letters, and threatened individual patrons who subscribed to *ONE* or received private letters that indicated a homosexual relationship. H. Ernest Stokes of Hartsville, South Carolina, for example, asked the ACLU if his civil liberties had been violated when, in a "most humiliating experience," a postal inspector summoned him to the post office, instructed him to open and read letters received from and written to a male friend, and asked him bluntly, "Are you a homosexual?" After the inspector threatened to obtain a warrant to search Stokes's home unless he returned to the post office with samples of other material, Stokes brought him several magazines, was required to initial each photo of men in "posing straps," and finally allowed to leave but warned that his mail would be watched. "I've been under this constant threat ever since," Stokes wrote, "and my day by day life is a hell, never knowing when I may be accosted again." In response, Watts assured Stokes that the postal inspector had acted without authority and offered to help him resist any future invasions of his privacy.[46]

Den Nichols, a college student in Kalamazoo, Michigan, wrote the ACLU with a similar complaint, explaining that his postal inspector threatened to search his parents' farm, asked him "how long have you been this way," and forced him to sign a statement that he would cancel his subscriptions to *ONE* and *Mattachine Review*. Fearing expulsion if college officials learned of his encounter with postal authorities, Nichols tried to preempt trouble by reporting the incident to his residence hall director and the dean of men, both of whom proved understanding and supportive. Still, Nichols worried. He feared his parents would find out, and he wanted to continue receiving his magazines. "Those items fulfill a meaningfulness in my life," Nichols wrote. Moreover, "I am willing to do what is necessary in order to protect our freedom." With characteristic empathy, Watts assured Nichols that the postal inspector had exceeded his authority on every count and that the ACLU would take up the issue with the postmaster general.[47]

Watts and Wulf enjoyed the support of homosexuals and homophile activists who joined ACLU affiliates. One who became quite prominent, Frank Kameny, a member of the ACLU since 1950, became a homophile activist after being fired for suspected homosexuality in 1957 from his position as Army Map Service astronomer. He helped to found the National Capitol Area ACLU in 1961 while suing the federal government for wrongful dismissal and demanding "a clear statement of the ACLU's policies in regard to the rights of homosexuals as a minority group." Homophile activist Vern Bullough, president of an Ohio chapter, urged Malin to address civil liberties violations based on "homosexuality and stigmatized sexual behavior in general." When he moved to Southern California in 1959, he brought these concerns to the local ACLU affiliate, established contact between it and area gay and lesbian organizations, and persuaded the director to assemble a "Sex and Civil Liberties Committee" to explore the civil liberties aspects of abortion, homosexuality, and other sexual behaviors. The leadership of other ACLU affiliates also included supporters of gay rights, including Albert Bendich of Northern California, W. Dorr Legg of Southern California, David Carliner of Washington, D.C., William Reynard and E. A. Dioguardi of Colorado, Richard Inman of Florida, and George Rundquist of the New York City affiliate.[48]

Policy statements and official documents indicate that the ACLU's approach to homosexuality changed little in the 1950s. Indeed, Merle Miller, a member of the Board of Directors at the time who later came out as a gay man, remembered that the ACLU was "notably silent" on the issue of homosexuality and that he himself was perhaps "most silent of all."[49] Still, a quiet revolution rumbled behind the scenes in the work of affiliates, the ALI, and ACLU leaders' correspondence with homosexual victims of persecution. Moreover, the ACLU's top leaders anticipated that the ongoing effort to overturn laws against birth control in Connecticut could, if successful in the Supreme Court, lead the ACLU to expand its defense of homosexual rights. "Once we have the high court's opinion" on birth control, associate director Alan Reitman noted, "we will be in a position to determine our policy on the civil liberties aspect of a variety of sexual practices, including homosexuality."[50]

By 1962, Connecticut activists had taken on the birth control case that would become *Griswold v. Connecticut*. ACLU leaders offered advice, planned their own privacy-oriented brief, and considered the case's relevance to laws regarding homosexuality and abortion. Wulf, Watts, and Reitman had discussed the issue for some time and would have pressed for new ACLU policy on "a variety of sexual practices including homosexuality" if the Supreme Court had upheld their privacy arguments in *Poe v. Ullman* (1961). With *Griswold* coming up through the courts, they hoped for a decision that would help them recast their entire approach to sexual issues. Harriet Pilpel's election to the Board of Directors that year promised to expedite the process.[51]

As a new ACLU board member with twenty-five years of civil liberties experience and more than a decade representing two of the most influential entities devoted to expanding sexual freedoms—the PPFA and Kinsey—Pilpel ap-

Figure 4.4 Catherine Roraback, Estelle Griswold, Dr. C. Lee Buxton, and unidentified woman, January 2, 1961, during the lower-court trial that would become *Griswold v. Connecticut*. (Courtesy, ©Bettmann/CORBIS)

proached the ACLU's 1964 Biennial Conference well positioned to push the organization into a more progressive stance on sexual rights. The conference met in Boulder, Colorado, where participants celebrated a number of recent landmark Supreme Court triumphs and planned for the future. A sense of optimism tempered by urgency pervaded the conference as attendees discussed new ways to "rewrite American Constitutional Law" while strategizing for the civil rights crisis in Mississippi, where violence threatened to overtake the voting rights project. The conference elected to allocate one million dollars to opening a Southern Regional Office in Atlanta before Harriet Pilpel turned its attention to matters of sexuality.[52]

Pilpel introduced the notion of sexual civil liberties in an unlikely session, "Civil Liberties and the War on Crime." The panel was organized by ACLU leaders who worried that the "war on crime" begun by John F. Kennedy's presidential administration in the early 1960s would bring with it wholesale abuses of civil liberties. To this effort at rethinking crime and criminality, Pilpel contributed an unexpected sexual twist. "It is up to the Union," Pilpel charged in her dramatic plenary presentation, "to draw out the civil liberties consequences of the American Law Institute's social policy position on sex laws." Urging her audience to recognize the importance of "a constitutionally protected right of privacy," she regretted that the ACLU had failed to take the lead on the most difficult issues of all, "namely abortion and homosexuality." Pilpel pointed out that board member Dorothy Kenyon had, for the past decade, exhorted her colleagues to recognize laws against abortion as violations of women's civil liberties, only to hear from them that abortion was not relevant to ACLU concerns. Laws against abortion and other "sex laws" constitute a form of "class legislation," Pilpel argued. They are applied primarily to the poor and underprivileged, and efforts to enforce them necessarily result in "wholesale violations of civil liberties" through surveillance, entrapment, arbitrary police action, speech repression, and intrusions on privacy. Furthermore, she maintained, under these laws, nine out of ten Americans qualified as sex criminals. "There's something wrong with the laws," Pilpel declared, when so many people violate them with impunity while others suffer prosecution and punishment. "The American Law Institute has pointed the way," she noted, to establishing a right of sexual privacy, but it is up to the ACLU to tease out and defend the civil liberties issues involved.[53]

Pilpel presented a compelling argument for bringing sexual conduct into the ACLU's civil liberties agenda by rooting it in ACLU tradition and due process, legitimating it with scientific findings, relating it to concerns about the "war on crime," and associating it with the criminal law reform undertaken by the ALI. She also presented her case in an environment and to an audience primed to accept it. So although the 1964 Biennial focused on civil rights,

Figure 4.5 Dorothy Kenyon at the pivotal 1964 American Civil Liberties Union Biennial Conference in Boulder, Colorado. (Courtesy, Princeton University Library)

Pilpel advocated a dramatic expansion of the ACLU's work on behalf of sexual privacy. Over the opposition of a vocal minority, the Biennial voted to adopt the ALI's recommendation to decriminalize private sexual conduct by consenting adults and instructed the ACLU to explore the constitutionality of abortion laws.[54]

For Pilpel, the ACLU's 1964 Biennial was notable for moving sexual rights onto the ACLU's national agenda, but also because it was there that she and Dorothy Kenyon began a friendship that would dramatically enhance their influence on the ACLU board. "One of the nice things" about the conference, Kenyon wrote Pilpel, "was the feeling of having become friends." The two attended panels together, debated issues, joined each other for sightseeing in the mountains, and later exchanged letters celebrating their newfound friendship. Thereafter, they vacationed together on Martha's Vineyard and joined forces to persuade the ACLU to recognize abortion as a civil liberties matter.[55] Their emerging friendship and rising influence portended a sea change within the ACLU as women individually and collectively gained ground in staff and policy-making positions that would take the ACLU's budding new privacy agenda in unexpected directions.

When the ACLU national office set its committee agendas for 1965 and 1966, issues of sexuality ranked high on the list of priorities. This shift was inspired by the 1964 Biennial but it also accorded with a number of broader developments. In a seven-to-two decision, the U.S. Supreme Court in *Griswold* recognized the constitutional right of privacy promulgated by Wulf, the ACLU, and Planned Parenthood. High-level federal policymakers, including ex-presidents Harry Truman and Dwight Eisenhower, had recently lent their names to population control and even Planned Parenthood. In the meantime, Lyndon Johnson's warnings about "the explosion in world population," declaration of a War on Poverty, signing of the Economic Opportunity Act (1964), and creation of the Office of Economic Opportunity (OEO) moved his administration toward providing federal funds for family-planning services. As birth control acquired respectability and sexual privacy obtained constitutional protection, the ACLU gained significant ground in its recent efforts to decriminalize private sexual behavior between consenting adults.[56]

Cultural events associated with the twentieth century's second sexual revolution created a local and national environment conducive to the ACLU's growing attention to sexual civil liberties. Many ACLU leaders lived and even more played in Greenwich Village, though ACLU offices had moved several blocks north. In the middle of the twentieth century, the Village that had provided a home for anarchists, free-lovers, and avant-garde writers and artists fifty years earlier now hosted the Beats and the creators of sexually and politically subversive art, music, poetry, and theater that gained prominence in the 1960s' counterculture. New sexual trends appeared on the national stage as well with Hugh Hefner's first Playboy Club in Chicago and Helen Gurley Brown's best-selling *Sex and the Single Girl* (1963), which promoted a "Playboy" lifestyle for women. These commercial enterprises joined go-go dancing, topless bars, swinger's parties, and Sexual Freedom Leagues on college campuses to announce the arrival of a cultural turn considered revolutionary by many, one that strengthened the ACLU's growing commitment to sexual civil liberties.[57]

Sexual practice did not join speech as an element of sexual civil liberties until the 1960s. It did so through a constitutional right to privacy that grew, not only out of the birth control movement, the sexual revolution, and the ACLU's long-standing defense of nudists, but from ACLU leaders' involvement in a constellation of organizations. A commitment to civil liberties broadly and free speech and due process in particular propelled ACLU attorneys into ongoing interactions with groups and individuals that expanded their thinking and commitments. Alfred Kinsey, women and men persecuted for homosexuality, American Law Institute reporters, and birth control advocates all prodded the ACLU to stretch its sexual civil liberties agenda to include sexual conduct. Interactions among leaders of these groups fueled a dynamic process of intellectual cross-pollination as attorneys like Harriet Pilpel, who represented multiple groups, served as conduits of information and ideas, spreading civil liberties language and values far and wide even as they brought different ways of thinking about sexual issues back to the ACLU. Catalyzed by this array of energetic individuals and their discussions of sexual issues, a new constitutional right to sexual privacy that protected sexual conduct began to emerge.

Some paths to sexual privacy, such as the one begun by nudists in the 1930s, failed to achieve any wider influence. Nudism, of course, did not offer the range of benefits and address the array of problems that birth control did. In addition, as a fringe movement of marginal and often competing organizations, nudism failed to interact with other movements and groups that might have broadened its constituency, raised its visibility, and brought it more fully into the mainstream of American law and culture. By contrast, the birth control movement found greater traction, gaining followers and supporters from a wide swath of the professional, medical, and legal community as well as a range of people from diverse economic, religious, and political backgrounds.

Timing mattered. The early 1960s proved more opportune than the 1930s for introducing the concept of privacy as a strategy for expanding sexual civil liberties. The intervening years had witnessed a marked loosening of restrictions on sexual display and also on contraception—a growing appreciation for non-procreative sexual pleasure. World War II and the postwar flowering of First Amendment consumer rights loosened strictures on sexual expression as government-issued pinups and later *Playboy* magazine transformed pictures of nude women from articles of obscenity into symbols of patriotism and personal freedom. Fears of overpopulation inspired by the Great Depression and later by the potential vulnerability of impoverished countries to Communist influence made contraception more socially acceptable, as did middle-class women's enthusiasm for it. The ascendance, in the early 1950s, of U.S. Supreme Court justices who privileged individual over states' rights invited arguments that prioritized the sexual civil liberties and privacy of citizens over the state's right to control their behavior. In addition, cultural events associated with the onset of the century's second sexual revolution indicated a more tolerant attitude toward a wide array of sexual behaviors. All of these developments increased the likelihood that efforts to expand sexual civil liberties would experience greater success in the 1960s.

Between the 1930s and 1960s, advocates for more liberal sex laws turned to the ACLU for advice and assistance. Under the ACLU's influence, proponents of criminal law reform, birth control, homosexual rights, and sexual freedom learned to think and talk about their main issues in constitutional terms even as they encouraged the ACLU to conceive of sexual civil liberties more broadly.[58] Considering disparate causes under a civil liberties umbrella inspired ACLU leaders to develop a coherent right to privacy in sexual matters. In so doing, they established the constitutional foundation for another sexual revolution.

Unsurprisingly, after the U.S. Supreme Court elevated privacy to the status of a constitutional right in *Griswold,* proponents and opponents of sexual freedom vied to shape the decision's impact. ACLU leaders once again confronted adversaries who—as with consumer rights—wielded weapons of the ACLU's own making. Privacy rights, they soon learned, could be invoked effectively by enemies as well as advocates of more liberal sex laws.

5

"To Produce Offspring without Interference by the State"

Making Reproductive Freedom, 1960s–1970s

William Bentley Ball was a civil libertarian—at least he thought he was. He was also a white man, a husband and father, an attorney, a devout Catholic, an advocate for civil rights, a supporter of President Lyndon Johnson's War on Poverty, and general counsel for the Pennsylvania Catholic Welfare Conference. In 1966, he opposed public funding for family-planning services. Some advocates of government-sponsored family planning services saw them as a population control strategy; others considered them essential for making the promise of *Griswold* a reality for poor women. Ball saw things differently. He warned Congress that federal funding for family-planning programs would result in widespread violations of the civil liberties of African Americans. He used words like genocide, spoke of racial eugenics, and predicted that federal involvement in family planning would bring massive violations of privacy—sexual privacy, bodily privacy, the sort of privacy recently awarded constitutional protection by the Supreme Court.[1] Ball's testimony opened an era of intense debate over what role the state should play in funding and regulating women's reproductive choices. The outcome of that debate would also help to shape the newly articulated right to privacy and determine whether and how it would make a full-blown civil liberty of sexual conduct.

Many in the ACLU responded positively to Ball, an eloquent spokesperson for civil rights and social justice and a skeptic of state power. Others in and out of the ACLU saw his vision as one that would curtail women's ability to determine their own reproductive destiny. No one anticipated the many ways that Ball's concerns would map the terrain of reproductive politics for the next several decades. Nor could anyone predict how women's rights activists in the ACLU would challenge Ball and fundamentally alter the landscape of reproductive rights and sexual civil liberties.

Griswold "cleared the way for government participation in family planning programs," ACLU leaders agreed. But was the government *obligated* to provide family-planning services? Harriet Pilpel and Dorothy Kenyon, ACLU board members who had long argued that laws against birth control effectively denied it only to the poor, answered yes and worked to establish a right to publicly funded birth control. If "constitutional guarantees are to be meaningful, mustn't they also imply an affirmative obligation on the part of government to make it possible for people to exercise their constitutional rights?" Pilpel asked in 1965, pointing out that this principle had already been applied to "Negro rights" and "the right of the accused to counsel." The newly formed Office of Economic Opportunity (OEO) had begun to make limited family-planning services available to married welfare recipients, but Pilpel and Kenyon demanded that it provide a full range of reproductive control options to needy women without regard to marital status. They argued that refusing to fund sterilizations and contraceptives for single women and unwed mothers represented an "invasion of the right of privacy."[2]

Most of their ACLU colleagues did not agree that the government was obligated to provide family-planning services to welfare recipients. If, however, the government chose to provide such services, the ACLU majority conceded that it must respect rights to equal protection, due process, and privacy. Accordingly, in collaboration with the Association for Voluntary Sterilization and various community action groups, the ACLU pressured OEO director Sargent Shriver to provide poor unmarried women the same family-planning services "available to the wealthy." Shriver's office retorted that "the Constitution is [not] violated every time OEO 'discriminates' against the poor by failing to support activities which can be financed privately by those who are more affluent." Moreover, Shriver pointed out, "unrestricted family planning aid" could destroy the entire program by provoking its opponents.[3]

Shriver's restrictions did not prevent challenges to the OEO's family-planning program. In 1965, critics aired their views in congressional hearings on two bills that would expand federal involvement in family planning. William Ball, the bills' most ardent foe, argued in a civil liberties idiom. "If the power and prestige of government is placed behind programs aimed at providing birth control services to the poor," he assured legislators, "coercion necessarily results and violations of human privacy become inevitable." Well-meaning caseworkers would query welfare recipients about their sexual histories, intimate practices, and personal beliefs to determine which family-planning strategies to recommend. Welfare recipients, whose livelihoods hung in the balance, would feel pressured to use contraceptives, agree to surgical sterilization, and even submit to abortions. Citing *Griswold,* Ball decried government encroachment on the privacy rights of citizens, declaring the sexual relationship "one of the most intimate and private of all human relationships." Citing recent ACLU-supported court opinions, he likened the welfare recipient offered family-planning services to the public schoolchild invited to pray but allowed to opt out. In such a "built-in coercive atmosphere," he maintained, "the availability of an exemption means very little indeed." More threatening still was the "racial eugenicism" likely to result from publicly funded family-planning services directed at a largely poor and black clientele.[4]

Ball's testimony commanded ACLU attention, because it drew the lines of debate in terms of civil liberties and civil rights. Many ACLU leaders were concerned about the possibility of coercion in government-sponsored family-planning programs. Several urged further study of Ball's privacy arguments and requested that Ball address the national board on these issues. Meanwhile, the ACLU testified against a bill that would provide family-planning services only to individuals whose religious and moral beliefs were compatible with family planning, arguing that the requirement would violate the privacy rights of aid recipients by forcing them to reveal their personal beliefs before gaining access to government aid.[5]

Whereas the ACLU emphasized the possibility of compulsion, Pilpel focused on the discriminatory impact of denying publicly funded family-planning services to the poor. She refuted Ball's testimony point by point in a legal memorandum for the hearing panel and took her argument on the televised *Today* show. "There is no coercion when you give people a free choice, which is what these programs do," she explained. "Hasn't the time come to recognize" that "many constitutional rights, including the right to plan your family, are no rights at all for many people, unless the government makes possible their exercise?" she asked. Without such affirmative action by public institutions, "equality under the law" would, she feared, remain little more than rhetoric.[6]

Pilpel demanded federal funding for sterilization as well as for birth control. A key legal adviser since the early 1950s to the two major advocacy groups for sterilization, the Association for Voluntary Sterilization (AVS) and the Human Betterment Association of America (HBAA), Pilpel understood that sterilization could be used for coercive purposes—as an aid to eugenic engineering, a measure for population control, and a means to reduce poverty. So she urged sterilization organizations and physicians to protect the civil liberties of patients by obtaining written consent even from "retarded or feeble-minded" patients and performing sterilizations only for the "medical well-being" of the patient, not to address "socio-economic" needs. At the same time—and in a somewhat contradictory vein—Pilpel linked sterilization to Lyndon Johnson's wars on crime and poverty, advocating public funding for birth control and sterilization to prevent the birth of "illegitimate, poverty-stricken children" who grow up in an environment that "breeds delinquency, unemployment, and ultimately, crime." Even so, Pilpel consistently framed the issue as one of civil liberties, declaring it "a violation of the rights of privacy of the recipients of OEO funds to deny them access to voluntary sterilization."[7]

Nevertheless, Ball's concept of privacy and his fears about racism and eugenics prevailed. They shifted the conversation away from the virtues of using affirmative government action to protect individuals from unwanted pregnancy and toward the necessity of safeguarding individuals from unwanted government interference in their reproductive lives. This approach addressed concerns raised by Catholic opponents of federal family-planning programs and also accusations by black activists that family planning served as a tool of race genocide. The black male militants who voiced these arguments most forcefully made up only a small minority of the African American population, but they exercised considerable influence even though black women continued to demand family-planning services. Black Muslims condemned the coupling of financial assistance with birth control in U.S. foreign aid programs to India, Africa, and Asia, criticized domestic social programs that placed a disproportionate number of birth control clinics in black neighborhoods, and charged that, if legalized, abortion too would be forced upon women of color.[8]

Disagreements among civil libertarians and their allies stymied Pilpel's and Kenyon's efforts to persuade the ACLU to support federally funded family-planning programs. They also frustrated the women's attempts to persuade their ACLU colleagues to support abortion rights.

Until 1956 most ACLU leaders did not even consider the possibility that abortion might be relevant to civil liberties. That year, persistent prodding by longtime board member Dorothy Kenyon and a seemingly unlikely individual, Jules E. Bernfeld, a hairstylist who lived in Virginia and contributed to the ACLU, finally put the issue on the table for the board's consideration. Bernfeld urged the ACLU to declare laws against "self-determination in childbearing" unconstitutional, explaining that legal abortion would help to reduce crime by preventing the birth of unwanted children or criminals-in-the-making. Like so many others who wrote to the ACLU, Bernfeld appreciated the advice and sympathetic ear of legal director Rowland Watts, who agreed that laws against abortion were archaic and lamented that the ACLU had taken no position on them. Watts referred Bernfeld to the American Law Institute (ALI) and the Planned Parenthood Federation of American (PPFA), but he also agreed to take the matter up with the ACLU board.[9]

Dorothy Kenyon had tried to raise the issue of abortion many times with the board, but she did not succeed until armed with Bernfeld's pragmatic argument and Watts's support. Nevertheless, board members concluded that, because they could not determine when life begins, they would leave the matter to "social agencies in the field" and consider addressing it only in the context of a "proper" abortion law reform campaign. Kenyon maintained that to focus on when life begins was to miss the point entirely, because women must have the "right to choose what shall happen to their bodies." Kenyon's declaration seemed to fall on deaf ears, but she appreciated that the board had finally begun to discuss the matter.[10] Kenyon gained a new ally in 1958 with the arrival of assistant legal director Melvin Wulf, who made no secret of his support for abortion rights as well as birth control. Perhaps his personal needs as a single but far from abstemious heterosexual man strengthened his commitment to both issues. If so, he was not alone. Many who supported abortion rights did so after having confronted the issue personally. In any case, after arguing in *Poe v. Ullman* (1960) that laws against birth control violated the right to privacy, Wulf contemplated defending abortion rights on the same grounds.[11]

Meanwhile, the emergence of a vigorous abortion law reform campaign in the early 1960s, one initially focused on therapeutic needs for abortion, called the ACLU's bluff. The campaign was a response, in part, to recommendations by the American Law Institute, the organization of leading lawyers and judges that had worked, since 1951, to develop a Model Penal Code that would guide criminal law reform at the state level. By the late 1950s, the ALI recommended the legalization of therapeutic abortions, defined as abortions performed by physicians who believed that continuing a pregnancy could jeopardize the "physical or mental health" of the woman or result in a severely physically or mentally impaired child. "Rape, incest, or other felonious intercourse" might also justify abortion, according to the Code, whose framers admitted that they would have made the abortion provisions even more lenient if not for political considerations.[12]

As ALI leaders hoped, the Model Penal Code inspired state legislatures to revise their criminal statutes and provided a prototype for doing so. Legislators around the country proposed laws that would allow therapeutic abortions, especially after the high-profile case of Sherri Finkbine exposed the difficulty of obtaining therapeutic abortions in the United States. A local television personality who hosted the children's program *Romper Room,* Finkbine flew to Sweden for an abortion after learning that the thalidomide she had taken to curb nausea caused severe fetal deformities. Concurrently, an epidemic of rubella, a disease that caused fetal defects, dramatically increased the number of women who sought therapeutic abortions. By the middle of the decade, liberalized abortion laws were supported by high-profile entities such as the *Christian Century,* National Council of Churches, state medical societies, members of state bar conventions, deans of law schools, the mainstream press, and law reviews. Abortion law reform groups formed all over the country. Calling themselves committees for "Humane Abortion Laws," they emerged first in California when the legislature considered bills to decriminalize therapeutic abortion.[13]

Supporters and opponents of abortion law reform urged the ACLU to take a stand on the issue. On abortion law reform, the ACLU would not at first be led by its affiliates, as it had been and would be on other issues; even the most adventuresome affiliate toed a narrow line on the issue. When, for example, one woman implored her local Southern California affiliate to support a therapeutic abortion bill in 1963, the director expressed personal support for her position but assured her that "there is no prospect that the ACLU will regard 'Therapeutic abortions' as a civil liberties matter."[14]

Just two years later, national ACLU leaders began to explore that possibility. In the interim, they had witnessed the emergence of an abortion law reform movement and received a demand from the 1964 Biennial Conference, addressed by Harriet Pilpel, that they explore the constitutionality of abortion laws. National ACLU leaders initiated the task by asking the Southern California affiliate—located in a hotbed of abortion law reform—to conduct a study and provide policy recommendations to the national office. The California affiliate assembled committees of psychiatrists, doctors, scholars, and attorneys to consider the issue. Many arguments surfaced, among them the claim that current abortion laws discriminated against women, especially poor women, arbitrarily permitted abortion by IUD but not by surgical methods, and failed to consider a woman's mental as well as physical health. Some members suggested that the laws deprived taxpayers of their property without due process by making it difficult for welfare recipients to obtain abortions. Others identified abortion as a possible remedy for the poverty and racial tensions exposed by the recent riots in Los Angeles's Watts neighborhood. Opponents of more liberalized abortion laws emphasized the rights of the fetus. After extended deliberations, the affiliate remained uncertain about the constitutional basis for abortion law reform, and the draft it finally sent to the national office presented an equivocal and tentative mishmash of possible claims.[15]

The Southern California affiliate's tune changed dramatically after the Supreme Court decided *Griswold v. Connecticut* in June 1965. With new confidence, it forwarded a proposal that condemned current abortion laws as unconstitutional, declared ALI reforms inadequate, and insisted on the individual's "right of privacy" to decide "when and whether to produce offspring without interference by the state." Pilpel, meanwhile, urged the national ACLU to revise its abortion policy quickly so that it could exert influence on the many legislative bills under consideration around the country.[16]

While the national ACLU deliberated, affiliates, state legislatures, and court cases moved forward. ACLU chapters in Florida, Iowa, and New York joined Southern California's to demand liberalized abortion laws. Legislatures in

Colorado, North Carolina, California, Florida, Illinois, Iowa, Michigan, Minnesota, Nevada, Oklahoma, Wisconsin, Hawaii, and Mississippi adopted therapeutic abortion laws to protect a woman's physical and mental health. Legislative reform efforts failed in other states—notably, Indiana, Arizona, Georgia, Maryland, Nebraska, and New York—while court challenges to abortion laws emerged around the nation. Meanwhile, the California Supreme Court endorsed a woman's "fundamental right" to decide whether or not to bear a child, rooting it in a "'right of privacy'" in *People v. Belous* (1969). The opinion relied heavily on *Griswold* and arguments made by the Southern California ACLU attorneys who represented Dr. Leon Belous.[17]

When the national ACLU board finally took up the question of abortion again, opinions among its leaders ran the gamut. Assistant legal director Joel Gora advocated that the ACLU whittle away at legal restrictions on abortion rather than assert a "blanket right." Others urged that the ACLU support the ALI approach of permitting therapeutic abortions. One affiliate leader urged the ACLU not to stretch privacy rights to include abortion because "a Court encouraged to take a flexible approach to questions of privacy may also be inclined to take a flexible approach when restraints upon free expression are involved." With so little agreement among them, board members solicited a policy proposal from their Due Process Committee.[18]

The ACLU's Due Process Committee cobbled together a draft policy that would allow a woman "unfettered discretion" to obtain an abortion within the first twenty weeks of gestation "with the consent of the husband, if any, if he is available." Board discussions over the draft grew heated when Pilpel objected to the requirement of a husband's consent, but men who asserted "the father's right to have a child" were defeated overwhelmingly. Pilpel's counterproposal that abortion be permitted without restrictions before twenty-six weeks gestation but thereafter only under a very limited number of circumstances attracted criticism from both ends of the spectrum. Kenyon maintained that a woman's right to abortion should be absolute and unrestricted. Others insisted that fetal viability and risks to the woman in late-term abortions should be considered. An eight-to-five vote favored a policy that would reflect concern for the woman rather than the fetus. Ironically, though, because fetal viability came at twenty-six weeks and abortions were judged safest for women before twelve weeks, this concern-for-the-woman-first approach moved the allowance for unfettered abortion back to the first trimester. In the end, board members sent their Due Process Committee back to the drawing board.[19]

A distraught Kenyon declared the ACLU board discussion "a shambles of irrelevance and illogic" with civil libertarians steadfastly refusing to apply civil liberties principles to abortion. Declaring herself "a Cassandra crying out in the A.C.L.U.

wilderness against the crime of our abortion laws and man's inhumanity to women," she denounced laws against abortion for holding women in "bodily slavery." A democracy in which women are "forced by the government to bear children against their will" is a mockery, she wrote. "Only Hitler could create the obscenity of women's bodies belonging (in this crucial function of theirs) to the state."[20]

On stage and behind the scenes some members dug in their heels; others came forward to support Kenyon or reconsidered their positions in light of her spirited arguments. Board member Lois Forer, who had missed the meeting, offered Kenyon her full support. Kenyon's friend and fellow board member George Soll agreed that a woman should have the right to "the sanctity of her own being," which included the "right to have an abortion at any time prior to actual birth." For practical reasons, however, he recommended that the ACLU policy stop short of that ideal and, reluctantly but hopefully, Kenyon and Pilpel agreed, a move that gained them two more allies by the time the committee reconvened. Opponents of abortion law reform argued for the rights of the unborn and the state's interest in preserving fetal life. Many laws, they pointed out, limit a person's dominion over his or her own body when exercise of that dominion affects others, as it does in cases of drug use, public intoxication, and public nudity. Kenyon argued that legalizing abortion would advance women's rights, help resolve the "population explosion," and prevent the tragedy of "unwanted" and "battered" children. A tied vote left Kenyon giddy and extraordinarily optimistic, and she and Pilpel made plans to push for public funding for abortions. Their opponents, meanwhile, began to study fetal viability and infanticide.[21]

By June 1967, Kenyon, who began her crusade for abortion rights as a lonely voice of one on the ACLU board, began to feel optimistic when colleagues on the Due Process Committee recommended that termination of pregnancy be decriminalized and made subject to the same laws and standards applied to other medical procedures. The statement criticized abortion laws for violating marital privacy, denying equal protection to poor women, interfering with physicians' professional judgment, and depriving women of life and liberty without due process of law. It came just two months after the National Organization for Women's call for the repeal of abortion laws.[22]

The Due Process Committee's recommendation that the ACLU support the repeal of abortion laws did not end debate on the board. Critics accused their colleagues of paving the way for infanticide and euthanasia and demanded the formation of an ad hoc committee on "Abortion and the Viable Fetus." The committee, made up of individuals from both camps, including Kenyon and Pilpel, agreed on the importance of extending privacy to "the results of sexual conduct," pregnancy among them, but struggled over how to deal with the viable fetus. A semantic solution, albeit a substantive one, came to them in the form of the term *abortion*. Medical dictionaries defined abortion as intentional termination of a pregnancy within the first twenty weeks, before fetal viability. By using the term *abortion* instead of "termination of a pregnancy," the ACLU could avoid commenting on late-term abortions. The policy adopted by the board changed little other than the use of this language. Despite the policy's compromises and contradictions—and the confusion even of board members who voted on it—the *New York Times* reported quite simply that under it, the ACLU sought to "abolish all laws imposing criminal penalties for abortions performed by licensed physicians, no matter what the reason."[23]

Reactions from outside the ACLU were mixed. Ready praise came from Nathan Rappaport, an abortion rights activist who had performed tens of thousands of abortions, spent nearly a decade in prison for doing so, and had failed in the 1940s to persuade the ACLU to assist him. "At long last," he wrote to *Playboy* magazine, the ACLU has declared that laws against abortion "invade the privacy of citizens." *Playboy* too commended the ACLU's new policy. New Yorkers for Abortion Law Repeal, however, considered the policy wholly inadequate. "Does the ACLU statement mean," the group's president asked, that as technology brings "the time of 'viability'... earlier and earlier... the woman's right to abortion becomes progressively diminished, and finally disappears completely?" Groups opposed to abortion rights complained that the ACLU's new position neglected children's rights and served the interests of population controllers. One critic feared that the goal of population control would "swiftly consume 'the woman's right.' "[24]

The ACLU ignored the criticism and turned to the task of implementing its policy through litigation. "Now that we have policy," declared Eleanor Holmes Norton, the ACLU's first black staff member and assistant legal director to Wulf, "we should be hot on abortion for 1969." Knowing of the Playboy Foundation's interest in overturning abortion laws, she appealed to it for financial assistance. "The issue is particularly ripe for litigation," she wrote a colleague impatiently. "Are there some bunnies we can get who have particular influence with the management?" Norton ended up depending not on bunnies but on Wulf and another ACLU colleague who impressed upon *Playboy*'s senior editor Nat Lehrman the importance of well-funded and timely action on abortion law reform. In reply, Lehrman suggested that "it would be immensely helpful... if I could tell Hefner that ACLU was willing to work with the Playboy Foundation not only on the abortion laws but in a study and challenge of some of the consensual sex laws." The ACLU was indeed moving in that direction but apparently not quickly enough to secure immediate and substantial donations for its abortion law reform from *Playboy*.[25]

Figure 5.1 Eleanor Holmes Norton, ACLU portrait. (Courtesy, Princeton University)

ACLU leaders could not afford to lose any time given the many legislatures reconsidering abortion laws. Wulf, Pilpel, and Norton discussed a possible test case with Roy Lucas, a young legal scholar and leader of the Association for the Study of Abortion. Meanwhile, ACLU associate director Alan Reitman helped to plan what would be a groundbreaking national conference on abortion laws to be held in February 1969, and the ACLU's director Jack Pemberton urged affiliates to report their abortion law reform activities for publication in the ACLU's newsletter. When one affiliate showed insufficient commitment to the cause, ACLU leaders chastised it but also sent a check to subsidize its abortion law work. Meanwhile, communiqués from the national office identified abortion as "a high priority" and urged affiliates to develop an abortion law reform strategy attentive to local conditions.[26]

As abortion law reform spread, many supporters began to demand outright repeal. They were motivated by optimism but also by the discovery, as one practitioner put it, that a significant proportion of women who wanted abortions did not fit into the categories that "most liberals conceded were justifiable." The trend toward repeal became evident at the 1969 "First National Conference on Abortion Laws: Modification or Repeal?" held in Chicago and cosponsored by the ACLU. The meeting featured such luminaries as Betty Friedan, cofounder of the National Organization for Women and author of *The Feminine Mystique*, and Alan F. Guttmacher, president of the Planned Parenthood Federation of America and founder of the Guttmacher Institute, an organization devoted to research, policy analysis, and public education regarding sexual and reproductive health and rights. Out of the conference grew the National Association for Repeal of Abortion Laws

(NARAL) and a new commitment to repeal. Despite the ambiguities of the ACLU's own abortion policy, leaders who participated in the conference characterized the repeal program adopted by the delegates as "basically in line" with ACLU policy. Pemberton began to refer to "our efforts for abortion law repeal," and Reitman too advocated repeal because "reform doesn't really help those most desperately in need of abortions, namely the poor and Negroes."[27]

Several of the ACLU's most ardent proponents of abortion rights—Pilpel, Kenyon, and Catherine Roraback—were not satisfied with the rhetoric of repeal in the absence of a clear policy. When they complained to executive director Jack Pemberton that the ACLU's policy should be revised yet again, he agreed but thought it "unwise" to return the policy to a board that had already considered it on four separate occasions. "What we should do," he suggested, "is clean up the staff interpretation of the Board policy." Together with Kenyon, Norton, and Reitman, Pemberton revised the policy to read:

> The Union asks that state legislatures abolish all laws imposing criminal penalties for abortions. The effect of this step would be that any woman could ask a doctor to terminate a pregnancy at any time.

As if to remove all doubt, Pemberton added: "Nothing short of total repeal of all such laws will meet these civil liberties criteria." Pemberton's revision was substantial. By retaining in a footnote the medical definition of abortion as "termination of a pregnancy prior to the time when a fetus could live outside of the mother's body," however, Pemberton employed language that prevented the ACLU from seeming to condone late-term abortion or even infanticide.[28] Kenyon expressed her pleasure to Bernfeld, the man whose support proved crucial in the 1950s. "I'm happy as can be that the end seems to be almost in sight. Isn't it fun to be almost prophets?" She also forwarded her original correspondence with Bernfeld to Reitman for preservation as "a footnote to history." It was to Bernfeld, she wrote Reitman, that "I first made my remark about women's right to control their own bodies," an idea that initiated the campaign to repeal abortion laws. "I am free now," she wrote gleefully to another colleague, "to shout abroad that this policy of mine is also that of the A.C.L.U."[29]

The ACLU's abortion policy aligned it closely with the emerging women's rights movement, but attorneys who worked on ACLU abortion cases were not necessarily governed by feminist instincts. When, for example, Philip Hirschkop, an attorney with the Virginia affiliate, set out to challenge state residency requirements for abortion, he sought a particular kind of plaintiff—"a young attractive" one who refrained "from fornicating because of pregnancy but otherwise would screw." We might find such a woman "in the Woman's Lib. groups" or on a college campus, he suggested to Wulf. "If you find the woman, the legal panel will deal with the technicalities of getting her pregnant," Hirschkop wrote, closing in mock exasperation, "Oh the things I do for civil liberties and science." Wulf joined the joke, advising Hirschkop, "If you can't get it up, let me know."[30]

In some ways, though, the joke was on men; "card-carrying feminists" had begun to "infiltrate and capture" the ACLU. For years Kenyon complained about the absence of women on the ACLU board, the tendency of male colleagues either to overlook or take credit for her contributions, and the organization's general failure to take women's rights seriously. When joined by other women and supported by a burgeoning feminist movement, Kenyon became more demanding and effective, as indicated by her successful behind-the-scenes collaborations with Pilpel, Norton, and Roraback to transform the ACLU's equivocal abortion policy into a call for repeal. Together, Kenyon, Pilpel, and Pauli Murray—a civil rights activist elected to the board in 1965 who later helped to found NOW—pushed the organization to challenge discrimination against women. This required that they take on skeptics like board member Floyd McKissick, who maintained that the focus should be "black male power" and that "equality for women" could wait until "tomorrow."[31]

Kenyon, Murray, and Pilpel fought hard for women's rights, but they did not identify publicly as feminists in the 1960s and early 1970s. When Murray complained in 1967 to the director of a legal organization whose board she had recently joined about the lack of women, she confessed to embarrassment at "express[ing] a point of view which labels me a 'feminist' in the eyes of some." The director refused to appoint another woman, but assured Murray that he enjoyed paying attention to her and other "attractive women, minds and all." In 1968, Kenyon informed colleagues on the ACLU board that "I am far from being a feminist and am not greatly interested in women," at least, "certainly not nearly as much as I am in men... [but I] care passionately for fair play, even for women and children." In 1970, Kenyon wrote a female friend, "I'm not a feminist at all. The reason? I adore men." And in a 1971 letter chastising Senator Edmund Muskie for failing to tackle sex discrimination she concluded, "Please don't take me to be a feminist. I am not. I am a board member and officer of the American Civil Liberties Union and have been for years. I am for human rights, and that happens to include men as well as women." Nor did Pilpel identify as a feminist, leading one new feminist board member to lament that Pilpel did not "consider Feminist concerns her own, or savor the bonds of sisterhood."[32] For some women who were committed to working with men on issues of civil liberties and women's rights in the late 1960s and early 1970s, feminism smacked of man-hating, undermined the camaraderie necessary to win men over to the cause, and also threatened to remove women's rights from the broader categories of human rights and civil liberties.

Even so, thanks in part to the groundwork laid by Kenyon, Murray, and Pilpel as well as Roraback and Norton, women who did identify as feminists

Figure 5.2 Pauli Murray, September 27, 1971. (Courtesy, AP Photo/Frank C. Curtin)

found the ACLU an increasingly receptive home in the early 1970s. They included Wilma Scott Heide, chair of the board of directors for NOW; Suzanne Post, founder of the Kentucky Women's Political Caucus; Brenda Feigen Fasteau, cofounder of *Ms.* magazine and the National Women's Political Caucus; Faith Seidenberg, NOW officer; Margie Pitts Hames, vice president of the Georgia Women's Political Caucus; and Ruth Bader Ginsburg, Rutgers law professor and future Supreme Court justice. In response to the growing influence of such women, at least one female old-timer—Pauli Murray—began to identify as a feminist but still worried that the younger women would consider her an "Aunt Thomasina," because she continued to play the role of "centrist." For Murray, this approach was a strategic effort "to use creative feminism on our male-dominated ACLU, by disarming them and then 'leading them.'"[33]

Sincere efforts to overcome the ACLU's own history of sex discrimination also attracted feminists. In 1970, his last year as director, Pemberton issued a memo acknowledging that his office had underpaid female staff members and overlooked women for high-level positions. "While we are going about the country as busy-bodies attacking other people's faults," he wrote, "we might well look to the consistency of our own practices." Indeed, women made up only 7 percent of national board members and were no better represented on affiliate boards. Women were excluded from planning for the biennial meetings, and very few women had ever occupied policymaking or executive positions on the national staff. Thus, Pemberton set in motion a plan of attack against sex discrimination within the ACLU that would be expanded upon under his successor.[34]

Aryeh Neier, elected by a very narrow margin to succeed Pemberton as director in 1970, also brought an ambitious plan to pursue foundation funds more aggressively and to engage the ACLU more fully with the flourishing women's movement. A New York Civil Liberties Union firebrand and longtime proponent of abortion law repeal, he saw in the day's protest movements great opportunities for the ACLU. "Civil liberties fare best in our society when organized minorities insist on the exercise of their rights," he explained to a foundation representative. The ACLU could maximize its influence by supporting grassroots activists mobilized on their own behalf—consumers, he called them. Identifying the women's rights movement as "by far the strongest and healthiest of today's 'consumer' movements for rights," he identified it as one of the ACLU's strongest allies in defending civil liberties and hoped to use its "muscle" to advance a broader civil liberties agenda. Courts respond to grassroots movements, Neier insisted, and even a conservative Supreme Court will expand individual rights when it feels pressure from "the organized power of a consumer movement." Under Neier's leadership and the influence of a large number of new feminist members, the ACLU board voted to make women's rights a priority on the 1972 agenda.[35] It was a move that would dramatically complicate the ACLU's sexual civil liberties agenda.

The ACLU launched its Women's Rights Project (WRP) in 1972 using seed money provided by the Ford and Playboy foundations. The Ford Foundation added the WRP to a list of organizations it sponsored to challenge sex discrimination, treating this investment as an extension of its longtime support for civil rights litigation. Playboy Foundation officers hoped their contribution to the WRP would help to rehabilitate the enterprise's reputation with feminists and strengthen its bond with the ACLU; both were in question since the Chicago-based ACLU affiliate held a fund-raiser at Hugh Hefner's mansion in 1969. A number of celebrities and local ACLU staff attended, but so did several disgruntled affiliate members who also belonged to the newly formed Chicago Women's Liberation Union. Angry that the ACLU would "legitimize Hefner by holding a benefit" at his home—one that included nude swimming at four in the morning—the women considered boycotting the event but opted instead to engage in guerilla theater. "We could protest both Playboy's portrayal of women as mindless sex objects for huge profits," they schemed, "and the ACLU's eager attachment to Hefner, also for money." Equipped with pinups of men in bunny suits, cards showing men as naked Playmates of the Month, and revealing posters of men with messages like "He's got a nice ass, but he's kind of dumb," the women posted their propaganda around Hefner's mansion before armed guards ousted them.[36]

These women were neither the first nor the last to challenge *Playboy* on feminist grounds. In 1963, Gloria Steinem criticized the enterprise in an expose written from a "bunny's" perspective. Two years later journalist Diana Lurie published a feminist critique of the magazine in *Life*, and feminists who demonstrated against the 1968 Miss America Pageant in Atlantic City dumped copies of *Playboy* into their "freedom trashcan," while students at Grinnell College stripped in a public protest against *Playboy*'s recruiting on campus. Feminist protests against *Playboy*'s portrayal and treatment of women would only escalate in the 1970s.[37]

Hefner fought back, and the ACLU figured prominently in his carrot-and-stick approach. He hired Morton Hunt to produce a "devastating piece that takes the [feminist] militants apart." "These chicks are our natural enemy," Hefner told Hunt. "The society they want is an asexual one." But even as Hefner attacked "militant" feminists in his magazine, he aimed to bolster his reputation among less radical feminists by advocating and funding more mainstream efforts on behalf of women's rights. The ACLU seemed an especially good bet for the Playboy Foundation. Chicago's ACLU director derided the feminist protest at Hefner's mansion as "Bull—." Moreover, the ACLU and its affiliates had long collaborated with *Playboy* against censorship, and many of their leaders subscribed to, read, and wrote laudatory letters to the magazine. In addition, an Illinois ACLU attorney, Burton Joseph, who assisted in the ACLU's *Tropic of Cancer* cases a few years earlier, had just become executive director and special counsel to *Playboy* and the new Playboy Foundation.[38]

When Aryeh Neier made formal application to Joseph for Playboy funds in 1971, he showcased the organization's impressive record in cases likely to appeal to Hefner—sexual civil liberties cases involving abortion, voluntary sterilization, birth control, and "bralessness." Within a month, Neier had the $40,000 he needed for the ACLU's Women's Rights Project. The Playboy Foundation also provided printing services for ACLU pamphlets and manuals on abortion rights. In the October issue of 1971, it ran a very complimentary seven-page article praising the ACLU as "the nation's chief defender of personal liberty" and urging readers to join or donate to it. One month later, Hugh Hefner hosted a black-tie benefit at his new California mansion and, with Ralph Nader, Arthur M. Schlesinger Jr., and Jules Feiffer in attendance, raised a reported $100,000 for the ACLU of Southern California.[39]

Playboy deflected some feminist criticism by contributing to women's rights causes, but it could not stop the attacks altogether. Feminists disrupted Hefner's television appearances, picketed his mansions and clubs, obstructed his efforts to recruit new "bunnies," and threatened his life. Meanwhile, they debated among themselves whether to accept *Playboy* money, with some eager to liberate Hefner's money as "reparations" and others to reject it as blood money. Similar disputes emerged over whether feminists should submit to interviews by *Playboy* staff, allow their writing to be published in the magazine, or accept honors from it. For many feminists, *Playboy*s contributions to women's rights causes could not make up for the magazine's treatment of women as sexual playthings—literally, things to be screwed, as depicted on a 1972 cover showing a naked woman shaped like a wine bottle with a corkscrew at the ready. ACLU board member, Catherine Roraback, protested the ACLU's acceptance of funds from *Playboy*, citing "the exploitative nature of the magazine in its portrayal of women." Other critics noted *Playboy*'s investment in women's rights focused on issues like birth control, sterilization, and abortion that were designed to serve "the convenience of the playboy, who does not wish to assume responsibilities."[40]

Brenda Feigen Fasteau and Ruth Bader Ginsburg, codirectors of the ACLU's Women's Rights Project (WRP), were more than happy to take *Playboy*'s money. Like Pilpel before them, they complimented *Playboy* for its reports on reproductive and sexual issues as well as its financial support for efforts to liberalize laws regarding sexuality, but they did not necessarily approve of the magazine itself. Fasteau, a lifelong opponent of pornography, thought the magazine "denigrated women," and she criticized the ACLU for holding fund-raisers at *Playboy* clubs and mansions, events that publicized and legitimized the magazine. But to Fasteau and presumably Ginsburg as well, applying for and accepting money from *Playboy* to litigate for women's rights seemed a different matter altogether.[41]

By the early 1970s, the women's rights and sexual civil liberties agendas of the ACLU prioritized abortion rights and brought leaders into a trio of cases that would soon make history. The political and cultural scene had changed considerably since the ACLU began drafting its policy on abortion six years earlier. Seventeen states had liberalized their abortion laws, and polling data suggested that an increasing majority of Americans favored making abortion more available. ACLU attorneys worked with abortion rights groups, wrote amicus briefs, argued cases, and served as advisers on the sidelines. When the U.S. Supreme

Court accepted its first abortion case, *United States v. Vuitch*, board members Mel Wulf and Norman Dorsen wrote the ACLU brief, arguing that the privacy rights accorded users of birth control in *Griswold* should extend to abortion patients as well. They persuaded only one justice, and in a five-to-two decision, the Supreme Court affirmed the constitutionality of criminal laws against abortions that were not essential to preserving a woman's psychological and physical health.[42]

Two other abortion cases were already working their way up through the courts—*Roe v. Wade*, instigated by the Women's Liberation Birth Control Information Center at the University of Texas at Austin, and *Doe v. Bolton*, led by attorneys from the ACLU's Georgia affiliate. As soon as the Supreme Court accepted the cases, the ACLU's Pilpel, Wulf, and Norman Dorsen got involved. They appointed Pilpel to recruit and coordinate amicus briefs, hoping thereby to present a stronger case for a woman's right to abortion, one bolstered by social science research and arguments from the medical and legal professions as well as agencies representing the poor, women's rights, and other "public spirited organizations." They planned and executed moot court sessions with the local attorneys who would argue the cases to prepare them for the aggressive questioning they would encounter before the Court. The ACLU did not appear amicus in either case because it considered *Doe* its own given that it was led by national board member Marjorie Hames. Moreover, ACLU leaders injected their arguments and perspectives into the cases by working closely with counsel and writing briefs for other groups.[43]

Meanwhile, Pilpel and Wulf filed influential amicus briefs for cases related to what Pilpel called "compulsory pregnancy laws" that restricted women's access to contraceptives. By spring 1972, Pilpel and Wulf celebrated a new extension of the right of privacy beyond married couples to individuals when the Supreme Court, in *Eisenstadt v. Baird*, overturned the Massachusetts statute that denied single women access to birth control. "If the right of privacy means anything," wrote Justice William Brennan for the majority, "it is the right of the *individual*, married or single, to be free from unwarranted governmental intrusion into ... the decision whether to bear or beget a child." Pilpel and her colleagues eagerly anticipated that the opinion would influence abortion rights and also cases involving "sexual acts between competent consenting adults in private."[44]

The ACLU also continued to wrestle with issues of government involvement in family-planning services. The board approved the policy recommendation made by the ACLU's 1970 Biennial Conference that it consider "the right to practice any birth control procedure by either women or men, including contraception, abortion, and sterilization" a matter of individual choice that should be exercised without "governmental intervention," "compulsion," or "coercion." It rejected, however, a recommendation that would have held the government responsible for funding these choices. "Affirmative government action," the board noted, could easily be perceived as "coercing the poor, and committing 'genocide' against black citizens." Thus, even as the ACLU embraced the repeal of abortion and birth control laws, it stopped short of advocating that the state fund abortions, contraception, or voluntary sterilization.[45]

Privacy cut many ways in the 1970s, and on January 23, 1973, it cut straight through state criminal abortion laws. With a seven-to-two majority in *Roe v. Wade* and *Doe v. Bolton,* the U.S. Supreme Court declared the "right of privacy... broad enough to encompass a woman's decision whether or not to terminate her pregnancy." At the same time, the Court imposed limits on a pregnant woman's rights, condoning state intrusion on her privacy to "safeguard health," "maintain medical standards," and "protect potential life." To balance a pregnant woman's rights with a state's interests, the Court created a trimester timetable according to which the woman's privacy would diminish as the state's interests in preserving her health and the life of the fetus increased. The Court also struck down statutes that restricted abortions to particular types of hospitals, required external approval, and imposed residency requirements. The opinions immediately invalidated abortion laws in forty-three states, including thirteen that had recently adopted ALI-type reform legislation. Even the four states whose laws complied most closely with the Supreme Court's new rulings contained questionable language about residency and hospital requirements. The *Roe* and *Doe* opinions halted thirty other abortion cases with which the ACLU and its affiliates were involved and sent every single state legislature back to the drawing board, some to challenge the Supreme Court's holdings and others to bring their laws into compliance. At the same time, *Roe* and *Doe* provoked a virulent antiabortion movement that would inspire the ACLU to develop a long-term strategy for preserving and expanding a central component of its sexual civil liberties agenda, one it would come to call reproductive freedom.[46]

"Reproductive control" was the ACLU's original terminology for its work on behalf of rights to birth control, abortion, and sterilization. It began to reconsider that language, however, as the federal government's war on poverty evolved. In 1970, Congress passed the Family Planning Services and Population Research Act, which devoted nearly $73 million to making "comprehensive voluntary family planning services readily available to all persons desiring such services." Furthermore, in 1971, the Office for Economic Opportunity (OEO) reversed its ban on providing funds for voluntary sterilization. So in 1972, when the ACLU's Board of Directors reconsidered its policy against government funding for birth control, abortion, and sterilization, it did so after the federal government had already begun to provide these services.[47]

This new state of affairs empowered board members who advocated public funding for reproductive control services. One member echoed Pilpel's earlier claims, arguing that "once we have accepted the right of control over one's own body, we are committed to requiring government provision of the resources to implement this." Otherwise, "poor people will have no effective freedom of choice." Another suggested that the ACLU drop its opposition to government family-planning programs and instead monitor them to ensure that they avoided coercion and maximized freedom. Only David Carliner of the Washington, D.C., affiliate condemned this approach, claiming that it privileged "white middle class, non-Catholic views of what families should be." An overwhelming majority voted to hold government responsible for making "freedom of choice" meaningful by providing "information, services, and facilities respecting birth planning."[48]

In response to the new policy, the ACLU Women's Rights Project expanded its reproductive control agenda to include monitoring government-sponsored family-planning programs in order to reduce restrictions on abortion and establish the right to choose or decline sterilization. Ginsburg and Fasteau worked with ACLU affiliates to coordinate litigation across the nation, and in their first year as directors of the WRP, they identified forty ACLU-sponsored reproductive control cases in the courts. The number of abortion cases escalated as individuals and institutions on all sides of the issue fought to shape the aftermath of *Roe* and *Doe*. Between 1973 and 1977, the ACLU became the preeminent litigator on abortion rights, bringing more than one hundred lawsuits.[49] But even as ACLU leaders defended abortion rights, they encountered a state campaign to control women's reproduction that fundamentally altered their understanding of the issue and exposed an unexpected dilemma regarding sexual civil liberties, one that centered on issues of federal funding and informed consent.

In 1973, twenty-seven-year-old Nial Ruth Cox, a nurse's aide in Suffolk County, New York, entered Fasteau's WRP office in a dilapidated ACLU suite in New York City. Fasteau read from a dog-eared slip of paper Cox pulled from her purse as the young black woman waited: "bi-lateral tubal ligation." When Fasteau asked Cox if she understood what the words meant, Cox teared up and nodded uncertainly before pouring out her story. Only seventeen when she became pregnant in 1963, Cox was living on public assistance with her mother and eight siblings in a housing project in Plymouth, North Carolina. When the social worker assigned to her family learned of Cox's condition, she threatened to cut off the family's funds unless Cox agreed to undergo a "temporary" sterilization procedure. Ashamed to have put her family's welfare in danger, Cox stood by helplessly while her mother signed a shaky X to the state's barebones form, thereby consenting for her young daughter to undergo an operation whose name she could not read and whose meaning she could not comprehend. This was legal in North Carolina and had been since 1929, when the state passed its first eugenics law. In the 1930s and 1940s, the law was directed primarily at residents of state mental institutions, prisons, or reformatories who exhibited signs of epilepsy, feeble-mindedness, or some other ailment considered to be genetic. But after World War II, North Carolina expanded and reoriented its eugenic sterilization program, and by the late 1960s, the majority of people sterilized under it were poor black women.[50]

Fasteau took Cox's case on behalf of the ACLU, working with its southern regional office to sue the North Carolina Eugenics Commission for $1 million. She relayed Cox's story to Gloria Steinem, a close friend with whom she had recently founded *Ms.* magazine, and the two traveled south to investigate further. When they asked prominent civil rights activist Fannie Lou Hamer about the problem, she seemed surprised. "Girls don't you know this goes on all the time?" she asked. "It happened to me too." It happened, they soon discovered, to tens of thousands of women, most of them black and all of them poor. As the ACLU shepherded Cox's case through the courts, the Southern Poverty Law Center, an organization founded in 1971 to ensure the implementation of civil rights laws, sued the OEO and the Department of Health, Education, and Welfare on behalf of fourteen-year-old Mary Alice and twelve-year-old Minnie Relf—sisters who were forcibly sterilized a year earlier in Montgomery, Alabama. Like Cox, the Relfs survived on public assistance and watched as their mother signed an X to the state's consent form.[51]

As the Cox and Relf cases worked their way through the courts, Fasteau transformed the WRP's passive policy against compulsory sterilization into an active effort to end the practice. *Ebony*, a magazine geared toward African American readers, published a feature on Fasteau, Cox, the Relfs, and their attorneys, and announced that the WRP and the Southern Poverty Law Center would provide free legal representation to victims of forced sterilization. Fasteau sought additional publicity by holding a major press conference and joining Cox in a *60 Minutes* interview with Mike Wallace. The media attention attracted more cases of compulsory sterilization to the ACLU and its affiliates, but only a tiny percentage of those that might have been brought. Without a doubt, the impoverishment and isolation of most victims as well as their reluctance to expose publicly an experience about which most felt deep humiliation prevented the vast majority from seeking legal assistance.[52]

Desperate to protect the many women who remained vulnerable to compulsory sterilization while litigation proceeded, the WRP worked to inform welfare recipients of their rights. It sent a clear explanation of these rights for publication in *Ebony* and also printed and distributed its own pamphlets. Publicity around the suits grabbed the attention of federal authorities in the Department of Health, Education, and Welfare (HEW), who immediately issued, for the first

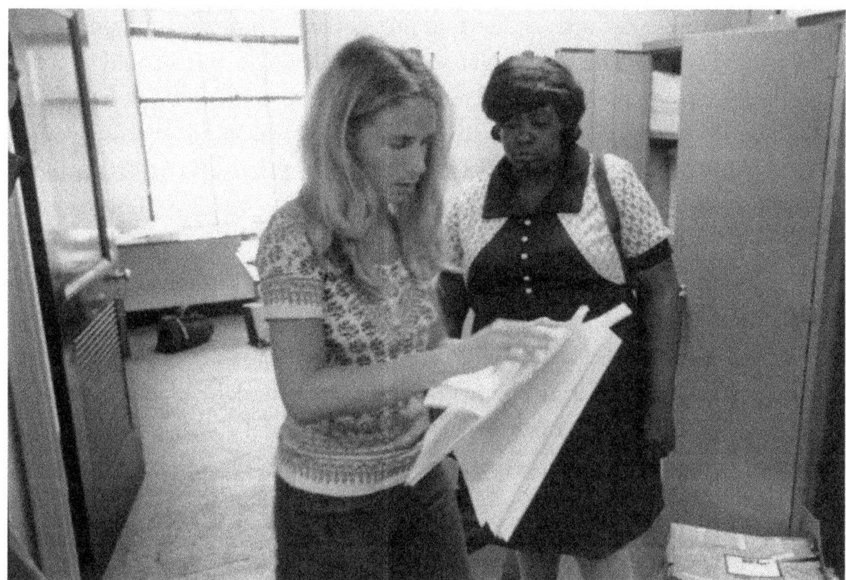

Figure 5.3 Brenda Feigen Fasteau and Nial Ruth Cox discussing their lawsuit against North Carolina's Eugenics Commission, October 1973, *Ebony* magazine. (Courtesy, Johnson Publishing Company, LLC. All rights reserved.)

time, regulations on federal sterilizations to require informed consent and a multilevel process of review for individuals unable to consent due to age or mental ability.[53] Thus, the Cox and Relf cases brought improvements to the system even before they reached the courts.

Cox lost her case on the grounds that the three-year statute of limitations had expired on her 1965 sterilization. The Relfs achieved a more satisfactory outcome. In *Relf v. Weinberger*, Judge Gerhard A. Gesell demanded an immediate halt to all federally funded sterilizations until regulations required that sterilization candidates be fully informed about the nature of the procedure (including the likelihood that it would permanently end fertility), be notified that declining the operation would not jeopardize public assistance benefits, and be capable of giving consent. WRP staff celebrated, but those who had watched states and hospitals ignore the *Roe* and *Doe* rulings worried that the *Relf* decision too might go disregarded.[54]

Dealing with compulsory sterilization and a flood of abortion cases at the same time led the WRP staff to think about freedom of choice in new ways that shaped the Reproductive Freedom Project (RFP) the ACLU created in 1974. When the project's founding director, Judith Mears, named it, she deliberately replaced the ACLU's earlier language of control with freedom. Control, after all, evoked the very eugenic hierarchy that had led to compulsory sterilization. Mears also developed a broad agenda that stretched well beyond abortion rights, in part, to diminish the appearance that the RFP *advocated* abortion per se, but also to cast reproductive freedom as something that all women could support, even those personally opposed to abortion. She did so by using the project to defend women subjected to forced sterilization as well as to support women who sought help with infertility and those who merely wanted the father in the delivery room.[55] By identifying the goal as freedom, not control, Mears also tapped into the language and ideals of the civil rights movement, signaling that the RFP would embrace the needs of the poor, women of color, and conservative women in addition to liberal, middle-class white women.

The fledgling RFP set out to determine whether Judge Gesell's ruling in *Relf* and the new HEW regulations it inspired were being implemented. It circulated a two-page survey to department heads of 154 accredited obstetrics-gynecology residency programs. The survey results indicated that, of the fifty-one institutions that responded, only three used consent forms that complied with HEW regulations. Most consent forms were confusing or ambiguous. Very few followed Judge Gesell's instructions to place prominently, at the top of each form, the following statement—"Notice: Your decision at any time not to be sterilized will not result in the withdrawal or withholding of any benefits provided by programs or projects." The RFP concluded that HEW had enforced neither its own regulations nor the court's ruling, given that 94 percent of the randomly chosen major teaching hospitals were in "gross noncompliance with existing federal regulations on sterilization."[56]

The RFP survey went further than Gesell's ruling and HEW's regulations to question hospitals about specific provisions that RFP staff considered essential for protecting patients' rights and ensuring informed consent. These included mandating a waiting period before the surgery, prohibiting hospital staff from offering sterilization to women in labor, recognizing that multiple cesarean deliveries did not present a medical indication for sterilization, presenting an audiovisual description of the procedure and its effects, and providing counseling through a patient advocate. Questions about these issues elicited even more disappointing responses, and the RFP concluded that hospitals did not provide information or an opportunity to deliberate that would allow patients to "give informed and knowledgeable voluntary consent."[57]

The RFP's "Hospital Survey on Sterilization Policies" exerted an unexpected amount of influence. The Committee to End Sterilization Abuse (CESA)—an organization founded in New York City in 1974 to fight forced sterilization in Puerto Rico until activists discovered it in their own backyard—connected with the RFP and worked to publicize the results of its survey. The survey began to influence judicial, administrative, and legislative approaches to sterilization almost immediately, appearing as evidence in a major sterilization case, *National Welfare Rights Organization v. Weinberger*

(1974), and prompting HEW officials to ask the RFP to withdraw or soften its findings. Failing that, HEW conducted its own survey, but was disappointed when its findings matched the RFP's.[58] The RFP survey led New York City Health and Hospitals Corporation (HHC), the largest municipal health care organization in the country, to overhaul its sterilization guidelines and forms. It did so in consultation with RFP staff and a racially diverse Advisory Committee on Sterilization that included leaders of CESA, the National Black Feminist Organization, and *Ms.* magazine. Their collaborative efforts concluded when new HHC guidelines went into effect in late 1975.[59]

Feminists in and out of the ACLU argued over New York City's HHC guidelines. Opponents feared that they would set precedents antagonistic to women's rights—especially rights to abortion—by treating medical procedures involving women's reproductive capacities differently from other operations. They complained that the guidelines would compromise women's rights by prioritizing "a woman's right to be a mother" over her right to control her own body. Many criticized the waiting period for imposing extra burdens on poor women who desired sterilizations by forcing them to undergo multiple surgeries and sustain extra child care and travel expenses. Feminists in the RFP defended the guidelines, arguing that the history of sterilization abuse erased distinctions between "voluntary and involuntary sterilizations" for Medicaid patients and wards of the state. Because of this history, they maintained that sterilization should be treated differently than abortion. Moreover, "since the pressures on the sterilization choice are in no way as great as the time pressures in the abortion choice," they argued, "regulation of voluntary sterilization does not burden the individual's right to choos[e] to the extent that regulation of abortion does." Given the historical and physiological differences between sterilization and abortion, they argued, "in abortion cases we rely on the doctor to protect the women from the state," but "in sterilization cases we should rely on the state to protect the woman from abuses by the doctors." Above all, they asserted, "no set waiting period or consent form is sacred"; all regulations must be evaluated according to history and current conditions.[60]

Despite serious opposition from some feminists and also physicians, the RFP-approved HHC guidelines were soon extended by law to all New York City hospitals and clinics that performed sterilizations. Even more important, these guidelines were reflected in the final set issued by HEW to take effect in 1979. They mandated a thirty-day waiting period, required clear explanations of the procedure and its permanency, and prohibited sterilization of any patient under the age of twenty-one or otherwise incompetent to consent. These significant achievements did not end sterilization abuse, though they did reduce its occurrence. At the same time, as many feminists feared, they also provided new bases for attacks on abortion rights.[61]

Even as challenges to *Roe* began to reach the U.S. Supreme Court by 1976, Judith Mears expressed great confidence in the status of abortion rights. As litigants and lobbyists, RFP staff had helped to establish the principle that hospitals offering obstetrical and gynecological services must also perform elective abortions; in most states Medicaid patients and minors were guaranteed access to abortions, and abortion clinics were allowed to advertise their services. "Since *Roe* and *Doe*," Mears announced to the ACLU's Biennial Conference in Philadelphia, "the lower federal courts have... transformed the original principle that the state cannot interfere with a woman's right to abortion (within the first two trimesters) into the principle that the state must affirmatively provide a woman with the means by which... she can exercise her right to an abortion." As she awaited the U.S. Supreme Court's ruling in an abortion case on which she served as cocounsel with an attorney for Planned Parenthood, an optimistic Mears anticipated that the court would continue its "consistent" and "vigorous" extension of the right to abortion.[62]

The decision in *Planned Parenthood of Central Missouri v. Danforth* (1976) pointed to a more complicated future. The Court upheld, among other things, the right of a minor and/or a married woman to an abortion with or without the consent of parent or spouse. However, it allowed states to require that patients give written consent to abortion, a requirement that the ACLU declared "overbroad," "vague," "an extra layer and burden of regulation on the abortion decision," and a violation of *Roe*. The Court allowed this requirement in part because certain other medical procedures required written consent, as did, ironically, surgical sterilizations performed under the HEW and HCC regulations approved by the ACLU's RFP.[63]

Federal funding for elective abortions represented the next major battleground for the RFP. Many ACLU leaders had feared, rightly as it turned out, that government involvement in family planning would lead to coercion. With regard to abortion though, leaders in the ACLU and its Reproductive Freedom Project worried less about the government coercing poor women to get abortions than about the government refusing to fund their abortions. Because *Roe* and *Doe* had established abortion as a constitutional right, they argued that "when a medical benefits system pays the expenses of women who choose to terminate their pregnancies by childbirth, it must also pay the expenses of women who choose to terminate their pregnancies by abortion." However, opponents of abortion rights recognized the public funding issue as a weak link in the abortion rights agenda, especially at a time when public officials struggled to cut spending as they confronted a ballooning deficit and a stagnant but inflationary economy. In 1976, Congress overrode President Gerald Ford's veto to pass the Hyde Amendment which prevented Medicaid from funding elective abortions or any in which the woman's life was not in danger. The flurry of court cases that challenged the

Hyde Amendment in 1977—*Maher v. Roe, Beal v. Doe,* and *Poelker v. St. Louis*—failed in a combined Supreme Court decision characterized by some as a "devastating retreat" from *Roe* and *Doe* because it allowed poor women to be forced into "bearing unwanted children."[64]

RFP leaders considered the Hyde Amendment's withdrawal of federal funding for most abortions only the latest method used by the government to coerce the reproductive lives of poor women, especially poor women of color. The amendment would leave stranded the approximately 300,000 women who sought Medicaid-funded abortions annually. Significantly, whereas women of color made up 13 percent of the population, they obtained 32 percent of legal abortions, suffered 82 percent of the deaths from illegal abortions, and relied on Medicaid at a rate approaching 40 percent—compared to 7 percent of white women. Women of color would, therefore, be disproportionately affected by the Hyde Amendment.[65]

Connections between abortion and sterilization were striking. The RFP's new director, Janet Benshoof, argued that without access to abortion, many poor women would resort to the only Medicaid-funded method guaranteed to control fertility—surgical sterilization. Coercion necessarily resulted from withholding federal funds for abortion but providing them for sterilization, she argued, and, as a result, abortion rights should provide "an issue around which all women can and should unite." Anticipating as much, the ACLU announced in 1977 that the right of all women to obtain an abortion would be its main priority. With regard to abortion, it challenged as violations of privacy the very requirements it advocated as protections of reproductive freedom in sterilization cases. These included certification by two or more physicians, written consent, mandatory information sessions and waiting periods, and limitations on the availability of the procedure to minors. Insisting on the same requirements for sterilization that it opposed for abortion left the RFP vulnerable to charges of hypocrisy while opening the door to the sort of incremental attacks on abortion rights that feminist opponents of the RFP-approved HHC sterilization guidelines had predicted.[66]

Abortion moved to the top of the ACLU's agenda at a time when the organization, hurting for members and funds, looked once again to the women's movement. In 1977, the ACLU's membership renewals fell by 15 percent, and its income plummeted. Facing a $300,000 shortfall, the ACLU laid off ten staff members and ended its monthly newsletter. Some blamed the drop-off in members on disenchantment with the ACLU following its defense of a Nazi march in Skokie, Illinois. Others speculated that the conclusion of the Watergate crisis, in which the ACLU had played a leading role, led many who had joined only for this issue to drift away. Still others blamed a chaotic and inefficient membership department. Neier wondered if members remained committed to the ACLU only "as long as one of the great struggles of the last decade and a half was underway: the civil rights movement in the South, the anti-war movement, Nixon, impeachment and then the revelations about the FBI and the CIA." By 1976, Neier acknowledged that "the only surviving rights movements with a high energy level are, first and foremost, the movement for women's rights and, a distant second, the gay rights movement"—the two movements that would drive much of the ACLU's agenda in the coming decades.[67]

The women's movement became more vital as the crisis over abortion rights grew increasingly urgent. Since 1968, women had been making up an ever larger percentage of the ACLU's membership. Ruth Bader Ginsburg fueled that growth when she sent out tailored membership recruitment letters. Meanwhile, Neier urged ACLU colleagues and affiliates to "build a campaign around the right to obtain abortions," acknowledging that "our efforts to retain and recruit members" have been helped more by "the abortion issue" than by anything else. Some members complained that the ACLU should devote at least as much attention to defeating the death penalty as to preserving and expanding abortion rights. Still others worried that focusing on abortion rights might undermine the ACLU's campaign for the Equal Rights Amendment. In the end, though, the board agreed with Neier that the abortion rights campaign furthered the ACLU's principles and also addressed its organizational needs.[68]

Critics began to portray the organization as a handmaiden of the women's rights movement, even though most ACLU resources continued to focus on issues that pertained primarily to men. In 1978, a peak year for the ACLU's emphasis on women's rights, it budgeted the same amount of money for the National Prison and Capital Punishment Projects as it did for the WRP and RFP. Moreover, the RFP also served men's interests to the extent that it was, as one staff member remembered, "consistent with everything *Playboy* believed in." In addition, under Ginsburg's deft leadership, the WRP pursued many of its cases on behalf of male plaintiffs—a strategy that proved stunningly effective, and one that highlighted ways that men too stood to benefit from the ACLU's women's rights agenda.[69]

When the ACLU's Reproductive Freedom Project inaugurated a "Campaign for Choice" in 1977 with the aim of safeguarding "reproductive choice" for all women and restoring it to poor women, it employed an array of strategies that went far beyond the ACLU's now-standard approach of working behind the scenes and filing amicus briefs. RFP leaders realized that they could no longer depend on the increasingly conservative federal courts and began to invest more heavily in public education, publishing brochures and pamphlets, placing articles in mainstream periodicals, issuing frequent press releases, and seeking opportunities to appear in the media. They also worked closely with affiliates,

Planned Parenthood, the National Abortion Rights Action League, and other groups to build local pro-choice coalitions, lobby legislators, and fight proposals for state constitutional conventions. Equally important, they struggled to wrest control over the terms of the debate from the "right-to-life" movement by using the language of choice as a proxy for the right to abortion. In 1971, Harriet Pilpel wrote an essay entitled "Legal Obstacles to Freedom of Choice in the Areas of Contraception, Abortion, and Voluntary Sterilization," and Wilma Scott Heide, ACLU board member and president of NOW, recommended that the ACLU substitute choice for control, because "choice is more consistent with civil liberties." One year later, Jimmye Kimmey, the executive director of the Association for the Study of Abortion (ASA), cast about for a monosyllabic word that would rival the catchy phrase "Right to Life," deflect the antiabortion movement's efforts to cast advocates of abortion rights as proabortion, and convey support for individual decision-making about reproduction. Kimmey settled on "Right to Choose," a phrase that would catch on like wildfire among abortion rights defenders. Choice was also a word that sat nicely alongside other new civil liberties such as privacy, consent, consumer rights, and women's rights.[70]

For the ACLU's RFP, meaningful choice must be unfettered, free of financial constraints and burdensome requirements, and available to any pregnant woman no matter her age, race, economic status, marital situation, or geographic location. The most vulnerable women in each of these categories were the first to suffer when, after failing to overturn *Roe* and *Doe*, opponents of abortion rights worked to restrict abortion incrementally. They did so by mimicking, unintentionally or not, RFP provisions designed to protect poor women from sterilization abuse. So they sought to deprive poor women of the right to abortion by denying Medicaid funds, to underage and unhappily married women by requiring parental and spousal consent, to rural and needy women by imposing a waiting period, and to conflicted and emotionally troubled women by requiring them to attend right-to-life counseling sessions. The RFP countered with lawsuits, lobbying, testimony before Congress, studies of the impact of antiabortion laws on women, training for lawyers interested in abortion litigation, and massive public education campaigns.[71]

In stark contrast to its advocacy work regarding sterilization, with respect to abortion the RFP demanded generous government funding and condemned the so-called "Akron Ordinances"—passed by the city of Akron, Ohio—that imposed waiting periods, restrictions on minors, and onerous paperwork and counseling, all in the name of informed consent. The ACLU initially opposed public funding for sterilization because state involvement could prove coercive and invade the privacy of welfare recipients, but by the middle of the 1970s it shifted gears, which allowed it to challenge the Hyde Amendment on grounds that denying public funds for abortion resulted in "compulsory pregnancy" and invaded the privacy of poor women by withholding from them the means to choose. Other aspects of its policy were less flexible. For example, the RFP continued to insist on a lengthy mandatory waiting period for sterilizations but vigorously opposed even brief waiting periods when opponents used them to make abortions more difficult to obtain. The RFP also demanded that no federal funds be used to sterilize any woman under the age of twenty-one even as it condemned policies—including parental consent and notification laws—that hindered the ability of minors to obtain abortions. Finally, the RFP lobbied for a robust policy of informed consent for sterilization patients, one that involved a counseling session with a "patient advocate," an informational audiovisual presentation that described the operation's advantages and disadvantages, and a signed consent form that described sterilization as a procedure that would permanently and irreversibly end fertility. But it fought against abortion opponents' efforts to establish parallel informed consent procedures, denouncing them as "compulsory propaganda programs."[72]

The RFP's various challenges to restrictions on abortion rights met with mixed results. No states called a constitutional convention or passed a human life amendment, and several continued to cover abortions for poor women. But by the late 1970s, the withdrawal of federal funding and imposition of a dizzying array of regulations made choosing abortion increasingly difficult. The RFP was besieged with abortion cases—sixty different ones by 1980—rendering it the veritable "center of abortion litigation."[73]

That year, the U.S. Supreme Court again upheld the Hyde Amendment in *Harris v. McRae*, including its refusal of federal funds for "medically necessary abortions." The decision was, in RFP director Janet Benshoof's words, "a total disaster" and a foretaste of life under an increasingly conservative Supreme Court. But three years later, Benshoof and her colleagues in the RFP celebrated "the most far-reaching victory on reproductive rights since *Roe v. Wade*" when, in *City of Akron v. Akron Center for Reproductive Health*, the U.S. Supreme Court struck down the Akron ordinances that set strict standards of informed consent for abortion patients. The ever-shifting legal terrain kept open nearly endless possibilities for litigation, and in such an uncertain environment doctors became fearful of performing abortions. The growing violence of the antiabortion movement only added to their fears as clinic bombings and murders of abortion providers overwhelmed mere legal concerns. The ascendance of the New Right amid the election of a succession of presidents who publicly disavowed abortion rights culminated in President Ronald Reagan's proclamation in 1984 of a National Sanctity of Human Life Day. Decrying abortion as the killing of "unborn children," Reagan called for citizens to reclaim the rights of "the unborn" and rededicate themselves to protecting "the weakest of our fellow human beings." By the middle

Figure 5.4 Janet Benshoof standing in front of the U.S. Supreme Court, no date. (Courtesy, Janet Benshoof)

of the 1980s, the RFP was fighting a defensive war against federal funding for anti-abortion activity and efforts to hold pregnant women responsible for fetal deaths. Although it won court battles on these particular issues, RFP leaders realized that with regard to abortion rights no victory was final and no achievement secure.[74] Merely holding the line would occupy all of their resources.

As the fetus became the proverbial poster-child of the New Right, abortion moved to the center of its agenda. RFP leaders suspected, however, that the New

Right's aims went well beyond revoking abortion rights. Indeed, the Reagan administration showed its hand in amicus briefs filed by its Justice Department in Supreme Court abortion cases. Assistant Solicitor General Samuel Alito recommended that the Justice Department file a brief in *Thornburgh v. American College of Obstetricians and Gynecologists* (1986), a Pennsylvania case involving state regulations similar to the Akron ordinances. He advised it to make an argument that would strike a delicate balance between questioning *Roe*'s validity by contending that the Constitution provided no right to privacy, and resting on its authority by insisting that the states may regulate abortion to further their interest in protecting prenatal life. Abortion involved not just medicine but also morality, he maintained, and the states should be allowed to require that abortion patients be counseled on the moral dimensions of their decision and alternatives to it. Alito's goal was not only to erode abortion rights but also to make way for a particular perspective on morality to shape state policy.[75] The government's side lost, but that it lost in a five-to-four decision put abortion rights activists and civil libertarians on notice that a sea change was in the works, one likely to curtail abortion rights and also to roll back—or dramatically redefine—the right to privacy so essential to protecting sexual conduct as a civil liberty.

Birth control and abortion claimed the attention of ACLU leaders from the 1950s through the 1980s, helping to transform their understanding of the Constitution and sexual freedom. As important as these causes were, however, ACLU attorneys realized early on that these alone would not protect women's control over their own reproduction. The right to avoid reproducing did not necessarily convey the right to reproduce, a right denied women who were surgically sterilized without their consent. As Ball, Black Muslims, and other militants in the racial power movements had predicted, federal funding for family-planning services did lead to coercion, particularly of black women. When cases of involuntary sterilization began to appear on the ACLU's doorstep by the middle of the 1970s, WRP leaders took action, formulating as they did so a new constitutionally grounded concept of reproductive freedom that drew from the experiences of women of color and welfare recipients.[76]

Why then did the RFP legal docket remain dominated by abortion with only a sprinkling of compulsory sterilization cases in the 1970s and 1980s? Most victims of compulsory sterilization shunned public attention, and, numerous though they were, their numbers did not approach the numbers of women with unwanted pregnancies. In addition, after the major court victory in *Relf*, the movement against policies that allowed compulsory sterilization often seemed most effective behind the scenes and at the administrative level where the RFP did much of its work.[77] Moreover, the 1970s brought a political and cultural climate hostile to compulsory sterilization. In stark contrast, the very successes of

Roe and *Doe* inspired the emergence of a powerful antiabortion movement that quickly claimed the moral high ground by advocating for "life" and cleverly turning civil liberties ideals away from women's rights and toward the rights of the fetus. Moreover, no serious efforts were made to pass a constitutional amendment requiring sterilization of welfare mothers, but many attempts were made to amend the Constitution to treat the fertilized egg as a person. Few if any activists aimed to reinstitute compulsory sterilization through state law, but countless "pro-life" activists and legislators drafted and presented bills designed to erode abortion rights. Finally, while advocates of compulsory sterilization took few cases to court after 1974, opponents of abortion rights filled court dockets with challenges to *Roe*.[78]

Scholars have identified the abortion rights movement with white women and the antisterilization movement with women of color. But in the ACLU black and white women worked together to establish policies on abortion. Working with and for victims of sterilization abuse shaped the ways that women in the ACLU thought and talked about the civil liberties aspects of reproduction. They borrowed from their knowledge of compulsory sterilization and eugenic control, for example, to rename pro-life activists "compulsory pregnancy" advocates and turn reproductive control into reproductive freedom. In addition, the greater understanding they gained of the difficulties experienced by women on public assistance heightened their appreciation of poor women's vulnerability to the abortion restrictions that proliferated after *Roe*. Overturning those restrictions became the main focus of the RFP's abortion litigation.[79]

The ACLU and RFP treated sterilization and abortion differently, demanding protections for sterilization that they denounced as unconstitutional restrictions when applied to abortion patients. Detractors considered the ACLU's differential treatment of sterilization and abortion evidence of hypocrisy. But for the RFP, sterilization and abortion were very different, due to the U.S.'s history of sterilization abuse and also because the procedures themselves were very different. Sterilization was permanent and abortion temporary—sterilization ended a woman's fertility and abortion ended only one particular pregnancy. Assuming that one pregnancy was much like any other and that a woman who underwent an abortion could later conceive, sterilization constituted a much more serious and irreversible procedure. In addition, as founding RFP director Judith Mears persuaded one judge, restrictions and protections that might prove "unduly burdensome" in abortion cases due to "the need for prompt surgical intervention" would not be so for sterilization cases, which could proceed on a more leisurely schedule.[80]

RFP attorneys noticed that even when government and hospital authorities did not pressure poor women to undergo sterilization, they accomplished the same result by allocating resources in ways that removed choice from the equation. By funding sterilizations but not abortions and by providing so meagerly for poor families, the federal government limited the options of poor women in ways that encouraged them to "consent" to sterilization. Thus, RFP activists fought for federally funded abortions in part to relieve poor women of economic pressures to be sterilized. With regard to informed consent and waiting periods, the RFP shaped its approach to the realities of the situation, listening to the stories of women who had undergone involuntary sterilizations as well as those who could not obtain abortions and formulating policy accordingly. Finally, as RFP director Janet Benshoof pointed out, because only women need abortions, while both women and men can be sterilized, the Constitution's equal protection guarantees might permit sterilization for women *and* men to be treated differently from other medical procedures but nevertheless require that abortion be governed by the same regulations applied to standard medical procedures undergone by men and women equally.[81]

Women's rights activists like those who headed the ACLU's WRP and RFP clearly changed the organization in ways that enhanced its attention to women's rights and its sensitivity to women's experiences. An earlier generation of women—including Pilpel, Kenyon, Norton, Murray, and Roraback—exercised influence in the ACLU by rallying Biennial Conference participants, pressing their points in board discussions, prevailing upon senior staff to implement new policies, maneuvering behind the scenes to shape policy, and occasionally throwing temper tantrums. By contrast, WRP and RFP leaders chose and litigated cases, negotiated deals with administrative agencies, managed budgets, and planned strategies.

The influence and unity of women's rights activists in the ACLU should not be overstated. Women had different ideas about what sexual civil liberties should look like, and they disagreed sharply, for example, over whether the ACLU should accept *Playboy* support. They also argued over what sort of informed consent should be required for sterilization and abortion and whether age restrictions and waiting periods should be the same for each procedure. Moreover, women's rights activists operated within a civil liberties paradigm that others in the ACLU would allow to be stretched only so far, and they ascended to positions of leadership just before a conservative turn in American politics and law would raise new barriers to their work even as this turn presented unexpected opportunities. Whereas the constitutional concept of privacy proved wonderfully elastic in ways that benefited the RFP's agenda, that very elasticity invited uses by individuals and groups with very different goals. William Ball would not be the last person to invoke privacy in service to an agenda that seemed, to many, hostile to women's rights and/or inimical to sexual civil liberties.

6

"What's Happening to Sexual Privacy?"

Easing Access to Sexual Expression, 1960s–1970s

"What's happening to sexual privacy?" Frank Trippett, senior editor of *Look* magazine, asked in 1970. His article appeared just five years after the Supreme Court established a constitutional right to privacy, but Trippett did not wonder why sexual privacy was becoming more important. He wondered instead why it was dying.[1] His question hinted at a relationship between emerging rights to sexual privacy and the ever greater exposure of sexuality in public. It was a relationship marked by unexpected twists and turns and a great deal of irony—a relationship illuminated by the ACLU's ongoing efforts to establish sexual civil liberties on the foundation of a right to privacy.

The most troubling privacy issues revolved around questions of access to wanted versus protection from unwanted sexual expression. ACLU leaders increasingly supported the efforts of homosexual rights activists—along with purveyors and consumers of sexual material—to expand access. Meanwhile, moral reformers, feminists, and other consumers demanded greater protection from unwanted sexual expression, including unsolicited mail, public sexual displays, and later sexual harassment and rape. Prioritizing the various civil liberties involved required ACLU leaders to make hard choices that strengthened their alliances with some groups and weakened their connections with others. By the dawn of the 1980s, they had formulated a new and expansive but also very specific right to sexual privacy that would draw the lines of the coming culture war over sex.

As a constitutional right, sexual privacy grew out of the ACLU's defense of the right to use and sell birth control and initiated the organization's first sustained effort to make a civil liberty of sexual conduct, an effort it soon redirected to the needs of homosexuals victimized by repressive laws and policies. The ACLU at first defended only homosexuals whose rights to due process, free speech, or other well-established civil liberties were violated. However, as ACLU staff members began to receive more requests for help from homosexuals who suffered from discrimination that went well beyond these conventional civil liberties claims, they began to consider the perspective of persecuted homosexuals. This transformed their thinking about sexual civil liberties and made their earlier approach seem unacceptably limited.

The ACLU's first interventions on behalf of homosexuals often involved neither the courts nor the law. Instead, they counseled individual victims of discrimination, and chastised media outlets that rejected advertisements submitted by homophile organizations. Refusing publication privileges was not technically a violation of the First Amendment, ACLU leaders recognized; but according to a consumer-oriented approach, these refusals represented a "denial of information to the public."[2] However sensitive ACLU leaders were to possible violations of speech rights, most did not consider it a civil liberties matter when homosexuals were denied federal employment or charged with criminal sodomy unless due process rights, unrelated to sexual orientation, seemed to be involved.[3]

Concerns about possible due process violations led ACLU legal director Melvin Wulf to challenge postal harassment of homosexuals in 1965. Years earlier, Wulf's predecessor, Rowland Watts, counseled individuals who were hassled by postal authorities for receiving or sending material with homosexual content, but in the 1960s, these incidents began to seem part of a systematic effort to intimidate gay men. Postal authorities were known to report recipients of "homosexual mail" to their employers, claiming that the employee posed a "security risk" or endangered children. Richard Schlegel was one of the lucky ones. When a postal inspector informed Schlegel's employer about the mail he received from homosexual organizations, his boss simply asked him to arrange for unmarked envelopes. A Maryland college professor was less fortunate. The president of his institution fired him after postal officials exposed letters he had written to a male "pen pal." Likewise, an official with the Pennsylvania State Department of Highways lost his job after postal inspectors told his supervisor about mail he received from the Janus Society, an early homophile organization. These and many other cases of harassment by postal inspectors came to light in the middle of the 1960s due to the growing prominence of the homophile movement amid escalating concerns about privacy. Revelations about the extent of these practices outraged ACLU leaders, who demanded an end to the post office's violations of patrons' privacy. In June 1965, the House of Representatives responded, assembling a Special Subcommittee on Invasion of Privacy to examine the government's use of "police state techniques," including postal surveillance, wiretapping, and "peepholes" in women's and men's restrooms. Within one year, post office surveillance of private mail collapsed under ACLU pressure, public exposure, congressional rebuke, threats of legislation, and a landmark Supreme Court decision, *Lamont v. Postmaster General* (1965). The Court held the post office's refusal to deliver Communist propaganda unconstitutional on the grounds that the postal patron—or consumer—had a First Amendment right to receive it.[4]

By 1965, a number of developments led the ACLU to reconsider an eight-year-old policy that committed it merely to defend even homosexuals whose rights to due process and freedom of speech were violated. At board member Harriet Pilpel's urging, the 1964 ACLU Biennial recommended that all consensual sexual behavior between adults in private be decriminalized; the 1964 Civil Rights Act provided new federal tools for dealing with discrimination; the Supreme Court affirmed a constitutional right to privacy in *Griswold v. Connecticut*; and an increasing number of affiliates demanded that the national ACLU take a stronger stand on the rights of homosexuals.

In the 1960s, ACLU affiliates began, as they had with other issues, to get out ahead of the national organization on the matter of homosexual rights. The Southern California affiliate challenged laws that criminalized sexual contact between males as violations of Title VII of the Civil Rights Act because they did not apply to women. The Washington, D.C., affiliate—inspired by charter member Frank Kameny, a onetime federal employee fired for homosexuality—called for an end to the federal policy of rejecting employees on grounds of sexual orientation and provided legal counsel for test cases. Other affiliates urged the national ACLU to challenge, as "an invasion of the right to privacy," federal policies against employing homosexuals. Many insisted that sexual activity conducted in private between consenting adults should be protected under the Constitution as long as it excluded "physical injury or torture." Some opposed this expansion of constitutional rights, fearing that it would dilute the ACLU's commitment to due process, freedom of speech, and other civil liberties. Others worried that protections for homosexuals would open public spaces to homosexual activity. Nevertheless, thanks largely to the work of affiliates, by January 1966, *Newsweek* identified the ACLU as the only group "apart from the homophile organizations" that actively opposed laws against homosexual acts. Nine months later, the national ACLU earned that designation when it denounced government regulation of "private homosexual behavior between consenting adults."[5]

ACLU leaders nevertheless remained ambivalent on issues that troubled the divide between public and private. They acknowledged as legitimate, for example, laws against prostitution and solicitation for sexual contact on the assumption that commercialized sex was ipso facto no longer private and therefore constituted behavior subject to public regulation. They also declined to condemn federal rules against employing homosexuals because such rules, ostensibly, governed only public sexual behavior. As the U.S. Civil Service Commission explained, as long as an employee's homosexuality remained private, it would not be investigated or acted upon. But when private homosexual behavior became known to others, it was thereby public and subject to government scrutiny and action. When one board member defended this position, reasoning that when "an employer has learned about such behavior... it is no longer private," Harriet Pilpel retorted that privacy refers to where the behavior takes place, "not whether it is secret." In the end, Pilpel's vision of privacy prevailed, and the ACLU revised its policy to protect all private sexual behavior between consenting adults.[6] The ACLU's new policy on homosexuality would prove unexpectedly momentous for the ongoing development of sexual civil liberties.

Not all homophile activists celebrated the ACLU's new policy on homosexuality. Frank Kameny and Clark Polak, president of the Janus Society, criticized it for continuing to condone laws against public solicitation. "The overwhelming majority of arrests of homosexuals," Kameny pointed out, are not for sodomy, per se, "but for solicitations of one sort or another," including behavior as innocuous as "a glance" or simply "a conversation in a bar." Public solicitation laws, he argued, were aimed at behavior that represents "merely a matter of a private business arrangement between two consenting adults." Kameny also defended prostitution, claiming that "there is no rational distinction... between a woman's hiring out her hands for stenography or her genitals for intercourse." ACLU founder Roger Baldwin weighed in from the sidelines, suggesting that the ACLU had construed the issue too narrowly by failing to recognize the unique problems faced by "bi-sexuals," especially married fathers charged with committing a homosexual act. But it was the dissatisfaction of ACLU devotee Arthur Cyrus Warner that eventually persuaded the ACLU to invest more fully in homosexual rights.[7]

At fifty years of age, Warner brought to homophile activism a law degree and Ph.D. in history from Harvard, considerable financial resources, an outsider's perspective as the son of Russian Jewish immigrants, and painful recollections of his first sexual experiences. Harsh punishments for masturbating, feeling attracted to other boys, and learning that Nazis killed homosexuals made for a traumatic adolescence. Finding sexual partners among anonymous men in theaters and restrooms and acquiring a painful case of gonorrhea did little to help. After being arrested for public solicitation in the weeks before he sat for the bar exam, Warner's legal career ended before it began and, in a "wrenching" move, he prepared to enter the more forgiving profession of academia. Throughout the 1950s and 1960s, Warner taught history while serving as an active member of the Civil Liberties Union of New Jersey, the Mattachine Society of New York, and other homophile groups. After twelve years of teaching at various institutions, Warner resigned in 1968 to devote himself to reforming laws affecting homosexuals.[8]

Comfortable financial circumstances allowed Warner to dedicate himself to homosexual law reform, but he was also motivated by the powerful mixture of hope and disappointment he experienced as he watched the American Law Institute (ALI) and the ACLU consider laws affecting homosexuals. Like the ACLU's 1967 policy, the ALI's Model Penal Code recommended decriminalizing consensual sodomy, but it also retained provisions against public solicitation commonly used to prosecute homosexual men. In 1968, Warner represented the Civil Liberties Union of New Jersey when he visited Professor Louis B. Schwartz, the Model Penal Code's chief reporter, to argue for the removal or modification of the offending section on public solicitation. Thus began a long and productive relationship that shaped Schwartz's thinking on the issue and his later attempts to revise the Federal Criminal Code.[9]

Warner hoped to make the ACLU more attentive to the needs of homosexuals, but he also aimed to lessen the dependence of homosexuals on the ACLU by developing a new organization focused on their legal needs. At one point, he willed the ACLU his estate for the purposes of removing "legal, political, economic, social and religious sanctions against homosexuals." With his friend Walter E. Barnett, also a law professor, he created the National Committee for Sexual Civil Liberties (NCSCL), an organization modeled on the ACLU but focused on the "special field of sexual civil liberties" and dedicated to overturning laws against fornication, adultery, sodomy, and other private sexual conduct between adults as well as statutes against public solicitation and prostitution.[10]

The NCSCL consisted of a small group of elite attorneys and scholars dedicated to homosexual law reform. In addition to cofounders Warner and Barnett, the group included ACLU legal director Melvin Wulf, William Reynard of the ACLU's Colorado affiliate, and two young, openly gay law school graduates from California and Ohio, respectively, Thomas Coleman and Craig Patton. Prominent social scientists also joined the NCSCL, namely Evelyn Hooker, whose work helped to persuade the American Psychiatric Association to remove homosexuality from its list of disorders, and Laud Humphreys, whose groundbreaking *Tearoom Trade: Impersonal Sex in Public Places* became a cause célèbre for documenting the participation of apparently heterosexual as well as homosexual men in public restroom sex.[11]

Commitment to homosexual law reform united the group, but it deliberately chose a generic name that referred to sexual freedom broadly. "In these days when the questions of birth control, abortion, pre-marital sex, and pornography are all of public concern," Warner explained, "belonging to a committee with a name such as ours should not carry any adverse effect." In addition, it allowed Warner, who advocated on behalf of homosexuals under the pseudonym Austin Wade, to work under his own name, and allowed the committee to recruit a number of individuals who might have shied away from an organization clearly associated with gay rights. The generic name also reflected Warner's strategy of pursuing rights for heterosexuals that would benefit homosexuals. Courts would be more likely to decriminalize private consensual conduct between heterosexual than between homosexual plaintiffs, Warner believed, but they would then find it difficult to uphold criminal sanctions against homosexuals who engaged in the same behavior. Defeating laws against fornication, sodomy, birth control, and abortion, for example, would challenge the law's tendency to permit only potentially procreative sex between spouses in ways that could erode sanctions against homosexuals.[12]

Decriminalizing sodomy was foundational to challenging discrimination against homosexuals, because as long as sodomy remained illegal, homosexuals—men in particular—were presumed to be lawbreakers and thus uniquely vulnerable to blackmail. Presumably, in the absence of sodomy laws, federal and state policies against employing homosexuals would become irrelevant and/or unconstitutional.[13] This approach mirrored the one employed by Ruth Bader Ginsburg, who, as director of the ACLU's Women's Rights Project, often defended individual male plaintiffs penalized by discriminatory policies that usually disadvantaged women. By taking on carefully selected cases involving men and heterosexuals respectively, Ginsburg and Warner aimed to persuade legislatures and courts to establish rights and liberties that benefited women and homosexuals.

Warner insisted that the NCSCL maintain a cool distance from the emerging homophile movement, not only to maintain the organization's image as a defender of sexual freedom for all, but also because Warner associated the movement with a "'ghetto' mentality." Warner considered the "homosexual subculture," not a genuine expression of common values and aesthetics, but a manifestation of "discrimination and bigotry" that would, with any luck, soon disappear, clearing the way for homosexuals to enter "the mainstream of American life." He criticized, as a disservice to "homosexual liberation," people who "prattl[e] about" and "try to organize courses on gay 'culture.'" Remaining aloof from gay activism and its showier variants also helped the NCSCL avoid publicity, another goal of Warner's. "Publicity in the area of homosexual law reform," Warner explained, "often amounts to nothing but a 'kiss of death.'"[14]

Stealth proved especially useful in the NCSCL's campaign to reform state and federal penal laws. In 1971, NCSCL members identified states that had begun to revise their penal codes, visited the chairs of state revision committees, submitted briefs, and worked with the ACLU and local affiliates to persuade legislators to liberalize or eliminate laws affecting homosexuals. Covert operations were the order of the day. "To publicize some of our successes" would, Warner believed, undermine the NCSCL's effectiveness and possibly even invite "tragic backlash" by provoking opponents. Publicity led one state to reverse its liberalized sodomy law, Warner believed. After the *Advocate*, a gay journal, celebrated Idaho's legislature for repealing laws against homosexual behavior between consenting adults and reducing penalties for homosexual solicitation, the state's legislators confronted a hue and cry that sent many scurrying back to retract their votes. As a result, convicted sodomists in Idaho could once again expect sentences up to life imprisonment. Warner subsequently declared the *Advocate* a menace and professed not to care "how 'happy' it makes all the little gay brothers and sisters to be able to read a national gay newspaper; the editors of that sheet have already done enough damage to homosexual law reform that they should hang their heads in perpetual shame and silently steal away." By contrast, the NCSCL's low-profile testimony and briefs helped to eliminate laws against sodomy in Ohio and sexual solicitation in Nebraska, while low-visibility NCSCL appearances before penal code commissions in Massachusetts, New Jersey, and California laid groundwork for later reform.[15]

The NCSCL did sponsor some public strategies. In Colorado, William Reynard brought two lawsuits on behalf of the NCSCL, resulting in "the first successful constitutional challenge anywhere to a sexual solicitation statute." NCSCL members also sought influence within the American Bar Association (ABA) and by 1973, the NCSCL—with the help of ACLU attorneys and leaders of the newly formed Lambda Legal Defense and Education Fund—persuaded the conservative ABA to call for the repeal of laws against sodomy.[16]

Warner anticipated even greater things from his furtive attempts to influence the federal criminal law reform effort. In 1966, President Johnson appointed a National Commission on Reform of Federal Criminal Laws directed by Louis B. Schwartz, the ALI Model Penal Code reporter whom Warner began to lobby in 1968. By 1971, Warner exulted to learn that a brief he wrote with the ACLU's Melvin Wulf and Spencer Coxe convinced the commission to remove "the odious solicitation section" that appeared in its original draft. Still, Warner urged his colleagues to keep "as quiet as possible" in order to avoid provoking opposition. Within two years, however, the NCSCL realized the victory's temporary nature when Congress restored the offensive provisions, public battles broke out over the entire document, the Watergate crisis derailed reform efforts, and subsequent administrations failed to take up the cause. By 1982, the code reform effort would collapse and with it Warner's influence over federal criminal law.[17]

Warner's commitment to homosexual law reform and a low profile did not prevent the NCSCL from attracting the attention of Margaret Standish of the Playboy Foundation in 1970. Standish read about the NCSCL in a Mattachine

Midwest newsletter and contacted Warner about their shared interest in "equitable sex laws." Warner saw in her overture an opportunity to influence people "in the heterosexual mainstream" but also the possibility of "some meaningful financial assistance." He assured Standish that the NCSCL shared the Playboy Foundation's goal of establishing "the inalienable right of consenting adults privately to engage in any form of sexual activity they please." Warner informed Standish that the NCSCL had attracted top legal and scholarly talent from around the country, and that its efforts to reform the sex laws were hampered only by limited finances.[18]

Warner and *Playboy* shared a common cause in the broad concept of sexual privacy for consenting adults. As *Playboy* head and founder Hugh Hefner had recently argued, the law had no business regulating sex, the most "private" act engaged in by human beings. Hefner focused on laws against fornication, adultery, and sodomy, and admitted to "a strong personal prejudice in favor of the boy-girl variety of sex," but he also opposed laws against homosexual activity. Thus, by the late 1960s, a publication responsible for making sex more public than ever, and one that had, since its founding, strategically positioned itself as antithetical—and perhaps even an antidote—to homosexual perversion, advocated sex law reform that would protect sexual privacy and decriminalize homosexual activity.[19]

Playboy's interest in homosexual law reform inspired Warner, Wulf, and a new ACLU staff attorney, Marilyn Haft. The ACLU's initial courtroom forays on behalf of such reform had proven disappointing, resulting in outright defeat, victory only for heterosexual married couples, or success at the lower-court level followed by appeal and reversal. But after *Roe v. Wade* extended privacy rights to abortion in 1972, Warner, Wulf, and Haft saw new hope for using privacy to defeat sodomy laws. Together, they prepared a proposal to seek funding from the Playboy Foundation for a project to coordinate a national litigation strategy for homosexuals.[20]

Unlike Warner, whose identity and experience as a homosexual motivated his activism, Haft came to her work inspired by a general passion for civil liberties. As a six-year-old child in Hebrew school, Haft recalled watching a film on the Holocaust that began her lifelong commitment to "make sure that this never happens again to anybody." This dedication led her to pursue a degree at New York University Law School and volunteer with the New York Civil Liberties Union before being hired by the national ACLU. As an attorney with the ACLU's Prisoners' Rights Project, Haft struggled to represent appeals that had been poorly developed in the lower courts. Frustrated, she began to seek out a new field of civil liberties law that would allow her to guide and shape key cases at an earlier stage in preparation for appealing them to higher courts. A field that needed trial attorneys badly enough would, she surmised, welcome a novice and

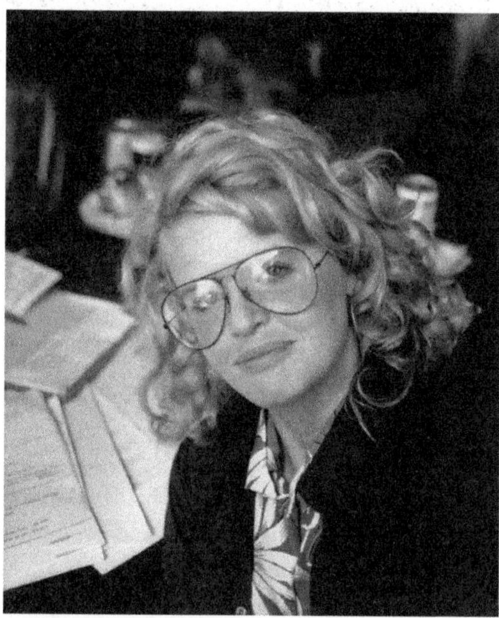

Figure 6.1 Marilyn Haft working on the ACLU's Sexual Privacy Project, circa 1974. (Courtesy, Marilyn Haft)

allow her to learn on the job. "I thought of gays," she recalled, "because they were beginning to make noise, but there were no real lawyers for them." Warner would have disagreed with that assessment, having personally assembled a group that included ten leading attorneys from around the country, but he was pleased that someone in the ACLU was finally eager to focus on homosexual law reform.[21]

Together, Haft and Warner proposed to the Playboy Foundation a Sexual Privacy Project that would draw on recent Supreme Court rulings on abortion to launch a "full scale attack" on laws that criminalized private, consensual, sexual conduct between adults. The project would coordinate a national litigation strategy, develop and circulate case materials, serve as an information clearinghouse, survey and report on existing laws and their discriminatory effects, and lobby legislatures, penal law revision commissions, and other interested bodies. A two-year budget of $150,000 would get the project off the ground under the direction of NCSCL cofounder Walter Barnett. A law professor at the University of New Mexico School of Law and graduate of Yale and Columbia University Law School, Barnett had recently completed a monumental study of the possibilities for homosexual law reform, *Sexual Freedom and the Constitution*, with support from the Harlan Fiske Stone Fellowship of Columbia University School of Law and the Ford and Playboy foundations.[22]

Burton Joseph, executive director of the Playboy Foundation, liked the proposal, but he offered only partial funding and, to the great disappointment of

Warner and Barnett, personally selected Haft to direct it. In so doing, he cut the NCSCL out of the project in any but the volunteer capacity that had always characterized its work. Joseph explained that he had only $40,000 to invest in the project, an amount that would not even cover Barnett's annual salary. Because Haft was married to a wealthy man and had previously worked for the New York City ACLU as a volunteer, Joseph assumed that she would accept a more modest sum. Moreover, by keeping the project in New York City, where Haft lived, the venture could benefit from the ACLU's offer of secretarial help, rent-free space, and telephone and Xeroxing services. Before Joseph selected Haft, he brought her to Chicago, where she impressed him as "a capable lawyer and a dignified and attractive spokesperson." Young and stylish, Haft also projected *Playboy*'s values more closely than the forty-year-old homosexual Barnett.[23]

Haft's identity as a heterosexual woman aided her work on behalf of gay rights in more substantive ways. Never having lived "in a closet" or felt like an "outcast," Haft was not weighed down by "the baggage" that sometimes prevented her gay colleagues from insisting on their full rights. Moreover, simply by supporting gay rights as a prominent, well-heeled, conventionally attractive, heterosexual woman, Haft brought the movement credibility. Although Barnett and Warner lamented that the "considerable expertise" found among NCSCL members had been overlooked in favor of "a novice in this particular field," and even though they regretted that the NCSCL would "remain starved financially" while "this supplementary endeavor gets all the money," neither doubted that Haft was "an extremely able attorney." At the end of the day, they felt lucky to have her on their side.[24]

With considerable excitement and energy, Haft launched the ACLU's Sexual Privacy Project in June 1973. Directing the project allowed her to shape a discrete field of law, and she cast her net widely to encompass prostitution and public solicitation as well as sodomy and discrimination against homosexuals. Haft paid little attention to the criminal law reform that occupied the NCSCL and relied instead on litigation, education, publicity, and collaboration with gay rights organizations.[25] Before she could invest in her work fully, though, Haft had to wrestle with ACLU policy.

After Haft sent out a mass mailing introducing herself and the Sexual Privacy Project, ACLU assistant director Alan Reitman identified discrepancies between the project's goals and current ACLU policy. "We have no policy," he wrote, on a number of matters listed as project priorities, including "decriminalizing prostitution" and "public solicitation for sexual acts," and he insisted that Haft "operate within the bounds of ACLU policy."[26] Haft looked to the ACLU's Biennial Conference in Milwaukee, Wisconsin, to obtain approval for her plans. There, she reached out to the local gay community and rode a wave of support for the new concept of victimless crimes.

Victimless crimes had become "an urgent issue" for liberals as successive wars on crime increased the incarceration rate across the board, including for offenses such as prostitution, sodomy, pot-smoking, and other drug use. The phrase emerged in the early 1970s, but the ideas harkened back to John Stuart Mill, whose influential 1859 essay, "On Liberty," acknowledged the legitimacy of government power "to prevent harm to others," not to protect from self-harm. This idea became a slogan for civil libertarians in the 1970s and gained cachet as reporters, scholars, and politicians blamed the overcrowding of prisons and overburdening of courts on the criminalization of behavior that victimized no one. The American Bar Association contributed to the movement when it established a Victimless Crimes Committee in 1973, the same year that prostitutes created their own rights-based organization, COYOTE (Call Off Your Old Tired Ethics), and the ACLU's Northern California affiliate created a Victimless Crimes Project. The timing was perfect for Haft's proposals, and she secured a strong Biennial Conference recommendation that the ACLU revise its policies on victimless crimes, including those on prostitution and public solicitation. Haft gained two more powerful allies when, one month later, Ruth Bader Ginsburg and Brenda Feigen Fasteau completed a report that recommended decriminalizing prostitution and public solicitation as "consensual act[s] between adults" that occur "within the zone of privacy protected by recent constitutional decisions."[27]

The national ACLU board debated these issues over a twelve-month period during which Haft proceeded with her original agenda for the Sexual Privacy Project. At times, she collaborated with Warner, who, despite his discomfort with some of Haft's publicity-seeking strategies and his abiding regret that her appointment had wrested the project away from the NCSCL, enthusiastically supported her work. She and Warner created the Victimless Crimes Reporter, later renamed the Sexual Law Reporter, which published current information on legal and political developments in the area of human sexuality for use by law students, law librarians, lawyers, judges, and activists. The NCSCL's Tom Coleman led the project with the assistance of unpaid law student interns, an annual donation of $1,000 from the ACLU, and publication and distribution expenses covered by the Playboy Foundation. Haft collaborated with others to write *The Rights of Gay People: The Basic ACLU Guide to a Gay Person's Rights* for the ACLU handbook series. Her national docket included cases that went beyond ACLU policy by including, for example, "solicitation for lewd acts." Accordingly, Haft agreed to testify for the ACLU on behalf of a Minnesota bill that would decriminalize prostitution. The Minnesota Civil Liberties Union's executive director, Matthew Stark, however, put a stop to her plans and complained to

Reitman that "a paid staff person" should not lobby on issues for which there was no national policy.[28] Thus, despite overwhelming support from the 1974 Biennial, Haft continued to face obstacles to her agenda at the affiliate and national level.

Public solicitation for prostitution vexed ACLU board members, because it implicated commercial as opposed to "pure" speech and also because it involved boundaries between private and public. Since 1967, when the ACLU advocated constitutional protection for "sexual behavior between consenting adults in private," it had distinguished carefully between such behavior and "solicitation" or other "acts in public." Haft countered these arguments by pointing out that most laws against prostitution were enforced discriminatorily, only against women. Moreover, because of the private and consensual nature of the acts involved in prostitution, effective law enforcement required entrapment methods that trampled rights to due process—a complaint voiced by longtime board member Dorothy Kenyon years earlier when she called prostitution law "one mass of undue process discriminatory as hell." Haft maintained that solicitation should be decriminalized along with prostitution because solicitation represented nothing more than an invitation to engage in a "relationship which is protected by the constitutional right of privacy."[29]

Warner worked, as usual, behind the scenes. While Haft lobbied the ACLU board, he took his case against criminal sanctions for sexual solicitation and sodomy to Model Penal Code reporter Louis B. Schwartz. Warner explained that solicitations—which he characterized as simply invitations to "engage in perfectly legal conduct"—do not offend the public as they might have in "the Victorian age." An adult today should be able to say no "to an unwanted sexual proposal without the aid of penal sanctions." He also insisted that solicitations are not "public acts." Like other private conversations, solicitations can take place in public locations without thereby becoming public acts. Warner convinced Schwartz, who also composed "an exceedingly helpful" letter for the NCSCL to use in its legal reform work, including the successful 1975 effort to pass a "consenting adults" bill in California.[30]

The conversation among ACLU board members over prostitution, homosexuality, and public solicitation had shifted by 1975, but echoes of earlier debates emerged. The board voted easily to support decriminalizing prostitution and eliminating "government and private discrimination against homosexuals," but the issue of public solicitation proved more contentious. Minors and unwilling adults could be exposed to solicitations, some argued. Others emphasized that solicitation invades "the public's privacy" with commercial speech about sex. Some countered that solicitations would remain unobtrusive because they "pertain to private sexual conduct." Yet others took a different approach entirely, arguing that treating public solicitation for sex as protected speech "trivializes the First Amendment and weakens its application to other subjects."[31]

As the ACLU board debated these issues, it received letters on the subject from around the country. "Public solicitation is a kind of 'thrusting'" that contains an element of coercion, wrote Lawrence Herman, a national board member from the Ohio affiliate. It subjects passersby to communications that belong in the private realm, he explained. Another agreed that a "right of individual privacy" should protect people "from offensive importunities" on "the public streets." Others countered that privacy rights have never protected people from "unwanted solicitation," and that "laws against public solicitation discriminate against poor prostitutes, who must operate in the streets."[32]

The most difficult issue regarding public solicitation remained the fact that the ACLU had long treated commercial as fundamentally different from noncommercial speech. "Commercial speech," one board member declared, "is the ACLU's obscenity"—in other words, a category of speech treated as less deserving of First Amendment protection. But ACLU efforts to distinguish between commercial and noncommercial speech were never clear. From its first decades of operation, the ACLU defended birth control and sex education entrepreneurs, as well as broadway theater playwrights and producers, and it continued to support nudist educational newsletters even after they morphed into glossy entertainment magazines. Differentiating between commercial and noncommercial material became increasingly difficult as the postwar era's growing attention to consumers' rights brought to the commercial realm the sheen of democracy, the demands of the constituent, and the rights of the citizen. But for many, solicitation for prostitution still highlighted stark differences between communication for communication's sake and communication for profit. It also increased the likelihood that the public would be exposed to sights and sounds that belonged, many believed, in the private sphere. In a telling move, the board tabled the question of public solicitation for sex until it could resolve the thorny issue of commercial speech, especially as it related to sexual expression.[33]

When the ACLU returned to its policies on commercial speech and sexual expression, it did so in a time of heightened concerns about privacy and consumer rights amid free-flowing sexual entertainment that had reached unprecedented dimensions. Erotic books and magazines circulated widely, often through the garishly labeled "adult" bookstores that emerged in cities and along the nation's highways. Moreover, the rating system adopted by the Motion Picture Association of America in 1968 led to a new genre of X-rated movies and public exhibitions of what became known as "hard-core." In retrospect, it was pornography's "golden age," the beginning of the era that would make way for *Deep Throat* and

The Devil in Miss Jones, shamelessly explicit feature films that found their way into middle-class culture through respectable theaters and reviews in the *New York Times*.[34]

Recent Supreme Court cases changed the landscape of obscenity law further by building on the privacy and consumer rights arguments first introduced by the ACLU. *Redrup v. New York* (1967) overturned the conviction of a New York City newsstand clerk prosecuted under state law for selling sexually explicit books to a plainclothes police officer. The Court suggested, however, that it would have upheld a statute narrowly drawn to protect juveniles or prevent "an assault upon individual privacy" that made it "impossible for an unwilling individual to avoid exposure." Limited as *Redrup* was, during the next eighteen months the Court relied on it to reverse thirty-five state and federal obscenity convictions. Only two years later, the Court articulated a standard of privacy that better reflected ACLU values when it overturned the conviction of Robert Eli Stanley for possessing obscene material in violation of Georgia state law. "If the First Amendment means anything," Justice Thurgood Marshall wrote, "it means that a State has no business telling a man, sitting alone in his own house, what books he may read or what films he may watch." Thus, in a ringing endorsement of the individual's "right to read or observe what he pleases—the right to satisfy his intellectual and emotional needs in the privacy of his own home," the Court held in *Stanley v. Georgia* (1969) that the Constitution "prohibit[s] making mere private possession of obscene material a crime."[35] Together, *Redrup* and *Stanley* reaffirmed the First Amendment rights of adult consumers and charted a new task for privacy as a civil liberty that could draw constitutional boundaries for obscenity law.

Privacy considerations also shaped public discussions when postal patrons continued objecting to unwanted sexually explicit mail. Renewed calls for more stringent laws were inspired by the circulation of an unprecedented amount of direct-mail advertising in the 1960s and 1970s. Complaints from the grass roots were joined by demands from the highest levels of government. In 1969, President Richard Nixon called for stronger legislation to curb obscene mailings, and in 1970, Chief Justice Warren Burger pointed out, in *Rowan v. Post Office Department,* that "every man's mail today is made up overwhelmingly of material he did not seek from persons he does not know. And all too often, it is matter he finds offensive." Burger insisted that "the right of every person 'to be let alone' must be placed in the scales with the right of others to communicate." In this context, Congress held more hearings to consider strengthening postal laws. ACLU leaders who had testified on postal policy in the 1960s did so again in the 1970s as the ongoing "junk-mail controversy" joined ever louder calls for the federal government to do something about the proliferating and increasingly public nature of obscenity. To be sure, some of these calls were provoked by cynical politicians anxious to provoke a furor and harness it to their own agendas. But the groundswell of anxiety about obscenity documented in the files of congressmen, letters to editors of newspapers and magazines, the lengthening membership rosters of grassroots pressure groups, and even the writings of public intellectuals and scholars can hardly be attributed to the skillful maneuvering of a handful of crafty politicians.[36]

The bill under consideration in 1970 would force material that fit a broad definition of obscenity to bear the label "sexually oriented advertising." Senders of such material would be forced to pay postal costs for items returned by recipients and also a substantial fine for doing so repeatedly. Lawrence Speiser, director of the ACLU's Washington, D.C., office, tried to persuade Congress to strike a balance between privacy and consumer rights. This bill goes "too far toward protecting the right of privacy," he testified, "at the expense of the freedom to send and to *receive* material protected by the First Amendment." Speiser's argument failed to attract support, and the bill passed as part of the Postal Reorganization Act of 1970.[37]

ACLU leaders returned to the policy drawing board after observing how privacy arguments supported growing demands for new laws against sexual material. In accordance with their decades-old consumer rights approach and the Supreme Court's recent endorsement of it, they revised their obscenity policy to oppose any statutory restraint "on the right to create, publish or distribute materials to adults, or the right of adults to choose the materials they read or view."[38] They then turned to the difficult issue of how to deal with sexually explicit material that is thrust at the public or displayed in a manner impossible for an unwilling viewer to avoid.

Several ACLU leaders drew on recent Supreme Court opinions to argue that thrusting, as they called it, violated the privacy of unsuspecting passersby. They enjoyed support from Thomas I. Emerson, a leading First Amendment scholar who had helped to craft the ACLU's privacy argument in *Griswold* v. *Connecticut* (1965). Emerson defended laws designed to protect captive audiences from exposure to uninvited sexual messages and material. Unwanted sexual communication can, he argued, elicit a "shock effect" strong enough to render it more like action than like speech. ACLU proponents of an antithrusting policy were also inspired by Denmark, a leader among European countries in casting off restrictions on obscenity but one that prohibited thrusting. Others supported an antithrusting policy to prevent children from being exposed to "lascivious" and "obscene" material on billboards and even bookstore display windows. As a practical matter, one argued, the courts will never "allow the unrestricted dissemination of material to children" anyway.[39] Advocates of an antithrusting policy spoke from a position of pragmatism, personal experience, and a sincere desire to preserve or restore a public sphere free of sexual images they associated with private behavior. They conceived of this public sphere as a place where involuntary exposure to sexual communications violated an individual's right to privacy.

Other board members insisted not only that "there is no right of privacy for people in the public arena" but that any restrictions on speech in public violate the First Amendment. Never having accepted the proposition that obscenity could be defined, the ACLU could not sanction laws that would protect the public from it, one argued. Board member Harriet Pilpel answered these arguments by suggesting that the ACLU accept laws against public depictions of "sexual intercourse and deviant sexual behavior involving the genitalia," while another member suggested simply the phrase "hard core pornography." Concerns about children, privacy, and the "unwilling audience" loomed large for many, but others resisted any restrictions on sexual displays, a suggestion that did not sit well with Pilpel. Would the ACLU call for no restraints on "six people having intercourse in a store window" that children pass on their way to school? Her colleague Charles Rabkin replied that "parents have the responsibility of bringing up their own children." Another member disagreed and pointed to the demoralizing influences over which parents exercised little or no control. Especially in large urban areas, "it is much harder to separate the private from the public sectors," and the ACLU should not oppose legislative efforts to do so.[40]

By February 1970, Pilpel's side led by a narrow margin, and the ACLU board adopted a new policy that would accept narrowly drawn laws to "prohibit the thrusting of hard-core pornography on unwilling audiences in public places." The policy excluded unsolicited mail from its definition of thrusting and continued to oppose measures that would allow customers to reject sexually oriented mail or alert them to it by labeling it with a special symbol. Such a mark, several argued, would eliminate "free choice" especially in small towns "since everybody would know what the symbol indicated" and people might reject such matter simply to avoid "social disapproval."[41] Even so, the ACLU's 1970 antithrusting policy indicated how complicated matters of sexual privacy had become.

Obscenity laws designed explicitly to protect children proved even more controversial for the ACLU board. Such laws required adult customers to make special efforts to obtain sexually oriented material by requesting it from behind the counter and presenting identification. Many members argued that these laws violated consumers' rights to "choose the materials they read or view." Several board members wondered if "a child should be allowed to buy any kind of pornography." On a more pragmatic note, they argued that repealing laws designed to protect children would prove so unacceptable to the general public that it could "torpedo everything else we are trying to do." Most, however, considered laws against distributing or selling particular material to minors a violation of the

First Amendment, mainly because such laws restricted the ability of adults to acquire such materials.[42]

By 1970, the ACLU's focus on consumer rights and privacy led it to oppose laws aimed at protecting children from sexually oriented material because such laws invariably restricted adult access. But these same concerns led the ACLU to recognize the right of individuals to avoid consuming or even encountering such material when in public, a place where individual privacy rights should protect one from unwilling exposure to sexual imagery. It was a precarious balance to strike and one that would not hold for long.

While ACLU leaders debated their own policies, they watched closely as the President's Commission on Obscenity and Pornography considered these and other issues. Convened by Lyndon Johnson in 1967 but completed in 1970 under Richard Nixon, the ACLU opposed the creation of the commission on the grounds that government should not be involved in such issues. Nevertheless, the commission's 1969 progress report echoed ideas evident in recent court decisions approved by the ACLU—notably *Redrup v. New York* (1967) and *Stanley v. Georgia* (1969)—when it suggested that most obscenity laws should be eliminated and those remaining drawn more narrowly to protect children and prevent "assaults upon individual privacy" by "offensive public displays." After the release of this preliminary report, commissioners Morton Hill, president of Morality in Media, and Charles Keating, founder of Citizens for Decency, denounced the commission as a pawn of the ACLU. "While Congress was unaware," Hill testified before a congressional subcommittee, "the ACLU gained control of the Commission" through its chair, William Lockhart, and commissioner Paul Bender, both ACLU members. The commission will "urge you to legalize obscenity for adults," he assured his audience, "since this has always been the ACLU's goal." Keating called attention to the college professors on the commission, pointing out their "ivory-tower outlook, alienated views, and libertine philosophies." No one realized it, but the commission's strongest link to the ACLU was actually Barbara Scott Preiskel, one of only two women on the commission and general counsel to the Motion Picture Association of America (MPAA). Preiskel provided the ACLU board with confidential information about the commission's work and advice about how to respond to it effectively. At her suggestion, ACLU leaders lodged a complaint about Keating with the White House and formed an ad hoc coalition of national organizations dedicated first to monitoring and later to defending the commission's conclusions.[43]

The ACLU-led ad hoc coalition on the President's Commission on Obscenity and Pornography was chaired by Harriet Pilpel and met for the first time in the fall of 1969, shortly after the Johnson Commission issued its progress report. By design, a majority of the members represented nonprofit or trade organizations, and only two spoke for commercial interests. Initial meetings aimed to find common ground. All criticized the postal bills and regretted that they applied even to material distributed by "socially worthwhile organizations" that offered advice on marriage or population control. They lamented the conservative "temper of the times," dreaded the "Supreme Court which will be sitting two years from now," and agreed on the need for strategic cooperation among advocates of free speech. Given the disparate perspectives represented, members did not reach a consensus easily, but they eventually converged on their commitment to consumers' rights. In other words, they agreed that an adult should not be prohibited "from reading books or seeing motion pictures that he chooses to read or view."[44]

Consumer rights figured prominently in testimony before the Johnson Commission in the spring of 1970. Pilpel testified on behalf of the ACLU and, guided by advice from Preiskel, emphasized the importance of consumer rights under the First Amendment and challenged accusations that the ACLU had exercised inappropriate influence over the commission. "The ACLU believes that there does exist a right in the individual to make a private decision as to what material he wishes to read or possess," Pilpel declared. That right had recently been applied to the home by the Supreme Court in *Stanley v. Georgia* (1969) and extended into public spaces by a federal court in *Karalexis v. Byrne* (1969). "If a rich Stanley can view a film, or read a book, in his home," the Court explained, "a poorer Stanley should be free to visit a protected theatre or library." In an ironic and novel twist that reversed the original equation used to argue for consumers' rights under the First Amendment, the Court also posited the consumer's right to view and read as the basis for a producer's right to create, arguing that "a constitutional right to receive a communication would seem meaningless if there were no coextensive right to make it." This logic was echoed by Pulitzer Prize–winning author and playwright Jerome Weidman, who testified before the Johnson Commission that "if the author can be prevented from writing what he chooses," then "the public's right to read is impaired." Similarly, he pointed out, "if an adult's right to read is restricted, then the author's freedom of expression becomes meaningless."[45] Clearly, the rights of adult consumers to access any material they might want had become firmly established in First Amendment jurisprudence and also made its way into popular thought.

The message was not lost on the Johnson Commission, whose final report reflected a strong commitment to the First Amendment rights of adult consumers. As many expected, the commission advocated repealing all laws that regulated the circulation of obscenity among consenting adults. It found no causal connection between obscenity and criminal or antisocial conduct, reaffirmed the right of individuals to read and view whatever they want, and encouraged comprehensive sex education as a tool for demystifying sex and reducing interest in pornography. The report did, however, endorse legislation—including laws against unsolicited mail—to prevent the unwilling exposure of children and the general public to sexually explicit material.[46]

The Johnson Commission's report triggered strong objections from around the country and within the nation's capital, including Vice President Spiro Agnew, members of Congress, and three of the eighteen commissioners. The Senate voted to condemn the commission's work in a resolution authored by Senator John McClellan (D-Ark.), who sponsored the bill to create the commission. McClellan told his colleagues that Congress "might just as well have asked the pornographers to write this report... although I doubt that even they would have had the temerity and effrontery to make the ridiculous recommendations that were made by the commission." President Nixon too repudiated the report as "morally bankrupt."[47]

ACLU leaders characterized attacks on the commission's report as an "assault on the freedom to read" and rallied their own troops. In another ironic twist, they strategized with the ad hoc coalition to defend the report of a commission whose formation they had initially opposed. The ad hoc group hoped to encourage serious public consideration of the commission's work by refuting critical editorials—such as the editorial in the *News-Sentinel* (Fort Wayne, Indiana) that characterized the report as "an unscientific piece of tripe produced by the American Civil Liberties Union"—and releasing a signed statement by prominent individuals who supported the report, including film star Charlton Heston.[48] In the end, the ad hoc coalition's painstakingly crafted statement itself mattered little, but by bringing important national groups together to find common cause against censorship, it helped to spread the ACLU's broad consumer rights understanding of the First Amendment to influential opinion-makers.

The Johnson Commission's report probably accomplished little that most commissioners intended in the short term, though it enjoyed a great deal of influence in the long term. At the outset, the report inspired a fierce backlash as citizens' groups and local officials mobilized to demonstrate that the American public supported stronger, not weaker, obscenity laws. Indeed, by many measures, it "widened the cultural divide and made the debate more rancorous than ever." But even as courts made frequent reference to the report, the Supreme Court continued to deny constitutional protection to obscenity. Over time, however, the report provided liberal defenders of pornography with a scientific and political basis for their arguments against obscenity laws. Moreover, studies funded by the commission dominated social science publishing on the subject for many years.[49]

The Johnson Commission's studies and report were not without their flaws. At least one careful analysis of the studies discovered that many of the researchers dismissed contradictory evidence, employed categories of analysis inconsistently, and neglected to use control groups. The commissioners themselves displayed a marked tendency toward holding pornography harmless in their selective use of the data presented to them. Follow-up studies later challenged the commission's findings and set new standards for social science in the field by rejecting many of the methods employed by the commissioned researchers. Indeed, this wave of scholarship found evidence that exposure to pornography, especially violent pornography, affected attitudes and behavior, laying the groundwork for critics of the Johnson Commission to demand that the issue of obscenity be revisited.[50]

The commission's conclusions did not align perfectly with ACLU policy either. Indeed, the commission endorsed regulations that the ACLU condemned as interfering with the rights of adult consumers, including restrictions on the sale of "so-called pornographic material" to children. Moreover, the commission's support for laws against "thrusting" of sexual material on television sent the ACLU back to reconsider its own approval of laws against thrusting.[51] Nevertheless, ACLU leaders defended the report because its broader claims confirmed their beliefs and also because implementing its suggestions would have eased access to sexual material by repealing many obscenity laws.

By 1973, as concerns about thrusting and privacy strengthened postal laws and threatened to influence the regulation of television, ACLU leaders reconsidered their recently revised obscenity policy. They were prodded by Franklyn S. Haiman, chair of the Illinois affiliate, national board member, and First Amendment scholar, who ridiculed the concept of thrusting. Haiman approached the debate armed with a fully developed and recently published argument against efforts to create a right to privacy from sexual speech. Individuals could use "selective perception" to avoid material they would rather not see, he maintained. Laws and policies against public thrusting treated "erotic communication" as a unique category of speech by letting the consumer's right to avoid it trump the producer's right to speak it and the consumer's right to access it with ease. Haiman argued for a much more limited right to avoid unwanted speech. "Privacy will be adequately safeguarded," he insisted, as long as we protect "our right to escape from one another after the first exposure to unwelcome communication." Pilpel objected, comparing "obscenity in public places" to a "physical assault" on a captive audience. Like shouting "fire" in a crowded theater or uttering "fighting words," displays of sexually explicit imagery in public places have a "non-speech" effect, she argued. But Haiman warned of the dreaded slippery slope. "If we open the door with regard to pornography, it could work to undermine the entire free speech concept," he suggested, then criticized the notion of a "so-called 'captive audience.'" Pilpel retorted that laws against thrusting were less about protecting a captive audience than about allowing people to frequent public spaces without being assaulted by sexually explicit displays. Few if any new ideas emerged in the debate that followed, but most participants sided with Haiman. "There are dangers," several concluded, in allowing privacy doctrine to grow "in directions never intended." An overwhelming majority on the board agreed and voted to rescind the ACLU's three-year-old policy on thrusting.[52] Traditional ACLU efforts to distinguish between commercial and noncommercial speech would not be far behind.

When ACLU board members revisited the issue of commercial speech in 1974, Reitman opened the discussion with the claim that commercial speech "is part of the sphere of 'public debate' which the First Amendment is designed to protect." Several board members objected, arguing that commercial speech "is not so much speech as it is the conduct of a business." Others, including Mel Wulf, worried that bringing commercial speech under First Amendment protection would dilute protection for "ideational" speech whose primary purpose was to convey ideas. These suggestions were defeated when Pilpel reminded the group of the ACLU's recent amicus brief in *Bigelow v. Virginia* (1974) which argued that commercial advertising for contraceptives and abortions provided essential information to consumers. Barbara Scott Preiskel and others agreed with Pilpel, pointing out that consumer "decisions are at least as vital to the day-to-day lives of most people as political choices" and that advertising and other forms of commercial speech equip consumers to participate knowledgably in the marketplace. After lengthy debate, the board finally brought its policy into line with trends long evident in ACLU practice by declaring commercial and noncommercial speech equally protected by the First Amendment.[53]

Under the ACLU's new policy recognizing full constitutional protection for commercial speech, Haft's proposal to decriminalize public solicitation for sex faced few obstacles. Haft explained to the board that, by endorsing the decriminalization of prostitution, it had cleared the way to opposing laws against public solicitation. Moreover, because prostitution relied on solicitation, restricting solicitation would unconstitutionally inhibit a form of sexual activity that should be protected by the right to privacy. Those who continued to express concerns about the impact of solicitation on the unsuspecting public, were met by claims that such solicitations were "usually unobtrusive" and would remain so "since the solicitation pertains to private sexual conduct." Lurking between the lines of the debate was the unspoken possibility that permitting such wide latitude to sexual communication in public might in fact deprivatize it, leading to sexual interactions that were no more private than a haircut in a salon, a meal at a cafe, or a stroll through a park. Nevertheless, Haft's proposal to protect public solicitation for sex under the First Amendment won a majority on the board and wide acclaim from the Biennial that met two months later when it endorsed "total sexual freedom among consenting adults in private."[54]

Victory over ACLU policy did not mean victory in court, and here the Sexual Privacy Project and the National Council for Sexual Civil Liberties experienced disappointment after disappointment. Under Haft, the ACLU joined *North Carolina v. Enslin* at the trial level with the aim of challenging the constitutionality of sodomy laws. In a classic case of entrapment, Eugene Enslin, owner of a local massage parlor and bookstore in Jacksonville, North Carolina, was approached for sex by Herbert P. Morgan, a seventeen-year-old marine and decoy for the local police. After committing fellatio and sodomy with Morgan, Enslin was arrested and phoned Frank Kameny, who brought the case to Haft's attention. Haft poured herself into the case, attending carefully to facts, argument, and presentation with the aim of establishing that the sexual activity under consideration was private and consensual. In an effort to appear appropriately feminine in a southern court, she "literally wore a gingham dress." To no avail. The lower court sentenced Enslin to one year in prison, a decision affirmed by the state supreme court, and left standing by the U.S. Supreme Court's refusal to hear the case.[55]

Doe v. Commonwealth's Attorney developed alongside *Enslin* but under the guidance of Philip Hirschkop, an ACLU attorney in Virginia who represented gay activists in a class-action suit against the state's antisodomy law. Hirschkop employed many of the same legal arguments and strategies that Haft used and achieved similar results, this time at the highest level. The U.S. Supreme Court took the case only to affirm the lower court's refusal to recognize sodomy as constitutionally protected behavior.[56]

"The year 1976 was terrible for sexual privacy," Haft wrote in the *ACLU Annual Report*, citing widespread state and municipal crackdowns on prostitution and recent court decisions on sodomy laws. "I thought [*Enslin*] was the most perfect case," she recalled several decades later, but perhaps the timing was wrong. Warner thought as much at the time. Furious that the ACLU had taken on the "premature" cases of Enslin and Doe, he believed they had asked the court to "take too great a leap." "The way must first be prepared," he explained, "by having the court extend *Griswold* to certain non-homosexual areas—fornication, for example—where there is less unwillingness on the part of judges" to extend privacy rights. "An impressive record was in the process of being built up," he wrote, through penal code reforms and state judicial action, but the U.S. Supreme Court decision in *Doe* would frustrate further efforts. Had Haft and others followed the NCSCL's lead, Warner argued, by eschewing publicity and working "quietly and effectively within the mainstream" instead of impulsively pushing cases through the courts, the "disaster" of the recent Supreme Court sodomy case would not have happened.[57]

More bad news arrived as a newly politicized Christian Right, emboldened, Warner suspected, by the results of *Enslin* and *Doe*, mobilized to roll back homosexual law reform. These efforts came to a head in Arkansas in 1977. Two years after the state legislature adopted a new penal code without sodomy laws, an Arkansas senator promoted a new antisodomy bill as "aimed at wierdos and queers who live in a fairyland world and are trying to wreck family life." When a local NCSCL member learned of efforts to reinstate Arkansas' sodomy laws, he asked the state's attorney general, Bill Clinton, to declare the bill unconstitutional. Clinton did not consider that position tenable in the wake of *Enslin* and *Doe*, but he promised to "discourage the criminalization of acts which have no business being part of the criminal law." Clinton recruited Nick Wilson (D), chair of the Senate committee assigned to the sodomy bill, to strangle the bill by holding it until the session adjourned. Wilson tried, but with only fifteen minutes left in the session, a powerful senator engaged him in some pork barrel politics that led to the bill's passage. Clinton felt "sick" about what had transpired. "I did my best to kill [the bill] and thought I had it done," he wrote the NCSCL representative, Keeston Lowery. "I told the Gov. I would publicly support him if he vetoed the bill," Clinton wrote. But I "could not say categorically that the bill is unconstitutional because the U.S. Sup. Ct. has refused to extend the right to privacy to homosexual partners in private, although I think their decision was wrong." After the state senate passed the antisodomy bill unanimously and Governor David Pryor signed it into law, Clinton assured Lowery, "I am more disappointed than you know."[58]

When Warner found this correspondence twenty years later during Clinton's first term as president, he was delighted to rediscover evidence of Clinton's "earnestness and sense of commitment" to the rights of homosexuals. In 1977, though, his mood was anything but light. That year the ACLU's Sexual Privacy Project ended. *Playboy* funds dried up, and Haft left the ACLU to work with Midge Costanza, assistant to the president for public liaison under Jimmy Carter. With her departure, the ACLU's homosexual rights agenda flagged for nearly a decade.[59]

As the 1970s drew to a close, homosexuals in America continued to come out of the closet, lobby for rights, and demand respect even as opposition to gay rights grew increasingly vicious. Anita Bryant's "Save Our Children" campaign accused homosexuals of recruiting defenseless children into homosexuality because they could not reproduce their own and cited the Bible to recommend the death penalty for sodomists. Amid such fanaticism, the appearance of "Kill a Queer for Christ" bumper stickers was hardly surprising—nor was the emergence of a new tool for discriminating against homosexuals, the public voter referendum. In 1977 and 1978, petitioners called for the heterosexual majority to vote on the rights of the homosexual minority in Dade County, Florida; Wichita,

Kansas; St. Paul, Minnesota; and Eugene, Oregon, among other cities. The assassinations of San Francisco Mayor George Moscone and the first openly gay elected official in California, Harvey Milk, brought the hatred to a bloody climax.[60] By the closing days of the seventies, many gay activists wondered whether sexual civil liberties would ever apply to them.

When asked, in 2010, what the short-lived Sexual Privacy Project accomplished, Marilyn Haft laughed. "You know we lost every case," she admitted. But court victories are not the only measure of success. Haft guided substantial revisions of the ACLU's policies on homosexuality, prostitution, and public solicitation, moving it into position to lead and shape the privacy revolution that ultimately made sex a civil liberty. As Haft sees it, her efforts were ultimately vindicated when the U.S. Supreme Court declared laws against sodomy unconstitutional in *Lawrence v. Texas* (2003). "I set the constitutional arguments that are still being used to this day," Haft observes. Equally noteworthy, she helped to "legitimize the gay rights movement" by bringing to it the support and legal credibility of the ACLU. Suspecting that younger people today do not appreciate the extent of discrimination against homosexuals, Haft points out that many of the issues she worked on have "sort of become second nature," but at the time, "they were all new and every single one of them was breaking ground."[61]

Arthur Warner's behind-the-scenes work also proved critical. Partly because he shunned publicity and opposed the emerging gay subculture, but also because he was irascible, pompous, and not widely liked, Warner has yet to appear in histories of the gay rights movement. Nonetheless, he inspired the ACLU to take sexual civil liberties more seriously, developed legal strategies that attracted *Playboy* funding by interrelating homosexual and heterosexual rights, and persuaded the influential legal scholar Louis B. Schwartz to reconsider his position on public solicitation and use his influence to sway legislators and federal policymakers. Through the NCSCL network, Warner brought arguments against the criminalization of sodomy to the attention of Bill Clinton as attorney general of Arkansas. He helped younger activists network and learn from an older generation, instilling in them a sense of confidence in their common mission. The reverberations of that work are apparent in the ongoing efforts of Warner's protégés, Thomas Coleman and Jay Kohorn, whose Los Angeles law practices litigate for homosexual rights; William B. Kelley, an attorney involved in gay and lesbian activism in Chicago; Professor Anthony Silvestre of the University of Pittsburgh, who researches AIDS prevention; and Professor Wayne Dynes of Hunter College, who writes on the history of same-sex love.[62]

The influence of Haft and Warner can also be seen in the ACLU's lasting commitment to gay rights and sustained opposition to laws against prostitution and public solicitation. By 1978, the ACLU had litigated more gay rights cases than all other organizations combined, and that year it also began to provide rent-free office space to the Lambda Legal Defense Fund. In 1986, the ACLU secured a substantial grant from James C. Hormel—a prominent gay rights activist and heir to the Hormel Foods family fortune—that underwrote the development of a Lesbian and Gay Rights Project headed by Nan Hunter. Today, the ACLU's Lesbian, Gay, Bisexual, Transgender and AIDS Project supports same-sex marriage using the careful legal strategy suggested by Warner. It urges allies to "make change, not lawsuits" by conducting grassroots public education efforts and working at the state level before turning to the federal courts.[63]

Just as the ACLU fought for the rights of consenting adults to engage in private sexual relations with whomever they pleased, by the 1970s it also ardently defended the right of adults to access sexual material with ease. Both agendas rested on particular understandings of freedom of speech and the right to privacy. Solicitation became a straightforward First Amendment issue when ACLU leaders erased the distinctions they had traditionally drawn between commercial and noncommercial speech. Public solicitation for sex then became a matter not only of free speech but also privacy because it involved—according to some rather tautological reasoning—sexual behavior assumed to be private and protected as such. For a while, a vocal contingent argued that, because sexual behavior was by definition private, public displays or images of it violated the privacy rights of unsuspecting passersby. A policy against thrusting marked their success, but it lasted no more than a few years, doomed by its inconsistency with the ACLU's growing emphasis on the First Amendment rights of consumers to access, unimpeded, sexual expression of all kinds.

"Public sex pops up everywhere," Frank Trippett noted in his 1970 ruminations on the disappearance of sexual privacy.[64] Ironically, constitutional sexual privacy played a major role in that phenomenon. By pursuing an understanding of privacy rights that included sexual conduct and consumer rights, ACLU leaders helped to constitutionalize this blurring of the boundaries between public and private and ease access to sexual expression of all kinds. But their efforts did not go unopposed and were, in fact, met by demands for greater protection from unwanted sex, including sexual harassment and rape—two issues that forced the ACLU to confront head-on apparent conflicts between civil liberties and women's rights and to recalibrate its sexual civil liberties agenda accordingly.

7

"Solutions Must Be Found within Civil Libertarian Guidelines"

Protecting against Rape and Sexual Harassment, 1970s–1990s

"I have been deceived by a bait and switch technique," radical feminist Andrea Dworkin wrote angrily. She felt betrayed after having been recruited into the ACLU in 1975 by a solicitation letter that touted the organization's commitment to women's rights and bore the signature of Ruth Bader Ginsburg. Dworkin, like many other feminists in the 1970s, had hoped that the ACLU would become the legal arm of the women's rights movement. Instead, by 1981, Dworkin considered the ACLU "a handmaiden of the pornographers," one that treated cries of "rape the women" as protectable speech. The ACLU's "First Amendment absolutis[m]" and blind loyalty to principle has trumped its defense of women's rights, she argued, especially rights to be free from unwanted sex.[1] Dworkin overstated her case, but she was right about one thing. Civil liberties principles shaped and constrained ACLU leaders' commitments to women's rights. Many of the sharpest conflicts between women's rights and civil liberties concerned issues of sexuality, especially access to versus protection from unwanted sexual expression, most notably rape and sexual harassment.

The ACLU did not assume leadership on rape law reform or sexual harassment law. And when it did eventually take up these issues, internal disagreements prevented it from speaking in a strong, unified voice. Even so, by debating the issues, testifying at congressional hearings, negotiating with administrators, filing legal briefs, and speaking to the press, ACLU leaders introduced civil libertarian perspectives on rape and sexual harassment that influenced judges, legislators, and the general public. The arduous process of formulating policy required them to hammer out compromises that exposed their core principles. That these negotiations took place against a backdrop of rising moral and political conservatism complicated matters by closing down old sources of funds and power and introducing new but thorny opportunities for coalition building. In the end, some would accuse the ACLU of privileging men's over women's rights and liberty over equality, while others would charge it with selling out to feminism. What really happened was much more complicated and involved the ACLU's long-standing commitments to racial justice and newer concerns about privacy, consumer rights, and sexual expression—central components of the ACLU's sexual civil liberties agenda.

Rape was not an entirely new issue for the ACLU, though before the 1970s, traditional civil libertarian priorities restricted its involvement to the due process rights of defendants—issues most likely to surface in cases of black men accused by white women. Such cases often devolved into classic examples of Jim Crow justice, complete with kangaroo court proceedings, discriminatory sentencing, and mob violence. Accordingly, ACLU lawyers challenged procedural irregularities, questioned the racial composition of juries, protested harsh sentences, and collaborated with local activists and the National Association for the Advancement of Colored People (NAACP) to protect defendants from vigilantes. They frequently employed the most common rape defense strategy of the day—seeking to discredit complainants as sexually promiscuous women.[2]

Take the case of the Scottsboro Boys, a rape case that became a cause célèbre for progressives in the 1930s. ACLU attorneys involved in the case cast doubt on the testimony of two white women who charged nine black teenage boys with rape by suggesting that the women were prostitutes who frequently entertained black customers. Most people simply assumed that the reputations and sexual activities of the complainants were relevant to the case. Few people wondered whether privacy rights should protect the women from being identified publicly or having their sexual activities scrutinized in court. On the contrary, in cases that involved a black man charged with rape by a white woman, the deck seemed so stacked against the defendant that few progressives even considered the rights of the complainant.[3]

The privacy of rape victims would not become a serious political issue until the 1970s, but as early as 1950 prominent individuals raised concerns about it. That year, J. Edgar Hoover, director of the Federal Bureau of Investigation, enlisted the media in his war on crime by urging newspaper editors to headline sex crimes and identify alleged offenders but exhorting them to withhold the names of victims. Ignaz Rothenberg, a media scholar and advocate for professional newspaper standards, issued an impassioned plea for media outlets to respect the privacy of rape victims, in part to encourage them to report the crime. In the 1950s, not only did publicizing a rape victim's name hinder her efforts to forget the incident—something psychiatrists of the day advised her to do—but it also jeopardized her reputation and chances for marriage, further discouraging women from coming forward.[4]

The 1950s witnessed a major development in rape law when the American Law Institute (ALI) drafted its Model Penal Code. The ALI produced a code that treated rape as fundamentally different from other crimes. In addition to upholding the marital exemption for rape that allowed husbands to coerce sex from wives, it required corroboration of the victim's testimony, imposed an unprecedentedly brief three-month statute of limitations, and downgraded the crime if the victim and perpetrator had a prior sexual relationship. The Code also explicitly permitted as a defense evidence that the victim was a prostitute or had engaged in "promiscuous sex relations." Code drafters were guided by a number of assumptions that later research would dispute, including that rapists were rarely repeat offenders, that most heinous rapes were committed by strangers, that women often did not know whether or not they wanted to have sex, and that women frequently misremembered their consent as coercion when the encounter led to unwanted pregnancy or other unpleasant consequence. Unlike robbery, assault, and fraud, rape required corroboration beyond the victim's word because, as code drafter Morris Ploscowe explained later, "Ladies lie."[5]

The 1970s brought more calls for law and order from Richard Nixon along with an emergent feminist antirape movement and a wave of rape reform legislation, all of which required the ACLU to reconsider the civil liberties involved in rape cases. As with abortion and sodomy, affiliates addressed the issue first, in response to a flurry of legislative proposals for rape law reform at the state level. In 1974, the Michigan legislature set the standard for what would be known as rape shield laws when it limited the admissibility of the victim's sexual history as evidence. When California legislators considered a rape shield bill, the ACLU of Northern California requested a study of the issue by prominent constitutional law scholars Anthony Amsterdam and Barbara Babcock.[6]

Personal experiences and commitments shaped Amsterdam and Babcock's joint memo for the Northern California affiliate. Amsterdam, a former prosecutor, became dedicated to abolishing the death penalty after he led an NAACP study in the 1960s that documented extreme racial bias in sentencing, especially in rape cases involving black defendants and white complainants. With regard to rape, "It was all about race initially," he recalled. Babcock, former head of the Public Defender's Office in Washington, D.C., brought the perspective of a defense attorney who represented a primarily black clientele. Introduced to the civil rights movement through her close friend and Yale Law School roommate, Eleanor Holmes Norton, Babcock was also attuned to sex discrimination, having endured countless incidents of it as one of a handful of women admitted to the 1960 class and the first woman hired at Stanford University Law School in 1969.

The memo she and Amsterdam wrote represented "a conscious effort to compromise between women's rights and the rights of criminal defendants," and as such, it "suited almost no one," Babcock remembered. But even as it inspired controversy inside and outside of the ACLU, the memo set the terms of debate.[7]

"The women's movement has brought to the attention of the nation," it began, "the fact that laws against rape are administered in ways which discriminate against women," subjecting them to "unnecessary indignities and invasions of privacy." Police officers and medical professionals treat complainants with suspicion, assuming that women lie about being raped, desire it, or deserve it, the memo declared. In public courtrooms, prosecutors subject complainants to wide-ranging questions about their sexual histories and juries receive unique instructions to treat the complainant's testimony with suspicion because rape charges are easy to make and difficult to refute. In addition, juries are instructed to consider a complainant's "unchaste" behavior as evidence of possible consent. Thus, Amsterdam and Babcock maintained, the treatment of complainants in rape cases raises civil liberties concerns regarding equal protection of the laws, the right to privacy, and "the right to claim protection of law without harassing and humiliating consequences." Their goal, they insisted, was not to increase convictions, but they nonetheless recommended that the ACLU oppose a number of prosecutorial strategies that made rape convictions more difficult to obtain. "Evidence of 'unchaste character' should not be admitted for any purpose," they insisted, and any evidence related to the complainant's sexual behavior or values should be shielded from open court until the judge deemed it relevant and thus admissible using appropriate standards. "There *are* situations in which the sexual history of the complainant is relevant to the issues in a rape prosecution," they argued, pointing to *Giles v. Maryland* (1967) as a prime example.[8]

Giles was a touchstone for the ACLU; like *Scottsboro* thirty years earlier, it involved black male defendants charged with rape by a white woman. In 1961, twenty-six-year-old Joseph Johnson joined brothers James and John Giles, nineteen and twenty-one respectively, on a fishing trip where they encountered the complainant. No one disputed the claim of sixteen-year-old Joyce Roberts that John Giles attempted and that Joseph Johnson and James Giles succeeded in having intercourse with her. What remained unclear was whether Roberts consented. The all-white jury for the Giles brothers and nearly-all-white jury for Johnson declared the men guilty and all three were sentenced to death, a penalty rarely if ever imposed on white men convicted only of rape. While all three men appealed, a defense committee convened on their behalf; their sentences were commuted to life in prison, and in 1967 the U.S. Supreme Court heard the case. According to the court's majority, the men's right to due process had been violated because the prosecutor suppressed evidence related to Roberts's sexual history. Apparently, five weeks after the alleged rape but before the trial, Roberts "had sexual relations with two men at a party," claimed that they too had raped her, and attempted suicide. Five jurors from the Giles' trial signed affidavits stating that, had this evidence been available, they would have found the men not guilty. The Supreme Court also considered the suppressed evidence relevant and instructed the Maryland Court of Appeals to reconsider the case in light of it. When Roberts, who had relocated to Florida, refused to return for a new trial, the state dropped the case and released the men.[9]

In the heyday of civil rights activism and with the memory of *Scottsboro* still fresh, *Giles* ignited fury against a racist justice system. To many observers, the men had been convicted of rape and sentenced to death because they were black, the complainant was white, and her sexual history had been concealed. Equally important, the men were freed only because the woman's sexual history, when it came to light, indicated to some that she had probably consented. Susan Brownmiller, who reported on the case for *Esquire*, also sympathized with the men. "No one will ever know with certainty exactly what happened that night," Brownmiller admitted, before going on to identify the complainant by name and report the story as one of three feckless black men who innocently accepted a promiscuous young white woman's invitation to sexual intercourse.[10] To Brownmiller, Amsterdam, Babcock, and many ACLU leaders, the lesson was clear: if a rape complainant's sexual history might persuade a jury to reach a verdict of not guilty, it must be admitted as evidence to protect the due process rights of defendants.

Race continued to loom large in ACLU discussions of rape laws in the 1970s. One member, "having grown up in the South where rape charges were often brought against blacks," argued against rape shield laws, because they would make it more difficult for black men to obtain justice in the courts. References to the *Giles* case were frequent. Indeed, the case served as shorthand for the relevance of the complainant's sexual history to determining consent. Even representatives of the ACLU Women's Rights Project (WRP), who urged the ACLU to support rape shield laws, treated *Giles* as a case of innocent defendants and a lying complainant whose actual consent was proven by the fact "that she had had intercourse with strangers on many other occasions."[11] "Most rape cases are not *Giles* cases," one ACLU leader objected, yet no one raised the possibility that Roberts's sexual history did not necessarily indicate that she had consented to sexual intercourse with Johnson and the Giles brothers.[12] Thus, ACLU leaders, deeply familiar with the nation's record of racist adjudication in rape cases, considered the men's release an unequivocal victory for justice.

The long shadow cast by *Giles* shaped the ACLU's approach to the issue of rape, as did the organization's strong tradition of supporting defendants' rights.

"Our purpose is not to increase convictions and the likelihood of prison terms for rapists," many ACLU board discussions of rape began. Some members insisted that even considering a policy that might ease convictions and incarcerations in rape cases placed the ACLU in a "prosecutorial" role. Many believed that if rape law were to be reformed at all, it should make convictions more, not less, difficult to obtain.[13]

By contrast, the feminist antirape movement that emerged in the early 1970s aimed to increase convictions. For women who had cut their activist teeth in the civil rights movement, this perspective on rape did not come easily. Before 1970, for example, Susan Brownmiller, who would become the most prominent voice in the feminist antirape movement, treated rape accusations as tools of racial oppression, and her research on *Giles* seemed only to confirm this. But after a member of her feminist consciousness-raising group described being gang-raped fifteen years earlier, Brownmiller began to think about rape differently. Her group joined others to sponsor a speak-out on rape in which thirty women narrated their experiences at the hands of rapists, the police, doctors, attorneys, judges, boyfriends, and parents. Harrowing in their unique details, the stories were just as terrifying in their similarities. Rape was clearly a "crime of power that crossed all lines of age, race, and class," they realized. Most importantly, it was a crime that men committed against women.[14]

The Conference on Rape held three months later brought the power of scholarship to a movement emerging out of personal experience. It also provided the seedbed for a number of feminist classics, including Brownmiller's *Against Our Will* (1976), an instant bestseller that profoundly influenced rape reform efforts. Many feminists applauded Brownmiller's effort to prevent concerns about race from hijacking the rape law reform movement. But some liberal critics accused Brownmiller of racism, charged her with setting back "the cause of civil rights and civil liberties," and branded her an ally of "law and order" conservatives.[15] These criticisms foreshadowed the protracted arguments over feminist rape reform that would surface in ACLU debates.

Shortly after *Against Our Will* appeared, feminists in the ACLU demanded a policy on rape, although they had yet to resolve a number of issues among themselves. Many of their disagreements revolved around whether rape should be treated the same as or differently from other criminal assaults. Those who insisted that rape should be regarded as just another assault aimed to demystify rape. Faith Seidenberg, ACLU board member and legal counsel for the National Organization for Women (NOW), argued that current law mythologized rape, treating "a woman's vagina as her most vital asset" and rape as if it detracted from a woman's worth. To counter this, Seidenberg argued for treating rape as a subclass of assault, calling it "sexual assault" rather than "rape," using the rules of

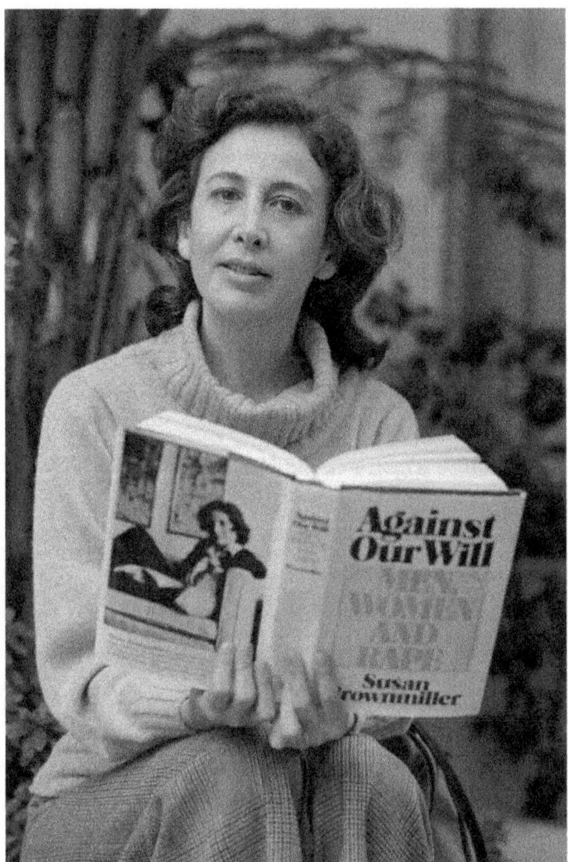

Figure 7.1 Susan Brownmiller with a copy of her best-selling book *Against Our Will: Men, Women, and Rape,* November 23, 1973. (Courtesy, ©Bettmann/Corbis/AP Images)

evidence and penalty structure applied in assault cases, and abandoning all efforts to "shield" the complainant from any particular line of questioning.

In stark contrast, the ACLU Women's Rights Project argued that rape law—and the ACLU's rape policy—should take into account "the real situation" of sexual inequality. A neutral rape law would not make public officials and the wider society treat rape like any other assault and rape victims like any other victims. Nor would it render the experience of rape the same as assault. Seidenberg's strategy would accomplish nothing but reduced penalties for convicted rapists, they argued. Rape should be treated differently from simple assault because it *was* different. It involved the most intimate and private parts of a woman's body, exposed victims to possible venereal disease and pregnancy, and, whatever anyone might say, left victims traumatized and stigmatized. Given the current tendency to question the complainant's veracity and assume that she got what she asked for, the WRP argued that the burden of proof should be shifted to require the defendant to prove consent rather than forcing the complainant to prove nonconsent.[16]

Rape shield laws proved controversial among ACLU feminists, because they limited the defense attorney's ability to probe a complainant's sexual history. Some insisted that a complainant's past behavior could not indicate consent in a particular situation any more than the conduct of a wrestler suggested a desire to be beaten up or the generosity of a benefactor signaled a willingness to be robbed. A few feminists threatened to quit the ACLU over the issue. Most, however, conceded that rape was different from other forms of assault in ways that might render a complainant's sexual history—particularly her past relationship with the defendant—relevant to determining consent. Many supported a compromise policy that would require *in camera*—literally, in chambers—hearings before the judge to determine the relevance of a complainant's sexual history before it could be admitted as evidence in court. Others, however, argued that such a closed-door procedure would change nothing; it would be administered by the same male judges who had long allowed defense attorneys free range to expose the sexual histories of complainants. Some judges "believe that a woman who has intercourse with anyone," they pointed out, is willing to have "intercourse with everyone."[17] Thus, even those who recommended that rape be classified as simply another type of sexual assault recognized that it differed from other criminal assaults because it involved activity to which one might legitimately consent.

Feminist concerns were not paramount for all women in the ACLU. Board member Jeannette Hopkins warned that white women had historically claimed the role of rape victim to gain power over black men and secure the approval and protection of white men. Because "a disproportionately large percentage of the defendants in rape prosecutions are black men," she declared, the ACLU must protect rape defendants' rights as part of its effort to achieve racial equality. Board member Hanna B. Weston argued simply that "solutions [for women's problems] must be found within civil libertarian guidelines." That argument would gain an enthusiastic following among ACLU leaders who worked to persuade feminists that women's rights depended on a particular understanding of rights to due process even as they formulated a rape policy that diverged sharply from the recommendations of their own Women's Rights Project.[18]

Rape shield laws did not undermine the defendant's right to due process, the WRP argued; they laid the groundwork for a fair trial. A fair trial "does not include the 'right' to introduce irrelevant and inflammatory evidence," a right enjoyed by criminal defendants only in rape trials. A fair trial would honor the defendant's civil liberties while respecting the complainant's right to privacy and to an unbiased procedure. A fair trial served the interests not just of the defendant and the complainant but of the broader public represented by the prosecution. As WRP staff attorney Jill Laurie Goodman explained, "when a legal system places undue burdens on the prosecution of a certain crime, as it traditionally has with rape," it is not just the complainant but "the public that loses."[19]

The WRP proposed a strong rape shield law that treated the complainant's sexual history as irrelevant except when it involved the defendant. The proposal received little attention within the ACLU and outright ridicule from board member Lawrence Herman in the ACLU newsletter, *The Civil Liberties Review*. According to Herman, rape shield laws provoked a "conflict between sexual privacy and fair trial." Because "the difference between intercourse and rape is consent," he argued, a court must determine the likelihood that the complainant consented, something on which only a complainant's sexual history could shed light. Herman insisted on a policy that would admit a complainant's entire sexual history as evidence if it "tends, even slightly, to increase or decrease the probability that a certain event occurred." If, for example, a woman who charged rape had previously consented to sexual intercourse with a stranger, a building employee, a casual acquaintance, or a group of men, a jury should be able to consider that when determining whether or not she consented to the same activity with a *particular* stranger, maintenance man, casual acquaintance, or group of men. A woman who had in the past consented to sexual activity under particular circumstances and with particular types of individuals could, he argued, be assumed more likely to engage in similar behavior in the future. Furthermore, the defendant's intent, not the complainant's experience, should determine whether or not a rape took place, according to Herman. The law should not treat a person who "mistakenly, albeit stupidly" believes that a woman consents to sexual intercourse when in fact she does not, the same as a person who knows that a woman does not consent but proceeds to have sexual intercourse with her anyway. Rape trials must focus on the defendant's perspective and complainant's sexual past, he argued, or the law must treat "all nonmarital intercourse [as] criminal."[20]

Herman's article angered many readers. One man declared a complainant's sexual history irrelevant to the crime of rape in part because rape was not about sex but about power. The involvement of genitalia is tangential to the perpetrator's goal of humiliating and subjugating the victim, he argued. ACLU member Dan Koestner characterized Herman's examples as permeated by "sexism" and accused him of seeking to punish women who exercise sexual freedom by preventing the law from protecting them from coercion. To Koestner, Herman's message seemed clear: sexual freedom was anything but free. It came at the cost of women's presumed consent and men's unpunished coercion. Two of Herman's colleagues at the Ohio State University College of Law also weighed in. The proper standard for the relevance of evidence is not whether it might possibly persuade a prejudiced jury that the complainant consented, they argued, but whether the persuasiveness of the evidence is legitimate and fair. "Stereotypical views" of women's sexuality make some men and some jurors think that a sexually experienced woman cannot be raped, they pointed out. "Unless women who engage in consensual sexual acts may be reasonably judged to consent to all such acts, there is no logical nexus between the evidence [of a woman's sexual past] and the inference" that she must have consented in the case at hand.[21]

These arguments also emerged in ACLU efforts to develop a rape policy. Leaders tended to follow Herman's lead by treating rape shield laws as the makings of a "classic civil liberties dilemma" rather than as tools for ensuring a fair trial. For them, the dilemma involved the "competing principles" of "due process for defendants and the right of privacy for women." The most vociferous opponents of rape shield laws argued that such laws undermined presumptions of innocence. "A civilized society," one man argued, "presumes that the crime did not take place." Challengers countered that this approach unfairly placed the complaining witness and her entire sexual history on trial. The ACLU should defend "the impartiality of the criminal process" with "due process for *all*, including rape victims and other plaintiffs," they argued. Opponents of rape shield laws decried the possibility that legal reform could divest an innocent defendant of "*real*, physical freedom" merely to alleviate a complainant's embarrassment and protect her "psychological state." Only by sharing the complainant's sexual history could a defendant explain why he believed that she consented, they insisted. A defendant's "reasonable" belief that the complainant consented often proved exculpatory, even absent her actual consent, so the point was a critical one.[22]

Fears that feminists might capture the debate infused many ACLU discussions. Several members tried to redirect the debate away from terms set by feminists, insisting that rape was "not a women's issue" because men could be raped too. Many opponents of rape shield laws blamed feminists for turning the ACLU from its traditional commitment to principle toward a new zeal for ideology. "God and the Women's Rights Project alone know," one wrote, "what *civil liberties* interest... is served by limiting admissibility of evidence in rape trials." Some accused feminists of forming an unholy alliance with "law-and-order advocates." Another argued that "sexist judges" may be a problem, but not a greater one than "prosecution-minded judges." Several insisted that women made false rape accusations because they "fantasize sexual assaults." White women were especially untrustworthy, because they charged black men with rape after enjoying consensual sexual relations with them simply to escape the condemnation of racist friends and family members.[23]

While the national ACLU debated its way toward a compromise policy, affiliates staked out a wide variety of positions on the matter. The ACLU of

Maryland opposed all bills that would limit the evidence allowed in rape trials. As director John Roemer III explained, while the affiliate supported "privacy and the rights of women," it could not allow those to compromise a defendant's rights. "How else can he show consent," Roemer asked, "except by attempting to demonstrate that the woman has consented to others in similar situations? The notorious Giles case," he pointed out, "turned precisely on evidence that the 'victim' had intercourse with strangers on many occasions." The Minnesota Civil Liberties Union also took an uncompromising stance against rape shield laws, maintaining that defendants must be allowed to show how the complainant's pattern of behavior indicated the likelihood of consent on the occasion in question. The Texas Civil Liberties Union and the Arizona, Northern and Southern California, Iowa, Ohio, Hawaii, Wisconsin, New Mexico, and National Capital Area affiliates took a more ambivalent approach that would allow *in camera* hearings to determine relevance and admissibility of evidence about the complainant's sexual past. By contrast, ACLU affiliates in Kansas, New Jersey, Oregon, and, for a time, New York endorsed rape shield laws that restricted jury consideration of the complainant's sexual history to relations only with the defendant and only if deemed relevant by a judge in an *in camera* proceeding.[24]

Many individual ACLU members pursued rape law reform outside of the organization. Marge Gates of the National Capital Area affiliate developed a handbook to guide police, prosecutors, medical agencies, and community organizations in treating rape victims with greater fairness and sympathy. Joan Glantz, director of the Houston affiliate, formed a coalition with local women's groups to teach public officials how to treat rape victims with sensitivity. Leaders of the Southern California affiliate's Women's Rights Project took to the streets to protest the California Court of Appeals' characterization of a rape victim as having asked for it. In this case, individual ACLU activists' efforts brought about a revision of the California court's opinion and inspired the passage of laws that mandated special rape training for police and nurses, public funding for rape kits to gather and preserve evidence, and limitations on the admissibility of evidence regarding a complainant's sexual history.[25]

By 1976, when the ACLU adopted its first rape policy, many states had already passed rape shield laws that limited inquiry into a complainant's sexual history. The ACLU's belated policy called attention to the conflict between the defendant's right to a fair trial and the complainant's right to privacy. Hewing closely to the line drawn by Herman and other opponents of rape shield laws, the policy deemed no aspect of a complainant's sexual history off limits but suggested that closed hearings—"administered fairly and free from sexist assumptions"—be used to determine the relevance of such evidence. The policy included another nod to the concerns of at least some feminists by suggesting that rape be treated as "but one form of sexual assault." The rape policy passed easily, but many

ACLU feminists considered it wholly inadequate. Following in the footsteps of Harriet Pilpel with regard to consensual sex and Marilyn Haft regarding sexual privacy, they took their concerns to the ACLU's Biennial meeting, and obtained a resolution demanding that the ACLU reconsider its definition of rape and policies on consent, spousal rights, sentencing, and the treatment of rape victims by public officials and the press.[26]

National ACLU leaders addressed the issue of marital rape for the first time in response to that Biennial resolution. State statutes and common law had long treated marriage as a "sexual contract," establishing a notion of marital unity that, under the legal doctrine of *coverture,* denied a woman's individual rights. Lawmakers and reformers who dismantled many aspects of *coverture* in the nineteenth century left intact the notion of conjugal rights or the assumption of a spouse's consent to sexual relations. In the 1950s and 1960s, the American Law Institute recommended no change to this aspect of the law and even reaffirmed that "coercion of a wife to submit to conjugal embrace is not rape."[27]

As late as 1973, the chair of the ACLU's Washington, D.C., affiliate declared that "it would be bad as a civil liberties matter to extend the jurisdiction of the courts to the privacy of the marital bed." When ACLU leaders debated the issue between 1976 and 1977, none of the fifty states recognized marital rape as a concept, let alone a crime. Women's Rights Project codirector Brenda Feigen Fasteau exhorted the ACLU to call for laws that would criminalize marital rape. Another colleague joined her, insisting that marriage does not imply consent "to every kind of sexual activity on every occasion." Individuals should be able to marry, she claimed, without sacrificing the right to "bodily self-determination." Otherwise, only the sodomy laws currently under attack by the ACLU and gay rights groups could protect a married woman from being "forced to submit to anal or oral intercourse."[28]

Several ACLU board members objected to criminalizing marital rape. Consistently prodefendant on the subject of rape law, Jeannette Hopkins argued that proof would be impossible to obtain unless a wife's claim against her husband were deemed sufficient. Michael Meyers, board member and assistant director of the NAACP, wondered if the marital state might imply consent. What about a "harmonious marriage in which the husband forced the wife to have sex on an evening when she is reluctant to participate," he asked. "Is that rape?" One member thought not; the marriage contract implies consent, which is why "withholding sex is considered grounds for divorce," he explained. Hopkins agreed, asserting that "aggression is sometimes in the nature of the sex act between married persons."[29]

Board members in favor of criminalizing marital rape stood their ground. Marc Fasteau, attorney and husband of Brenda Feigen Fasteau, argued that every sexual encounter, whether in or out of marriage, should require explicit consent from each participant. Jewel Bellush, a political science professor at Hunter College, agreed, declaring marital status irrelevant in rape cases. In reply to several members who claimed that past consent implies future consent, attorney Judith Bregman countered with an anecdote. She might frequently loan a friend money, but if that friend takes money that has been denied her, "that is theft." "The 'NO' on the particular occasion invalidates all the prior history." A majority agreed. The low likelihood that racial discrimination would play a role in a marital rape case eased the board's decision and, in 1977, it voted to eliminate the marital exemption for rape even as it noted that consent might be inferred "when the complainant and defendant are married."[30]

Addressing issues related to media coverage of rape proved even more difficult, because for many, it raised First Amendment concerns. The question of whether newspapers should reveal the names of rape victims had come to ACLU leaders' attention years earlier in the context of encouraging victims to report crimes, but not until the 1970s did feminists raise the matter as one of women's rights. By then, many, if not most, media outlets already followed a policy of withholding the names of rape complainants in response to entreaties by law-and-order advocates and changing professional standards. Several states, including Georgia and Florida, made it a misdemeanor to publish or broadcast the names of rape victims.[31]

When Georgia's law against publishing the names of complainants in rape cases came under fire in the early 1970s, ACLU leaders considered their position on what appeared to them another civil liberties dilemma, one that pitted "the First Amendment rights of the news media" against "the privacy rights of a rape victim." At immediate issue was the Supreme Court case *Cox Broadcasting v. Cohn,* in which the father of a young girl who was raped and murdered sued an Atlanta television station for broadcasting his daughter's name. In 1974, legal director Melvin Wulf and executive director Aryeh Neier took opposite sides on the matter. If the press can be prohibited from publishing a rape victim's name, Wulf argued, surely it could be prevented from publishing classified information like that found in the Pentagon Papers. Neier, on the other hand, claimed that when civil liberties come into conflict, the ACLU should seek to balance them, not just allow the First Amendment to trump all. "The First Amendment interest in knowing the names of rape victims seems miniscule to the point of non-existence," he insisted, while "the privacy interest seems very large." In the end, the ACLU declined to participate in *Cox Broadcasting v. Cohn* (1975) because leaders could not agree on which side to support. The Supreme Court decided in favor of the broadcasters and declared Georgia's law unconstitutional.[32]

ACLU leaders reconsidered media coverage and sentencing guidelines against the larger question of whether rape should be treated differently from other violent crimes. Some continued to urge the ACLU to treat rape as unique and caution the press against naming rape victims in order to protect their privacy. But those who argued that rape should be treated as a gender-neutral crime with regard to press coverage and sentencing won. The resulting policy statement noted that rape had achieved "a near-mystical status" as a uniquely heinous crime but recommended that it be reduced to the level of other aggravated assaults by imposing similar penalties and using the language of "sexual assault."[33]

In 1976, the ACLU presented its position to Congress as one of only five groups to testify on whether the Federal Rules of Evidence should be revised "to provide for the privacy of rape victims." Elizabeth Holtzman (D-N.Y.), an ACLU member who introduced the federal rape shield law in question, had survived her own "close call[s]" with would-be rapists and became enraged after reading, in Brownmiller's *Against Our Will,* about the criminal justice system's treatment of victims. Holtzman's bill rendered most but not all evidence of a complainant's sexual history inadmissible in court, and some feminists considered it too weak, but the ACLU opposed it as a violation of defendants' rights. Testifying on behalf of the ACLU was Dovey Roundtree, a prominent African American criminal lawyer with decades of experience representing men charged with rape and murder. Her own grandmother had, at the age of thirteen, escaped being raped but at great physical cost when her father's white employer retaliated by stomping on and crushing her feet, leaving her with lifelong pain, deformity, and an awkward gait. Roundtree's experiences and identities combined many of the elements that the ACLU tried to balance in the long wake of *Scottsboro* and *Giles.*[34]

Tensions between race and gender discrimination roiled beneath the surface of congressional hearings on Holtzman's rape shield bill. Most witnesses endorsed the bill, including representatives for NOW and the American Bar Association, leaving the ACLU practically alone in opposing it. Roundtree opened with the ACLU's standard claim that rape shield legislation raised conflicts between the complainant's right to privacy and the defendant's right to due process. Holtzman's bill "does not adequately ensure the defendant's right to a fair trial," Roundtree argued. It would, for example, have barred the evidence that led to the freeing of the Giles brothers. Holtzman, herself an ACLU member, probed for inconsistencies. The ACLU considered a *defendant's* criminal record inadmissible in court, she pointed out, but it supported admitting a *complainant's* sexual history. "If a defendant's prior conviction for rape should not be introduced as evidence in a rape trial," she asked, "how do you argue that a woman's prior sexual history ought to be spread all over the record?" Roundtree emphasized the high stakes for defendants in rape trials. A conviction for rape could lead to a life sentence or even execution, she pointed out, hinting at the severe penalties often imposed on black men convicted of rape. As a result, "every possible safeguard for the defendant must be given." Holtzman countered that the ACLU opposed allowing a defendant's criminal record into a rape trial precisely because of the information's "prejudicial effect" on a jury. "I would hope," she closed, "that the A.C.L.U. would be as aware of the prejudicial effect on the jury of discussion of a woman's past history and as sensitive to a woman's constitutional rights to privacy."[35]

The Privacy Protection for Rape Victims Act passed in 1978. Holtzman was pleased, though the act permitted greater use of a complainant's sexual history than her original bill would have allowed. For example, it included a "catch-basin" provision that allowed into court evidence of a complainant's past sexual behavior if a judge thought it might convince a jury that the complainant actually consented or that the defendant had reason to believe so. Once again, a rape shield law, this time a federal one, prioritized the defendant's rights and intentions over the victim's experience and perspective. Some people argued that a federal rape shield law was of little importance anyway given that only 42 of the 55,000 rapes committed between 1974 and 1976 were federal offenses. But the law also served as a model for a number of state rape shield laws as well as for the U.S. military.[36]

A majority of states and even the federal government passed rape shield laws of some sort, but many feminists considered them cosmetic measures at best. Most were quite weak and none held a complainant's prior relationship with the defendant inadmissible—a notable omission given that most rapes occurred on dates or between acquaintances. Prosecutors continued to find ways to bring the complainant's sexual history with third parties into rape trials, and judges permitted it. Although most states passed laws against marital rape, they still recognized marriage as implicit consent to sexual intercourse. Moreover, most reform laws recast rape as sexual assault, removing gender from the legislative language and thereby lowering the standards by which the constitutionality of the statutes would be judged. Because the law applied equally to women and men—despite the fact that nearly all rapists were male and nearly all victims female—the reform laws were assessed only according to a "rational basis" test rather than the "heightened scrutiny" that laws couched in gender-specific language required. Other critics pointed out that to the extent that rape reform focused on protecting the privacy of the victim—rather than achieving a truly fair trial by omitting irrelevant evidence—it upheld the idea that legal protection from sexual assault required women's sexual modesty. By focusing on sexual privacy, in other words, rape shield laws rested on assumptions that public attention to a woman's sexual history degraded her and that a woman whose sexual behavior had already received public notice deserved less sexual privacy in court.[37]

In the end, the legal system continued to privilege defendants with constitutional rights denied to complainants in rape cases. These rights included access to a defense attorney who served as an advocate—as opposed to the prosecutor who represented not the complainant but the state; the right to appeal—a right denied the complainant by prohibitions against double jeopardy; and the right to suppress evidence of past criminal behavior—a right denied complainants, who were required to reveal even noncriminal sexual behavior.[38] Thus, many of the civil libertarian limits that the ACLU advocated remained in effect despite the flurry of rape shield laws that might have shifted the balance of power toward the complainant. As with consumer rights and privacy, a civil liberties approach to rape privileged access to sexual expression—in this case, physical expression—over protection from it.

If rape occupied the extreme end on a continuum of sexual violence, sexual harassment followed close behind, and it too commanded the attention of ACLU leaders in the 1970s. Indeed, the ACLU Women's Rights Project helped to launch Karen Sauvigne, a key figure responsible for naming sexual harassment and launching the movement against it. Sauvigne's work with the WRP in 1972 helped her network with other women's rights activists, including Eleanor Holmes Norton, and provided her with a legal and civil rights framework for conceptualizing sexual harassment. The ACLU also provided temporary office space and equipment for Sauvigne's brainchild, Working Women United Institute (WWUI), one of the first organizations to focus on fighting sexual harassment in the workplace. The movement against sexual harassment caught fire, ignited by the resurgence of women's rights activism generally and fueled by feminist efforts against rape, domestic violence, and pornography. Within a few years, the movement won its first major court victory, *Williams v. Saxbe* (1976); *Ms.* magazine ran a cover feature entitled "Sexual Harassment on the Job and

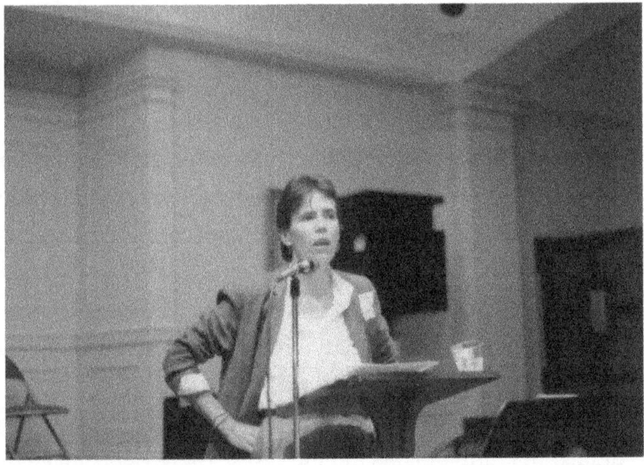

Figure 7.2 Karen Sauvigne speaking on sexual harassment, circa 1982. (Courtesy, Karen Sauvigne)

How to Stop It" (1977); and journalist Lin Farley and law professor Catharine MacKinnon published pathbreaking books on the subject.[39]

Black women's support was key to the success of the movement against sexual harassment. Unlike the antirape movement, which raised the specter of *Scottsboro*, *Giles*, and the victimization of black men, the movement against sexual harassment evoked memories of the unwanted sexual attention black women suffered under slavery and since. It attracted the support of black women's groups—including the National Council of Negro Women and the Black Women's Organizing Collective—and prominent individuals like Eleanor Holmes Norton, who, as head of the Equal Employment Opportunity Commission (EEOC), declared sexual harassment a violation of Title VII of the Civil Rights Act and drafted influential policy on the matter. Equally important, individual black working women filed and won the first major sexual harassment cases. The ACLU's growing support for women's rights and ongoing commitment to workplace equality and racial justice demanded that it take the issue seriously. That the movement against sexual harassment spoke to the needs and concerns of black women and emerged unburdened by a legacy of racist violence directed against black men, helped it gain faster traction with ACLU leaders than rape law reform had.[40]

The ACLU began to consider its own policy on sexual harassment in 1981, shortly after the EEOC chaired by Eleanor Holmes Norton released its guidelines. In contrast to discussions of rape in which the ACLU board virtually ignored the recommendations of its own Women's Rights Project, with regard to sexual harassment the new director of the WRP, Isabelle Katz Pinzler, led the conversation. Her hand was strengthened by the fact that prohibiting sexual harassment did not raise the specter of racism or involve criminal law. In addition, as long as the ACLU focused on quid pro quo harassment, in which an employer required sexual favors of an employee, laws and policies against it did not seem to threaten civil liberties. That changed when the discussion turned to hostile environment sexual harassment, which usually involved speech.[41]

Pinzler and other proponents of laws and policies against hostile environment sexual harassment confronted the ACLU's First Amendment—an expansive provision that protected not only consumer rights and commercial speech but also sexual expression thrust at unwilling and captive audiences. When some ACLU board members demanded that "pure speech" be excluded from the ACLU's sexual harassment policy, Pinzler resisted. She pointed out that ACLU policy allowed a number of infringements on so-called pure speech, including statutes that prohibited employers from circulating intimidating or antiunion statements and bans on "purely verbal racial harassment in the workplace." Pinzler explained that "abusive language of a sexual nature, written epithets and pictures" are used to discourage women from entering male-dominated occupations by creating a "hostile and intimidating atmosphere." She agreed, however, that the ACLU should protect some types of speech banned under EEOC guidelines. Words like "fuck" and "screw" no longer refer only to sex acts and should therefore be permitted, Pinzler admitted, even though they might offend particular individuals. The long process of formulating policy on a new civil liberties issue had begun.[42]

Between 1981 and 1984, while ACLU committees worked to develop a policy on sexual harassment, the cultural and political landscape changed dramatically. The "Reagan Revolution" ushered in a conservative, overtly antifeminist administration that actually copied feminists by politicizing cultural issues related to gender roles, sexuality, and reproduction, though it did so to very different ends. The Equal Rights Amendment supported by the ACLU since 1970 and passed by Congress in 1972 expired in 1982 when it failed to obtain support from the necessary thirty-eight states. The feminist and civil libertarian issues that gained political traction in this climate were often those that attracted moral conservatives by emphasizing gender differences through protective attitudes toward women and repressive approaches to sexuality.[43]

Feminist activism against pornography dated back to the 1960s, but it took a new form in the 1980s as activists relied more heavily on legal solutions approved by antifeminists on the right. By 1983, feminist antipornography activists developed municipal ordinances designed to create a civil rights remedy for victims of pornography. Because this legislation challenged the sexual expression associated with liberalism, it too stood to attract support from the New Right. The antipornography ordinance developed by feminist law professor Catharine MacKinnon and activist Andrea Dworkin, for example, obtained the endorsement of local decency groups and conservative politicians as well as feminists and liberals. But it also provoked a wave of opposition from other feminists who assembled the Feminist Anti-Censorship Taskforce (FACT), a group that included ACLU staff attorney Nan Hunter. FACT members objected to the antipornography ordinance as a form of censorship but also decried its association with antifeminist conservatives.[44]

"The feminist porn wars," as they became known, did not just provide a backdrop to ACLU discussions of sexual harassment policy; they shaped the debate when Karen Sauvigne made a presentation to the ACLU's Equality Committee in 1983. Sauvigne considered herself "on the free speech side" of the feminist pornography debate, and she tried to distance the movement against sexual harassment from the one against pornography, a tricky maneuver given the overlapping concerns and the prominence of high-profile feminist Catharine MacKinnon in each. Sauvigne defined sexual harassment broadly as "unwanted attention of a sexual nature in the context of work relationships which make the recipient uncomfortable or deny her opportunity." In contrast to rape law, which focused on the intent and perceptions of the defendant, Sauvigne insisted that sexual harassment be determined by its effect on the complainant. "Men will say it was 'not intended to be harassing,'" she acknowledged, "due to a socialized difference in their orientation to sex and sexuality." But to achieve equality, the law must take into account the different ways that women and men experience the workplace. A friendly exchange indicated that Sauvigne's position was being favorably received until law professor William Forbath objected to the possibility that sexual harassment policy would infringe on the First Amendment. People interpret sexual messages differently, he argued. A woman joined in, to ask if "the office prude" should set the standards for the workplace. Another wondered whether Sauvigne's goal was an androgynous workplace, and committee member Elaine Spitz argued that some professional women "would be offended if their sexuality were not recognized."[45]

"Calendar pinups" in the workplace soon dominated the discussion. Committee member Carolyn Simpson argued that pinups were as threatening to women as photos of lynchings were to black men. Spitz asked Simpson if she thought car mechanics should be forced to take down their pinups, and when Simpson said yes, Forbath charged her with class bias for assuming that blue-collar men used pinups to intimidate women. Pinups alone, in the absence of "other harassing behavior," should not be considered a form of sexual harassment, Forbath and Spitz maintained. But Vicki Been, a recent law school graduate and ACLU staff member, suggested that, whatever the intent of the men who posted them, pinups could create an intolerable environment, especially for a lone woman in a male-dominated workplace. Spitz countered that treating pinups at work as sexual harassment would put the ACLU on the wrong side of "the pornography issue." But others insisted that sexual imagery should be prohibited at work where employees represented a captive audience. Widespread agreement that antipornography ordinances violated the First Amendment provided common ground among them but also increased the likelihood that banning pornography from the workplace would be labeled censorship rather than good sexual harassment policy.[46]

ACLU discussions about standards for actionable harassment also took place in the shadow of the 1977 Nazi march defended by the ACLU in Skokie, Illinois. What is the difference, associate director Alan Reitman asked, between the "psychic distress" caused by sexual harassment and the "emotional harm" inflicted by the Nazi march in Skokie? Should a complainant have to prove that the harassment was "unreasonable," caused psychological pain, or interfered "substantially" or "significantly" with her productivity? Several members questioned the comparison, pointing out that, whereas Skokie residents could steer clear of the Nazi event, employees cannot avoid the workplace.[47] Nevertheless, along with concerns about the First Amendment, determination to craft a policy consistent with ACLU support for the Nazi demonstrators ensured that the final proposal would contain little recognition of hostile environment sexual harassment.

Much of the debate turned on concerns that also plagued rape law—whose perspective to privilege and what to do about false claims. Was it the harasser's intent or the victim's experience that should determine sexual harassment? Several board members worried about "the rights of the harassers" and the danger that even unfounded accusations could ruin careers. Others countered with cautions against "trivializing the problem of sexual harassment" and assuming that "hysterical women" will bring baseless charges.[48]

In 1984, the ACLU finally adopted a policy that defined sexual harassment as "intentional unwanted physical contact of a sexual nature which is clearly offensive" and "intentional unwanted" requests for sexual favors accompanied by rewards or punishments—quid pro quo sexual harassment. The policy accepted limits on "sexual expression" in the workplace only when "directed at a specific employee" and resulting in "definable consequences" that "demonstrably hinders or completely prevents" the victim from functioning at work. In a clear rejection of the hostile environment concept, the ACLU policy stated explicitly that it did not apply to "verbal harassment that has no other effect on its recipient than to create an unpleasant working environment."[49] Thus, the ACLU's first policy on sexual harassment in the workplace prioritized the First Amendment and, as with rape, defined harassment according to the intentions of the perpetrator rather than the experience of the victim.

The ACLU took a similar approach to the hate speech codes that proliferated in response to an alarming wave of racist incidents at colleges and universities in the 1980s. The codes troubled ACLU leaders as much as the racism did, and some suspected that rising social and political conservatism escalated racial tensions while encouraging inclinations toward censorship. Threatening and insulting messages against African American students were slipped under dormitory room doors, scrawled on classroom blackboards, delivered verbally in face-to-face confrontations, and conveyed through racist performances and displays on campuses around the nation. That white students at some of the country's most elite institutions were responsible for many of these incidents proved even more troubling, and college administrators joined with faculty to draft hate speech codes that would allow them to punish violators and discourage recurrences. The ACLU and its affiliates negotiated the codes with university officials, sued recalcitrant schools, and collaborated with political conservatives to challenge campus policies against hate speech.[50]

Like feminist proponents of laws against sexual harassment and pornography, ACLU leaders' opposition to hate speech codes sometimes allied them with erstwhile foes on the right. One of these, Representative Henry Hyde (R-Ill.), a fierce opponent of abortion rights and most other aspects of the ACLU's civil libertarian agenda, became a comrade-in-arms against campus speech codes. Together, the "unlikely duo" of Hyde and the ACLU sponsored the ill-fated Collegiate Speech Protection Act that promised to withhold federal funding from any college or university—public or private—that imposed hate speech codes. In the political climate of the 1980s and 1990s, just as feminist movements against sexual harassment and pornography enjoyed support from social conservatives, "free-speech liberals and First Amendment absolutists" found common cause against hate speech codes with conservatives whose main objections were less to censorship than to "supercharged multicultural sensitivity."[51]

Meanwhile, the conservative political environment that buoyed movements against pornography and sexual harassment began to show its potential to undercut them as well. When Clarence Thomas replaced Eleanor Holmes Norton as chair of the Equal Employment Opportunity Commission, EEOC support for sexual harassment complainants plummeted. Indeed, in *Meritor Savings Bank v. Vinson* (1986), the first sexual harassment case to reach the U.S. Supreme Court, Thomas's EEOC filed an amicus brief on behalf of the bank, arguing that employers could not be held liable for a hostile environment created by supervisors. Thomas's position to the contrary, many political and moral conservatives continued to oppose sexual harassment for their own reasons, and the Supreme Court disagreed with the EEOC in a unanimous opinion written by the leader of the Court's conservative bloc, Chief Justice William Rehnquist. His landmark decision declared hostile environment sexual harassment actionable under Title VII of the 1964 Civil Rights Act.[52]

But the Reagan administration leveled a sharp though indirect blow at feminist activism against sexual harassment when it cut federal funds for social services and attacked *Roe v. Wade* (1972). In response, leading liberal foundations redirected their money away from organizations like Sauvigne's Working Women United Institute and the ACLU Women's Rights Project and toward agencies that fought for abortion rights and provided alternatives to the crumbling federal social safety net. Sauvigne left WWUI in 1984, the same year its sister organization in Boston—Alliance Against Sexual Coercion—closed its doors. The WWUI limped along without Sauvigne until 1987, when it, too, folded. The Women's Rights Project struggled to remain afloat. Meanwhile, prominent antifeminist Phyllis Schlafly promoted a contradictory set of ideas that appealed to many critics of sexual harassment policies: working women invited sexual harassment by dressing provocatively, lied about it to get revenge against men who rejected them, and deserved it as interlopers on men's turf. The ascendance of such conservative politics divided feminists over matters of strategy. Some warned of the difficulties of "fight[ing] sexual harassment without being antisexual" and advised that "when a right-wing antifeminist backlash is attempting to reinstitute prudish and repressive limits on sexual freedom, it is more important than ever that feminists not project antisexual attitudes."[53] Clearly, the socially and morally conservative politics of the day had contradictory and divisive effects on feminist efforts to eliminate sexual harassment and they would continue to trouble the development of ACLU policy on the matter.

When Lois Robinson, a first-class welder at an overwhelmingly male shipyard in Jacksonville, Florida, charged her employer with sexual harassment for subjecting her to "sexually explicit pornography" and "sexually suggestive and humiliating comments," some applauded her for advancing gender equality in the workplace. Others criticized her for attempting to repress freedom of speech and sexual expression. U.S. District Judge Howell Melton decided in Robinson's favor, declaring the First Amendment irrelevant because the case concerned "discriminatory conduct" that created a "hostile work environment" directed at a "captive audience." Melton ordered Jacksonville Shipyards to adopt a sexual harassment policy in consultation with the NOW Legal Defense and Education Fund that represented Robinson. He also ordered the removal of all sexually oriented pictures, including *Playboy* centerfolds, from the workplace but, consistent with EEOC guidelines, he awarded Robinson only one dollar in damages. NOW praised the opinion as "groundbreaking," but the Florida ACLU affiliate criticized it as a violation of workers' rights to free expression.[54]

Shortly after Judge Melton released his decision in *Robinson*, the ACLU elected its first female president, Nadine Strossen, professor of constitutional law at New York Law School and national board member since 1983. Strossen assumed leadership of the ACLU's eighty-three-member board in the wake of significant strides toward gender parity but also at a time of serious disagreement over how the organization should handle apparent conflicts between gender equality and civil liberties.[55] Hostile environment sexual harassment cases forced the ACLU to take sides on these issues, requiring that Strossen mediate between warring factions.

When Robinson and Jacksonville Shipyards both appealed Judge Melton's decision—the former hoping for back pay and the latter eager to escape the injunction—debates over which side to support broke out among the national ACLU and two of its strongest affiliates. Robyn Blumner, executive director of the Florida affiliate and well-known "free speech purist," was incensed to hear that a district court judge ordered an employer to "redecorat[e] an office." Her position was clear: the expression prohibited in *Robinson* did not meet the ACLU's standards for sexual harassment, because it did not target Robinson directly or

Figure 7.3 Nadine Strossen, new ACLU director, 1991. (©Faye Ellman)

deprive her of job benefits like pay, training, or promotion. "Lois Robinson was not sexually harassed," Blumner declared. Jeanne Baker, the affiliate's interim legal director, agreed, but their colleague Mary Coombs thought the Florida affiliate should support Robinson. The three tried to draft a compromise brief that would reflect Blumner and Baker's First Amendment perspective while taking into account Coombs's concerns about women's rights, but ultimately the brief still backed the shipyard against Robinson, and Coombs refused to sign it.[56]

Meanwhile, the Southern California affiliate, which tended toward "the equality side of things" when confronted with competing civil liberties principles, urged the national ACLU to support Robinson. When the national office instead joined the Florida affiliate's brief supporting the shipyard, open warfare broke out. Coombs rallied eighty lawyers and law professors around the country to sign a competing brief, among them a number of prominent ACLU leaders, including Janet Benshoof, director of the Reproductive Freedom Project (RFP); Sylvia Law, member of the RFP advisory board; Nan Hunter, former director of the Gay and Lesbian Rights Project and cofounder of FACT; Nadine Taub, former director of the Women's Rights Project; Erwin Chemerinsky, board and executive committee member of the Southern California affiliate; Susan Estrich, former national board member and former president of the Civil Liberties Union of Massachusetts; and national board members Joan Mahoney, Margaret Russell, and Mary Ellen Gale. The media loved the spectacle of ACLU v. ACLU and devoted a great deal of ink to what some termed a "tug-of-war between civil liberties and the politics of the left" and others called a conflict between "First Amendment purists" and equality advocates.[57]

Some interpreted the defections from the ACLU's official position less charitably. Baker felt "knifed in the back" and regretted that she and Blumner had compromised their First Amendment principles on the brief in an effort to placate Coombs. Blumner accused Robinson's supporters of making an "end run" around the First Amendment by separating the workplace out as uniquely unprotected by the U.S. Constitution. "Every place is a workplace to someone," she argued. Street cleaners and mail carriers work on public byways; house cleaners and plumbers work in private homes. Must pornography also be removed from these spaces? At bottom, Blumner suspected that Robinson's allies were advancing the feminist antipornography agenda through backdoor sexual harassment victories.[58]

The national ACLU's *Robinson* brief focused on the First Amendment. It did not deny hostile environment sexual harassment but suggested an extremely tough standard of review. To be actionable, the "expressive activity" in question must be clearly directed at a particular employee and have "definable consequences for the individual that demonstrably hinder or completely prevent continued functioning as an employee." The brief accused the lower court's *Robinson* ruling of inappropriately treating merely "offensive" expression as harassment and criticized it for characterizing pornography as "a visual assault." The First Amendment does not permit equating "expression, by itself, with 'assault,'" the ACLU argued. Judge Melton's order that all sexually suggestive materials must be removed from the workplace represented an unconstitutional ban on "possessing, reading, and privately displaying 'sexually suggestive' materials." Throughout, the ACLU brief treated the workplace as little different from a public thoroughfare or a private bedroom. It criticized the court for trying "to 'cleanse' the workplace" and thereby cleanse "the minds of Ms. Robinson's coworkers." Pornographic pictures of women may be "offensive," the brief acknowledged, but the First Amendment protects "expressive activity that has no other effect on its recipient than to create an unpleasant working environment."[59]

By contrast, the brief submitted on behalf of Robinson by Coombs and the eighty other lawyers, ACLU leaders among them, denied that the First Amendment governed the workplace. First Amendment principles simply do not apply to workplaces in the same way that they apply to "speech in the public forum."

Courts had established that "the workplace is not a free marketplace of ideas" by allowing employers to limit employees' workplace expression. Moreover, because of hierarchical relationships and economic necessity, job sites were unique spaces where "economic coercion limits workers' ability to escape offensive expression." In the lawyers' brief, the victim's perspective and experience determined whether the behavior in question constituted harassment. The brief supported the lower court's order with one key exception: it opposed the ban on "private possession" of pornography on company property. Employees should, the lawyers' brief suggested, be able to keep sexual materials in their backpacks and lockers in "areas that female employees ordinarily could and would avoid."[60]

Like the lawyers' brief, many feminists and social conservatives criticized the ACLU's claim that *Robinson* should be treated as a First Amendment case. Alison Wetherfield, director of NOW's legal defense fund, pointed out that "nobody is stopping anybody from reading what they like when they're on their own," but different standards must prevail "in the communal workplace." The Women's Legal Defense Fund accused the ACLU of privileging the harasser's over the victim's perspective in claiming that a "visual onslaught of naked female bodies" did not constitute sexual harassment. Another critic accused the ACLU of "sleeping with the enemy" by "siding with men who posted nude centerfolds" rather than supporting women's efforts to eliminate sex discrimination in the workplace. Morality in Media spokeswoman Patty McEntee also considered the ACLU's First Amendment arguments misplaced. "Pornography in and of itself is sexual harassment," McEntee declared.[61]

Robinson provoked a pitched battle that split the ACLU, uniting some feminists with social conservatives on one side and aligning First Amendment purists with employers on the other. Many expected the case to reach the Supreme Court, where the constitutional dimensions of sexual harassment law would be clarified. Instead, after oral arguments before a three-judge panel in the Eleventh Circuit, the two sides resolved their differences in a confidential settlement and the case ended without fanfare in 1992.[62]

The unceremonious and quiet resolution of *Robinson* might have rendered it an inconsequential footnote to the history of sexual harassment law. But *Robinson*'s importance lay in the opportunity it afforded the ACLU to introduce First Amendment concerns into the adjudication of sexual harassment. ACLU leaders considered First Amendment issues paramount when they formulated their policy on sexual harassment in 1984, but they were virtually alone in doing so. During sexual harassment law's first fifteen years of development, the fact that speech was involved did not raise First Amendment concerns for the courts. Nor, before *Jacksonville Shipyards,* did defendants claim protection under the First Amendment. As one legal scholar explained, "the presence of speech in the harassing act" was not seen as implicating the First Amendment any more than "the presence of speech in virtually every act of unlawful price-fixing, unlawful gambling, or unlawful securities fraud." But after ACLU leaders brought their long-held speech concerns to the fore in *Robinson*, many legal scholars, defense attorneys, journalists, and members of the general public began to contend that laws against hostile environment sexual harassment violated rights to free speech.[63]

As the First Amendment entered considerations of sexual harassment law, the terrain of the debate altered in unexpected ways when Anita Hill testified about her own experience of sexual harassment as an employee of conservative Supreme Court nominee Clarence Thomas. Between 1981 and 1983 Hill worked as Thomas's assistant at the Department of Education and then the EEOC. In the fall of 1991, before the Senate Judiciary Committee and a vast television audience, Hill recounted Thomas's relentless requests for dates, gratuitous comments on her appearance, and persistent and graphic talk about pornographic videos and his own sexual prowess. Intimidated and unnerved, Hill ended up hospitalized for acute stomach pain before leaving the EEOC for a job at Oral Roberts University.[64]

Riveted by the spectacle of an African American woman accusing an African American man of undignified and potentially unlawful discriminatory behavior toward a federal employee—conducted before a panel of white male senators—observers around the country argued over whose testimony was more credible and what the unfolding drama indicated about sex and race in America. A clear gap delineated in complicated ways by gender, race, and class emerged as a vocal majority of white and black professional women threw their support behind Hill, charging that men "just don't get it," while men of both races joined other black women in accusing Hill of aiding liberals and racists in an effort to derail Thomas's nomination.[65]

The First Amendment, notably absent from the hearings themselves, appeared elsewhere. Its most outspoken defender, the ACLU, made no official statement on the Thomas-Hill hearings. Before Hill's charges became public, the ACLU voted by a one-vote majority to remain neutral on Thomas's nomination and maintained that position throughout. But where the national ACLU declined to tread, others stepped boldly and employed arguments long popularized by the organization. Many wrote to local newspapers to question where one draws the line "between normal male-female banter" and "lascivious overtures." "When we draw this line," one man asked, "don't we also risk obscuring the line of freedom of speech and expression?" A *USA Today* reporter lamented that "the free speech issue" wasn't raised in the hearings but anticipated that sexual harassment law would crumble under a serious First Amendment challenge.

Jeffrey Rosen, writing for the *New Republic*, suggested that if courts considered the behavior recounted by Hill to be actionable sexual harassment, it would represent "the most serious threat to the First Amendment of the past decade." The Florida ACLU's Robyn Blumner made light of Hill's testimony even as she acknowledged that Thomas's persistent requests for dates and sexual comments—including the infamous "Who put a pubic hair on my Coke can?" and descriptions of porn star "Long Dong Silver"—might create an unpleasant work environment. "But what about freedom of speech?" she asked. "Doesn't a law which punishes offending words, indelicate language and graphic verbiage violate the First Amendment?"[66]

By raising awareness and drawing attention to sexual harassment, the Thomas-Hill hearings exercised a major if indirect impact on the ACLU. Sexual harassment complaints filed with the EEOC nearly tripled between 1990 and 1995. ACLU affiliates around the country honored Hill with various civil liberties awards that recognized her role in raising awareness about sexual harassment. In this climate, ACLU leaders anticipated that another case would soon make its way to the highest court, so they worked to resolve their differences by revisiting their 1984 policy. Some aimed to avoid a replay of the dueling briefs in *Robinson*. Others hoped to expand the ACLU's support for women subjected to hostile environment sexual harassment. Those who prioritized the right to equal employment in a nondiscriminatory workplace squared off against others who considered absolute freedom of speech paramount. Strossen insisted that neither approach need trump the other and urged the board to preserve freedom of speech and equality in the workplace. After vigorous debate and several close votes, the board modified ACLU policy to make hostile environment sexual harassment charges easier to bring by eliminating the requirement that the harassment be targeted at a specific individual—and recognizing harassment directed at a gender or group—and by reducing the standard of harm the harassment must meet. Critics of the new sexual harassment policy accused it of transforming the ACLU from a civil liberties into a civil rights organization, but fans credited it with more realistically addressing inequality and power issues so that civil liberties principles would not disadvantage the already disadvantaged.[67]

The ACLU's new sexual harassment policy pleased many feminists but provoked a great deal of opposition among other civil libertarians who watched with dismay as feminists worked to extend sexual harassment law into new arenas. Benson Wolman, national board member and former director of the Ohio affiliate, criticized the new policy for failing to protect employee speech rights. Where, he wondered, would demands for greater sexual equality end? His question was a good one. Lori Peterson, a Minnesota attorney, took aim at sexist television advertisements when she cited the "Swedish Bikini Team" beer commercials as evidence that Stroh's Brewery encouraged sexual harassment in its plants. Law professor Cynthia Grant Bowman charted a legal strategy for eliminating sexual harassment on the street, because "in order to participate as equal citizens in the polis, women must reclaim the public space." These efforts did not surprise Wolman, Blumner, Baker, and other civil libertarian critics of sexual harassment law. Instead, they demonstrated a basic truth: minor concessions would lead to ever greater encroachments on freedom of speech. Hoping to pull the ACLU back before it lost its footing on this slippery slope, Baker gave an "impassioned speech" at the 1993 Biennial that resulted in a binding resolution requiring the national board to reconsider the First Amendment implications of its revised sexual harassment policy.[68]

The ACLU's position on sexual harassment was in flux when the U.S. Supreme Court heard its second sexual harassment case, *Harris v. Forklift Systems* (1993). Clarence Thomas sat in judgment as the High Court considered Theresa Harris's claims that her employer, Charles Hardy, subjected her to "an abusive work environment" on the basis of her gender. No one contested the facts—that, among other things, Hardy repeatedly insulted Harris as "a dumb ass woman," invited her in front of other coworkers to negotiate her raise with him at the Holiday Inn, made sexual innuendos about her clothing and other women's as well, and suggested, again in the presence of coworkers, that her professional success derived from granting sexual favors to customers. The lower court decided against Harris on the grounds that the harassment she experienced was merely offensive, not severe enough to harm her "psychological well-being."[69]

The ACLU's brief recommended reversal, arguing that, although the expression in question merely interfered with Harris's ability to do her job—rather than making it impossible for her to function—it was nonetheless actionable. Even so, just as it had in *Robinson* and under enormous pressure from its Florida affiliate, the ACLU devoted nearly half of its brief to urging the court to consider the freedom of speech implications of the case. "This case presents the Court," the ACLU brief began, "with the difficult task of defining sexual harassment, and distinguishing unlawful behavior in the workplace from protected expression under the First Amendment." "It is essential," the brief argued, "that the effort to eradicate discrimination not ignore First Amendment rights." A merely "intimidating, hostile, or offensive" work environment should not be actionable. Unanimously, the Court decided in favor of Harris in an opinion that made no mention of the First Amendment but eased the burden of proof on plaintiffs by denying that they must show "tangible effects" from the harassment.[70]

The ACLU publicly praised the Supreme Court's opinion in *Harris* as one that balanced the right to speak freely with the right to be free from sexual harassment, but the organization remained deeply divided and its position on the issue ambivalent. Many feminists were angered to find that the ACLU's *Harris* brief came nearly as close to undermining as to supporting Harris's claim. Women's Rights Project attorney Susan Deller Ross observed that, although the WRP had submitted briefs in every major case regarding sex discrimination, it played no role in the ACLU's *Harris* brief. Ross complained that the ACLU brief provided employers with a "respectable" First Amendment argument for allowing sexual harassment. Sexual harassment law does not implicate the First Amendment, she explained, because it does not ban the harasser's speech but merely requests that he "express himself elsewhere," at home or on a public street. He should not, however, "be able to hound a woman off the job or force her to endure humiliation in silence as a price for keeping her job."[71] Clearly, neither the ACLU's recently revised policy nor its single brief in *Harris* established a stable consensus on sexual harassment.

Just one month after the Supreme Court handed down its opinion in *Harris,* ACLU leaders confronted another sexual harassment case with great potential to further divide an already deeply divided organization. *Johnson v. County of Los Angeles Fire Department* also involved one of the ACLU's strongest affiliates, the fiercely independent Southern California group known for its progressive positions on civil rights and equality. The stage was set for another major internal confrontation.

Captain Steven W. Johnson liked to read *Playboy* magazine at the Los Angeles County fire station where he worked. So after the county fire department adopted a sexual harassment policy that banned such materials from firehouses, Johnson appealed to *Playboy* for help. *Playboy* attorney Burton Joseph eagerly joined the case and also involved the ACLU of Southern California. Firefighters are expected to risk their lives, he noted, but "when it comes to selecting what they want to read, they are treated like children." Assuming that feminists had created the fire department's sexual harassment policy, Joseph argued that they should not target *Playboy,* a forty-year-old magazine that supports "equality between the sexes." Moreover, feminists should be especially wary of allowing an official body to "ban the possession and reading of *Playboy,*" given the importance of broad First Amendment rights to their own movement for sexual and reproductive freedom.[72]

The ACLU of Southern California had developed a reputation for defending equality and advocating strict policies against hostile environment sexual harassment. It objected to centerfolds and other sexualized images of women posted in the workplace, but Johnson's case seemed different because it involved private consumption of these images. After much anguished discussion, the affiliate voted to support Johnson. Ramona Ripston, executive director of the affiliate, announced the decision, declaring, "you cannot ban what people can read" without violating the First Amendment. "This is not a case of pinups or posters on the wall," explained Paul Hoffman, the ACLU attorney who represented Johnson. "A firefighter has a right to read." The First Amendment rights of consumers loomed large and also appeared prominently in the brief coauthored by Hoffman and Joseph. "Every citizen," they asserted, "has a constitutionally protected right of access to read and view any material he or she chooses."[73]

As the case unfolded, public responses to it demonstrated that the ACLU's consumer-oriented interpretation of the First Amendment had taken firm root. The *Daily News of Los Angeles* editorialized that "the freedom to read should not be sacrificed on the altar of gender sensitivity." The *Washington Post* announced that even critics of *Playboy* should "accept another's right to read it," as did an *Orlando Sentinel* editor who considered the magazine "pornography and a polluter of minds" but nevertheless recognized Johnson's "right to read" it at the firehouse. A columnist for the *Sun-Sentinel* stated simply that according to the U.S. Constitution, "no adult can tell any other adult what to read," and a University of California, Los Angeles law professor declared it a "simple case" because Johnson "has a right to read what he wants." Newspapers around the country reported that Johnson's lawsuit against the County of Los Angeles Fire Department was a defense of his "right to read," and the Freedom to Read Foundation declared its support for Johnson. In addition, Feminists for Free Expression—an anticensorship organization formed in 1992—filed a brief on behalf of Johnson, arguing that the right to privacy also protects "intimate personal decisions such as the choice to read or view sexual materials."[74]

No one questioned the right to read—not even Johnson's opponents, including the County of Los Angeles Fire Department. Instead, they challenged the right to bring sexually explicit material into the workplace on the grounds that it created a hostile environment for the eleven female firefighters who worked and slept in fire stations among nearly 2,400 men. For them, context was crucial. The first female firefighter was hired by the department in 1985, and women made up less than 2 percent of all firefighters nationwide. Even Johnson admitted that female firefighters were "chided and poked and teased" more than male firefighters, "but nothing they couldn't survive." Reminders that the firehouse remained a male preserve were plentiful and included stacks of *Playboy* magazines on the backs of toilets, the *Playboy* television channel running in common spaces, and the mysterious and unwelcome appearance of sanitary napkins on women's beds and dildos in their lockers. Several experienced sexual assault by coworkers while sleeping in the firehouse. Patricia Vaughan, the Employee Relations Representative for the fire department, drafted its sexual harassment policy after visiting a fire station well supplied with *Playboy* magazines. Cynthia Barbee and Janet Babcock, two County of Los Angeles firefighters, testified to "a constant barrage of abusive and suggestive sexual remarks made by male firefighters while reading magazines with nude pictures." Barbee, the first woman to join the department, said that she found the magazines degrading to women and, especially under a fire station's conditions of "forced intimacy," felt that they created "an offensive, unprofessional and intimidating atmosphere." A former firefighter turned journalist, Angelo Figueroa, agreed that Johnson had a "right to ogle centerfolds," as long as he indulged in private and off-duty, but not in the fire station. "Equal rights for women" requires that such activity be banned from the workplace, he insisted. Similarly, Tammy Bruce, president of the Los Angeles NOW chapter, argued that Johnson's case does not implicate "freedom of speech" because firefighters "can read and do whatever they want when they are not on the job." The issue, according to attorneys for the county, was sexual harassment and the fact that the presence of skin magazines in the fire station created a hostile environment for female firefighters.[75]

The battle lines were drawn and, while the ACLU, *Playboy*, and Johnson contended that the ban on sexually oriented material violated the First Amendment, NOW and the County of Los Angeles Fire Department insisted that the ban was necessary for maintaining equal working conditions. At the end of the one-day trial, U.S. District Judge Stephen Wilson declared the county's sexual harassment policy in violation of the First Amendment. His decision echoed ACLU concerns by claiming that the county was trying to control the thoughts of its employees by restricting their right to read *Playboy* in the fire station. As long as readers refrained from exposing the magazine's contents to unwilling viewers and making lewd comments and gestures, Wilson affirmed their right to read it at work.[76]

Johnson and his coworkers celebrated by taking a *Playboy* magazine to work while local NOW leaders, female firefighters, and county officials criticized the court's decision. "The workplace is not a free marketplace of ideas," Bruce declared. John Hill, the county's affirmative action officer, worried that other public employees would claim a "First Amendment right to read *Playboy*" at work, though he believed that "reading a magazine in the county work force is a privilege, not a right." Barbee meanwhile worried about a return to the environment that greeted her as a rookie nine years earlier when "firefighters watched adult sex movies on a big screen and sex magazines were everywhere." County fire department officials considered filing an appeal but dropped it, fearing the possibility of a broader ruling against them. Instead, they carefully retooled their sexual harassment policy so that it would exclude private, quiet, and consensual viewing of sexual material.[77]

For the ACLU, the *Johnson* victory was especially sweet. After a decade of infighting over sexual harassment law, the case brought the Florida and Southern California affiliates together with the national ACLU in defense of consumers' rights under the First Amendment. This newfound unity did not erase earlier disagreements such as those that emerged over *Robinson* and *Harris*. Indeed, Ripston made that clear when she announced that the affiliate would not defend a firefighter who "takes the centerfold and opens it up for all to see." "We would agree that pictures on a wall create a hostile working environment," Ripston explained, "but we don't think that reading something does."[78] Disagreements remained, but *Johnson* helped the ACLU establish a limit on the extent to which sexual harassment policy could encroach upon speech rights—the consumer's right to read, see, and hear—a limit that even the more equality-minded affiliates and leaders respected.

That the right to read *Playboy* in a workplace trumped concerns about gender equality even for ACLU proponents of strict sexual harassment law indicates the extent to which consumer rights shaped their understanding of the First Amendment. By 1994, this was true not only for the ACLU but—thanks to decades of public education and litigation on behalf of the right to read, see, and hear—also its opponents. Neither NOW leaders nor County of Los Angeles attorneys challenged the right to read. They simply argued that this right must bend to the equality demands of the workplace.

In the wake of *Johnson*, the ACLU board prepared its response to the 1993 Biennial's demand that it reconsider its sexual harassment policy. Strossen appointed a special sexual harassment committee. The committee quickly agreed to update the policy to include sexual harassment based on sexual orientation, but then broke into two opposing factions. The group that wrote the majority report was headed by board members Wendy Kaminer and Jeanne Baker, who aimed to make the ACLU's policy more protective of workplace speech by excluding "speech that is not intended to harass." Focusing on intent would, they hoped, break the "presumed link between sexually explicit speech and harassment" and distance the policy from the feminist antipornography movement.[79]

"At the heart of the debate about sexual harassment," Kaminer and Baker argued, "is a debate about women's response to whatever is defined as pornography. Do we presume that sexually explicit magazines or posters in the workplace demean, threaten or simply unsettle women and constitute harassment?" they asked. "Do we presume that women are harassed as well by sexual remarks?" Their answer was a resounding no. Sexual expression does not always threaten sexual equality. Nor, they insisted, does "a pornographic image of a woman" have the same impact on a female employee as "an image of a lynching" has on a black one. "The picture of a murdered black man sends a clear and unmistakable message," they insisted, while "the message of pornography is ambiguous." Statements like "Let's get the cunt," they agreed, should be prohibited at work but not, "You look sexy in that dress."[80] By focusing on the intent of the alleged harasser, Kaminer and Baker hoped to challenge the theoretical underpinnings of antipornography feminism and retain possibilities for sexual expression in the workplace.

The opposing bloc, led by Joan Mahoney and Mary Ellen Gale—signers of the competing lawyers' brief in *Robinson*—refused to focus on the harasser's intent and resisted efforts to confuse sexual harassment with "a debate about the value of sexual expression or of pornography." The relevant issue was not "intent or directedness" but "disparate impact." What mattered was whether particular conduct and expression created unequal working conditions based on sex. Cautioning against "First Amendment correctness," they decried the "cynical politics and spurious principles" of individuals—including right-wing enemies of civil liberties—who attempted to deploy the First Amendment in ways that would erode gains in workplace equality. Their minority report urged the board to refrain from weakening the current policy.[81]

The board meeting to consider the majority and minority reports of the sexual harassment committee was tense and acrimonious. The authors of each report accused each other of employing underhanded tactics—from repeating and distorting personal stories shared with the committee to persuading the board to consider the minority before the majority report. Issues of sexuality typically provoked strong feelings, and these also targeted core ACLU values. Some members treated the First Amendment as the trump card of civil liberties, while others insisted on balancing it against equality and civil rights. One member approved of the focus on intent, thinking it would "allow room for normal sexual expression" in the workplace. Another member considered intent irrelevant because "sexual harassment is often unconscious." To Kaminer, this seemed like an effort not to "just police people's thoughts but police thoughts that they don't even know that they have." Others reminded the board that it was nearly impossible to enforce civil rights laws requiring a showing of intent. "In civil rights litigation, intent means unenforceable," one member asserted.[82]

Mary Ellen Gale recalled that more women and minorities favored her position and that the board as a whole proved "more respectful of equality concerns" than she had anticipated. The board refused to incorporate intent into the policy, though it did include sexual orientation, as both sides requested. In the end, Kaminer and Baker's majority report lost decisively, and the gains won by women's rights advocates in the 1993 policy stood.[83]

The issues of rape and sexual harassment pulled civil libertarians out of their comfort zone. Rape law reform and sexual harassment law involved, not protections of individual rights from the state, but protections *by* the state *from* other individuals. In addition, advocates of rape law reform and robust sexual harassment law demanded not the easier access to sexual expression that civil libertarians had long sought but greater protection from it. ACLU leaders could not avoid these issues, because they had positioned the organization as a proponent of women's rights and also because many considered rape law reform and sexual harassment law potential threats to civil liberties. Moreover, by the late 1970s, the ACLU leadership included a substantial number of women and people of color—many recruited from the women's and civil rights movements—whose perspectives had begun to reshape ACLU approaches to sexual civil liberties.

The rape policies adopted by the ACLU in 1976 and 1977 remained in effect in 2010. The ACLU participated in the feminist rape law reform project by recognizing marital rape, embracing the language of sexual assault, decrying "sexist assumptions," and questioning the relevance of a complainant's sexual history. Nevertheless, traditional civil libertarian concerns about defendants' rights and the historical role of rape charges and prosecutions in perpetuating white supremacy meant that ACLU policy continued to support wide latitude for defense attorneys anxious to exploit the complainant's sexual history.[84]

Civil libertarian concerns also guided the ACLU's evolving positions on sexual harassment. Between 1984 and 1996, the ACLU formulated its first sexual harassment policy and revised it twice to enhance its appeal to feminists. As potential threats to the First Amendment, expressive and hostile environment sexual harassment triggered the most controversy as members debated targeted versus nontargeted harassment and intent versus impact. Some wondered whether the ACLU would ever be able to settle on a sexual harassment policy. At two key moments, opposing camps found common ground. In the 1994 *Johnson* case, they identified it in a shared commitment to the consumer's First Amendment rights. In 1995, they located it again when, amid rancorous debate, they agreed to incorporate into their policy same-sex harassment and harassment based on sexual orientation. The sexual harassment policy they finalized then proved the most durable yet; it remained in effect and unchanged fifteen years later. That consumer speech rights and gay rights bridged two hostile factions in the sexual harassment debate speaks to how central these had become to the ACLU's sexual civil liberties agenda.[85]

In the end, ACLU leaders adopted policies on rape and sexual harassment despite their many disagreements and resistance to any sort of state regulation of sexual expression. By bringing their particular civil liberties perspectives on these issues to the media, Congress, the courts, and beyond, the ACLU influenced the adjudication, enforcement, and public discussion of rape and sexual harassment law in ways that were often at odds with feminist efforts. That the ACLU was changed in the process cannot be denied. In the end, the ACLU compromised on some of its core principles, most notably the defendant's rights to due process and freedom of speech in the workplace. The compromises it made did not satisfy many feminists. That the ACLU compromised at all on rape and sexual harassment is, nevertheless, testament to the influence feminists had gained in the ACLU as well as to the close relationship between sexuality and civil liberties that the ACLU had forged.

What did the ACLU's limits on rape law reform and sexual harassment policy mean for sexual civil liberties? As with consumer rights and privacy, they indicated that a civil liberties paradigm privileged access to overprotection from sexual expression, whether that expression came in the form of unsolicited sexual mail, unwanted sexual intercourse, or unwelcome sexual material at work. At the close of the twentieth century, sexual civil liberties were not necessarily the same as sexual freedom.

Conclusion

More than a half-century after helping to found the ACLU, Roger Baldwin reflected on the state of the nation's sexual culture and the ACLU's contributions to it. "Nudity is accepted, complete and unadorned," Baldwin noted in 1974, thinking no doubt of the recent fad of streaking but pointing out that "we always defended" nudism. "The ACLU discovered a lot of new rights along the road in fifty years," he mused. "We discovered privacy. We always knew there should be a line beyond which law should not interfere with private conduct," but "we did not begin to carve out a private area formally until we took on the birth control cases." That is, he said proudly, "when the Supreme Court discovered privacy too. Now we have a doctrine and we are fast developing a whole series of prohibitions against snooping of all sorts." Our goal is no more "looking into bedrooms to see what sort of sex is going on," he said. Nevertheless, he noted that even as the ACLU had helped to establish sexual privacy as a constitutional right, it also defended public sexual display that has "gone far beyond good taste into the 'prurient and salacious.'" Still, "the censors we so long fought in the [A] CLU" are gone. "The smut-hunters, the Legion of Decency, the league for clean literature (or something) and the private motion picture review boards" have all fallen away. Indeed, he observed, "there seem to be no prudes left among us." But "is it better?" he wondered.[1]

Much has changed in American sexual culture since Roger Baldwin and Crystal Eastman founded the ACLU, and many of those changes were initiated or shaped by leaders of the organization and their contributions to evolving ideas about civil liberties. In 1920, few people considered the possibility that obscenity laws might violate the First Amendment let alone entertained the prospect that individuals might have a right to consume it. Sexual imagery, expression, and information were largely confined to private spaces and particular venues, where they were nonetheless often targeted for suppression by reformers and law enforcement officials. Leaders of the young ACLU defended select individuals—playwrights, birth control activists, sex educators, and nudists—who had personal connections to the organization, seemed to be victims of political bias, and were motivated more by seriousness of purpose than commercial intent. Defending these people and their causes changed the ACLU in important ways.

Early on, nudism inspired ACLU leaders to experiment with notions of sexual privacy and to recognize the blurriness of boundaries between speech and practice. Rights to privacy should, they argued, prevent laws against indecent exposure from affecting nudism practiced on privately owned property or among family members. Similarly, First Amendment rights should protect nudist photographs because they were intrinsic to nudist advocacy and educational efforts. Thus, long before ACLU leaders formulated a constitutional right to privacy and defended sexual conduct along with speech, they flirted with these ideas in their various defenses of nudism as early as the 1930s.

The ACLU dramatically changed its standards for the speech it would defend when it began to focus on the rights of consumers. Establishing a consumer's rights under the First Amendment addressed important challenges identified by ACLU leaders. Publishers, authors, editors, and other producers of speech often declined to defend their First Amendment rights out of fear for their reputations and costs associated with litigation, but consumers represented by the ACLU had relatively little to lose. Moreover, while pressure groups could argue rightly that their boycotts against vendors of *Playboy*, for example, did not violate the right to produce the magazine, they could not deny that an effective boycott reduced consumer access to it. Indeed, that was their goal. Reorienting the First Amendment around consumer rights and moving consumers into the vanguard as defenders of free speech helped the ACLU recruit complainants and recast the antiobscenity work of pressure groups as censorship.

Positioning consumers as the First Amendment's primary clients was a revolutionary move that expanded the amendment's constituency to include everyone who might want to "read, see, and hear." It worked so well in part because it went unnoticed. It seemed to articulate what had always been the case by echoing the individualistic, consumer-oriented ethos of the postwar era and resonating with a public eager to consume after a decade and a half of war and depression-induced privation. However familiar it might have seemed, the idea of a First Amendment right for consumers transformed the law and the ways that people thought and felt about their rights. ACLU leaders spread the notion of "a right to read, see, and hear" far and wide through public education efforts and collaborations with other organizations. As a result, whereas few if any would-be readers in the 1930s protested the banning of James Joyce's *Ulysses*, when Hugh Hefner's *Playboy* and Henry Miller's *Tropic of Cancer* were censored in the early 1960s, consumer demands for the "right to read" were deafening—and music to ACLU leaders' ears.

The ACLU was shaped by the people who led it—mostly attorneys who ferried information and ideas back and forth among their other professional affiliations and relationships. Just as nudists shaped the ACLU's approaches, so did the American Birth Control League, the Planned Parenthood Federation, the Kinsey Institute, the American Law Institute, *Playboy* magazine, and individual homosexuals and victims of involuntary sterilization who appealed to the organization for help. These groups and their members encouraged the ACLU to broaden its agenda to include sexual practices while they themselves learned to frame their concerns in terms of civil liberties. Together, they developed rights, including a right to privacy, that would reshape constitutional law and exercise a profound influence over American culture.

The importance of personal interactions and experiences cannot be overstated. The ACLU's agenda was, from the very beginning, shaped less by some logic inherent in the Constitution than by the particular values, desires, and experiences that individual ACLU leaders brought to their work. Launched by bohemian free-lovers, it is hardly surprising that the ACLU so quickly took up the cause of sexual rights and liberties. That the organization was led by men and women who loved, lusted, and struggled with each other's demands for sexual freedom and sexual equality helps to explain why birth control became such an important cause to ACLU leaders so early; it mediated their disagreements and held out the possibility of more full and equal sexual freedom for women, even if that reality remained painfully elusive for most. Personal experiences brought other issues onto the ACLU's agenda. Casual nudism and close associations with more serious nudists predisposed the ACLU's early leaders to defend this marginal group. Interactions with homosexuals and women subjected to coerced sterilization encouraged ACLU leaders to learn about their difficulties and develop civil liberties strategies to address them. The very phrases "sexual privacy" and "reproductive freedom" grew out of these encounters.[2] The arrival of a second generation of Greenwich Village free spirits steeped in the values of the civil rights and later women's rights movements would also reshape the ACLU in the latter decades of the twentieth century.

In some ways, ACLU leaders defended rights as old as the Constitution—and much older, some would argue—but they created new ones as well, and all were subject to appropriation by opponents who sought very different ends. For example, the ACLU's notion of consumer rights under the First Amendment was designed to maximize diversity and ease consumer access in the marketplace of ideas. So the ACLU resisted when others invoked consumer rights to call for restrictions on sexually explicit material, because these would limit marketplace diversity and consumer access. Similarly, ACLU leaders who intended for the right to privacy to increase access to birth control and abortion, fought against privacy-based efforts to omit these services from public assistance programs. Likewise, ACLU leaders who advocated "informed consent" to make reproductive freedom meaningful for women vulnerable to involuntary sterilization, resisted when opponents of their overall goals seized on their language and methods to reduce women's access to abortion.

This balancing act teetered when the ACLU recommended incongruous guidelines for the provision of sterilization and abortion services. Because abortion had been denied to women, they endeavored to make it more accessible, but because sterilization had been forced on women, they worked to make it more difficult to obtain. Despite the different histories, medical requirements, and personal consequences associated with abortion and sterilization, this position was a precarious one to maintain, and the ACLU did so with limited success. Where it gained the most traction, though, was in advancing and expanding the notion of privacy that underwrote reproductive freedom.

When a constitutional right to privacy became firmly established as the basis for reproductive freedom in *Griswold* and *Roe*, the ACLU and homophile organizations worked to extend it to sexual behavior more broadly. ACLU leaders had long wrestled with the distinctions they had traditionally recognized between speech and conduct, public and private, commercial and noncommercial. By the middle of the 1970s, they abandoned most of these distinctions and advocated the decriminalization of all private consensual sexual conduct between adults and the removal of all impediments to adult access to sexual material, including those designed to shield children and unwilling audiences from it. Increasingly, privacy and First Amendment rights became the basis of consumer access to sexual expression of all kinds, behavior as well as speech.

While the ACLU worked to expand access to sexual expression, many people demanded protection from it. Consumers who called for movie ratings and protection from unsolicited sexually explicit mail were followed by feminists who demanded freedom from unwanted sexual attention, including rape and sexual harassment. Rape, as a criminal matter, triggered the ACLU's longtime dedication to the rights of defendants, but sexual harassment involved civil proceedings and coincided with the ACLU's commitment to equal employment. Racial history and politics help to explain the discrepancies between how the ACLU treated rape and how it treated sexual harassment; policies against sexual harassment did not raise the specter of racist "southern justice" evoked by rape law reform.[3] For many ACLU leaders, however, hostile environment sexual harassment raised concerns about freedom of speech. That gay rights and the First Amendment rights of consumers helped bridge internal disagreements over sexual harassment policy bespoke the central position these issues assumed on the organization's civil liberties agenda by the 1990s. Moreover, that the ACLU assumed leadership in the movements for reproductive and gay rights but was often at odds with the movements against rape and sexual harassment exposes some of the limits that its civil libertarian principles and priorities imposed on feminist influence.

The ACLU's evolving approach to sexual civil liberties was shaped by fierce debates among leaders over what issues involved civil liberties and how to prioritize when the civil liberties of one group seemed to clash with those of another. Thus, ACLU leaders' understandings of the relationship between the Constitution and sexuality were highly contingent, shaped by circumstances, personalities, and relationships, as well as by sharp conflicts among dedicated civil libertarians who were often influenced by allegiances to other groups, movements, and issues.

Forces outside the ACLU also influenced its work. The focus on consumers inspired by the New Deal, World War II, and postwar environment fueled ACLU efforts to develop a First Amendment approach to consumers' rights. Contemporaneous anxieties about population pressures assisted the ACLU's defense of birth control even as they raised new civil liberties concerns regarding possible coercion. The civil rights and women's rights movements forced ACLU leaders to pay more attention to issues of racial and gender equality to remain relevant, attract young members, and also to tap new sources of funding. The rise of the New Right encouraged ACLU leaders to partner with conservatives on particular issues. Thus, while individual personalities and the dynamics among them molded the ACLU's approach to civil liberties, so too did the social and political context in which they operated.

The ACLU has had a profound effect on American law, politics, and culture with regard to sexuality. Not only do the ideas and language of its leaders show up in court opinions, legal treatises, and laws, but they also pervade the realm of popular culture and civil society, where political pundits, media representatives, and leaders of public interest groups and trade associations give voice to phrases popularized by the ACLU. Phrases such as "informed consent," "reproductive freedom," "the right to privacy," and "the right to read" roll easily off the tongues of many if not most American adults today, conservatives as well as liberals. Yet another measure of the ACLU's influence can be found in the prodigious and often successful efforts of its adversaries to appropriate and redeploy its own language and principles. That groups and individuals with very different aims have found political utility in these civil libertarian values attests to the hegemonic status they have attained.

Of the new rights formulated by the ACLU, only the "right to read"—or the consumer's rights under the First Amendment—has, until now, lacked any sort of history at all. Its timelessness and constitutional lineage has gone unquestioned. Whatever scholars might try to divine about the hazy intentions of the framers, consumers' rights under the First Amendment were carefully constructed by leaders in the ACLU who used them to expand popular understandings of what activities might constitute censorship and to motivate individual consumers to demand a First Amendment right of unfettered access to anything they might want to read, see, or hear. Because it resonated so powerfully with the individualistic ethos stoked by post–World War II consumer culture, this consumerist understanding of free speech took firm root and grew to exercise a profound impact on American sexual culture.

It also smoothed the ACLU's transition from defending noncommercial speech alone to including commercial speech as well. In a Cold War society in which consumption and capitalism became as important as voting and democracy to defining American freedom, the First Amendment must cover commercial speech as well as the rights of consumers to access it easily.

The more widely historicized right to privacy also reshaped American sexual culture in unexpected ways. Granted constitutional status by the Supreme Court in *Griswold v. Connecticut* (1965), the right has taken on a life of its own, invoked to protect not only sexual behavior between consenting adults that takes place in spaces long considered private but increasingly stretched to encompass sexual expression and conduct in places once thought public—among them workplaces, restrooms, theaters, and city streets.[4]

Although these changes—many of them propelled by the ACLU—have been momentous, cultural critics and scholars disagree about the current state of American sexual rights and culture. Some bemoan what they see as today's culture of sexual repression, one in which the religious Right has declared a "war on sex" and liberals have failed to "articulate a defense of sexual rights."[5] These observers acknowledge that 50 million American consumers have voted with their credit cards to make "adult entertainment" fabulously profitable. They lament, nonetheless, that shame often prevents those same consumers from defending their rights when zoning laws, the Children's Internet Protection Act (2000), the Broadcast Decency Enforcement Act (2005), community pressure, consumer boycotts, and the pragmatic decisions of broadcast media restrict access to sexual content. Examples abound. 7-Eleven stores have refused to sell *Playboy*, *Penthouse*, and similar magazines since 1986; Omni hotels discontinued in-room pornography channels in 2000; public libraries that receive federal funds must equip their public-access computers with filtering devices that require adult patrons to request permission to access pornographic websites as of 2000; and Clear Channel Communications dropped Howard Stern's radio show in 2004. Some critics believe that we need laws to protect "the rights of people offended by the neurotic stripping of human eroticism from workplaces and civic spaces across America."[6] Their complaints about sexual repression include ongoing discrimination against homosexuals with regard to marriage, child custody, adoption, public solicitation for sex, and (until recently) military service. They also point to legal protections for pharmacies and physicians who refuse to dispense emergency contraception or perform abortions, the Supreme Court's upholding of the Partial Birth Abortion Act in *Gonzales v. Carhart* (2007), and also recent efforts to pass the Blunt amendment that would allow employers and health plans to refuse to cover contraceptive services as evidence that reproductive freedom and sexual privacy more generally are under sustained attack.[7]

Other scholars and cultural critics decry a contemporary American sexual culture that recognizes few boundaries, legal or normative, on expression or behavior. They emphasize that free-flowing video and Internet pornography has become mainstream, setting the standards for female beauty, and writing the script or substituting for human sexual relationships. They argue that pornography has distorted relationships between women and men, adults and children, by teaching viewers to respond sexually to unhealthy, exploitative, and even dangerous stimuli. At the same time, they point out the many ways that young women in particular reenact what they see in pornography and do so to their own detriment, posting nude pictures of themselves on the Internet, flashing their breasts in bars and other public places à la *Girls Gone Wild*, creating pornographic magazines with photographs of their own and their friends' bodies, and engaging in sexual conduct that they neither desire nor enjoy with men concerned only about their own pleasure.[8] They lament that the U.S. Supreme Court overturned the Child Pornography Prevention Act (1996) as too broad and ruled the Child Online Protection Act (1998) unconstitutional.[9] "We have protected the rights of those who wish to live in a pornified culture," journalist Pamela Paul declares, "while altogether ignoring the interests of those who do not."[10]

Both sides paint a grim picture of American sexual culture in the first two decades of the twenty-first century. But their concerns could not be more different. Do we live in a sexually repressive culture or one saturated with sex? And how does the work of the ACLU help explain what has happened and why?

The ACLU has challenged most if not all of the restrictions on sexual expression and behavior mentioned above. It played crucial roles in the Supreme Court decisions that overturned the Child Pornography Prevention Act and brought the lawsuits and made the consumer rights arguments that triumphed in *Ashcroft v. ACLU* (2004), the case that overturned the Child Online Protection Act. The ACLU argued that requiring pornographic websites to provide access only to visitors who submit credit card numbers on adult verification screens would deter access to speech and rights to privacy, "depriv[ing] adults of material they are constitutionally entitled to receive." The Court overturned the law on the grounds that it imposed an "undue burden" on consumers who "have a constitutional right to receive" pornographic material on the Internet.[11]

The ACLU and many other public interest groups—including the American Library Association, the American Book Sellers Association, Feminists for Free

Expression, the National Book and Children's Literacy Alliance, and the National Council of Teachers of English—have fought so effectively for the First Amendment rights of consumers that consumers need not organize on their own behalf. Commercial entities, too, claim to represent consumers' rights, from Playboy Enterprises to the local bookseller who resists collective efforts to remove *Playboy* magazine from the shelves on the grounds that doing so would violate the consumer's right to "decide what to see, read... and think about."[12] Ironically, by individualizing consumer rights to speech, the ACLU may have contributed to the reluctance of consumers to defend their rights through collective action. In other words, by casting as censorship the activities and boycotts of pressure groups, the ACLU has encouraged consumers to think about their rights in individual terms that may also deter collective demands for greater access to proscribed material. Consumers may rarely mobilize to defend their First Amendment rights, but those rights are nevertheless being defended effectively and with gusto.

Sexual privacy of different sorts is actually under attack by both sides in this debate. Conservatives target the privacy rights of women and homosexuals by seeking to impose limits on reproductive freedom and gay rights. Civil libertarians take aim at sexual privacy of a different sort. By demanding that consumers enjoy the easiest possible access to sexual expression, they have contributed to an increasingly sex-saturated public sphere that renders sex anything but private. In a sharp critique of this development, a number of feminist writers criticize the "pornification" or "porning" of America, pointing out that it is neither a gender-neutral nor an equal-opportunity phenomenon.[13] The most casual glance at a magazine rack at the grocery store or even a quick perusal of the girls' and boys' sides of the children's clothing section will convince most observers that it is primarily through the bodies of girls and women that this culture's sexual expression takes place. And it is largely the bodies and lives of girls and women that suffer the consequences through their vulnerability to unwanted pregnancy, greater susceptibility to venereal disease, pressure to look and act like a porn star, and more frequent victimization by sexual assault, rape, and sexual harassment.[14] It is worth considering the sobering fact that, were both sides of these debates to win their battles with sexual privacy simultaneously, women would lose the ability to control their reproductive lives at the exact moment that they began to inhabit a free-for-all sexual culture premised on the sexualization of women's and girls' bodies.[15]

Civil libertarian approaches to sexuality have blurred older boundaries between public and private in many ways, including several less obvious ones. Just as personal experiences and values shaped the public policies that ACLU leaders pursued, so also did ACLU leaders take civil libertarian ideals back into their personal and private lives. And just as the sexualization of American culture has had profoundly different consequences for women and men, so the more private version of sexual civil liberties practiced by the ACLU's earliest leaders more often than not empowered men at the expense of their female partners. Yet out of that crucible emerged a commitment to defending birth control that would eventually culminate in a sweeping ACLU movement for women's reproductive freedom. Out of it also came a precedent for importing concepts of civil liberties into the private realm and private relationships.

In 1995, Nadine Strossen, president of the ACLU, published *Defending Pornography: Free Speech, Sex, and the Fight for Women's Rights*. The book stretched the definition of censorship well beyond state suppression, obscuring the boundaries between public and private by arguing that simply criticizing pornography or boycotting a vendor of sexually explicit materials might constitute censorship—especially if the criticism or the boycott resulted in impediments to consumer access. Underlying her argument was an assumption that individuals have the right to consume sexual material. Surely if employees had the right to read *Playboy* at their workplace—as demonstrated by the ACLU-supported *Johnson* case—an individual had the right to read it at home. And that right, that consumer's right to pornography, has grown to exceed the right of any individual to escape pornography in private or in public.[16]

But "is it better?" Roger Baldwin wondered. To be sure, Americans have created a culture that honors, with constitutional guarantees, particular rights to

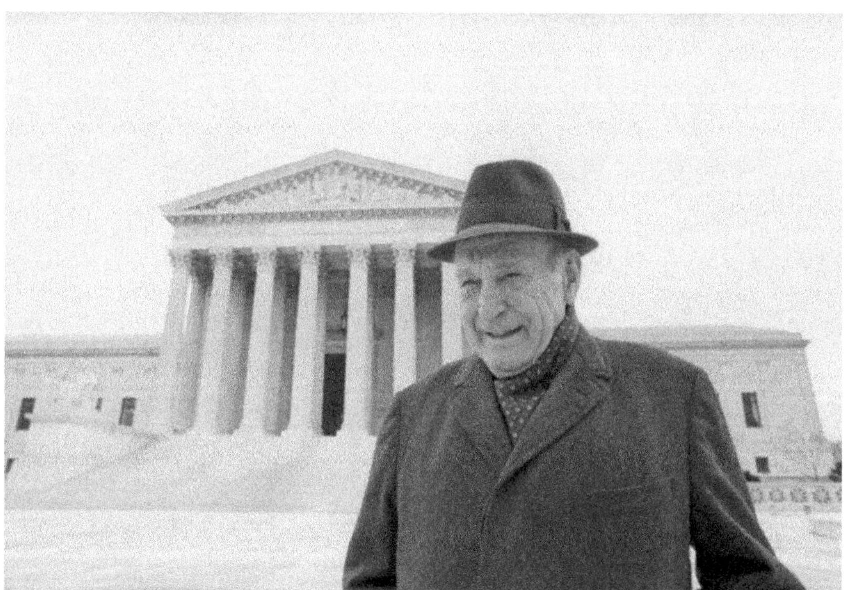

Figure 8.1 Roger Baldwin in front of the U.S. Supreme Court on the occasion of his eighty-sixth birthday and the fiftieth anniversary of the ACLU, January 20, 1970. (Courtesy, ©Bettmann/Corbis/AP Images)

free speech and sexual privacy including, within certain limits, access to birth control, abortion, sexually explicit material, and private, consensual sexual relationships between adults. But it is also a culture that leaves to legislative and regulatory whim the rights of adults to escape and to protect their children from unwanted sexual expression and attention—from sexually provocative advertisements and broadcast media to sexual harassment and rape. Disagreements over these very issues have given rise to intermittent but ongoing "culture wars" over sex and morality that seem to pit diametrically opposed groups against each other. A closer look, though, reveals that Americans have also achieved a broad consensus on the sanctity of freedom of speech and sexual privacy—concepts the ACLU moved to the very core of American constitutionalism but also into more widespread and popular understandings of civil liberties and individual rights.[17] Disagreements about the parameters of free speech and sexual privacy abound. But the fact that people who disagree on ends share a commitment to means and employ a common civil liberties idiom speaks to the exalted status that freedom of speech and sexual privacy achieved in the twentieth century, in large measure as a result of the ACLU's sexual rights odyssey.

NOTES

Introduction

1. Barnett, *Sexual Freedom and the Constitution*, v.
2. See analysis and polls cited in McClosky and Brill, *Dimensions of Tolerance*, 199–203; The Harris Poll #47, April 12, 2011; Gallup's Annual Values and Beliefs poll, May 5–8, 2011; quotes from Herzog, *Sex in Crisis*, 182; see also Klein, *America's War on Sex*, 177; Stein, *Sexual Injustice*, 1, 18.
3. Other scholars track the evolutionary nature of sexual revolutions in the twentieth-century United States. See for example Bailey, *Sex in the Heartland*.
4. Article-length contributions to scholarship on women in the ACLU focus on women's rights. They include Strossen, "American Civil Liberties Union"; Gale and Strossen, "The Real ACLU"; Epstein, "The Impact of the ACLU Reproductive Freedom Project"; Campbell, "Raising the Bar"; Hartmann, "Litigating Feminist Principles: The American Civil Liberties Union," in *The Other Feminists*, 53–91.
5. Haag, *Consent*, xix; Gurstein, *The Repeal of Reticence*, 3–7.
6. Rosen, *The Unwanted Gaze*; O'Harrow, *No Place to Hide*; Etzioni, *The Limits of Privacy*; Schneider, "Synergy of Equality and Privacy"; Nussbaum, "What's Privacy Got to Do With It?" This book, like other scholarship, suggests that, although most Americans today consider the ACLU itself left-of-center, much of its traditional civil liberties agenda has become mainstream. Bean, "Pressure for Freedom"; Garey, *Defending Everybody*; Markmann, *The Noblest Cry*; Murphy, *Meaning of Freedom of Speech*; Kutulas, *American Civil Liberties Union*; Walker, *In Defense*.
7. One of the ACLU's earliest publications stated that "much of the work we do does not appear with our names because the primary responsibility for it rests with others." See "The Fight for Free Speech" (New York: American Civil Liberties Union, September 1921), 11. On the ACLU's later turn to litigation as one of its primary strategies, see Zackin, "Early ACLU."
8. Author interview with Michael Meyers, November 24, 2010.

Chapter 1

1. "The Fight for Free Speech" (New York: American Civil Liberties Union, September 1921).
2. First quote from "Times Square to Have a Million-Dollar Town Hall," *New York Times*, April 27, 1919; second quote from "Town Hall Forum Radical, He Says," *New York Times*, April 7, 1921; Lucille B. Milner to Sanger, November 14, 1921, MSP-MF, series 2, reel 57;

Albert DeSilver to Richard Enright, November 14, 1921; third quote from "Police Veto Halts Birth Control Talk," *New York Times*, November 14, 1921; "Mrs. Sanger is Jailed," *New York Call*, November 14, 1921; "Mrs. Sanger is Freed," *New York Call*, November 15, 1921; "Mrs. Sanger Urged to Sue Enright for False Arrest," *New York Call*, November 15, 1921; DeSilver to Enright, November 14, 1921; Enright to DeSilver, November 16, 1921; Lahey to DeSilver, November 17, 1921; Milner to Sanger, November 17, 1921; ACLU to Rev. Patrick Hayes, November 17, 1921, ACLU-MF, reel 25. See also Chesler, *Woman of Valor*, 203–204; Sanger, *Margaret Sanger*, 301–315; Sanger, *My Fight for Birth Control*, 212–237; Douglas, *Margaret Sanger*, 158–162; last quotes from Milner, *Education of an American Liberal*, 157.

3. Walker, *In Defense*, 22, 31–32, 82; Cottrell, *Roger Nash Baldwin*, 166–167; Trimberger, "Women in the Old and New Left," 433. Most scholars assume that the ACLU's founders were "extremely puritanical" and even "squeamish about sex," language that originated with ACLU attorney Morris Ernst. See Ernst to Clifford Forster, June 15, 1948, HRC-ERC, box 84.
4. Witt, *Patriots and Cosmopolitans*, 157–208; Stansell, *American Moderns*, 244–245; Wetzsteon, *Republic of Dreams*, 192–202.
5. Rinehart, ed., *One Woman Determined*.
6. The editor of Doty's autobiography dismisses Doty's crushes on women as meaningless. See Rinehart, ed., *One Woman Determined*, 27, 41, 49, first two quotes from 36; third quote from 48.
7. Long sections of Doty's autobiography seem to be taken directly from her diary entries. Quotes from Rinehart, ed., *One Woman Determined*, 45, 47–49; see also 40, 41, 44. Judith Bennett's *History Matters* convinced me that, even if the "lesbian-like" behavior I noted was not central to my point, I should include it. Leila Rupp treats the discomfort with lesbianism experienced by a contemporary of Doty's as evidence of limits placed on female friendships by the first sexual revolution. Bennett, *History Matters*, 108–127; Rupp, "Feminism and the Sexual Revolution," 300–302.
8. Rinehart, ed., *One Woman Determined*, 49–50, 58.
9. Wetzsteon, *Republic of Dreams*, 193; Rinehart, ed., *One Woman Determined*, 62; McFarland, *Inside Greenwich Village*, 130–131.
10. Wetzsteon, *Republic of Dreams*, 193; Rinehart, ed., *One Woman Determined*, 62; McFarland, *Inside Greenwich Village*, 130–131.
11. All quotes from Rinehart, ed., *One Woman Determined*, 70.
12. "The Child Welfare Exhibit," *New York Times*, March 3, 1910; Rinehart, ed., *One Woman Determined*, 71–75.
13. "Phillips Dies of His Wounds," *New York Times*, January 25, 1911; Rinehart, ed., *One Woman Determined*, 75.
14. Clues to Hugh Cabot's identity can be found in the following sources: Rinehart, ed., *One Woman Determined*; Crenner, *Private Practice*; correspondence between Doty and the Cabots, SSC-MZD; Ward, "The Medical Brothers Cabot"; McDougal et al. "Hugh Cabot—1872–1945"; correspondence cited below. Richard Cabot would later help to establish the ACLU's Boston affiliate.
15. Quotes from Rinehart, ed., *One Woman Determined*, 86.
16. Quotes from Rinehart, ed., *One Woman Determined*, 86 and 88; Richard C. Cabot to Doty, October 9 (no year); Hugh Cabot to Doty, October 31, 1911; January 27, 1919; February 17, 1919; February 25, 1920; July 3, 1920, SSC-MZD, box 2; Doty to W.K.A. (Richard Cabot), n.d., HUA-RCC, box 37; McDougal et al., "Hugh Cabot—1872–1945," 649; Ward, "The Medical Brothers Cabot," 30–39. Doty's lack of empathy for Mary Cabot resembles that of her contemporary, Doris Stevens, whose feminism produced no sisterly feelings of understanding for the wives of the men who fell in love with her. See Rupp, "Feminism and the Sexual Revolution."

17. Quotes from Rinehart, ed., *One Woman Determined*, 117–118, 204; see also 116–128; and Doty, *Society's Misfits*. On gay and lesbian relationships in prisons, see Kunzel, *Criminal Intimacy*.
18. McFarland, *Inside Greenwich Village*, 31; Witt, *Patriots and Cosmopolitans*, 165–172.
19. First two quotes from Cook, ed., *Crystal Eastman*, 3; O'Neill, *The Last Romantic*, 21–24; Wetzsteon, *Republic of Dreams*, 195; third quote from Eastman, *Enjoyment of Living*, 356; see also Cook, "Radical Women of Greenwich Village," 246; Eastman, "Marriage Under Two Roofs," *Cosmopolitan*, December 1923, in Cook, ed., *Crystal Eastman*, 76–83; "Suffragette Lawyer Married," *New York Times*, May 6, 1911; Fishbein, "Freud and the Radicals." Just one day later, brother Max wed Eastman's former roommate Ida Rauh.
20. "Wisconsin Defeats Suffrage," *New York Times*, November 7, 1912; Aronson, "Taking Liberties"; Witt, *Patriots and Cosmopolitans*, 172–182; Dawley, *Changing the World*, 92–96; Cook, ed., *Crystal Eastman*, 4–6, 24, 29; Cook, "Radical Women," 243–257; Stansell, *American Moderns*, 313–317.
21. "Roger Baldwin, 1-12-72," "Baldwin, 5-17-72," and "Herbert Baldwin, 10-26-71," Joseph Lash notes, FDR-JPL, box 49. All other quotes from "The Reminiscences of Roger Nash Baldwin," 17, interviewed by Dr. Harlan B. Phillips, November 1953–January 1954, CUOHP-MF.
22. The nature of the contraception Baldwin used is unknown. He later claimed that he first learned about condoms in college. "Roger Baldwin, 1-12-71," Joseph Lash notes, FDR-JPL, box 49. See also Cottrell, *Roger Nash Baldwin*, 11; Twelfth Census of the United States, 1900, Norfolk, Massachusetts, rev. June 15, 2009, http://www.ancestry.com (August 4, 2011).
23. First quote from Lamson, *Roger Baldwin*, 25; second quote from "Roger Baldwin, 1-12-72," Joseph Lash notes, FDR-JPL, box 49.
24. Quotes from "Roger Baldwin, 11-4-71, 12-24-71, 2-14-71," and "Herbert Baldwin and Robert Baldwin, 10-26-71," Joseph Lash notes, FDR-JPL, box 49. See also Lamson, *Roger Baldwin*, 21–22, 26–27; Cottrell, *Roger Nash Baldwin*, 17–18; transcripts of Roger Baldwin "Recollections Tape 7, Side B," PML-PLC, box 1.
25. Shortly before Baldwin's arrival, a major "civic cleanup" led by district attorney Joseph W. Folk had wrested St. Louis government from the control of a political machine and returned it to the "'better' elements," soon to include Baldwin himself. Piott, *Holy Joe*; Geiger, "Joseph W. Folk"; quote from "Reminiscences of Roger Nash Baldwin," 23–24, CUOHP-MF, see also 6–12, 25–35, and "Roger Baldwin, 12-21-71," "Roger, 10-4-71," "Roger, 1-8-72," and "Baldwin, 10-11-71," Joseph Lash notes, FDR-JPL, box 49; Lamson, *Roger Baldwin*, 32–36; Flexner and Baldwin, *Juvenile Courts and Probation*, vii–viii.
26. The married man with whom Strong was involved was noted reformer Judge Benjamin Barr Lindsey. Strong and Keyssar, *Right in Her Soul*, 51, 54, 55–60; Lamson, *Roger Baldwin*, 42–43. For a different interpretation of Baldwin and Strong's intimate relations see Ogle, "Anna Louise Strong," 81–85. See also "Roger Baldwin, 1-7-72, 1-8-72, and 1-12-72," Joseph Lash notes, FDR-JPL, box 49. On Baldwin's social life in St. Louis, see Interviews with Baldwin, PML-PLC, box 1.
27. Quotes from *Much Ado*, n.d., FDR-JPL, box 49; see also "Roger Baldwin, 1-8-72," Joseph Lash notes, FDR-JPL, box 49; Lamson, *Roger Baldwin*, 8–9, 40–42 and Lamson Transcripts, "Recollections Tape 3, Side 2," January 15, 1973, PML-PLC, box 1.
28. Lamson, *Roger Baldwin*, 45–48.
29. "Roger Baldwin, 10-4-71, 1-7-72, 1-12-72," Joseph Lash notes, FDR-JPL, box 49. See also Graber, *Transforming Free Speech*, 53–54; Rabban, *Free Speech in Its Forgotten Years*, 65–67; Falk, *Love, Anarchy, and Emma Goldman*, 11–12; "Reminiscences of Roger Nash Baldwin," 36–38, 40–41, CUOHP-MF; Cottrell, *Roger Nash Baldwin*, 30–31. On Baldwin's relationship with Goldman, see Baldwin, "Recollections of a Life in Civil Liberties-I," 56–57; Drinnon, *Rebel in Paradise*, 253; Goldman, *Living My Life*, 665; Baldwin to Goldman,

June 1, 1928, RNB-MF, reel 7. Sanger and Goldman were allies as well as rivals, vying for center stage and competing over attentions from Alexander Berkman. See Chesler, *Woman of Valor*, 141–142.

30. Doty seems to have become acquainted with Sanger by 1915. See Sanger to Mrs. How Martin, July 17, 1915, and Sanger to Friends and Comrades, January 5, 1916, in Sanger, *Selected Papers*, vol. 1, 150–151 and 175. Perhaps Baldwin subscribed to *The Woman Rebel*; a similar circular, sent two years earlier, went out to the periodical's 2,000 subscribers. See Sanger, *My Fight for Birth Control*, 94, 140; Chesler, *Woman of Valor*, 102; quotes from Baldwin to Sanger, February 1, 1916, RNB-MF, reel 14.
31. Sanger reported the event differently, usually omitting Baldwin entirely. See for example, Sanger, *My Fight for Birth Control*, 146–147; Sanger, *Margaret Sanger*, 199–201; Sanger to Charles and Bessie Drysdale, August 9, 1916, in Sanger, *Selected Papers*, 187 n. 12, 191. Baldwin dated the event in 1912, but documentary evidence places it four years later, in 1916. "Reminiscences of Roger Nash Baldwin," 48–49, CUOHP-MF. See also "Roger Baldwin, 3-7-72," Joseph Lash notes, FDR-JPL, box 49; AUAM Meeting Minutes, February 10, 1917, AUAM-MF, reel 1; Dennett to Mrs. Holt, May 14, 1917, MWD-MF, reel 33. Most scholarly accounts place Baldwin at the scene. See Douglas, *Margaret Sanger*, 97; Chesler, *Woman of Valor*, 141; Walker, *In Defense*, 33–34; Cottrell, *Roger Nash Baldwin*, 43, 46–48; Lamson, *Roger Baldwin*, 54–55; Johnson, *Challenge to American Freedoms*, 195. An exception is Kennedy, *Birth Control in America*, 81.
32. The AUAM struggled on for another year. See Oswald Garrison Villard to Dear Friend, April 2, 1918; Dennett to Dear Friend, January 5 and 9, 1918; American Union Against Militarism letterhead, June 16, 1916, MWD-MF, reel 32; "Roger Baldwin, 3-4-72," Joseph Lash notes, FDR-JPL, box 49; Walker, *In Defense*, 11–20; Milner, *Education of an American Liberal*, 39, 65; Dawley, *Changing the World*, 95, 103, 117.
33. Dennett to Mrs. Holt, May 14, 1917, MWD-MF, reel 33; AUAM Meeting Minutes, February 10, 1917; June 4, 1917; AUAM Executive Committee Minutes, June 15, 1917, AUAM-MF, reel 1; Lamson, *Roger Baldwin*, 84–95; Cook, ed., *Crystal Eastman*, 4–6, 24, 29; Cook, "Radical Women," 243–257; Stansell, *American Moderns*, 313–317; Cottrell, *Roger Nash Baldwin*, 41, 46–48.
34. Lamson, *Roger Baldwin*, 27–57. For an interpretation less focused on personal experiences, see Weinrib, "Sex Side of Civil Liberties," esp. 328–339.
35. Quote from Walker, *In Defense*, 43. See also Murphy, *World War I*, 248–272; McGerr, *A Fierce Discontent*, 304–308.
36. For a well-developed treatment of this Progressive twist on civil libertarianism, see Graber, *Transforming Free Speech*.
37. The phrase "matters of public concern" was common among the day's First Amendment scholars, many of whom used it to determine the compass of constitutionally protected speech. Quote from Lamson, *Roger Baldwin*, 126; see also Milner, *Education of an American Liberal*, 67–68. In a 1972 reminiscence Baldwin resisted being characterized as a "Greenwich Village Left[ist]," though his biographer considered the designation accurate. Cottrell, *Roger Nash Baldwin*, 107. Artists in the early twentieth century used the word "fauve," French for "wild beast," to refer to a postimpressionist painting style that employed bold colors and distortion to convey rebelliousness and disorder. See also Stansell, *American Moderns*, 76–78, 159. Donald Johnson argues that only war could have brought unity on issues of free speech by creating common needs among diverse groups, including conscientious objectors. Johnson, *Challenge to American Freedoms*, 194–199.
38. Tone, *Devices and Desires*, 22–24, 37–39, 48–63.
39. ACLU to Reverend Patrick Hayes, November 17, 1921, ACLU-MF, reel 25. Robyn Rosen suggests that Dennett considered the ACLU's support for birth control weak. More likely, Dennett was dissatisfied with the ACLU's refusal to side with her against Sanger. See Dennett to Baldwin, January 31, 1930; Dennett to Baldwin, December 8 and 11, 1934; Baldwin to Dennett, December 10 and 13, 1934, MWD-MF, reel 16; Rosen, *Reproductive Health*,

Reproductive Rights, 103–104; "Woman's Own Story of Her Night in Jail," *New York Times*, November 20, 1921; "Arrest Mrs. Rublee for Views on Birth Control," *New York Times*, December 3, 1921; "Plan to Test Police Power Over Speech," *New York Times*, December 4, 1921; "Drops Mrs. Sanger's Case," *New York Times*, February 19, 1916; Sanger, *Margaret Sanger*, 309; "Police Veto Halts Birth Control Talk," *New York Times*, November 14, 1921; "Mrs. Sanger Urged to Sue Enright for False Arrest," *New York Call*, November 15, 1921; Milner to Sanger, 11-14-21; Albert DeSilver to Richard E. Enright, November 14, 1921; Milner to Sanger, November 17, 1921; Baldwin to William Sanger, November 18, 1921; "Birth Control Suit Waits on Police Inquiry," *New York Times*, November 19, 1921; "Filled Theater Applauds Talks on Birth Control," *New York Tribune*, November 19, 1921; Albert DeSilver to Richard Enright, November 21, 1921; DeSilver to William O. Lahey, November 22, 1921; "Police Probing Own Raid on Sanger Rally," *New York Call*, November 23, 1921; "Demands Police Quiz Mgr. Dineen," *New York Call*, November 25, 1921; "Arrests Mrs. Rublee, Witness at Birth Control Inquiry," *New York Post*, December 2, 1921; "Birth Control Aid Set Free After Arrest at Inquiry," *New York Herald*, December 3, 1921, ACLU-MF, reel 25; "Plan to Test Police Power Over Speech," *New York Times*, December 4, 1921; "See Plot by Police to Bar Free Speech," *New York Times*, December 10, 1921; Sanger to Henry John Gibbons, December 7, 1921, in Sanger, *Selected Papers*, 331–332; "Police Admit Error in Town Hall Raid," *New York Times*, February 18, 1922; "Hirshfield Inquiry Ends Up in the Air," *New York World*, February 8, 1922, ACLU-MF, reel 29. One public official, Michael M. Dolphin, Assistant Corporation Counsel of the City of New York, endured a yearlong investigation and possible censure by the American Bar Association for his role in the arrests. See "In the Matter of Michael M. Dolphin," 208 AD 223 (March 7, 1924), and 240 N.Y. 89 (March 31, 1925), and "Court Ruling Curbs Bar Association," *New York Times*, April 1, 1925.

40. Quote from DeSilver to Herbert L. Satterlee, January 7, 1922; "Civil Liberties Union Protests Banning of Birth Control Rallies at Cooper Union," *New York Call*, January 15, 1922, ACLU-MF, reel 25; "Calls Witnesses Over Birth Control," *New York Times*, February 2, 1922; "Albany Mayor's Ban Draws Fire," *New York Call*, January 25, 1923, ACLU-MF, reel 29; ACLU Executive Committee Minutes, January 29, 1923; February 5, 13, 19, 24, and 26, 1923; "Report on Civil Liberty Situation for Week Ending. . . January 27, 1923," ACLU-MF, reel 31; "Mayor Defied on Sanger Ban; Test Tonight," *Albany News*, February 20, 1923; "Sanger Meeting in Albany" (February 21, 1923), *New York Times*, April 23, 1923, ACLU-MF, reel 33; Sanger to Civil Liberties Union, telegram, February 20, 1924; ACLU to Mayor Walrath, telegram, February 20, 1924; William M. Marlow to Walrath, February 20, 1924; Baldwin to Sanger, February 21, 1924; Field Secretary to Anne Kennedy, February 23, 1924; Sanger to Baldwin, February 23, 1924; Kennedy to Baldwin, March 6, 1924, ACLU-MF, reel 37; "Vetoes Birth Control Ban," *New York Times*, February 26, 1924; "Topics of the Times," *New York Times*, February 27, 1924.
41. Baldwin, "Memo on the CLU," n.d., PML-PLC, box 1.
42. First two quotes from Baldwin to Mrs. Cannon, unknown date, 1924; third quote from Baldwin to Dr. Alice Hamilton, October 14, 1924; fourth quote from Baldwin to Richard C. Cabot, October 26, 1924; John S. Codman to Cannon, March 21, 1924; Baldwin to Codman, unknown date, 1924; March 13, 1924, and April 10, 1924; Codman to ACLU Gentlemen, April 21, 1924; Codman to Kennedy, April 16, 1924; Baldwin to Kennedy, April 22, 1924, and September 9, 1924; unknown to Baldwin, no date; Codman to Baldwin, November 4 and 18, 1924 and December 5, 1924; Baldwin to Codman, n.d.; "Instructions," February 13, 1925; Baldwin, "Memorandum re: Birth Control Meeting," November 6, 1924; Rosa H. Roemer to Baldwin, November 9, 1924; Codman to Baldwin, November 18, 1924, and January 28, 1926; quote from November 19, 1925; Baldwin to Anna Levin, unknown date; Baldwin to Hilbert F. Day, November 11, 1924; Day to Baldwin, November 12 and 13, 1924; Baldwin to Kennedy, unknown date, November 1924; Baldwin to Anne Kennedy, September 9 and 26, 1924, ACLU-MF, reel 37; "Birth Control Talk Tonight,"

Boston Massachusetts American, September 16, 1923; "Birth Control is 'Degenerate' Says Boston Mayor; 'Nonsense' Says Union," *Telegraph American*, April 10, 1924; "Will Defy Curley Ban on Meeting," *Boston Post*, February 13, 1925, ACLU-MF, reel 43; ACLU Executive Committee Meeting Minutes, January 5 and 12, 1925; February 9 and 16, 1925; March 2, 1925, ACLU-MF, reel 40.

43. Ironically, Mayor Curley was a member of the Board of Trustees for Old South but was outvoted on the ACLU's application to use the hall for a free speech meeting. Sanger spoke to a private Boston group at the Young Men's Hebrew Association. First quote from "Liberty Union is Scored by Mayor" (unidentified newspaper), May 10, 1925, and "Curley Calls 'Civil Liberties' A Pest," *Springfield Massachusetts Republican*, May 14, 1925; "Old South Speakers Score Curley Ban on 'Free Speech,'" *Boston Herald*, May 13, 1925; second and third quotes from "Protest 'Liberty' Meeting," *Boston Massachusetts Post*, May 12, 1925; ACLU Executive Committee Meeting Minutes, May 4, 1925; "Birth Control Head to Defy Mayor," *Boston Massachusetts American*, February 17, 1925; "Mayor Holds Up Birth Control Talk," *Boston Massachusetts Morning Globe*, March 3, 1925; "Free Speech for Boston," *Boston Transcript*, May 9, 1925; "Controversy Over Mayor's Birth Control Ban Revived," *Boston Herald*, May 10, 1925; "Sizzling Shot for Curley," *Boston Globe*, May 13, 1925, ACLU-MF, reel 43; ACLU Executive Committee Meeting Minutes, March 16 and 30, 1925, and July 20, 1925; ACLU Executive Committee Meeting Minutes, March 9, 1925, ACLU-MF, reel 40; "Statement by Roger Baldwin . . . concerning the proposed meeting of Mrs. Sanger," February 16, 1925; "Instructions," February 13, 1925, SSC-AFP, box 89; Codman to Mr. Dunn, March 18, 1924; Lawrence G. Brooks to Baldwin, April 3, 1924; Baldwin to Codman, April 9, 1924; Lawrence G. Brooks to Baldwin, April 3, 1924, ACLU-MF, reel 37; Walker, *In Defense*, 60–62.

44. Codman to Baldwin, November 19, 1925; Codman to Baldwin, February 18, 1926, ACLU-MF, reel 49; "Remove Dolphin, Liberties Union Urges Hylan," *New York Call*, December 4, 1921, ACLU-MF, reel 25; Sanger, *My Fight for Birth Control*, 236–237.

45. Meeting minutes suggest that Flynn brought Tresca's case to the attention of the ACLU. ACLU Executive Committee Minutes, September 4, 1923, p. 3, ACLU-MF, reel 31. See also Chief Inspector, Post Office Department to Mr. W. J. Burns, August 30, 1923; Chief Inspector, Post Office Department, Memorandum, August 23, 1923; Marguerite Tucker, "Carlo Tresca," *Greenwich Villager*, April 22, 1922; Burns, "Memorandum for Mr. Hoover in re: Carlo Tresca and Umberto Nieri," March 22, 1924; Frank R. Welsh to J. R. Hoover, Esq., March 12, 1925; Wm. J. West Memorandum, May 5, 1922; William Loughlin Report, March 12, 1923, #8222, FOIA-FBI, Carlo Tresca file. See also Pernicone, *Carlo Tresca*, 152–158; Gallagher, *All the Right Enemies*, 98–109; Sanger, *Selected Papers*, 417–418; Shaw, *The Body Taboo*, 317–324; "Seek Clemency for Carlo Tresca," January 10, 1925, *New York Times*; "Conviction of Anti-Fascist 'Persecution,' Liberties Union Says," January 6, 1925, *New York Times*.

46. Quotes from Bailey to Codman, August 24, 1927; see also Milner to John Codman, May 12, 1927; Bailey to H. C. Wellman, March 31, 1927; Milner to Walter Frank, August 4, 1927, ACLU-MF, reel 52. Bailey led the ACLU during Baldwin's sabbatical between 1926 and 1929. Historians have noted but misinterpreted the ACLU's subdued role in censorship fights during these years. See Walker, *In Defense*, 82–83; Boyer, *Purity in Print*, 202–203. ACLU leaders watched for an opportunity to challenge Boston's strict censorship regime. With the election of Mayor Malcolm Nichols in 1926, they saw hope for change, and urged Sanger to return to the beleaguered city to hold a birth control meeting cosponsored by the ACLU. But Sanger was in England, causing a delay that would extend even further because of the ACLU's involvement with the Sacco and Vanzetti cases. ACLU Executive Committee Meeting Minutes, December 28, 1925, ACLU-MF, reel 40; Codman to Baldwin, January 28, 1926, February 18 and 25, 1926; Baldwin to Codman, February 1, 18, and 25, 1926, ACLU-MF, reel 49; Baldwin to Sanger, November 30, 1926, ACLU-MF, reel 52; "Boston Cases 1920–1929: Interference with Meetings," ACLU-MF, reel 57.

47. Paul Cravath to Albert DeSilver, January 10, 1922, ACLU-MF, reel 25; quote from Federal Bureau of Investigation Report on American Civil Liberties Union, p. 7, October 3, 1924, FOIA-FBI, ACLU file.
48. Walker, *In Defense*, 31–32, 82–83; Schmidt, "Socialist-Feminism," 195, 199–200, 202; Cook, ed., *Toward the Great Change*, 90–96; Lamson, *Roger Baldwin*, 126; Cottrell, *Roger Nash Baldwin*, 106, 112, 166; Roger Baldwin, "For the children and grand-children and their kin," unpublished manuscript (1962), RNB-MF, reel 3; Rice, *Minority Report*, 6, 83–84, 102, 158, 181, 359–360, 371, 379, 384–385, 387, 396–397 (on Rice's involvement with the ACLU, see pp. 346–348); Rinehart, ed., *One Woman Determined*, 72, 87–88, 213, 239, 245, 250, 258–259, 262; Chen, *"Sex Side of Life,"* 78–79, 83, 113, 120–121; Pernicone, *Carlo Tresca*, 238–239, 243–247, 152–158; Gallagher, *All the Right Enemies*, 27–28, 40, 95, 98–109, 113, 147; Flynn, *The Rebel Girl*, 333–334; Marguerite Tucker, "Carlo Tresca," *Greenwich Villager*, April 22, 1922, and Chief Inspector, Post Office Department to Mr. W. J. Burns, Director, Bureau of Investigation, August 30, 1923, FOIA-FBI, Carlo Tresca file.
49. Witt, *Patriots and Cosmopolitans*, 203–208; Aronson, "Taking Liberties," 8–10.
50. First four quotes from "Roger Baldwin, March 4, 1972," Joseph Lash notes, FDR-JPL, box 49; fifth quote from Baldwin to Doty, September 26, 1918; sixth and seventh quotes from Baldwin to Doty, October 14, 1918; eighth quote from Baldwin to Doty, undated, SSC-MZD, box 2; all other quotes from Rinehart, ed., *One Woman Determined*, 233–234, see also 217, 232–233, 261–262, and "Roger Baldwin, March 4, 1972"; "Roger Baldwin, 3-7-72," Joseph Lash Notes, FDR-JPL, box 49; Lamson, *Roger Baldwin*, 115–117.
51. First two quotes from Baldwin to Doty, July 27, 1921; fifth quote from Baldwin to Doty, July 27, 1921; sixth, seventh, and eighth quotes from Baldwin to Doty, undated; see also Baldwin to Doty, October 2, 1919, and July 27, 1921, SSC-MZD, box 2; quotes three and four from Rinehart, ed., *One Woman Determined*, 239, see also 87–88, 213, 245. Doty complained that "Roger's ideal of freedom applied to everything," while to her, freedom was "intellectual and spiritual." She admitted that her "views had changed and were often not in accord with Roger's." "This [total independence of each partner] was the ideal of that time," she wrote. Rinehart, ed., *One Woman Determined*, 87–88, 213, 236, 239, 245, quotes from 239. See also "Morris Ernst, 2-7-72"; "Roger Baldwin, 2-14-71," Joseph Lash notes, FDR-JPL, box 49. When Doty's contemporary, feminist Doris Stevens, was urged by her husband to "act like a modern woman" by entertaining herself with other men, Stevens complied, but then sought to marry the men with whom she had extramarital affairs. Rupp, "Feminism and the Sexual Revolution," 296.
52. First two quotes from "Roger Baldwin, 10-21-71," Joseph Lash notes, FDR-JPL, box 49; third quote from "Roger Baldwin, 3-7-72"; fourth and fifth quotes from "Lucille Milner, 3-22-72"; see also "Anna Friedkin, 1-16-72"; "Roger Baldwin, 5-24-72"; "Clifton Read, 9-25-72"; "Phil Taft, 10-12-72," Joseph Lash notes, FDR-JPL, box 49. Baldwin admitted to the affair with Tucker and alluded to others but dismissed them as unimportant because they "didn't function in any relationship that marked my life"; "I was not living with any of them," and "there were no scandals or anything like that." With Doty in Europe, Baldwin remembered, "I had lady friends[;] of course I had them when I wasn't living with my wife—to one degree or another." See Transcript of "Recollections, Tape 10 Side A," PML-PLC, box 1. Contemporaneous documentation confirms Doty's worries about Strong. See Baldwin to Doty, October 2, 1919; June 14, 1921, SSC-MZD, box 2.
53. Quotes from Hugh Cabot to Doty, February 25, 1920, July 3, 1920; Hugh Cabot to Doty, February 25, 1920; see also Martha Baldwin to Doty, October 24, 1920, and November 2, 1934, SSC-MZD, box 2. Nearly sixty years later, Baldwin remembered that Doty "had one pregnancy during our early marriage but it was terminated—I never found out how. It was not her first." Quote from Baldwin's 1978 "Reminiscences," reproduced in Rinehart, ed., *One Woman Determined*, 258. Preston's close friends and family were less accepting than she and sometimes expressed "outrage" at Baldwin's behavior. "Helen

Mannoni, 10-31-72"; "Roger Baldwin, 3-7-72"; "Roger Baldwin, 9-24-71," Joseph Lash notes, FDR-JPL, box 49. Baldwin reported the birth of his daughter, Helen Thompson Baldwin, to Doty in a letter that indicated a rather marked change in him. "I'd like to go [abroad]," he wrote, "but I do not think Evelyn wants to leave a new baby, and I would hardly go without her." Quote from Baldwin to Doty, May 5 ["about 1936"], SSC-MZD, box 2. Correspondence between Doty and Baldwin extended through the year of her death in 1963. Baldwin often sent Doty money, and the two remained in contact and continued to care about each other throughout their lives.

54. The reverse may also have been the case. In an effort to explain what made Baldwin such a great ACLU leader, Morris Ernst wrote, "His inner repulsions against restraint produced the impetus for his public fights." Ernst to Holmes, November 16, 1949, HRC-MEC, box 44.

55. On the appointment of Wolcott Pitkin as ACLU counsel, see "Free Speech in 1924" (New York: American Civil Liberties Union, 1925), 32–33, 40, in MSP-MF, series 2, subseries 1 (S3.82), and "The Reminiscences of Roger Nash Baldwin," 127, CUOHP-MF. For more on Kenyon, see Weigand and Horowitz, "Dorothy Kenyon," and "Material Collected by Mildred Adams Kenyon: Biography draft," unpublished manuscript, pp. 88–89, SSC-DK, box 3. On Gertrude Besse King, see Walter Lippman's introduction to King, *Alliances for the Mind*, vii–ix, 153. First and second quote from King to Kenyon, October 19, 1920; third and fourth quote from King to Kenyon, October 27, 1920; fifth and sixth quotes from Pitkin to Kenyon, 1920, SSC-DK, box 15; seventh quote from Kenyon to Pitkin, Autumn 1921; eighth quote from Pitkin to Kenyon, May 6, 1924; see also Kenyon to Pitkin, March 9, 1922; April 23 and 25, 1923, May 4, 1923, June 12, 1923, August 15, 1923, SSC-DK, box 16. Very few of Kenyon's letters to Pitkin or King have survived, and the few that have may very well have been saved because they were never sent. See correspondence in SSC-DK, boxes 15 and 16. Kenyon refers to Pitkin as Peter, Pat, Patsy, Parsons, and Wolcott. In a particularly pointed letter, Pitkin advised Kenyon that "if we are to survive on a basis of real freedom," she must stop burdening him with unreasonable demands and expressing such pain when he failed to meet them. "I really don't want any more requests . . . with such disproportionate results," he warned. Quote from Pitkin to Kenyon, October 21, 1921; see also Pitkin to Kenyon, August 17, 22, and 27, 1921, SSC-DK, box 16. Like Doty, as a student at Smith College, Kenyon may also have felt attracted to other women. They were "quite the rage," Kenyon recalled of crushes between women in a 1971 interview. Prompted by the interviewer, she agreed that "it was an atmosphere that would breed that sort of thing." See Kenyon Interview, June 14, 1971, SSC-DK, box 4.

56. Quotes from Rice, *Minority Report*, 102; see also 84, 183, 184, 224; see also 10, 83–84, 102, 158, 181, 359–360, 371, 379, 384–385, 387, 396–397. After marriage, both men seemed more comfortable pursuing sexual relationships with women of their own class. Did attaining the "respectable" status of husband open up new sexual opportunities? Or had birth control and sexual "freedom" become more acceptable among their female peers by the time they married? See Rice to Frank Harris, August 17, 1920; see also October 7, 1920; February 17, 1921, HRC-ERC, box 111.

57. First quote from Rice to Frank Harris, June 23, 1921; second quote from Rice to Harris, May 29, 1925, HRC-ERC, box 111; third and fourth quotes from Rice to Bertram Bloch, September 7, 1925, HRC-ERC, box 110; fifth, sixth, and seventh quotes from Rice, *Minority Report*, 182–183; see also 181 and 184; Ruth to Rice, n.d., HRC-ERC, box 59.

58. Quotes from Rice, *Minority Report*, 84, 102, 183, 184, 224; see also 83, 158, 181, 359–360, 371, 379, 384–385, 387, 396–397. Rice's assertions along these lines are plentiful. "I live, primarily, for myself, for the exploitation of my I-ness," he wrote. "In all vital things, I let nothing or nobody stand in the way of what seems to me fulfillment." Rice to Harris, n.d.; see also Rice to Harris, December 7, 1941, HRC-ERC, box 111; Harris to Rice, December 13, 1941, HRC-ERC, box 59; Baldwin to Rice, March 31, 1942, HRC-ERC, box 89; Rice to Bertram Bloch, April 6, 1927, HRC-ERC, box 110. Hazel Rice disappeared from the historical record after leaving the ACLU in 1942.

59. Quote from Chen, *"Sex Side of Life,"* 113; see also 78–79, 83, 113, 120–121. On heterodoxy, see Schwarz, *Radical Feminists of Heterodoxy;* Stansell, *American Moderns;* and Wetzsteon, *Republic of Dreams.*
60. One scholar has referred to Tresca's relentless infidelity as a "cancer" on his relationship with Flynn. Flynn's depression was exacerbated, no doubt, by a number of recent political disappointments. Pernicone, *Carlo Tresca,* 238–239; 243–247; see also Gallagher, *All the Right Enemies,* 27–28, 40, 95, 113, 147; Flynn, *The Rebel Girl,* 333–334. Albert DeSilver died tragically when he fell from a moving train in 1924. See "Fall Off Train Kills Albert De Silver," *New York Times,* December 8, 1924; Nelles, *A Liberal in Wartime.* According to one scholar, Margaret DeSilver's jealousy about Flynn's earlier relationship with Tresca may have inspired her to call for Flynn's ouster from the ACLU board in 1939, one year before Flynn's formal expulsion for her membership in the Communist Party. See Camp, *Iron in Her Soul,* 158–159. On Flynn's expulsion, see Lamont, ed., *Trial of Elizabeth Gurley Flynn;* Baxandall, *Words on Fire,* 30–31, 268; Camp, *Iron in Her Soul,* 125–137; Margaret DeSilver to Baldwin, January 3, 1939, ACLU-MF, reel 167; DeSilver to Baldwin, December 8, 1939; DeSilver to Rice, December 8, 1939; John Haynes Holmes to Rice, January 3, 1940, HRC-ERC, box 84.
61. First and fourth quotes from Holmes to Cecil A. Damon, December 5, 1938, SSC-MSP, box 30; second quote from "Pastor for Birth Control," *New York Times,* December 4, 1916; third quote from "Ten Women Named As Greatest Living," *New York Times,* May 18, 1931. See also "Mrs. Byrne to Have a Feeding Schedule," *New York Times,* January 29, 1917, and "Tells Future of Marriage," *New York Times,* January 24, 1927; Voss, *Rabbi and Minister,* 107, 109. On Dennett's early relationship with Holmes, see Holmes to Dennett, April 19, 1917, and July 19, 1917, MWD-MF, reel 33. On Holmes's involvement with the VPL, see Dennett to Holmes, June 9, 1917; "Minutes of meeting called by Mrs. Leslie J. Tompkins," January 3, 1922; "Meeting of Governing Body of the Voluntary Parenthood League," January 3 and 19, 1922; unknown to Margaret, January 10, 1922; "Meeting of the Executive Committee," May 20, 1922; June 1, 1922; January 25, 1923; May 17, 1923; Holmes to Mrs. Kennedy, December 8, 1925; Holmes to Mrs. Bronson, December 8 and 11, 1925, MWD-MF, reel 13. When the VPL asked Holmes to support Dennett's birth control bill and oppose Sanger's, Holmes refused to get involved, characterizing the split as "a personal matter" between the two and announcing that he simply "believe[d] in birth control" and would continue supporting both women and their organizations. Holmes failed to convince his congregation to host Sanger in 1925, but in 1929 the church sponsored a talk by the medical director of the American Birth Control League. "Today's Programs in City's Churches," *New York Times,* November 10, 1929; Minutes, ACLU Executive Committee, January 12, 1925; Minutes, ACLU Executive Committee, February 9, 1925, ACLU-MF, reel 40. Holmes's support for birth control did not derive from the fear of overpopulation that motivated many others. Nor was it limited to opposing laws against birth control—a position that would have accorded with his belief that law could not act as a moral agent. Holmes actually recommended the use of birth control, not just the repeal of laws against it. Holmes, *Religion for To-day,* 220–221; Voss, *Rabbi and Minister,* 190; Baldwin, "John Haynes Holmes—Preacher and Prophet, 1879–1964," May 3, 1964, RNB-MF, reel 7; Donald Szantho Harrington, "Dr. John Haynes Holmes, 1879–1964," April 5, 1964, http://members.fortunecity.com/hobeika/unitarians/holmes.html (retrieved August 6, 2011); American Birth Control Conference, *Birth Control,* 188–189.
62. Dennett to Albert DeSilver, May 12, 1918; DeSilver to Dennett, May 15, 1918, MWD-MF, reel 33; "Meetings of the Executive Committee," September 15, ca. 1922; "Meeting of the Executive Committee of the V.P.L.," November 3, 6, 17, and 28, 1922; December 13, 1922; January 10, 17, 25, and 29, 1923; February 16, 1923; March 5 and 27, 1923; April 3, 1923; "Facts re: Misunderstanding of DeSilvers, V.P.L. and M.W.D.," Dennett to DeSilver, March 28, 1923; April 21 and 25, 1923; DeSilver to Dennett, April 27, 1923, MWD-MF, reel 13. A major disagreement between Dennett and the DeSilvers regarding the use of donated

funds ended their collaboration in 1923. Margaret DeSilver did not join the ACLU executive board until 1925. ACLU Executive Committee Minutes, January 12, 1925, ACLU-MF, reel 40; Pernicone, *Carlo Tresca*, 246–247.

63. See for example Walker, *In Defense*, 31, 83. The appearance of civil libertarian language and values in the private lives of ACLU founders parallels their efforts to use Freudianism to "resolve their personal problems." Quote from Fishbein, "Freud and the Radicals," 186. Recent examples of public officials and religious leaders who denounce marital infidelity in public but practice it in private abound. See "Mysteries Remain After Governor Admits an Affair," *New York Times*, June 24, 2009; "GOP's Senator's Sex Scandal Brings Us Back to the Glory Days of 2006," *Village Voice*, June 16, 2009; "Spitzer is Linked to Prostitution Ring," *New York Times*, March 10, 2008; "Church Minister Resigns After Sex Scandal in US," *Telegraph.co.uk*, May 20, 2008; "Haggard's Church Discloses More on Sex Scandal," *New York Times*, January 26, 2009.
64. Gordon, *Woman's Body, Woman's Right*, 193; quote from Rupp, "Feminism and the Sexual Revolution," 304.

Chapter 2

1. For examples of similar rhetoric among antiobscenity activists, see Wheeler, *Against Obscenity*, 99, 104. Baldwin to John Casey, April 27, 1931; "Memorandum on Censorship Situation in Boston," April 20, 1931; Baldwin to Hiram Motherwell, June 17, 1931, ACLU-MF, reel 88; "Theatre Gag Stirs Civil Liberties to Aid Gotham's Stage," *Industrial Solidarity*, December 23, 1930, ACLU-MF, reel 71. See also Walker, *In Defense*, 82–84.
2. See Walker, *In Defense*, 22, 31–32, 82, and Cottrell, *Roger Nash Baldwin*, 166–167, both of whom characterize early ACLU leaders in these terms. Their language (and perhaps their interpretation) seems borrowed from Morris Ernst, who wrote to another ACLU officer in 1948, "The Union has always been squeamish with respect to matters sexual." His role in the organization will be discussed later in the chapter. Ernst to Clifford Forster, June 15, 1948, HRC-ERP, box 84.
3. See chapter 1 regarding the Sacco and Vanzetti case. Milner to Codman, August 4, 1927, October 20, 1927; Codman to Milner, August 11, 1927; "(COPY) Commonwealth of Massachusetts vs. Warner V. Williams," n.d.; Circulars for *The Great Secret of Freemasonry*, ACLU-MF, reel 52. Williams advertised his book as the "most immoral Book in print." Milner to Roewer, September 29, 1927; Codman to Milner, October 4, 1927; ACLU telegram to Roewer, October 5, 1927; Codman to Bailey, October 18, 1927; Milner to Codman, October 20, 1927, ACLU-MF, reel 52.
4. Joseph P. Lash Interview with Roger Baldwin, March 6, 1972, in Cottrell, *Roger Nash Baldwin*, 166 n. 45; Boyer, *Purity in Print*, 203–204; Hays, *Let Freedom Ring*, 159, 163; Rice to Harry Dana, December 22, 1930, HRC-ERP, box 88.
5. Dennett to Ernst, December 6, 1928; Dennett to Ernst, August 27, 1928; September 1, 1928; October 20, 1928; November 8, 1928; December 6 and 19, 1928; Ernst to Dennett, August 30, 1928; October 2, 1928; December 17, 1928, MWD-MF, reel 23; "Mrs. Dennett Inquiry By Congress Urged," *New York Times*, May 7, 1929. On the Civic Club, see Chen, *"Sex Side of Life,"* 187, 302. See also Walker, *In Defense*, 82; Craig, "Sex Side of Life," 149–152; Dennett, *Who's Obscene?* 46–47, 188–189, 195–198; *United States v. Dennett*, 39 F. 2d 564; Dennett to "Dearest People," May 2, 1929; Hays to Dennett, May 21 and 25, 1926; September 20, 1926; February 14, 1927; October 4, 1927; Dennett to Hays, May 22, 1926; September 17, 1926; February 10, 1927; October 1, 1927; MWD-MF, reel 21. Evidence suggests that the timing of Dennett's plan to challenge the post office ban and her criminal indictment for mailing obscenity were indeed coincidental. As she explained in a letter to friends, "In his original proposal [Ernst] would have been bringing an injunction

against the government, while now he is simply counselor for the defense in a criminal case." Dennett to "Beloved Vine and Myra," March 1, 1929, MWD-MF, reel 21.

6. Baldwin to the National Committee, February 7, 1929, ACLU-MF, reel 71; Hays, *Let Freedom Ring*, 139; "Debate Between John Haynes Holmes, D.D. and Dr. Elmer Rice," January 28, 1931, HRC-ERP, box 88; Lindey to Mr. Stein et al., June 11, 1929; Lindey to Dennett, June 20, 1929, HRC-MEC, box 287; Dennett to Ernst, August 27, 1928; Lindey to Dennett, June 13 and 20, 1929; Bailey to Dennett, January 17, 1929; March 4, 1929; Dennett to Bailey, January 18, 1929, MWD-MF, reel 23. See also Chen, *"Sex Side of Life,"* 227–229, and Weinrib, "Sex Side of Civil Liberties," 325.
7. Quotes from Walker, *In Defense*, 83; see also Boyer, *Purity in Print*, 204; Friedman, *Prurient Interests*, 256 n. 48; Baldwin, "Oral History," 199; Rodell, "Morris Ernst." Dennett called the organization of the defense committee a "grand uprising." By the late 1920s, she had "assumed that such spontaneity was impossible,—a sort of 'before the war' spirit." See Dennett to Bailey, February 21, 1929, and November 3, 1930; see also Ernst to Dennett, February 18, 1929; Bailey to Dennett, May 3, 1929; American Civil Liberties Union, "The Prosecution of Mary Ware Dennett for 'Obscenity,'" June 1929, MWD-MF, reel 23; American Civil Liberties Union, Monthly Bulletin for Action, December 1929, 384, 4, ACLU-MF, reel 71; Baldwin to John Casey, License Commissioner, Boston, April 27, 1931; "Memorandum on Censorship Situation in Boston," April 20, 1931, ACLU-MF, reel 88; Dennett to "Beloved Vine and Myra," March 1, 1929; Dennett to Vine, March 1, 1929, MWD-MF, reel 21; Chen, *"Sex Side of Life,"* 269–303. The ACLU was also inspired to invest more of its resources in litigation because, by the end of the 1920s, it had won, almost by accident, a number of free speech victories, including several promising Supreme Court decisions. Leaders sensed that the judicial system was beginning to shift in their favor. This development empowered attorneys already in the ACLU and attracted new ones to the group. Walker, *In Defense*, 72–81; Baldwin to Bailey, December 12, 1927; Baldwin to Pitkin, December 12, 1927; Baldwin to Samuel Untermyer, November 8, 1927, ACLU-MF, reel 52.
8. "Scores Dennett Verdict," *New York Times*, January 10, 1929.
9. Quotes from Samuel Cummins to Mrs. Dennett, May 16, 1929, and Meyer Stein, "Memo for Mr. Ernst, Mr. Lindey, In re: Mary Ware Dennett," May 23, 1929; see also "Memorandum for Mr. Lindey," May 17, 1929; Alexander Lindey to Mrs. Dennett, May 21, 1929, MWD-MF, reel 23; Chen, *"Sex Side of Life,"* 297.
10. First quote from Mary Ware Dennett, "Regarding the Verdict of 'Guilty' in 'The Sex Side of Life' Case," undated, MWD-MF, reel 21; second quote from Sumner to Forrest Bailey, May 20, 1929; Bailey to Sumner, May 31, 1929; Bailey to Dennett, May 17, 1929; Chase to Bailey, May 20, 1929; Sumner to Bailey, May 20, 1929; Donnelly to Bailey, May 21, 1929; "Memorandum for Dr. Edward L. Keyes, Chairman, at Town Hall, Wednesday evening," May 22, 1929; "Mary Ware Dennett Defense Committee: Town Hall Meeting, May 22, 1929"; "Mary Ware Dennett Defense Committee Minutes," June 13, 1929; "Public Hearing on Sex Education—Freedom or Censorship under Auspices of The Mary Ware Dennett Defense Committee at Town Hall, New York City, May 21st, 1929," MWD-MF, reel 23; "Mrs. Dennett Decries Postal Censorship," *New York Times*, May 23, 1929.
11. Bob Marshall to Mrs. Dennett, March 3, 1930, MWD-MF, reel 20; Alexander Lindey to Dennett, June 9, 1930; July 2, 1930, MWD-MF, reel 23; *United States v. Dennett*, 39 F. 2d 564–569.
12. "Planks of Nudism," n.d.; Ilsley Boone, "Why Nudism?" n.d.; SCA-ACLU, box 17; Ilsley Boone, "On the Non-Obscenity of Nudist Pictures" (reprinted from *Sunshine & Health*, October 1942), ACLU-MF, reel 220. See also Unknown (redacted) to J. Edgar Hoover, February 19, 1945, FOIA-FBI, Ilsley Boone file.
13. First three quotes from Cottrell, *Roger Nash Baldwin*, 241 (see also 243) and Lamson, *Roger Baldwin*, viii; fourth quote from "Corliss Lamont, 3-7-72," Joseph Lash notes, FDR-JPL, box 49; last two quotes from Baldwin, "For the children and grand-children

and their kin," 1962; see also Baldwin, "Appendix to my memo on Evie and myself," 1962, RNB-MF, reel 3; Lash interviews with Baldwin, October 4, 1971, and November 5, 1971, FDR-JPL, box 49; Baldwin, "A Memo for Peggy Lamson," October 1974, PML-PLC, box 1. Baldwin also practiced casual nudism at Dell Brook, his farm in Oakland, New Jersey. See also Joseph Lash notes on dinner with Baldwin and friends, December 5, 1971; Lash interview with Baldwin, March 7, 1972, FDR-JPL, box 49; Lamson interview with Baldwin, July 25, 1974, Tape 21, PML-PLC, box 1; Baldwin, "Appendix to my memo on Evie and myself," 1962; Baldwin, "Evie: for the children," July 1978, RNB-MF, reel 3; Andrea Sachs, "Martha's Vineyard vs. Nantucket: What's the Diff?" *Washington Post*, July 23, 2000.

14. "Dies in the Spring," *The Nation*, April 4, 1942, 385–386; "Dr. Maurice Parmelee, Pioneer Nudist," n.d., ANRL—Personalities Files: Maurice Parmelee; "Maurice Parmelee, Economist Ousted for Nudism Stand, Dies," *New York Times*, March 28, 1969; Maurice Parmelee, "Results of Investigation" (June 11, 1948), 1–34, FOIA-FBI, Parmelee file; Gibbons, "Say, Whatever Became of Maurice Parmelee." H. C. Stewart to Greenbaum, Wolff & Ernst, December 24, 1927, HRC-MEC, box 390; Parmelee, *The New Gymnosophy*; Parmelee, *Nudism in Modern Life*; Baldwin to Ernst, November 20, 1929; Ernst to Baldwin, November 21, 1929, HRC-MEC, box 399; C. R. Lewis to Parmelee, August 3, 1933; Julius H. Parmelee to Lewis, August 8, 1933; Lewis to Parmelee, October 26, 1933; Parmelee to Honorable John M. Woolsey, October 26, 1934; Baldwin to Ernst, February 2, 1934; Lindey to Baldwin, August 8, 1934; Baldwin to Lindey, February 16, 1934; Lindey to Lewlie C. Garnett, April 16, 1934; *U.S. v. 6 Books Entitled "Nudism in Modern Life,"* District Court of D.C.; Ed Campbell to Lindey, October 25, 1934; Lindey to Campbell, November 7, 1934 and December 16, 1936; Lindey to Joe, December 1, 1934; David L. Rosston & Co., to Greenbaum, Wolff and Ernst, January 10, 1935, HRC-MEC, box 390. Boone tried to avoid legal trouble by submitting page proofs of his magazine to John S. Sumner, secretary of the New York Society for the Suppression of Vice, and modifying issues according to Sumner's suggestions. Frederick Woltman, "'Ban' on Nudist Magazine Charged to License Trick," *New York City World-Telegram*, June 23, 1934, ACLU-MF, reel 106; NCFC Minutes, March 14, 1934, and April 11, 1934, ACLU-MF, reel 107; "Enter Uncle Danny," unidentified magazine article, n.d., ANRL: Personalities File: Donald Johnson; "Defense Statement at post office Hearing Re: Sunshine & Health," July 29, 1947, ACLU-MF, series 3, reel 43. On the Fellerman case see *New York v. Maurice Fellerman*, 276 N.Y.S. 198 (December 24, 1934); *New York v. Fellerman*, 268 N.Y. 514 (June 4, 1935); *New York v. Fellerman*, 269 N.Y. 629 (January 7, 1936); NCFC Minutes, November 14, 1934, March 14, 1934, ACLU-MF, reel 107; Lee Hazen to Florina Lasker, January 5, 1935, ACLU-MF, reel 115; Baldwin to Clifton Read, June 5, 1936; Boone to Baldwin, April 24, 1937; NCFC Minutes, May 13, 1937, ACLU-MF, reel 141; *People v. W.C. Spangler*, March 31, 1937, NCA-ACLU, box 25.

15. Quotes from *New York v. Vincent Burke*, 276 N.Y.S. 402 (December 24, 1934); see also "Legal Nudism," *Time*, January 7, 1935; section 1140 in Fitzpatrick, *Penal Law*, 221; sections 1530 and 1533 in Committee of Fourteen, *Social Evil*, 139; untitled magazine article, n.d., ANRL: Personalities Files: Donald Johnson; "24 Seized in Raid on Nudist Cult Here," *New York Times*, December 8, 1931; "Frees 19 Nudists in Gymnasium Raid," *New York Times*, December 15, 1911; "24 Freed in 'Nudist' Case," *New York Times*, January 3, 1932; "Nudists Rollick About Big Farm at Scotchtown," *Middletown Times Herald*, August 8, 1933; William W. Newcomb to ACLU, October 3, 1932, ACLU-MF, reel 97; Lee Hazen to Florina Lasker, January 5, 1935, ACLU-MF, reel 115; "Nudists to Invade City, With Sites Kept Secret," *Pittsburg Pennsylvania Post*, August 8, 1934, ACLU-MF, reel 106. For a first-hand account of the raid by a member of the Olympian League, see Major Lyman Barry, "The Good Old Days," *Nude & Natural*, 14.1, n.d., 50, ANRL, Subject Files: History of American Nudism. See also Lester, *Godiva Rides Again*, 52–59; Ilfeld and Lauer, *Social Nudism in America*, 33–35; Merrill, *Among the Nudists*, 278, 297.

16. Quote from *New York v. Vincent Burke,* 276 N.Y.S. 402 (December 24, 1934); "Legal Nudism," *Time,* January 7, 1935. Burke's confident assessment of the decision and sensational media coverage of it by nationally circulated magazines such as *Time* may also have helped to mobilize antinudists. Quote in "Legal Nudism," *Time,* January 7, 1935, and "Policeman Dances for Court in Vain," *New York Times,* December 27, 1934.
17. Smith to Dunnigan, January 4, 1935, NYSL-AESC, box 50.
18. First quotes from "Catholics Begin Fight on Nudism," *New York Times,* January 3, 1935; last quote from "Nudists See Smith 'Inconsistent' Foe," *New York Times,* January 4, 1935; see also "Catholics Deny Wide Reform Aim," *New York Times,* January 15, 1935; Ilfeld and Lauer, *Social Nudism in America,* 34; "Nudists Appeal to Smith," *New York Times,* January 14, 1935; Carlos A. Gardiner to Smith, January 3, 1935, NYSL-AESC, box 50; "The New Crusade," *The Nation,* January 16, 1935, 62. *The Nation* interpreted Smith's apparent shift from "realistic statesman" to puritanical moralist, along with his recent failed bid for the presidency, as evidence that he had lost his once-solid political moorings. One scholar sees Smith's efforts to pass antinudism legislation as an effort to revive his political viability. Hoffman, "Making Private Parts Public," 43–45. Biographies of Smith insinuate that these activities might reflect his deepening connection to the Catholic Church. See Josephson, *Al Smith,* 466; Finan, *Alfred E. Smith,* 332–333. On Smith's refusal, as governor, to allow Catholic teachings to guide his hand, see Pringle, *Alfred E. Smith,* 338–339.
19. "Oppose Anti-Nudist Bill," *New York Times,* February 3, 1935.
20. First quote from John H. N. Potter to Smith, January 17, 1935, and "The Discipline of the Flesh," unidentified newspaper article, n.d., NYSL-AESC, box 50; last quote from "Nudists See Smith 'Inconsistent' Foe," *New York Times,* January 4, 1935; Boone to Smith, January 12, 1925 (misdated—should be 1935); Boone, "An Open Letter to Alfred E. Smith," January 14, 1935, NYSL-AESC, box 50.
21. Quotes from "Remarks by Mrs. Ryskind at Albany—February 5, [1935]," HRC-MEC, box 896; "Anti-Nudist Bill Obtains No Backing," *New York Times,* February 6, 1935. An abridged version of Ryskind's testimony can be found in Shaw, *The Body Taboo,* 235–236. Information on Mary Ryskind is scarce. On her work for the ACLU office, see Baldwin to A. A. Heist, October 7, 1946, ACLU-MF, reel 234. On her efforts to attract leaders of organized women to the NCFC and ACLU, see Ryskind to Mrs. Charles H. Sabin, January 15 and 29, 1934; Ryskind to Mrs. William Baldwin Smith, February 17, 1934; Ryskind to Mrs. John Beal, February 23, 1934; March 14, 1934, ACLU-MF, reel 107. Henry S. Huntington, vice chair of the International Nudist Conference, begged the ACLU to send an NCFC representative to the hearings in Albany and even offered to provide the delegate with transportation. Huntington to Barrett Clark, January 12, 1935, ACLU-MF, reel 115.
22. First, second, sixth, and seventh quotes from "Nudismo," *The Nation,* February 20, 1935, 210; third, fourth, fifth, eighth and ninth quotes from "Anti-Nudist Bill Obtains No Backing," *New York Times,* February 6, 1935, and Shaw, *The Body Taboo,* 230, see also 229; last quote from Clifton Read to Alexander Lindey, February 14, 1935, ACLU-MF, reel 115; see also "Religion: Pope on Nudism," *Time,* March 18, 1935; Charles E. Gay, "Nudism as Viewed by the American Magazines," undated and unpublished manuscript, ANRL—Subject File: Histories-Articles.
23. First quote from "Pope Pius Bitterly Assails Nudism Cults," *Spokane Daily Chronicle,* March 5, 1935; second and third quote from "Nudism in Germany Suppressed by Nazis," *New York Times,* March 8, 1933; see also "Pope Denounces Nudism as Pagan," *New York Times,* March 6, 1935; "Pope Hits at Nudism," *Los Angeles Times,* March 6, 1935; "Cult of Nudism Scored by Pope," *Evening Independent,* March 5, 1935. For contradictory interpretations of nudism under the Nazis, see Williams, *Turning to Nature*; and Ross, *Naked Germany.*
24. Quotes from Read to Lehman, sent to NCFC for signatures, April 18, 1935, HRC-ERC, box 84; see also American Civil Liberties Union, bulletin #662, ACLU-MF, reel 115; "Nudist Bill Reported," *New York Times,* March 14, 1935; "Anti-Nudist Bill Voted," *New York Times,* April 9, 1935; "Albany Votes Bill Outlawing Nudism; Leaders Wrangle,"

New York Times, April 16, 1935. Other nudists criticized Burke for commercializing nudism. See Kurt Barthel, "Facts About the Origin of Nudism Abroad and in the United States," unpublished manuscript, 1952, ANRL—Subject Files: History of American Nudism.

25. "Anti-Nudism Bill Signed by Lehman," *New York Times*, May 14, 1935; "North Jersey Area Haven for Nudists," *New York Times*, July 28, 1935; untitled magazine article, "Religion Communities," 13–14, ANRL—Subject Files: History of American Nudism; "Sunshine Park," *Nudism Today*, No. 11, n.d., 11–12, ANRL—Personalities Files: Donald Johnson. ACLU leaders also stepped forward when, in an ironic twist on Vincent Burke's hopes that other states would follow the New York State Supreme Court in recognizing the legality of nudism, several midwestern and southern states instead moved toward adopting antinudist laws similar to New York's new law. The ACLU's underdeveloped midwestern affiliates could offer little direct assistance. Baldwin advised Boone from afar and provided him with the names of sympathetic local attorneys. Together, they prevented the passage of antinudist legislation in Michigan and Indiana. The Ohio State Legislature passed the Keller Bill, modeled on New York's antinudist law, after the Ohio attorney general announced that nudism did not violate state law. By contrast, the Michigan legislature's refusal to pass an antinudist bill was, in part, a reaction against an unpopular antinudist court decision, *People v. Ring*, 267 Mich. 657 (June 4, 1934); NCFC Agenda, October 8, 1937, ACLU-MF, reel 141; Baldwin to Boone, January 31, 1939; Boone to Baldwin, February 2 and 3, 1939, ACLU-MF, reel 167; "The Deadly Triangle: Michigan, Indiana, Ohio," unidentified magazine, n.d., ANRL: Personalities Files: Donald Johnson. On ACLU affiliates in Indiana, Michigan, and Ohio, see Walker, *In Defense*, 118, and Leis, *History of ACLU in Ohio*. See also Nevitt, "Legal Aspects of Nudism," 57–61. "*People v. Hildabridle*: Voelker and the Art of Crafting an Opinion," *Supplement from the Michigan Supreme Court Historical Society*, February 2009, 6–9.

26. Quote from *Parmelee v. United States*, 113 F. 2d 729 (May 14, 1940); see also Lindey to Edmund Campbell, January 10, 1935, and December 16, 1936; Lindey to Clifton Read, January 10, 1935, ACLU-MF, reel 115; Harry F. Ward to "Our Friends," November 1938, ACLU-MF, reel 167. An appeal seemed likely to succeed, because the decision defied a higher court precedent established five years earlier in *United States v. One Book Called Ulysses* (1933), a case argued and won by Ernst. See Lindey to Baldwin, December 2, 1938; Baldwin to Lindey, December 3, 1938; Lindey to Campbell, December 9 and 16, 1938; Campbell to Lindey, December 1, 1938, ACLU-MF, reel 156; Lindey to Ernst, December 3, 1938; Boone to Campbell, December 5, 1938; Campbell to Boone, December 6, 1938; Campbell to Lindey, December 6, 1938; Lindey to Campbell, December 7, 1938, and March 29, 1939; Lindey memo, December 15, 1938, HRC-MEC, box 390.

27. Lindey to Hazel Rice, November 7, 1940; September 11, 1940; Hazel Rice to Lindey, May 27, 1940; Campbell to Lindey, January 11, 1940; Harry Hibschman to Lindey, May 25, 1940, HRC-MEC, box 390; Lindey to Baldwin, May 16, 1940; Baldwin to Lindey, May 17, 1940; ACLU Board of Directors Minutes, May 20, 1940; NCFC Minutes, January 23, 1941; Lindey to Clarice Brows, May 18, 1941, ACLU-MF, reel 192; "Dr. Maurice Parmelee, Pioneer Nudist," n.d., ANRL-Personalities Files: Maurice Parmelee.

28. "Offers Aid in Fight on Stage Censors," *New York Times*, December 9, 1930; "Stage Censoring Fought as Source of New Rackets," *New York Times*, December 9, 1930, ACLU-MF, reel 71; Edward Childs Carpenter, "Stage Censorship," *New York Times*, December 6, 1930, 14.

29. First quote from Houchin, *Censorship of the American Theatre*, 93; see also 6–9, 14–15, 19–22, 26, 28–30, 34, 41; Friedman, *Prurient Interests*, 96–104; Witham, "The Play Jury." All other quotes from Elmer Rice to the *New York Times*, January 29, 1922.

30. Quote from Houchin, *Censorship of the American Theatre*, 116, 118, 127–128; see also Wheeler, *Against Obscenity*, 98–100, 129, 135–138; Graber, *Transforming Free Speech*, 54; Friedman, *Prurient Interests*, 62–94. The motion picture industry developed its own system of self-censorship in the 1920s under Will Hays.

31. According to historian Andrea Friedman, in the 1930s, voluntary or self-censorship began to represent, not a democratic alternative to, but the equivalency of, state censorship. Juries were considered the new democratic option. Friedman, *Prurient Interests*, 170–173. "Offers Aid in Fight on Stage Censors," *New York Times*, December 9, 1930; "Liberties Union Offers Help in Censorship War," *New York City News*, December 9, 1930; "Stage Censoring Fought as Source of New Rackets," *New York Herald Tribune*, December 9, 1930; "Theatre Gag Stirs Civil Liberties to Aid Gotham's Stage," *Industrial Solidarity*, December 23, 1930; "New York Dramatists' Guild Prepares for Censors," *Citizen* (Schenectady), December 26, 1930, ACLU-MF, reel 71. See also Elmer Rice, "The Theatre Again Faces the Censorship Problem," *New York Times*, December 14, 1930.
32. First and second quotes from Arthur to Bailey, January 29, 1931; third and fourth quotes from Kenyon to Bailey, February 9, 1931; fifth, sixth, and seventh quotes from Goldstein to Bailey, January 30, 1931; see also Bailey to Goldstein, February 2, 1931, ACLU-MF, reel 88; Bailey to Arthur, January 28, 1931; Gordon W. Moss to Frank Gilmore, March 29, 1932, ACLU-MF, reel 88; Friedman, *Prurient Interests*, 112–113; "Group of 100 Ready in Censorship Fight," *New York Times*, December 16, 1931; Schwarz, *Radical Feminists of Heterodoxy*, 14, 32, 55, 62, 64–65, 117, 121; Wetzsteon, *Republic of Dreams*, 108–158, 176.
33. First two quotes from "Agree that Stage Must Purge Itself," *New York Times*, January 29, 1931; third quote from "Leading Churchmen Scored on Theatre," *New York Times*, February 19, 1931; see also "Moving for Censorship," *New York Times*, January 30, 1931, and "Stage Censoring Fought as Source of New Rackets," *New York Times*, December 9, 1930, ACLU-MF, reel 71; Holmes, "No Stage Censorship," *New York Tribune*, February 26, 1931, ACLU-MF, reel 97; "Dr. John Haynes Holmes," transcript of memorial service, April 5, 1964, "John Haynes Holmes—Preacher and Prophet, 1879–1964," RNB-MF, reel 7; Holmes, *Religion for To-Day*, 220; Voss, *Rabbi and Minister*, 69. Rice would echo many of Holmes's criticisms of the theater when his career as a playwright floundered years later, and he declared that only government sponsorship could save the theater. Rice to Herbert Kline, December 1, 1936, HRC-ERP, box 106; "What's the Matter with Broadway," *Dalton Bulletin*, May 1957, HRC-ERP, box 93; see also Rice, *Minority Report*, 340–341.
34. Bailey to Lewis Mumford, February 11, 1931, ACLU-MF, reel 88. On Morris Ernst's adamant opposition to any sort of self-regulation, see "Education Here Called Innocuous," *New York Times*, March 29, 1931.
35. Quote from Bailey to the Members of this Committee, April 1, 1931; Louise Stevens Bryant to Bailey, May 11, 1931; Bailey to Bryant, May 12, 1931, ACLU-MF, reel 88. The most extensive treatments of the NCFC can be found in Friedman, *Prurient Interests*, 4–5, 170–180, and Walker, *In Defense*, 85, 155, 228.
36. Moss to Editor, *Christian Endeavor World*, October 6, 1931; Baldwin to Hiram Motherwell, June 17, 1931; Baldwin to John Casey, April 27, 1931; "Memorandum on Censorship Situation in Boston," April 20, 1931, ACLU-MF, reel 88; "Theatre Gag Stirs Civil Liberties to Aid Gotham's Stage," *Industrial Solidarity*, December 23, 1930, ACLU-MF, reel 71; see also Walker, *In Defense*, 82–84.
37. First three quotes from Lewis Gannett, "Books and Things," *New York Herald-Tribune*, January 15, 1937; fourth and fifth quotes from unsigned to John J. Spencer, November 24, 1938, ACLU-MF, reel 156; sixth quote from Zechariah Chafee, "The Censorship in Boston," n.d., ACLU-MF, reel 67; see also Baldwin to Casey, April 27, 1931; "Memorandum on Censorship Situation in Boston," April 20, 1931; Baldwin to Hiram Motherwell, June 17, 1931; Secretary to Mr. L. L. Dantzler, July 7, 1931, ACLU-MF, reel 88; "Theatre Gag Stirs Civil Liberties to Aid Gotham's Stage," *Industrial Solidarity*, December 23, 1930, ACLU-MF, reel 71. See also Walker, *In Defense*, 82–84; Boyer, *Purity in Print*, 163, 195; Friedman, *Prurient Interests*, 105–106, 109–113.
38. Quotes from Baldwin to Casey, April 27, 1931 and "Memorandum on Censorship Situation in Boston," April 20, 1931; Moss to Frank Gilmore, March 29, 1932; Moss to

George D. Leonard, March 29, 1932; April 11 and 26, 1932; Gilmore to Moss, April 1 and 26, 1932; Moss to Rose, April 4 and 16, 1932; Moss to Arthur Le Sueur, April 6, 1932; Moss to Mrs. L. N. Scott, April 6, 1932; Hatcher Hughes to Catheryne Cooke Gilman, April 6, 1932; Moss to Mrs. George S. Cavanaugh, April 11, 1932; Moss to Kittleson, April 12, 1932; "Suggested Procedure in Organizing Freedom from Censorship Committee in Minneapolis," April 24, 1932; Moss to "Our Friends in Minneapolis," April 28, 1932; Moss to Dennett, May 18, 1932; Hyman Edelman to Moss, June 7, 1932; Moss, "Memo on Minneapolis Censorship legislation," July 20, 1932, ACLU-MF, reel 88. Later, when the Old Howard Theater was attacked by city officials for staging obscene burlesque shows, Baldwin and the ACLU were the only theater defenders not financially invested in its survival. Heywood Broun, "It Seems to Me," *New York World Telegram*, May 13, 1937.

39. Moss to Rose, March 29, 1932; Hughes to William Anderson, March 29, 1932; "Memorandum on Censorship Situation in Boston," April 20, 1931, ACLU-MF, reel 88; secretary to David Niles, January 18, 1934; Hughes, et al. to Board of Censors, January 17, 1935, ACLU-MF, reel 115; Rice to Gilman, August 30, 1932, MHS-GFP, box 18. On the Minneapolis "Crazy Quilt" controversy, see Wheeler, *Against Obscenity*, 129–132.
40. Dennett, "Excerpts from Address at the Conference of the A.B.C.L., Hotel Astor, New York: On Birth Control and the Law," November 19, 1929, SSC-MSP, box 5; ACLU Minutes of the Board of Directors and the National Council on Freedom from Censorship, February 15, 1932, ACLU-MF, reel 88; Ernst to Mrs. Hazel Moore, March 8, 1939, HRC-MEC, box 363; Moss to Dennett, February 23, 1932, ACLU-MF, reel 87; Dennett to Hon. Walter M. Pierce, February 19, 1934; Sanger, "A Few Important Reasons for Amending Existing Birth Control Laws," n.d.; Dennett to Baldwin, December 8, 1934, ACLU-MF, reel 107. The rivalry between Dennett and Sanger has been covered elsewhere. See especially Rosen, *Reproductive Health, Reproductive Rights*. In principle, ACLU leaders preferred Dennett's repeal approach. See Baldwin to Dennett, August 4, 1931; Moss to Dennett, August 17, 1931; Myra P. Gallert and Dennett to Dear Friend, n.d.; Dennett to Baldwin and Moss, July 28, 1931, ACLU-MF, reel 86; Baldwin to Ernst, December 31, 1931, ACLU-MF, reel 87. On the personal animosity between Sanger and Dennett, see Dennett to Sanger, February 15, 1930, SSC-MSP, box 5.
41. First three quotes from Dennett to Baldwin, December 11, 1934; Baldwin to Dennett, December 13, 1934, ACLU-MF, reel 107; see also Moss to Dennett, August 17, 1931; Baldwin to Dennett, August 4, 1931, ACLU-MF, reel 86.
42. Sanger's 1934 national conference, Birth Control and National Recovery, aimed to draw attention to the link between contraception and the nation's economic health. Contemporary birth control activists, scholars, media sources, and New Deal policymakers also made this connection. Others, like founding ACLU board member and Socialist presidential candidate Norman Thomas, objected to blaming the Depression, unemployment, and poverty on overpopulation or the inability of the poor to limit the size of their families, claiming that such arguments failed to place blame where it belonged, on "the old capitalist order." Historian Linda Gordon echoed Thomas when she suggested that for some people birth control became a tool for improving the economy without redistributing wealth. In any case, the number of birth control clinics in the United States increased during the Depression from 29 in 1929 to 374 by 1938. See "Birth Control," *World Tomorrow*, April 1923, 131; Sanger, "A Few Important Reasons for Amending Existing Birth Control Laws," n.d.; Alexander Lindey to Dennett, January 30, 1934; Hannah Stone notes on "Hotel Annapolis" letterhead, n.d.; Baldwin to Stone, December 10, 1934, ACLU-MF, reel 107; "American Conference on Birth Control and National Recovery," January 15–17, 1934, NYPL-NTP, reel 2; Gordon, *Moral Property of Women*, 221, see also 240–242; Eleanor Dwight Jones to the American Fund for Public Service, June 22, 1931, NYPL-AFPS, reel 33; "Medicine: Birth Control Raid," *Time*, April 29, 1929; "Medicine: Abortion," *Time*, January 4, 1932; "Medicine: Relief & Babies," *Time*, April 8, 1935; "The Accident of Birth," *Fortune* 17 (February 1938), 83–86, 108; "Medicine: Voluntary Parenthood," *Time*,

December 2, 1929; "Medicine: Birth Control's 21st," *Time*, February 18, 1935; "Medicine: Birth Controllers on Parade," *Time*, January 29, 1934; "Medicine: Controller," *Time*, February 7, 1938; Norman Thomas to Sanger, December 19, 1933, NYPL-NTP, reel 2.

43. Gordon, *Moral Property of Women*, 225.
44. Chesler, *Woman of Valor*, 270; first quote from "Religion: Birth Control's Week," *Time*, May 18, 1936; second quote from "Medicine: Birth Control Astride," *Time*, May 4, 1931; "Medicine: Birth Controllers on Parade," *Time*, January 29, 1934; "Medicine: Birth Control's 21st," *Time*, February 18, 1935.
45. Dennett asked the ACLU to donate the funds remaining from her own Defense Committee to Midgard's case. First quote from Bailey to Dennett, September 6, 1930, see also September 24, 1930, and October 1930; second quote from "In Federal Court, Seattle, Washington, April 28th, 1931: Digest of Judge Bourquin's opinion"; see also Dennett to Bailey, October 3 and 19, 1930; Adele Parker-Bennett to Baldwin, August 5, 1930; "Importer Ready to Go to Bat for Book," *Seattle Star*, May 14, 1930; C. E. Midgard to Dennett, May 30, 1930; Dennett to Midgard, June 29, 1930; Dennett to Baldwin, August 2, 1930, MWD-MF, reel 21; Bailey to Dennett, October 7, 1930; Bailey to Ernst, October 10, 1930; Dennett to Bailey, October 19 and 20, 1930; Midgard to Dennett, November 1, 1930; Midgard to Bailey, April 29, 1931; "Moral Censors Ban Scientific Medical Work," *Industrial Worker*, August 23, 1930; "The New Censorship," *Indianapolis, Indiana Times*, July 25, 1930, ACLU-MF, reel 71; Dennett to Lindey, July 3, 1930; "Memorandum for Files," July 3, 1930, MWD-MF, reel 23.
46. AMA stands for American Medical Association. First four quotes from "Chicago Yokels Ready Victims of Ancient 'Men Only' Stuff," *Chicago Tribune*, December 13, 1927; fifth quote from Mrs. Robert S. Huse to Olin West, M.D., March 15 and 23, 1929, AMA-MST.
47. First four quotes from "Chicago Yokels Ready Victims of Ancient 'Men Only' Stuff," *Chicago Tribune*, December 13, 1927; fifth quote from Mrs. Robert S. Huse to Olin West, M.D., March 15 and 23, 1929; sixth and seventh quotes from S. Dana Hubbard, M.D. to Dr. Morris H. Kahn, June 17, 1929, AMA-MST; eighth and ninth quotes from "Bureau of Investigation: M. Sayle Taylor, 'America's Doctor of Matrimony' Who Claims to Reveal the Mysteries of Sex," *Journal of the American Medical Association* 98, 11 (March 12, 1932), 908–909. In the 1920s, Taylor, a former medical student, left a career in social work to serve as William Jennings Bryan's traveling debate partner, arguing against Christian fundamentalism and for science and evolution. Given the ACLU's involvement in the famous 1925 Scopes case involving Bryan, it is possible that ACLU leaders knew of Taylor from these touring debates. See La-Fon Laboratories to Dear Madam, n.d.; "Taylor's La-Fon Perfumed Douche Powder" label; Taylor, "Secret of Youth and Charm"; Taylor, *The Male Motor*; Taylor, "Natural Birth Control"; Taylor, "Sex Vigor"; Taylor, "Facts for Wives"; B. O. Halling to AMA, June 25, 1930, AMA-MST. On "feminine hygiene" as a term for eluding legal proscriptions on birth control, see Tone, *Devices and Desires*, 151–182; on the *Married Love* case see Walker, *In Defense*, 86.
48. First quote from Baldwin to Gordon Ward, March 22, 1932; Ward to Baldwin, March 20, 1932; Hatcher Hughes to Taylor, March 22, 1932; Gordon W. Moss to Mrs. Roland T. Hamner, April 20, 1932; second, third, and fourth quotes from Bureau of Investigation, AMA telegram to Moss, May 24, 1932; Albert P. Van Dusen telegram to Moss, date illeg.; Moss to Florence Rose and Sanger, May 25, 1932; Taylor to National Council on Freedom from Censorship, May 24, 1932; Moss to D. Martin, Esq., May 25 and 31, 1932; Moss to Taylor, May 26, 1932; June 2 and 7, 1932; Moss to Philip H. Hickson, June 2, 1932; Moss to J. Bolling Jones, June 10, 1932; Hamner to Moss, June 13, 1932; Baldwin to Hamner, June 14, 1932; Taylor to Moss, May 24, 1932; Philip H. Hickson to Moss, June 6, 1932, ACLU-MF, reel 86. Little has been written about M. Sayle Taylor, who died prematurely in 1942. See Munson, *All Talk*, 26–27; Dunning, *On the Air*, 74; Wood, *Forbidden Fruit*; Fowler and Crawford, *Quacks*; "M. Sayle Taylor of Radio, 53, Dies," *New York Times*, February 2, 1942; "Taylor, Marion Sayle," biographical card, AMA-MST.

49. By 1933, Taylor became a national radio persona, the "Voice of Experience," and received invitations to speak before civic groups like the Kiwanis, synagogues, women's clubs, and state governors. As one of the nation's first talk-radio therapists, he employed several dozen secretaries to help him answer and vet the thousands of letters he received each week. David C. Roberts, M.D. to Dr. Arthur J. Cramp, January 22, 1933; "The Voice of Experience," "Radio Mystery Man Unmasks," *Radio Guide*, unidentified, undated; Samuel Cummings to Morris Fishbein, June 24, 1933; Mr. F. E. Spicer to AMA, March 15, 1936; AMA Bureau of Investigation to Dr. Milton L. Sorock, August 16, 1938, AMA-MST; "Stage Sex Lecturer Not on Air as 'Voice,'" February 21, 1935, unidentified, ACLU-MF, reel 115; "Art: Radio Plugs," *Time*, March 18, 1935; Harriman, "Profiles: The Voice"; "Airs Academic Sanctity," *Harvard Crimson*, April 16, 1936; "Radio: V.O.E.," *Time*, January 2, 1939; "Nation Hears Plea for Paralysis Aid," *New York Times*, January 26, 1937; "Events Today," *New York Times*, June 16, 1937; "Religious Services," *New York Times*, November 18 and 19, 1938; "M. Sayle Taylor of Radio, 53, Dies," *New York Times*, February 2, 1942; Taylor to Hatcher Hughes, April 23, 1932, ACLU-MF, reel 86; Tone, *Devices and Desires*, 169–170.
50. For another example of birth control activists' objections to a sensationalized exhibit on "feminine hygiene," see Judith J. Breakey to Sanger, HRC-MEC, box 267. On birth control activists' intolerance for commercial as opposed to medical birth control providers, see Gordon, *Moral Property of Women*, 225–226.
51. Hughes to Stella Hanau, March 21, 1932 (note from Hanau attached); Mrs. F. Robertson Jones to Hughes, May 16, 1932; Dorr to Jones, May 11, 1932, SSC-PPFA I, box 28.
52. Quote from Pilpel and Ernst, "A Medical Bill of Rights," *Journal of Contraception*, February 1937, 35–37; see also James H. Moyle to Collectors of Customs and Others Concerned, February 10, 1937, ACLU-MF, reel 156; see also "Correspondence: Contraceptive Advice, Devices and Preparations," *Journal of the American Medical Association* 108, 21 (May 22, 1937), 1819–1820.
53. First quote from Brief for Claimant-Appellee in *U.S. v. One Package* (October 5, 1936), MWD-MF, reel 19; second quote from William L. Laurence, "Birth Control Is Accepted by American Medical Body," *New York Times*, June 9, 1937; third and fourth quotes from Pilpel to Hazel Rice, October 30, 1937, HRC-MEC, box 364; Sanger to Senator Warren Austin, January 10, 1933; Lindey to Dr. Ira S. Wile, November 2, 1935, HRC-MEC, box 69. The Tariff Act of 1930 prohibited importation of any "article whatever for the prevention of conception or for causing unlawful abortion." *U.S. v. One Package*, 86 F.2d 737 (December 7, 1936). Ernst and Lindey's brief pointed out that a physician's exception to the 1873 Comstock Act was originally slated for inclusion but, perhaps mistakenly, dropped without notice or debate. The court of appeals victory did not instantly translate into a reformed Customs Office, and ACLU attorneys worked tirelessly to free many contraceptive materials that Customs officials continued to seize. See Lindey to Huntington Cairns, May 11, 1939; Pilpel to Mr. Woodbridge Morris, June 24, 1940; Beatrice Richards to Pilpel, June 28, 1940, HRC-MEC, box 266. By 1940, the Federal Trade Commission began to crack down on manufacturers who sold ineffective birth control devices and information, including companies that sold calendars to help women follow the so-called rhythm method often recommended by Catholic clergy. "Medicine: Birth Control by Rule?" *Time*, March 25, 1940. See also Kennedy, *Birth Control in America*, 249–252; Hanau to Ernst, n.d.; Ernst to Hanau, March 19, 1934, HRC-MEC, box 267; Woodward, "Contraceptive Advice"; Benjamin, "Lobbying for Birth Control"; Dennett to Mrs. Thomas N. Hepburn, January 9, 1936, MWD-MF, reel 18; Greenbaum, Wolff & Ernst to Groff Conklin, April 21, 1937, HRC-MEC, box 390; Greenbaum, Wolff & Ernst, "Memorandum: *United States v. Marriage Hygiene, United States v. Parenthood*," June 24, 1938, ACLU-MF, reel 156.
54. Ernst to Sanger, April 30, 1940, HRC-MEC, box 363. On Sanger, see Chesler, *Woman of Valor*, 371–387, 391–393; Kennedy, *Birth Control in America*, 255–257; "Medicine: Birth Controllers Demobilized," *Time*, July 12, 1937.

55. Pilpel helped to word the questions for this Gallup Poll. See Pilpel, "File Memorandum: Birth Control Federation," December 7, 1939, HRC-MEC, box 266; Benjamin, "Lobbying for Birth Control"; Stix, "Birth Control"; "Medicine: Birth Control," *Time,* March 31, 1941.
56. Tone, *Devices and Desires,* 117.
57. Laura Briggs makes a compelling argument for the inadequacy and indeed wrongheadedness of the claim that overpopulation caused Puerto Rico's poverty, but the perceived link between population control and anti-Communism would extend into the 1960s. See Schoen, *Choice and Coercion,* 62; Gordon, *Moral Property of Women,* 238–240, 284; Briggs, *Reproducing Empire,* 81–89, 110, 146–147; Stycos and Hill, "Prospects of Birth Control"; Graham, *Toward a Planned Society,* 149–159. Although Briggs implies that the U.S. team—including Morris Ernst, Margaret Sanger, and Clarence Gamble—foisted birth control onto Puerto Ricans, correspondence between Ernst and Puerto Rican activists suggests that local activists appealed to the U.S. group for assistance. On the involvement of Pilpel and the Birth Control Federation in the population control movement, see Pilpel file memoranda, December 19, 1940; January 31, 1941; Pilpel to Morris Lewis, January 23, 1941, HRC-MEC, box 266. Lindey to Ernest Gruening, December 6, 1938; Florence Rose to Ernst, January 24, 1938; Lindey to Estella A. Torres, January 25, 1939; "Copy: Birth Control," n.d.; Executive Committee Minutes, Birth Control Federation of America, November 26, 1940, HRC-MEC, box 267.

Chapter 3

1. Quote from J. P. McGlynn to Hugh Hefner with note to Pat Malin, February 8, 1961, ACLU-MF, series 3, reel 59. This chapter responds to calls "to discover how consumption became a cultural ideal, a hegemonic 'way of seeing' in twentieth-century America." Fox and Lears, *The Culture of Consumption,* x–xi.
2. Legal scholars have lamented that the slippage from the rights of speakers to the rights of listeners has gone largely unremarked. Thomas, "Listener's Right to Hear"; "Case Note: The First Amendment and the Right to Hear," and Steel, "Comments: Freedom to Hear."
3. The best and most comprehensive treatment of twentieth-century consumerism remains Cohen, *Consumers' Republic.*
4. Quotes from Baldwin to Gentlemen, March 12, 1931; see also Gordon Moss to W. I. Griffith, March 25, 1931, ACLU-MF, reel 88; Moss to Judge Henry Neil, April 7, 1931, ACLU-MF, reel 87; Friedman, *Prurient Interests,* 155; "Statement of Policy Concerning the Ownership of Radio Stations by Newspapers," March 11, 1942, ACLU-MF, reel 220; Toro, "Standing Up for Listeners' Rights," 10, 46–49, 74–75, 81–82, 149–161; Ernst, *First Freedom,* 179; McChesney, *Telecommunications,* 236; Starr, *Creation of the Media,* 327–384.
5. See Friedman, *Prurient Interests,* 101–103, 136–138; Wheeler, *Against Obscenity,* 37–38, 45, 54–55, 66.
6. First quote from "Sermons Give Film Campaign Added Impetus," *New York City World-Telegram,* July 16, 1934; see also "Warn Film Reformers, Liberty Union Calls Hand," *New York American,* July 16, 1934; "Censorship," *New Orleans LA. Tribune,* July 20, 1934; second quote from Clifton Reed to Rabbi William F. Rosenblum, August 16, 1934; third quote from Holmes, "Statement in Dissent"; see also Holmes to Baldwin, September 6, 1934; "Statement of the American Civil Liberties Union on the Agitation Against the Movies," n.d.; Harry F. Ward et al., to Rev. Sidney Goldstein et al., September 28, 1934, ACLU-MF, reel 107; "Proposed Statement by Dr. John Haynes Holmes"; Holmes to Rice, July 25, 1934; A. L. Wirin to Rice, September 12, 1934, HRC-ERC, box 86; "Liberties Union Raises Question," *Des Moines Register,* September 30, 1934; Ingram Bander, "Suppression, A Modern Problem: An Interview with John S. Sumner," April 18, 1932, and "Suppression,

A Modern Problem: An Interview with Morris Ernst," April 20, 1932, *Campus* (City College of New York Magazine); Ernst to George Jean Nathan, March 18, 1931, HRC-MEC, box 387; Rice to Covici Friede Inc., January 17, 1929, HRC-ERC, box 85; Rice to Forrest Bailey, May 21, 1931, ACLU-MF, reel 87; Rice, "Organized Charity"; Walker, *In Defense*, 100.

7. Walker, *In Defense*, 159–160; Arthur H. DeBra to Baldwin, March 9 and 14, 1945; Baldwin to DeBra, March 12, 1945, ACLU-MF, reel 232.
8. First quote from Rice to Forrest Bailey, May 21, 1931, ACLU-MF, reel 87; see also Rice, *Minority Report*, 274–277; Rice, "Organized Charity." All other quotes from Ernst, "Memorandum by Morris Ernst Prepared at the Request of the Board of Directors at the Special Meeting Held Thursday, October 9, 1941," ACLU-MF, reel 192; and Ernst, "So-Called Market Place"; see also Ernst, *Too Big*, 132–160; "Memorandum of the Associated Press Case: Mr. Ernst's Comment," September 23, 1942; Ernst to Holmes, April 14, 1942, ACLU-MF, reel 203.
9. First quote from Baldwin to John C. Flinn, August 17, 1942, HRC-ERC, box 86; second quote from Dorothy Kenyon, "Brief on Behalf of American Civil Liberties Union, Amicus Curiae," Supreme Court of the United States, *Thelma Martin v. City of Struthers, Ohio* (October Term, 1942), 9, SSC-DK, box 25; third quote from *Martin v. City of Struthers*, 319 U.S. 141 (May 3, 1943). Later Supreme Court opinions that cite *Martin* in establishing the rights of consumers of speech include *Thomas v. Collins*, 323 U.S. 516 (1945); *Lamont v. Postmaster General*, 381 U.S. 301 (1965); *Stanley v. Georgia*, 394 U.S. 557 (1969), and *Kleindienst v. Mandel*, 408 U.S. 753 (1972). Laura Wittern-Keller brought the *Kleindienst* case to my attention. See also Steel, "Comments: Freedom to Hear," 335–336; "Memorandum of Eduard C. Lindeman in reply to Morris Ernst's Memorandum on Present Day Threats to Civil Liberties," October 30, 1941; Arthur Garfield Hays, "Comment on Mr. Ernst's Memorandum," November 27, 1941, ACLU-MF, reel 192; R. W. Riis to Holmes, October 12, 1942, ACLU-MF, reel 203; Ernst to Holmes, April 2 and 14, 1942, ACLU-MF, reel 20; Ernst to Forster, April 23, 1942, HRC-MEC, box 404.
10. FDR quote from "Presidential Memorandum for Fly, Hon. James Lawrence," September 30, 1943; see also "Fly, Hon. James Lawrence, Chairman, Federal Communications Commission," November 1, 1943, FDR-Official File, 1770–1779, box 1; Fly, "Freedom of Communications," July 9–13, 1945, ACLU-MF, reel 227; Edwardson, "James Lawrence Fly's Fight," and Toro, "Standing Up for Listeners' Rights," 47; *Associated Press v. U.S.*, 326 U.S. 1 (June 18, 1945); "Freedom in Our Time," *Time*, March 6, 1944; Hocking, *Freedom of the Press*, 161–162, 164; Fones-Wolf, "Defending Listeners' Rights"; United Nations Declaration of Human Rights, December 10, 1948, http://www.un.org/en/documents/udhr/ (retrieved May 26, 2012).
11. Baldwin to Ernst, December 11, 1944, ACLU-MF, reel 228; Ernst, "Memorandum on the Problems of Freedom and Diversity in Communications," December 1944; Baldwin to Board of Directors, January 4, 1945; ACLU Board of Directors Minutes, January 8, 1945; Baldwin to the National Committee and Affiliated Committees, January 17, 1945, ACLU-MF, reel 227.
12. Quotes from Baldwin to Mr. C. E. Boyer, May 19, 1945; and "Are you FREE to READ—SEE—HEAR?" n.d., ACLU-MF, reel 232; see also Chicago Division, ACLU, "Statement on Censorship of Indecent and Obscene Literature," February 28, 1949, ACLU-MF, reel 261.
13. First quote from Jim Farrell to Baldwin, March 26, 1947; see also E. A. Ross to Baldwin, January 25, 1945; Alexander Meiklejohn to Baldwin, January 30, 1945, ACLU-MF, reel 227; J. B. Milgram to ACLU, November 24, 1947, ACLU-MF, reel 242; second quote from Herbert Babb to ACLU, August 2, 1946; see also Raymond L. Wise, "Minority Report of Special Committee to Consider Certain Aspects of Free Speech," December 26, 1946; Harry Eckstein, et al. to ACLU Board of Directors, May 23, 1946, ACLU-MF, reel 234; Milner, "Memorandum of Telephone Conversation with Morris Ernst," November 30, 1944; Baldwin to Ernst, December 11, 1944, ACLU-MF, reel 228; Ernst, "Memorandum on the Problems of

Freedom and Diversity in Communications," December 1944; ACLU Board of Directors Minutes, January 8, 1945; Holmes to Baldwin, January 11, 1945; Baldwin to Holmes, January 12, 1945; Baldwin to members of the ACLU National Committee and Affiliated Committees, January 17, 1945, ACLU-MF, reel 227; Ernst to Holmes, April 2, 1942, ACLU-MF, reel 203; "Are you FREE to READ—SEE—HEAR?" n.d., ACLU-MF, reel 232; Archer Winston, "Movie Talk: Meeting on Movie Censorship Discusses the Problems," *New York Post*, March 7, 1945, ACLU-MF, reel 228; Baldwin to Mr. C. E. Boyer, May 19, 1945; ACLU news release, June 7, 1945, ACLU-MF, reel 232; Baldwin to John C. Flinn, August 17, 1942, ACLU-MF, reel 220; Farrell to Baldwin, March 26, 1947, ACLU-MF, reel 242; Arthur Jenner to ACLU, December 5, 1950, ACLU-MF, reel 41; Rice to Rev. William Howard Melish, April 14, 1948, ACLU-MF, reel 40; Mrs. E. L. Wilson to Malin, February 5, 1953, ACLU-MF, reel 46. On motion picture exhibitors' resistance to censorship, see Wittern-Keller, *Freedom of the Screen*. The ACLU struggled to persuade exhibitors, booksellers, and publishers to take cases to court. See Hazel Rice to Screen Writers' Guild Executive Secretary, December 4, 1941, ACLU-MF, reel 192; Ernst to Forster, March 2, 1944; Frederic Melcher, February 16, 1944, ACLU-MF, reel 220; Andrew Heiskell to Rice, Holmes, and Baldwin, November 26, 1946, ACLU-MF, reel 234.

14. First quote from "Memorandum on the Limits of Boycott: Adopted by the Board of Directors," March 8, 1948, ACLU-MF, reel 252; ACLU news release, December 7, 1942, ACLU-MF, reel 203; Forster to Luther Knight Macnair, November 25, 1953, ACLU-MF, reel 47; Baldwin to William Goldman, December 8, 1947; Hays to Harold W. Seidenberg, December 1, 1947, ACLU-MF, reel 242; second and third quotes from ACLU Press Release, June 7, 1945; Hays to Fitelson & Mayers, June 25, 1945; Pilpel to Forster, January 23, 1945; "After Censorship?" *Motion Picture Herald*, May 19, 1945; "Memorandum on Motion Picture Censorship," February 19, 1945; Quincy Howe to Norman Thomas, February 21, 1945; DeBra to Baldwin, March 9, 1945; "Memorandum on the Meeting on Motion Picture Censorship," March 6, 1945; ACLU Board of Directors Minutes, March 19, 1945; Henry Eckstein, "Memorandum of conversation (April 5, 1945) with Mr. Arthur Mayer on Mr. Morris Ernst's memo re: Movie Censorship," April 6, 1945, ACLU-MF, reel 232; Baldwin and Harold Sherman amicus briefs in *U.S. v. Paramount Pictures*, October 1, 1945 and September 29, 1945, ACLU-MF, reel 234; Ernst to Levy, April 14, 1949; Levy to Forster, April 21, 1949; Baldwin to Sidney Schreiber, April 29, 1949; "Memorandum of Conference Between Sidney Schreiber, Phillip O'Brien and . . . for the Motion Picture Association, and Herbert M. Levy and Clifford Forster for the American Civil Liberties Union, March 29, 1949"; Levy to Mr. R. F. Windron, June 20, 1950, ACLU-MF, reel 270; Reitman to Barry Marks, July 17, 1952, ACLU-MF, reel 44; "Statement on Codes Which Restrict Freedom of Expression," January 28, 1953, ACLU-MF, reel 46.
15. Quotes from "Memorandum on the Limits of Boycott: Adopted by the Board of Directors, March 8, 1948," ACLU-MF, reel 252; see also Richard Fuller to Ernst, March 14, 1946, HRC-MEC, box 44; Ernst, "Freedom to Read"; Ernst to Governor Thomas Dewey, March 9, 1949, ACLU-MF, reel 238; Lincoln R. Melville to ACLU, November 29, 1947, ACLU-MF, reel 242; Frederick Lewis Allen to National Publishers Association, January 16, 1947, HRC-MEC, box 147; Baldwin to Bosley Crowther, October 5, 1945, ACLU-MF, reel 232; "To Survey Associates," n.d., ACLU-MF, reel 227; Paul Kellogg to Baldwin, October 5 and 26, 1945, ACLU-MF, reel 228.
16. Quote from "Memorandum and Outline on the Study of Freedom in Communication," July 28, 1945, ACLU-MF, reel 227; see also "Resolution to be Submitted at the Close of the Conference," November 14, 1945; Rice, "Memorandum," May 25, 1945, ACLU-MF, reel 232; Harry Eckstein et al., to the Board of Directors, May 23, 1946, ACLU-MF, reel 234; Ernst, untitled memo, May 2, 1945; "To the Members of the Board of Directors," May 16, 1945; ACLU Board of Directors Minutes, n.d., 1945; "Memo from Morris Ernst in Response to Objections Raised to His Proposal," June 8, 1945; Hays to Baldwin, June 29, 1945, ACLU-MF, reel 227; McChesney, *Telecommunications*, 236.

17. Quote from Walker, *In Defense*, 208, see also 175–207; Cottrell, *Roger Nash Baldwin*, 325–329; Ernst to Holmes, March 31, 1949; Ernst to Walter Gellhorn, February 17, 1949, HRC-MEC, box 44; Osmond Fraenkel Diary, February 22, 1950 and February 14, 1954, PML-OFD; see also Toro, "Standing Up for Listeners' Rights"; Kutulas, *American Civil Liberties Union*, 136–162.
18. For cases refused by the ACLU because they involved questionable material or individuals, see for example, Hazel Rice to Mr. G. Gazulis, January 20, 1936; Hazel Rice to Baldwin, January 9, 1938; Baldwin to Mr. Syd Pierce, September 7, 1938, ACLU-MF, reel 156; Hays to ACLU, August 2, 1937, ACLU-MF, reel 141. See also Talese, *Thy Neighbor's Wife*, 93–111; Ernst to Pilpel, August 5, 1947, HRC-MEC, box 44; Ernst to Pilpel, n.d.; Pilpel to Ernst and File, January 21, 1957, HRC-MEC, box 272; Bailey to Arthur Fisher, June 24, 1931; Baldwin to Upton Sinclair, July 2, 1931; Secretary to Mr. L. L. Dentzler, July 7, 1931; Moss to Mr. Robert P. Anderson, September 11, 1931, ACLU-MF, reel 88; Memo by James, July 9, 1940, HRC-MEC, box 390.
19. Quote from Levy to Hugh R. Manes, November 4, 1955, ACLU-MF, reel 49; see also Stanley Fleishman to ACLU, September 1, 1954; Levy to Fleishman, September 8, 1954, ACLU-MF, reel 48; Levy to Roth, May 27, 1949, July 11, 1949; Roth to Levy, June 5, 1949, ACLU-MF, reel 261. In 1941, the ACLU declared it "impracticable" to distinguish between "commercial and non-commercial literature." See "Statement with Regard to the Sale of Literature in Public Places and House to House," August 1941, ACLU-MF, reel 192. See also Gertzman, "Strange Story of Samuel Roth"; SAC, New York to Director, FBI, January 30, 1956, FOIA-FBI, Samuel Roth file.
20. Quotes from *U.S. v. Roth*, 237 F. 2d 796 (September 18, 1956); Rowland Watts to Erwin B. Ellman, Esq., October 16, 1956, ACLU-MF, reel 51; Ernst to Fleischman, February 4, 1957; Ernst to Frank, February 25, 1949, and January 14, 1949; Pilpel to Frank, July 16, 1956; Frank to Ernst, July 26, 1956; Ernst to Rankin, March 13, 1957, HRC-MEC, box 216.
21. Quote from Rice to Frank, November 19, 1956; see also Watts to Censorship Panel, October 25, 1957; Levy to Rice, November 23, 1956, HRC-ERC, box 85; Minutes, Censorship Panel Meeting, October 24, 1956, UCLA-SCACLU, box 1; Joughin to Affiliates, October 29, 1956, ACLU-MF, reel 534; Watts to Erwin B. Ellmann, October 16, 1956, ACLU-MF, reel 51; George A. Dreyfous to Joughin, November 15, 1956, ACLU-MF, reel 534.
22. Quotes from *Roth v. U.S.*, Brief of American Civil Liberties Union as Amicus Curiae (submitted by Emanuel Redfield), October term 1956, ACLU-MF, reel 534; see also Minutes, Free Speech Association Committee, January 16, 1957, HRC-ERC, box 89; Osmond Fraenkel Diary, January 21, 1957, PML-OFD; Reitman to Levy, July 20, 1959, ACLU-MF, reel 252; Reitman to Morton Icove, March 28, 1957, ACLU-MF, reel 52; ACLU News Release, April 19, 1957, UCLA-SCACLU, box 1; Censorship Panel Meeting, November 28, 1956, NCA-ACLU, box 25; Foster, "Comstock Load"; *Roth v. U.S.*, Brief of Morris L. Ernst, October Term 1956, HRC-MEC, box 272. See also Pilpel to Ernst, January 22, 1957; Pilpel to File, January 23, 1957; Pilpel to Florence and Barbara Frank, March 22, 1957, HRC-MEC, box 272.
23. First quote from Justice Potter Stewart in Dickson, ed., *Supreme Court in Conference*, 356; other quotes from Warren's concurrence in *Roth v. United States*, 354 U.S. 476; 77 S. Ct. 1304 (June 24, 1957).
24. First four quotes from *Model Penal Code, Tentative Draft No. 6* (Philadelphia: American Law Institute, May 6, 1957). This draft explicitly acknowledged the status of *U.S. v. Roth* before the U.S. Supreme Court (pp. 12–13). All other quotes from *Roth v. United States*, 354 U.S. 476; 77 S. Ct. 1304 (June 24, 1957). *Roth* was decided with a companion case, *Alberts v. California*. Schwarz to Malin, June 8, 1955; Levy to Schwartz, June 15, 1955; Schwartz to Levy, June 16, 1955; Levy to Schwartz, July 11, 1955; Schwartz to Levy, February 22, 1956; Schwartz to O'Meara, February 22, 1956, PML-ACLU, box 345; "Material Prepared by the American Civil Liberties Union for Members of the American Law

Institute Concerning Tentative Draft No. 1 of A Model Code of Pre-Arraignment Procedure" (New York: ACLU, May 1966); Joseph O'Meara to Levy, February 4, 1956, PML-ACLU, box 342; Ernst to Bok, December 17, 1948, HRC-MEC, box 154; *Commonwealth v. Gordon*, 1949 Pa. Dist. & Cnty. Dec. (March 18, 1949); Watts to Censorship Panel, October 25, 1957, HRC-ERC, box 85; Wechsler, "The Challenge of a Model Penal Code," 1097–1133; Wechsler, "Codification of Criminal Law"; Hixson, *Pornography and the Justices*, 21.

25. Reitman to Soll, June 2, 1959, ACLU-MF, reel 59; Reitman to Censorship Panel, December 13, 1957, HRC-ERC, box 85; O. K. Armstrong to Dear Friend, August 29, 1957, ACLU-MF, reel 54; O.K. Armstrong to Publishers, *Dude* and *Gent* Magazines, August 29, 1957, ACLU-MF, reel 51.
26. The ACLU's 1957 support for *One, Inc.* rested squarely on the First Amendment and did not extend to other rights sought by homosexuals. Reitman to Watts, June 21, 1957, ACLU-MF, reel 54; Watts to William Lambert, July 17, 1957; Watts to Spencer Coxe, August 1, 1957, SC-ACLU, box 17; see also *One, Inc. v. Olesen*, 241 F.2d 772 (February 27, 1957); *One, Inc., v. Olesen*, 355 U.S. 371 (January 13, 1958); Mezey, *Queers in Court*, 21–22; Cain, "Litigating for Lesbian and Gay Rights"; "Policy Guide of ACLU," July 5, 1966, SC-DK, box 30; Bullough, "Lesbianism, Homosexuality," 23–24. Not everyone in the ACLU considered nudist practice a civil liberties matter. See for example, Reitman to Armand Charland, December 16, 1957, ACLU-MF, reel 52.
27. Quote from Baldwin to O. John Rogge, January 16, 1958, ACLU-MF, reel 479; see also *Sunshine v. Summerfield*, 355 U.S. 372 (January 13, 1958); *Sunshine Book Co. v. McCaffrey*, 168 N.Y.S. 2d 268 (December 3, 1957); *Sunshine v. Summerfield*, 184 F. Supp. 767 (May 20, 1960); Harold Leventhal to Forster, August 13, 1948, and November 26, 1948; Forster to Leventhal, October 6, 1948; Baldwin to Forster, September 14, 1948; Forster to Boone, September 22, 1948; Baldwin to Leventhal, May 18, 1948, ACLU-MF, reel 42; Leventhal to Baldwin, March 5, 1948, ACLU-MF, reel 41; Edward de Grazia, "Brief of American Civil Liberties Union, Amicus Curiae," *Summerfield v. Sunshine Book Company*, U.S. Court of Appeals, May 5, 1954; de Grazia to Levy, May 14, 1954, and December 16, 1954, ACLU-MF, reel 480; Rogge to Levy, April 15, 1955; Watts to Irving Ferman, October 10, 1957; Watts to de Grazia, November 5, 1957, ACLU-MF, reel 479; Rogge to Levy, May 12, 1955; Boone to Baldwin, June 21, 1955; Watts to Rogge, August 2, 1956, PML-ACLU, box 603; Watts to Roland Brooks, October 29, 1957, ACLU-MF, reel 53; Berton M. Boone, "A First Class Magazine at Second-Class Rates," unidentified publication, ANRL-Subject Files: Nudist History. Through the ACLU, Boone enjoyed first-class legal representation and assistance by Harold Leventhal, O. John Rogge, and Edward de Grazia, all prominent attorneys with impressive political connections. See special issue on Harold Leventhal, *Columbia Law Review* 80, 5 (June 1980), 879–930; Deery, "A Divided Soul"; "O. John Rogge, 77, Anti-Nazi Activist," *New York Times*, March 23, 1981. On ACLU efforts to get Roth's unusually harsh five-year imprisonment and $5,000 fine reduced, see Levy to Reitman, January 13, 1958; Reitman to Levy, January 17, 1958; Malin to William P. Rogers, January 17, 1958, ACLU-MF, reel 54; *Samuel Roth v. U.S.*, 255 F. 2d 440 (May 22, 1958); "Petition for Writ of Certiorari to the United States of Appeals for the Second Circuit," *Roth v. U.S.*, October term, 1957, ACLU-MF, reel 534; Harriet Pilpel to Roger Smith, November 6, 1957, HRC-MEC, box 272.
28. Quotes from *Excelsior Pictures v. Regents of the University of the State of New York*, 165 N.Y. 2d 237 (July 3, 1957); see also Watts to Craig Morton, June 7 and 19, 1957; Morton to Watts, October 22, 1957, ACLU-MF, reel 51; Walter Bibo to Reitman, April 3, 1958; Reitman to the Files, n.d.; Norval Packwood to Malin, September 25, 1956; Packwood to Reitman, October 9, 1956; Watts to Stuart Dunnings, November 7, 1956, ACLU-MF, reel 53; Packwood to ACLU, May 14, 1957; Watts to George G. Iggers, May 20, 1957; Watts to Gene Lary, June 13, 1957, ACLU-MF, reel 52; "*People v. Hildabridle*: Voelker and the Art of Crafting an Opinion," *Supplement from the Michigan Supreme Court Historical Society*,

February 2009, 6–9; *People v. Hildabridle*, 353 Mich. 562 (September 9, 1958). See also Hoffman, "Making Private Parts Public," 204–215, 249–259.

29. When the military faced criticism, in the 1960s, for producing and distributing increasingly sexy publications—*Overseas Weekly* and *Stars and Stripes*—the ACLU defended it on the grounds that "one of the basic principles of the First Amendment" is "the right of all men to select what they wish to read." Quote from John de J. Pemberton to Hon. Robert S. McNamara, April 24, 1962; "Military Cold War Education and Speech Review Policies: United States Senate, Special Preparedness Subcommittee of the Committee on Armed Services," March 8, 1962, ACLU-MF, reel 60; *Hearings Before the Committee on Armed Services, United States Senate*, S. Res. 191 (September 6–7, 1961); see also Breazeale, "In Spite of Women"; Ehrenreich, *Hearts of Men*; Osgerby, *Playboys in Paradise*; Fraterrigo, *Playboy and the Making.*
30. Boyer, *Purity in Print*, 288–289; Strub, "Perversion for Profit," 20–22; Kielbowicz, "Origins of the Junk-Mail Controversy," 248–272.
31. First three quotes from "Testimony of Patrick Murphy Malin . . . Before Gathings Select Committee on Current Pornographic Materials," December 5, 1952, ACLU-MF, reel 243. See also "Testimony of Herbert Monte Levy, Staff Counsel of the American Civil Liberties Union, Before the Gathings Select Committee," December 5, 1952, SC-ACLU, box 1; Joughin to Edward H. Meyerding, June 21, 1954, ACLU-MF, reel 47; ACLU Press Release, May 9, 1955, ACLU-MF, reel 49; "Testimony of Ernest Angell, Chairman of the Board of Directors of the American Civil Liberties Union," July 31, 1959, ACLU-MF, reel 55; fourth quote from Spencer Coxe to Reitman, July 13, 1959; Reitman to Dan Lacy, August 5, 1959, ACLU-MF, reel 252; fifth quote from Boyer, *Purity in Print*, 288; see also 287 and Nyberg, *Seal of Approval.*
32. First quote from Rice to Joseph Meyers, February 25, 1953, HRC-ERC, box 85; second quote from ACLU Press Release, April 26, 1951; third quote from Reitman to Leon Goldstein, May 3, 1951 ("Spot Announcement" enclosed); see also "Statement of Brig. General David Sarnoff," April 30, 1951; ACLU, Colorado Chapter, "Censors Without Portfolio: Keep Right to Choose for Ourselves," *Denver Post*, April 23, 1953; "Speech for Miss Lillian Gish at Censorship Meeting," 1951, ACLU-MF, reel 43; all other quotes from Forster to Gentlemen, November 26, 1952, and Forster to All Affiliates, November 26, 1952; see also ACLU Press Release, November 12, 1952, ACLU-MF, reel 45, and ACLU Press Release, February 21, 1953, ACLU-MF, reel 47; Rice to Theodore N. Lewis, September 15, 1948, ACLU-MF, reel 49; Forster to Members of the Censorship Committee, March 12, 1948, ACLU-MF, reel 252; NCFC Minutes, April 2, 1948, HRC-ERC, box 84; Rice to Dear ——, May 10, 1948; Minutes, Discussion on Freedom of Expression, May 21, 1948; NCFC, "Proposal for more effective organization of the forces opposing censorship," June 4, 1948, ACLU-MF, reel 40; Levy to Editor, *Goshem Indiana News*, February 27, 1950, ACLU-MF, reel 270; Rice to Malin, March 24, 1950; "By-Laws of National Council for Freedom of Expression," n.d.; Rice to Malin, February 13, 1950, ACLU-MF, reel 269; "Pressure Group Censorship: The Policy of the American Civil Liberties Union," November 1951, SC-ACLU, box 2; Forster, "Memorandum on the projected 'National Council for Freedom of Expression,'" May 1949, PML-ACLU, box 77; Malin to Arthur Summerfield, September 30, 1959, ACLU-MF, reel 252; Reitman to Charles F. Murphy, January 3, 1955; Spencer Coxe to H. J. Maxwell, June 15, 1955; Coxe to Philip Lopresti, September 15, 1955, ACLU-MF, reel 49; Malin to Mrs. Guy Percy Trulock, October 10, 1956; Ken Douty, "Spot Check of Bookstores for Censorship Pressures," August 1, 1957; Marvin Mirsky, "Report on Spot Check on Chicago Bookstores for Censorship Pressures, June 1957," ACLU-MF, reel 52; Rice to Publishers, February 25, 1953, HRC-ERC, box 85; Benjamin Roth, "Statement for Immediate Release," January 2, 1954, ACLU-MF, reel 48; Joughin to Douty (Illinois Division, ACLU), June 17, 1955, and July 8, 1955; Tom Murray to Bill Sanborn (Ohio Civil Liberties Union), December 17, 1956, ACLU-MF, reel 51; Morris H. Rubin to Forster, December 22, 1953, ACLU-MF, reel 46; Malin to Douty, June 6, 1957,

ACLU-MF, reel 53; Martha Thomas (Ohio Civil Liberties Union) to Joughin and Reitman, July 19 and 25, 1958, ACLU-MF, reel 54.

33. First quote from Marie McColgan to Ernest Angell, August 8, 1959, ACLU-MF, reel 252; second and third quotes from Dorothy Dunbar Bromley to Joughin, May 27, 1954; see also Hugh Strong to ACLU, May 12, 1954, and June 13, 1954; Livonna Herzog to Malin, May 8, 1954; Ray Past to Angell, May 28, 1954; Norman Thomas to Angell, May 7, 1954; Thomas to ACLU, May 21, 1954; Joughin to Strong, May 25, 1954, ACLU-MF, reel 47; Paul Pfeiffer to Angell, May 10, 1954, and July 2, 1954, NC-ACLU, box 24; Rosemary Kiefer to ACLU, February 14, 1955, and April 14, 1955; ACLU Press Release, May 9, 1955; Alfred Lewis to Malin, May 9, 1959; Jane Loeb to ACLU, August 24, 1955; "Censorship of Comic Books: A Statement in Opposition on Civil Liberties Grounds" (New York: ACLU, May 1955), ACLU-MF, reel 49; NCFC Minutes, May 28, 1954, PML-ACLU, box 79; ACLU Board Minutes, June 7, 1954, HRC-ERC, box 85. An affiliate leader in Indiana joined Thomas and Bromley in requesting that the ACLU reconsider its policy. See Joseph O'Meara to Malin, December 23, 1955; O'Meara, "Concluding Portion of Remarks . . . before the Legal Panel of the American Civil Liberties Union, Illinois Division," May 10, 1957, ACLU-MF, reel 52. Ernest Besig to Forster, January 8 and 13, 1953, PML-ACLU, box 78; Doyle, "What Nobody Knows"; Reitman to *Harper's*, August 1, 1956, PML-ACLU-DC, box 7-10. Media industry leaders who declined to collaborate with the ACLU include Leon Shimkin (Pocket Books, Inc.) to Rice, March 5, 1953; Ralph Daigh (Fawcett Pubs., Inc.) to Rice, March 10, 1953; Oscar M. Schiff to ACLU, February 24, 1953, ACLU-MF, reel 47; Joseph B. Ullman (New American Library of World Literature) to Rice, March 12, 1953, ACLU-MF, reel 46.

34. First four quotes from "Texts of Librarians' Manifesto and Resolution on Book Curbs," *New York Times*, June 26, 1953, and "Working Paper, ALA/ABPC Conference on the Freedom to Read, Westchester Country Club, Rye, New York, May 2–3, 1953," April 23, 1953; sixth and seventh quotes from "Recent Developments in the Censorship Field," September 2, 1953, ACLU-MF, reel 45; fifth quote from "Council's Statement on Censorship," 1, 2 *Censorship Bulletin* (March 1956), ACLU-MF, reel 50; eighth quote from "Storm Center" advertisement; see also "Story of the Story of 'Storm Center'"; Reitman to Jonas Rosenfield, Jr. et al., May 25, 1956, and June 28, 1956; Reitman to Affiliates, July 2, 1956; Reitman to Daniel Taradash, July 9, 1956; ACLU, Greater Philadelphia Branch, July 24, 1956, ACLU-MF, reel 51; ninth quote from Reitman to Sanray Smith, May 27, 1957, ACLU-MF, reel 53. See also Tom Murray to Ohio Civil Liberties Union, December 17, 1955, ACLU-MF, reel 51; "The American Civil Liberties Union notes the 10th anniversary of the American Book Publishers Council," n.d.; Frank K. Kelly, "President and Press, Librarians and Lawyers, Courts and Citizens Beat Censors on Many Fronts in 1953," *American Book Publishers Council Bulletin*, January 3, 1954, ACLU-MF, reel 47; "Can Minnesota Escape Censorship," *Minneapolis Star*, January 17, 1957; "Statement of the [Freedom-to-Read Citizens'] Committee," n.d., ACLU-MF, reel 57; Bob Sykes, "Right to Read" [The New Jersey Committee for the Right to Read], n.d., ACLU-MF, reel 63; Donald G. Paterson (MN ACLU) to Stewart H. Benedict, March 6, 1958, ACLU-MF, reel 54; "Radio Book Festival," *New York Times*, March 29, 1953; Robins, *Censorship and the American Library*, 22–25; Thomison, *History of American Library Association*, 184–191; "Bar Favors Books and Bricker," *Life* 35, 10 (September 7, 1953), 40; Blanshard, *Right to Read*; Gellhorn, McKeon, and Merton, *Freedom to Read*; Small, "What Censorship Keeps You from Knowing"; Small, "Too Many Self-Appointed Censors." ACLU leaders attended ALA meetings to discuss censorship issues as early as 1940. Thomison, *History of American Library Association*, 144. ACLU leaders suggested that affiliates consider adopting some of the Right-to-Read committees' strategies. Reitman to Leanne Golden, September 16, 1964, ACLU-MF, reel 63. Some scholars simply assume that the right to read equates to the right to speak. See for example, Payne, "Changing Right to Read."

35. First quote from Forster to Rice, April 16, 1953; see also Rice to Forster, April 18, 1953, HRC-ERC, box 86; Lamont to Rice, April 28, 1953, HRC-ERC, box 85. Second and third quotes from "ACLU Objects," *Catholic Standard and Times*, January 18, 1957; fourth quote from Spencer Coxe to the *Catholic Standard and Times*, March 1, 1957, ACLU-MF, reel 52; fifth quote from Forster to Luther Knight Macnair, November 25, 1953, ACLU-MF, reel 47. See also Joughin to Douty, May 11, 1955, ACLU-MF, reel 51; Reitman to Walter Frank, May 2, 1955, ACLU-MF, reel 49; Reitman to Ernst, July 1, 1955; Reitman to Lillian Smith, April 5, 1956; Levy to Files, August 1, 1955; Reitman to Emil Oxfeld, March 26, 1956, ACLU-MF, reel 50.
36. First quote from Forster to Affiliates, State and Local Correspondents, November 5, 1952; all other quotes from "Statement on Censorship Activity by Private Organizations and the National Organization for Decent Literature," January 30, 1957, SC-ACLU, box 1; see also Malin to Monsignor Thomas J. Fitzgerald, September 25, 1958, ACLU-MF, reel 54; Rice and Malin to Board of Directors, April 10, 1951, ACLU-MF, reel 44; Malin and Rice telegram to Rev. William A. Scully, January 2, 1957, ACLU-MF, reel 52.
37. First quote from ACLU press release, May 2, 1957; see also Reitman to *Times-Journal* Editor, June 7, 1957; "ACLU Censorship Panel Meeting," October 24, 1956, PML-ACLU, box 80; Morris Ernst, "Your *Freedom to Read* is in Danger," n.d., ACLU-MF, reel 53. Second and third quotes from Malin to Monsignor Thomas Fitzgerald, May 5, 1958; see also Reitman to Malin, May 2, 1958, ACLU-MF, reel 54; Reitman to H. David Leventhal; Reitman to Paul Obler, September 9 and 11, 1957, ACLU-MF, reel 53. Reitman suggested that the mere existence of powerful pressure groups—whether or not they used boycotts—intimidated booksellers and motion picture exhibitors.
38. First three quotes from M. W. to "Dear Men," January 8, 1957, ACLU-MF, reel 52; fourth quote from Frank Jeanette to ACLU, May 7, 1957; fifth quote from Ruth Glaser to ACLU; sixth quote from F. A. Fink, "NODL vs. Bennnett Cerf," from "Our Sunday Visitor," Huntington, Ind.; see also Jack Feltz to Malin, May 29, 1958, and July 10, 1958; W. B. Haugh, May 7, 1957; Breig, "Declaration of Civil Liberty"; Breig to Malin, July 23, 1957, ACLU-MF, reel 53; later quotes from Rosemary Kieer to ACLU, February 14, 1955, ACLU-MF, reel 49.
39. First two quotes from Elaine Mates to ACLU, June 10, 1957; all other quotes from Edward Dixon to ACLU, June 10, 1957, and July 31, 1957; see also Matthew K. Clarke to Ernest Angell et al., June 12, 1957; G. W. C. Ross to Donald G. Paterson, November 14, 1957, ACLU-MF, reel 53.
40. First quote from Meiklejohn to Ernest Angell, July 17, 1957; Malin to Persons Signing 1957 Statement on NODL and Private Pressure Group Censorship, February 17, 1958; see also Lewis Galantiere to Reitman, October 9, 1957; Reitman to Rice, September 9, 1957, HRC-ERC, box 85; Osmond Fraenkel Diary, October 21, 1957, PML-OFD; see also Nelson, *Education and Democracy*.
41. First two quotes from Lillie Caldwell to ACLU, May 7, 1957; see also Roy L. Stamp Sr. to ACLU, May 6, 1957; Francis Hackett to Reitman, May 15, 1957; fourth quote from Shirley Aime Colin to ACLU, June 10, 1957, ACLU-MF, reel 53; third quote from "15 Clergymen Oppose 'Pressure' Used in Banning of 'Baby Doll,'" unidentified newspaper article, n.d., ACLU-MF, reel 52; final two quotes from Eric Saunders to ACLU, February 28, 1953, ACLU-MF, reel 47; see also Blackwood, "Show Biz and the Censor"; and editorials, *The Churchman*, May 15, 1957. Although Ernst contributed to this tendency to associate Catholics with censorship, by 1958 he worried about "an increasing amount of anti-Catholic bigotry" and sought opportunities to open communication between Catholics, Jews, and Protestants. Ernst to Karl Menninger, April 2, 1958, HRC-MEC, box 540.
42. First two quotes from "The Mike Wallace Interview" with Bennett Cerf, November 30, 1957, http://www.hrc.utexas.edu/multimedia/video/2008/wallace/cerf_bennett.html (retrieved September 7, 2009). See also William Peters, "What You Can't See on TV," *Redbook*, July 1957, ACLU-MF, reel 51; Arnold Grossman, "A Disturbing Report on Why

More and more Librarians are Taking Books Out of Circulation," *Redbook*, April 1960, ACLU-MF, reel 56; The Editors, "How to Deal with Obscene Books," *Redbook*, November 1957, ACLU-MF, reel 52; Frank J. Fogarty to *The Bergen Evening Record*, October 28, 1955, ACLU-MF, reel 50; Leslie M. Zatz to Malin, January 1, 1957; Mrs. Burton D. Wechsler to Ruth Smith, January 27, 1957; Smith to Wechsler, January 30, 1957, ACLU-MF, reel 52; Paul Obler to Sirs, September 9, 1957; H. David Leventhal to ACLU, October 11, 1957; Reitman to Lee Swartzbereg, December 11, 1957, ACLU-MF, reel 53; Steven S. Schwarzschild to Louis Joughin, April 2, 1957; Stewart H. Benedict to ACLU, February 18, 1958; Malin to Fitzgerald, March 11, 1958, ACLU-MF, reel 54; Esther Rubinstein, May 9, 1959, ACLU-MF, reel 55; Clarke Shabino telegram to ACLU, March 22, 1963, SC-ACLU, box 65; Morris Lowenthal to "Those Interested in Protecting the 'Freedom to Read,'" April 9, 1965, NCA-ACLU, box 35; LeRoy Charles Merritt to Samuel Rapport, March 17, 1958, NCA-ACLU, box 25; L. R., Boston to *drum: sex in perspective*, July 1965, 33. Frustrated consumers also formed Right-to-Read committees. The New Jersey Right to Read Committee was mobilized by a "housewife" who became angry when she learned that James Baldwin's *Another Country* was being removed from her local bookstore at NODL's behest. The Freedom to Read Committee of Black Hawk County formed in reaction to a Citizens for Decent Literature film, *Pages of Death*, that blamed "dirty magazines" for causing rape. "Right to Read" (with Reitman to Leanne Golden, September 16, 1964), ACLU-MF, reel 64; see also "Freedom to Read," *Playboy*, December 1967, 89.

43. First quote from Msgr. Thomas J. Fitzgerald, "NODL States Its Case," *America*, June 1, 1957, 280–282; second quote from Fitzgerald to Malin, February 18, 1958; see also Jeffrey Fuller to Fitzgerald, June 17, 1957; Fitzgerald to Fuller, July 1, 1957; Malin to Fitzgerald, July 19, 1957; March 11, 1958, and May 5, 1958; Fitzgerald to Reverend R. E. Van Mullekom, March 26, 1958; Mullekom to Fitzgerald, March 29, 1958; Reitman to Malin, May 2, 1958; Peter S. Jennison to Reitman, June 10, 1958; "Let's Abolish Lurid Magazines," *The Clubwoman*, February 1957; Malin to Mrs. Stephen J. Nicholas, December 10, 1957; Reitman to Dan Lacy, December 16, 1957; Reitman to Ann G. Wolfe, December 16, 1957; Lacy to Reitman, December 23, 1957; Malin to Millicent C. McIntosh, January 13, 1958; McIntosh to Malin, March 4, 1958; O. K. Armstrong to American Book Publishers Council, Inc., September 7, 1957; Reitman to Armstrong, September 13, 1957; January 3, 1958; Reitman to George W. Cornell, January 14, 1958; Reitman to Malin, January 30, 1958; "Newsletter: Churchmen's Commission for Decent Publications," June 5, 1958; Clyde W. Taylor to Friend, November 17, 1958, ACLU-MF, reel 54; final three quotes from "Summary Report: Special Study on Decency in Literature and Other Mass Media," January 14, 1959, SC-ACLU, box 1; Reitman to Censorship Panel, December 13, 1957; Malin to Persons Signing ACLU 1957 Statement on NODL and Private Pressure Group Censorship, February 17, 1958, HRC-ERC, box 85; Fitzgerald to Fuller, June 10, 1957, ACLU-MF, reel 53; O'Connor, "The National Organization for Decent Literature," 405–406. *Playboy*'s editorial staff and letters to the editors praised the ACLU for drawing out the First Amendment implications of boycotts. "Applause for ACLU," *Playboy*, October 1964, 63–64.

44. The Office to Censorship Committee, October 15, 1965, SC-ACLU, box 115; O'Connor, "National Organization for Decent Literature," 409–410.

45. First three quotes from Rice to Soll, March 31, 1960, ACLU-MF, reel 59; second two quotes from John E. Coons to Leanne Golden, April 5, 1969; final two quotes from O'Meara to Reitman, July 29, 1960, ACLU-MF, reel 58. See also Reitman to John Preston Ward, September 1, 1959; Reitman to Sidney Schreiber, September 4, 1959; Raymond Gray to Schreiber, September 21, 1959, ACLU-MF, reel 55; Reitman to Soll, September 4, 1959, and October 9, 1959; Paul Gebhard to Reitman, September 22, 1959; Frank J. Curran to Reitman, October 6, 1959; Reitman to Curran, October 9, 1959; Philip Q. Roche to Spencer Coxe, November 20, 1959; Soll to Benjamin Karpman, March 9, 1960; Karpman to Soll, March 14, 1960; "The Potentiality of a Comic-Book to increase the aggressive behavior and Motivation of Adolescents," with Julius Mark to Reitman, September 2, 1959;

Jean A. Thompson to Reitman, October 14, 1959, ACLU-MF, reel 59; Richard Lichtman, "Sex and Censorship in a Free Society," n.d., ACLU-MF, reel 56; Lichtman, "Pornography & Censorship"; Arthur E. Summerfield, "Let's Stop Filth," *Lowell Sun*, August 2, 1959, 44; Osmond Fraenkel Diary, April 11 and 23, 1960; November 1, 1960; June 19, 1961; March 19, 1962; April 2 and 16, 1962, PML-OFD.

46. First quote from George A. Dreyfous, "Comment by ACLU Affiliates," p. 5, ACLU-MF, reel 534; second quote from Betsy McDonald to Leanne Golden, September 30, 1960; third quote from George C. Whitney, "Comments on Draft Copy of ACLU Pamphlet on Obscenity, Censorship and Free Speech," received October 5, 1960; see also Sprayregen to Reitman, July 27, 1960, ACLU-MF, reel 58.
47. First two quotes from Lloyd M. Smith to Reitman, April 4, 1960; see also Fleishman to Eason Monroe, April 5, 1960, ACLU-MF, reel 58; second quote from Levy to William E. Sanborn, October 18, 1955, ACLU-MF, reel 50; final quotes from Soll to O'Meara, August 22, 1960, ACLU-MF, reel 59.
48. Quotes from "Statement of Harriet F. Pilpel Re Obscenity Legislation," April 11, 1962, SC-ACLU, box 55; Pemberton to Board of Directors, April 11, 1962, HRC-ERP, box 84; "Obscenity and Censorship: Two Statements of the American Civil Liberties Union," March 1963, SC-ACLU, box 1; ACLU Press Release, May 28, 1962, ACLU-MF, reel 59; Reitman to Rice, n.d., HRC-ERC, box 85. Rice criticized his own committee's conclusions when he represented it before the board. When Pilpel questioned him, Rice explained, "I went along with the clear and present danger idea because it seemed the only way to get *anything* passed so that the matter could come up to the Board." Rice then presented his own proposal as an alternative to his committee's handiwork. Rice to Pilpel, April 17, 1962, HRC-ERC, box 84. Absenteeism at ACLU board meetings often shaped the organization's policies and resolutions. See Louis Joughin to Malin, June 28, 1954, PML-ACLU, box 79. According to ACLU historian Sam Walker, even the ignominious 1940 resolution that led the ACLU to purge Communists from its ranks can be explained in part by "the vagaries of attendance at board meetings." Walker, *In Defense*, 130–133.
49. Quotes from Hilde L. Mosse, "The Influence of Mass Media on the Mental Health of Children," 3, 2 *National Association for Better Radio and Television* (Summer 1963), ACLU-MF, reel 62; see also Beaty, *Fredric Wertham*, 186–194; Rifas, "'Especially Dr. Hilde L. Mosse'"; Wheeler, *Against Obscenity*, 139–143; Jowett, ed., *Children and the Movies*.
50. Henry Miller, "Defense of the Freedom to Read," *Evergreen Review*, Summer 1959, quoted at length in Martin, "The King of Smut"; Forster to Ernest Besig, September 15, 1952; Levy to Forster, November 13, 1953, ACLU-MF, reel 47; and *Two Obscene Books v. United States of America*, 92 F. Supp. 934 (October 23, 1953); Miller to Rosset, summer 1960, quoted in McCord, "American Avant-Garde," 88–89, 91–92, 96; Phyllis Bellows to Ernst, March 7 and 23, 1961; Ernst to Bellows, March 9, 1961, HRC-MEC, box 530; Thomas, "Most Dangerous Man"; Katz, "*Tropic of Cancer* Trials"; McCord, "American Avant-Garde," 90, 95. One of Grove's attorneys, Charles Rembar, explains that *Tropic* ended up in court so often partly, ironically, because the Customs Department and post office had lifted their bans on the book, allowing for no "federal criminal prosecution in which the question of *Tropic*'s obscenity might be litigated." Rembar, *The End of Obscenity*, 168–169. Examples of local *Tropic* cases that involved the ACLU include *Dorothy Upham v. Robert W. Dill*, 195 F. Supp. 5 (June 27, 1961), represented by Ephraim London and Melvin Wulf; *Attorney General v. The Book Named "Tropic of Cancer"* 345 Mass. 11 (May 16, 1952), amicus brief submitted by the Civil Liberties Union of Massachusetts; *Yudkin v. State*, 229 Md. 223 (July 5, 1962), amicus briefs submitted by the ACLU and the Maryland Civil Liberties Union; *California v. Bradley Smith*, Calif. Sup. Ct. (February 1962), represented by Stanley Fleishman with amicus brief submitted by A. L. Wirin and Fred Okrand; *William J. McCauley v. Tropic of Cancer*, 20 Wis. 2d 134 (May 20, 1963), amicus brief submitted by the Wisconsin chapter of the ACLU; *Grove Press, Inc. v. Gerstein*, 378 U.S. 577 (June 22, 1961), represented by Edward de Grazia; and *Jacob Zeitlin v. Roger Arnebergh*, 59 Cal. 2d 901 (July 2, 1963),

represented by A. L. Wirin and Fred Okrand with amicus brief submitted by Stanley Fleishman.

51. Radio industry representatives were among the first to try to expand standing in the 1940s, but they did so to fight a federal regulatory apparatus they loathed. As a result, New Deal liberals viewed the notion of a media consumer's standing with suspicion until, in the 1950s, various groups of radio listeners attempted to claim standing before the Federal Communications Commission in order to challenge the discriminatory practices of particular radio stations. See Toro, "Standing Up for Listeners' Rights," 161–169, 172–173, 175, 178, 180, 220–223. See also Levy to Alfred A. Albert, July 12, 1954, ACLU-MF, reel 47; "Note: Standing to Protest and Appeal the Issuance of Broadcasting Licenses: A Constricted Concept Redefined," *Yale Law Journal* 68 (1959), 783; Jaffe, "Standing to Secure," and "Notes: Government Exclusion of Foreign Political Propaganda," *Harvard Law Review* 68, 8 (June 1955), 1393–1409. Relevant case law includes the aforementioned *Martin v. City of Struthers* 319 U.S. 141 (May 3, 1943) and *Associated Industries v. Ickes*, 134 F. 2d 694 (February 8, 1943).

52. "Who Is to Censor What We See, Hear, Read?" *Kalamazoo Michigan Gazette*, January 25, 1961; "Your Right to Read, to Know," unidentified Alabama newspaper, December 28, 1962, ACLU-MF, reel 59; "Big Brother Will Read For You," *Portland Reporter*, February 27, 1963, ACLU-MF, reel 61; "'The Right to Read': The NCTE Speaks Out on Censorship!" *Modern Language Journal* 47, 2 (February 1963), 70–71; Peter Jennison, "Freedom to Read," Public Affairs Pamphlet, No. 344, 1963; "Freedom-to-Read Bulletin," 5, 1 (March 1962), ACLU-MF, reel 60; "Audience Unlimited News," May–June 1966, ACLU-MF, reel 64; final quotes from *Dorian Book Quarterly*, January–February–March 1964; see also advertisement cited in Meeker, "Behind the Mask of Respectability," 78–116, esp. 101.

53. First quote from author interview with Sprayregen, January 21, 2010; second quote from Charles W. Gray to Elmer Gertz, quoted in Gertz to Henry Miller, February 16, 1962, in Gertz and Lewis, *Henry Miller*, 41; see also McCord, "American Avant-Garde," 102–105; "Statement in Support of Freedom to Read," *Evergreen Review* (July–August 1962), 6, 25, reprinted in Kaufman, Ortenberg, and Rosset, eds., *Outlaw Bible*, 630–631; Rosset to Rice, April 5, 1962, HRC-ERC, box 86; Eberly, *Citizen Critics*, 70, 90–92.

54. First and last quotes from author interview with Sprayregen, January 26, 2010; second quote from Sprayregen to Spencer Coxe, December 7, 1961, ACLU-MF, reel 58; see also Sprayregen to Louis L. Jaffe, October 26, 1961, UCL-ACLU, box 32. Sprayregen credited the following two influential law review articles with his ideas: Jaffe, "Standing to Secure," and "Notes: Government Exclusion of Foreign Political Propaganda." On ACLU frustration with booksellers' reluctance to sue for the right to sell *Tropic of Cancer*, see Gordon Young to ACLU, October 30, 1961; R. Vance Fitzgerald to Reitman, December 12, 1961; Reitman to Fitzgerald, December 18, 1961, ACLU-MF, reel 58; Reitman to Mr. E. R. Hutchison, October 9, 1964, ACLU-MF, reel 62; ACLU Censorship Committee Report, n.d., PML-ACLU, box 83.

55. Author interview with Sprayregen, January 26, 2010; author interview with Joseph Ronsley, January 26, 2010; *Haiman v. Morris*, 61 S. 19718, Superior Ct. of Cook County Ill. (1962); *Wilson v. Haiman*, Ill. Sup. Ct. (October 1961) in Osmond K. Fraenkel and Ann Fagan Ginger, eds., "Civil Liberties Docket," 7, 4 (July 1962), http://sunsite.berkeley.edu/meiklejohn/meik-7_4/meik-7_4-4.html (retrieved May 27, 2012); "Notes: Government Exclusion of Foreign Political Propaganda," *Harvard Law Review* 68, 8 (June 1955), 1393–1409; Gertz and Lewis, *Henry Miller*, xx; Eberly, *Citizen Critics*, 65–66; "Illegal Seizures of Books Charged," *New York Times*, October 17, 1961; "Verified Complaint for a Temporary and Permanent Injunction," *Haiman v. Morris*, October 13, 1961, PML-ACLU-DC, box 14; "Amended Verified Complaint for a Permanent Injunction," *Haiman v. Morris*, January 25, 1962, NUA-FHP, box 23; ACLU Illinois Division News Release, October 16, 1961; Alexander Polikoff and Burton Joseph, "Memorandum in Opposition to Defendants' Motion to Strike Complaint and Dismiss Action," in *Ronsley v. Stanczak*, n.d., LOC-EGP, box 258.

56. Sprayregen quotes from "Brief and Argument for Plaintiffs-Appellees," *Haiman v. Morris* (September 1952), NUA-FHP, box 11; Epstein quotes from *Haiman v. Morris* (February 21, 1962), NUA-FHP, box 23; see also Gertz to Henry Miller, February 22, 1962, reprinted in Gertz and Lewis, *Henry Miller,* 52–54. Grove Press's lead attorney, Gertz, did not initially approve of the ACLU's focus on the right to read. See Gertz, *A Handful of Clients,* 231, 256–257; "Tropic of Cancer Wins," *New York Times,* February 22, 1962; Stephen Wise Tulin to Milton Stanzler, December 27, 1961, ACLU-MF, reel 60; Norris, "'Cancer' in Chicago"; "Freedom to Read is Upheld," *Chicago Daily News,* February 23, 1962; Sprayregen to Haiman et al., July 9, 1964, NUA-FHP, box 23; *Chicago Daily Law Bulletin,* February 22, 1962, 1.
57. Quote from Sprayregen to President, West Publishing Company, March 13, 1962, UCL-ACLU, box 32. See also Gertz and Lewis, *Henry Miller,* 28–29, 51–52; Gertz, *A Handful of Clients,* 280–281, 301; Eberly, *Citizen Critics,* 91, 102–103 n. 12; "Suppression of 'Tropic of Cancer' Spreads as ACLU Continues to Fight," February 5, 1962, ACLU-MF, reel 60; Jean Shanberg to Larry Speiser, October 24, 1961, PML-ACLU-DC, box 14; Gertz to Henry Miller, February 1 and 15, 1962; Rosset to Rice, April 5, 1962, HRC-ERC, box 86; "Statement in Support of the Freedom to Read," in Kaufman, Ortenberg, and Rosset, eds., *Outlaw Bible,* 630–631; "Judge Epstein Rules 'Tropic' Is Not Obscene," *Chicago Daily Law Bulletin,* February 22, 1962.
58. The defendants filed a motion to dismiss the case, arguing that Ronsley lacked standing to sue in part because he stood to suffer no damage to his property. First three quotes from Alexander Polikoff and Burton Joseph, "Memorandum in Opposition to Defendants' Motion to Strike Complaint and Dismiss Action," in *Ronsley v. Stanczak,* n.d.; final three quotes from Judge Bernard M. Decker, "Memorandum of Opinion," *Ronsley v. Stanczak* (April 6, 1962); see also Brief for the Plaintiffs-Appellees, *Haiman v. Morris* (September Term 1962), NUA-FHP, box 23; Gertz to Sprayregen, April 9, 1962; Gertz to Polikoff and Joseph, April 9, 1962; "Motion to Strike Complaint and Dismiss Action," in *Ronsley v. Stanczak* (February 15, 1962), LOC-EGP, box 258; see also "Uphold Citizen's Right to Challenge Censorship by Public Official," n.d., ACLU-MF, reel 60. Sixteen years later, Decker would side with the ACLU in ruling that the town of Skokie, Illinois, must permit a neo-Nazi march. "Judge Bernard M. Decker; OKd Neo-Nazi March," *Los Angeles Times,* November 6, 1993.
59. First quote from "Freedom Through Dissent," ACLU 42nd Annual Report, July 1, 1961, to June 30, 1962 (New York: Oceana Publishers, 1962), 5–7; second quote from Brennan's concurrence in *Lamont v. Postmaster General,* 381 U.S. 301 (May 24, 1965). The ACLU filed influential amicus briefs in *Lamont* and *Martin v. City of Struthers,* the two key Supreme Court cases that wrote consumer rights into the First Amendment. See *Martin v. City of Struthers,* 319 U.S. 141 (May 3, 1943). Many legal scholars at the time were unaware of the lower-court rulings that laid the groundwork for *Lamont.* See for example Klein, "Towards an Extension of the First Amendment," 141. Shortly after the U.S. Supreme Court decided *Grove Press,* the Supreme Court of Illinois, to which Morris appealed after his defeat before Judge Epstein, quietly reversed its holding that *Tropic of Cancer* was obscene. See *Grove Press v. Gerstein,* 378 U.S. 577 (June 22, 1964); Sprayregen to Haiman et al., July 9, 1964, NUA-FHP, box 23; third quote from "Text of Kennedy's Message to Congress on Protections for Consumers," *New York Times,* March 16, 1962. See also *Jacobellis v. Ohio,* 378 U.S. 184 (June 22, 1964); Cohen, *Consumers' Republic,* 345; "Kennedy Submits a Broad Program to Aid Consumer," *New York Times,* March 16, 1962.
60. First two quotes from Sandra Silverman to Richard F. Morton, July 19, 1966; see also Silverman to Shel Silverstein, May 4, 1966; Silverman to Anson Mount, May 4, 1966, UCL-ACLU, box 6. All other quotes from undated drafts and Theodore Berland to Dear Friend, July 15 and 19, 1966; August 3 and 10, 1966; Theodore Berland to "You know," August 10, 1966, UCL-ACLU, box 6.

61. Quotes from "Hearings before the Committee on post office and Civil Service, House of Representatives, Eighty-Eighth Congress" on H.R. 142, H.R. 319, and Similar Bills, June 25–27 and July 10 and 24, 1963, pp. 7–8, 11, 17, 20, 27, 34, 35, 48, 56, 64, 75–81, 85, 106, 110, 114–115. See also Strub, "Perversion for Profit," and Schaefer, "Plain Brown Wrapper." ACLU members also wrote to the national office to complain about the organization's approach to unsolicited mass mailings of sexually titillating material. See for example Paul D. Hubbe to ACLU, April 2, 1962, ACLU-MF, reel 59.
62. Quotes from "Hearings before the Committee on post office and Civil Service, House of Representatives, Eighty-Eighth Congress" on H.R. 142, H.R. 319, and Similar Bills, June 25–27 and July 10 and 24, 1963, pp. 66–93.
63. First two quotes from "Statement of Timothy J. May, General Counsel, United States Post Office Department Before United States Senate Special Subcommittee on Juvenile Delinquency," February 17, 1967, quotes from 7 and 9; third quote from "Statement of Lawrence Speiser," April 13, 1967; all other quotes from "Testimony of Lawrence Speiser," October 30, 1967; see also Speiser to Pemberton, Reitman, and Marvin Karpatkin, March 1, 1967; Karpatkin to Pemberton, et al., March 27, 1967, ACLU-MF, reel 65. Speiser rallied *Playboy* editors to the cause by characterizing the bill as a threat to the magazine, claiming that it was aimed at "nonobscene mail matter." See "Postal Pandering," *Playboy*, January 1968, 61–62, 66. On Ginzburg see Boyer, *Purity in Print*, 300–305.
64. First quote from 39 USCS section 3008; 39 USCS section 4009 (1964 ed., Supp. IV); and Title III of the Postal Revenue and Federal Salary Act of 1967, 39 USCS section 4009; second and third quotes from "Summary of May 28, 1969 Meeting of National Organization on Legislative Proposals to Curb Mailing of Obscene Materials," June 30, 1969, PML-ACLU, box 194; fourth, fifth, and sixth quotes from *Rowan v. U.S. post office*, 397 U.S. 728 (May 4, 1970). See also Kielbowicz, "Origins of the Junk-Mail Controversy."
65. Rice to Eric Johnston, June 11, 1953; Forster to DeBra, September 21 and December 30, 1953; Forster to Kenneth Clark, December 3, 1953; Forster to Johnston, December 30, 1953, ACLU-MF, reel 46; Forster to Schreiber, January 21, 1954, ACLU-MF, reel 48; Patrick Malin to Johnston, December 5, 1955; ACLU Press Release, December 5, 1955, ACLU-MF, reel 50; Malin to Johnston, November 23, 1956; Reitman to Manning Clagett, September 14, 1956; Claggett to Reitman, September 20, 1956, ACLU-MF, reel 51; Schreiber to Reitman, May 26, 1959, ACLU-MF, reel 56. "Production Code Revised," December 12, 1956; "New Motion Picture Association of America Code," February 7, 1957; LJ (Louis Joughin) to AR (Alan Reitman), March 6, 1957; Malin to Johnston, April 18, 1957, ACLU-MF, reel 52.
66. First quote from *Times Film v. Chicago*, Brief of American Civil Liberties Union, Illinois Division, as Amicus Curiae, October 10, 1960; see also Watts to Charles Davis, January 27, 1961, ACLU-MF, reel 60; second quote from *Jacobellis v. Ohio*, Brief of American and Ohio Civil Liberties Unions as Amici Curiae, October Term, 1962; see also Berkman to unknown, November 3, 1962; Wulf to Berkman, February 18, 1963; de Grazia to Leroy Charles Merritt, March 16, 1965, ACLU-MF, reel 63; third quote from *Jacobellis v. Ohio*, 378 U.S. 184 (June 22, 1964). By 1965, movie censorship boards could be found in Maryland, New York, Virginia, Kansas, and several cities, including Chicago, Illinois; Detroit, Michigan; Providence, Rhode Island, and Forth Worth, Texas. See ACLU Office to Censorship Committee, "Memorandum prepared by Barbara Scott," n.d., SC-ACLU, box 115; *Times Film Corp. v. City of Chicago*, 365 U.S. 43 (January 23, 1961); Tim Clagett to Reitman, February 3, 1961, ACLU-MF, reel 59; Reitman to Clagett, February 28, 1961, ACLU-MF, reel 60; Barbara Scott to Reitman, March 6, 1963; Reitman to Ernest Mazey, March 8, 1963; "Summary of Present Status of Film Censorship and Classification," March 18, 1963, ACLU-MF, reel 61; Randall, *Censorship of the Movies*, 177. Pressure group action against movies increased sevenfold between 1962 and 1965, but the final blow to state movie censorship came in *Freedman v. Maryland*, 380 U.S. 51 (1965).

67. First quote from "Kit for Use Against Censorship Legislation," Council of Motion Picture Organizations, Inc., January 13, 1960; "'COMPO' Formed to Combat Attacks on Filmdom," *New York Times*, October 29, 1950, ACLU-MF, reel 56; "Statement to: The State of New York Joint Legislative Committee . . . The Judiciary Committee of the New York Assembly, The Public Education Committee of the New York Senate," The Council of Motion Picture Organizations, Inc., January 21, 1960, ACLU-MF, reel 57; The [ACLU] Office to the Board of Directors, February 28, 1963, ACLU-MF, reel 61.
68. Wheeler, *Against Obscenity*, 54–58, 82–85; Cross, *Kids' Stuff*, 147–187; Cohen, *Consumers' Republic*, 292–344.
69. Quotes from "Minutes, Communications Media Committee," October 29, 1968; The Office to Communications Media Committee, December 11, 1968; "Minutes, Communications Media Committee," December 18, 1968, ACLU-MF, reel 65. In 1971, the ACLU of Northern California announced that it had received "complaints from parents who desire to have their children see movies which someone has decided they should not see." Paul N. Halvonik, "Notice to the Legal Committee, ACLUNC and Legal Coordinators," May 19, 1971, NCA-ACLU, box 13.
70. First three quotes from "Minutes, Communications Media Committee," October 29, 1968; final two quotes from "ACLU Policy Statement on Voluntary Motion Picture Classification," March 10, 1969; see also Office to Communications Media Committee, December 11, 1968; "Minutes, Communications Media Committee," December 18, 1968; Reitman to Pilpel, March 10, 1969, ACLU-MF, reel 65. Negative reaction to the ACLU's criticism of the MPAA came swiftly. David Wolper, president of an independent production company, declared, "you have just lost me because of your recent attack" on the MPAA rating system. It "*does not*," he insisted, pose a "prior restraint on the creative process." In response, Reitman admitted that the ACLU had no proof that the MPAA Code or its new rating system would diminish the free expression of moviemakers but quoted one producer's claim that "under cover of the 'X'-rating, the industry faces the worst and most insidious censorship in its history." Quotes in "ACLU Policy Statement on Voluntary Motion Picture Classification," March 10, 1969; Wolper to ACLU, April 14, 1969; June 10, 1969; Reitman to Wolper, July 8, 1969, ACLU-MF, reel 65. See also Peter Bart, "Hollywood's Morality Code Undergoing First Major Revisions in 35 Years," *New York Times*, April 7, 1965; MPAA to Rev. Roderick J. Wagner, September 22, 1965, ACLU-MF, reel 63; "Hollywood is Preparing a Broad Film Classification System," *New York Times*, September 21, 1968; "As Nation's Standards Change, So Do Movies," *New York Times*, October 8, 1968; "Ratings to Bar Some Films to Children," *New York Times*, October 8, 1968; Lewis, *Hollywood v. Hard Core*, 149.
71. Quote from *Ginsberg v. New York* 390 U.S. 629 (April 22, 1968). See also Reitman to Pemberton, January 15, 1965, HRC-ERC, box 88; "Statement of Lawrence Speiser . . . before the Committee on Commerce, United States Senate," June 11, 1968, ACLU-MF, reel 65; "Plan to Classify Movies Debated," *New York Times*, June 12, 1968; Bosley Crowther, "Towards a New Order," *New York Times*, April 4, 1965. On the death of the MPAA Production Code and the creation of a movie rating system, see Leff and Simmons, *Dame in the Kimono* and Brisbin, "Censorship, Ratings, and Rights"; Lewis, *Hollywood v. Hard Core*; Wyatt, "The Stigma of X."
72. Quotes from Vincent Canby, "For Better or Worse, Film Industry Begins Ratings," *New York Times*, November 1, 1968. The *New York Times* predicted that the rating system would encourage the production of more films with adult themes. Canby, "Bishops Applaud Eased Film Code," *New York Times*, September 28, 1966; Canby, "New Production Code for Films Endorsed by Theater Owners," *New York Times*, October 1, 1966; "Catholics Criticize a Film Code Ruling," *New York Times*, November 17, 1966; Motion Picture Association of America Press Release, September 20, 1966, ACLU-MF, reel 65; "Mature Audiences Only," *New York Times*, October 7, 1966; Reitman to Scott, September 14, 1966, and October 3, 1966; Scott to Reitman, September 16, 1966, ACLU-MF, reel 65.

73. In 2008, the law prevented a mailer from continuing to send material to a patron who complained that it is "erotically arousing or sexually provocative." 39 USC section 3008. On the current rating system, see the MPAA's own website, http://www.mpaa.org/ratings (retrieved July 1, 2011). The MPAA continues to adapt to external pressure. For example, in response to Kirby Dick's damning documentary expose *This Film is Not Yet Rated* (2006), MPAA CEO Dan Glickman tweaked the rating system. See David M. Halbfinger, "Rating (and Finding) the Movie Raters" and "Hollywood Rethinks Its Ratings Process," *New York Times*, January 16 and 18, 2007; A. O. Scott, "Some Material May Be Inappropriate or Mystifying, and the Ratings May Be as Well," *New York Times*, September 1, 2006.
74. By the end of the first decade of the twenty-first century, lead ACLU staff attorney Chris Hansen averred that consumers' rights under the First Amendment are so well established today that the ACLU would readily bring a lawsuit on behalf of consumers, but rarely needs to do so, because such censorship has become so rare. Author interview with Chris Hansen, November 24, 2009. Examples of recent ACLU cases argued in part on behalf of consumers include *Ashcroft v. Free Speech Coalition*, 535 U.S. 234 (April 16, 2002); *Ashcroft v. ACLU*, Brief for the Respondents, 542 U.S. 656 (June 29, 2004). Legal scholars have expressed frustration at courts' unwillingness to distinguish between producers' and consumers' rights under the First Amendment. See for example, Wagner, "The First Amendment and the Right to Hear," and Thomas, "The Listener's Right to Hear."

Chapter 4

1. First two quotes from Stone and Pilpel, "Social and Legal Status of Contraception"; all other quotes from "Civil Liberties and the War on Crime," May 1964, SSC-DK, box 30.
2. What I call intellectual cross-pollination was not a deliberate ACLU strategy. It is worth noting, though, that in 1964, one board member suggested that the ACLU could spread its influence more effectively if members would join the boards of other organizations to "push our point of view." Dan Lacey quoted in Osmond Fraenkel Diaries, January 2, 1964, PML-OFD.
3. Quotes from "A Lawyer Who Loves Challenges," *Boston Globe*, April 10, 1983; Eleanor Jackson Piel interview with Harriet Pilpel, March 20, 1972; author interview with Judith and Alan Appelbaum, May 27, 2010.
4. Quotes from Eleanor Jackson Piel interview with Harriet Pilpel, March 20, 1972, and author interview with Judith and Alan Appelbaum, May 27, 2010. See also Reitman to Pilpel, June 26, 1963, ACLU-MF, reel 196; Silverman, "Pursuing Celebrity," 29. On Pilpel, see also Richard D. Heffner radio interview with Harriet Pilpel, October 16, 1979; Swiger, *Women Lawyers at Work*, 152–168; Gerson, "Renaissance Woman"; Law, "Harriet Fleischl Pilpel"; "Remembering Harriet Pilpel," *National Review*, May 27, 1991, 63; Wheeler, "Harriet Pilpel"; "Harriet Pilpel on Women, Law and Social Change," *On the Issues* 8 (1987), 5; Robert Pilpel to author, August 2, 2005; September 12, 2005; October 27, 2005; Kenyon to ACLU Board, June 8, 1971, SSC-DK, box 15; Mary Ratcliffe to Pilpel, August 15, 1973, SSC-HFP, box 5.
5. See Pilpel and Zavin, *Your Marriage*; Pilpel, Zuckerman, and Ogg, *Abortion*; Pilpel and Norwick, *When Should Abortion be Legal?*; Stone and Pilpel, "Social and Legal Status of Contraception"; Pilpel, "Problem Box"; Pilpel and Zavin, "Birth Control"; Pilpel and Zavin, *Your Marriage and the Law*; Pilpel and Zavin, "Sex and the Criminal Law"; Pilpel, "But Can You Do That?" See also Pilpel to Hazel Rice, October 30, 1937, ACLU-MF, reel 141.
6. D. Kenneth Rose to Ernst, January 6, 1943, HRC-MEC, box 363; Ernst to Baldwin, April 10, 1941; ACLU Board of Directors Minutes, September 14, 1942, ACLU-MF, reel 203.
7. Quotes from Margaret Sanger, "Birth Control and Civil Liberties," October 13, 1941, MSP-MF, reel S72; see also Clifford Forster to William Prickett, April 17, 1947, ACLU-MF, reel 234.

8. Quote from Garrow, *Liberty and Sexuality*, 120; see also 116; Forster to Prickett, April 17, 1947, ACLU-MF, reel 234; Mrs. Clayton Whitehill to Baldwin, July 5, 1943; Simon M. Newman to ACLU, June 1, 1943, ACLU-MF, reel 211; Adele Gleason to Baldwin, March 15, 1948, ACLU-MF, reel 256; "Birth Control Information Cases Arise in the States," n.d.; Planned Parenthood newsletter, January–February 1952; ACLU News Release, February 6, 1952; Weekly Bulletin, April 6, 1953; Levy to Malin, ACLU-MF, reel 316. "I'd be willing to bet," wrote Pilpel's son Robert, "that in many ways large and small she took every opportunity to bring Planned Parenthood and the ACLU closer together." Robert Pilpel to author, August 10, 2005.
9. Quote from PPLC "Special Legislative Edition," Spring 1955, ACLU-MF, reel 50; see also Garrow, *Liberty and Sexuality*, 135–136.
10. Quotes from Levy to Malin, April 26, 1955, ACLU-MF, reel 50. The PPFA regularly requested that its keynote speakers circulate their lectures in advance. Ernst to Rose, February 5, 1945; Ernst to Charles E. Scribner, March 7, 1945; Sanger to Ernst, March 14, 1945, HRC-MEC, box 267; Ernst to Sanger, February 5, 1945, HRC-MEC, box 894; see also Garrow, *Liberty and Sexuality*, 139.
11. Quote from Malin, "Civil Liberties and the American Family," May 6, 1955, PPFA II, 104.21; see also Frederick S. Jaffe, Planned Parenthood Press Release, May 6, 1955; Robert Satter to Louis Joughin, May 12, 1955; Joughin to Satter, May 16, 1955; Ralph S. Brown to Louis Joughin, May 19, 1955; Joughin to Brown, May 24, 1955; Joughin to Brown, February 2, 1956, ACLU-MF, reel 50; "Memorandum of Roger Baldwin on the 'Clear and Present' Danger Test," January 13, 1949; "The Clear and Present Danger Test," July 21, 1949, ACLU-MF, reel 260.
12. First quote from NYCLU News Release, July 18, 1958; second quote from News Release, February 16, 1959; see also Finn, "Controversy in New York"; ACLU Greater Philadelphia Branch News Release, April 21, 1959; "Birth Control Cases Arise in the States," n.d.; Phila. Branch's INTERIM REPORT, July 1, 1959"; "ACLU Units View Ban on Birth Control Information as Limiting Free Speech," *York, Pennsylvania Gazette & Daily*, May 1, 1959; Gaynor and Tauber to Executive Board, October 13, 1958; Reitman to Gordon, November 12, 1958; Thomas to Golden, February 6, 1959; March 6, 1959, ACLU-MF, reel 316; Watts to Brown, March 10, 1959, ACLU-MF, reel 393.
13. Quotes from author interview with Melvin Wulf, May 27, 2010. See also James, *The People's Lawyers*, 24–31.
14. Author interview with Melvin Wulf, May 27, 2010; James, *The People's Lawyers*, 24–31; Wulf quotes from David Garrow interview with Melvin Wulf, March 19, 1992; Wulf to Theodore Botter, Esq., March 6, 1959; "Birth Control Information Cases Arise in the States," n.d.; Botter to Wulf, March 11, 1959, ACLU-MF, reel 316; Pilpel to Harper, April 16, 1959; Pilpel to Jaffe, May 5, 1959, SSC-PPFA II, box 184.
15. First two quotes from Joughin to Burton T. Wilson, June 17, 1958; last two quotes from Minutes, Due Process Committee, July 15, 1959, SSC-PPFA II, box 104; see also Minutes, ACLU Board of Directors Meeting, August 17, 1959; second and third quotes from Malin to ACLU Staff, June 9, 1958; see also Joughin to Brown, June 10 and 18, 1958; "Intra-Office Buck Sheets," Joughin to Staff, June 16, 1958; Reitman to Brown, July 14, 1958; Brown to Reitman, September 5, 1958; Jerome Caplan to ACLU, January 19, 1960; ACLU News Release, September 23, 1959; ACLU Weekly Bulletin, #2013, October 12, 1959; Roraback to Watts, September 24, 1959, October 20, 1959; Brown to Reitman, September 30, 1959; Connecticut Planned Parenthood newsletter, December 1959, ACLU-MF, reel 393; Osmond Fraenkel Diary, August 17, 1959, PML-OFD; "Birth Control Law Hit," *New York Times*, June 7, 1958; David Garrow interview with Melvin Wulf, March 19, 1992; David Garrow interview with Catherine Roraback, September 17, 1991; Reitman to Jules H. Gordon, November 12, 1958; Martha Thomas to Leanne Golden, February 6, 1959; Thomas to Ohio Civil Liberties Union Chapter Chairmen, February 5, 1959; "News Release," February 20, 1959; "ACLU in Policy Statement Scores State Laws Barring Birth

Control Devices," n.d.; Fern Babcock to Reitman, September 28, 1959; Felix Morrow to Malin, November 12, 1959; Stuart B. Barber to ACLU, January 15, 1960; Wulf to Barber, March 1, 1960, ACLU-MF, reel 316; Watts to Roraback, August 28, 1959; October 5, 1959; Jaffe to Campbell, September 2, 1959, PPFA II, box 184; Wulf to Sheldon Mitchell, January 22, 1960; February 29, 1960; Nancy Wechsler to Mitchell, January 26, 1960; Mitchell to Wulf, February 5, 1960; Alice Grailcourt to Jeffrey E. Fuller, May 16, 1960, ACLU-MF, reel 57; see also Garrow, *Liberty and Sexuality*, 154–155.

16. Pilpel to Campbell, October 29, 1958; "Outline of Points Discussed at Conference . . . November 14, 1958"; Ernst, Memo on "PPFA—Conn. Birth Control Suit," December 9, 1958; quotes from Pilpel to Harper, November 10, 1958; June 19, 1959; July 6, 1959, SSC-PPFA II, box 184. On *Roth*, see chapter 3. See also Walker, *In Defense*, 235, and Wittern-Keller, *Freedom of the Screen*, 197–213. The Connecticut attorneys often resented critical oversight by New York City outsiders. They also worried that Connecticut courts would not respond well to involvement by New York City–based organizations and requested that the ACLU and PPFA refrain from filing amicus briefs until the case left the state courts. See Harper to Watts, March 19, 1959, ACLU-MF, reel 393; Lorraine Campbell to Bill Fitzgerald, May 19, 1959; Campbell to Mrs. Sidney Hessel, July 1, 1959; Fifield Workum to William Vogt, July 8, 1959, SSC-PPFA II, box 184; see also Garrow, *Liberty and Sexuality*, 151–228.

17. "Medicine: Family Planning," *Time*, August 12, 1957; Jack Nelson to ACLU, August 8, 1959; Leon Arnold Muller, "Free Contraceptives for Poor People," June 22, 1955, ACLU-MF, reel 316; Ernst to E. R. Michaud, September 28, 1959, HRC-MEC, box 566. See also Lord, *Condom Nation*, 93; Solinger, *Wake Up Little Susie*, 205–231; Gordon, *Moral Property of Women*, 279–285; and Connelly, *Fatal Misconception*, 155–194.

18. Quotes from Brief for Planned Parenthood Federation of America, *Poe v. Ullman*, October Term, 1960; see also Pilpel to Harper, November 14, 1960; Pilpel to Mary Calderone et al., May 25, 1960; Calderone to Pilpel, June 14, 1960, PPFA II, box 184; *Poe v. Ullman* and *Buxton v. Ullman*, 362 U.S. 987 (May 23, 1960); *Buxton, Doe, Hoe, and Poe v. Ullman*, 147 Conn. 48 (December 8, 1959). The Court declined to overturn the birth control statute in part because the legislature had refused to do so.

19. The ACLU and Connecticut Civil Liberties Union (CCLU) collaborated on one brief written by Wulf and Ruth Emerson. Emerson was a Yale Law School graduate and wife of Tom Emerson, an attorney who had been collaborating with Roraback and Harper on the Connecticut case. Because of their junior status, Emerson and Wulf, who wrote the ACLU/CCLU brief in *Poe v. Ullman*, appeared last on a list of five attorneys named as counsel. Even ACLU press releases attributed the brief to senior attorneys who played little or no role in its creation. According to Wulf, Emerson wrote the final section on due process rights of physicians, though when interviewed by Garrow in 1991, Emerson had no memory of her role in writing the brief. Wulf quotes from amicus brief for ACLU and CCLU in *Poe v. Ullman*, October Term, 1960; see also ACLU News Release, September 22, 1960; Wulf to Ruth Emerson, August 22, 1960; Ruth Emerson to Wulf, August 25, 1960; Watts to Ashton L. Sommers, October 11, 1960; Nancy Wechsler to Wulf, September 21, 1960; Roraback to Wulf, September 26, 1960, ACLU-MF, reel 393; David Garrow interview with Melvin Wulf, March 19, 1992; author interview with Melvin Wulf, May 27, 2010; Harper quotes from Brief for Appellants, *Poe v. Ullman*, October Term, 1960, PPFA II, box 184.

20. First quote from author interview with Melvin Wulf, May 27, 2010; second quote from Long, *Mapp v. Ohio*, 27, see also 5–9, 26–28, 67–69; final two quotes from *Mapp v. Ohio*, 367 U.S. 643 (June 19, 1961); see also Stewart, "Road to *Mapp*"; Walker, *In Defense*, 249–250. Scholars disagree about whether Harper or Wulf introduced privacy as a constitutional right to the Supreme Court. Garrow and Johnson imply that Harper preceded the others in developing a privacy basis for birth control. More implausibly, Hull and Hoffer credit the privacy argument to a law review article published two years after the three submitted their briefs to the Supreme Court. In Wulf's favor, in 1960, just before the U.S.

Supreme Court heard *Poe*, the *Yale Law Journal* attributed the privacy argument primarily to the ACLU brief written by Wulf and Emerson. Furthermore, in Wulf's request for permission to file an amicus brief in the *Poe* case, he explained his intention to claim that the Connecticut birth control statutes "invade the privacy" of the appellants in violation of the Fourteenth Amendment. In 1991, Wulf claimed to have been the first to introduce the "notion of a modern constitutional right of privacy to the Supreme Court," and Catherine Roraback agreed that "the privacy question was really just treated tangentially up until Mel filed the ACLU brief." Wulf to Honorable John J. Bracken, August 24, 1960, ACLU-MF, reel 393; see also Wulf, "On the Origins of Privacy"; Garrow, *Liberty and Sexuality*, 147, 166–168, 170–172; David Garrow interview with Catherine Roraback, September 17, 1991; "Connecticut's Birth Control Law: Reviewing a State Statute under the Fourteenth Amendment," *Yale Law Journal* 70, 2 (December 1960), 322–334; Johnson, *Griswold v. Connecticut*, 44–45; Hull and Hoffer, *Roe v. Wade*, 82–83; Redlich, "Are There Certain Rights."

21. Historians tend to treat search-and-seizure and sexual privacy separately and have, as a result, not appreciated the connections between them, though attorneys and judges at the time did. See Weisberg, "Control of Her Own Destiny"; Schroeder, "Keeping Police out of the Bedroom."
22. First quote from "Connecticut Contraceptive Law Upset by High Court Predicted," *Cleveland Plain Dealer*, April 11, 1961; all other quotes from Justice John Harlan's dissent in *Poe V. Ullman*, 376 U.S. 497 (June 19, 1961); see also Wulf, "On the Origins of Privacy"; Dickson, ed., *Supreme Court in Conference*, 797–799; Schroeder, "Keeping Police out of the Bedroom."
23. Oral arguments can be heard at the Oyez Project, *Poe v. Ullman*, 367 U.S. 497 (1961), http://oyez.org/cases/1960-1969/1960/1960_60 (retrieved July 5, 2010). See also Jaffe to Cass Canfield, April 21, 1961, PPFA II, box 184; "Pike Condemns Contraceptive Ban as Illegal," May 26, 1960, unidentified newspaper clipping; "Catholics Need Not Promote Laws Against Birth Control," *The Pilot*, June 10, 1960, ACLU-MF, reel 316; "Conn. MDs Tell About 'Law We Don't Obey,'" *New York Post*, September 22, 1960; Ernst, *Touchwood*, 283; Schoen, *Choice and Coercion*, 62; Watkins, *On the Pill*, 32–33.
24. Quote from "Bench and Bar Unite to Clarify the Law," *New York Times*, January 12, 1923. No early ACLU leaders seem to have been involved with the ALI, but they undoubtedly knew about it, if not from reading the *New York Times*, then from board member Dorothy Kenyon, who discussed the Institute with Elihu Root Jr. at the time it was cofounded by his father, Elihu Root. By the 1960s, Pilpel provided an even stronger ACLU connection to the ALI through her legal assistant, Nancy Wechsler, whose brother-in-law, Herbert Wechsler, led the drafting of the Model Penal Code. In addition, Nancy Wechsler's father, Osmond Fraenkel, was ACLU general counsel. See also S. R. [Elihu Root Jr.] to Kenyon, October 21, 1924, SSC-DK, box 16; Wechsler, "Challenge of a Model Penal Code," 1103; Hull, "Restatement and Reform"; Robinson and Dubber, "American Model Penal Code"; "About the American Law Institute," http://www.ali.org/doc/thisIsALI.pdf (retrieved July 5, 2011); Wechsler, "Codification of Criminal Law"; Goodrich and Wolkin, *Story of the American Law Institute*.
25. First quote from Kinsey to Ernst, August 24, 1943; Ernst to Kinsey, August 26, 1943; September 21, 1943, KI-KC, Ernst file 1. See also Ernst, "1.; Introductory statement . . . ," March 2, 1948, HRC-MEC, box 773. A *Life* magazine feature on Ernst noted his "overpowering preoccupation with sex" and also his tendency toward "bottom pinching," a characterization that one of Ernst's friends considered an understatement and that may explain Catherine Roraback's veiled complaints about Ernst in Garrow, *Liberty and Sexuality*, 153, 158–159. Like so many of the ACLU's founders, Ernst too participated in extramarital affairs, and his wife may have done so as well. See Silverman, "Pursuing Celebrity," 226–227, 230; Rodell, "Morris Ernst," 106. Ernst's major writings focus on issues of sexuality and sex provided Ernst's one moment of sympathy with the only group of people he

detested and feared enough to advocate depriving them of speech rights—Communists. "Sex is one of the mainsprings of a Communist's motivations just as it is for everyone else," he wrote in a 1952 analysis of the sexual behavior of American Communists. Quote from Ernst and Loth, *Report on the American Communist*, 162; see also 163–180.

26. Stone and Pilpel, "Social and Legal Status of Contraception," and Pilpel and Zavin, "Marriage Counseling Section." See correspondence in KI-KC, Morris Ernst and Harriet Pilpel files.
27. Kinsey, *Sexual Behavior in the Human Male*, 223–225, 263–265, 389–393, 447, 664–665; Kinsey to Alan Gregg, April 2, 1949, RAC-RFC, box 40; George W. Corner to Gregg, December 29, 1948; Kinsey, "Annual Report: Institute for Sex Research," April 15, 1954, RAC-RFC, box 39; Kinsey to Pilpel, March 30, 1950, KI-KC, Pilpel file 1; Linsky, "Most Critical Opinion"; Jones, *Alfred C. Kinsey*, 527, 619–620.
28. First two quotes from *U.S. v. 31 Photographs*, 156 F. Supp. 350 (October 31, 1957); all other quotes from Pilpel to Gebhard and Pomeroy, November 21, 1958; see also Pilpel to Kinsey, November 2, 1950; September 15, 1955; January 18, 1956; Kinsey to Pilpel, November 23, 1951; January 14 and 16, 1956; "Academic Freedom Cited in Kinsey Case," *New York World Telegram & Sun*, July 17, 1957; "Kinsey Institute Seeks to Save Erotic Brands from Burning," *New York Post*, July 17, 1957; Pilpel, "But Can You Do That?"; Pilpel to Gebhard, July 22, 1957; November 21, 1958; Gebhard to Pilpel, July 25, 1957, KI-KC, Pilpel files; RSM, "Dr. Alfred Kinsey," April 18, 1955, RAC-RFC, box 39; Jones, *Alfred C. Kinsey*, 669–670, 767; Gathorne-Hardy, *Kinsey*, 345–346, 436, 442. On Pilpel's relationship with Kinsey, see Eleanor Jackson Piel interview with Harriet Pilpel, September 1975; Kinsey to Ernst, September 22, 1949, KI-KC, Ernst file 2; Kinsey to Ernst, February 1, 1955; Ernst to Kinsey, February 4, 1955; August 21, 1926, KI-KC, Ernst file 4; quote from Pilpel to Kinsey, October 29, 1953; Pilpel to Kinsey, January 6 and 31, 1950; February 15 and 28, 1950; March 22, 1950; April 7, 1950; Kinsey to Pilpel, February 7 and 23, 1950; March 3 and 30, 1950, KI-KC, Pilpel file 1; Pilpel to Pomeroy, September 22, 1956; Pilpel to Gebhard et al., September 24, 1956, KI-KC, Pilpel file 2; Gerson, "Renaissance Woman," 1, 24–25. After the Rockefeller Foundation withdrew its support for the Kinsey Institute, Pilpel took advantage of a social event with foundation officers to plead the Institute's case. JM to RSM, January 30, 1957, RAC-RFC, box 39. See also Stevens, "*United States v. 31 Photographs*," 316–318.
29. Ernst to George Corner, January 6, 1950; Kinsey to Ernst, January 26, 1950; April 6, 1950; first quote from Ernst to Kinsey, March 2, 1948; see also February 15, 1950; Ernst to Kinsey, March 2 and 26, 1948; March 24, 1949; April 12, 1949; Kinsey to Ernst, March 4 and 8, 1948; March 19, 1949; April 2, 6, and 28, 1949, KI-KC, Ernst files 1and 2; second quote from Ernst and Loth, *American Sexual Behavior*, 126; see also 109–127; Ernst, "Law," 19; Ernst, "The Kinsey Report"; Ernst and Loth, "What Kinsey Will Tell"; "Excerpt from A[lan] G[regg] Diary," April 12, 1949, RAC-RFC, box 40.
30. Ernst to Bok, December 17, 1948, HRC-MEC, box 154; *Commonwealth v. Gordon*, 1949 Pa. Dist. & Cnty. Dec. (March 18, 1949); Ernst to Frank, February 25, 1949; January 14, 1949; Pilpel to Frank, July 16, 1956; Frank to Ernst, July 26, 1956; Ernst to Rankin, March 13, 1957, HRC-MEC, box 216; *U.S. v. Roth*, 237 F. 2d 796 (September 18, 1956); Watts to Erwin B. Ellman, Esq., October 16, 1956, ACLU-MF, reel 51; Ernst to Stanley Fleishman, February 4, 1957; Ernst to Kinsey, January 31, 1949; February 2, 1949; April 12, 1949; Kinsey to Ernst, April 6 and 28, 1949; Ernst to Gregg, April 4, 1949, KI-KC, Ernst file 2; Ernst to Kinsey, August 21, 1956, KI-KC, Ernst file 4; "Excerpt from AG Diary," April 12, 1949, RAC-RFC, box 40. Bok also worked closely with those drafting the ALI Model Penal Code. See Herbert F. Goodrich to Joseph H. Willits, February 20, 1952; February 5, 1953, RAC-RFC, box 303. By 1951, Kinsey was cited in a U.S. district court, a U.S. court of appeals, and lower courts in Illinois, San Francisco, and South Bend, Indiana. See Deutsch, "What Dr. Kinsey is up to now!"; *Ikalina Shumate v. Johnson Publishing Company*, 139 Cal. App. 2d 121 (February 9, 1956); Robert Velt Sherwin, "Are Americans Sex Hypocrites?" *Coronet* (1954), ACLU-MF, reel 47; Lockridge, *Sexual Conduct*, 19; "Medicine: Behavior,

After Kinsey," *Time*, April 12, 1948; "Moral Lapse Laid to Kinsey Report," *New York Times*, October 21, 1950; Jones, *Alfred C. Kinsey*, 575; Geddes, *Analysis of the Kinsey Reports*, 268; Palmore, "Published Reactions"; Gathorne-Hardy, *Kinsey*, 351–353, 411; Linsky, "The Most Critical Option"; "Medicine: 5,940 Women," *Time*, August 24, 1953; John B. Danby to Kinsey, August 2, 1953, KI-KC, Redbook file.

31. Alexander Lindey to Kinsey, November 26, 1951; Kinsey to Lindey, November 23, 1951, HRC-MEC, box 391; Levy to Pilpel, April 24, 1956; Pilpel to Kinsey, May 1, 1956, KI-KC, Pilpel file 2; Gebhard to Reitman, September 22, 1959; Watts to Kinsey, August 2, 1956; Reitman to Gebhard, September 17, 1959; Reitman to Pomeroy, October 6, 1959, KI-KC, ACLU file; George E. Rundquist to Hon. Louis B. Heller, September 2, 1953; New York Civil Liberties Union News Release, September 2, 1953; Kinsey to Edward de Grazia, December 20, 1955; Reitman to de Grazia, February 20, 1956, ACLU-MF, reel 46; Watts to Ernest Harms, August 13, 1956; Reitman to Pilpel, July 25, 1957, ACLU-MF, reel 54.
32. Quote from Lawrence S. Kubie to Alan Gregg, June 16, 1948; WW to RSM [Robert S. Morrison], May 3, 1949, RAC-RFC, box 40; WW to AG, March 8 and 12, 1951; WW to CBA, May 7, 1951, RAC-RFC, box 41; "RSM Diary," February 11, 1957, RAC-RFC, box 39; Palmore, "Published Reactions."
33. "Excerpt from diary of November 6, 1953, AJWarren"; "RSM Diary," April 2, 1956, quote from May 3, 1956; RSM to JCB et al., June 5, 1956, RAC-RFC, box 39; CIB to WW, June 21, 1951, RAC-RFC, box 41.
34. Quotes from *Model Penal Code, Tentative Draft No. 6* (Philadelphia: American Law Institute, May 6, 1957), 10–57, 189–192. On the reporters' exposure to Kinsey's work see Schwartz, review of Kinsey et al., *Sexual Behavior in the Human Male*; also *Model Penal Code, Tentative Draft No. 4* (Philadelphia: American Law Institute, 1955), Kinsey: 206–208, 213, 233, 252, 259, 276, 279, 281–283; Ploscowe: 243–244, 246, 252, 254, 283, 286; Tappan: 277–278; 204–216; Wechsler, "Codification of Criminal Law"; ALI Minutes, March 16–20, 1955; see also March 17–20, 1948; March 14–17, 1951, and May 18, 1951; May 22, 1953; March 15–17, 1956; December 11–15, 1956; December 11–13, 1958; March 11–14, 1959; March 17–19, 1960; December 14–16, 1961; December 14–16, 1961; March 15–17, 1962, UPLS-ALIA. Scholarly articles that discuss Kinsey's influence over the ALI include Allyn, "Private Acts/Public Policy," and Denno, "Why the Model Penal Code's Sexual Offense Provisions." More ideologically driven works that link Kinsey and the ALI include Jeffrey and Ray, "American Law Institute's Model Penal Code"; Reisman, *Kinsey*; Jeffrey, "Restoring Legal Protections." The ALI's approach to birth control featured prominently in briefs filed in *Griswold v. Connecticut.* See Pilpel to Jaffe and Nancy Wechsler, January 22, 1965, SSC-PPFA II, box 184; *Model Penal Code, Tentative Draft No. 4* (Philadelphia: American Law Institute, 1955), 276–280; ALI Minutes, March 16–20, 1955, UPLS-ALIA. On sodomy, see *Model Penal Code, Tentative Draft No. 4*, 276–280; Ploscowe to Joseph H. Willits, October 27, 1950; Thorsten Sellin to Willits, November 1 and 2, 1950; Willits, "Judge Morris Ploscowe," October 30, 1950; "Interviews: JHW, Judge Morris Ploscowe," November 1, 1950; "Interviews: JHW, Herbert F. Goodrich, Director American Law Institute," November 17, 1950; RSM to JHW, July 19, 1951; "Interviews: HAD, Professor Herbert Wechsler," February 11, 1953, RAC-RFC, box 303; Wechsler, "Challenge of a Model Penal Code," 1106, 1133; Ploscowe, *Sex and the Law*, 130; Kinsey to Pilpel, February 7, 1950; March 30, 1950, KI-KC, Pilpel file 1; Reisman, *Kinsey*, 202–203. Scholars disagree about when, exactly, the ALI council approved of removing consensual adult sodomy from the criminal code. See for example D'Emilio, *Sexual Politics*, 112 and n. 9; "Resolution in Support of the Model Penal Code," *Mattachine Review*, November–December 1955; Richards, *The Sodomy Cases*, 149; Eskridge, "Privacy Jurisprudence," 774.
35. Ernest Besig to District Attorney, Amador County, November 22, 1946; Gard Chisholm to Besig, November 26, 1946; December 18, 1946; Besig to Chisholm, December 4, 1946; Besig to A. A. Heist, April 3, 1947; Heist to Besig, April 9, 1947; Besig to Frederick Robin,

May 27, 1947, NCA-ACLU, box 6; Edward E. Odom to Frederick E. Robin, May 24, 1946, ACLU-MF, reel 303; Reitman to Menninger, June 23, 1950; Menninger to Reitman, July 10, 1950, HRC-MEC, box 44; Canaday, *The Straight State*, 146–150; see also Johnson, *Lavender Scare*.

36. Quotes from Barbara J. Scannell to ACLU, February 15, 1951, ACLU-MF, reel 303.
37. Watts to Spencer Coxe, March 5, 1958, PML-ACLU, box 345; quotes from June Fusca to ACLU, March 16, 1951; Levy to Fusca (including a copy to Scannell who provided no forwarding address), April 4, 1951, ACLU-MF, reel 303. Fusca refers to receiving a "general discharge," a term that was used interchangeably with "undesirable discharge." See "Liberty Is Always Unfinished Business: 36th Annual Report of the American Civil Liberties Union, July 1, 1955 to June 30, 1956" (New York, ACLU), 62.
38. William J. Klausner to ACLU, April 7, 1953; quotes from "John Sheldon," to ACLU, February 27, 1956; Robert S. Falk to Elmer Davis, February 7, 1957; Nelson Stone to Malin, November 8, 1957; C. R. Hedenstad to ACLU, June 27, 1958; Rev. Robert W. Wood to Reitman, September 27, 1956; Golden to LJ's secretary, Philadelphia, ONE, October 4, 1956; on Joughin see "From LJ, Philadelphia, ONE," May 22, 1956; Joughin to Watts, May 24, 1956; Coxe to Joughin, October 1, 1956, ACLU-MF, reel 303; Bill Colvig to Ernest Besig, March 4, 1958, NCA-ACLU, box 7; Levy to Klausner, April 17, 1953, ACLU-MF, reel 303. Homophile activist Vern Bullough recalled discussing "homosexuality and stigmatized sexual behavior" in the late 1950s with Malin, who replied that ACLU policy would address these issues "over his dead body." See Bullough, "Lesbianism, Homosexuality." See also Raj Ayyar interview with Vern Bullough, n.d.
39. Wood to Malin, September 7, 1956; "From LJ, Philadelphia, 'One' etc.," November 7, 1956, ACLU-MF, reel 303; Johnson, *Lavender Scare*, 131–144.
40. "Nomination of Rowland Watts for the Durfee Award," n.d., PC-LW; author interview with Linda, Lannie, and David Watts, June 13, 2010.
41. Quotes from "ACLU Position on Homosexuality," January 7, 1957; see also Wood to Malin, September 7, 1956; "From LJ, Philadelphia, 'One' etc.," November 7, 1956; Reitman to Levy, June 25, 1951; Levy to Veterans Administration, June 29, 1951; Edward E. Odom to Levy, July 9, 1951; Spencer Coxe to Joughin, October 1, 1956; "Greater Phila., *One* (Homosexual magazine)," May 7, 1956; "From LJ, Philadelphia, ONE," May 22, 1956; Joughin to Watts, May 24, 1956, ACLU-MF, reel 303; Reitman to Watts, June 21, 1957, ACLU-MF, reel 54; ACLU Due Process Committee Minutes, December 19, 1956, PML-ACLU, box 80. Edward Sagarin, a professor of sociology and criminology at the City University of New York, wrote *The Homosexual in America* under the pseudonym Donald Webster Cory. As testament, perhaps, to the dearth of support homosexuals received outside their own networks, in 1957, *The Ladder*—a three-year-old newsletter for "female homophiles" and the first national publication of its kind in the United States—commended the ACLU for even this rather weak statement of concern about the rights of homosexuals. "The ACLU Takes a Stand on Homosexuality," *The Ladder* 1, 6 (March 1957), 8–9. See also Esterberg, "From Illness to Action"; D'Emilio, *Sexual Politics*, 112.
42. Levy to Wertham, May 11, 1951; July 2, 1951; Wertham to Levy, June 12, 1951; first and second quotes from Watts to Robert S. Falk, February 27, 1957; Francis Martin Ruland to ACLU, May 5, 1958; third quote from Watts to Ruland, May 13, 1958; H. E. Stokes Jr. to ACLU, January 9, 1959; Watts to Stokes, February 13, 1959; Watts to Master Sgt. John Raymond Carey, April 18, 1957; May 19, 1957; Watts to Ralph Rudd, May 10, 1957; Martha Thomas to Watts, May 14, 1957; Kenneth F. Beall to ACLU, January 15, 1958; July 14, 1958; Watts to Beall, July 8, 1958; August 28, 1958; Watts to Selig Goodman, March 6, 1958, ACLU-MF, reel 303; Wolfenden et al., *Report of the Committee*; Watts to William Lambert, July 17, 1957; SC-ACLU, box 17. On *One, Inc. v. Oleson* (1957) see chapter 3.
43. Watts to Coxe, March 5, 1958; Coxe to Watts, March 7 and 25, 1958; Watts to Schwartz, May 9, 1958, PML-ACLU, box 345.

44. Gonzalo Segura, Jr. to B. W. Huebsch, November 21, 1957; first quote from Reitman to Segura Jr., November 29, 1957; second and third quotes from Watts to Selig Goodman, March 6, 1958; all other quotes from Unsigned to Gentlemen, January 19, 1959; see also Judith M. Saunders, "Stella Rush a.d.a., Sten Russell (1925–)," in Bullough, *Before Stonewall*, 135–144; Intra-Office Buck Sheets, January 21, 1959, ACLU-MF, reel 303.
45. Quote from Wulf to J. D. Mercer, March 25, 1959, ACLU-MF, reel 54. American media may have greeted the Wolfenden Report more approvingly than did the British media. See Williams, "Sex Offenses," 354–355; "The Wolfenden Report," *Time*, September 16, 1957.
46. Quotes from Stokes to ACLU, November 21, 1960; February 2, 1962; see also Watts to Stokes, November 25, 1960; Speiser to Stokes, February 9, 1962, ACLU-MF, reel 60.
47. Quotes from Den Nichols to ACLU, February 27, 1961; March 6, 1961; see also R. A. Weidauer to Nichols, January 11, 1961; Nichols to ACLU, August 17, 1962; Watts to Nichols, March 2, 1961, ACLU-MF, reel 59; Wulf to Nichols, August 27, 1962, ACLU-MF, reel 60. A therapeutic culture pervaded college campuses in the postwar era, and punitive measures gave way to psychiatric treatment for homosexuals and other sexual "deviants." See Bailey, *Sex in the Heartland*, 63–74.
48. First quote from Kameny to ACLU, May 15, 1962; see also Stuart Simon to Charlie Johns, February 5, 1959; Leanne Golden to Howard Dixon, February 10, 1959; "FCLU Hits at Johns," *Miami News*, February 16, 1959; Janette Rainwater to Golden, May 20, 1959; "Statement: The Legislative Committee of the American Civil Liberties Union . . .," n.d.; "Report of the Florida Legislative Investigation Committee to the 1959 Session of the Legislature"; Reitman to Kameny, May 28, 1962; Kameny to Reitman, June 18, 1962; Coxe to E. A. Dioguardi, May 11, 1962; see also W. Dorr Legg to Reitman, September 8, 1967; Richard A. Inman, "Atheneum Viewpoint," February 1965; Inman to Leanne Katz, March 6, 1965; E. A. Dioguardi to Dear Gentlemen, April 4, 1965; Legg to Reitman, September 8, 1967, ACLU-MF, reel 303. Second quote from Bullough, "Lesbianism, Homosexuality"; Gallo, *Different Daughters*, 244 n. 23. See also Alfred R. Lindesmith to ACLU, January 31, 1961; Rembert L. Butterfield to Malin, April 6, 1961; Wulf to Butterfield, April 10, 1961, and newspaper clippings, ACLU-MF, reel 59; Bullough to Monroe, February 7, 1964, SC-ACLU, box 124. The committee seems to have been quickly renamed and reoriented as the "ACLU Committee on Civil Liberties and Unusual Sex or Gender Behavior." See "ACLU Committee on Civil Liberties and Unusual Sex or Gender Behavior, Notes of meeting held April 1" (no year—probably 1964 or 1965), SC-ACLU, box 124. Several affiliates expressed markedly less enlightened ideas on homosexuality. As late as 1962 the Philadelphia branch's executive director, Spencer Coxe, assured one correspondent that laws against homosexual behavior did not raise civil liberties questions. Coxe to Norman Cousins, April 17, 1964; May 6, 1964, ACLU-MF, reel 62. See also Boyd, *Wide Open Town*, 217–218; "Homosexuality as Bar to U.S. Job Challenged," *Washington Evening Star*, April 24, 1963; *Bruce C. Scott v. John W. Macy, et al.*, "Complaint for Declaratory Judgment and Review of Determination of Suitability for Federal Employment," SC-ACLU, box 17; Gallo, *Different Daughters*, 13–15; Miller, *On Being Different*, 11; Eskridge, *Dishonorable Passions*, 152–153; Bullough, *Before Stonewall*, 209–218; D'Emilio, *Sexual Politics*, 117, 155–156; Johnson, *The Lavender Scare*, 192.
49. Quote from Merle Miller, "What It Means to be a Homosexual," *New York Times*, January 17, 1971.
50. Quotes from Reitman to Dioguardi, May 10, 1962, and Reitman to Kameny, May 28, 1962, ACLU-MF, reel 303. As late as 1963, when Wulf asked the ACLU's Due Process Committee to consider revising its policy on homosexuality, he was told that issues involving homosexuality were "not a pressing problem in civil liberties terms." Wulf to Due Process Committee, November 7, 1963; ACLU Due Process Committee Minutes, December 18, 1963, PML-ACLU, box 84.
51. Quote from Reitman to Dioguardi, May 10, 1962, ACLU-MF, reel 303; see also Wulf to Edward M. Levine, February 23, 1962; Pilpel to Jaffe, November 27, 1961, SSC-PPFA II,

box 184; Wulf to David H. Bremer, December 11, 1961, ACLU-MF, reel 393; Wulf to Edward M. Levine, February 23, 1962, ACLU-MF, reel 316. On abortion, see Ernst to Cass Canfield, August 21, 1962; Ernst to Mary Calderone, August 28, 1962; October 3, 1962, HRC-MEC, box 528; Jules E. Bernfeld to Ernst, May 10, 1961, HRC-MEC, box 530; Wulf to Norman Redlich, January 15, 1963; ACLU Press Release, March 9, 1965, ACLU-MF, reel 196. ACLU leaders were less certain that birth control rulings would impact federal wiretap policy. "Wiretap v. Privacy," *New York Times*, June 15, 1965. In most scholarly accounts, Pilpel makes but a cameo appearance at the ACLU's 1964 Biennial. See for example Walker, *In Defense*, 267–268; Garrow, *Liberty and Sexuality*, 296, 795 n. 52; Hartmann, *The Other Feminists*, 68–69.

52. Walker, *In Defense*, 236; Pilpel, "Civil Liberties and the War on Crime," *Biennial Conference of the American Civil Liberties Union*, June 21–24, 1964, SC-ACLU, box 124. According to board member Osmond Fraenkel, election to the board was, for Pilpel, "an ambition of many years standing." Quote from Osmond Fraenkel Diaries, January 22, 1962, PML-OFD.
53. Regarding the war on crime, see Gilbert, *Cycle of Outrage;* Beaty, *Fredric Wertham*; Nyberg, *Seal of Approval*; Simon, *Governing Through Crime*. Quotes from Pilpel, "Civil Liberties and the War on Crime," *Biennial Conference of the American Civil Liberties Union*, June 21–24, 1964 (document dated May 1964), UCLA, SC-ACLU, box 124.
54. Meeting of the Due Process Committee, ACLU, November 18, 1965, ACLU-MF, reel 317; Reitman to Eleanor Holmes Norton, PML-ACLU, box 87; "The American Civil Liberties Union," *drum: sex in perspective*, October 1964, 15–16. Osmond Fraenkel comments at great length on Pilpel's session and the audience's response to it. See Osmond Fraenkel Diaries, June 21–22, 1964, PML-OFD.
55. Kenyon to Pilpel, July 3, 1964; March 16, 1965; March 22, 1965; October 29, 1968; Pilpel to Kenyon, July 7, 1964; August 3, 1964; March 18, 1965, SSC-DK, box 15; ACLU Due Process Committee Minutes, December 19, 1956; October 15, 1958; PML-ACLU, box 80.
56. "Supreme Court's Birth Control Decision Accepts ACLU Points," unidentified newspaper, n.d.; Reitman to Ernst, January 10, 1966, ACLU-MF, reel 196; Brief for Appellants, *Griswold v. Connecticut*, October Term, 1964, SSC-PPFA II, box 184; Brief for the ACLU, *Griswold v. Connecticut*, February 1965, SSC-HFP, box 7; *Griswold v. Connecticut*, 381 U.S. 479 (June 7, 1965); Graham, *Toward a Planned Society*, 152–154, quote from 154; Gordon, *Moral Property of Women*, 289; Freedman and D'Emilio, *Intimate Matters*, 250; "Population Crisis: Hearings Before the Subcommittee on Foreign Aid Expenditures of the Committee on Government Operations, United States Senate, 89th Congress Second Session on S. 1676," Part 1 (January 19, 26 and February 9, 1966), 2–4; "Matters for Consideration of ACLU Subject-Matter Committees," September 1965, HRC-ERC, box 84; Wulf to Jack Pemberton and Reitman, December 20, 1965, ACLU-MF, reel 64; Norton to Reitman, July 7, 1966, PML-ACLU, box 87; ACLU Due Process Committee Minutes, November 18, 1965, ACLU-MF, reel 317.
57. D'Emilio and Freedman, *Intimate Matters*, 302–308; Allyn, *Make Love, Not War*, 25–29, 44–47, 207–210.
58. Until the ALI began drafting the Model Penal Code, few states had even attempted to revise their legal codes, but in the 1960s and 1970s many states formed legislative commissions to update their codes, consulting with ALI attorneys and calling on members of Kinsey's staff for assistance on laws regarding sex offenses. By 1978, thirty-five states had revised their penal codes, using the ALI Model Penal Code as a guide. Watts to Coxe, March 5, 1958, PML–ACLU, box 345; Robinson and Dubber, "The American Model Penal Code," 320, 322–323, 326–327; ALI Minutes, March 17–20, 1948; March 10–13, 1971; December 13–16, 1978, UPLS-ALIA. For an extensive if biased treatment of state penal code revisions see Jeffrey and Ray, "American Law Institute's Model Penal Code," 57–154; Ernst, "Kinsey Report," 281; Goodrich and Wolkin, *Story of the American Law Institute*, 24.

Chapter 5

1. Quotes from Ball, "Statement Prepared for Presentation Before the Subcommittee on Foreign Aid Expenditures of the Senate Committee on Government Operations," August 24, 1965, ACLU-MF, reel 317; see also Ball, "Population Control."
2. First quote from CLU Bulletin #2256, February 14, 1966, ACLU-MF, series 3, reel 63; second, third, and fourth quotes from Pilpel, "A Right Is Born"; fifth quote from Pilpel to Kenyon and Reitman, November 9, 1965, SSC-DK, box 29.
3. First quote from Pemberton to Shriver, July 27, 1966; second quote from Donald M. Baker to Pemberton, August 18, 1966; third quote from Shriver to Pemberton, June 21, 1966; "Sargent Shriver Charged with 'Counting Angels on Head of Pin' in Birth Control Debate as World Faces Starvation," August 25, 1966; ACLU Due Process Committee Minutes, n.d.; ACLU Equality Committee Minutes, November 4, 1965; Pilpel to Pemberton and Reitman, March 28, 1966; ACLU Board Minutes, February 14, 1966; Hal Witt to Reitman, April 4, 1966; Reitman to Witt, April 13, 1966; ACLU Bulletin #2263, "ACLU Assails Restrictions"; "Proposed Statement on OEO Ban on Voluntary Sterilization," n.d., ACLU-MF, reel 317; Anthony Partridge to John Rague, July 13, 1966; William G. Phillips to John Sherman Cooper, June 1, 1966, SWHA-AVS, box 52; ACLU Equality Committee Minutes, October 13, 1965, SSC-DK, box 29; Pemberton to Shriver, March 24, 1966; "Association for Voluntary Sterilization, Inc.: Fact Sheet on Voluntary Contraceptive Sterilization," July 1966; Pilpel to Equality Committee, October 4, 1965; Office to Board of Directors, November 4, 1965; Reitman to Rague, March 24, 1966; Rague to Reitman, May 20, 1966, SWHA-AVS, box 47. Some community action groups rejected OEO funds that were restricted in these ways, declaring them "obnoxious invasions of privacy associated with the man-in-the-house rule which is so hated by the population we serve." Quote from James G. Banks to Shriver, February 25, 1966, ACLU-MF, reel 318.
4. Quotes from Ball, "Statement Prepared for Presentation Before the Subcommittee on Foreign Aid Expenditures of the Senate Committee on Government Operations," August 24, 1965, ACLU-MF, reel 317. Ball was not alone. See *Population Crisis: Hearings Before the Subcommittee on Foreign Aid Expenditures of the Committee on Government Operations, United States Senate, 89th Congress Second Session on S. 1676*, Part 2 (February 16, March 2 and 3, 1966), 389–390, 398; Part 5-B (June 15, 1966), 1331, 1374, 1399–1400, 1409; Part 3 (February 1, 1968), 626–627; Ball, "Population Control"; Graham, *Toward a Planned Society*, 154–156.
5. Planned Parenthood objected to the ACLU's approach. See Reitman to Jeannie Rosoff, June 7, 1966; Speiser to Hon. Lester Hill, March 22, 1966; Reitman to Pilpel, April 7, 1966; Reitman to Speiser, April 18, 1966; Wechsler to Reitman, June 3, 1966; "Memorandum Submitted in Behalf of American Civil Liberties Union on S. 2993"; "Memorandum Submitted by American Civil Liberties Union to Senate Committee on Labor and Public Welfare Re: S. 2993," July 1966, ACLU-MF, series 2, reel 18; "Proposed Statement by ACLU Regarding OEO Ban on Voluntary Sterilization," July 7, 1965, PML-ACLU, box 87; Pemberton to Shriver, March 24, 1966, SWHA-AVS, box 47; Office to Equality Committee, November 1, 1965, ASL-PMC, box 55.
6. First quote from Transcript of *Today* show, January 14, 1966; see also Ball to Pemberton, January 17, 1966; Reitman to Ball, January 20, 1966; Rowland Evans and Robert Novak, "Birth De-Control Problems Hamstring Poverty Project," *Lawrence Journal-World*, December 11, 1965; Reitman to Pilpel, September 9, 1965; Coxe to Pemberton, January 13, 1966; Reitman to Wulf, January 20, 1966; Anne H. Strickland to Mrs. Edward H. Harte, January 24, 1966, ACLU-MF, reel 317; all other quotes from Pilpel to Equality Committee, October 4, 1965; see also Office to Equality Committee, November 1, 1965, PML-ACLU, box 86; Pilpel, "A Right is Born"; Greenbaum, Wolff & Ernst, general counsel, "Memorandum of Law on Constitutional Liberties and Publicly Supported Family Planning Programs," and Alanson W. Willcox, "On Support of Family Planning Services—Constitutional

Issues," in *Population Crisis: Hearings Before the Subcommittee on Foreign Aid Expenditures of the Committee on Government Operations, United States Senate, 89th Congress Second Session on S. 1676*, Part 5-B (June 15, 1966), 1518–1524 and 4 (April 7, 8, and 11, 1966), 802–805, 811.

7. First three quotes from Pilpel to Smith, May 14, 1957; October 7 and 19, 1960; fourth and fifth quotes from "Statement to be Presented by Harriet Pilpel . . . at Illinois State Birth Control Commission Hearing on March 4, 1964"; Smith to Charles Potter, October 7, 1964; sixth quote from Harriet Pilpel, "Proposed Statement by ACLU Regarding OEO Ban on Voluntary Sterilization," June 29, 1965; see also Irene Headley Armes to Pilpel, May 12, 1953; Pilpel to Ruth Proskauer Smith, May 14, 1957; October 7 and 19, 1960; April 8, 1963, and November 15, 1963; Smith to Pilpel, October 10, 1960; April 9, 1963; Pilpel and Wechsler to Rague, May 14, 1965; Pilpel to Baker, May 20, 1965; Pilpel to Rague, June 2 and 29, 1965; December 14, 1965, and April 7, 1966; Rague to Pilpel, June 30, 1965; December 20, 1965, and February 5, 1969; Pilpel signature on form to receive information on Human Betterment Association of America, April 30, 1953; Pilpel File Memorandum, October 22, 1963; Helen Schmidt to Jack I. Lipman, October 25, 1963; Lipman to Pilpel, October 30, 1963, SWH-AVS, box 35; Office to Board of Directors, November 4, 1965; Rague to Reitman, April 19, 1965, and May 20, 1966; Reitman to Rague, May 27, 1966, and March 24, 1966; Rague to Executive Committee, December 1, 1965, SWHA-AVS, box 47; Baker to Pilpel, May 25, 1965, SWHA-AVS, box 43. Pilpel exercised influence on the American Bar Association as vice chair of the Committee on Inter-Professional Liaison of the Family Law Section. See Rague to Pilpel, March 30, 1966, SWHA-AVS, box 52; Dowbiggin, *The Sterilization Movement*, 11, 101, 146.

8. Reitman to Pilpel, April 14, 1972, ACLU-MF, reel 319; Ward, *Poor Women, Powerful Men*, 27, 39, 91–95, 133; Critchlow, *Intended Consequences*, 109–110, 144–145; Nelson, *Women of Color*, 85–111; Gordon, *Moral Property of Women*, 289–290.

9. Quote from Bernfeld, *Hairdresser's Odyssey*, 128, see also 1, 37, 38–40, 127–176; Bernfeld to Ernst, May 10, 1961; Ernst to Bernfeld, May 15, 1961, HRC-MEC, box 530; Lawrence Lader to Kenyon, June 23, 1964, SSC-DK, box 12; Kenyon to Reitman, December 9, 1969; Kenyon to Bernfeld, December 9, 1969, SSC-DK, box 28; Sarat, "Abortion and the Courts."

10. First two quotes from ACLU Due Process Committee Minutes, December 19, 1956, and October 15, 1958, PML-ACLU, box 80; second quote from Kenyon, "The Legal Concept of Equality," April 2, 1959, SSC-DK, box 22; Bernfeld to Watts, May 1, 1957; October 12, 1958, reprinted in Bernfeld, *Hairdresser's Odyssey*, 132–133.

11. Wulf to Judson Crews, October 31, 1960, ACLU-MF, reel 57; author interview with Melvin Wulf, May 27, 2010; David Garrow interview with Melvin Wulf, March 19, 1992. Planned Parenthood leaders were more reluctant to envision birth control on a continuum with abortion after having worked for decades to establish birth control as abortion's antithesis. See "Release from the Comstock Era," *Birth Control Review*, December 1939, 24–25, cited in Garrow, *Liberty and Sexuality*, 274, 790 n. 8, 284, 393–394, 335–336. In 1960, Bernfeld despaired because "even the American Civil Liberties Union will not come face to face with the issue and say either 'this is' or 'is not' a civil liberties' matter." See Bernfeld to Kenyon, August 31, 1960, reprinted in Bernfeld, *Hairdresser's Odyssey*, 139. Alan F. Guttmacher described his personal experiences with abortion clients in Guttmacher, "A Defense of the Supreme Court's Abortion Decision." Sarah Weddington, the lawyer for Roe in *Roe v. Wade*, and Pat Maginnis, founder of Citizens' Committee for Humane Abortion Laws, one of the movement's first advocacy groups, both underwent abortions in Mexico. Roy Lucas, author of a tremendously influential law review article and brief on abortion rights, helped his girlfriend obtain an abortion long before he began to challenge laws against it. Various ACLU leaders—including Baldwin, Doty, and possibly Kenyon as well—also experienced or aided their partners and friends in obtaining abortions, and Pilpel recalled knowing, as a child, that friends of her parents obtained illegal abortions. On *Poe v. Ullman*, see chapter 4.

12. Quotes from *Model Penal Code, Proposed Official Draft* (Philadelphia: American Law Institute, May 4, 1962), 189–192; "Legal Abortions Proposed in Code," *New York Times*, May 22, 1959. On the ALI, see chapter 4.
13. Guttmacher, "A Defense of the Supreme Court's Abortion Decision"; Schwartz, "Morals Offenses and the Model Penal Code," 683–686; Garrow, *Liberty and Sexuality*, 281–284; "Statement by Deans of California Schools of Law and Members of the California Bar on Proposed Humane Abortion Act," n.d., NC-ACLU, box 21; "California Bar Convention Calls for Abortion Reform," *CCTA (California Committee on Therapeutic Abortion) Newsletter*, November 1966, SC-ACLU, box 193; "State Assembly—By the Committee of Women for a Humane Abortion Law," September 29, 1964; "Statement Presented to the Criminal . . . Committee of the California State Assembly by the Committee for a Humane Abortion Law," September 29, 1964, SC-ACLU, box 124; "Bill Introduced by Assemblyman Beilenson," February 18, 1965, NC-ACLU, box 21; "Minutes of First Meeting of Organizing Committee on Therapeutic Abortion Legislation," September 2, 1965, SC-ACLU, box 193. The ALI's approach to birth control featured prominently in briefs filed in *Griswold v. Connecticut*. See Pilpel to Fred Jaffe and Herbert Wechsler, January 22, 1965, SSC-PPFA II, box 184; Hartmann, *The Other Feminists*, 68.
14. Quote from Eason Monroe to Linda Beck, April 26, 1963; see also Beck to Monroe, n.d.; SC-ACLU, box 65; Cyril Means to Pemberton, April 21, 1965, SC-ACLU, box 193; Peter Colt Josephs to William G. McLoughlin, December 2, 1965; Carl Reiterman to Pemberton, March 4, 1967, ACLU-MF, reel 317; Michael M. Gask to Reitman, September 25, 1966; Thomas L. Shaffer to Pemberton, March 21, 1967, ACLU-MF, reel 318; Kenyon to Robert E. Hall, SSC-DK, box 33.
15. Quote from "Notes on Meeting of Lawyers Study Group of Abortion Sub-Committee of Sex and Civil Liberties Committee," April 20, circa 1965; Eugene E. Epstein to Reitman, August 22, 1966; "The Case for Abortion," unidentified author, n.d.; "Minutes, Abortion Sub-Committee on Sex, Mental Health and Civil Liberties Committee," April 1, 1965; "Notes on Meeting of Lawyers Study Group of Abortion Sub-Committee of Sex and Civil Liberties Committee," n.d., SC-ACLU, box 160; Reitman to Monroe, March 16, 1965; Reitman to Affiliates, February 23, 1965, SC-ACLU, box 124. On the 1964 Biennial, see chapter 4.
16. Quotes from ACLU of Southern California, "Policy Statement on Abortion," September 21, 1966, SC-ACLU, box 220; see also Osmond Fraenkel Diaries, June 9, 1965, PML-OFD; George Slaff to Kenyon, April 5, 1968, SSC-DK, box 28; Norma G. Zarky to Carolyn Bloomberg with "Draft of ACLU Working Paper on Abortion," September 24, 1965; Zarky to Monroe, November 18, 1965, SC-ACLU, box 160; Zarky to Monroe, July 18, 1966, SC-ACLU, box 26; William Kopit and Pilpel, "Abortion and the New York Penal Laws," April 20, 1965, SC-ACLU, box 193; "Testimony of Harriet F. Pilpel for the New York Civil Liberties Union," March 7, 1966, ACLU-MF, reel 317; Kopit and Pilpel, "Abortion and the New York Penal Laws," December 7, 1966, ACLU-MF, reel 318; Minutes, ACLU Board of Directors, February 14, 1967, SSC-DK, box 30. The national ACLU office began its own study of abortion laws after losing patience with its Southern California affiliate. See Reitman to Norton, July 7, 1966, PML-ACLU, box 87.
17. Quotes from *People v. Belous*, 71 Cal. 2d 954 (September 5, 1969); see also "Memorandum on Abortion," May 26, 1967; Reitman and Trudy Hayden to Board of Directors, October 31, 1967, ACLU-MF, reel 318.
18. Joel Gora to Reitman, October 2, 1966; Office to Due Process Committee Re: Abortion Working Papers, December 9, 1966; Office to Due Process Committee Re: Statement by Benjamin S. DuVal, January 6, 1967, ACLU-MF, reel 318.
19. First two quotes from Office to Board of Directors, February 8, 1967; see also Edward J. Ennis to Due Process Committee, February 20, 1967, ACLU-MF, reel 318; third quote from Minutes, ACLU Board of Directors, February 14, 1967, SSC-DK, box 30.

20. Quotes from Kenyon to Fellow Board Members, February 21, 1967, SSC-DK, box 30; see also Garrow, *Liberty and Sexuality*, 313–314.
21. Forer to Kenyon, February 27, 1967; see also Edward Ennis to Fellow Board Members, February 24, 1967, SSC-DK, box 30; first and second quotes from Soll to Due Process Committee, March 7, 1967; see also Soll to Ennis, March 3, 1967; Kenyon and Soll to the Board, June 9, 1967; Reitman and Hayden to Board of Directors, October 31, 1967, ACLU-MF, reel 318; Kenyon to Pilpel, April 13 and 25, 1967; Kenyon to Reitman, April 19, 1967; Kenyon to Peter Josephs, May 10, 1967; Kenyon to Gordon Meyerhoff, May 10, 1967, SSC-DK, box 28; Pilpel to Kenyon, April 18, 1967, SSC-DK, box 29; ACLU Board Minutes, June 15, 1967, PML-ACLU, box 20; third, fourth, and fifth quotes from Soll, Pilpel, and Kenyon to Due Process Committee, March 7, 1967, SSC-DK, box 29; Ennis to Soll with cc: message to Reitman, March 6, 1967; ACLU Due Process Committee Minutes, March 8, 1967, SSC-DK, box 30. "Described as an infanticider and hater of poor little fetuses," Kenyon wrote, "I regard myself as their benefactor." My goal is to save those "pitiful little 'unwanted' creatures upon whom our wicked abortion laws have conferred the 'precious' gift of life." Her efforts to obtain evidence of this from a friend who served as a judge in family court faltered when her friend pointed out that many abused children were quite wanted. Several years later, Pilpel cited a recent study that found killings of newborns associated with unwanted pregnancies. See Pilpel, Zuckerman, and Ogg, *Abortion*, 20. Other quotes from Kenyon to Robert E. Hall, SSC-DK, box 33 and Kenyon to Ira Glasser, July 9, 1969, SSC-DK, box 28; see also Kenyon to Judge Nanette Dembitz, January 29, 1970; Dembitz to Kenyon, February 4, 1970, SSC-DK, box 14.
22. See sources cited in preceding note and Hartmann, *The Other Feminists*, 70.
23. Kenyon seems to have introduced this linguistic solution after being alerted to it by Robert E. Hall, President of the Association for the Study of Abortion. See Kenyon to Hall, December 20, 1967, SSC-DK, box 33. First quote from Ad Hoc Committee on Abortion and the Viable Fetus to Board of Directors, November 22, 1967; see also Peter Colt Josephs to Kenyon, April 2, 1967; Baldwin to Wulf, April 15, 1968; Norton to Baldwin, April 19, 1968; Pilpel to Reitman, March 31, 1969; Reitman to Pilpel, April 10, 1969, ACLU-MF, reel 318; Pemberton to Kenyon, June 24, 1969; Kenyon to Pilpel, November 4, 1968; ACLU Office to Board of Directors, January 11, 1968; Kenyon to Pemberton, January 15, 1968; Reitman to Kenyon, October 20, 1967; November 9, 1967, SSC-DK, box 28; second quote from "A.C.L.U. Asks End to Abortion Bans," *New York Times*, March 25, 1968; Thomas L. Shaffer to Reitman, November 6, 1967, ACLU-MF, reel 318; ACLU Board Minutes, January 25, 1968, PML-ACLU, box 91; ACLU Board Minutes, December 2–3, 1967; Office to Board of Directors, January 18, 1968; Equality Committee Minutes, February 3, 1966, SSC-DK, box 29. See also Murray, *Pauli Murray*, 363. Murray served on the ACLU board between 1965 and 1973 and joined its Due Process Committee in 1966. Pemberton to Board of Directors, December 21, 1967, SSC-DK, box 30; Osmond Fraenkel Diaries, February 14, 1967; December 2–3, 1967; January 25, 1968, PML-OFD. Two other treatments of these ACLU policy discussions include Garrow, *Liberty and Sexuality*, 313–314, 349; Meehan, "ACLU v. Unborn Children," and Donohue, *Politics of the American Civil Liberties Union*, 95–103.
24. First two quotes from Nathan Rappaport to A. C. Spectorsky, July 4 and 9, 1968, ACLU-MF, reel 606; third, fourth, and fifth quotes from James Clapp to Reitman, October 6, 1969; final quote from Terry Ashe Croft to Pilpel, May 1, 1972; see also Reitman to Croft, June 15, 1972, ACLU-MF, reel 319. Reitman acknowledged that women were underrepresented as decision makers in the ACLU, but assured Croft that the organization was taking steps to rectify the gender imbalance at the affiliate and national level. See also "A.C.L.U. and Abortion," *Playboy*, July 1968, 7, and on Rappaport, see Garrow, *Liberty and Sexuality*, 315, 361.
25. First four quotes from Norton to Reitman, July 3, 1968; see also December 5, 1967; Reitman to Norton, December 6, 1967; fifth and sixth quotes from Lehrman to Wulf, July 19, 1968; John Fordon to Nat Lehrman, July 9, 1968, ACLU-MF, reel 318; Wulf to Lehrman,

July 16, 1968, ACLU-MF, reel 606. *Playboy* ran articles and letters to the editor (many apparently written by its own staff) that advocated abortion rights. See Fraterrigo, *Playboy and the Making*, 156; Lester, *Eleanor Holmes Norton*, 106. Murray described her ambivalence about abortion later in life, after becoming a priest. "I have some moral and spiritual problems about abortion," she told Leila Rupp and Verta Taylor in 1983. "I am beyond the age where it is a personal problem for me so I am not active in any pro-choice movements but I would not speak against it. I see it as an individual choice, I don't think the state should be involved in telling a woman what she should do in her life but [due to] my own internal personal problems with it . . . I would not be a public advocate." Quote from Leila Rupp and Verta Taylor interview with Pauli Murray, June 16, 1983; see also Murray to Dear Skipper, April 22, 1950, and Skipper to Dear Pixie, April 26, 1950, in Scott, ed., *Pauli Murray and Caroline Ware*, 55–60.

26. Quote from Bruce Clayton to Affiliates, March 25, 1969, SSC-DK, box 30; see also "Fact Action Urged on Abortion Bills," *Inside ACLU*, March 31, 1969; "Abortion Law Liberalized," *Inside ACLU*, May 5, 1969, SC-ACLU, box 156; Norton to Fordon, July 3, 1968; Reitman to Pemberton, March 4, 1969; Pemberton to Ivan Shapiro, March 4, 1969, ACLU-MF, reel 318; Wulf to Lehrman, July 16, 1968; Roy Lucas to Wulf, July 4, 1968; Jimmye Kimmey to Pilpel, July 22, 1968; Wulf to Tobias Simon, March 24, 1969, ACLU-MF, reel 606; Garrow, *Liberty and Sexuality*, 335–339.
27. First quote from Garrow, *Liberty and Sexuality*, 351; second quote from Edgar B. Keemer Jr., "Report of First National Conference on Abortion Laws: Modification or Repeal?" March 24, 1969, SC-ACLU, box 193; third quote from Pemberton to Shapiro, March 4, 1969; fourth quote from Reitman to Mazey, March 6, 1969, ACLU-MF, reel 318; see also Pemberton to Kenyon, June 24, 1969, SSC-DK, box 28.
28. Kenyon, a longtime repeal advocate, helped women in her neighborhood organize Chelsea Women for Repeal of State Abortion Law and demonstrated at the New York State Legislature's abortion law reform hearings in Albany. "Chelsea Women for Repeal of State Abortion Law," August 1968, SSC-DK, box 30; Kenyon to Lillian Wachtel, March 13, 1969; Kenyon, "On Abortion," *Chelsea Clinton News* (March 6, 1969), SSC-DK, box 17; *Inside ACLU* (January 27, 1969), SC-ACLU, box 156; Reitman to Lawrence Lader, February 11, 1969; Ivan Shapiro to Pemberton, February 28, 1969; Pemberton to Shapiro, March 4, 1969; Reitman to Pemberton, March 4, 1969; Reitman to Ernest Mazey, March 6, 1969, ACLU-MF, reel 318; "New Group Will Seek Changes in Abortion Laws," *New York Times*, February 17, 1969; Cassidy, "The Abortion Controversy."
29. First three quotes from Pemberton to Kenyon, June 24, 1969; final five quotes from Kenyon to Reitman, December 9, 1969; see also Kenyon to Jules E. Bernfeld, December 9, 1969; Kenyon to Pemberton, July 27, 1969; Kenyon to Mrs. Lee Gidding, June 30, 1969; Kenyon to Pemberton, July 22, 1969, SSC-DK, box 28; fourth quote from drafts of "Policy Statement of American Civil Liberties Union on State Laws Prohibiting Abortion," n.d.; fifth and sixth quotes from Pemberton to Kenyon, July 14, 1969; Pilpel to Reitman, March 31, 1969; Kenyon to Pemberton, April 29, 1969; Roraback to Pemberton, May 6, 1969, ACLU-MF, reel 318; Kenyon to Clapp, December 9, 1970, and January 5, 1971, SSC-DK, box 14; Hayden to Reitman, October 23, 1969, ACLU-MF, reel 319. Despite these changes in 1969, the ACLU abortion policy retained its 1968 date and, as of 2010, had not been substantially revised. See *ACLU Policy Guide* 2010. Later Kenyon complained that Pemberton took credit for her work. See Kenyon to Pilpel, January 5, 1970; Pilpel to Kenyon, January 19, 1970, SSC-DK, box 29.
30. Quotes from Hirschkop to Wulf, April 8, 1970, and Wulf to Hirschkop, April 15, 1970, ACLU-MF, reel 318.
31. First two quotes from Hartmann, *The Other Feminists*, 56; final three quotes from Equality Committee Minutes, December 28, 1967; see also April 26, 1966; February 21, 1968; March 28, 1968; April 16, 1968; ACLU Board Minutes, December 14–15, 1968; January 8, 1969; Kenyon to Henry Schwarzschild, February 8, 1967; April 7, 1967; Kenyon to

Reitman, January 7, 1970; Kenyon to Dorsen, April 24, 1970; Plenary Meeting of Board of Directors Minutes, January 29–30, 1966, SSC-DK, box 29; Alan Reitman and Susan Goldstein to the Board, September 19, 1968, NCA-ACLU, box 30; Kenyon to Schwarzschild, March 13, 1967; Kenyon to Rolland O'Hare, July 18, 1968, SSC-DK, box 28. Murray and Kenyon initially opposed the ERA, preferring the Fourteenth Amendment as the basis of legal equality for women. By 1970, failure to persuade the courts to adopt their interpretation, as well as the growing conservatism of the Supreme Court and the groundswell of women's rights activism and support for a new ERA, changed their minds. See Murray to Equality Committee, March 30, 1970; Office to Board of Directors, September 21, 1970, ACLU-MF, reel 318; "Statement of Pauli Murray on the Equal Rights Amendment Submitted to the Senate Judiciary Committee," September 16, 1970, ACLU-MF, reel 319; Kenyon to Mrs. W. H. Van Voris, June 22, 1972, SSC-DK, box 4; Kenyon's handwritten notes on Office to Board of Directors, September 21, 1970, SSC-DK, box 29; Kenyon and Murray to Board, September 24, 1970, SSC-DK, box 30; Murray to Pemberton, July 16, 1970, ASL-PM, box 55.

32. First two quotes from Murray to Schwarzchild, February 5, 1967; third quote from Schwarzschild to Kenyon, cc: Murray, March 14, 1967; fourth, fifth, and sixth quotes from Kenyon to ACLU Board, December 23, 1968, SSC-DK, box 28; seventh quote from Kenyon to Louise Noun, March 26, 1970, SSC-DK, box 29; eighth quote from Kenyon to Edmund S. Muskie, August 27, 1971, SSC-DK, box 14; last quote from Suzy Post to Murray, February 5, 1973, ASL-PM, box 56. Here I part company with the trend popular among many women's historians to identify as feminist women from the past who would not have self-identified as such and, in some cases, even explictly rejected the term. I believe we are better able to understand women on their own terms if, rather than labeling them according to ours, we closely examine their contexts, tease out their perspectives, and ultimately respect their choices about what to call themselves.
33. Quotes from Murray to Post, February 2, 1973, ASL-PM, box 56; see also Murray, *Pauli Murray*, 184, 214, 217, 416.
34. Quotes from Pemberton to Members of the national and affiliate boards, department heads, affiliate executives, July 9, 1970, SSC-DK, box 29; Reitman to Executive Directors, October 25, 1972; Charles Lam Markman, "Women and the American Civil Liberties Union," n.d., ACLU-MF, reel 319; Office to Board of Directors, November 20, 1970, SSC-DK, box 30; Nancy Phillips to Kenyon, September 5, 1969, SSC-DK, box 14; "1972 Biennial Conference Report of the American Civil Liberties Union," PC-MF. In 1967, the ACLU board consisted of seventy-two men and six women. "New Dimensions . . . New Challenges: 46th Annual Report," July 1, 1965 to January 1, 1967 (New York: American Civil Liberties Union, 1967), 59.
35. Quotes from Neier to Eli Evans, March 8, 1973; see also Equality Committee to Board of Directors, November 16, 1971; Neier to Noun, October 6, 1971, ACLU-MF, reel 319; Walker, *In Defense*, 314–315; Neier, *Taking Liberties*, xxvi–xxviii, 13. Kenyon considered Neier "aggressive and divisive." See Kenyon to O'Hare, September 29, 1970; Kenyon to Neier, January 8, 1971; Marvin Karpatkin to Kenyon, November 22, 1971; Ennis to Kenyon, December 7, 1971; Hayden to Kenyon, December 15, 1971, SSC-DK, box 29.
36. Quotes from Moore et al., "Up Against the Wall, Hugh Hefner"; see also "No Women's Rights in Playboy Mansion," *Hyde Park Herald*, December 31, 1969; author interview with Joel Sprayregen, January 26, 2010; Jody [Parsons] Howard obituary, *Chicago Tribune*, February 7, 2010. Sprayregen believed that Hefner appreciated the publicity incited by the women's protest. See also J. Anthony Lukas, "The 'Alternative Life-Style' of Playboys and Playmates," *New York Times*, June 11, 1972; Epstein, "The Impact of the ACLU," 25 n. 59.
37. Quotes from Fraterrigo, *Playboy and the Making*, 174–175. For more on Playboy and the women's movement see Weyr, *Reaching for Paradise*, 225–247, and Pitzulo, *Bachelors and Bunnies*. See also Hodgdon, "Chicago Women's Liberation Union."

38. Quotes from Fraterrigo, *Playboy and the Making*, 177–179, see also 193–199. Members of the ACLU board and leaders of its affiliates wrote supportive letters to *Playboy* as early as 1960, and *Playboy* praised the ACLU in return. See Ernst to Editor, *Playboy*, December 1960, 9–10; Nick Landacre to Editor, *Playboy*, August 1966, 145; Jay A. Miller to Editor, *Playboy*, February 1968, 46–47; and April 1968, 66; Pilpel to Editor, *Playboy*, January 1969, 51; Charles A. Penn to Editor, *Playboy*, October 1964, 65, 166; "Postal Pandering," *Playboy*, January 1968, 61–62; "A.C.L.U. and Abortion," *Playboy*, July 1968, 47. For evidence that many ACLU leaders read *Playboy* regularly, see Larry Speiser to Pemberton, July 24, 1969, ACLU-MF, reel 65, and Speiser to Lehrman, February 13, 1969, ACLU-MF, reel 66; videotaped interview with Burt Joseph, March 30, 2010; Neier to Joseph, February 1, 1971, ACLU-MF, reel 319.
39. Quote from "Women's Rights Cases," February 1971; see also Neier to Joseph, February 1, 1971; "Playboy to Put Up $$ For Lib Gals," unidentified newspaper article, March 10, 1971; Equality Committee to Board of Directors, November 16, 1971, ACLU-MF, reel 319; "Playboy Fete Gains $100,000 for A.C.L.U.," *New York Times*, November 22, 1971; J. Anthony Lukas, "The 'Alternative Life-Style' of Playboys and Playmates," *New York Times*, June 11, 1972; Trudi to Ira and Suzanne, November 3, 1981, PML-ACLU, box 370; Kenyon to Dorsen, April 24, 1970; Kenyon to Neier, February 4, 1971; Neier to Kenyon, February 1, 1971; Kenyon to Karpatkin, November 12, 1971, SSC-DK, box 29; Murray and Kenyon to ACLU Board, September 23, 1970, SSC-DK, box 30; Andrews, "A.C.L.U.—Let There Be Law," 119, 122, 222–224, 226, 228.
40. First quote from "1976 Biennial Conference Report of the ACLU," June 10–13, 1976, 100, ACLU-MF, series 3, reel 2; second quote from Fraterrigo, *Playboy and the Making*, 193; see also 179–181, 194–204; Pitzulo, *Bachelors and Bunnies*; Mackinnon, *Feminism Unmodified*, 134–145, 193, 199; J. Anthony Lukas, "The 'Alternative Life-Style' of Playboys and Playmates," *New York Times*, June 11, 1972. Fasteau recalled, and the documentary record confirms, that the Playboy grant came with "no strings attached." Author interview with Feigen (Fasteau), June 23, 2010.
41. Quote from author interview with Brenda Feigen (Fasteau), June 23, 2010; Pilpel, "Contraception and Freedom," 51; Pilpel, "Abortion Laws Challenged," 60; Ginsburg et al., "Equality for Women," 52; Feigen, *Not One of the Boys*, 214–235; Walker, *In Defense*, 305, 338; Cowan, "Women's Rights Through Litigation"; Berger, *Litigation on Behalf of Women*; George and Epstein, "Women's Rights Litigation." Judith Mears, founding director of the ACLU's Reproductive Freedom Project, also approved of seeking funds from *Playboy* and requested financial assistance for an ongoing abortion case. Mears to Burton Joseph, October 28, 1975, ACLU-MF, reel 393.
42. Kenyon to Clapp, December 9, 1970, SSC-DK, box 14. The New York Civil Liberties Union and Pilpel were a driving force behind this repeal victory. See Neier to Kenyon, January 7, 1971; Kenyon to Neier, January 8, 1971, SSC-DK, box 29; Garrow, *Liberty and Sexuality*, 470, 489–490; Walker, *In Defense*, 302–303; see Justice Douglas's partial dissent in *United States v. Vuitch*, 402 U.S. 62 (April 21, 1971).
43. Quote from Lucas to Ad Hoc Group, May 7, 1971; see also Fred Okrand to Pilpel and Lucas, June 11, 1971, ACLU-MF, reel 319; ACLU-MF, reel 606; Garrow, *Liberty and Sexuality*, 389–404, 422–428; *Doe v. Bolton*, 410 U.S. 179 (January 22, 1973). Pilpel and Norma Zarkey, of the Southern California Civil Liberties Union, both filed briefs on behalf of other organizations.
44. First quote from Pilpel and Peter Ames, "Legal Obstacles to Freedom of Choice in the Areas of Contraception, Abortion, and Voluntary Sterilization in the United States," September 15, 1971, SSC-HFP, box 4; second and third quote from *Eisenstadt v. Baird*, 405 U.S. 438 (March 22, 1972); fourth quote from Pilpel, Wechsler, and Jane Zuckerman, "Memorandum Re: United States Supreme Court Decision in Massachusetts Birth Control Case," April 14, 1972, SSC-HFP, box 7; see also Garrow, *Liberty and Sexuality*, 517–520, 541–542.

45. Quotes from Reitman to Pilpel, April 14, 1972, ACLU-MF, reel 319, and Equality Committee to Board of Directors, September 10, 1973, SSC-DK, box 29. In 1971, ACLU Committees were overwhelmingly male and white. The Communications Media Committee consisted of thirty men and only three women with just one black member. The Free Speech/Association Committee was made up of twenty men and two women, all of them white, and the Due Process Committee included nine men and four women, two of them black. By contrast, the Equality Committee was composed of sixteen men, and thirteen women, including seven black members. See Beatrice Gelfand to Reitman, December 8, 1971; Hayden to Reitman, January 7, 1972; and Gora to Reitman, n.d., PML-ACLU, box 115; Reitman to Norton, April 9, 1969, ACLU-MF, reel 318; "S.C. Sterilization Case Lost," *Civil Liberties*, September 1975; Feigen, *Not One of the Boys*, 251–256; Kluchin, *Fit to Be Tied*, 73–113, 148–183.
46. Quotes from *Roe v. Wade*, 410 U.S. 113 (January 22, 1973); see also *Doe v. Bolton*, 410 U.S. 179 (January 22, 1973); Walker, *In Defense*, 302–303; Pilpel et al., "Summary of United States Supreme Court Decisions Regarding Abortion Rendered on January 22, 1973," January 26, 1973, SSC-HFP, box 8; "Women's Rights Project Legal Docket: Affiliate and National Litigation" (January 1973), SC-ACLU, box 201; "Memorandum Re: Existing Policies Within the Federal Government Which are in Conflict with the 1973 Supreme Court Decisions on Abortion," May 5, 1975, PML-ACLU, box 370; Ruth Jane Zuckerman, "Abortion and the Constitutional Rights of Minors," July 1973, SSC-HFP, box 4; *Nyberg v. City of Virginia*, 495 F. 2d 1342 (February 19, 1974); "Abortion," *Civil Liberties*, May 1974; Mears to Wulf, February 6, 1973; Wulf to Mears, February 20, 1973; Ed Doerr to Reitman, April 2, 1973; Reitman to Doerr, April 19, 1973, ACLU-MF, reel 319.
47. Quotes from Reitman to Pilpel, April 14, 1972, ACLU-MF, reel 319, and Equality Committee to Board of Directors, September 10, 1973 (contains excerpts from ACLU 1971 board minutes), SSC-DK, box 29. The WRP monitored litigation in the area of voluntary sterilization, and ACLU affiliates often represented clients directly. See "ACLU Women's Rights Project," April 17, 1972, SC-ACLU, box 201; Wilma Scott Heide to Equality Committee, November 2, 1971, ASL-PM, box 55; Kluchin, *Fit to Be Tied*, 23, 126, 132; Nelson, *Women of Color*, 75–76; Dowbiggin, *The Sterilization Movement*, 157.
48. First two quotes from Equality Committee to Board of Directors, September 10, 1973, SSC-DK, box 29; all other quotes from Board of Directors Meeting Minutes, September 29–30, 1973, PML-ACLU, box 26; see also Ward, *Poor Women, Powerful Men*, 92; Kluchin, *Fit to Be Tied*, 96.
49. Quote from "Proposal for the Women's Rights Project of the American Civil Liberties Union Foundation," December 1972, PML-ACLU, box 240; see also Women's Rights Project Legal Docket, December 15, 1972, PML-ACLU, box 383; "Proposal for the Women's Rights Project of the American Civil Liberties Union," December 1972, PML-ACLU, box 240; Women's Rights Project Legal Docket: Affiliate and National Litigation, January 1973, SC-ACLU, box 201; "The ACLU's Campaign for Choice: The Right of a Woman to Control Her Own Body," n.d., ACLU-MF, series 6, reel 4.
50. Quote from "$1 Million Sterilization Suit is Filed," *Lewiston (Maine) Daily Sun*, July 13, 1973; Feigen, *Not One of the Boys*, 251–256; *Cox v. Stanton*, 381 F. Supp. 349 (August 22, 1974); Schoen, *Choice and Coercion*, 244, 247; Begos and Railey, "Sign This or Else"; Torgesen, "N.C. Eugenics Survivors"; *Policy Guide of ACLU*, July 5, 1966, #245, SSC-DK, box 30.
51. Quotes from author interview with Brenda Feigen (Fasteau), June 23, 2010; see also Equality Committee to Board of Directors, September 10, 1973, SSC-DK, box 29; Feigen, *Not One of the Boys*, 251–256; Lee, *For Freedom's Sake*, 21; Joseph J. Levin, Jr. et al., *Relf v. Weinberger*, Complaint, July 31, 1973, http://www.splcenter.org/sites/default/files/Relf_Original_Complaint.pdf (retrieved July 10, 2011); "The Law: Sterilized: Why?" *Time*, July 23, 1973; Slater, "Sterilization."

52. Prior to 1973, only one ACLU case seems to have involved involuntary sterilization. The case was brought on behalf of Gloria Cavitt, an inmate of Beatrice State Home for the Retarded in Nebraska whose release depended on submitting to sterilization. The case was lost in the Supreme Court of Nebraska but won in the state legislature which repealed the law that allowed Cavitt's sterilization. *In re Cavitt*, 182 Neb. 712 (March 8, 1968); *In re Cavitt*, 183 Neb. 243 (June 14, 1968); "Women's Rights Project Legal Docket: Affiliate and National Litigation," January 1973, SC-ACLU, box 201; Slater, "Sterilization," 151; "The Law: Sterilized: Why?" *Time*, July 23, 1973; "Suit Seeks to Void Sterilization Law," *New York Times*, July 13, 1973; Babcock, "Sterilization"; Feigen, *Not One of the Boys*, 252–253. According to Kluchin, "at least thirty-three lawsuits involving coercive sterilization were filed in the late 1960s and 1970s." Many of these were represented by the ACLU, its cooperating attorneys and affiliates. Quote from Kluchin, *Fit to Be Tied*, 151–152.
53. "Proposal for the Women's Rights Project of the American Civil Liberties Union Foundation," December 1972, PML-ACLU, box 240; Kluchin, *Fit to Be Tied*, 180.
54. *Relf v. Weinberger*, 372 F. Supp. 1196 (March 15, 1974); Kluchin, *Fit to Be Tied*, 180–183; "Memorandum re: Existing Policies Within the Federal Government which are in Conflict with the 1973 Supreme Court Decisions on Abortion," May 5, 1975, PML-ACLU, box 70.
55. Author interview with Mears, July 21, 2010; "Judith Mears, called as a witness, being first duly sworn . . . ," two pages from court record in *Tuozzoli v. Killian*, 386 F. Supp. 9 (April 24, 1974), PC-JM. As historian Philippa Strum reminded me, some scholars have suggested that the Reproductive Freedom Project was created to handle abortion cases that the Ford Foundation would not allow the Women's Rights Project to take. See Epstein, "ACLU Reproductive Freedom Project," 13.
56. Quotes from Elissa Krauss, "Hospital Survey on Sterilization Policies," March 1975, PML-ACLU, box 370. Tellingly, all hospitals surveyed distributed a statement designed to absolve the attending physician and participating hospital personnel of responsibility for the outcome of the operation.
57. Quote from Elissa Krauss, "Hospital Survey on Sterilization Policies," March 1975, PML-ACLU, box 370; Kluchin, *Fit to Be Tied*, 184–189.
58. Kluchin, *Fit to Be Tied*, 186–187, 205–206; Mears to Pilpel, May 22, 1975, PML-ACLU, box 238; see also Nelson, *Women of Color*, 200, fn. 27; "Statement of Pamela S. Horowitz, Legislative Counsel American Civil Liberties Union Washington Office on Proposed Restrictions Applicable to Sterilizations Funded by the Department of Health, Education, and Welfare," January 17, 1978, PML-ACLU, box 356.
59. Mears to Pilpel, May 22, 1975; Mears and Ira Glasser to Lowell Bellin, June 2, 1975; Mears to Neier et al., June 3, 1975, PML-ACLU, box 238. Antisterilization organizations emerged in response to local conditions around the country. In California, for instance, where Chicanas suffered the highest rates of compulsory sterilization, the issue moved to the center of a nascent Chicana rights movement. Other groups included the Chicago Committee to End Sterilization Abuse and the Committee for Abortion Rights and Against Sterilization Abuse (CARASA). "Sterilization Abuse: A Task for the Women's Movement," January 1977, http://www.uic.edu/orgs/cwluherstory/CWLUArchive/cesa.html (retrieved July 10, 2010); Nadine Brozan, "The Volatile Issue of Sterilization Abuse," *New York Times*, December 9, 1977; Kluchin, *Fit to Be Tied*, 187, 198–203.
60. Quotes from "1976 Biennial Conference Report of the ACLU," June 10–13, 1976, ACLU-MF, series 3, reel 2. Mears tried to persuade the ACLU to address the rights of parents or legal guardians to consent to the sterilization of their "retarded and mentally disturbed" children or wards. Mears to Neier et al., June 3, 1975; Mears to National Board Members et al., June 27, 1975, PML-ACLU, box 238; Diane Henry, "Parents of 3 Retarded Girls Fight Hospital Refusal to Sterilize Them," *New York Times*, October 2, 1977; "Sterilization Regs Get ACLU Support," *Civil Liberties Alert*, 2, March 1, 1978, ACLU-MF, series 6, reel 3. In another failed ACLU sterilization case, *Pierce v. Walker*, judges exonerated Dr. Clovis Pierce

even though he required Medicaid patients to "undergo tubal ligation if they were delivering a third living child," because he obtained written consent from his patients. See *Pierce v. Walker*, 560 F. 2d 609 (July 26, 1977); Kluchin, *Fit to Be Tied*, 161–168; Paul et al., "Pregnancy, Teenagers and the Law, 1974."

61. NOW, PPPFA, and others opposed the guidelines. "Suit Challenges Curbs on Sterilization of Women," *New York Times*, January 11, 1976; Irwin H. Kaiser, "Against Sterilization Policy Here," *New York Times*, January 12, 1976; "New York City Health Dept. Opposes Measure on Sterilization Control," *New York Times*, March 25, 1977; Nadine Brozan, "The Volatile Issue of Sterilization Abuse: A Tangle of Accusations and Remedies," *New York Times*, December 9, 1977; Kluchin, *Fit to Be Tied*, 192–196, 203–224; Nelson, *Women of Color*, 140–189; "Statement of Pamela Horowitz, Legislative Counsel, American Civil Liberties Union on Proposed Restrictions Applicable to Sterilizations Funded by the Department of Health, Education, and Welfare," January 17, 1978, PML-ACLU, box 356; Reproductive Freedom Project to Women's Rights Liaisons, October 7, 1975, SSC-HFP, box 4.
62. Quotes from Judith Mears, "Status of Abortion Litigation," June 10–13, 1976, ACLU-MF, series 3, reel 2; "The ACLU's Campaign for Choice," ACLU, n.d., ACLU-MF, series 4, reel 4; *Bigelow v. Virginia*, 421 U.S. 809 (June 16, 1975). Regarding what determined whether or not a case was designated as an ACLU case, see Mears to Joyce Armstrong, April 7, 1975; on Mears's request that *Playboy* contribute funds to the case, see Mears to Burton Joseph, October 28, 1975; on Mears's role as cocounsel, see Mears to Joan Dunlop, October 29, 1975, ACLU-MF, reel 393.
63. Quotes from *Planned Parenthood of Central Missouri v. Danforth*, 428 U.S. 52 (July 1, 1976).
64. First quote from Ellen Leitzer, "Facts About Abortion," December 1976, ACLU-MF, reel 320; second and third quotes from "Recent Abortion Decisions," *Women's Rights Project Newsletter*, July 1977, 1, 3, SCA-ACLU, box 66; Leitzer to Affiliates, October 4, 1976, PML-ACLU, box 370; "Reproductive Freedom Project Quarterly Report, October 1976," PML-ACLU, box 385; ACLU Board of Directors Minutes, October 2–3, 1976, ACLU-MF, series 3, reel 1; *Beal v. Doe*, 432 U.S. 438 (June 20, 1977); *Maher v. Roe*, 432 U.S. 464 (June 20, 1977); *Poelker v. St. Louis*, 432 U.S. 519 (June 20, 1977); Pilpel to Colleagues, October 4, 1974, SSC-HFP, box 3.
65. Benshoof, "Mobilizing for Abortion Rights," *Civil Liberties Review*, September–October 1977, ACLU-MF, series 9, reel 4; Patricia Beyea to Affiliate Directors et al., February 10, 1978, PML-ACLU, box 47.
66. Quote from Benshoof, "Mobilizing for Abortion Rights," *Civil Liberties Review*, September–October 1977, ACLU-MF, series 9, reel 4; Patricia Beyea to Affiliate Directors et al., February 10, 1978, PML-ACLU, box 47; "The ACLU's Campaign for Choice: The Right of a Woman to Control Her Own Body," ACLU, n.d., ACLU-MF, series 4, reel 4; Neier to Board of Directors, September 22, 1977, PML-ACLU, box 356.
67. Quotes from Aryeh Neier to Affiliates, July 22, 1977, ACLU-MF, series 2, reel 1; Neier, "Today's Civil Liberties Battle Fronts," June 10–13, 1976, ACLU-MF, series 3, reel 2.
68. Quotes from Neier to Affiliates, July 22, 1977; see also Neier to Board of Directors, September 22, 1977, and November 22, 1977, ACLU-MF, series 2, reel 1; "To Members of the American Civil Liberties Union and the New York Civil Liberties Union," May 1969; Ernest Angell to Ernst, June 2, 1969, HRC-MEC, box 773; Ernst to Soll, May 12, 1969; Ernst to Baldwin, October 16, 1973, HRC-MEC, box 886; Bishop, "Politics and the ACLU"; Neier to the *Wall Street Journal*, January 17, 1972, SC-ACLU, box 220; "American Civil Liberties Union Finds Itself in the Midst of Wrenching Internal Debate on Goals and Methods," *New York Times*, February 20, 1977; Mann, "Hard Times"; Tom Goldstein, "The A.C.L.U. Finds Another Issue: Itself," *New York Times*, April 23, 1978; J. Anthony Lukas, "The A.C.L.U. Against Itself," *New York Times*, July 9, 1978; ACLU Board of Directors Minutes, September 24–25, 1977, ACLU-MF, series 1, reel 1; Neier to Affililates, September 28, 1977, PML-ACLU, box 356.

69. Quotes from author interview with Brenda Feigen (Fasteau), June 23, 2010; see also Critchlow, *Intended Consequences,* 285 n. 42. Landmark women's rights cases fought by the WRP on behalf of male clients include *Frontiero v. Richardson,* 411 U.S. 677 (1973), and *Weinberger v. Wiesenfield,* 420 U.S. 636 (1975); see also "Transcription of the Clinical Legal Education Oral History Interview with Associate Justice Ruth Bader Ginsburg," August 17, 2007, http://lib.law.cua.edu/nacle/Transcripts/Ginsburg.pdf (retrieved July 10, 2011); Greenhouse, "Celebrating the Jurisprudence"; Dukart, "Geduldig Reborn."
70. First quote from Beyea to Affiliate Directors et al., October 7, 1977; "Draft: Supplement to 'ACLU "Right to Choice" Campaign,'" n.d., PML-ACLU, box 356; Dorsen to ACLU board of Directors, February 17, 1977; ACLU/PPFA Meeting, December 5, 1977, ACLU-MF, reel 606; Beyea to Affiliate Directors et al., October 7, 1977; Beyea to Dorothy Davidson et al., October 13, 1977; Beyea to Neier et al., June 2, 1978; Beyea to Neier et al., March 7, 1978, PML-ACLU, box 356. For a critique of this shift toward education see Ernst to Ennis, September 16, 1974; "Statement of Aryeh Neier . . . on Final Language of the 1978 'Hyde Amendment,'" December 7, 1977; Beyea to National Board et al., February 3, 1978; Ira Glasser to ACLU Staff et al., October 6, 1978; Reitman, "Brief Comments on ACLU Directions in 1970s," n.d., PML-ACLU, box 47; "A Proposal to Support the Litigation and Public Education Efforts of the Reproductive Freedom Project of the American Civil Liberties Union Foundation," 1980, PML-ACLU, box 382; Beyea to Affiliate Directors et al., November 1, 1977; ACLU/PPFA Meeting, December 5, 1977, PML-ACLU, box 47. Longtime ACLU board member Rolland O'Hare and an internal report both objected to the RFP's blanket opposition to a constitutional convention. O'Hare to Neier, November 7, 1977, PML-ACLU, box 47; Marjorie M. Smith to Campaign for Choice, November 8, 1977, ACLU-MF, reel 606; Eve Paul to Pilpel, November 14, 1975, SSC-HFP, box 7; ACLU Due Process Committee Minutes, December 19, 1956; October 15, 1958, PML-ACLU, box 80; Pilpel and Peter Ames, "Legal Obstacles to Freedom of Choice in the Areas of Contraception, Abortion, and Voluntary Sterilization in the United States," September 15, 1971, SSC-HFP, box 4; last three quotes from Heide to Equality Committee, November 2, 1971, ASL-PM, box 55; and Greenhouse and Siegel, eds., *Before Roe v. Wade,* 33–34; see also Hull and Hoffer, *Roe v. Wade,* 4. For a critique of the language of choice and an explanation of how it may have encouraged condemnation of women who "chose" to reproduce despite their poverty, see Nelson, *Women of Color,* 182–189; Solinger, *Beggars and Choosers.*
71. See the sources cited in the preceding note. The RFP also arranged to have a visible presence at the International Women's Year Conference in Houston, Texas. *Notes from the Women's Rights Project,* 1, 7 (October 1977), ACLU-MF, series 9, reel 4.
72. Indeed, many of these policies instructed the doctor to call the fetus a human being, describe its anatomy and sensations of pain in great detail, and explain that an abortion might cause future sterility or psychological disturbances. The policies did not require the doctor to discuss the more serious dangers associated with pregnancy and childbirth. Elissa Krauss, "Reproductive Freedom Project: Hospital Survey on Sterilization Policies," March 1975, PML-ACLU, box 370; quotes from "A Proposal to Support the Litigation and Public Education Efforts of the Reproductive Freedom Project of the American Civil Liberties Union Foundation," 1980, PML-ACLU, box 382; Beyea to Neier et al., June 2, 1978, PML-ACLU, box 356; Benshoof and Judith Levin, "Current Legal Issues in Abortion Litigation," June 16–19, 1979, ACLU-MF, series 3, reel 2.
73. Quote from Beyea to Neier et al., June 2, 1978, PML-ACLU, box 356; "ACLU Campaign for Choice 1981 'CON CON' Project Final Report," n.d., PML-ACLU, box 357. Less positive assessments of the RFP's achievements focus narrowly on litigation and federal funding for abortion to the neglect of legislation, amendments, state funding, and sterilization. See, for example, Epstein, "ACLU Reproductive Freedom Project"; Benshoof and Judith Levin, "Current Legal issues in Abortion Litigation," June 16–19, 1979, ACLU-MF, series 3, reel 2; Lourdes Soto et al., to Women's Rights Liaisons and Lawyers et al., June 18, 1980, PML-ACLU, box 387.

74. First quote from Beyea to Neier, et al., June 2, 1978, PML-ACLU, box 356; second quote from "Hyde Encourages Efforts to Curtail All Abortions," *New York Times*, July 1, 1980; third quote from Linda Greenhouse, "Court Reaffirms Right to Abortion and Bars Variety of Local Curbs," *New York Times*, June 16, 1983; final quotes from Ronald Reagan, Proclamation 5147—National Sanctity of Human Life Day, January 13, 1984, Woolley and Peters, *The American Presidency Project*. See also Beyea to Affiliate Directors, et al., October 7, 1977; January 5, 1978; "Statement of Norman Dorsen . . . on Public Funding of Abortion Under the Fiscal 1979 Labor-HEW Appropriations Bill," April 19, 1978, PML-ACLU, box 47; Sylvia Law to Dorsen, February 14, 1978; Dorsen to John T. Noonan Jr., March 13, 1978, PML-ACLU, box 47; Margo Krupp to Henrietta H. Marshall, March 15, 1978, SSC-PPFA II, box 104; "ACLU Report: The Impact of the Hyde Amendment on Medically Necessary Abortions," October 1978; "ACLU Report Documents End of Medicaid Abortions," October 24, 1978, ACLU-MF, series 6, reel 4; *Harris v. McRae*, 448 U.S. 297 (June 30, 1980); Edna D. Wells, "Case Notes," *ACLU Lawyer: The Newsletter of the Legal Department of the ACLU*, 6 (July 31, 1980), SSC-HFP, box 4; "Statement of Norman Dorsen . . . on Public Funding of Abortion Under the Fiscal 1979 Labor-HEW Appropriations Bill," April 19, 1978, PML-ACLU, box 47; *Harris v. McRae*, 448 U.S. 297 (June 30, 1980); Benshoof to Sustaining Members, July 11, 1983, PML-ACLU, box 370; *City of Akron v. Akron Center for Reproductive Health*, 462 U.S. 416 (June 15, 1983); "Reproductive Freedom Project Proposal," 1980; "A Proposal to Support the Litigation and Public Education Efforts of the Reproductive Freedom Project of the American Civil Liberties Union Foundation," 1980, PML-ACLU, box 382. Richard Nixon refrained from commenting publicly on *Roe v. Wade* but expressed dissatisfaction privately, acknowledging only that abortion might be legitimate in the case of rape or to end a mixed-race pregnancy. Gerald Ford clearly stated his opposition to *Roe v. Wade* but considered abortion legitimate in the case of rape and to save the life of the pregnant woman. Jimmy Carter worked to keep federal funds from being used for abortion, though he also criticized the movement for a "human life amendment." Charlie Savage, "On Nixon Tapes, Ambivalence over Abortion, Not Watergate," *New York Times*, June 24, 2009; Gerald R. Ford to Archbishop of Cincinnati, September 10, 1976; Gerald R. Ford, "The President's News Conference," July 19, 1976; Jimmy Carter, "Clinton, Massachusetts Remarks," March 16, 1977; Jimmy Carter Interview with the National Black Network, July 18, 1977; Carter, "Yatesville, Pennsylvania Remarks," October 15, 1980, all from Woolley and Peters, *The American Presidency Project*. In 1974, Pilpel predicted that treating a fetus as a person would result in the policing of women's bodies. A fetal life amendment could easily lead to mandatory monthly pregnancy tests for all women of reproductive age, prescribed behavior regimens for pregnant women, and criminal investigations of all women whose pregnancies ended in a stillbirth or miscarriage. Pilpel, "The Fetus as Person." See Benshoof to Roger Willson, May 3, 1984, PML-ACLU, box 47; Marcia Chambers, "Dead Baby's Mother Faces Criminal Charge on Acts in Pregnancy," *New York Times*, October 9, 1986; Benshoof, "Fetal-Rights Case Attacks Civil Liberties of Women," *New York Times*, November 10, 1986; Chambers, "Charges Against Mother in Death of Baby are Thrown Out," *New York Times*, February 27, 1987; Reproductive Freedom Project Annual Report, 1987, PML-ACLU, box 390.

75. "The Women's Rights Project: A Proposal for Funding, March 1, 1982–February 28, 1984," January 1982, PML-ACLU, box 388; Reproductive Freedom Project Annual Report, 1985, PML-ACLU, box 389; Samuel A. Alito to the Solicitor General, May 30, 1985; Charles Fried to Alito et al., June 3, 1985, reproduced from the National Archives and Records Administration, Record Group 60, Department of Justice Files of the Deputy Assistant Attorney General, Charles Cooper, 1981–1985, box 20, http://www.archives.gov/news/samuel-alito/accession-060-89-216/Thornburgh-v-ACOG-1985-box20-memoFriedtoAlito-June3.pdf (retrieved July 10, 2011); Reproductive Freedom Project Annual Report, 1985, PML-ACLU, box 389; Brief for the United States as Amicus Curiae in Support of

Appellants in *Thornburgh v. American College of Obstetricians and Gynecologists*, http://www.justice.gov/osg/briefs/1985/sg850181.txt (retrieved July 10, 2011).

76. Reitman to Pilpel, April 14, 1972, ACLU-MF, reel 319; Ward, *Poor Women, Powerful Men*, 27, 39, 91–95, 133; Critchlow, *Intended Consequences*, 109–110, 144–145; Nelson, *Women of Color*, 85–111; Gordon, *Moral Property of Women*, 55–83, 289–290; Nadasen, *Welfare Warriors*, 217.
77. In the 1980s and 1990s, black women were sterilized twice as often as similarly situated white women. See Roberts, *Killing the Black Body*, 97.
78. Ironically, Judith Mears brought a lawsuit in 1977, two years after she left the ACLU's Reproductive Freedom Project, to allow compulsory sterilization. The case involved three families who wanted to sterilize their "severely retarded" daughters. On their behalf, Mears sued the Connecticut hospitals that refused to perform the procedures on the grounds that the law was unclear on whether parents could consent to the sterilization of a minor child. Mears, convinced that the parents cared deeply for their daughters and that sterilization would be in their best interests, disguised the girls' identities by naming them after gemstones: Rebecca Ruby, Denise Diamond, and Priscilla Pearl. Mears persuaded Judge M. Joseph Blumenfeld to allow the sterilizations to proceed. See Wheeler interview with Judith Mears, July 21, 2010; "Parents of 3 Retarded Girls Fight Hospital Refusal to Sterilize Them," *New York Times*, October 2, 1977; *Ruby v. Massey*, 452 F. Supp. 361 (May 16, 1978); Blumenfeld to Mears, December 20, 1979, PC-JM; Ellen Leitzer, "What's Happening on the Hill," January 1975, ACLU-MF, reel 320.
79. Quote from Mears to Affiliates and Liaisons, February 21, 1975, PML-ACLU, box 370. Even poor women whose benefits covered abortion found that the slow-moving tangle of welfare bureaucracy frustrated their efforts to meet the trimester requirements of *Roe*.
80. First quote from "Catching the Lifeline: Update on ACLU Abortion Tie," *National Right to Life News*, November 1978, SSC-HFP, box 1; second quote from Judge M. Blumenfeld in *Ruby v. Massey*, 452 F. Supp. 361 (May 16, 1978); see also Paul and Pilpel, "Teenagers and Pregnancy," 301–302.
81. See Nadine Brozan, "The Volatile Issue of Sterilization Abuse: A Tangle of Accusations and Remedies," *New York Times*, December 9, 1977; Davis, *Women, Race and Class*, 206, 215; author interview with Janet Benshoof, August 2, 2010.

Chapter 6

1. Trippett, "What's Happening to Sexual Privacy?"
2. Spencer Coxe to Norman Cousins, April 17, 1964; May 6, 1964; Reitman to Cousins, July 29, 1964, ACLU-MF, reel 62; Frank Kameny to Gentlemen, July 26, 1969, ACLU-MF, reel 303.
3. "The American Civil Liberties Union," *drum: sex in perspective*, October 1964, 15–16; "How to Handle a Federal Agent," *drum: sex in perspective*, December 1964, 15–16.
4. *Lamont v. Postmaster General*, 381 U.S. 301 (May 24, 1965). Reitman was disappointed that he was not able to locate more cases of postal harassment against homosexuals. Reitman to Coxe, February 15, 1966; Coxe to Reitman, January 21, 1966, ACLU-MF, reel 65; Coxe to Wulf, April 23, 1965; quotes from "Senator Urges Ban on U.S. Mail Checks," *New York Times*, March 12, 1964; "Postmaster General Promises Tighter Control of Mail Covers," n.d.; Coxe to Reitman, August 5, 1965; Reitman to Affiliates, September 1, 1965; Ernest Mazey to Reitman, September 10, 1965; Gerald H. Goldberg to Wulf, May 4, 1965; William C. Sewell to Dear Sir, August 26, 1965, ACLU-MF, reel 64; Judson Townley to Eleanor Blue, September 5, 1964; Marlin Brown to Wulf, October 5, 1964, ACLU-MF, reel 63; Reitman to Justice Samuel H. Hofstadter, January 19, 1965; February 2, 1965; Hofstadter to Reitman, January 23, 1965, ACLU-MF, reel 303; Wulf to Eugene E. Epstein, February 2, 1965, SC-ACLU, box 124; "Senators Demand Names of 24,000 Under Mail

Watch," *New York Times*, February 24, 1965; "High Court Voids Mail Law Curbing Red Propaganda," *New York Times*, May 25, 1965; D'Emilio, *Sexual Politics*, 213–214.

5. Chapter 4 discusses the ACLU's first policy on homosexuality. In 1966, the Southern California branch issued one of the first official ACLU declarations that "the right to privacy in sexual relations is a basic constitutional right," excluding "rape, coercion, fraud, assault, prostitution or the corruption of minors." See "Sex-Civil Liberties Statement Passed," *Open Forum* 63, 1 (January 1966); Office to Board of Directors, November 24, 1965, ASL-PMC, box 54; Ralph Royal Gore to Dear Sirs, February 8, 1957; E. A. Dioguardi to Seymour H. Bucholz, October 31, 1965; Reitman to Coxe, September 17, 1965; Samuel H. Hofstadter to Reitman, January 23, 1965; ACLU Due Process Committee Minutes, n.d. (soon after November 24, 1965), ACLU-MF, reel 303; "Resolution of the National Capital Area Civil Liberties Union on Federal Employment of Homosexuals," August 7, 1964; first quote from A. Harry Levitan and Benjamin Schoenfeld, "Should Homosexuals Be Excluded from Federal Employment," June 1965, PML-ACLU, box 86; second quote from Vern Bullough, "Statement of ACLU Policy Regarding Sexual Behavior," October 1, 1965; "ACLU Committee on Civil Liberties and Unusual Sex or Gender Behavior: Preliminary Report to the Board of Directors, May 18, 1965," SC-ACLU, box 232; Clore Warne to Eason Monroe, November 15, 1965, SC-ACLU, box 124; ACLU Due Process Committee Minutes, June 8, 1966, PML-ACLU, box 87; "ACLU Hits Treatment of Homosexuals," *Atlanta, GA. Journal*, January 10, 1966; "The Homosexual in America," *Newsweek*, January 21, 1966; last two quotes from Reitman to Eleanor Norton, September 28, 1966, including policy statement titled "Sex and Civil Liberties," ACLU-MF, reel 303. See also Office to Due Process Committee, April 6, 1966, and May 31, 1966, ASL-PMC, box 54; Johnson, *The Lavender Scare*, 190–191; D'Emilio, *Sexual Politics*, 155–156.
6. Reitman to Norton, September 28, 1966, including policy statement titled "Sex and Civil Liberties"; quotes from "Due Process Committee Recommendations on Sexual Behavior," n.d.; E. A. Dioguardi to Gentlemen, January 22, 1967; Reitman to Norton, February 16, 1967; "ACLU Statement on Homosexuality," August 31, 1967, ACLU-MF, reel 303. The Civil Service Commission claimed that it treated homosexuality the same as cases of an employee's adultery, "incest, illegal fornication, prostitution, or other sexual acts which are criminal and offensive to our mores and our general sense of propriety," corroborating the claims of many homophile activists that criminal sodomy laws underlay federal policies against employing homosexuals. Quote from John W. Macy, Jr. to Mattachine Society of Washington, February 25, 1966, LOC, https://ecf.cand.uscourts.gov/cand/09cv2292/evidence/PX2566.pdf (retrieved May 27, 2012).
7. First quotes from Clark P. Polak to Reitman, August 31, 1967; Kameny to Lynn Rosner, September 17, 1967; last quote from Baldwin to ACLU Legal Dept., n.d.; Wulf to Baldwin, April 3, 1969; Alan Reitman to W. Dorr Legg, August 29, 1967; W. Dorr Legg to Reitman, September 8, 1967; ACLU Press Release, August 31, 1967; "End of Criminal Sanctions for Homosexuality Sought by Union," *Weekly Bulletin*, October 9, 1967, ACLU-MF, reel 303. That ACLU leaders heard and considered these criticisms can be seen in Reitman to Jack Pemberton, March 17, 1969, PML-ACLU, box 621. Some of Baldwin's friends suspected that he was bisexual. See Cottrell, *Roger Nash Baldwin*, 369–370; Joseph Lash interview with Phil Taft, October 12, 1972, FDR-JPL, box 49.
8. Warner to Robert N. Wilentz, August 17, 1992, PML-ACW, box 18; Bill Gardner to Abby Rubenfeld, July 7, 1984, PML-ACW, box 30; John Lauritsen, "Arthur Cyrus Warner (1918–)," in Bullough, ed., *Before Stonewall*, 282–290.
9. Schwartz also presented at a 1982 NCSCL meeting. See "Agenda: 1982 Meeting of the National Committee for Sexual Civil Liberties, Philadelphia, Pennsylvania," PML-ACW, box 5; Warner to Schwartz, June 12, 1968; Warner to John Van Pelt Lassoe Jr., February 24, 1969, PML-ACW, box 36; Barnett to Warner, February 11, 1971; Warner to Bill Kelley, n.d.; Warner to Sheldon Glueck, March 11, 1971; Warner to Kelley, November 22, 1972,

PML-ACW, box 31; Warner to Schwartz, March 13 and 26, 1975; April 25, 1977; Schwartz to Warner, April 1, 1975, PML-ACW, box 35.

10. Eventually, Warner hoped to address housing, employment, licensing, insurance, child custody, and adoption difficulties confronted by homosexuals. First quote from Warner, "A fundamental measure of a free society . . . ," n.d., ACLU-MF, reel 303; Warner to Jene Chandler, September 12, 1972; Warner to William F. Reynard, September 30, 1970, PML-ACW, box 31; second quote from Warner, "Memorandum for Mr. Aryeh Neier," February 17, 1973; Warner to Sandra Kurjiska, March 25, 1983, PML-ACW, box 36; "The National Committee for Sexual Civil Liberties consists of . . . ," n.d., no title, PML-ACW, box 6.
11. When the local bar association tried to withhold Patton's license to practice law on the grounds that his homosexuality made him a sodomist and therefore a criminal, Patton challenged the decision and won. Warner to Reynard, September 30, 1970; Warner to Foster, Summer Solstice 1972, PML-ACW, box 31; Warner, "Memorandum for Aryeh Neier," February 17, 1973, PML-ACW, box 36; Eskridge, *Dishonorable Passions*, 173–174; "A final word—about formation of NCSCL . . . ," n.d., PML-ACW, box 5; Coleman, *Domino Effect*, 9, 15–18.
12. Quotes from "A final word—about formation of NCSCL . . . ," n.d., PML-ACW, box 5. The organization was originally named the National Committee for Homosexual Law Reform. Warner to Herbert E. Selwyn, December 28, 1970; Warner to Tom W. Parker, October 16, 1970; Warner to Herbert E. Selwyn, December 28, 1970, PML-ACW, box 31; Eskridge, *Dishonorable Passions*, 173–174.
13. Warner to Kelley, November 3, 1970, PML-ACW, box 31; "Project Narrative: Oral History of Arthur C. Warner, New Jersey Leader for Lesbian and Gay Civil Rights," n.d., no author, PML-ACW, box 8; quote from *American Law Institute Model Penal Code and Commentaries*, Part II (Philadelphia: American Law Institute, 1980), 357.
14. First quote from Warner to Herbert E. Selwyn, December 28, 1970; Warner to Foster, Summer Solstice, 1972; last two quotes from Warner to Rob Cole, May 30, 1972; all other quotes from Warner to Kelley, February 27, 1971, PML-ACW, box 31. Warner charged Frank Kameny with seeking publicity and attention to further his own agenda at the broader movement's expense. See Austin Wade to Marc Jeffers, April 28, 1969; Wade to Kameny, April 28, 1969; Wade to Jeffers, May 14, 1969, PML-ACW, box 36.
15. Warner, "Memorandum for Mr. Aryeh Neier," February 17, 1973, PML-ACW, box 36; Warner to Dear Contributor, n.d.; Barnett to Warner, n.d.; first two quotes from Warner to Rob Cole, May 30, 1972; "Idaho Sex Reform: Adult Consent Law Adopted; Nation's Third," *The Advocate*, June 22, 1971; all other quotes from Warner to Foster, Summer Solstice, 1972; Warner to Rob Cole, May 30, 1972, PML-ACW, box 31. Eskridge indicates that the *Advocate* may indeed have played a role in provoking opposition to the revised law. See Eskridge, *Dishonorable Passions*, 180, 182–184, and Eskridge, "Challenging the Apartheid of the Closet," 847 n. 123. New Jersey and California repealed their sodomy laws later in the 1970s. See "Getting Rid of Sodomy Laws: History and Strategy that Led to the Lawrence Decision," http://www.aclu.org/lgbt-rights_hiv-aids/getting-rid-sodomy-laws-history-and-strategy-led-lawrence-decision (retrieved July 19, 2011). On New Jersey see Warner to Barnett, November 11, 1971; Warner to Foster, Summer Solstice 1972, PML-ACW, box 31.
16. Quote from Warner to Ralph Temple, June 15, 1972; Warner and Barnett to Dear Contributor, n.d.; Warner to Margaret Standish, April 27, 1971; Warner to Cole, May 30, 1972, PML-ACW, box 31; Warner, "Memorandum for Mr. Aryeh Neier," February 17, 1973; Craig Patton to Warner, February 26, 1973, PML-ACW, box 36; Warner, "Forward," March 7, 1973, PML-ACW, box 35; author interview with Marilyn Haft, August 9, 2010; author interview with Thomas Coleman, August 9, 2010; Coleman, *Domino Effect*, 18–19; Eskridge, *Dishonorable Passions*, 175–176.
17. Gainer, "Federal Criminal Code Reform"; first quote from Walter E. Barnett and Warner to Dear Contributor, n.d.; second quote from Warner to Tom, January 17, 1971; Warner

to Stephen M. Nagler, February 16, 1971; Barnett to Dear Committee Member, July 29, 1971, PML-ACW, box 31; Kelley to Warner, January 25, 1973, PML-ACW, box 36. By 1980, the ACLU faced off against Louis B. Schwarz in opposition to the code. See Schwartz, "Civil Liberties vs. the ACLU"; Ira Glasser to the Editor, *New Republic*, September 6 and 13, 1980, 7, 40.

18. On *Playboy* and heterosexuality, see Fraterrigo, *Playboy and the Making*, 40–41, and Ehrenreich, *Hearts of Men*, 42–51. First quote from Standish to Austin Wade, October 20, 1970; August 16, 1971; second and third quotes from Warner to Bill Kelly, November 2, 1970; fourth quote from Warner to Margaret Standish, November 2, 1970, PML-ACW, box 31. In private correspondence, Warner admitted that the NCSCL was "almost entirely concerned with homosexuality." Quote from Warner to LeRoy Schultz, October 16, 1972, PML-ACW, box 31.
19. Warner to Burton Joseph, February 27, 1971, PML-ACW, box 31; quotes from Hefner, "The Legal Enforcement of Morality." See also Fraterrigo, *Playboy and the Making*, 40–41.
20. See for example *Buchanan v. Batchelor*, 308 F. Supp. 729 (January 21, 1970); *Schlegel v. United States*, 397 U.S. 1039 (April 20, 1970). See also Barnett and Warner to Dear Contributor, n.d.; Warner to J. Thomas Menaker, September 14, 1971; Warner to Cole, May 30, 1972; Warner to Ralph Temple, June 15, 1972; Warner to Barnett, August 22, 1972; Barnett to John O'Loughlin, September 13, 1972, PML-ACW, box 31; Eskridge, *Dishonorable Passions*, 154–158; "Gay Males Ask Court to Void D.C. Sodomy Law," *The Advocate*, October 13, 1971; Judith M. Mears to Wulf, n.d.; Temple to Mears, March 21, 1972; Wulf to Mears, May 1, 1972, ACLU-MF, reel 303; ACLU, Special Docket: Homosexuals, May 1, 1972, SC-ACLU, box 225; "ACLU News," press release, August 11, 1972, ACLU-MF, reel 319; Warner to Barnett, January 15, 1973, PML-ACW, box 36; "Sexual Privacy Project: A Joint Project of the American Civil Liberties Union Foundation and the National Committee for Sexual Civil Liberties," March 1973, PML-ACW, box 35.
21. Quotes from author interview with Marilyn Haft, August 9, 2010; Warner to Kelly, n.d.; Barnett and Warner to Dear Contributor, n.d., PML-ACW, box 31.
22. Quote from "Sexual Privacy Project: A joint project of the American Civil Liberties Union Foundation and the National Committee for Sexual Civil Liberties," March 1973, PML-ACLU, box 236; author interview with Thomas Coleman, August 9, 2010. Barnett secured early funding by couching his project as one that would investigate the "untoward effect" on population growth of discrimination against unmarried people. Even before publication, Barnett's book was cited in a court of appeals dissent, which recognized that courts and legislatures had begun to follow the "social revolution on the subject of private consensual sexual relations between two consenting adults" and concluded that "New Mexico should follow this trend." *State v. Trejo*, 83 N.M. 511 (February 4, 1972); Barnett, *Sexual Freedom and the Constitution*, v. See also Barnett to Joseph, January 11 and 26, 1973; Barnett to Warner, January 27, 1973; Coleman to Barnett, February 17, 1973; Warner to Coleman, March 5, 1973, PML-ACW, box 36; Neier to Joseph, March 6, 1973, PML-ACW, box 35.
23. Barnett earned approximately $26,000 a year as a law professor. Quotes from Joseph to Barnett, April 4, 1973 and May 7, 1973, PML-ACW, box 35; see also author interview with Marilyn Haft, August 9, 2010; Cole, "ACLU Launched."
24. First three quotes from author interview with Marilyn Haft, August 9, 2010; last quote from Warner to Barnett, October 16, 1972, PML-ACW, box 31; all other quotes from Barnett to Joseph, April 20, 1973, PML-ACW, box 35.
25. Haft remembers the instigation and naming of the Sexual Privacy Project a bit differently. She recalls suggesting a gay rights project to Wulf and the ACLU board, at which point Ruth Bader Ginsburg suggested that she couch the project in terms of sexual privacy and include prostitutes in order to avoid the perception that the ACLU discriminated against heterosexuals. Author interview with Marilyn Haft, August 9, 2010; Haft to Dear People,

June 11, 1973; Bill Kelley to Warner and Barnett, June 15, 1973, PML-ACW, box 35; R. Michael Wetherbee to Kelley, April 19, 1974, PML-ACW, box 29.

26. Haft to Dear People, June 11, 1973, PML-ACW, box 35; quotes from Reitman to Haft, June 20 and 21, 1973, ACLU-MF, reel 319.
27. American Civil Liberties Union, *Sexual Privacy Project*; R. Michael Wetherbee to William B. Kelley, April 19, 1974; Kelley to Wetherbee, April 24, 1974, PML-ACW, box 29; first quote from Halvonik, "Hope and Affection," 132–135; second quote from Hill, "Constitutional Status of Morals Legislation," 1. The phrase "victimless crime" does not appear in *Time* until 1970 and the *New York Times* until 1971, although a 1973 article claimed that pressure to remove "victimless crimes" from the law books dated back at least a decade. Ira Glasser, executive director of the New York Civil Liberties Union, used the phrase as early as 1969. See Glasser to Dorothy Kenyon, June 30, 1969, SSC-DK, box 28; see also Elizabeth Drew, "The Rule of Lawyers," *New York Times* (October 7, 1973); "The Law: The Scandal of Court Congestion," *Time*, November 9, 1970; Eric Pace, "Reform in 'Victimless Crime' Laws Urged at Legislative Hearings," *New York Times*, September 14, 1971; Boruchowitz, "Victimless Crimes," 69; Stanmeyer, "Victimless Crimes and Public Morality," 369. On the ABA see Robert L. Burnham to Haft, December 26, 1973; Haft to Burnham, January 11, 1974, PML-ACW, box 31; on COYOTE see Weitzer, "Prostitutes' Rights"; Haft, "Hustling for Rights." See also Haft, "Sexual Privacy: A Paper Prepared for Discussion at a Policy-Implementation Workshop at the June 13–16, 1974 Biennial Conference at the University of Wisconsin, Milwaukee," PML-ACLU, box 700; "Memo: Due Process Committee to Board of Directors re: Biennial Conference and Committee Recommendations on Victimless Crimes," September 19, 1975, ACLU-MF, series 2, reel 2. Last two quotes from Ginsburg and Fasteau, "The Legal Status of Women Under Federal Law: Report of Columbia Law School Equal Rights Advocacy Project," September 1974, ACLU-MF, reel 319.
28. Haft tried to interest the American Bar Association in sponsoring the project under the title of "Victimless Crimes Reporter." Burnham to Haft, December 26, 1973; Warner, "Memorandum," October 20, 1973; Haft to Burnham, January 11, 1974; Haft to Warner, January 14, 1974, PML-ACW, box 31; Coleman, *Domino Effect*, 46, 48–50; "Sexual Law Reporter: Proposal Submitted by National Committee for Sexual Civil Liberties and American Civil Liberties Union," January 1974, PML-ACW, box 14; Boggan et al., *Rights of Gay People*; American Civil Liberties Union, *Sexual Privacy Project*; Haft to Nancy Olkon, February 13, 1975; Matthew Stark to Reitman, March 31, 1975; Reitman to Stark, April 9, 1975; quotes from Stark to Reitman, April 29, 1976, PML-ACLU, box 114.
29. First four quotes from *Policy Guide of the American Civil Liberties Union* (July 5, 1966), 246, SSC-DK, box 30; fifth and seventh quotes from "Memo: Due Process Committee to Board of Directors Re: Biennial Conference and Committee Recommendations on Victimless Crimes," September 19, 1975, ACLU-MF, series 2, reel 2; sixth quote from Dorothy Kenyon to Ira Glasser, June 26, 1969, SSC-DK, box 28. See also Kenyon to *New York Times*, July 14, 1971, SSC-DK, box 17; Kenyon to Stanwood Kenyon, August 5, 1971, SSC-DK, box 14.
30. R. Michael Wetherbee to Warner, July 3, 1974, PML-ACW, box 35; Wetherbee to Kelley, April 19, 1974, PML-ACW, box 29; first four quotes from Warner to Schwartz, March 13 and 26, 1975; see also Schwartz to Warner, April 1, 1975, PML-ACW, box 35; Coleman, *Domino Effect*, 42–43. According to historian William Eskridge, after California repealed its sodomy laws, "sodomy reform seemed like an idea whose time had come." By decade's end, nearly 90 percent of Americans resided in the thirty-five states that had "substantially decriminalized sodomy." Sexual solicitation laws were another matter. Quotes from Eskridge, *Dishonorable Passions*, 200–201, see also 197–199.
31. First quote from ACLU Board of Directors Statement, April 13, 1975, "National Gay Task Force, Gay Civil Rights Support Statements and Resolutions Packet," ACLU-MF, reel 303; *1976 Policy Guide of the American Civil Liberties Union*, 179–180, 232–233; all other quotes

from Cole, "ACLU Launched"; "Gay Rights Policy Updated," *Civil Liberties Review*, January 1976; and "Memo: Due Process Committee to Board of Directors Re: Biennial Conference and Committee Recommendations on Victimless Crimes," September 19, 1975, ACLU-MF, series 2, reel 2.

32. First quote from Lawrence Herman to Reitman, December 17, 1974, PML-ACLU, box 113; second quote from Brian Heffernan to Due Process Committee, April 9, 1975, ACLU-MF, reel 320; all other quotes from Reitman to Board of Directors, January 29, 1976, ACLU-MF, series 2, reel 1.
33. Quote from Communications Media and Free Speech Association Committees to Board of Directors, November 24, 1975, ACLU-MF, series 2, reel 2; see also Howard W. Goldstein, "Commercial Advertising and the First Amendment: A Working Paper for the Free Speech-Association Committee and the Communications-Media Committee," January 1973, ACLU-MF, series 4, reel 37; Free Speech/Association Committee to the Board, February 17, 1965; "Excerpts from Free Speech Committee Minutes of April 16, 1965"; ACLU Press Release, November 17, 1965; ACLU-MF, reel 63; Communications Media Committee Minutes, November 19, 1969, PML-ACLU, box 195; Richard Yale Feder to Reitman, April 23, 1969; Reitman to Wulf, May 5, 1969, ACLU-MF, series 3, reel 65.
34. Allyn, *Make Love, Not War*, 184–185; Lewis, *Hollywood v. Hard Core*, 188–191, 205; Foster Hirsch, "He's Happy in His 'Blue' Heaven," *New York Times*, January 24, 1971; Corliss, "That Old Feeling."
35. Quotes from *Redrup v. New York*, 386 U.S. 767 (May 8, 1967), and *Stanley v. Georgia*, 394 U.S. 557 (April 7, 1969). See also Hixson, *Pornography and the Justices*, 75, 91.
36. Strub, "Perversion for Profit," 258–259; quotes from *Rowan v. Post Office Department*, 397 U.S. 728 (May 4, 1970).
37. Speiser to Ad Hoc Group of National Organizations, November 12, 1970; ACLU-MF, reel 66; quotes from "Statement of Lawrence Speiser," November 18, 1970, PML-ACLU, box 195; see also Fowler, *Unmailable*, 196–202.
38. Quote from Communication Media Committee Minutes, June 25, 1969, PML-ACLU, box 195. See also "Grandfather Goldwater Asks Ban on Obscene Mail," *New York Times*, October 2, 1969. On debates over postal policy see Kielbowicz, "Origins of the Junk-Mail Controversy"; Fowler, *Unmailable*, 182–186. On antiobscenity movements of the day see Zurcher and Kirkpatrick, *Citizens for Decency*; Boyer, *Purity in Print*, 291–293, 298–300, 304–306. On attributing antiobscenity activism to political maneuvering, see Strub, "Perversion for Profit."
39. First quote from Haiman, "Speech v. Privacy," 191; all other quotes from Communications Media Committee Minutes, May 14, 1969, and June 25, 1969, PML-ACLU, box 195; see also Dorsen, "In Memory of Tom Emerson."
40. First quotes from Communications Media Committee Minutes, June 25, 1969; last quote from Reitman to Ad Hoc Group of National Organizations Meeting to Discuss Legislative Proposals to Curb Distribution of Obscene Materials, November 3, 1969, PML-ACLU, box 195.
41. First quote from "Text of Statement of Policy on Obscenity and Censorship Adopted by ACLU Board of Directors," February 14, 1970, ACLU-MF, reel 66; Bea Gelfand to Reitman, February 25, 1970, PML-ACLU, box 194; Communications Media Committee to Board of Directors, September 10, 1973, ACLU-MF, series 4, reel 204; all other quotes from Communications Media Committee Minutes, October 22, 1969, PML-ACLU, box 195.
42. First and third quotes from "Text of Statement of Policy on Obscenity and Censorship Adopted by ACLU Board of Directors," February 14, 1970, ACLU-MF, reel 66; second quote from Communications Media Committee Minutes, June 25, 1969, PML-ACLU, box 195; Office to Board of Directors, January 29, 1970, PML-ACLU, box 194.
43. First quote from "Commission on Obscenity and Pornography: Progress Report," July 1969, ACLU-MF, reel 65; other quotes from Harriet Pilpel, "Statement of American Civil

Liberties Union Before President's Commission on Obscenity and Pornography," May 11, 1970, PML-ACLU, box 194, and Citizens for Decent Literature press release, November 17, 1969, ACLU-MF, reel 66. See also Osmond Fraenkel Diaries, March 15, 1965, PML-OFD; Communication Media Committee Minutes, October 22, 1969; Reitman to Ad Hoc Group of National Organizations Meeting to Discuss Legislative Proposals to Curb Distribution of Obscene Materials, November 3, 1969; "Summary of May 28, 1969 meeting of National Organization on Legislative Proposals to Curb Mailing of Obscene Materials," June 30, 1969; PML-ACLU, box 195; Reitman to Speiser et al., January 19, 1970; Reitman to Speiser, January 12, 1970; Reitman to Barbara Scott (Preiskel), March 3, 1970; Betsy Nolan to Dear Editor, September 25, 1970, PML-ACLU, box 194; Reitman to Cody Wilson, September 2, 1969; "Persons Attending Meeting on Administration's Anti-Obscenity Policy," November 14, 1969, ACLU-MF, reel 65; Speiser to Brad Patterson, January 21, 1970, ACLU-MF, reel 66. On Keating's role on the commission see Strub, "Perversion for Profit," 231–237.

44. First quotes from "Summary of May 28, 1969 meeting of National Organization on Legislative Proposals to Curb Mailing of Obscene Material," June 30, 1969; "Summary of the Second Meeting September 24, 1969 of National Organizations on Legislative Proposals to Curb Distribution of Obscene Materials," October 3, 1969; "Persons Attending Meeting on Administration's Anti-Censorship Policy," September 24, 1969, PML-ACLU, box 195; and "Summary of Third Meeting of National Organizations on Legislative Proposals to Curb Distribution of Obscene Materials, November 14, 1969," December 19, 1969; last quote from Bea Gelfand to Alan Reitman, November 25, 1970, PML-ACLU, box 194.
45. Pilpel and Weidman quotes from "Commission on Obscenity and Pornography: Statement of Jerome Weidman, for the Authors League of America," May 13, 1970; Mark P. Robinson, "Prepared Statement for Commission on Obscenity and Pornography," n.d.; see also Judith Krug, "Statement of the American Library Association Prepared for the Commission on Obscenity and Pornography," May 4, 1970; Krug to Alan Reitman, May 26, 1970; Lockhart to Pemberton, April 6, 1970; Reitman to Speiser, April 14, 1970; Reitman to Lockhart, April 14, 1970, ACLU-MF, series 3, reel 66; second quote from Pilpel, "Statement of American Civil Liberties Union Before President's Commission on Obscenity and Pornography," May 11, 1970; "Background Information for Use with Report on President's Commission on Obscenity and Pornography," n.d., PML-ACLU, box 194; all other quotes from *Karalexis v. Byrne*, 306 F. Supp. 1363 (November 28, 1969). See also Lockhart and McClure, "Censorship of Obscenity."
46. It included a blistering minority report written by Keating, Hill, and another commissioner. Other critics called the report a "magna carta for the pornographer," and attacked the scientific basis of the commission's studies, the liberal biases of the commissioners themselves, and the overrepresentation of ACLU members among them. Packer, "The Pornography Caper"; quote from "Excerpts from Panel's Majority Report, Dissenting Opinions and Other Views," *New York Times*, October 1, 1970. On female antiobscenity activists' much earlier use of sex education as an antidote to obscenity, see Wheeler, *Against Obscenity*.
47. Strub, "Perversion for Profit," 235, 238–239; "Psychologist Disputes Report on Smut," *New York Times*, August 12, 1970; Packer, "The Pornography Caper"; first quote from "Senate Votes, 60 to 5, to Reject and Censure Obscenity Report," *New York Times*, October 14, 1970; second quote from "Nixon Repudiates Obscenity Report as Morally Void," *New York Times*, October 25, 1970; see also "Psychologist Disputes Report on Smut," *New York Times*, August 12, 1970; Edwards, "Politics and Pornography."
48. First quote from Alan Reitman to Freeman Lewis, October 28, 1970; second quote from "$2 Million Wasted on Tripe," *News-Sentinel*, October 16, 1970; see also Reitman to Philip Jacobson, November 4, 1970; "Agenda for November 9 Meeting," November 5, 1970; Reitman to Scott (Preiskel), November 3, 1970; "Editorials on Report of the Commission on

Obscenity & Pornography," n.d.; "WCBS Editorial Reply," n.d.; Reitman to Claire Cooper, November 12, 1970; Scott (Preiskel) to Reitman, November 25, 1970; December 10, 1970; "Draft of reply by Harriet F. Pilpel . . . to WCBS-TV editorial of October 28, 1970," n.d.; Pilpel to Reitman, December 10, 1970; "Text of Coalition Statement on the Report of the Federal Commission on Obscenity and Pornography," January 21, 1971; W. L. Smith to Morton A. Hill, S.J., March 23, 1971, ACLU-MF, reel 66; "Statement of the American Civil Liberties Union on S. 3736 to Establish a Commission on Noxious and Obscene Matters and Materials," September 1, 1960; Reitman to Ernest Angell, January 22, 1965; Angell to Hon. Ernest Gruening, January 29, 1965; Gruening to Angell, February 4, 1965; Gruening to Speiser, February 10, 1965; Speiser to Gruening, February 10, 1965; Board of Directors Minutes, March 15, 1965; "Statement of Lawrence Speiser," September 2, 1965, ACLU-MF, reel 63; Elmer Rice to Rex Stout, March 2 and 20, 1965, HRC-ERC, box 85. Preiskel provided the names of organizations and individuals whose testimony before the commission indicated that they might support the ACLU. See "Summary of November 8 meeting of Ad Hoc Committee of National Organizations," November 10, 1970; "Summary of the Second Meeting of the Ad Hoc Committee of National Organizations Concerned About Attacks on the Report of the President's Commission on Obscenity and Pornography," November 23, 1970; "Summary of the Third Meeting of the Ad Hoc Committee of National Organizations concerned about attacks on the report of the President's Commission on Obscenity and Pornography," February 17, 1971; "Coalition of Organizations Calls for Fair Debate on Porn Report," *Jackson, Mississippi News*, January 25, 1971; Coalition of Organizations Calls for Fair Debate on Porn Report," *Providence Journal*, January 25, 1971; "Let's Give it a Hearing," *Kansas City Star*, January 24, 1971; Stanton Peckham, "Readers' Roundup," *Denver Post*, January 31, 1971; John McClellan to Neier, April 8, 1971; Reitman to Ad Hoc Committee on Federal Commission on Obscenity and Pornography, April 15, 1971, PML-ACLU, box 194; "Senate Votes, 60 to 5, to Reject and Censure Obscenity Report," *New York Times*, October 14, 1970.

49. The Supreme Court decision in *Miller v. California* (1973) provided evidence of the report's limited immediate impact and the growing influence of conservative justices appointed by Richard Nixon. Scott (Preiskel) to Reitman, December 17, 1970, ACLU-MF, reel 66; Allyn, *Make Love, Not War*, 194–195; Strub, "Perversion for Profit," 241; quote from Boyer, *Purity in Print*, 309–311. See also Packer, "The Pornography Caper"; *Miller v. California*, 413 U.S. 15 (June 21, 1973). For a contrasting interpretation see Strub, "Perversion for Profit," 297–302. Liberal opponents of obscenity law who rely on the authority of the Johnson Commission report include Strossen, *Defending Pornography*, 263; Duggan and Hunter, *Sex Wars*, 20–21; Williams, *Hard Core*, 16; and Amitai Etzioni "'Porn is Here to Stay,'" *New York Times*, May 17, 1977. See also Diamond, "Pornography and Repression." Published studies funded by the commission include Cook et al., "Pornography and the Sex Offender"; Ware et al., "Semantic Meaning"; Amoroso et al., "Effects of Physiological Measurement"; and Zurcher and Kirkpatrick, *Citizens for Decency*.
50. Packer, "The Pornography Caper"; Diamond, "Pornography and Repression"; "Summary of Meeting to Plan the ACLU Response to the Reagan Commission on Pornography," September 24, 1984, ACLU-MF, reel 67; see literature cited in Donnerstein and Hallam, "Facilitating Effects of Erotica"; and Donnerstein and Barrett, "Effects of Erotic Stimuli."
51. Quotes from Communications Media Committee Minutes, November 9, 1970, PML-ACLU, box 194.
52. Haiman quotes from Communications Media Committee to the Board of Directors, September 10, 1973; Haiman to National Board of Directors, September 4, 1973, ACLU-MF, series 4, reel 204; and Haiman, "Speech v. Privacy"; all other quotes from Minutes of Board of Directors Meeting, September 29–30, 1973, PML-ACLU, box 26.
53. First and third quotes from Communications Media Committee and Free Speech/Association Committee to Board of Directors, April 11, 1974; second quote from Howard

W. Goldstein, "Commercial Advertising and the first Amendment: A Working Paper for the Free Speech-Association Committee and the Communications-Media Committee," January 1973; see also Max Gitter to Carol Jennings, February 28, 1973; "Proposal by Committee member Tom Emerson," in Communications Media Committee and Free Speech/Association Committee to Board of Directors, April 11, 1974; John H. Henn to Wulf, February 14, 1974, ACLU-MF, series 4, reel 37; all other quotes from Communications Media and Free Speech Association Committees to Board of Directors, November 24, 1975; Reitman to Board of Directors, December 12, 1975, ACLU-MF, series 2, reel 2; Wulf, Joel Gora, Judith Mears, et al., Brief for Appellant in *Bigelow v. Virginia*, October term, 1974, ACLU-MF, series 4, reel 38.

54. Quotes from Reitman to Board of Directors, January 29, 1976; see also Board of Directors Minutes, April 10–11, 1976, ACLU-MF, series 2, reel 1, and 1976 Biennial Conference Report of the ACLU, June 10–13, 1976, ACLU-MF, series 2, reel 2.
55. First quote from Reitman to Board of Directors, January 29, 1976; see also Board of Directors Minutes, April 10–11, 1976, ACLU-MF, series 2, reel 1; second quote from author interview with Marilyn Haft, August 9, 2010; see also Eskridge, *Dishonorable Passions*, 184–186; *North Carolina v. Enslin*, 25 N.C. App. 662 (May 7, 1975); *Enslin v. North Carolina*, 425 U.S. 903 (March 29, 1976).
56. Eskridge, *Dishonorable Passions*, 186; *Doe v. Commonwealth's Attorney*, 403 F. Supp. 1199 (October 24, 1975); *Doe v. Commonwealth's Attorney*, 425 U.S. 901 (March 29, 1976). The Court issued no written opinion.
57. First quote from *ACLU Annual Report*, 1976, ACLU-MF, series 9, reel 4; second quote from author interview with Marilyn Haft, August 9, 2010; all other quotes from Warner, "The disaster which occurred . . . ," n.d.; see also Bruce Voeller to *The Advocate*, May 14, 1976, PML-ACW, box 31. Warner's critique represented an implicit criticism of the legal strategies employed by Haft and the ACLU, but Warner strove to absolve them both of any responsibility for the cases by placing blame squarely on the shoulders of Kameny, his longtime nemesis and rival. Calling the failed cases "the crowning achievement of Frank Kameny," Warner identified him as the incompetent puppeteer behind the scenes and the irresponsible instigator who encouraged the parties to bring suit. Bruce Voeller, executive director of the National Gay Task Force, objected strenuously to Warner's characterization of the cases, insisting that they were "the best possible cases" and were designed to preempt "bad" cases that would block access to the courts and set damaging precedents. He insisted that ACLU attorneys directed both cases expertly and benefited from Kameny's involvement.
58. First quote from Eskridge, *Dishonorable Passions*, 202; other quotes from Clinton to Keeston Lowery, February 18, 1977; March 22 and 30, 1977; Lowery to Clinton, February 3, 1977 and March 29, 1977, PML-ACW, box 35; and Clinton, *My Life*, 246–248.
59. Quote from Warner to Coleman, August 26, 1996, PML-ACW, box 35.
60. Quotes from Eskridge, *Dishonorable Passions*, 202, 211, 213; see also Bruce Voeller, "We are deeply concerned . . .," January 3, 1978; "NGTF Conference on Public Referenda on Civil Rights," January 12, 1978, ACLU-MF, reel 303; Robert A. Davis, "Relevance of Gay Issues to Initiatives and Referenda: A statement prepared for discussion at a plenary session at the June 16–19, 1979, Biennial Conference at Mount Vernon College in Washington, D.C.," ACLU-MF, series 3, reel 2.
61. Quotes from author interview with Marilyn Haft, August 9, 2010.
62. Author interview with Melvin Wulf, August 2, 2010; author interview with Thomas Coleman, August 9, 2010.
63. Weitzer, "Prostitutes' Rights in the United States," 34; author interview with Thomas Coleman, August 9, 2010; Bruce J. Ennis to Shepherd Raimi, February 1, 1978, PML-ACLU, box 47; Peter Thomas Judge, "Gay Rights: A paper prepared for discussion at a policy-implementation workshop at the June 14–16, 1979 Biennial Conference at Mount Vernon College, Washington D.C.," ACLU-MF, series 3, reel 2. Nan D. Hunter, "'a hell of a month to start a gay rights project': First Annual Report, June 1986–June 1987," PML-ACLU, box

389; author interview with Nan Hunter, November 1, 2010; quote from Julia Duin, "Gay Leaders Counsel Against Federal Suits," *Washington Times*, May 28, 2009.

64. Quote from Trippett, "What's Happening to Sexual Privacy?" Trippett attributed the emergence of "public sex" to the ability of technology to invade privacy but also to technology's depersonalizing and dehumanizing effects that lead people to rebel by asserting basic human instincts. Scholars too have posited a dynamic relationship between pornography and technology. See for example Barss, *The Erotic Engine*; and Johnson, "Pornography Drives Technology."

Chapter 7

1. Dworkin, "The ACLU: Bait and Switch," 37–39.
2. When Recy Taylor, a black woman, charged four white men with rape in 1949 and local Alabama authorities refused to prosecute, ACLU leaders saw no grounds for their involvement. "There is nothing . . . that we can do," they wrote in response to a plea on Taylor's behalf. Quote from Henrietta Buckmaster to Kate Crane Gartz, January 11, 1945; Forster to Gartz, January 24, 1945, ACLU-MF, reel 232. See also McGuire, *Dark End of the Street*; Jacquet, "The Giles-Johnson Case," and, for a definitive treatment of the long and tangled history of race and rape in the nineteenth-century American South, Sommerville, *Rape and Race*.
3. On the ACLU and rape see William Pickens, "Lynching and Debt-Slavery" (New York: American Civil Liberties Union, 1921), ACLU-MF, reel 7; Milner to Sheriff, January 28, 1922, ACLU-MF, reel 25. The *Baltimore Evening Sun* challenged the ACLU's assumptions that charges brought by women known to have participated in prostitution might not be credible, asking, "Are prostitutes to be deprived of the usual protection of law?" Quote in Hamilton Owens to Forrest Bailey, August 25, 1951; see also Bailey to Hollace Ransdall, April 29, 1931; Walter White to Bailey, May 3, 1931; Ransdall to Bailey, May 6, 1931; "Excerpt from a Confidential Report on the Scottsboro Cases," May 7, 1931; Ransdall, "Report on the Scottsboro Case," May 27, 1931; Bailey to David H. Pierce, June 9, 1931, ACLU-MF, reel 76; "For Immediate Release," July 26, 1950; Soll to Dear ——, n.d.; Levy, "Re: Willie McGee Case," April 1951, PML-ACLU, box 579; Levy to John C. Walters, February 29, 1952, PML-ACLU, box 587; R. Jess Brown and Wulf, "Motion to Quash the Panel of Grand Jurors," in *State of Mississippi v. Richard Bass*, November 1967; Wulf, et al., Brief for Appellant in *Richard Bass v. State of Mississippi*, October 1965; Wulf to Brown, October 15, 1968; February 6, 1969, and April 11, 1969, ACLU-MF, series 4, reel 325; Watts to Walter Harwood, July 28, 1959, ACLU-MF, reel 190; Walker, *In Defense*, 91; Dorr, *White Women, Rape, & the Power of Race in Virginia*, 254 n. 29, ACLU-MF, reel 76. Osmond Fraenkel, who would serve as the ACLU's chief counsel from 1954 to 1977, joined the organization in the 1930s because he supported its work on behalf of the Scottsboro defendants. Fraenkel diary entry, November 11, 1954, PML-OFD.
4. "Press Is Warned on Welfare State," *New York Times*, April 27, 1950; Rothenberg and Steffens, "The Rape Victim"; Rothenberg, *The Newspaper*. Nine years later Rothenberg informed the ACLU that most newspapers had begun to protect the anonymity of rape victims. Rothenberg to Malin, January 16, 1960; Ernst to Rothenberg, February 3, 1960; Reitman to Rothenberg, February 2, 1960, HRC-MEC, box 566.
5. *Model Penal Code, Draft No. 5* (Philadelphia: American Law Institute, 1955), 241–265, first quote from p. 254; second quote from Lesley Oelsner, "Law of Rape: 'Because Ladies Lie,'" *New York Times*, May 14, 1972; Estrich, "Rape"; see also Denno, "Why the Model Penal Code's Sexual Offense Provisions."
6. Amsterdam and Babcock to Women's Rights Committee et al., n.d.; Eve Cary to Wulf, October 5, 1971; "Statement of David B. Isbelle, Chairman American Civil Liberties Union of the National Capital Area Before the Public Safety Committee of the District of Columbia

City council on the Report of the Task Force on Rape," October 16, 1973, ACLU-MF, reel 319; Minutes Executive Meeting, March 18, 1974, SC-ACLU, box 225.

7. First quote from Labi, "Man Against the Machine," 19; see also Meltsner, *Cruel and Unusual*, 75, 78–105; and Amsterdam e-mail to author, October 16–17, 2010. Later quotes from Babcock e-mail to author, October 21, 2010; see also LaDoris Hazzard Cordell interview with Babcock, March 13, 2007; Lester, *Eleanor Holmes Norton*; memo reprinted in Babcock, Freedman, and Norton, *Sex Discrimination and the Law*; Amsterdam and Babcock to Women's Rigths Committee et al., n.d., ACLU-MF, reel 319.
8. Quotes from Amsterdam and Babcock to Women's Rights Committee et al., n.d., ACLU-MF, reel 319. According to Amsterdam and Babcock, admissible evidence must show one of the following: (1) the complainant had consensual sexual intercourse with the defendant within six months of the alleged rape, (2) the defendant "knew of prior sexual activity of the complainant which would reasonably lead him to believe that she was consenting to sexual intercourse under the circumstances of their encounter," (3) the complainant "misrepresented the nature of her sexual experience on occasions other than that of the alleged rape," (4) the complainant led the defendant to believe that she consented in the past to sexual activity "sufficiently similar to those of the encounter with the defendant so as to establish that she consented to sexual intercourse with the defendant," and (5) the complainant had a motive to fabricate a rape charge.
9. Quotes from *Giles v. Maryland*, 386 U.S. 66 (February 20, 1967); see also *State v. Giles and Giles*, 239 Md. 458 (July 13, 1965); Chip Brown, "James Giles' Lessons Lost on His Son," *Washington Post*, March 1, 1980; David Snyder, "When Racial Justice was Young," *Washington Post*, March 28, 2003; "3 Doomed in Rape Win Commutation," *New York Times*, October 25, 1963.
10. Brownmiller, "Rashomon in Maryland."
11. First quote from Due Process Committee Minutes, May 5, 1975; second quote from Deborah Rothman to Due Process Committee, March 12, 1975, ACLU-MF, reel 320; see also "Statement of David B. Isbell," October 16, 1973, ACLU-MF, reel 319.
12. First quote from Due Process Committee Minutes, May 5, 1975; second quote from Rothman to Due Process Committee, March 12, 1975; John Roemer III to Delegate Joseph Owens, March 17, 1975, ACLU-MF, reel 320; third quote from Due Process Committee et al., to Board of Directors, January 27, 1976, ACLU-MF, series 2, reel 1; see also "Statement of David B. Isbell," October 16, 1973, ACLU-MF, reel 319.
13. First quote from "Statement of American Civil Liberties Union of Northern California on the Administration of Laws Against Rape," n.d., SC-ACLU, box 308; second quote from Herman to Reitman, April 15, 1975; Privacy Committee Minutes, October 15, 1975, ACLU-MF, reel 320.
14. Quote from Brownmiller, *In Our Time*, 200. See also Brownmiller, *Against Our Will*, 198–201, 215–217, 234; Edwards, "Rape, Racism"; Whitfield, *Death in the Delta*, 113–114; Bronstein, *Battling Pornography*, 44–52.
15. Quote from Brownmiller, *In Our Time*, 247. See also Edwards, "Rape, Racism"; Whitfield, *Death in the Delta*, 113–114.
16. Seidenberg quotes from "Report of the Due Process, Privacy and Equality Committees on Prior Sexual History of Complainant in Criminal Proceedings for Rape," February 14–15, 1976; WRP quote from Board of Directors Minutes, March 5–6, 1977, ACLU-MF, series 1, reel 1.
17. Jill Laurie Goodman to Equality Committee, November 5, 1976; Equality Committee Minutes, December 9, 1976, PML-ACLU, box 114; Barbara Sommer to Edward J. Ennis, May 22, 1974; quote from Amsterdam and Babcock to Women's Rights Committee et al., ACLU-MF, reel 319; Sommer e-mail to author, October 15, 2010; Deborah Rothman to Due Process Committee, March 12, 1975; Due Process Committee Minutes, September 26, 1975, ACLU-MF, reel 320.
18. On the ACLU Women's Rights Project see chapter 5. First quotes from Equality Committee Minutes, February 12, 1976; March 2, 1976, PML-ACLU, box 114; last quote from Hanna

B. Weston, "Libertarian First, Feminist Second," *Civil Liberties Review*, February–March 1977, ACLU-MF, series 9, reel 4; see also Strossen, "American Civil Liberties Union."

19. First quote from Due Process Committee, Privacy Committee, Equality Committee to Board of Directors, January 27, 1976, ACLU-MF, series 2, reel 1; see also Office to Due Process Committee, June 11, 1975, ACLU-MF, reel 320; last quotes from Goodman to Equality Committee, November 5, 1976, PML-ACLU, box 114. The point has since been made by legal scholars. See Galvin, "Shielding Rape Victims."
20. Due Process Committee Minutes, October 24, 1975, ACLU-MF, reel 320; quotes from Herman, "What's Wrong with the Rape Reform Laws?"
21. Quotes from James C. Walsh to editor; Koestner to editor; and Louis A. Jacobs and Victoria Anne Manley to editor, *Civil Liberties Review*, May–June 1977, 4–6.
22. First three quotes from "List of Issues Before Subject Matter Committees, 1975–1976 Season," August 26, 1975, ACLU-MF, series 2, reel 2; Privacy Committee Minutes, October 15, 1975; "The Right to Fair Trial Should not be Qualified," *Civil Liberties*, April 1976; fifth and sixth quotes from Due Process Committee Minutes, May 5, 1975; see also September 26, 1975; Brian Heffernan to Due Process Committee, June 6, 1975; Herman to Reitman, April 15, 1975, ACLU-MF, reel 320; fourth, seventh, and eighth quotes from Lawrence K. Karlton to Charles C. Marson, April 8, 1974, ACLU-MF, reel 319.
23. First and final three quotes from Lawrence K. Karlton to Charles C. Marson, April 8, 1974, ACLU-MF, reel 319; fourth and fifth quotes from John Roemer III to Brian Heffernan, April 15, 1975; Due Process Committee Minutes, April 17, 1975, ACLU-MF, reel 320; sixth quote from Herman, "What's Wrong with the Rape Reform Laws?" See also author interview with Monroe Freedman, October 12, 2010; Mari Goldman to Editor, "Capitol Alert," 4, 4 (May 8, 1974), SC-ACLU, box 309.
24. Quotes from John Roemer III to Delegate Joseph Owens, March 17, 1975; Privacy Committee Minutes, October 15, 1975; "Press Release, MCLU Calls for Defeat of Proposed Trial Bill," March 16, 1975; Katie Hauser to Reitman, November 5, 1975, ACLU-MF, reel 320; "Appendix B: Compendium of ACLU Affiliates' Positions or Testimony on Legislation"; Due Process Committee to Board of Directors, February 5, 1976; ACLU-MF, series 2, reel 1. The New York affiliate soon rescinded its rape shield policy.
25. 1976 Biennial Conference Report of the ACLU, University of Pennsylvania, June 10–13, 1976, ACLU-MF, series 2, reel 2; "Court Bows to Pressure," unidentified newspaper article; "Court Modifies Sexist Language in Hitchhiking Rape Case," *Women's Rights Project Newsletter* 1, 4 (November 1977), SC-ACLU, box 66. See also Compton, *Call of Duty*, 238–239.
26. Herman, "What's Wrong with the Rape Reform Law?" 64; *1976 Policy Guide of the American Civil Liberties Union* (New York: American Civil Liberties Union, 1976), 198–199; "Resolutions Proposed by Workshops Discussing Today's Civil Liberties Battlefronts," June 10–13, 1976; 1976 Biennial Conference Report of the ACLU, June 10–13, 1976, ACLU-MF, series 2, reel 2. For another interpretation of the ACLU's rape policy discussions, see Donohue, *Politics of the American Civil Liberties Union*, 95. For an analysis of state rape shield laws see Spohn and Horney, *Rape Law Reform*; Marsh, Marsh, Geist, and Caplan, *Rape and the Limits of Law Reform*; Anderson, "From Chastity Requirement to Sexual License."
27. First two quotes from Ryan, "The Sex Right"; all other quotes from *Model Penal Code, Tentative Draft No. 4* (Philadelphia: American Law Institute, 1955), 244, 279. Behind the ALI's reluctance to recognize marital rape lay concerns about marital privacy—the same privacy that would underwrite women's rights to birth control and abortion. Indeed, drafters of the code eliminated criminal sanctions for all consensual sexual activity between adults in part because they objected to law that "would thrust the prospect of criminal sanctions into the ongoing process of adjustment in the marital relationship. . . . Retaining the spousal exclusion avoids this unwarranted intrusion of the penal law into the life of the family." Quote from *Model Penal Code and Commentaries,* Part II (Philadelphia: American Law Institute, 1980), 345.

28. First quote from "Statement of David B. Isbelle, Chairman American Civil Liberties Union of the National Capital Area Before the Public Safety Committee of the District of Columbia City Council on the Report of the Task Force on Rape," October 16, 1973, ACLU-MF, reel 319. See also Equality Committee Minutes, February 12, 1976; all other quotes from Goodman to the Equality Committee, November 5, 1976, PML-ACLU, box 114. The WRP relied heavily on Brownmiller's *Against Our Will*, which used the language of "bodily integrity" and "self-determination" to argue for laws against marital rape. See also extensive use of the book in Privacy Committee, Equality Committee, Due Process Committee to Board of Directors, February 24, 1977, ACLU-MF, series 2, reel 1.
29. Quotes from Equality Committee Minutes, December 9, 1976, PML-ACLU, box 114.
30. Quotes from Privacy Committee, Equality Committee, Due Process Committee to Board of Directors, February 24, 1977, ACLU-MF, series 2, reel 1; Equality Committee Minutes, December 9, 1976, PML-ACLU, box 114; *1977 Supplement to the American Civil Liberties Union Policy Guide* (Lexington, Mass.: D.C. Heath, 1978), 67.
31. Estelle Freedman suggested that newspaper's evolution from sensational to professional reporting was accompanied by a decline in the printing of rape victims' names. Freedman e-mail to author, October 6, 2010. See also Gara LaMarche to Equality Committee, November 30, 1976, PML-ACLU, box 114.
32. First two quotes from Gara LaMarche to Equality Committee, November 30, 1976, PML-ACLU, box 114. The debate between Wulf and Neier took place in 1974 but was reported at length in minutes for 1977. All other quotes from Privacy Committee, Equality Committee, Due Process Committee to Board of Directors, February 24, 1977, ACLU-MF, series 2, reel 1; see also *Cox Broadcasting v. Cohn*, 420 U.S. 469 (March 3, 1975).
33. First three quotes from Privacy Committee, Equality Committee, Due Process Committee to Board of Directors, February 24, 1977; last two quotes from Minutes, Board of Directors Meeting, March 5–6, 1977, ACLU-MF, series 1, reel 1; Brownmiller, "Rashomon in Maryland," 130. Two books designed to vindicate the Giles brothers referred to the complainant by pseudonym. See Smith and Giles, *An American Rape*, vii; Strauss, *Where Did the Justice Go?*
34. Quotes from Holtzman, *Who Said It Would Be Easy?* 146–147. Roundtree provided research assistance for Pauli Murray. See Murray, *States' Laws on Race and Color*, 1. See also McCabe and Roundtree, *Justice Older Than the Law*, 3–4, 83–88; Kathleen McCabe e-mail to author, October 26, 2010.
35. Quotes from *Privacy of Rape Victims: Hearing Before the Subcommittee on Criminal Justice of the Committee on the Judiciary House of Representatives, Ninety-fourth Congress, second session, on H.R. 14666 and other bills ... July 29, 1976* (Washington, D.C.: U.S. Govt. Printing Office, 1977). Legal scholars have struggled to understand the ACLU's resistance to rape shield laws given its support for women's rights. See Haxton, "Comment: Rape Shield Statutes."
36. Galvin, "Shielding Rape Victims"; Goldstein, "Tenth Annual Review"; Reeves, "Time to Fine-Tune"; Tilley, "Feminist Repudiation"; Testimony of Roger A. Pauley in *Privacy of Rape Victims: Hearing Before the Subcommittee on Criminal Justice of the Committee on the Judiciary House of Representatives, Ninety-fourth Congress, second session, on H.R. 14666 and other bills ... July 29, 1976* (Washington, D.C.: U.S. Govt. Printing Office, 1977). As the chief opponent of Holtzman's original bill, Roundtree and the ACLU probably contributed to weakening the bill before it became law.
37. Quotes from "Rape Legislation," *Women's Rights Project Newsletter: American Civil Liberties Union of Southern California*, April 1977, SC-ACLU, box 66. Legal scholars have written extensively about the impact of rape law reform with most arguing that the celebrated but limited reform in the 1970s and 1980s actually brought little change in the adjudication of rape. See Tilley, "Feminist Repudiation"; Bryden and Lengnick, "Rape in the Criminal Justice System"; Spohn and Horney, *Rape Law Reform*, 174; Hasday,

"Contest and Consent"; Anderson, "Chastity Requirement"; Gruber, "Rape, Feminism, and the War on Crime."

38. Some scholars argue that the Michigan rape shield law—which was actually drafted by feminists and came closest to representing feminist demands—brought a substantial increase in convictions for rape. Marsh, Geist, and Caplan, *Rape and the Limits of Law Reform*, 105–119.
39. Sauvigne to Neier, July 12, 1976; "Statement of Purpose," n.d., PML-ACLU, box 240; Baker, *Women's Movement Against Sexual Harassment*, 21–26, 29–30, 34, 116–117, 181, 184, 188–189; author interview with Karen Sauvigne, November 14, 2010; MacKinnon, *Sexual Harassment of Working Women*; Farley, *Sexual Shakedown*; Lindsey, "Sexual Harassment on the Job."
40. Baker, *Women's Movement Against Sexual Harassment*, 21–26, 116–117, 181, 188–189.
41. Equality Committee Minutes, February 10, 1983, PML-ACLU, box 185.
42. Pinzler was thinking no doubt of *Cohen v. California* (1971), in which the U.S. Supreme Court affirmed the ACLU's argument for a citizen's right to wear a jacket emblazoned with "Fuck the Draft." A later EEOC ruling reassured Pinzler that the guidelines would not be used to ban all "vulgar language" especially in situations where "the language was part of customary business practice and not a function of the presence of the plaintiff." Quotes from Pinzler to Alan Reitman, May 26, 1981 and June 22, 1981, PML-ACLU, box 185; *Cohen v. California*, 403 U.S. 15 (1971).
43. Evans, *Tidal Wave*, 176–177; Bronstein, *Battling Pornography*, 279–335; Dworkin, *Pornography*; Lederer, ed., *Take Back the Night*, and Griffin, *Pornography and Silence*. Critical observers noted the increasing misogyny and violence of the genre, and antirape activists began to theorize a relationship between the practice and depiction of sexualized violence against women.
44. Duggan and Hunter, *Sex Wars*, 29–64, 239–275; author interview with Nan Hunter, November 1, 2010; Downs, *New Politics of Pornography*, 95–143; Bronstein, *Battling Pornography*, 323-331; Walker, *In Defense*, 351. Walker credits the ACLU with organizing FACT, but Hunter insists that the ACLU played no role.
45. First quote from Duggan and Hunter, *Sex Wars*, 9; second quote from author interview with Karen Sauvigne, November 14, 2010; all other quotes from Equality Committee Minutes, February 10, 1983 and March 20, 1983, PML-ACLU, box 185.
46. Quotes from Equality Committee Minutes, February 10, 1983 and March 20, 1983, PML-ACLU, box 185; author interview with Mary Ellen Gale, December 3, 2010.
47. Quotes from Equality Committee Minutes, March 10, 1983, PML-ACLU, box 185.
48. Quotes from Equality Committee Minutes, March 10, 1983, PML-ACLU, box 185.
49. First three quotes from ACLU Board Minutes, April 14–15, 1984, provided by Nadine Strossen; all other quotes found in excerpt from ACLU Board Minutes, June 1984, PML-ACLU, box 185.
50. Walker, *Hate Speech*, 127–134, 143–148; ACLU Board Minutes, October 13–14, 1990, provided by Nadine Strossen; quotes from "Free Speech and Bias on College Campuses," Policy 72a, Thomas Hilbink to Persons Holding Policy Guides, March 1, 1992, PML-ACLU, box 1910.
51. Quotes in Elaine S. Povich, "ACLU Joins Hyde in Free-Speech Fight," *Chicago Tribune*, March 12, 1991, and Anthony Flint, "Political Correctness: Unlikely Alliances Form Over Speech Issues on Campus," *Seattle Times*, April 2, 1991.
52. Baker, *Women's Movement Against Sexual Harassment*, 138; *Meritor Savings Bank v. Vinson*, 477 U.S. 57 (1986).
53. Quote from Gordon, "Politics of Sexual Harassment," 12; see also Bronstein, *Battling Pornography*, 299; author interview with Karen Sauvigne, November 14, 2010; author interview with Isabelle Katz Pinzler, December 2, 2010; Baker, *Women's Movement Against Sexual Harassment*, 146; 152–154, 239 n. 86, 299–300, 310.

54. Quoted in Taylor, "Sexual Harassment," 189; *Robinson v. Jacksonville Shipyards, Inc.*, 76 F. Supp. 1486 (January 18, 1991); "Nude Photos on Job Ruled Harassment," *Chicago Tribune*, January 24, 1991; "Pinups Ruled Harassment: NOW Cheers Judge's Ruling; ACLU Might Appeal," *Dallas Morning News*, January 24, 1991; Tamar Lewin, "Nude Pictures Are Ruled Sexual Harassment," *New York Times*, January 23, 1991; Lewin, "Ruling on Pinups as Sexual Harassment: What Does it Mean?" *New York Times*, February 8, 1991.
55. After setting a goal of a fifty-fifty gender ratio, the ACLU went from a board of 7 percent to 30 percent women between 1970 and 1990. See David Gonzalez, "A.C.L.U. Chooses a New President," *New York Times*, January 27, 1991.
56. Quotes from author interview with Robyn Blumner, November 29, 2010; see also author interviews with Jeanne Baker, December 12, 2010, and Mary Coombs, December 3, 2010.
57. Author interviews with Joan E. Mahoney, November 23, 2010; Robyn Blumner, November 29, 2010; Mary Coombs, December 3, 2010; Mary Ellen Gale, December 3, 2010; Isabelle Katz Pinzler, December 2, 2010; and Nadine Strossen, November 22, 2010. See also Dennis Cauchon, "Harassment, Free Speech Collide in Florida," *USA Today*, November 20, 1991; Brief of 80 Individual Law Professors and Lawyers in *Robinson v. Jacksonville Shipyards* (August 5, 1992); Walker, *In Defense*, 368. According to Blumner, the WRP objected to the ACLU brief in *Robinson*. Quotes from Cauchon, "Civil Dispute Within the ACLU," *USA Today*, March 31, 1993; Strossen, "Regulating Workplace Sexual Harassment."
58. First quote from author interview with Jeanne Baker, December 12, 2010; other quotes from "NOW, ACLU Disagree on Pin-Ups," *Orlando Sentinel*, April 28, 1992, and author interview with Robyn Blumner, November 29, 2010.
59. Quotes from ACLU brief in *Robinson v. Jacksonville Shipyards* (March 26, 1992).
60. Quotes from Brief of 80 Individual Law Professors and Lawyers in *Robinson v. Jacksonville Shipyards* (August 5, 1992), 5, 7, 18.
61. First two quotes from Howard Troxler, "What More Unlikely Foes? NOW vs. ACLU," *St. Petersburg Times*, November 4, 1991; Wetherfield et al., Brief for Appellant Lois Robinson in *Robinson v. Jacksonville Shipyards*, January 22, 1992; third quote from Judith L. Lichtman et al., Brief Amicus Curiae of the Women's Legal Defense Fund in *Robinson*, August 5, 1992; fourth and fifth quotes from "ACLU Misses Boat in Pinup Case," *Sun-Sentinel*, November 11, 1991; last quote from Larry Witham, "Pinup Ruling Splits ACLU, Feminists," *Washington Times*, November 2, 1991.
62. Quote from Cauchon, "Harassment, Free Speech Collide in Florida," *USA Today*, November 20, 1991; see also Irvine, "Alternative Dispute Resolutions Symposium."
63. Quotes from Schauer, "The Speech-ing of Sexual Harassment." Nadine Strossen agrees that, until the mid-1990s, potential conflicts between sexual harassment policy and the First Amendment received virtually no scholarly attention despite the ACLU's concerns about them a full decade earlier. See Strossen, "Kenneth M. Piper Lecture," and Strossen, "Regulating Workplace Sexual Harassment." For examples of law review articles that considered these issues after *Robinson*, see Robbins, "When Two Liberal Values Collide"; Volokh, "How Harassment Law Restricts"; Karner, "Political Speech"; Jaffe, "Walking the Constitutional Tightrope"; Balkin, "Free Speech and Hostile Environments."
64. "Testimony of Anita F. Hill, Professor of Law, University of Oklahoma, Norman, OK, 10/11/91," http://www.mith2.umd.edu/WomensStudies/GenderIssues/SexualHarassment/hill-thomas-testimony (retrieved July 29, 2011).
65. Quote from Evans, *Tidal Wave*, 225; see also Mansbridge and Tate, "Race Trumps Gender."
66. The Southern California affiliate broke ranks to oppose the nomination. See Karen De Witt, "A.C.L.U. to Remain Neutral on Nomination of Thomas," *New York Times*, August 19, 1991; "A.C.L.U. Dissent on Thomas," *New York Times*, August 30, 1991; author interview with Nadine Strossen, November 22, 2010; author interview with Joan E. Mahoney, November 23, 2010; first three quotes from Joseph E. Leicht to editor, *St. Louis Post-Dispatch*, October 15, 1991; fourth quote from Cauchon, "Harassment, Free Speech Collide in

Florida," *USA Today*, November 20, 1991; fifth quote from Rosen, "Reasonable Women"; all other quotes from Blumner, "Sexual Harassment v. Freedom of Speech," *St. Petersburg Times*, March 13, 1994, and "Sexual Harassment Law Erodes Freedom of Speech," *Milwaukee Journal Sentinel*, November 30, 1997. See also Stephen T. Wyckoff to editor, *Syracuse Post-Standard*, October 10, 1991.

67. Cauchon, "Civil Dispute within the ACLU," *USA Today*, March 31, 1993; Neil A. Lewis, "At A.C.L.U., Free-Speech Balancing Act," *New York Times*, April 4, 1993; Philip Gailey, "ACLU Weakens Its Commitment to Free Speech," *St. Petersburg Times*, April 11, 1993. Whereas the earlier 1984 policy required that actionable expression include "definable consequences for the individual that demonstrably hinders or completely prevents" functioning as an employee, the revised version prohibited expression shown to "hinder significantly" an employee's ability to perform at work or "significantly adversely effect [*sic*] mental, emotional, or physical well-being on the basis of sex." See ACLU Policy Guide, 1992, 400, PML-ACLU, box 1910; and "Sexual Harassment in the Workplace," policy #315, passed April 3–4, 1993, PC-MEG; National Board Minutes, April 3–4, 1993, PC-MM; author interviews with Robyn Blumner, November 29, 2010, and Mary Ellen Gale, December 3, 2010. The 1993 National ACLU Board included forty-nine men and thirty women. National Board of Directors Attendance, April 3–4, 1993, PC-MM; see also Baker, *Women's Movement Against Sexual Harassment*, 173; Mandy Welch, "ACLU to Honor Anita Hill," *Tulsa World*, December 10, 1991; "New York ACLU to Honor Anita Hill," *Lancaster New Era* (Pa.), April 23, 1992; Anne Burke, "Streisand, Hill Get Honors," *Daily News of Los Angeles*, December 12, 1992; *Meritor Savings Bank, FSB v. Vinson*, 477 U.S. 57 (June 10, 1986); Cauchon, "Civil Dispute within the ACLU," *USA Today*, March 31, 1993; author interviews with Wendy Kaminer, November 29, 2010; Robyn Blumner, November 29, 2010; Michael Meyers, November 24, 2010; Mary Ellen Gale, December 3, 2010; Nadine Strossen, November 22, 2010; and Isabelle Katz Pinzler, December 2, 2010; quote from Blumner, *St. Petersburg Times*, October 24, 2010; Ira Glasser to ACLU Executive Committee, March 22, 1993; National Board Minutes, April 3–4, 1993, PC-MM.

68. On the Stroh's case brought by attorney Lori Peterson on behalf of eight employees see Lanpher, "A Bitter Brew." On street harassment see Bowman, "Street Harassment"; "A Move to Protect Women From 'Street Harassment,'" *New York Times*, July 2, 1993; and Nielsen, *License to Harass*. See also 1993 Biennial Resolution on Sexual Harassment, June 1993, PC-MEG; "Hate Crimes, Harassment Split ACLU," *ABA Journal*, July 1993, 17, 20; Blumner e-mail to author, December 6, 2010; author interview with Jeanne Baker, December 12, 2010; National Board Minutes, April 3–4, 1993, PC-MM.

69. Quotes from *Harris v. Forklift Systems*, U.S. dist. LEXIS 20115 (November 27, 1990). The brief filed by Thomas's EEOC spoke of "the naturalness, the pervasiveness, and what might be called the legal neutrality of sexual attraction (as contrasted to racial prejudice)." Quoted in Baker, *Women's Movement Against Sexual Harassment*, 165; see also Cochran, *Sexual Harassment and the Law*, 98–100.

70. Despite the new policy that applied to nontargeted expression, the ACLU placated Blumner and the Florida affiliate by including a footnote that distinguished *Harris* from *Robinson* by insisting that only *Harris* concerned targeted expression. This concession prevented the feisty Florida affiliate from submitting a competing brief—something it considered doing even though filing before the Supreme Court without national ACLU approval would have terminated its affiliate status and its share of revenue. Author interviews with Jeanne Baker, December 12, 2010; Robyn Blumner, November 29, 2010; "Hate Crimes, Harassment Split ACLU," *ABA Journal*, July 1993, 17, 20. First quotes from ACLU brief in *Harris v. Forklift Systems*, 1992 U.S. Briefs 1168 (April 30, 1993), and Susan Deller Ross, "Workplace Harassment," in LaMarche, *Speech and Equality*, 109; last quote from *Harris v. Forklift Systems*, 510 U.S. 17 (November 8, 1993). See also Linda Greenhouse, "Court, 9-0, Makes Sex Harassment Easier to Prove," *New York Times*, November 10, 1993.

71. Quotes from Susan Deller Ross, "Workplace Harassment," in LaMarche, *Speech and Equality*, 108–110, 112, 121. See also "A Standard is Set: Plaintiffs Needn't Show Psychological Harm or Job Impairment," *New York Times*, November 10, 1993; ACLU brief (filed jointly with the American Jewish Congress) in *Harris v. Forklift Systems*, April 30, 1993. Neither john a. powell [sic] nor Steven Shapiro (current legal director for the ACLU) responded to the author's request for an interview.
72. "ACLU Sues for Right to *Playboy*," *San Jose Mercury News*, December 17, 1993; quotes from Keith Stone, "ACLU, *Playboy*, Firefighter Sue: County Ban on Adult Magazines in Stations Challenged," *Daily News of Los Angeles*, December 17, 1993," and Paul Hoffman, Burton Joseph, et al., Memorandum in Support of Motion for Preliminary Injunction in *Johnson v. County of Los Angeles Fire Department*, January 10, 1993, PC-NL.
73. First quote from Keith Stone, "ACLU, *Playboy*, Firefighter Sue: County Ban on Adult Magazines in Stations Challenged," *Daily News of Los Angeles*, December 17, 1993, and author interviews with Nadine Strossen, November 22, 2010, and Mary Ellen Gale, December 3, 2010; second quote from "Firehouse Ban on '*Playboy*' Challenged in 1-Day Trial," *Daily Breeze* (Torrance, Calif.), June 8, 1994; last quote from Hoffman, Joseph et al., Memorandum in Support of Motion for Preliminary Injunction in *Johnson v. County of Los Angeles Fire Department*, January 10, 1993, PC-NL.
74. First quotes from "Editorial—It's Nobody Else's Business," *Daily News of Los Angeles*, December 19, 1993; "Defending the Right to Read," *St. Petersburg Times*, June 27, 1994; "A Fireman and His Magazine," *Washington Post*, June 13, 1994; Ray Recchi, "Sex-in-Reading Rules: Will Bible Be Next?" *Sun-Sentinel*, June 9, 1994; "'Playboy' Ruling Strikes Balance," *Daily Breeze*, June 12, 1994; and "Freedom to Read Foundation News," 19 (1994), 2–3. Different versions of Associated Press articles on Johnson's suit for the "right to read" showed up in newspapers around the country. See "Proposal Would End Racy-Magazine Ban," *Philadelphia Inquirer*, September 23, 1994; "Rules Allow Playboys at L.A. Firehouse," *Chicago Tribune*, September 23, 1994; "Firefighter Returns to Work—Without Playboy," *San Francisco Chronicle*, June 14, 1994; "LA Fireman May Read *Playboy*, Judge Rules," *Boston Globe*, June 10, 1994. Last two quotes from Cathy E. Crosson, counsel for Feminists for Free Expression, amicus brief in *Johnson v. County of Los Angeles Fire Department*, January 24, 1994, PC-NL.
75. First two quotes from Levinson, *Outspoken*, 282, 290; Sandy Banks, "Firehouse Culture an Ordeal for Women," *Los Angeles Times*, December 3, 2006; third, fourth, and fifth quotes from *Johnson v. County of Los Angeles Fire Department*, 865 F. Supp. 1430 (October 25, 1994); sixth and seventh quotes from Angelo Figueroa, "Folding in the Center," *Miami Herald*, June 22, 1994; eighth and ninth quotes from "NOW Backs Fire Station Ban," *Daily Breeze* (Torrance, Calif.), January 11, 1994. See also County of Los Angeles Fire Department policy, PC-MEG.
76. Janet Gilmore, "Firefighter Contends Magazine Ban is Unconstitutional," *Daily News of Los Angeles*, June 8, 1994; *Johnson v. County of Los Angeles Fire Department*, 865 F. Supp. 1430 (October 25, 1994).
77. First quote from "Judge OKs *Playboy* at Firehouse," *Chicago Tribune*, June 10, 1994; "'*Playboy*' Fire Captain Back—Locker Not Bare," *Daily Breeze* (Torrance, Calif.), June 14, 1994; all other quotes from Janet Gilmore, "*Playboy* Magazine Ruling Leads to Policy Re-Evaluation," *Daily News of Los Angeles*, June 12, 1994; Gale Holland, "*Playboy* Allowed Back in Firehouses," *Daily Breeze* (Torrance, Calif.), June 10, 1994; Patricia Vaughan to Nan Levinson (1998 sexual harassment policy attached), June 5, 2001, PC-NL.
78. Quotes from "ACLU Sues for Right to Playboy," *San Jose Mercury News*, December 17, 1993, and "NOW Backs Fire Station Magazine Ban," *Daily Breeze* (Torrance, Calif.), January 11, 1994. See also "ACLU/SC Policy on Sexual Harassment," September 21, 1994, PC-MEG.
79. Quotes from "Special Committee on Sexual Harassment—Majority Report," April 1995, PC-MEG.

80. Quotes from "Special Committee on Sexual Harassment—Majority Report," April 1995, PC-MEG; Majority Subcommittee on Sexual Harassment to ACLU Board, October 5, 1995; Kaminer, "Draft of presentation to the ACLU national board re: proposed sexual harassment policy," April 26, 1995, PC-WK.
81. Quotes from Gale to Baker, et al., April 14, 1995; "Special Committee on Sexual Harassment: Minority Report," April 14, 1995; Gale to ACLU National Board, October 4, 1995, PC-MEG; author interview with Mary Ellen Gale, December 3, 2010. Gale recalled being influenced by Toni Morrison, *Race-ing Justice, En-gendering Power: Essays on Anita Hill, Clarence Thomas, and the Construction of Social Reality* (New York: Pantheon, 1992).
82. Author interviews with Joan E. Mahoney, November 23, 2010, and Nadine Strossen, November 22, 2010; first three quotes from interview with Wendy Kaminer, November 29, 2010; last quote from Excerpt from April 1995 Board Meeting Minutes, PC-MEG.
83. Quote from author interview with Mary Ellen Gale, December 3, 2010; see also author interviews with Jeanne Baker, December 12, 2010, and Wendy Kaminer, November 29, 2010.
84. *ACLU Policy Guide*, 2010.
85. *ACLU Policy Guide,* 2010. By the dawn of the twenty-first century, the ACLU had become one of the most ardent defenders of the right to be free from same-sex sexual harassment or sexual harassment based on sexual orientation. See ACLU and affiliate briefs in *Hopkins v. Baltimore Gas & Electric Company* (April 5, 1995); *Oncale v. Sundowner Offshore Services, Inc.* (August 11, 1997); *Donovan v. Poway Unified School District* (March 14, 2007); Juniper Lesnik to Mary Bull, January 17, 2008, http://www.aclunc.org/news/press_releases/asset_upload_file866_8170.pdf (retrieved July 29, 2011); Tina Forde, "ACLU Says it Wants to Help Tehachapi School District," *Tehachapi News*, December 16, 2010.

Conclusion

1. Quotes from Roger Baldwin, "Memo for Peggy Lamson on the state of civil liberties today 1974"; Roger Baldwin, "memo on the CLU," n.d., PML-PLC, box 1.
2. See chapters 4 and 5.
3. On "southern justice," see "Breaching the White Wall of Southern Justice," *Time*, April 15, 1966; Norman Rockwell painting, *Southern Justice*, *Look*, June 21, 1964.
4. See the ACLU brief on behalf of Senator Larry Craig in *State of Minnesota v. Larry Edwin Craig*, September 2007.
5. Quotes from Herzog, *Sex in Crisis*, xi–xii; see also Strub, "Perversion for Profit," 491–530.
6. Quote from Klein, *America's War on Sex*, 122.
7. Klein, *America's War on Sex*, 29–45, 61–62, 124, 126, 168–171; Herzog, *Sex in Crisis*, 168–169; "Report to Congress: Children's Internet Protection Act," August 2003; *United States v. American Library Association*, 539 U.S. 194 (June 23, 2003); N. C. Aizenman and Rosalind S. Helderman, "Birth Control Exemption Bill, 'the Blunt Amendment' Killed in Senate," *Washington Post*, March 1, 2012. On abortion in particular see Emily Bazelon, "The New Abortion Providers," *New York Times Magazine*, July 18, 2010, 30–37, 44, 46–47.
8. Paul, *Pornified*, 133; Jensen, *Getting Off*; Dines, *Pornland*; Alexander, *America Unzipped*; Levy, *Female Chauvinist Pigs*; Sarracino and Scott, *The Porning of America*; Levin and Kilbourne, *So Sexy So Soon*; Durham, *The Lolita Effect*; Opplinger, *Girls Gone Skank*. See also Brumberg, *The Body Project*, xxii–xxiii, 141–192; Stacey, "Stupid Boob Behavior"; whatboyswant.com/; Alexandra Jacobs, "Campus Exposure," *New York Times Magazine*, March 4, 2007, 44–49.
9. Paul, *Pornified*, 206–207; Dines, *Pornland*, 142–143.
10. Paul, *Pornified*, 253.

11. See ACLU briefs in *Ashcroft v. ACLU* (2004); *Ashcroft v. Free Speech Coalition* (2001); *Gonzales v. Carhart* (August 2006); ACLU pretrial brief in *American Library Association v. United States* (March 20, 2002); *Ashcroft v. ACLU*, 542 U.S. 656 (June 29, 2004).
12. "Minutes of Bull's Head *Playboy* Panel Discussion," University of North Carolina, Chapel Hill, September 10, 2007, provided by Chadwick Roberts.
13. On antipornography feminism as antisex see for example Strossen, *Defending Pornography*, 19–29, 106–120. On the ubiquity and gendered nature of pornography in particular see for example Paul, *Pornified;* Jensen, *Getting Off;* Dines, *Pornland;* Sarracino and Scott, *The Porning of America*; Levin and Kilbourne, *So Sexy So Soon*; Durham, *The Lolita Effect*; Opplinger, *Girls Gone Skank.* See also Brumberg, *The Body Project*, xxii–xxiii, 141–192; Stacey, "Stupid Boob Behavior"; whatboyswant.com/; Alexandra Jacobs, "Campus Exposure," *New York Times Magazine*, March 4, 2007, 44–49.
14. Paul, *Pornified*, 163.
15. Atwood, *The Handmaid's Tale.*
16. According to a 2004 Harris Poll, 23 percent of Americans consider "full access to pornography" a basic constitutional right. Quote from Paul, *Pornified*, 249.
17. Anthony Lewis makes a similar point about the First Amendment, but notes that sexual privacy—as represented by the Supreme Court's decision in *Roe v. Wade*—has enjoyed considerably less stability. Lewis, *Freedom for the Thought*, 169–181.

BIBLIOGRAPHY

Secondary Literature

Alexander, Brian. *America Unzipped: In Search of Sex and Satisfaction.* New York: Harmony Books, 2008.

Allyn, David. *Make Love, Not War, The Sexual Revolution: An Unfettered History.* New York: Routledge, 2001.

Allyn, David. "Private Acts/Public Policy: Alfred Kinsey, the American Law Institute and the Privatization of American Sexual Morality." *Journal of American Studies* 30 (1996), 405–428.

The American Law Institute: Seventy-fifth Anniversary, 1923–1998. Philadelphia: American Law Institute, 1998.

Anderson, Michelle J. "From Chastity Requirement to Sexual License: Sexual Consent and a New Rape Shield Law." *George Washington Law Review* 70 (February 2002), 51.

Andrews, Peter. "A.C.L.U.—Let There Be Law." *Playboy,* October 1971, 119, 122, 222–224, 226, 228.

Aronson, Amy Beth. "Taking Liberties: Crystal Eastman, Media Ethics and the Exercise of a Free Press." Association for Education in Journalism and Mass Communication, December 22, 1998. http://list.msu.edu/cgi-bin/wa?A2=ind9812D&L=AEJMC&P=1105 (retrieved August 4, 2011).

Atwood, Margaret. *The Handmaid's Tale.* New York: Anchor Books, 1998.

Bailey, Beth. *Sex in the Heartland.* Cambridge: Harvard University Press, 2002.

Baker, Carrie N. *The Women's Movement Against Sexual Harassment.* New York: Cambridge University Press, 2008.

Balkin, J. M. "Free Speech and Hostile Environments." *Columbia Law Review* 99 (December 1999), 2295–2316.

Barss, Patchen. *The Erotic Engine: How Pornography Has Powered Mass Communication, from Gutenberg to Google.* Toronto: Doubleday Canada, 2010.

Baxandall, Rosalynn Fraad. *Words on Fire: The Life and Writing of Elizabeth Gurley Flynn.* New Brunswick, N.J.: Rutgers University Press, 1987.

Bean, Barton. "Pressure for Freedom: The American Civil Liberties Union." Ph.D. diss., Cornell University, 1954.

Beaty, Bart. *Fredric Wertham and the Critique of Mass Culture: A Re-Examination of the Critic Whose Congressional Testimony Sparked the Comics Code.* Jackson: University Press of Mississippi, 2005.

Begos, Kevin, and John Railey. "Sign This or Else . . ." http://extras.journalnow.com/againsttheirwill/parts/two/story2.html (retrieved May 5, 2012).

Bennett, Judith. *History Matters: Patriarchy and the Challenge of Feminism.* Philadelphia: University of Pennsylvania Press, 2006.

Berger, Margaret A. *Litigation on Behalf of Women: A Review for the Ford Foundation*. New York: Ford Foundation, 1980.
Boyd, Nan Alamilla. *Wide Open Town: A History of Queer San Francisco to 1965*. Berkeley: University of California Press, 2003.
Boyer, Paul. *Purity in Print: Book Censorship in America from the Gilded Age to the Computer Age*. Madison: University of Wisconsin Press, 2002.
Breazeale, Kenon. "In Spite of Women: 'Esquire' Magazine and the Construction of the Male Consumer." *Signs* 20, 1 (Autumn 1994), 1–22.
Briggs, Laura. *Reproducing Empire: Race, Sex, Science, and U.S. Imperialism in Puerto Rico*. Berkeley: University of California Press, 2002.
Brisbin, Richard A. "Censorship, Ratings, and Rights: Political Order and Sexual Portrayals in American Movies." *Studies in American Political Development* 16 (Spring 2002), 1–27.
Bronstein, Carolyn. *Battling Pornography: The American Feminist Anti-Pornography Movement, 1976–1986*. New York: Cambridge University Press, 2011.
Brumberg, Joan. *The Body Project: An Intimate History of American Girls*. New York: Vintage, 1997.
Bryden, David P., and Sonja Lengnick. "Rape in the Criminal Justice System." *Journal of Criminal Law and Criminology* 87 (Summer 1997), 1194–1384.
Bullough, Vern. "Lesbianism, Homosexuality, and the American Civil Liberties Union." *Journal of Homosexuality* 13, 1 (Fall 1986), 23–33.
Bullough, Vern, ed. *Before Stonewall: Activists for Gay and Lesbian Rights in Historical Context*. New York: Harrington Park Press, 2002.
Cain, Patricia A. "Litigating for Lesbian and Gay Rights: A Legal History." *Virginia Law Review* 79 (October 1993), 1551–1641.
Camp, Helen C. *Iron in Her Soul: Elizabeth Gurley Flynn and the American Left*. Pullman: Washington State University Press, 1995.
Campbell, Amy Leigh. "Raising the Bar: Ruth Bader Ginsburg and the ACLU Women's Rights Project." *Texas Journal of Women and the Law* 11 (2002), 157–241.
Canaday, Margot. *The Straight State: Sexuality and Citizenship in Twentieth-Century America*. Princeton, N.J.: Princeton University Press, 2009.
"Case Note: The First Amendment and the Right to Hear: *Urofsky v. Allen*." *The Yale Law Journal* 108, 3 (December 1998), 669–676.
Cassidy, Keith. "The Abortion Controversy as a Problem in Contemporary American History: Some Suggestions for Research." *Journal of Policy History* 1, 4 (October 1989), 440–460.
Chauncey, George. *Gay New York: Gender, Urban Culture, and the Making of the Gay Male World, 1890–1940*. New York: Basic Books, 1994.
Chen, Constance. *"The Sex Side of Life": Mary Ware Dennett's Pioneering Battle for Birth Control and Sex Education*. New York: New Press, 1996.
Chesler, Ellen. *Woman of Valor: Margaret Sanger and the Birth Control Movement in America*. New York: Simon and Schuster, 1992.
Cochran, Augustus B., III. *Sexual Harassment and the Law: The Michelle Vinson Case*. Lawrence: University Press of Kansas, 2004.
Cohen, Lizbeth. *A Consumers' Republic: The Politics of Mass Consumption in Postwar America*. New York: Vintage, 2003.
Connelly, Matthew James. *Fatal Misconception: The Struggle to Control World Population*. Cambridge: Harvard University Press, 2008.
Cook, Blanche Wiesen. "The Radical Women of Greenwich Village: From Crystal Eastman to Eleanor Roosevelt." In *Greenwich Village Culture and Counterculture*, ed. Rick Beard and Leslie Cohen Berlowitz. New Brunswick, N.J.: Rutgers University Press, 1993, 229–257.
Corber, Robert J. *Homosexuality in Cold War America: Resistance and the Crisis of Masculinity*. Durham, N.C.: Duke University Press, 1997.
Corliss, Richard. "That Old Feeling: When Porno Was Chic." *Time*, March 29, 2005.

Cottrell, Robert. *Roger Nash Baldwin and the American Civil Liberties Union*. New York: Columbia University Press, 2000.

Cowan, Ruth B. "Women's Rights Through Litigation: An Examination of the American Civil Liberties Union Women's Rights Project, 1971–1976." *Columbia Human Rights Law Review* 8 (1976), 373–412.

Craig, John. "'The Sex Side of Life': The Obscenity Trials of Mary Ware Dennett." *Frontiers* 15 (1995), 145–166.

Crenner, Christopher. *Private Practice: In the Early Twentieth-Century Medical Office of Dr. Richard Cabot*. Baltimore: Johns Hopkins University Press, 2005.

Critchlow, Donald T. *Intended Consequences: Birth Control, Abortion, and the Federal Government in Modern America*. New York: Oxford University Press, 1999.

Cross, Gary. *Kids' Stuff: Toys and the Changing World of American Childhood*. Cambridge: Harvard University Press, 1997.

D'Emilio, John. *Sexual Politics, Sexual Communities: The Making of a Homosexual Minority in the United States, 1940–1970*. Chicago: University of Chicago Press, 1983.

Dawley, Alan. *Changing the World: American Progressives in War and Revolution*. Princeton, N.J.: Princeton University Press, 2003.

Deery, Phillip. "'A Divided Soul'? The Cold War Odyssey of O. John Rogge." *Cold War History* 6, 2 (May 2006), 177–204.

Denno, Deborah W. "Why the Model Penal Code's Sexual Offense Provisions Should be Pulled and Replaced." *Ohio State Journal of Criminal Law* 1 (2003), 207–218.

Dines, Gail. *Pornland: How Porn Has Hijacked our Sexuality*. Boston: Beacon Press, 2010.

Dorr, Lisa Lindquist. *White Women, Rape, and the Power of Race in Virginia, 1900–1960*. Chapel Hill: University of North Carolina Press, 2004.

Dorsen, Norman. "In Memory of Tom Emerson." *Yale Law Journal* 101, 2 (November 1991), 317–320.

Douglas, Emily Taft. *Margaret Sanger: Pioneer of the Future*. New York: Holt, Rinehart and Winston, 1970.

Dowbiggin, Ian. *The Sterilization Movement and Global Fertility in the Twentieth Century*. New York: Oxford University Press, 2008.

Downs, Donald Alexander. *The New Politics of Pornography*. Chicago: University of Chicago Press, 1999.

Drinnon, Richard. *Rebel in Paradise: A Biography of Emma Goldman*. Chicago: University of Chicago Press, 1961.

Duggan, Lisa, and Nan D. Hunter. *Sex Wars: Sexual Dissent and Political Culture*. New York: Routledge, 1995.

Dukart, Jennifer Yatskis. "Geduldig Reborn: Hibbs as a Success [sic] of Justice Ruth Bader Ginsburg's Sex-Discrimination Strategy." *California Law Review* 93 (March 2005), 541–586.

Dunning, John. *On the Air: The Encyclopedia of Old-Time Radio*. New York: Oxford University Press, 1998.

Durham, M. Gigi. *The Lolita Effect: The Media Sexualization of Young Girls and What We Can Do about It*. New York: Overlook, 2009.

Eberhardt, Charles N. "Note: Integrating the Right of Association with the *Bellotti* Right to Hear." *Cornell Law Review* 72 (November 1986), 159–194.

Eberly, Rosa A. *Citizen Critics: Literary Public Spheres*. Urbana: University of Illinois Press, 2000.

Edwards, David M. "Politics and Pornography: A Comparison of the Findings of the President's Commission and the Meese Commission and the Resulting Response." http://home.earthlink.net/~durangodave/html/writing/Censorship.htm (retrieved July 20, 2011).

Edwardson, Mickie. "James Lawrence Fly's Fight for a Free Marketplace of Ideas." *American Journalism* 14, 1 (Winter 1997), 19–39.

Ehrenreich, Barbara. *The Hearts of Men: American Dreams and the Flight from Commitment*. New York: Anchor Books, 1987.

Epstein, Lee. "The Impact of the ACLU Reproductive Freedom Project." Paper presented at the Midwest Political Science Association Meeting, April 15–18, 1981, Cincinnati, Ohio. http://epstein.law.northwestern.edu/research/conferencepapers.1981MPSA.pdf (retrieved July 20, 2010).

Eskridge, William N., Jr. "Challenging the Apartheid of the Closet: Establishing Conditions for Lesbian and Gay Intimacy, Nomos, and Citizenship, 1961–1981." *Hofstra Law Review* 25 (1997), 817–970.

Eskridge, William N., Jr. *Dishonorable Passions: Sodomy Laws in America, 1861–2003*. New York: Viking, 2008.

Eskridge, William N., Jr. "Privacy Jurisprudence and the Apartheid of the Closet, 1946–1961." *Florida State University Law Review* 24 (1997), 703–840.

Esterberg, Kristin Gay. "From Illness to Action: Conceptions of Homosexuality in *The Ladder*, 1956–1965." *Journal of Sex Research* 27, 1 (February 1990), 65–80.

Estrich, Susan. "Rape." *Yale Law Journal* 85, 6 (May 1986), 1087–1184.

Etzioni, Amitai. *The Limits of Privacy*. New York: Basic Books, 1999.

Evans, Sara. *Tidal Wave: How Women Changed America at Century's End*. New York: Free Press, 2003.

Falk, Candace. *Love, Anarchy, and Emma Goldman*. New York: Holt, Rinehart and Winston, 1984.

Finan, Christopher M. *Alfred E. Smith: The Happy Warrior*. New York: Hill and Wang, 2002.

Fishbein, Leslie. "Freud and the Radicals: The Sexual Revolution Comes to Greenwich Village." *Canadian Review of American Studies* 12, 2 (Fall 1981), 173–189.

Fones-Wolf, Elizabeth. "Defending Listeners' Rights: Labour and Media Reform in Postwar America." *Canadian Journal of Communication* 31, 3 (2006), 499–518.

Fowler, Dorothy Ganfield. *Unmailable: Congress and the post office*. Athens: University of Georgia Press, 1977.

Fowler, Gene, and Bill Crawford. *Quacks, Yodelers, Pitchmen, Psychics, and Other Amazing Broadcasters of the American Airwaves*. Austin: University of Texas Press, 2002.

Fox, Richard Wightman, and T. J. Jackson Lears, eds. *The Culture of Consumption: Critical Essays in American History*. New York: Pantheon, 1983.

Fraterrigo, Elizabeth. *Playboy and the Making of the Good Life in Modern America*. New York: Oxford University Press, 2009.

Freedman, Estelle, and John D'Emilio. *Intimate Matters: A History of Sexuality in America*. 2nd ed. Chicago: University of Chicago Press, 1997.

Friedman, Andrea. *Prurient Interests: Gender, Democracy, and Obscenity in New York City, 1909–1945*. New York: Columbia University Press, 2000.

Gainer, Ronald L. "Federal Criminal Code Reform: Past and Future." *Buffalo Criminal Law Review* 2 (1998), 45–93.

Gale, Mary Ellen, and Nadine Strossen. "The Real ACLU." *Yale Journal of Law and Feminism* 2, 1 (Fall 1989), 161–187.

Gallagher, Dorothy. *All the Right Enemies: The Life and Murder of Carlo Tresca*. New Brunswick, N.J.: Rutgers University Press, 1988.

Gallo, Marcia M. *Different Daughters: A History of the Daughters of Bilitis and the Rise of the Lesbian Rights Movement*. New York: Carroll and Graf, 2006.

Galvin, Harriett R. "Shielding Rape Victims in the State and Federal Courts: A Proposal for the Second Decade." *Minnesota Law Review* 70 (April 1986), 763–916.

Garey, Diane. *Defending Everybody: A History of the American Civil Liberties Union*. New York: TV Books, 1998.

Garrow, David. *Liberty and Sexuality: The Right to Privacy and the Making of Roe v. Wade*. New York: Macmillan, 1994.

Gathorne-Hardy, Jonathan. *Kinsey: Sex the Measure of All Things*. Bloomington: Indiana University Press, 1998.

Geiger, Louis G. "Joseph W. Folk v. Edward Butler, St. Louis, 1902." *Journal of Southern History* 28, 4 (November 1962), 438–449.

George, Tracey E., and Lee Epstein. "Women's Rights Litigation in the 1980s: More of the Same?" *Judicature* 74, 6 (April–May 1991), 314–321.

Gerson, Ben. "Renaissance Woman." *National Law Journal* 5, 3 (September 27, 1982).

Gertz, Elmer, and Felice Flanery Lewis. *Henry Miller: Years of Trial and Triumph, 1962–1964.* Carbondale: Southern Illinois University Press, 1978.

Gertzman, Jay A. "The Strange Story of Samuel Roth: The Demon in Galicia, Its Exorcism and What Happened After." *Jewish Magazine*, April 2009. http://www.jewishmag.com/132mag/demons_roth/demons_roth.htm (retrieved January 16, 2012).

Gibbons, Don C. "Say, Whatever Became of Maurice Parmelee, Anyway?" *Sociological Quarterly* 15 (Summer 1974), 405–416.

Gilbert, James. *A Cycle of Outrage: America's Reaction to the Juvenile Delinquent in the 1950s.* New York: Oxford University Press, 1986.

Goldstein, Ben, ed. "Tenth Annual Review of Gender and Sexuality Law: Criminal Law Chapter: Rape, Sexual Assault and Evidentiary Matters." *Georgetown Journal of Gender and the Law* 10, 2 (2009), 457–480.

Goodrich, Herbert F., and Paul A. Wolkin. *The Story of the American Law Institute, 1923–1961.* St. Paul: American Law Institute Publishers, 1961.

Gordon, Linda. *The Moral Property of Women: A History of Birth Control Politics in America.* Chicago: University of Illinois Press, 2002.

Gordon, Linda. *Woman's Body, Woman's Right: Birth Control in America.* New York: Penguin, 1990.

Graber, Mark. *Transforming Free Speech: The Ambiguous Legacy of Civil Libertarianism.* Berkeley: University of California Press, 1991.

Graham, Otis, Jr. *Toward a Planned Society: From Roosevelt to Nixon.* New York: Oxford University Press, 1976.

Greenhouse, Linda. "Celebrating the Jurisprudence of Justice Ruth Bader Ginsberg [*sic*]: Learning to Listen to Ruth Bader Ginsburg." *New York City Law Review* 7 (Fall 2004), 213.

Greenhouse, Linda, and Reva B. Siegel, eds. *Before Roe v. Wade: Voices that Shaped the Abortion Debate Before the Supreme Court's Ruling.* New York: Kaplan, 2010.

Gruber, Aya. "Rape, Feminism, and the War on Crime." *Washington Law Review* 84 (November 2009), 581–658.

Gurstein, Rochelle. *The Repeal of Reticence: America's Cultural and Legal Struggles over Free Speech, Obscenity, Sexual Liberation, and Modern Art.* New York: Hill and Wang, 1996.

Haag, Pamela. *Consent: Sexual Rights and the Transformation of American Liberalism.* Ithaca, N.Y.: Cornell University Press, 1999.

Hartmann, Susan. *The Other Feminists: Activists in the Liberal Establishment.* New Haven: Yale University Press, 1998.

Hasday, Jill Elaine. "Contest and Consent: A Legal History of Marital Rape." *California Law Review* 88 (2000), 1373–1505.

Haxton, David. "Comment: Rape Shield Statutes: Constitutional Despite Unconstitutional Exclusions of Evidence." *Wisconsin Law Review* 1985 (September–October 1985), 1219.

Herzog, Dagmar. *Sex in Crisis: The New Sexual Revolution and the Future of American Politics.* New York: Basic Books, 2008.

Hill, John Lawrence. "The Constitutional Status of Morals Legislation." *Kentucky Law Journal* 98 (2009–2010), 1–66.

Hixson, Richard. *Pornography and the Justices: The Supreme Court and the Intractable Obscenity Problem.* Carbondale: Southern Illinois University Press, 1996.

Hixson, Walter L. *Parting the Curtain: Propaganda, Culture, and the Cold War, 1945–1961.* New York: St. Martin's Griffin, 1997.

Hocking, William Ernest. *Freedom of the Press: A Framework of Principle.* Chicago: University of Chicago Press, 1947.

Hodgdon, Tim. "The Chicago Women's Liberation Union: On the Cutting Edge of Protest Against Sexual Objectification." http://www.uic.edu/orgs/cwluherstory/CWLUAbout/abdoc5.html (retrieved July 10, 2011).

Hoffman, Brian. "Making Private Parts Public: American Nudism and the Politics of Nakedness, 1929–1963." Ph.D. diss., University of Illinois, Champaign-Urbana, 2009.

Houchin, John H. *Censorship of the American Theatre in the Twentieth Century.* New York: Cambridge University Press, 2003.

Hull, N. E. H. "Restatement and Reform: A New Perspective on the Origins of the American Law Institute." *Law and History Review* 8, 1 (Spring 1990), 55–96.

Hull, N. E. H., and Peter Charles Hoffer. *Roe v. Wade: The Abortion Rights Controversy in American History.* Lawrence: University Press of Kansas, 2001.

Ilfeld, Fred, Jr., and Roger Lauer. *Social Nudism in America.* New Haven, Conn.: College and University Press, 1964.

Irvine, Mori. "Alternative Dispute Resolutions Symposium: The Lady or the Tiger: Dispute Resolution in the Federal Courts." *University of Toledo Law Review* 27 (Summer 1996), 795–804.

Jacquet, Catherine. "The Giles-Johnson Case and the Changing Politics of Sexual Violence in the 1960s United States." Forthcoming, *Journal of Women's History.*

Jaffe, David M. "Walking the Constitutional Tightrope: Balancing Title VII Hostile Environment Sexual Harassment Claims with Free Speech Defenses." *Minnesota Law Review* 80 (April 1996), 979.

James, Marlise. *The People's Lawyers.* New York: Holt, Rinehart, and Winston, 1973.

Jeffrey, Linda. "Restoring Legal Protections for Women and Children: A Historical Analysis of the States' Criminal Codes." *The State Factor: Jeffersonian Principles in Action* (American Legislative Exchange Council), April 2004. http://www.drjudithreisman.com/archives/alec0404.pdf (retrieved May 5, 2012).

Jeffrey, Linda, and Colonel Ronald D. Ray. "A History of the American Law Institute's Model Penal Code: The Kinsey Reports' Influence on 'Science-based' Legal Reform, 1923–2003—A Work in Progress." Unpublished manuscript, First Principles, Inc., August 2003.

Jensen, Robert. *Getting Off: Pornography and the End of Masculinity.* Cambridge, Mass.: South End Press, 2007.

Johnson, David K. *The Lavender Scare: The Cold War Persecution of Gays and Lesbians in the Federal Government.* Chicago: University of Chicago Press, 2004.

Johnson, Donald. *The Challenge to American Freedoms: World War I and the Rise of the American Civil Liberties Union.* Lexington: University Press of Kentucky, 1963.

Johnson, John W. *Griswold v. Connecticut: Birth Control and the Constitutional Right of Privacy.* Lawrence: University Press of Kansas, 2005.

Johnson, Peter. "Pornography Drives Technology: Why Not to Censor the Internet." *Federal Communications Law Journal* 49 (November 1996), 217–226.

Jones, James H. *Alfred C. Kinsey: A Public/Private Life.* New York: Norton, 1997.

Josephson, Matthew, and Hannah Josephson. *Al Smith: Hero of the Cities.* Boston: Houghton Mifflin, 1969.

Jowett, Garth, ed. *Children and the Movies: Media Influence and the Payne Fund Controversy.* New York: Cambridge University Press, 1996.

Karner, Jessica M. "Political Speech, Sexual Harassment, and a Captive Workforce." *California Law Review* 83 (1995), 637–673.

Katz, Al. "The *Tropic of Cancer* Trials: The Problem of Relevant Moral and Artistic Controversy." *Midway* (Chicago), January 1, 1969, 99–125.

Kaufman, Alan, Neil Ortenberg, and Barney Rosset, eds. *The Outlaw Bible of American Literature.* New York: Thunder's Mouth Press, 2004.

Kennedy, David. *Birth Control in America: The Career of Margaret Sanger.* New Haven: Yale University Press, 1970.

Kielbowicz, Richard. "Origins of the Junk-Mail Controversy: A Media Battle Over Advertising and Postal Policy." *Journal of Policy History* 5, 2 (1993), 248–272.

Klein, Marty. *America's War on Sex: The Attack on Law, Lust and Liberty.* Westport, Conn.: Praeger, 2008.

Kluchin, Rebecca M. *Fit to Be Tied: Sterilization* and *Reproductive Rights in America, 1950–1980.* New Brunswick, N.J.: Rutgers University Press, 2009.

Kunzel, Regina. *Criminal Intimacy: Prison and the Uneven History of Modern American Sexuality.* Chicago: University of Chicago Press, 2008.

Kutulas, Judy. *The American Civil Liberties Union and the Making of Modern Liberalism, 1930–1960.* Chapel Hill: University of North Carolina Press, 2006.

Labi, Nadya. "A Man against the Machine." *The Law School Magazine: The New York University School of Law,* Autumn 2007, http://blogs.law.nyu.edu/magazine/2007/a-man-against- the-machine/ (retrieved May 30, 2012).

Lamson, Peggy. *Roger Baldwin: Founder of the American Civil Liberties Union. A Portrait.* Boston: Houghton Mifflin, 1976.

Law, Sylvia A. "Harriet Fleischl Pilpel: A Tribute." *Family Planning Perspectives* 23, 4 (July–August 1991), 182–183.

Lee, Chana Kai. *For Freedom's Sake: The Life of Fannie Lou Hamer.* Urbana: University of Illinois Press, 1999.

Leff, Leonard J., and Jerold L. Simmons. *The Dame in the Kimono: Hollywood, Censorship, and the Production Code.* Lexington: University Press of Kentucky, 2001.

Leis, Betsy. *A History of ACLU in Ohio.* Cleveland: ACLU of Ohio, 1995.

Lester, Hugh C. *Godiva Rides Again: A History of the Nudist Movement.* New York: Vantage Press, 1968.

Lester, Joan Steinau. *Eleanor Holmes Norton: Fire in My Soul.* New York: Atria Books, 2003.

Levin, Diane E., and Jean Kilbourne. *So Sexy So Soon: The New Sexualized Childhood and What Parents Can Do to Protect Their Kids.* New York: Random House, 2009.

Levinson, Nan. *Outspoken: Free Speech Stories.* Berkeley: University of California Press, 2006.

Levy, Ariel. *Female Chauvinist Pigs: Women and the Rise of Raunch Culture.* New York: Free Press, 2006.

Lewis, Anthony. *Freedom for the Thought That We Hate: A Biography of the First Amendment.* New York: Basic Books, 2007.

Lewis, Jon. *Hollywood v. Hard Core: How the Struggle Over Censorship Saved the Modern Film Industry.* New York: New York University Press, 2002.

Linsky, Mark. "The Most Critical Opinion: Sex Offenses and Castration in San Diego, 1938–1975." *Journal of San Diego History* 35, 4 (Fall 1989). https://www.sandiegohistory.org/journal/89fall/most.htm (retrieved July 5, 2010).

Long, Carolyn N. *Mapp v. Ohio: Guarding Against Unreasonable Searches and Seizures.* Lawrence: University Press of Kansas, 2006.

Lord, Alexandra M. *Condom Nation: The U.S. Government's Sex Education Campaign from World War I to the Internet.* Baltimore, Md.: The Johns Hopkins University Press, 2010.

Mackinnon, Catharine A. *Feminism Unmodified: Discourses on Life and Law.* Cambridge: Harvard University Press, 1987.

Markmann, Charles Lam. *The Noblest Cry: A History of the American Civil Liberties Union.* New York: St. Martin's Press, 1965.

Marsh, Jeanne C., Alison Geist, and Nathan Caplan. *Rape and the Limits of Law Reform.* Boston: Auburn House, 1982.

Martin, Jay. "'The King of Smut': Henry Miller's Tragical History." *Antioch Review* 35, 4 (1977), 342–367.

May, Elaine Tyler. *Homeward Bound: American Families in the Cold War Era.* New York: Basic Books, 1988.

May, Lary. *The Big Tomorrow: Hollywood and the Politics of the American Way.* Chicago: University of Chicago Press, 2000.

McChesney, Richard W. *Telecomunications, Mass Media, and Democracy: The Battle for the Control of America's Broadcasting Industry, 1928–1935.* New York: Oxford University Press, 1995.

McClosky, Herbert, and Alida Brill. *Dimensions of Tolerance: What Americans Believe About Civil Liberties.* New York: Russell Sage Foundation, 1983.

McCord, Brian. "An American Avant-Garde: Grove Press, 1951–1986." Ph.D. diss., Syracuse University, 2002.

McDougal, W. Scott, et al. "Hugh Cabot—1872–1945: Genitourinary Surgeon, Futurist, and Medical Statesman." *Urology* 50, 4 (1997), 648–654.

McFarland, Gerald W. *Inside Greenwich Village: A New York City Neighborhood, 1898–1918.* Amherst: University of Massachusetts Press, 2001.

McGerr, Michael. *A Fierce Discontent: The Rise and Fall of the Progressive Movement in America.* New York: Oxford University Press, 2003.

McGuire, Danielle L. *At the Dark End of the Street: Black Women, Rape, and Resistance—A New History of the Civil Rights Movement from Rosa Parks to the Rise of Black Power.* New York: Knopf, 2010.

Meehan, Mary. "ACLU v. Unborn Children." *Human Life Review*, Winter 2001. http://groups.csail.mit.edu/mac/users/rauch/nvp/consistent/aclu.html (retrieved June 1, 2010).

Meeker, Martin. "Behind the Mask of Respectability: Reconsidering the Mattachine Society and Male Homophile Practice, 1950s and 1960s." *Journal of the History of Sexuality* 10, 1 (January 2001), 78–116.

Meltsner, Michael. *Cruel and Unusual: The Supreme Court and Capital Punishment.* New York: Random House, 1973.

Mezey, Susan Gluck. *Queers in Court: Gay Rights Law and Public Policy.* New York: Rowman and Littlefield, 2007.

Michigan Supreme Court Historical Society. "*People v. Hildabridle*: Voelker and the Art of Crafting an Opinion." *The Verdict of History: The Mid-Twentieth Century: 1940–1970*, Supplement 2009, 6–10.

Munson, Wayne. *All Talk: The Talkshow in Media Culture.* Philadelphia: Temple University Press, 1993.

Murphy, Paul L. *The Meaning of Freedom of Speech: First Amendment Freedoms from Wilson to FDR.* Westport, Conn.: Greenwood Press, 1972.

Murphy, Paul L. *World War I and the Origin of Civil Liberties in the United States.* New York: Norton, 1979.

Nadasen, Premilla. *Welfare Warriors: The Welfare Rights Movement in the United States.* New York: Routledge, 2005.

Nelles, Walter. *A Liberal in Wartime: The Education of Albert DeSilver.* New York: Norton, 1940.

Nelson, Adam R. *Education and Democracy: The Meaning of Alexander Meiklejohn, 1872–1964.* Madison: University of Wisconsin, 2009.

Nelson, Jennifer. *Women of Color and the Reproductive Rights Movement.* New York: New York University Press, 2003.

Nevitt, Peter K. "The Legal Aspects of Nudism." *Journal of Criminal Law and Criminology* 41, 1 (May–June, 1950), 57–61.

Nielsen, Laura Beth. *License to Harass: Law, Hierarchy, and Offensive Public Speech.* Princeton, N.J.: Princeton University Press, 2004.

Nussbaum, Martha C. "What's Privacy Got to Do With It? A Comparative Approach to the Feminist Critique." In *Women and the United States Constitution: History, Interpretation, and Practice*, ed. Sibyl A. Schwarzenbach and Patricia Smith (New York: Columbia University Press, 2003), 153–175.

Nyberg, Amy Kiste. *Seal of Approval: The History of the Comics Code.* Jackson: University Press of Mississippi, 1998.

O'Connor, Thomas F. "The National Organization for Decent Literature: A Phase in American Catholic Censorship." *Library Quarterly* 65, 4 (1995), 386–414.

O'Harrow, Robert, Jr. *No Place to Hide: Behind the Scenes of Our Emerging Surveillance Society.* New York: Free Press, 2005.

O'Neill, William L. *The Last Romantic: A Life of Max Eastman.* New York: Oxford University Press, 1978.

Ogle, Stephanie Francis. "Anna Louise Strong: Progressive and Propagandist." Ph.D. diss., University of Washington, 1981.

Opplinger, Patrice A. *Girls Gone Skank: The Sexualization of Girls in American Culture.* Jefferson, N.C.: McFarland, 2008.

Osgerby, Bill. *Playboys in Paradise: Masculinity, Youth, and Leisure-Style in Modern America.* Oxford: Berg, 2002.

Paul, Pamela. *Pornified: How Pornography is Transforming Our Lives, Our Relationships, and Our Families.* New York: Times Books, 2005.

Payne, Jack B. "The Changing Right to Read: American Society, the Courts, and the Problem of Literary 'Decency.'" M.A. thesis, University of Wyoming, 1951.

Pernicone, Nunzione. *Carlo Tresca: Portrait of a Rebel.* New York: Palgrave Macmillan, 2005.

Piott, Steven L. *Holy Joe: Joseph W. Folk and the Missouri Idea.* Columbia: University of Missouri Press, 1997.

Pitzulo, Carrie. *Bachelors and Bunnies: The Sexual Politics of Playboy.* Chicago: University of Chicago Press, 2011.

Pringle, Henry F. *Alfred E. Smith: A Critical Study.* New York: Macy-Masius, 1927.

Rabban, David. *Free Speech in its Forgotten Years.* New York: Cambridge University Press, 1997.

Randall, Richard. *Censorship of the Movies: The Social and Political Control of a Mass Medium.* Madison: University of Wisconsin Press, 1968.

Redlich, Norman. "Are There 'Certain Rights...Retained by the People?'" *New York University Law Review* 37 (November 1962), 787–812.

Reeves, Major Shane R. "Time to Fine-Tune Military Rule of Evidence 412." *Military Law Review* 196 (2008), 47–90.

Reisman, Judith A. *Kinsey: Crimes and Consequences.* Arlington: Institute for Media Education, 1998.

Rembar, Charles. *The End of Obscenity: The Trials of Lady Chatterley, Tropic of Cancer, and Fanny Hill by the Lawyer Who Defended Them.* New York: Harper and Row, 1968.

Richards, David A. J. *The Sodomy Cases: Bowers v. Hardwick and Lawrence v. Texas.* Lawrence: University Press of Kansas, 2009.

Rifas, Leonard. "'Especially Dr. Hilde L. Mosse': Wertham's Research Collaborator." November 11, 2005, unpublished manuscript in author's possession.

Robbins, Wayne Lindsey, Jr. "When Two Liberal Values Collide in an Era of 'Political Correctness': First Amendment Protection as a Check on Speech-Based Title VII Hostile Environment Claims." *Baylor Law Review* 47 (Summer 1995), 789–814.

Roberts, Dorothy. *Killing the Black Body: Race, Reproduction, and the Meaning of Liberty.* New York: Vintage, 1998.

Robins, Louise S. *Censorship and the American Library: The American Library Association's Response to Threats to Intellectual Freedom, 1939–1969.* Westport, Conn.: Greenwood Press, 1996.

Robinson, Paul H., and Markus D. Dubber. "The American Model Penal Code: A Brief Overview." *New Criminal Law Review* 10, 3 (Summer 2007), 319–341.

Rosen, Jeffrey. *The Unwanted Gaze: The Destruction of Privacy in America.* New York: Random House, 2000.

Rosen, Robyn L. *Reproductive Health, Reproductive Rights: Reformers and the Politics of Maternal Welfare,* 1917–1940. Columbus: Ohio State University Press, 2003.

Ross, Chad. *Naked Germany: Health, Race, and the Nation.* New York: Berg, 2005.

Rupp, Leila. "Feminism and the Sexual Revolution in the Early Twentieth Century: The Case of Doris Stevens." 15, 2 Feminist Studies (Summer 1989), 289–309.

Ryan, Rebecca M. "The Sex Right: A Legal History of the Marital Rape Exemption." *Law and Social Inquiry* 20, 4 (Autumn 1955), 941–1001.

Salisbury, Harrison E. "The Strange Correspondence of Morris Ernst and John Edgar Hoover, 1939–1964." *The Nation,* December 1, 1984, 575–577.

Sarat, Austin. "Abortion and the Courts: Uncertain Boundaries of Law and Politics." In *American Politics and Public Policy: Seven Case Studies*, ed. Allan P. Sindler. Washington, D.C.: Congressional Quarterly Press, 1982.

Sarracino, Carmine, and Kevin Scott. *The Porning of America: The Rise of Porn Culture, What It Means, and Where We Go from Here*. Boston: Beacon Press, 2009.

Schaefer, Eric. "Plain Brown Wrapper: Adult Films for the Home Market, 1930–1969." In *Looking Past the Screen: Case Studies in American Film History and Method*, ed. Jon Lewis and Eric Smoodin. Durham, N.C.: Duke University Press, 2007.

Schauer, Frederick. "The Speech-ing of Sexual Harassment." In *Directions in Sexual Harassment Law*, ed. Catharine A. MacKinnon and Reva B. Siegel. New Haven: Yale University Press, 2004.

Schmidt, Cynthia Ann Bolger. "Socialist-Feminism: Max Eastman, Floyd Dell, and Crystal Eastman." Ph.D. diss., Marquette University, 1983.

Schneider, Elizabeth. "The Synergy of Equality and Privacy in Women's Rights." *University of Chicago Legal Forum* 2002, 137–154.

Schoen, Johanna. *Choice and Coercion: Birth Control, Sterilization, and Abortion in Public Health and Welfare*. Chapel Hill: University of North Carolina Press, 2005.

Schroeder, Andrew B. "Keeping Police out of the Bedroom: Justice John Marshall Harlan, *Poe v. Ullman*, and the Limits of Conservative Privacy." *Virginia Law Review* 86, 5 (August 2000), 1045–1094.

Schwarz, Judith. *Radical Feminists of Heterodoxy: Greenwich Village, 1912–1940*. Lebanon, N.H.: New Victoria Publishers, 1982.

Shaw, Elton Raymond. *The Body Taboo: Its Origin, Effect, and Modern Denial*. Washington, D.C.: Shaw, 1937.

Silverman, Joel Matthew. "Pursuing Celebrity, Ensuing Masculinity: Morris Ernst, Obscenity, and the Search for Recognition." Ph.D. diss. University of Texas at Austin, 2006.

Simon, Jonathan. *Governing Through Crime: How the War on Crime Transformed American Democracy and Created a Culture of Fear*. New York: Oxford University Press, 2007.

Solinger, Rickie. *Beggars and Choosers: How the Politics of Choice Shapes Adoption, Abortion, and Welfare in the United States*. New York: Hill and Wang, 2001.

Solinger, Rickie. *Wake Up Little Susie: Single Pregnancy and Race Before Roe v. Wade*. New York: Routledge, 1992.

Sommerville, Diane Miller. *Rape and Race in the Nineteenth-Century South*. Chapel Hill: University of North Carolina Press, 2004.

Spohn, Cassia, and Julie Horney. *Rape Law Reform: A Grassroots Revolution and Its Impact*. New York: Plenum Press, 1992.

Stansell, Christine. *American Moderns: Bohemian New York and the Creation of a New Century*. New York: Henry Holt, 2000.

Starr, Paul. *The Creation of the Media: Political Origins of Modern Communications*. New York: Basic Books, 2004.

Steel, John M. "Comments: Freedom to Hear: A Political Justification of the First Amendment." *Washington Law Review* 46 (1971), 323–334.

Stein, Marc. *Sexual Injustice: Supreme Court Decisions from Griswold to Roe*. Chapel Hill: University of North Carolina Press, 2010.

Stevens, Kenneth R. "*United States v. 31 Photographs*: Dr. Alfred C. Kinsey and Obscenity Law." *Indiana Magazine of History* 71, 4 (December 1975), 299–318.

Stewart, Potter. "The Road to *Mapp v. Ohio* and Beyond: The Origins, Development and Future of the Exclusionary Rule in Search-and-Seizure Cases." *Columbia Law Review* 83, 6 (October 1983), 1365–1404.

Strong, Tracy B., and Helene Keyssar. *Right in Her Soul: The Life of Anna Louise Strong*. New York: Random House, 1983.

Strossen, Nadine. "The American Civil Liberties Union and Women's Rights." *New York University Law Review* 66 (December 1991), 1940–1961.

Strub, Whitney. "Perversion for Profit: The Politics of Obscenity and Pornography in the Postwar United States." Ph.D. diss., University of California, Los Angeles, 2006.

Swiger, Elinor Porter. *Women Lawyers at Work*. New York: Julian Messner, 1978.

Talese, Gay. *Thy Neighbor's Wife*. Garden City, N.Y.: Doubleday, 1980.

Taylor, Joan Kennedy. "Sexual Harassment and the First Amendment." *CommLaw Connspectus* 4 (1996), 189.

Thomas, Geoffrey L. "The Listener's Right to Hear in Broadcasting." *Stanford Law Review* 22, 4 (April 1970), 863–902.

Thomas, Louisa. "The Most Dangerous Man in Publishing." *Newsweek*, December 6, 2008.

Thomison, Dennis. *A History of the American Library Association, 1876–1972*. Chicago: American Library Association, 1978.

Tilley, Cristina Carmody. "A Feminist Repudiation of Rape Shield Laws." *Drake Law Review* 51 (2002), 45.

Tone, Andrea. *Devices and Desires: A History of Contraceptives in America*. New York: Hill and Wang, 2001.

Torgesen, Lara. "N.C. Eugenics Survivors Seek Justice: The Ultimate Betrayal." http://www.indyweek.com/indyweek/nc-eugenics-survivors-seek-justice/Content?oid=1330583 (retrieved July 10, 2011).

Toro, Amy. "Standing Up for Listeners' Rights: A History of Public Participation at the Federal Communications Commission." Ph.D. diss., University of California, Berkeley, 2000.

Trimberger, Ellen Kay. "Women in the Old and New Left: the Evolution of a Politics of Personal Life." *Feminist Studies* 5, 3 (Autumn, 1979), 432–450.

Volokh, Eugene. "How Harassment Law Restricts Free Speech." *Rutgers Law Review* 47 (1995), 563.

Voss, Carl Hermann. *Rabbi and Minister: The Friendship of Stephen S. Wise and John Haynes Holmes*. New York: Association Press, 1964.

Wagner, Dana R. "The First Amendment and the Right to Hear: *Urofsky v. Allen*." *Yale Law Journal* 108, 3 (December 1998), 669–676.

Walker, Samuel. *Hate Speech: The History of an American Controversy*. Lincoln: University of Nebraska Press, 1994.

Walker, Samuel. *In Defense of American Liberties: A History of the ACLU*. New York: Oxford University Press, 1990.

Ward, Martha C. *Poor Women, Powerful Men: America's Great Experiment in Family Planning*. Boulder: Westview Press, 1986.

Ward, Patricia Spain. "The Medical Brothers Cabot: Of Truth and Consequence." *Harvard Medical Alumni Review* 56, 4 (1982), 30–39.

Watkins, Elizabeth Siegel. *On the Pill: A Social History of Oral Contraceptives, 1950–1970*. Baltimore: Johns Hopkins University Press, 1998.

Weigand, Kate, and Daniel Horowitz, "Dorothy Kenyon: Feminist Organizing, 1919–1963." *Journal of Women's History* 14, 2 (Summer 2002), 126–131.

Weinrib, Laura. "The Sex Side of Civil Liberties: United States v. Dennett and the Changing Face of Free Speech." *Law and History Review* 30 (2012), 325–386.

Weisberg, Jonathan T. "In Control of her Own Destiny: Catherine G. Roraback and the Privacy Principle." *Yale Law Report*, Winter 2004, 40–43.

Weitzer, Ronald. "Prostitutes' Rights in the United States: The Failure of a Movement." *Sociological Quarterly* 32, 1 (Spring 1991), 23–41.

Wetzsteon, Ross. *Republic of Dreams, Greenwich Village: The American Bohemia, 1910–1960*. New York: Simon and Schuster, 2002.

Weyr, Thomas. *Reaching for Paradise: The Playboy Vision of America*. New York: Times Books, 1978.

Wheeler, Leigh Ann. *Against Obscenity: Reform and the Politics of Womanhood in America, 1873–1935*. Baltimore: Johns Hopkins University Press, 2004.

Wheeler, Leigh Ann. "Harriet Pilpel: General Counsel, ACLU." In *Yale Biographical Dictionary of American Law*, ed. Roger Newman. New Haven: Yale University Press, 2009, 427–428.

Whitfield, Stephen. *A Death in the Delta*. Boston: Johns Hopkins University Press, 1991.

Williams, John Alexander. *Turning to Nature in Germany: Hiking, Nudism, and Conservation, 1900–1940*. Stanford, Calif.: Stanford University Press, 2008.

Witham, Barry B. "The Play Jury." *Educational Theatre Journal* 24, 4 (December 1972), 430–435.

Witt, John Fabian. *Patriots and Cosmopolitans: Hidden Histories of American Law*. Cambridge: Harvard University Press, 2007.

Wittern-Keller, Laura. *Freedom of the Screen: Legal Challenges to State Film Censorship, 1915–1981*. Lexington: University Press of Kentucky, 2008.

Wood, Brett. *Forbidden Fruit: The Golden Age of the Exploitation Film*. Baltimore: Midnight Marquee Press, 1999.

Wyatt, Justin. "The Stigma of X: Adult Cinema and the Institution of the MPAA Rating System." In *Controlling Hollywood: Censorship and Regulation in the Studio Era*, ed. Matthew Bernstein. New Brunswick, N.J.: Rutgers University Press, 1999, 238–263.

Zackin, Emily. "The Early ACLU and the Decision to Litigate." *Princeton University Library Chronicle* 67, 3 (Spring 2006), 526–551.

Published Primary Sources

American Birth Control Conference. *Birth Control: What It Is, How It Works, What It Will Do. The Proceedings of the First American Birth Control Conference Held at the Hotel Plaza, New York, November 11, 12, 1921*. New York: Birth Control Review, 1921.

American Civil Liberties Union. *Sexual Privacy Project Legal Docket*. New York: American Civil Liberties Union, 1974.

Amoroso, Donald M., et al. "The Effects of Physiological Measurement and Presence of Others on Ratings of Erotic Stimuli." *Canadian Journal of Behavioral Science* 4, 3 (1972), 191–203.

Babcock, Barbara, Ann E. Freedman, and Eleanor H. Norton. *Sex Discrimination and the Law: Causes and Remedies*. New York: Little, Brown, 1975.

Babcock, Richard F., Jr. "Sterilization: Coercing Consent." *The Nation*, January 12, 1974, 51–53.

Baldwin, Roger. "Recollections of a Life in Civil Liberties-I." *Civil Liberties Review* 2, 2 (1975), 39–72.

Ball, William B. "Population Control: Civic and Constitutional Concerns." *Religion and the Public Order* 4(1968), 128–169.

Barnett, Walter. *Sexual Freedom and the Constitution: An Inquiry into the Constitutionality of Repressive Sex Laws*. Albuquerque: University of New Mexico Press, 1973.

Benjamin, Hazel C. "Lobbying for Birth Control." *Public Opinion Quarterly* 2, 1 (January 1938), 48–60.

Bernfeld, Jules E. *Hairdresser's Odyssey: An Anthology by a Prophet and Rebel*. Ardmore, Pa.: Whitmore, 1976.

Bishop, Joseph W. "Politics and the ACLU." *Commentary*, December 1971, 50–58.

Blackwood, James R. "Show Biz and the Censor." *Presbyterian Life*, December 28, 1957, 11–13.

Blanshard, Paul. *The Right to Read: The Battle Against Censorship*. Boston: Beacon Press, 1955.

Boggan, E. Carrington, Marilyn G. Haft, Charles Lister, and John P. Rupp. *The Rights of Gay People: The Basic ACLU Guide to a Gay Person's Rights*. New York: E. P. Dutton, 1975.

Boruchowitz, Robert C. "Victimless Crimes: A Proposal to Free the Courts." *Judicature*, February 1, 1973, 69–78.

Bowman, Cynthia Grant. "Street Harassment and the Informal Ghettoization of Women." *Harvard Law Review* 106 (January 1993), 517.

Brownmiller, Susan. *Against Our Will: Men, Women and Rape*. New York: Fawcett Books, 1975.

Brownmiller, Susan. *In Our Time: Memoir of a Revolution*. New York: Dial Press, 1999.

Brownmiller, Susan. "Rashomon in Maryland." *Esquire*, May 1968, 130–132, 134, 145–147.

Clinton, Bill. *My Life*. New York: Knopf, 2004.

Cole, Rob. "ACLU Launched on Major Gay Rights Project." *The Advocate,* November 21, 1973.

Coleman, Tom. *The Domino Effect: How Strategic Moves for Gay Rights, Singles' Rights, and Family Diversity Have Touched the Lives of Millions: Memoirs of an Equal Rights Advocate.* Glendale, Calif.: Spectrum Institute Press, 2009.

Committee of Fourteen. *The Social Evil in New York City: A Study of Law Enforcement.* New York: Andrew H. Kellogg, 1910.

Compton, Lynn D. *Call of Duty: My Life before, during and after the Band of Brothers.* New York : Berkley Caliber, 2008.

Cook, Blanche Wiesen, ed. *Crystal Eastman on Women and Revolution.* New York: Oxford University Press, 1978.

Cook, Blanche Wiesen, ed. *Toward the Great Change: Crystal and Max Eastman on Feminism, Antimilitarism, and Revolution.* New York: Garland, 1976.

Cook, Royer F., et al. "Pornography and the Sex Offender: Patterns of Previous Exposure and Arousal Effects of Pornographic Stimuli." *Journal of Applied Psychology* 55, 6 (1971), 503–511.

Cory, Donald Webster. *The Homosexual in America: A Subjective Approach.* New York: Greenberg, 1951.

Dennett, Mary Ware. *Who's Obscene?* New York: Vanguard Press, 1930.

Deutsch, Albert. "What Dr. Kinsey is up to now!" *Look,* May 22, 1951, 85–90.

Diamond, Irene. "Pornography and Repression: A Reconsideration." *Signs* 5, 4 (Summer 1980), 686–701.

Dickson, Del, ed. *The Supreme Court in Conference (1940–1985): The Private Discussions Behind Nearly 300 Supreme Court Decisions.* New York: Oxford University Press, 2001.

Donnerstein, Edward, and Gary Barrett. "Effects of Erotic Stimuli on Male Aggression toward Females." *Journal of Personality and Psychology* 36, 2 (1978), 180–188.

Donnerstein, Edward, and John Hallam. "Facilitating Effects of Erotica on Aggression against Women." *Journal of Personality and Social Psychology* 36, 11 (1978), 1270–1277.

Doty, Madeleine Zabriskie. *Society's Misfits.* New York: Century Co., 1916.

Doyle, Ruth. "What Nobody Knows About Juvenile Delinquency." *Harper's,* August 1956, 47–50.

Dworkin, Andrea. "The ACLU: Bait and Switch." *Yale Journal of Law and Feminism*1, 1 (1989), 37–39.

Dworkin, Andrea. *Pornography: Men Possessing Women.* New York: E. P. Dutton, 1979.

Eastman, Max. *Enjoyment of Living.* New York: Harper and Brothers, 1948.

Edwards, Alison. "Rape, Racism, and the White Women's Movement." Chicago: Sojourner Truth Organization. http://www.sojournertruth.net/rrwwm.pdf (retrieved July 28, 2010).

Ernst, Morris L. *The Best is Yet*... New York: Harper and Brothers, 1945.

Ernst, Morris L. *The First Freedom.* New York: Macmillan, 1946.

Ernst, Morris L. "Freedom to Read, See, and Hear." *Journal of Educational Sociology* 19, 4 (December 1945), 230–235.

Ernst, Morris L. "The Kinsey Report and its Contributions to Related Fields: The Kinsey Report and the Law." *Scientific Monthly,* May 1950, 279–282.

Ernst, Morris L. "Law." *Saturday Review,* March 13, 1948, 19.

Ernst, Morris L. *A Love Affair with the Law: A Legal Sampler.* New York: Macmillan, 1968.

Ernst, Morris L. "The So-Called Market Place of Thought." *Bill of Rights Review* 2 (1942), 86–91.

Ernst, Morris L. *Too Big.* Boston: Little, Brown, 1940.

Ernst, Morris L. *Touchwood: A Year's Diary.* New York: Atheneum, 1960.

Ernst, Morris L. *Untitled: The Diary of My 72nd Year.* New York: Robert B. Luce, 1962.

Ernst, Morris L. *Utopia: 1976.* New York: Rinehart, 1953.

Ernst, Morris L., and Alexander Lindey. *Hold Your Tongue! Adventures in Libel and Slander.* London: Methuen, 1936.

Ernst, Morris L., and David Loth. *American Sexual Behavior and the Kinsey Report.* New York: Bantam, 1948.

Ernst, Morris L., and David Loth. *Report on the American Communist.* New York: Henry Holt, 1952.

Ernst, Morris L., and David Loth. "What Kinsey Will Tell." *Redbook*, May 1950, 37, 86–90.

Ernst, Morris L., and William Seagle. *To the Pure: A Study of Obscenity and the Censor*. New York: Viking Press, 1928.

Farley, Lin. *Sexual Shakedown: The Sexual Harassment of Women on the Job*. New York: McGraw-Hill, 1978.

Feigen, Brenda. *Not One of the Boys: Living Life as a Feminist*. New York: Knopf, 2000.

Finn, James. "Controversy in New York." *Commonweal*, September 12, 1958, 583–586.

Fitzpatrick, John T. *Penal Law and the Code of Criminal Procedure of the State of New York*. 8th ed. Albany, N.Y.: Matthew Bender, 1916.

Flexner, Bernard, and Roger N. Baldwin. *Juvenile Courts and Probation*. New York: Century Co., 1914.

Flynn, Elizabeth Gurley. *The Rebel Girl: An Autobiography, My First Life (1906–1926)*. New York: International Publishers, 1955.

Foster, Henry H., Jr. "The 'Comstock Load': Obscenity and the Law." *Journal of Criminal Law, Criminology, and Police Science* 48, 3 (September–October 1957), 245–258.

Geddes, Donald Porter. *An Analysis of the Kinsey Reports on Sexual Behavior in the Human Male and Female*. New York: New American Library of World Literature, 1954.

Gellhorn, Walter, Richard McKeon, and Robert K. Merton. *The Freedom to Read: Perspective and Program*. New York: R. R. Bowker, 1957.

Gertz, Elmer. *A Handful of Clients*. River Grove, Ill.: Follett, 1965.

Ginsburg, Ruth Bader, Brenda Fasteau, et al. "Equality for Women." *Playboy*, August 1973, 52.

Goldman, Emma. *Living My Life*. Vol. 2. New York: Dover, 1970.

Gordon, Linda. "The Politics of Sexual Harassment." *Radical America* 15, 4 (July–August 1981), 7–14.

Griffin, Susan. *Pornography and Silence: Culture's Revenge Against Nature*. New York: Harper and Row, 1981.

Guttmacher, Alan F. "A Defense of the Supreme Court's Abortion Decision." *The Humanist*, May–June 1973, 6–7.

Haft, Marilyn. "Hustling for Rights." *Civil Liberties Review* 1, 2 (Winter–Spring 1974), 8–26.

Haiman, Franklyn S. "Speech v. Privacy: Is There a Right Not to Be Spoken To?" *Northwestern University Law Review* 67, 2 (May–June 1972), 153–199.

Halvonik, Paul N. "Hope and Affection in Milwaukee." *Civil Liberties Review*, Fall 1974, 132–135.

Harriman, Margaret Case. "Profiles: The Voice." *New Yorker*, October 26, 1935, 26–29, and November 2, 1935, 24–28.

Hays, Arthur Garfield. *City Lawyer: The Autobiography of a Law Practice*. New York: Simon and Schuster, 1942.

Hays, Arthur Garfield. *Let Freedom Ring*. New York: Boni and Liveright, 1928.

Hefner, Hugh M. "The Legal Enforcement of Morality." *University of Colorado Law Review* 40 (1968), 199–221.

Herman, Lawrence. "What's Wrong with the Rape Reform Laws?" *Civil Liberties Review*, December 1976–January 1977, 60–72.

Holmes, John Haynes. *Religion for To-day: Various Interpretations of the Thought and Practice of the New Religion of Our Time*. Boston: Beacon Press, 1917.

Holtzman, Elizabeth, with Cynthia L. Cooper. *Who Said it Would Be Easy? One Woman's Life in the Political Arena*. New York: Arcade, 1996.

Jaffe, Louis L. "Standing to Secure Judicial Review: Public Actions." *Harvard Law Review* 74, 7 (May 1961), 1265–1314.

Katz, Esther, ed. *Selected Papers of Margaret Sanger*. Ed. Esther Katz. Vol. 1. Urbana: University of Illinois Press, 2003.

King, Gertrude Besse. *Alliances for the Mind*. New York: Harcourt, Brace and company, 1924.

Kinsey, Alfred C. *Sexual Behavior in the Human Male*. Philadelphia: W. B. Saunders, 1948.

Klein, Michael R. "Towards An Extension of the First Amendment: A Right of Acquisition." *University of Miami Law Review* 20 (1965), 114–147.

LaMarche, Gara, ed. *Speech and Equality: Do We Really Have to Choose?* New York: New York University Press, 1996.

Lamont, Corliss, ed., *The Trial of Elizabeth Gurley Flynn by the American Civil Liberties Union*. New York: Horizon Press, 1968.

Lanpher, Katherine. "A Bitter Brew." *Ms.*, November–December 1992, 36–41.

Lederer, Laura, ed. *Take Back the Night: Women on Pornography*. New York: William Morrow, 1980.

Lichtman, Richard. "Pornography & Censorship."*Commentary* 32, 2 (August 1961), 156.

Lindsey, Karen. "Sexual Harassment on the Job and How to Stop It." *Ms.*, November 1977, 47–51, 74–78.

Lockhart, William, and Robert McClure. "Censorship of Obscenity: The Developing Constitutional Standards." *Minnesota Law Review* 45 (1960), 5–121.

Lockridge, Norman. *The Sexual Conduct of Men and Women: A Minority Report*. New York: Hogarth House, 1948.

MacKinnon, Catharine. *Sexual Harassment of Working Women*. New Haven: Yale University Press, 1979.

Mann, Jim. "Hard Times for the ACLU." *New Republic*, April 15, 1978, 12–15.

Mansbridge, Jane, and Katherine Tate. "Race Trumps Gender: The Thomas Nomination in the Black Community." *PS: Political Science and Politics* 25, 3 (September 1992), 488–492.

McCabe, Katie, and Dovey Johnson Roundtree. *Justice Older Than the Law: The Life of Dovey Johnson Roundtree*. Jackson: University Press of Mississippi, 2009.

Merrill, Frances and Mason. *Among the Nudists*. New York: A. A. Knopf, 1931.

Miller, Merle. *On Being Different*. New York: Random House, 1971.

Milner, Lucille B. *Education of an American Liberal*. New York: New Horizon, 1954.

Moore, Nancy, Jody Parsons, and Kathy Roberts. "Up Against the Wall, Hugh Hefner." *Chicago Women's Liberation Union News*, January 1970.

Murray, Pauli. *Pauli Murray: The Autobiography of a Black Activist, Feminist, Lawyer, Priest, and Poet*. Knoxville: University of Tennessee Press, 1989.

Murray, Pauli, ed. *States' Laws on Race and Color: Studies in the Legal History of the South*. Athens: University of Georgia Press, 1997.

Neier, Aryeh. *Taking Liberties: Four Decades in the Struggle for Rights*. New York: Public Affairs, 2003.

Norris, Hoke. "'Cancer' in Chicago." *Evergreen Review*, July–August 1962, 41–66.

Packer, Herbert L. "The Pornography Caper." *Commentary*, February 1971, 72–76.

Palmore, Erdman. "Published Reactions to the Kinsey Report." *Social Forces* 31, 2 (December 1952), 165–172.

Parmelee, Maurice. *The New Gymnosophy: The Philosophy of Nudity as Applied in Modern Life*. New York: F. H. Hitchcock, 1927.

Parmelee, Maurice. *Nudism in Modern Life: The New Gymnosophy*. New York: Alfred A. Knopf, 1930.

Paul, Eve W., Harriet F. Pilpel, and Nancy Wechsler. "Pregnancy, Teenagers and the Law, 1974." *Family Planning Perspectives* 6, 3 (Summer 1974), 142–147.

Pilpel, Harriet F. "Abortion Laws Challenged." *Playboy*, April 1970, 60.

Pilpel, Harriet F. "But Can You Do That?" *Publisher's Weekly* 170, 26 (December 31, 1956), 2677–2680.

Pilpel, Harriet F. "Contraception and Freedom." *Playboy*, January 1969, 51.

Pilpel, Harriet F. "The Fetus as Person: Possible Legal Consequences of the Hogan-Helms Amendment." *Family Planning Perspectives* 6, 1 (Winter 1974), 6–7.

Pilpel, Harriet F. "Problem Box." *Marriage and Family Living*, August 1951, 137.

Pilpel, Harriet F. "A Right is Born: Privacy as a Civil Liberty." *Civil Liberties*, November 1965, 2.

Pilpel, Harriet F., and Kenneth P. Norwick. "When Should Abortion Be Legal?" New York: Public Affairs Committee, 1969.

Pilpel, Harriet F., and Theodora S. Zavin, "Marriage Counseling Section: Birth Control." *Marriage and Family Living* 14, 2 (May 1952), 117–124.
Pilpel, Harriet F., and Theodora Zavin. "Sex and the Criminal Law." *Marriage and Family Living* 14, 3 (August 1952), 238–244.
Pilpel, Harriet F., and Theodora Zavin. *Your Marriage and the Law*. New York: Rinehart, 1952.
Pilpel, Harriet F., Ruth Jane Zuckerman, and Elizabeth Ogg. *Abortion: Public Issue, Private Decision*. New York: Public Affairs Committee, 1975.
Ploscowe, Morris. *Sex and the Law*. New York: Prentice-Hall, 1951.
Rice, Elmer. *Minority Report: An Autobiography*. New York: Simon and Schuster, 1963.
Rice, Elmer. "Organized Charity Turns Censor." *The Nation*, June 10, 1931, 628–630.
Rinehart, Alice Duffy, ed., *One Woman Determined to Make a Difference: The Life of Madeleine Zabriskie Doty*. Bethlehem, Pa.: Lehigh University Press; Cranbury, N.J.: Associated University Presses, 2001.
Rodell, Fred. "Morris Ernst: New York's Unlawyerlike Liberal Lawyer is the Censor's Enemy, the President's Friend." *Life*, February 21, 1944, 96–98, 100, 102, 105–107.
Rosen, Jeffrey. "Reasonable Women." *New Republic*, November 1, 1993.
Rothenberg, Ignaz. *The Newspaper: A Study in the Workings of the Daily Press and Its Laws*. New York: Staples Press, 1946.
Rothenberg, Ignaz, and Mildred K. Steffens. "The Rape Victim." *American Mercury* 75, 334 (October 1951), 75–79.
Ryan, Rebecca M. "The Sex Right: A Legal History of the Marital Rape Exemption." *Law and Social Inquiry* 20, 4 (Autumn, 1955), 941–1001.
Sanger, Margaret. "Birth Control and Civil Liberties." *The Churchman*, November 1, 1941, 14–15.
Sanger, Margaret. *Margaret Sanger: An Autobiography*. New York: Dover Publications, 1971.
Sanger, Margaret. *My Fight for Birth Control*. New York: Farrar and Rinehart, 1931.
Schwartz, Louis B. "Civil Liberties vs. the ACLU." *New Republic*, July 26, 1980, 20–23.
Schwartz, Louis B. "Morals Offenses and the Model Penal Code." *Columbia Law Review* 63, 4 (April 1963), 669–686.
Schwartz, Louis B. Book Review (Alfred Kinsey et al., *Sexual Behavior in the Human Male*), *University of Pennsylvania Law Review* 96, 6 (June 1948), 914–918.
Schwarz, Judith. *Radical Feminists of Heterodoxy: Greenwich Village, 1912–1940*. Norwich, Vt.: New Victoria, 1986.
Scott, Anne Firor, ed. *Pauli Murray and Caroline Ware: Forty Years of Letters in Black and White*. Chapel Hill: University of North Carolina Press, 2006.
Slater, Jack. "Sterilization: Newest Threat to the Poor." *Ebony*, October 1973, 150–154, 156.
Small, Collie. "Too Many Self-Appointed Censors." *Reader's Digest*, September 1951, 109–112.
Small, Collie. "What Censorship Keeps You From Knowing." *Redbook*, July 1951, 22–24, 81–85.
Smith, A. Robert, and James V. Giles. *An American Rape: A True Account of the Giles-Johnson Case*. Washington, D.C.: New Republic Book Co., 1975.
Stacey, Michelle. "Stupid Boob Behavior." *Cosmopolitan*, October 2006, 198–201.
Stanmeyer, William A. "Victimless Crimes and Public Morality." *Modern Age* (Chicago) 18, 4 (September 1, 1974), 369–379.
Stix, Regine K. "Birth Control and the Public Health." *Milbank Memorial Fund Quarterly* 16, 2 (April 1938), 221–223.
Stone, Abraham, and Harriet F. Pilpel. "The Social and Legal Status of Contraception." *North Carolina Law Review* 22 (April 1944), 219–225.
Strauss, Frances. *Where Did the Justice Go? The Story of the Giles-Johnson Case*. Boston: Gambit, 1970.
Strossen, Nadine. *Defending Pornography: Free Speech, Sex, and the Fight for Women's Rights*. New York: Anchor Books, 1995.
Strossen, Nadine. "The Kenneth M. Piper Lecture: The Tensions Between Regulating Workplace Harassment and the First Amendment: No Trump." *Chicago-Kent Law Review* 71 (1995), 701–727.

Strossen, Nadine. "Regulating Workplace Sexual Harassment and Upholding the First Amendment—Avoiding a Collision." *Villanova Law Review* 37 (1995), 757–785.

Stycos, J. Mayone, and Reuben Hill. "The Prospects of Birth Control in Puerto Rico." *Annals of the American Academy of Political and Social Sciences* 285 (January 1953), 137–144.

Taylor, Marion Sayle. "Facts for Wives: Plain Truths about Marriage." Chicago: Hygienic Orificial Co., 1928.

Taylor, Marion Sayle. *The Male Motor: Its Uses and Abuses.* Steubenville, Ohio: Kirk Publishers, 1927.

Taylor, Marion Sayle. "Natural Birth Control and Pre-determination of Sex." Chicago: Hygienic Orificial Co., 1928.

Taylor, Marion Sayle. "The Secret of Youth and Charm: Plain Sex Truths for Women." Akron, Ohio: Commercial Ptg. & Litho., 1927.

Taylor, Marion Sayle. "Sex Vigor: How Retained, How Regained." Self-published, 1927.

Trippett, Frank. "What's Happening to Sexual Privacy?" *Look*, October 20, 1970, 50.

Ware, Edward E., et al. "The Semantic Meaning of Pornographic Stimuli for College Males." *Canadian Journal of Behavioral Science* 4, 3 (1972), 204–209.

Wechsler, Herbert. "The Challenge of a Model Penal Code." *Harvard Law Review* 65, 7 (May 1952), 1097–1133.

Wechsler, Herbert. "Codification of Criminal Law in the United States: The Model Penal Code." *Columbia Law Review* 68, 8 (December 1968), 1425–1456.

Williams, J. E. Hal. "Sex Offenses: The British Experience." *Law and Contemporary Problems* 25, 2 (Spring 1960), 334–360.

Williams, Linda. *Hard Core: Power, Pleasure, and the "Frenzy of the Visible."* Berkeley: University of California Press, 1989.

Wolfenden, Sir John, C.B.E., et al. *Report of the Committee on Homosexual Offences and Prostitution.* London: Her Majesty's Stationery Office, September 1957.

Woodward, W. C., M.D. "Contraceptive Advice, Devices and Preparations—Reply." *Journal of the American Medical Association* 108, 21 (May 22, 1937), 1820.

Woolley, John T., and Gerhard Peters. *The American Presidency Project.* http://www.presidency.ucsb.edu/ws/print.php?pid=39772 (retrieved July 10, 2011).

Wulf, Melvin L. "On the Origins of Privacy." *The Nation*, May 27, 1991, 700–704.

Zurcher, Louis A., Jr., and R. George Kirkpatrick. *Citizens for Decency: Antipornography Crusades as Status Defense.* Austin: University of Texas Press, 1976.

Oral Interviews

Judith and Alan Appelbaum, interview by the author, May 27, 2010.

Barbara Babcock Oral History Interview, conducted by LaDoris Hazzard Cordell, American Bar Association, Women Trailblazers in the Law Project. http://www.c-spanvideo.org/program/294200-1 (retrieved July 28, 2011).

Jeanne Baker, telephone interview by the author, December 12, 2010.

Janet Benshoof, interview by the author, August 2, 2010.

Mitchell Bernard, telephone interview by the author, November 18, 2010.

Mark Blassius, telephone interview by the author, October 25, 2010.

Robyn Blumner, telephone interview by the author, November 29, 2010.

Susan Brownmiller, telephone interview by the author, November 1, 2010.

Vern Bullough, interview by Raj Ayyar, "America's Foremost Historian of Sexuality: Vern L. Bullough, RN, Ph.D." *GayToday.com*, http://www.gaytoday.com/interview/010103in.asp (retrieved July 5, 2011).

Thomas Coleman, telephone interview by the author, August 9, 2010.

Mary Coombs, telephone interview by the author, December 3, 2010.

Brenda Feigen (Fasteau), telephone interview by the author, June 22, 2010.

Monroe Freedman, telephone interview by the author, October 12, 2010.

Mary Ellen Gale, telephone interview by the author, December 3, 2010.

Marilyn Haft, telephone interview by the author, August 9, 2010.
Chris Hansen, telephone interview by the author, November 24, 2009.
Trudy Hayden, telephone interview by the author, June 25, 2010.
Lawrence Herman, telephone interview by the author, November 3, 2010.
Nan Hunter, telephone interview by the author, November 1, 2010.
Burton Joseph, videotaped interview, unknown interviewer. http://www.youtube.com/watch?v=nodXszFU8jM (retrieved July 5, 2010).
Wendy Kaminer, telephone interview by the author, November 29, 2010.
Joan E. Mahoney, telephone interview by the author, November 23, 2010.
Judith Mears, telephone interview by the author, July 21, 2010.
Michael Meyers, telephone interview by the author, November 24, 2010.
Pauli Murray, transcribed oral interview by Leila Rupp and Verta Taylor, June 16, 1983.
Aryeh Neier, telephone interview by the author, August 19, 2010.
Harriet Pilpel, transcribed radio interviews by Richard Heffner, October 16, 1979; February 4, 1983, and May 9, 1984.
Harriet Pilpel, transcribed oral interview by Eleanor Jackson Piel, March 20, 1972; April 5, 1972; April 1975, and September 1975, HU-SL, SROHP.
Isabelle Katz Pinzler, telephone interview by the author, December 2, 2010.
Joseph Ronsley, telephone interview by the author, January 26, 2010.
Catherine Roraback, interview by David Garrow, September 10 and 17, 1991.
Susan Deller Ross, telephone interview by the author, November 19, 2010.
Karen Sauvigne, telephone interview by the author, November 14, 2010.
Joel Sprayregen, telephone interviews by the author, January 21 and 26, 2010.
Nadine Strossen, telephone interview by the author, November 22, 2010.
Samuel Walker, telephone interview by the author, July 6, 2010.
Linda, Lannie, and David Watts, telephone interview by the author, June 13, 2010.
Melvin Wulf, interview by David Garrow, March 19, 1992.
Melvin Wulf, interviews by the author, May 27, 2010 and August 2, 2010.

E-mail Correspondence

Anthony Amsterdam
Barbara Babcock
Estelle Freedman
Margaret Ellen Gale
Andrew Hacker
Kathleen McCabe
Robert Pilpel
Alexander Polikoff
Margaret Russell
Barbara Sommer
Joel Sprayregen
Ruth Jane Zuckerman

Archival Collections and Abbreviations

AMA—American Medical Association Historical Archives, Chicago, Ill.
MST—M. Sayle Taylor File
ANRL—American Nudist Research Library, Cypress Cove Nudist Resort, Kissimmee, Florida
Subject Files
Personalities Files
ASL—Arthur Schlesinger Library, Harvard University
PMC—Pauli Murray Collection

SROHP—Schlesinger-Rockefeller Oral History Project
SCA—Charles E. Young Research Library, University of California, Los Angeles
ACLU—American Civil Liberties Union of Southern California Records
EU—Emory University, Atlanta, Georgia
MPH—Marjorie Pitts Hames Collection
FOIA-FBI—Freedom of Information Act, Federal Bureau of Investigation Records (obtained through individual requests unless noted otherwise)
American Civil Liberties Union
Roger Baldwin
Ilsley Boone
Ralph Ginzburg
Henry S. Huntington
Dorothy Kenyon
Alfred Kinsey
Maurice Parmelee
Harriet Pilpel
Playboy
Elmer Rice
Samuel Roth (shared by Claire Culleton)
Carlo Tresca
FDR—Franklin Delano Roosevelt Presidential Library, Hyde Park, N.Y.
JPL—Joseph P. Lasch Papers
PPF—President's Personal File
HRC—Harry Ransom Center, University of Texas at Austin
MEC—Morris Ernst Collection
ERC—Elmer Rice Collection
AKC—Alfred A. Knopf Collection
HUA—Harvard University Archives, Harvard University Library, Cambridge, Mass.
RCC—Richard C. Cabot Papers
HU-SL—Harvard University, Schlesinger Library, Cambridge, Mass.
SROHP—Schlesinger-Rockefeller Oral History Project
KI—The Kinsey Institute for Research in Sex, Gender, and Reproduction, Inc., Indiana University, Bloomington, Ind.
KC—Kinsey Correspondence
LOC—Library of Congress Wash., D.C.
EGP—Elmer Gertz Papers
MHS—Minnesota Historical Society, St. Paul, Minn.
GFP—Robbins Gilman and Family Papers
NA—National Archives, Great Lakes Region, Record Group 21
NDO—Records of U.S. District Courts, Northern District of Ohio, Western Division, Toledo
NYPL—New York Public Library
AFPS—American Fund for Public Service Records
NTP—Norman Thomas Papers
NYSL—New York State Library, Albany
AESC—Alfred E. Smith Collection
NCA—North Baker Research Library, California Historical Society, San Francisco, Calif.
ACLU—American Civil Liberties Union of Northern California Archives
NUA—Northwestern University Archives, Evanson, Ill.
FHP—Franklyn Haiman Papers
PC—Private Collections
JB—Janet Benshoof
MF—Monroe Friedman
MEG—Meg Ellen Gale

LH—Lawrence Herman
WK—Wendy Kaminer
NL—Nan Levinson
JM—Judith Mears
MM—Michael Meyers
LW—Linda Watts
PML—Mudd Library, Princeton University, Princeton, N.J.
ACLU—American Civil Liberties Union Archives
ACLU-DC—National Capital Area ACLU Affiliate
ACW—Arthur Cyrus Warner Papers
OFD—Osmond Fraenkel Diaries
PLC—Peggy Lamson Collection
RAC—Rockefeller Archive Center, Sleepy Hollow, N.Y.
RFC—Rockefeller Foundation Collection
SWHA—Social Welfare History Archives, University of Minnesota, Minneapolis
ASV—Association for Voluntary Sterilization collection
SSC—Sophia Smith Collection, Smith College, Northampton, Mass.
AFP—Ames Family Papers
DK—Dorothy Kenyon Papers
HFP—Harriet Fleischl Pilpel Papers
PPFA—Planned Parenthood Federation of America Collections I and II
MZD—Madeleine Zabriskie Doty Papers
MSP—Margaret Sanger Papers
WRC—Women's Rights Collection
UCL—The University of Chicago Library, Chicago, Ill.
ACLU—ACLU: Illinois Division Records
YU—Yale University, New Haven, Conn.
MPP—Maurice Parmelee Papers

Microfilm Collections

ABCL-MF—American Birth Control League Papers
ACLU-MF—American Civil Liberties Union Collection
AUAM-MF—American Union Against Militarism Papers
CUOHP-MF—Columbia University Oral History Project
JHH-MF—John Haynes Holmes Papers
MSP-MF—Margaret Sanger Papers
MWD-MF—Mary Ware Dennett Papers
RNB-MF—Roger Nash Baldwin Papers

Online Collections

UPLS—University of Pennsylvania Law School, Philadelphia, Penn.
ALIA—American Law Institute Archives
http://www.law.upenn.edu/cf/biddle/ali/index.cfm (retrieved July 5, 2011).

INDEX

Page numbers in italics refer to figures.